SLAVERY & ISLAM

SLAVERY & ISLAM

JONATHAN A.C. BROWN

ONEWORLD ACADEMIC

Oneworld Academic

An imprint of Oneworld Publications

Published by Oneworld Academic, 2019

A CIP record for this title is available from the British Library

ISBN 978-1-78607-635-9
eISBN 978-1-78607-636-6

Cover image: A slave market in Zabid, Yemen, from a thirteenth-century illustrated copy of the *Maqamat* of al-Hariri (d. 1122). Courtesy of the Sonia Halliday Photo Library.

Typeset by Hewer Text UK Ltd, Edinburgh
Printed and bound in Great Britain by Clays Ltd, Elcograf S.p.A.

Oneworld Publications
10 Bloomsbury Street
London WC1B 3SR
England

MIX
Paper from responsible sources
FSC® C018072
www.fsc.org

Contents

Preface

Whenever I think of writing prefaces my first thought is always a flood of gratitude and the desire to express it sincerely and without the mediation of style. Gratitude to the God for my life, for all the blessings I've received. But when I'm on the road what I feel the strongest is immense appreciation for all the kind and hospitable souls who've hosted me, taken me in and guided me during my travels. And shame for not having reciprocated or kept in touch. Here in Sarajevo those people are too many for me to count with any ease. Faces and moments flood over me as I lean my head back against the wall in the courtyard. Gannady Vaziliev and Vadim Voronin, who hosted me for weeks in Moscow. In Tehran, the family of Faramarz Jahanbakhsh, who literally took me in – almost off the street – and let me live with them for months, refusing any payment. The brothers and friends on the train to Yazd who insisted I stay with them, and who took me to the mountain village of Taft for a BBQ. The cab driver in Rasht who let me sleep at his house when all the hotels were full. Hesham Benkirane and his family who brought me to their home in Tangier. Selda Kaplan's kind mother in Kayseri who bought me new underwear (not that I needed it! Apparently, that's something one does in Turkey) while her father made up for all the prayers he'd missed in his youth. The family in Jenne who let me and Charles Bartlett sleep on the roof of their house and served us millet porridge in the morning. The family of my old nanny Liberata who let us stay with them for days and days in Dakar. The mother in Jenin who invited me over and served me a huge lunch it must have taken her ages to prepare. Of course, Tariq, Rami, Iffat and their families in Cairo. The Alam Khan family, who picked Garrett and me up in a limo in Hyderabad and hosted us, arranging tours of Osmania University and whose noble and stylish patriarch inquired in a tone both imperious and endearing, 'Brown! What do you want to do in Hyderabad?!' I'm haunted by my failure to thank you all and remain in touch as I should. I long for forgiveness.

I go into my motivation for writing this book a bit in the Introduction, but here I'll add a few mundane details. I had originally intended to write a series of online essays on slavery and Islam for the Yaqeen Institute, with which I am associated, beginning in January 2017. I published one essay on the problem of defining slavery (the core of Chapter One of this book) and had a second one ready to go (it became Chapter Four and part of Chapter Seven), but I soon realized that this issue was simply too complicated and controversial to deal with piecemeal. In the meantime, Oneworld, a publisher with whom I had the wonderful experience of writing two books previously, suggested I do a whole book on the topic. During the spring semester of 2018 I taught an undergraduate course on Islam and Slavery, which helped me organize material and try out explanations with students. I am grateful to Oneworld for the suggestion. And I wish the Çarşe Mosque were open. There the enormous, creeping rose vines loom around you on creaking trellises and fan you with hints of fragrance that are truly signs of the God. But this noticeably roseless mosque will do.

Ghazi Husrev Beg Mosque
Sarajevo, August 12, 2018

Acknowledgments

More than any book I have written, this one is composed of the knowledge of others who were kind enough to aid me with their expertise. I am hesitant to thank them or involve anyone in this book because the subject is so contentious and because many likely do not agree with opinions or conclusions I express. I urge the reader not to hold them accountable for anything in this book but to blame only me, reserving for those who helped me the appreciation due to those generous with their knowledge to all who come asking. I am very grateful to Samer Akkach, Kecia Ali, Aun Hasan Ali, Chris Anzalone, Abdurrahman Atcil, Kevin Bales, Murteza Bedir, Dan Byman, Anne-Marie Carstens, Ahmed El Shamsy, Mohammad Fadel, Bernard Freamon, Mohamed Ghilan, Kyle Harper, David Hollenbach, Kyle Ismail, Pamela Klasova, Leo Lefebure, Rosabel Martin-Ross, Ann Mayer, Harry Morgan, Abdul Rahman Mustafa, Rasoul Naghavi Nia, Shlomo Pill, Yasir Qadhi, Jawad and Omar Qureshi, Muhammad Rofiq, Ahsan Sayed, Uri Simonsohn, Luke Sheridan, Sohaira Siddiqui, Nur Sobers-Khan, Abdallah Soufan, Omar Suleiman, Ali Tariq, Tariq Al-Timimi, Sarra Tlili, Aissata Wane, Bilal Ware, Zachary Wright, Saad Yacoub, Shafat Maqbool and Alden Young.

A few people deserve particular gratitude for the time they took to help me and the unusual degree of material and insight they shared. My student Said Saleh Kaymakci shared so much from his incredibly active mind and wide reading in Ottoman history, helping me with sources and checking my work for mistakes. My students Tesneem Alkiek and Rezart Beka assisted me a great deal with research and their creative contributions. Arnold Yasin Mol has been an energetic colleague who is always willing to share his observations, broad reading and discuss the toughest and most controversial issues with me – even on WhatsApp. Abbas Barzegar is so good at exactly the theoretical nonsense I can't manage. Joe Bradford is an *ʿallama.* Margarita Rosa was patient in helping me with my great ignorance and compassionate in her correction. Ahmed Abdel Meguid saved my *6eez* from a major, major, unforced Kant error. Ovamir Anjum, as usual, has been a teacher and thinker whose mind always operates several levels above mine and who, as usual, took the time to lift me up. Andrew March has been a true friend in the life of the mind. I have never met someone so exact in his thinking and exacting of those who think with him, and he has been one of the few people who has helped me with his time, energy and expertise through this whole process. Omar Anchassi remains, though younger than me, a great teacher and resource. His wide reading, solid insights, honesty and generosity with his knowledge have been pillars of this project. Muntasir 'The Machine' Zaman continues to astound me with his attention to detail, thoroughness and incredible ability to find mistakes in things I've written. As I worked on this book, the insults and accusations directed at me by others in the academy at times caused me to doubt my credentials as a scholar. As I write out these acknowledgments, however, seeing the talent, capacity and good intentions of those who eagerly offered me their help is all the affirmation I need.

A special debt of gratitude I owe to Professor Nathaniel Mathews, who has been so giving of his time and prodigious command of material on slavery in world history and in Islamic civilization. I am not an expert on this subject. He is, and he has guided me through much of what I've done in this book. I am almost certain he does not agree with me on a number of important points, but he always helped me nonetheless. Such is a committed scholar.

It's hard for me to know how to thank my family for their support. I was attacked a good amount for my work on this topic, and my wife suffered a great deal through that. But she never once said that I should abandon a topic that I thought was important. She has experienced me writing books before, with the late nights clacking away in the dark of our bedroom, the constant obsession, the duties left untended. She did not complain, and she compensated for my self-indulgence. That is the most an egghead academic could ask for. My children will read lots of awful things about their father. But at least they can read a good book, too. My parents-in-law, Dr. Sami and Nahla, my brothers- and sisters-in-law, Abdullah, Leena, Ali and Lama, they have all been a bulwark of support and great humor for which I am most grateful.

I started this book after the remaining pillars of my life had fallen into the mortal depths of memory. My father passed away in April 2016. He was a wonderful father who was loving and supportive. He taught me much, but what I remember most is that if I gave into fear or didn't stand up for justice I wouldn't be worth him talking to. He said becoming Muslim was the best thing I had done. Then just a few months later Aunt Kate Patterson died. My mom away from mom. When she moved to Berkeley in the eighties she became a foreign embassy of coolness and our link to a different, zanier and more advanced world, a world of sushi and electronic gadgets, of lawyer dolls that screeched 'My client is innocent!' when you squeezed them, of Tolkien and *Star Trek*, of 'mobile communicators' and picking up commuters to cross the Bay Bridge. An MA in Classics from Oxford was just one of the many things that made her the most interesting person I knew, always ready to help me out of cooking predicaments or listen to me complain about whatever. Her death left a gaping hole in my life.

And then there is that missing piece of me I can hardly speak of. It's been eight years since my mother, Dr. Ellen Brown, died in Ethiopia. My sisters and I, we put her shrouded body on a great pyre of eucalyptus logs and sesame seeds and watched for hours as the flames raged and the smoke danced past trees silhouetted by the pending darkness. She would just love this book. She's to blame for the part of me that couldn't not write it, the part I think is best. She would maybe say to a friend that I was just like her and be very proud, but she would be wrong. Whereas in me there is selfishness and thoughtlessness, in her there was nothing but endless love and sacrifice. Where in me there is arrogance, in her there was insufficient self-regard. One time she told me that if there was a God she had known it once, when she lay collapsed with dysentery in the back of a truck driving down a dirt road in the Chadian bush. A blue bird with radiant wings that flashed with the sunlight flew alongside her long enough to give her hope. I just realized I had almost the same experience in Mali. So this book's for you, Mommy. May the God that fills ill hearts with wonder and pulls back the earthly veil that clouds our sight bring us together one day in the Abode of Peace, in 'an assembly of Truth in the presence of an omnipotent Lord' (Quran 54:55).

Notes on Transliteration, Dates and Citation

I have used a minimum of transliteration in the body of the text in order to make this book as accessible as possible. In the main text, I have used the following transliterations for Arabic words. The ' character in the middle of a word represents a simple glottal stop, like the initial sounds of both syllables in 'uh-oh.' The ʿ symbol indicates the Arabic letter *ʿayn*, a sound absent in English but one that resembles the 'aaaah' noise a person makes when getting their throat checked by the doctor. In Arabic and Persian words, '**q**' represents a voiceless uvular sound produced at the back of the throat. It is non-existent in English, but one could most closely approximate this sound with the 'c' sound at the beginning of the crow noise 'Caw! Caw!' '**Gh**' indicates a sound similar to the French 'r,' and '**kh**' represents a velar fricative like the sound of clearing one's throat. '**Dh**' indicates the 'th' sound in words like 'that' or 'bother.' '**Th**' represents the 'th' sound in words like 'bath.' When providing transliterated words within parenthesis in the main text and in the Notes and Bibliography in general, I have used the Library of Congress system (see below).

In the main body of the book I have omitted the Arabic definite article 'al-' in proper names unless it is an essential part of a construction, like the name ʿAbd al-Rahman, or if it is part of a ruler's regnal name, like Al-Rashid (these seemed pathetic without the definite article). I have rendered the Arabic connective noun 'ibn' (son of) as 'bin'.

In the Notes and Bibliography, I have used the standard Library of Congress transliteration system for Arabic, with the non-construct *tāʾ marbuṭa* indicated by an '**a**.' I use **(s)** for the honorific Arabic phrase 'May the peace and blessings of God be upon him (*ṣallā Allāh ʿalayhi wa sallam*),' which is commonly said and written after Muhammad's name. For Persian I have used a slightly adjusted Library of Congress transliteration system that preserves the Arabic conventions for Arabic letters. I have used a dramatically altered Turkish system, preserving only the distinct Turkish vowel markings. 'Ibn' is abbreviated as 'b'.

Dates in this book will follow the Common Era format.

The only unusual citation conventions in this book are those for citing mainstay Sunni Hadith collections. I have followed the standard Wensinck system of citing to the chapter, subchapter of every book (e.g., *Ṣaḥīḥ al-Bukhārī*: *kitāb al-buyū*ʿ, *bāb dhikr al-khayyāṭ*) except the *Musnad* of Ibn Ḥanbal, which is cited to the common Maymaniyya print. All translations are my own unless otherwise indicated in the endnotes.

For my father, Jonathan Cleveland Brown, in long-due loving memory

. . . the segregationists put the white integrationist in a special category of hatred, for in their eyes he is a 'traitor to the white race.'

Jonathan C. Brown, nineteen, on being beaten by Klansmen and police during his integrationist work in St. Augustine, Florida. *Congressional Record* 110, n. 138 (July 20, 1964): 15723

Introduction

Can We Talk About Slavery?

If you do not like the past, change it.
William L. Burton, 'The use and abuse of history'[1]

The certainty of faith carries us over the fissures of doubt, but it does not resolve them. Memory marks well the questions we fail to answer. One moment I recall clearly. Not long after I had embraced Islam in my late teens I lay on my old bed in my old room reading a translation of the Quran. I remember the verse exactly. God compares the slave and the wealthy man, asking if they are alike.[2] The answer implied is no. This is a parable comparing powerless idols to the Almighty, but I was surprised that God was juxtaposing slave and free to make this point. Shouldn't slavery mean nothing because slavery is horrific and people are equal? I passed over the question and read on. In time, after I had become a professor and a Muslim scholar, I would occasionally be asked about slavery and Islam, but the question was too obscure to require me to master more than a perfunctory, stock answer.

In the summer of 2014 the fissure was opened wide, and Muslims had no idea how to mend it. Muslims in the West are used to bad news. But ISIS was the worst news. The headlines refreshed and reproduced: 'ISIS takes sex slaves,' 'ISIS and the theology of rape,' and so on and so on. Jihadist arguments for killing civilians had always been bad. ISIS's reasoning on slavery cut deep because it was so clean. ISIS claimed to be the caliphate reborn, re-establishing the Shariah according to the Book of God and the way of His messenger. The Quran had allowed slavery, the Prophet Muhammad had slaves, and this had all been allowed by the Shariah. So why shouldn't ISIS do it?

The conversations on social media and in person were passionate and combustible. Things were different back then, some Muslims pleaded. So slavery was okay in the past? Well, the Quran and the Prophet were wrong, other Muslims admitted. Then why should anyone follow them? Yes, Islam had allowed slavery, but it wasn't *that bad*. Are you saying some slavery is acceptable? All that could be said was that what ISIS was doing was not Islam. It had never been and never could be. ISIS was the bête noire long dreamed of by an Islamophobia industry that had recently broken into the mainstream of American politics (though it was already a fixture on the European scene). Even for those liberals who had long made excuses for Islam, Muslim slavery – especially sex slavery – was an ancient specter made flesh again, and it was simply a bridge too far. There was no appetite or room for Muslims to make sense of what ISIS's deeds and justification meant in their religion, what the communal consequences would be for condemning passages of the Quran and something done by the Prophet, or how Muslims could reclaim their faith without doing so.

The Trump era dawned and crowds flocked to airports to protest the US government's ban on Muslims entering the country. Muslims in the US found themselves welcome at tables still hunched over by the surviving giants of America's Civil Rights past, and many ordinary Muslims found pride and empowerment in doing what the more prescient among their leaders had long called for: joining the long train of the struggle for civil liberty and emancipation in America. Muslims, Black Lives Matter, Palestine, Feminism: these were called out now side by side. Here was no space for discussing the moral and theological challenge presented by slavery. Slavery was the apotheosis of everything being fought. Yet Muslims still read the same Quranic verse I had, and the fissure remained, obscured only by the swirl of denial and cognitive dissonance.

As the horror of ISIS filled the media, I decided I needed an answer to the 'Islam and slavery' question once and for all, so I started to research the topic. As a white, male, tenured university professor for whom a reasonable day means not moving forty feet from his own French press, the topic of slavery had been peripheral for me prior to this. But as I began to look into it I started to notice how often slavery appeared in the media. Kanye West suggested that American slavery had gone on too long not to have been 'a choice.' A Texas school teacher asked students to list slavery's pros and cons. A Filipino-American journalist admitted his family had brought a slave with them to America. Activists in the US denounced the 'modern-day slavery' of prison labor and called for statues of Thomas Jefferson to be taken down because he had owned slaves. White nationalists said their indentured-servant ancestors had been slaves too, and President Trump asked rhetorically if Americans were going to remove statues of the slave-owning George Washington as well. Someone at a Republican campaign rally in Alabama asked a reporter to 'show [him] where in the Bible it says slavery is wrong.' The problem with writing books is that you start to see your subject everywhere. Whether it was *Solo* or *Sorry to Bother You*, I kept having to turn to my wife and ask, 'Am I crazy or is this movie about slavery?'

ISIS had raised the question of whether enslaving non-Muslims was the real face of Islam and posed the perennial question in its most alarmed tone: 'Why can't those barbaric Muslims just join the modern world?!' But after only a few months of screen shots and link-saving I realized that Americans had the same problem Muslims did. Anne Norton has observed that the West's 'problem with Islam' is really a projection of its own enduring internal anxieties, and Roxanne Euben has shown how the Islamist ideologues that Western national security pundits love to demonize were engaged in many of the same critiques as twentieth-century Western philosophers.[3] With slavery, however, it is not a question of projection or some mimetic blockage. The moral and communal challenges that slavery poses to the traditions of Islam and America (both as a nation and part of the Christian West) are simply strikingly similar. If slavery is a manifest and universal evil, why did no one seem to realize this until relatively recently, and what does that mean about our traditions of moral reasoning or divine guidance? Why do our scriptures condone slavery and why did our prophets practice it? How can we venerate people and texts – the prophets, Founding Fathers, a scripture or founding document – that considered slavery valid or normal? And, if we see clear and egregious moral wrongs that those people and texts so conspicuously missed, why are we venerating or honoring them in the first place? This book is devoted to engaging and, hopefully, answering these questions, especially as pertains to the extreme case of sex slavery.

This is a book for people who want to understand how Muslims conceptualized, practiced and eventually abolished slavery in Islam. It is also a book for those interested in how traditions that venerate the past confront realizations of its profound moral failings and how they manage the crises that ensue. First, however, we look at the problem of defining exactly what slavery is and whether there is one thing we can call 'slavery' across history

(Chapter One). Then we tour how Islamic law and theology envisioned *riqq*, the system of slavery in Islamic law (Chapter Two), as well as how Muslims from Senegal to Sumatra actually practiced, purchased and employed various forms of servile labor (Chapter Three). Then we tackle the heart of what I term the 'Slavery Conundrum' (Chapter Four) before turning to Muslim debates over ending slavery and evaluating their convincingness (Chapters Five and Six). Finally, we address the painful topic of slave-concubinage in a concluding discussion (Chapter Seven).

As I was writing this book, my response to the routine social prompt of 'So what are you working on?' elicited varied reactions. My observation has been that most people – Muslims and non-Muslims – do not like talking about slavery. This is understandable. Some, including many academics, feel strongly that acknowledging – let along studying – the moral problems presented by it is unnecessary. I believe that what they mean is that the subject makes them uncomfortable. People are not uncomfortable with settled issues. They are uncomfortable when they sense that a thin layer of social consensus on a divisive and painful topic is being disturbed. Whether for Muslims or Americans (or both), the issues of slavery and the moral problem it presents lurk just below the surface and rear their heads again and again. As a brief scan of the media in the US reveals, they are not going away any time soon. For Muslims, ISIS made addressing the place of *riqq* in Islamic scripture and law essential. As Kecia Ali wrote, ISIS laid bare 'the untenable nature' of Muslims burying their heads in the sand and refusing to come to terms with slavery in Islam.[4] We cannot pretend it is not part of our religion; it is present in the Quran we read every day in prayer. But neither can we deny our visceral certainty that slavery is repugnant. How can we make meaningful and honest sense of what seems like an obvious contradiction?

WHAT I ARGUE IN THIS BOOK

Much contemporary Western, particularly American, discourse on slavery is trapped in the Slavery Conundrum. This is the insistence that 1) slavery is an absolute evil throughout history and 2) that there are no gradations within slavery that escape this verdict. Since every major religious and philosophical tradition either justified, defended or at least tolerated some form of slavery until the early modern period, this means that the traditions of moral and spiritual authority to which many still adhere were, and are, complicit in gross moral evil. Whether among Christian theologians in the nineteenth century, Muslim scholars in the twentieth or in public discussion about America's Founding Fathers today, several common arguments have been developed to explain how we modern folk have progressed morally beyond the authorities underpinning our past. But none of these can explain why authorities endowed with profound wisdom or divine guidance supported something that was as evil a millennium ago as it is today, at least not without us drastically reducing their moral or spiritual standing.

This conundrum is easily resolved, though the resolution is an uncomfortable one. There is near uniform agreement today that slavery is wrong. But that does not mean that everything we label as 'slavery' in history was always wrong in every time and every place. Confusion over this stems from two ambiguities. First, we use the word 'slavery' to refer to a vast spectrum of dramatically different relationships of labor and control that do not merit one, uniform moral judgment. In doing so, we project a morally charged category from our own Atlantic tradition onto other epochs and societies, condemning some and exonerating others, validating the suffering of some and ignoring others.

Second, there is ambiguity in our use of the word 'wrong,' which can mean both things considered negative or harmful in some societies but not in others as well as things that are wrong in all times and circumstances. There are undoubtedly elements of harm and suffering in any position of dependency, subordination or coercion. But only in the last two centuries did a significant number of observers conclude that slavery constituted a moral evil weighty enough to call for its end as an institution. While this perception arose in some societies over three hundred years ago, it appeared elsewhere later on and in some places only much more recently. This is because some societies developed the technologies and economies of production that allowed them to dispense with coerced human labor earlier than others. Moral condemnations of slavery are thus not reflections of eternal moral realities. Rather, they are moral sentiments produced by societies reorienting and adjusting their priorities and values with changing circumstances.

Some forms of servile labor have been so severe and exploitative that major religions and philosophical systems have branded them intrinsic, absolute wrongs. Eventually this was the opinion reached about the plantation slavery of the Americas and the Atlantic slave trade that supplied it. Other historical phenomena that we also refer to conventionally as 'slavery,' however, have been much less severe and were closer to forms of wage labor than to dehumanizing domination.

The practice of *riqq* among Muslims was as diverse as the polyglot civilization that grew up around the message of Islam and which stretched across thirteen centuries from Africa to the steppes of Russia, from the Balkans to Southeast Asia. Although the practice was certainly significantly informed by the Shariah, it was also strongly shaped by existing local traditions and shifting economic forces. These could even lead the practice of *riqq* to violate the clear dictates of Islamic law, such as the prohibition on enslaving Muslims and the mistreatment of slaves. According to the theory of *riqq* in Islam, however, slaves had rights to freedom of belief, religious practice, family relations, limited property, social involvement and physical protection that were similar to other dependent classes in society, such as children and wives. This is similar to the moderate servile status that Catholic natural law philosophers considered morally acceptable, as opposed to the absolute domination that they condemned as repugnant.

The one aspect of *riqq* that is completely irreconcilable with the regnant morals of today's global West is the right of male slave owners to have sex with their female slaves, a right clearly stated in the Quran and the teachings of the Prophet. The Islamic legal tradition that Muslim jurists articulated and that Muslim judges applied, however, restricted men's rights of sexual access to wives and slave-concubines if such conduct was harmful, a characterization that was determined by the customs of the particular society in question. Although legal slavery no longer exists and should not be revived, this presents us with a worthwhile hypothetical: in theory, the incongruity between the modern primacy of consent in sexual relationships and slave-concubinage in *riqq* could be bridged by this notion of harm (*ḍarar*). In a society that considered any non-consensual sex to be per se transgressive and harmful, a male owner's right to sexual access to his female slaves would be restricted.

Muslim clerics were courageous in upholding the Islamic law on who could rightfully be enslaved and were passionately committed to Islam's exhortation to emancipate slaves at the slightest pretense. Yet it was not until they encountered European abolitionism in the mid-nineteenth century that they considered eliminating *riqq* as an institution. Since then, Muslim scholars and intellectuals have developed a range of arguments, some mirroring Christian abolitionists, for justifying ending a practice that God and His prophet had allowed. One feeble claim was that Islam had never actually allowed slavery, while a second stronger one argued that banning slavery outright would have been impossible in the Prophet's day, so God set Muslims on the path to do so gradually. A third line of reasoning, which I find the most convincing, was that the Shariah, that ideal of God's law in Islam, had always aimed at maximizing emancipation. In the modern period, this goal can best be achieved by joining efforts to eliminate all forms of enslavement. This argument is particularly compelling because the same anti-slavery sentiment that gradually won over hearts and minds in the West has also become a sincere conviction among many, if not most, Muslims worldwide. Other Muslim scholars have suggested that *riqq* is impermissible today because the circumstances under which it had been allowed no longer apply in our multilateral world order. Still others defend *riqq* as a practice that Muslim states might legitimately choose to suspend at present but that could be brought back into operation in the future.

APOLOGY FOR SLAVERY?

Some might object to my referring to slavery as a conundrum: it's not a conundrum, it's evil, pure and simple, and any push to prolong the discussion is a move to defend it. This objection is understandable, but it misses the point. Slavery is not a conundrum because *we* feel some conflict about slavery's moral standing. I am prepared to assume that anyone reading this book feels slavery is evil. It is a conundrum because voices we still consider either infallible, venerable or authoritative all either condoned or defended it.

Slavery is an extremely sensitive topic. Applying a scholarly lens to any subject that has resulted in deep trauma and human suffering is inherently fraught. This is particularly true when the institution in question still shapes many of the parameters of injustice in a society, as is the case with slavery in the US and, indeed, with the legacy of slavery in Muslim countries like Mauritania. Beyond this, however, the study of slavery is structurally sensitive because the present abolitionist consensus – namely that slavery is a profound moral evil in all its forms and must be vanquished from the earth – was hard won. The millennia-old pro-slavery consensus that it eventually overcame had defended the institution by pointing out its internal diversity (with 'benign' slavery opposed to 'absolute' types), its ubiquity in human history and its overwhelming embrace in the loftiest towers of religious authority and moral philosophy. To defeat this colossal edifice, abolitionists had to show that none of this mattered. They did so by arguing that *all* slavery, anywhere, was so evil that no defense of it could be stomached.

Yet when historians or social scientists today study the history of slavery either in one region or globally, they inevitably uncover those same threads that defenders of slavery had cited before: that 'slavery' is an extremely diverse phenomenon, that some of its manifestations are more dramatic or severe than others, and that the finest minds and most enlightened hearts had offered a wide variety of explanations and justifications for it. In studying slavery, they seem to be unintentionally exhuming the demons that abolitionists had vanquished and placing the abolitionist consensus at risk.

All this has resulted in an unusual feature of scholarly discourse on slavery. Unlike almost any other subject I know of, scholars writing on slavery are expected to pause at some point to reaffirm slavery's moral abhorrence.[5] Not to do so, to raise the possible mildness of some instances of slavery, or, worst of all, to raise even the possibility of moral relativism in judging it, are all likely to be branded as an apology for slavery.[6]

I think this obscures a crucial point. The tremendous diversity of historical phenomena we call 'slavery' and the moral, philosophical and religious approval they enjoyed for the entirety of human history until the nineteenth century are not minor points that can be dismissed with an enlightened sigh about the backwardness of past generations. They are gigantic, indisputable and still influential realities. In the broad scope of humanity's experience, they are far more imposing than the comparatively upstart consensus that all slavery is evil. It should not be suspect to point this out, since this is fairly obvious to anyone who takes even a cursory look into history or premodern literature and philosophy.

The study of history is inherently destabilizing. The evil of slavery is a certainty for us. But such certainties of the present are threatened by the study of history precisely because it gives them a past. Our certainties are such because we convince ourselves either that those truths are self-evident and always have been, or that our latest attainment of moral progress deserves our full confidence. History shows that neither is the case. If other people were as certain as we are, just about other things, then our own certainties shrink in significance. And the fear that one day other certainties will take their place looms in the peripheries of our conscience. When a certainty of our present is not just something obvious to our minds but felt deeply in our hearts and souls, then historicizing it – making it part of history instead of either outside of history or its culmination – is all the more alarming.

What is even more morally disconcerting is that even our assessments of the past change with changing times. What we see when we look into the well of history is largely a reflection of ourselves, our beliefs, our categories and our assumptions. In his study of how classical Rome has been studied in the West, Niall McKeown shows how modern scholarship on Roman slavery has repeatedly been shaped just as much by whatever the social orthodoxies are at the time as by the historical evidence. 'Each generation seems to have produced interpretations that generally fitted their wider ethical and social beliefs,' he observes, and each interpretation is just as likely to be wrong as the next.[7]

One response to all this would simply be to say that all pro-slavery texts, traditions and individuals were simply wrong – horribly wrong – on the issue, and that any attempt to make excuses for them is an apology for slavery. Again, such an objection is orthogonal to the subject of this book. If one has even a modicum of esteem for these religious and philosophical traditions, one still has to explain how they could have allowed or defended something that deserves nothing more than the guillotine of total condemnation. If we still value and respect these texts and traditions, then refusing to discuss their affirmation of slavery is not 'moving on.' It is ignoring an enormous moral elephant in the room. Trying to answer these challenges is not an apology for slavery. It is recognizing a reality. Indeed, I think that these facts place a burden of proof on us as Westerners, Christians, Muslims, Jews, etc., to explain how those sources and traditions that we still consider morally authoritative, whether the Bible, the Quran, Aristotle, Buddhist scriptures, St. Augustine, Montesquieu, Locke and so on all condoned slavery in one form or another.

But can't we just conclude that the Bible, Quran, Aristotle, etc., were wrong on slavery but still have much else to offer us? We could certainly conclude that, but do we usually take moral, legal or spiritual advice from those who support slavery? Whatever the answer we come up with, the questions need to be asked and discussed. As I make clear in this book, I believe slavery is wrong. What interests me here is explaining how almost all moral authorities in human history thought it was right, and what this means for our view of history, moral philosophy and theology.

POWER AND THE STUDY OF SLAVERY

Beyond the sensitivity inherent in Americans discussing the history of slavery, this endeavor pushes us onto the charged axes of several longstanding disputes. These include the power dynamics involved in studying the post-colonial world as well as the pervasive knot of problems around race. To speak about the history of the Atlantic slave trade is inevitably to make or to be seen to make an assignment of responsibility. The study of the history of the slave trade remains locked in an explicit or implicit debate over who is to blame. As far back as John Locke (d. 1704), African internal warfare and enslavement of other Africans was used to justify the European trade in African slaves.[8] So when Western historians write about the (undeniable) role of African states and agents in the transatlantic slave trade, some scholars from the post-colonial world have read this as attempting to saddle non-Europeans with the burden of European sin.[9]

Slavery and Western-led abolition have long been intertwined with colonialism and the debates around power politics, security and demography that have followed. The long history of Western scholarship and governments projecting an image of barbarity onto the 'Eastern' or 'African' other as part of the construction of Western identity, or to justify colonial conquest, has greatly complicated making anything approaching objective assessment of the nature of slaver(ies) in the non-West. Since the 1970s, many Western scholars of Middle East and Islamic history have worried that Western disapproval of slavery in those traditions might be a continuation of colonial powers using the cause of slavery as a reason/excuse for intervention in native affairs. With Islamophobia proliferating in the West in recent decades, some scholars sincerely trying to combat inaccurate stereotypes of Muslims as regressive and dangerous might feel compelled to portray slavery in the Islamic world as 'not that bad.' Ironically, going back to the 1400s, an assortment of Europeans and Americans have painted a benign image of slavery in the Muslim world as well as in other African and Asian societies. Sometimes this was because they simply found this to be the case. But it often served other agendas. It fended off abolitionist objections to powerful overseas commercial or political interests in slave-holding regions by showing that slavery there was tolerable, or that the conditions of slaves in colonial holdings merited no real concern.[10]

If the production of knowledge is an exercise of power, then there are few subjects more susceptible to the subjectivities this involves than the study of slavery. Some readers might object (as some already have) that it is not appropriate for a white person (such as me) to write a book like this on slavery because I cannot possibly understand slavery's dehumanizing trauma. They might add that insisting on investigating the moral and theological dimensions of slavery rather than focusing on the suffering it has caused is a product of my privilege.

All of this is completely correct. I am a white, American male, who grew up in Chevy Chase, Maryland, in the 1990s, and I have enjoyed immense privilege in my life. Even the Islamophobia I have suffered has been the luxury brand. As I consider the many times in this book that I have used 'we' in a sentence, an undeniable theme emerges. Sometimes 'we' is Muslims today, sometimes it means (white?) Americans, and sometimes (white?) Westerners more generally. But 'we' are always the slavers, the repentant and reformed masters. This is an ineluctable failing of this book and of my voice. That I set about writing this book not as a white American examining slavery in US history but as a Muslim seeking an answer to the moral challenge that slavery presents to *my* religion might make little difference. As a white American man and a Muslim, I am twofold the slaver. I cannot exit my race or religion or set them aside, and neither is a pass for the historical failings of the other. I suppose I can only leave this book to stand or fall on its merits. Regarding slavery in the Americas, as a person who has benefited from the expropriated land, lives and labor of millions of Native Americans and Africans (many of whom were Muslims), it is the responsibility of me and others like me to pay reparations to their descendants (does this mean Muslims must pay reparations? This is a subject for another day).[11]

BLACKNESS, WHITENESS AND SLAVERY

Before a battle between Arabs from the mountains of Yemen and an Ethiopian army on Yemen's Red Sea coast in the mid-1000s CE, the Arab general addressed his troops. The Arabs in the coastal region had produced so many children by African slave women over the years, he said, that 'black skin subsumes both free and slave.' The only way to distinguish between Ethiopian and Arab combatants was by language, he warned.[12] The many layers folded into this comment will only be fully appreciated in later chapters, but among them is the key Islamic legal principle that children born of free fathers and slave-concubine mothers are born free and with full social standing. As a result, color did not *determine* servile status. But there are other subtle and unpleasant strata here as well. The general, an Arab from the mountains, is demeaning the Arabs of the coastal plain for becoming Black themselves.

The Prophet Muhammad had been very clear about discrimination, arrogance or denigrating others based on race. When one of his followers insulted a respected Ethiopian Muslim for his ancestry, the Prophet became irate. 'By Him who sent down the book upon Muhammad, no one has any virtue over anyone else except by deeds,' he inveighed.[13] During his farewell sermon, the Prophet preached that the Lord of mankind was one and that humanity's ancestor was one, so no race or nation could be better than any other except through piety (*taqwā*).[14] Throughout history, Muslims have regularly forgotten this foundational lesson. In this book I address anti-Black sentiments in Islamic civilization and their links to slavery and its justifications, but here at the beginning it is important to note that such racism is totally illegitimate in the religion of Islam.

The question of race does raise an important terminological choice. Clearly people have different skin colors. A person picked at random from Norway and a person picked at random from the Congo will probably look very different, and it is not surprising that one might draw on the vocabulary of lightness and darkness to describe their comparative features. This so far is a neutral process. But white/black and light/dark have also been synonymous with judgments about purity/pollution and good/evil in many civilizations, so employing a language of color rarely stays neutral for long.

Differences in skin tone and features exist, but groupings based on color are inevitably social constructs. They are thus products of power relations and laden with judgments of value, differing between cultures. Though in the US anyone with *any* of the phenotypical features common to Sub-Saharan Africa is commonly categorized as 'black,' that categorization is the product of centuries of social, economic and political construction, intimately bound to and shaped by the history of slavery in North America. In Brazil, racial groupings around the colors of white (*branca*), brown (*parda*) and black (*preta*) function very differently due to how the production of Brazilian cultural memory and identity has incorporated racial mixing and color blending much more than the US has.[15]

America is not the first society or civilization to have a construction of 'Blackness.' As Abdullah Hamid Ali has shown, the conception of 'Blackness' (and Whiteness) had its own history in Islamic thought. Unlike the simplistic regime of race in the US, color was not the only rubric under which the populations of Sub-Saharan Africa were categorized by Arab-Islamic high culture nor was it employed in binary terms. In medieval Islamic discourse from the Mediterranean to India, *Zanj* were people from the coast and interior of east Africa, *Habash* were the inhabitants of Ethiopia and the Horn of Africa, while *Sud* (Blacks) referred more generically to all the peoples of the Sahel region and south.[16] Medieval Muslims in the Mediterranean Middle East used a variety of colors to describe Sub-Saharan Africans, including blue, green and purple. Even in nineteenth-century Egypt, slaves being brought to market from Sub-Saharan Africa were described as either 'black,' 'brown' or 'Ethiopian.'[17] The famous Moroccan traveler Ibn Battuta (d. *circa* 1370) was typical when, voyaging through modern-day Mali and Niger, he constantly referred to Muslims from north of the Sahara as 'whites.' Because when we are discussing the phenotype of peoples from south of the Sahara in this book we are almost inevitably viewing them from either the perspective of an American construction of race or an Arab-Islamic one, we will use capital letters to describe them: Black Africans and the physical feature of Blackness.[18]

1

Does 'Slavery' Exist?
The Problem of Definition

Auda: The Arabs? What tribe is that?
Lawrence: They're a tribe of slaves. They serve the Turks.
Auda: Well, they are nothing to me.

Lawrence of Arabia (1962)

So goes the fictionalized conversation between the historical figures T. E. Lawrence and Auda Abu Tayi, the great Arab chieftain. A similar cinematic pronouncement was made nearly forty years later, when the protagonist of the science fiction classic *The Matrix* (1999) learns that humans are living in a computer-generated virtual reality while their bodies generate power for machines. 'You are a slave,' our hero is told, 'like everyone else, born into bondage.'[1]

These films raise an intriguing question: can one be a slave and not know it? Or, better put, is slavery in the eye of the beholder? *Ben-Hur* (1959), another blockbuster, had similarly touched on the nature of slavery. The young master Judah Ben-Hur welcomes home his family's skilled old slave, Simonides. 'My life belongs to the House of Hur,' Simonides coos sincerely before asking his master's permission for his daughter to marry. She too was Judah's property, Simonides reminds him, 'born the daughter of your slave.' 'When I inherited you,' Judah rejoins, 'I inherited a friend, not a slave.'[2] The question here is more controversial: can one be a slave and be happy about it?

In 1917, around the same time that Lawrence's admittedly absurd exchange with Auda would have taken place, the Ottoman wartime government issued a new family law. It introduced restrictions on marriage age that were unprecedented in Islamic law. A particularly outspoken and conservative Muslim jurist named Sadreddin Efendi (d. 1931) wrote a livid response. Muslims should know, he wrote, that this law would deprive them of their God-given rights under the Shariah and make them slaves (*köleler*) of the state.[3] This was an ironic complaint. Through the late 1800s, the upper administration of the Ottoman Empire had been in the hands of a bureaucratic class who were actually called 'slaves' (*kullar*).[4] But these 'slave' bureaucrats were 'slaves' in name only. Their title was merely a vestige of earlier times, when the master–slave relationship had been how the Ottoman rulers expressed and maintained loyalty and sovereignty. In fact, earlier Ottoman political writings had often used the phrase *kul* (slave) to convey what European authors after the sixteenth century expressed as citizen or subject.[5]

The Ottoman Empire was not alone in relying on the idiom of slavery. The soldiers and administrators of China's Manchu Qing dynasty (1644–1912) were also technically slaves (*aha*) of the dynasty and proudly referred to themselves as such. By the later Qing period, the title of slave was applied to anyone of Manchu descent in imperial China. But neither Ottoman subjects nor Qing Manchus lived in any servile condition.[6] Here we face a third, thorny question about slavery: what makes one a slave? Is it a label or a reflection of one's actual conditions?

Writing at the twilight of the Victorian era, of the Ottoman and the Qing empires alike, the Irish polymath John Kells Ingram (d. 1907) complained that 'careless or rhetorical writers use the words "slave" and "slavery" in a very lax way.' Tacking this complaint to the end of his influential 1895 history of slavery, Ingram did not have in mind Ottoman or Manchu lexical laxity. He was objecting to activists in Britain who were railing against the 'subjection of women' by equating it to slavery or protesting over workers toiling as 'wage-slaves.'[7] This was preposterous, he scoffed. Neither wives nor workers were subjected to serious mistreatment.[8]

A century later, in *Fight Club* (1999), the charismatic Tyler Durden disagreed. We are all 'slaves with white collars,' he tells his disgruntled disciples in the film, laboring for a capitalist system, pacified and driven mad simultaneously by our quest to buy 'shit [we] don't need.'[9] A British labor rights activist could not have described the situation better. Ingram and Durden pose our fourth and final question: who gets to decide when the word 'slave' is used, who counts as a slave and who does not?

Slavery is the ritual dictum of power. It is the metaphor and reality of domination, subordination and dependence. In practice, the word and its trove of connected images can be applied anywhere there is an asymmetry of power. Like an incantation, it can be directed upwards in reverence to pledge loyalty and assure belonging, as Simonides did with Ben-Hur. It can be invoked to critique domination or the usurpation of control, as with Sadreddin Efendi's objections. It can be used to alert others to their own powerlessness, as in the case of Lawrence and Auda. Or it can be shouted to protest one's own exploitation, as done by the activists who so annoyed Ingram. 'Slavery' can be deployed and inverted to communicate dominance and indomitability, having right or having being wronged. The final chorus 'Rule, Britannia! Britannia, rule the waves! Britons never, never, never shall be slaves' still reverberates with imperial pride. But it was first sung in 1740 in artistic opposition to the misguided policies of Britain's own government.[10] It became the rallying cry of an empire that helped bring the power imbalance of global slavery to its acme all while celebrating the imperial nation's impunity from subservience.

From ancient times through the heyday of the British Empire, the power of slavery was the very undeniability of domination and control. Yet before 'Rule, Britannia!' was a century old, influential voices within the British elite had turned 'slavery' from an index of power to a signifier of the ultimate injustice. Since the tipping point into abolition in the mid-nineteenth century, the power of 'slavery' has been the moral force of the word. It comes not from exploiting labor but from labeling specific practices and institutions with the mark of moral barbarism. Whoever controls its application determines whose suffering and subjugation matters enough to merit the brand of absolute moral condemnation that 'slavery' carries.

As our above examples from films, legal writing and social criticism all show, 'slavery' is a word that is easy to use but very hard to define. This difficulty stems from the very function and history of the word itself. For many centuries defining slavery was unimportant. When a person or a group manifestly dominated another person or group, there was little need to define what was happening. Definitions of slavery in Roman law were both brief and sparse because Roman jurists assumed it was an obvious reality that needed only to have its details described at times. It did not need to be theorized.[11] Similarly, as far as I know, there are no legal definitions of slavery offered by Muslim jurists within the first three centuries of Islam.[12] Defining 'slavery' becomes important only when the reality of its domination begins chaffing at important moral or, in the Islamic case, theological principles. It is contested only when the word acquires a moral force separate from the reality of domination, as occurred after the victory of abolitionism in the nineteenth century. Since then, to invoke 'slavery,' to call something 'slavery,' is to make a powerful moral claim about the nature of reality. We cannot understand this without investigating what lies behind and within this process of definition and contestation.

THE MAIN ARGUMENT

In this chapter I argue that there is no definition of slavery that covers everything we scholars in the West want to call slavery while excluding those things we do not want to call slavery. This is because the notion of 'slavery' as a transhistorical, global reality spanning centuries and civilizations is a projection of Western scholarship, which often seeks to fit the great variety of human experiences into its own categories, along with their accompanying judgments. The contemporary notion of 'modern-day' slavery is ethically admirable and aids the present and future pursuit of justice. But when projected backwards into history, its shadow is anachronistically all-encompassing. And its use in the present suffers from the same political biases and blindness as the study of slavery in the transhistorical past.

This does not mean, of course, that slavery did not or does not exist. Slavery as we understand it existed in Western civilization, and institutions similar to it have existed elsewhere. There have been in various times and places in history phenomena that have borne some degree or another of similarity to what we understand as slavery. But though they might resemble our understanding of slavery, they were not by any means the same thing. To place them in a category we have shaped according to our own historical memory and to brand them with the same moral judgment is inaccurate and imposing. More importantly, deploying the term 'slavery' is an eminently political act, meaning that it turns on certain communities deciding whose suffering or exploitation is worth marking out as unconscionable, whose exploitation or abuses are called out and whose remain anonymous.

DEFINITION: A CREATIVE PROCESS

The other day my wife asked me if I had cleaned the tables in the kitchen. I responded, 'What do you mean by tables?' (we don't have tables in our kitchen). 'The countertops,' she replied with a smile. 'Well, that depends what you mean by "cleaned",' I answered, deploying air quotes. That was not a wise response.

This short exchange presented two challenges. First, since my wife grew up speaking Arabic at home, sometimes when she talks about domestic matters she translates in her head from Arabic into English. The Arabic dialect she grew up speaking does not have a distinct word for countertop. It is just a 'table' (*ṭāwila*). So, when I asked her to define what she meant by that, she had to reconsider the linguistic equation that had gone through her head. '*Tawila* = table' had to be refined (and redefined) as '*tawila in this case* = countertop.' This is an instance of **nominal definition**, or defining *words* and what they mean, which we do when we write dictionaries but also when we translate from one language to another. As the case of *tawila*/countertop shows, there is often not a one-to-one equivalency between words in different languages. This has consequences. If my wife had asked me to clean all the 'tables' in the house before guests came over, I would not have understood that as applying to countertops. It would mean tables in the dining room, etc.

The second challenge in this exchange was a matter of **real definition**, or of defining things that we consider to be real outside of language and expression, either in the sense of a tangible, material reality or in the sense of a real concept or idea. Certainly, languages differ in their words for 'clean.' But that was not what was at issue in my second question or my wife's distinct displeasure with it. The issue was that my definition of 'clean' for kitchen counters is that all the food, etc., has been put away and that there are no visible spills or noticeable chunks of food on the countertops. For my wife, 'clean' countertops have been sprayed with cleaner and wiped down. My wife was (justifiably) annoyed by my response because this was not a problem of translation. For her 'cleanliness' was a reality that should be grasped by any reasonable, well-adjusted person.

Yet, of course, 'cleanliness' is not a distinct reality, existing 'out there' in the world and graspable by all. It is a concept defined by groups of people and, more appropriately, by different cultures and subcultures. American travelers in Japan find that US standards for a 'clean' restaurant bathroom would mortify Japanese diners, just as Americans visiting Egypt are shocked by Egyptian standards for 'clean' countertops (dust from the desert accumulates so quickly in Egypt that in all but hermetically sealed households a surface will build up a noticeable layer of dust after just a few hours).

The importance of defining words and concepts is not just a domestic or everyday matter. It also forms the first step in academic interaction or even higher-register informal discussions. Professors teaching a class on 'Islamic law' or 'love in English literature' will instinctively begin the first day of class by trying to offer or explore 'what we mean by' law or love. This notion that any investigation of a subject should begin by defining it goes back at least as far as Aristotle (d. 322 BCE) in the Western and Islamic traditions and Confucius (d. *circa* 500 BCE) in the East, and its priority has been consistently reaffirmed ever since.

But what are we really doing when we define things? Often, we engage in nominal definition for pure procedural practicality. We define things so that others know what we mean when we use a word. My wife explained to me what she meant by tables. Sometimes we might do so because we intend to use a word differently from how it is used in regular conversation.

Defining has more important and consequential dimensions as well. Going back as far as Aristotle, Western and Islamic philosophers alike have understood defining things as the process of identifying and grasping their essential natures as well as their contours and boundaries.[13] On the first day of class, the professor is not defining 'love' just so that everyone knows how the word is going to be used in class discussions. What the professor is trying to do is to move beyond our casual use of the term and pin down some crucial reality about the very essence of the concept of love, a concept that most people today understand to be a reality existing in our world.

Behind this whole process of definition is a perennial debate about the nature of reality in both Western, Islamic and even East Asian philosophies. Do the things, relationships and ideas we identify around us *really exist*, 'out there' in the world? Or do we conjure up their existence in our collective minds, as part of ordering the amorphous mass of reality around us? Are naming and defining merely acts of description or also acts of creation? In philosophy, this is often called the dichotomy between Realism (the theory that categories, ideas, etc., really do have an existence 'out there,' separate from our minds and cultures) and Nominalism (the claim that only particular things exist; categories, theories and ideas are all conjured up in our collective minds as an act of ordering the particulars around us). Realism is often associated with Plato (d. 347 BCE) and the Christian tradition of Augustine (d. 430 CE), who held that our material world is just a reflection of a higher realm of forms. Nominalism is advocated by the medieval scholars William of Ockham (d. 1347), Lorenzo Valla (d. 1457) and Ibn Taymiyya (d. 1328).

Obsessing over the Realism/Nominalism question can be a distraction. In fact, it can quickly yank the rug from under our feet and drop us into a rabbit hole. Try *really* pondering whether any important idea that comes to mind really, actually exists. Does 'freedom' exist? If human beings disappeared, would there still be 'freedom'? Indeed, try it in the scientific realm: does the 'Law of Gravity' really exist, as a law out there in the universe? Or is it just a heuristic, an observation that happens to (so far) accurately describe the behavior of objects?

Yet the Realism/Nominalism question has its uses. It asks us to consider whether whatever we are talking about is a reality undisputedly 'out there' in the world or something we have conjured into existence and projected as an idea or category on the world around us. It can be hard to tell the difference, a fact which reveals how much culture defines reality. Cancer is clearly a disease that exists apart from any culture, language or worldview. Cells malfunction, multiply out of control and form harmful tumors. It can be measured and detected. Pharaohs died of cancer over three millennia ago, and people die of it today.[14] But does the illness of depression 'exist' in a similar way? It is certainly treated as a material reality by medical professionals in most modern societies, thought to be caused by chemical imbalances in the brain.[15] But opinion among Americans is split over whether depression is an objective illness or just a function of personal weakness or self-indulgence.[16] How confident can we be saying that a historical figure like Alexander the Great or Martin Luther suffered from a mental illness like depression? Did those illnesses 'exist' back then?

Among certain social circles in the West, questioning whether depression exists outside of our own social conceptions would be met with opprobrium. But moving farther afield, the American Psychiatric Association recognizes the existence of certain 'culturally bound syndromes,' or illnesses that seem only to exist in specific cultures. These include *taijin kyofusho*, 'a Japanese syndrome of intense fear of offending others through bodily appearance or function' that is often permanently incapacitating.[17] This illness really 'exists' in Japanese culture. It does not in other cultures and languages.

The question becomes more complicated when applied to relationships or ideas. Looking at the biological relationship between a mother and the child she gives birth to, it seems uncontroversial to point to it and call it 'motherhood.' But what about a woman and her adopted child? Here it is the care, commitment and bond between the two that makes the relationship, not a material or biological reality. Would that be understood as 'motherhood' in all cultures? In Anglo-Saxon cultures, the relationship between a boy and his mother's brother is simply the ordinary family one of 'nephew/uncle.' But in matrilineal societies like that of the Trobriand Islands, it takes over many of the roles of the father/son relationship in most cultures.[18] If a Trobriand Islander with no idea about other cultures traveled to London and met a family there, the relationship he perceived as existing between an English boy and his uncle would exist only in the Trobriander's mind, not for anyone else. Beyond the relationship between things or people that we can see or sense around us, this question enters its ultimate complexity when applied to abstract ideas like freedom, democracy, good and evil.

Returning to definition, real definition can similarly involve things that seem to have undisputed, demonstrable existences and boundaries. If we look at a series of smallish, furry, carnivorous quadrupeds that walk on their toes (digitigrade), pant to cool themselves, and have snouts and extended ears, we might decide that, despite being different sizes and colors, they make up a family called Canidae (dogs). We could note that another set of animals are very similar, but they are larger, have longer noses, walk on four open feet (plantigrade) and are generally omnivorous. We could call this family Ursidae (bears). There are tangible and measurable realities being described here. Each of these families share significant genetic similarities within themselves and differences between each other. Canidae and Ursidae cannot interbreed with one another.

Yet what we are doing in defining these two families is not simply trying to understand the essential features of a thing, concrete and 'out there' in the world. We have moved from observing and comprehending myriad individual creatures to concluding that some of them should be grouped together into something we have decided to call a species, then that lots of these species can be grouped into a larger collection that we have called a genus, and then into families like Canidae, etc. This action of defining dogs (Canidae) and bears (Ursidae) is actually a process of **abstraction**, or drawing out a conceptual form or category from particulars.[19]

Real definition is thus often not the act of describing the essential nature of something that exists. It is itself an existential act, the act of creating an abstraction and asserting that this abstract concept, category or idea *exists*.

In the case of bears and dogs, to a great extent we have imposed this classification on an external reality that cares nothing for our words and definitions. Species of dog and bear do not organize their lives or interact with one another based on our taxonomies, and there are some species that do not fit very well into any group. Zoologists define species as sharing a gene pool, to the extent that, generally, if they breed with another species the offspring will be weak or infertile. But the countless crossbreeds of dogs and occasionally bears shows that this is not always a real division that exists in nature.[20] It is more a line we have drawn with some degree of arbitrariness to order our world. Gene pools are clumps on a continuum that has no definitive lines dividing it into segments. We draw those lines ourselves.

This existentially creative element of definition is even clearer in the case of something less material. When a Japanese psychiatrist says *taijin kyofusho* is 'a syndrome of intense fear of offending others through bodily appearance or function,' what they are really saying is, 'An illness called *taijin kyofusho* really exists, and it is characterized by an intense fear of . . . etc.'[21] Moreover, such a statement also brings with it an evaluative element. Defining *taijin kyofusho* is also a statement about how we should feel about it; it's an illness, so we should be concerned or feel informed of a potential malady. By contrast, when someone defines democracy, most people today feel a sense of approval and aspiration to that ideal.

DEFINITION TO DISCOURSE: A POLITICAL PROCESS

When defining concepts or categories, we see ourselves as discovering and explaining the essence of a real thing, 'out there' in the world, and tracing its contours, including and excluding. We are often, indeed, describing crucial features of demonstrable, measurable particulars. But we are also often calling concepts and categories into existence by abstracting them from those sensible, measurable particulars. In doing so we are not only creating something that may only be an extrapolation of our own minds or cultures, we are asserting that it exists in other times, places and cultures as well. And we are also passing judgment on the value of that thing.

This is an inherently political process, since it involves asserting and managing relationships of power. This is clear if we think of the example of *taijin kyofusho*. If Japanese doctors were to assert that this was, in fact, a real illness that existed in every society and needed to be combatted, and they started combing American campuses for signs of it, we would justifiably accuse them of imposing their own, unique culturally bounded categories on others.

That defining things, even in the philosophical sense we have discussed so far, is an act of projecting *our* reality rather than merely discovering *the* reality is revealed in what nominalists like Ibn Taymiyya pointed out as the circularity involved in abstraction and definition. Abstraction is based on observing a number of particular cases and then attempting to define an abstract category or concept on the basis of what we see as their shared, essential characteristics. We then test that definition by applying it to new, particular cases. But how do we know if the definition works or not? We only know this because we already know that the test case does or does not fall under the category we are defining. For example, we can observe a selection of small, furry carnivores and abstract from them the category of 'dog.' But if we come across another such animal, we will know it is a dog without applying this abstract definition, just as we knew that there were enough similarities within the individual group of animals for us to undertake an abstraction to begin with. And if we find that the definition technically applies to something we strongly feel is not a dog or does not technically apply to something we feel strongly is a dog, then we are liable either to adjust the definition to fit the new case or ignore the definition entirely.

So what purpose is definition actually serving? As Ibn Taymiyya notes, it does not seem to introduce any new knowledge.[22] The founding father of definition, Aristotle, defined definition itself as the process of identifying a thing's essence. But, ironically, he could only define essence as what is yielded by definition.[23] What is 'out there,' and how we define it, already exists in our minds. Abstraction and definition are not neutral or objective processes of discovering knowledge. They are more akin to rituals lending scholarly cover to assertions made by a particular viewpoint about the nature of reality.

Although we think of ourselves as defining concepts or categories by observing a selection of particulars and then abstracting from them a definition of that concept or category, we already know whether a new particular case should fall under the definition or not, and we adjust our definition accordingly. What we are really doing is not moving from the concrete realm of particulars up to the realm of abstract definition. We are really just grouping together particulars based on analogies – bundles of similarities we have noticed between particulars – to realities we already know.

Scholars have proposed that one way to avoid this circularity is to test a definition by inverting it: what is a small, carnivorous mammal with digitigrade feet, extended ears, a snout and which pants to cool itself? It's a dog. But this test of a definition produced by abstraction is only guaranteed to work in the abstract. It fails once a test case is not actually analogous to what we already know to be the core of the definition. Some cases are trivial. According to the scientific definition of fruits and vegetables, tomatoes are a fruit and bananas are a berry.[24] We are happy to leave that definition to scientists, because we all know that, for all intents and purposes, tomatoes are vegetables and bananas are . . . well, they're whatever bananas are.

Terrorism and its definition provide a more provocative demonstration. A common definition of terrorism (there is no agreed upon definition), similar to those used by the US government, is that it is the use or threat of violence by non-state actors against non-combatants for an ideological cause.[25] We can test our definition by inverting it: what is 'an act of violence by non-state actors against non-combatants for an ideological cause'? It's terrorism. That seems obvious enough, and the abstraction seems accurate. Except, as in the case of tomatoes, when it is not.

In 2015 Canadian police foiled the plot of several young, white Canadians to open fire in a crowd. When asked if law enforcement considered this an attempted act of terrorism, a police spokesman replied that these were individuals who 'had some beliefs and were willing to carry out violent acts against citizens' but that it was not terrorism. 'It's not culturally based,' he explained.[26] The next day Canada's Justice Minister reiterated this point: 'The attack does not appear to have been culturally motivated, therefore [it's] not linked to terrorism.'[27] In 2010 an American man seeking to strike a blow against government tyranny crashed his plane into an IRS building. When a government spokesperson announced that the attack was not terrorism, experts objected that this did indeed fit the standard definitions of terrorism. A Fox News anchor interjected to interpret the comment for the audience: 'This does not appear to be terrorism *in any way that that word is conventionally understood*' (emphasis mine).[28]

So why are definitions of terrorism as an abstract concept failing when applied to situations they should fit? Because the test for the 'correct' definition of terrorism is not whether it encompasses the essence of some external reality, an abstraction 'out there' in the world. Terrorism is a word that *we* have shaped and deployed. It is a category *we* have called into existence. The definition of terrorism is correct if, and only if, it corresponds to *what we mean* by terrorism and how *we* use the word, as the Canadian Minister of Justice, the US Department of Homeland Security and the Fox anchor showed. Even if we come up with a well-crafted definition for the abstract category of terrorism, it is whether a particular incident strikes our speech community as 'terrorism,' not whether it fits under our abstract definition, that ultimately governs how we label it.

'We' think of terrorism as a bundle of associated features, and 'we' identify something as terrorism when it is analogous to what 'we' have dubbed terrorism in the past. Scholarly definitions of terrorism, of which there are more than 109 by one count, are all abstractions.[29] They make no mention of the race, background, religion or culture of the actors. But when 'we' say terrorist 'we' think of non-whites and non-Christians, in short, not *real* Westerners.[30] Abstraction here is supposed to discover or inaugurate a category that transcends particular interests or loyalties. But definition carries with it an evaluation. And, as some scholars of terrorism have cynically observed, when 'we' think of terrorism what we really mean is 'violence of which we do not approve,'[31] or certainly violence done by people of whom we do not approve.

The act of assertion embodied in abstraction and definition is a preliminary step in a larger process, one by which we give shape and features to our reality. They form part of what Michel Foucault (d. 1984) and others have described as **discourses**, or those constellations of words, terms, propositions and maxims that form our thought and intellectual cultures. These discourses make up the reality that we 'know' around us. They are the background of our minds.[32] This is not a neutral process. Reality is made by powerful and dominant forces and interests. Terrorism as a defined concept makes up terrorism discourse, which is used to condemn and delegitimize events and actors. Terrorist is an eminently political label, used to draw lines, exclude and vilify. Governments and policy makers molded the term for just this purpose.[33] Of course, this does not mean that a violent act done by a 'terrorist' is fabricated or did not really occur, any less than an animal we call a dog does not exist simply because the category of dog is something that we have made up. But that we have a category called terrorism, with its own loaded meaning and purpose, and that we apply it to certain things and not others, is a reality we have manufactured.

DEFINING \ˈSLĀ-V(Ə-)RĒ\: WE KNOW IT WHEN WE SEE IT

Why discuss definition, Realism vs. Nominalism, dogs and terrorism in a book on slavery? Because it is with those words and categories that seem most basic that we are least aware that in using them we are constructing and shaping a reality that we expect others to recognize. In his effort to define hardcore pornography, American Supreme Court Justice Potter Stewart famously said, 'I know it when I see it.'[34] This epigram is not uncommonly invoked by scholars of terrorism to encapsulate the chronic problem of definition they face. It applies equally in the study of slavery.

There are few words in use today more provocative and loaded than terrorism. Slavery is one of them, and it has remained peerlessly fraught and upsetting for nearly two centuries. And, like the study of terrorism, the study of slavery has stumbled again and again on the problem of defining the term at its very center. As the leading scholar of slavery in Western civilization, David Brion Davis, observed, 'The more we learn about slavery, the more difficulty we have defining it.'[35]

This observation seems a straightforward recognition of a scholarly challenge. But, in light of our discussion of abstraction-as-creative-act and discourse formation, it conceals the circularity we noted above. If we cannot effectively define slavery, how do we know what constitutes slavery so that we know what we should look at when trying to define slavery? Try replacing 'slavery' with 'dogs': the more we learn about the family Canidae, the more difficulty we have defining it. But we already know what dogs are. That's how we know what animals belong in the group we are trying to produce an abstract definition for. Like dogs, we recognize the phenomena that we take into consideration when trying to define slavery because they look like what *we* think slavery is. So the study of slavery as a supposedly global, transhistorical phenomenon is really the study of things that look like slavery *to us*. This circularity was acknowledged by another leading scholar of slavery in the Atlantic world. Joseph C. Miller remarked that one of the biggest challenges facing historians and anthropologists interested in slavery is whether there is even some single institution of slavery that exists across time and space that they can study.[36] Circularity again rears its head. If there is not some transhistorical phenomenon of slavery, then what exactly is slavery studies studying?

Here the analogy between the discourses of terrorism studies and slavery studies stops working. Terrorism studies is part of security studies. Its scholars might nod to the use of the word 'terror' in the context of political violence during the French Revolution or in late nineteenth-century Russia, but those are not their concerns.[37] Terrorism is an immediate threat to 'us' today. Regardless of how much effort analysts expend trying to craft a global definition for terrorism, 'we' always know it when we see it because 'it' is an immediate security concern for us.

The study of slavery as a transhistorical phenomenon is quite the opposite. It seeks to study slavery across time and geographic expanse. One scholar of African slavery, James Watson, dismissed ongoing scholarly debates over the definition of slavery by insisting that what is slavery is obvious to 'sensible people,' and that dwelling on this question would reduce his classes to 'a dry, lifeless exercise in taxonomy.'[38] We all know what we're talking about when we talk about slavery, he seems to be saying, so let's just get on with it. For Watson and many others, the study of slavery as a transhistorical, global phenomenon is premised on the notion that 'sensible people' know what slavery is and would recognize it when they see it, wherever and whenever they went. To refer to the Justice Potter/pornography analogy again, for Watson, to study slavery transhistorically is to claim that we would not just know what constitutes hardcore pornography in *our* society. **We would recognize it anywhere and at any time.**

As 'sensible people,' let's test if that is true. Would we know slavery if we saw it? Imagine that, as *Doctor Who* fans, we hitch a ride in the TARDIS, a craft that allows us to travel across space and time. Our first stop is an exotic, desert land. We visit a well-off home, where we find certain people performing domestic work while an older man sits drinking tea. Everyone has the same dark skin color. Suddenly, the lounging tea-drinker flies into a rage, shouts at a young man leaning down to speak to him and smacks him hard with a fly swatter. Another, slightly older man rushes over, receives some instructions from the man along with a number of gold coins. The seated man shouts out, 'This disappointment, I know he wishes for my death!', pointing to the man he smacked. 'But you,' he says to the man to whom he gave the coins, 'you pray for my long life.' We are eager to know who all these people are. We ask the man who had received the coins – and the praise – and he says his name is Saffron and that he is one of the 'delicate folk' in the household. He has worked in this house for five years, but he tells us that, in one year's time, he will have saved enough money to move on and start his own business. We ask about the young man who was smacked. 'Oh, that poor boy . . . he'll be here till the old man dies.'

Back in the TARDIS, we voyage on through time and space, this time to meet the powerful prime minister of an expansive empire. The prime minister enters the throne room surrounded by dozens of armed guards, and we sense the trepidation in the hushed muttering of the audience around us. One voice whispers, 'The minister is worth eighty million gold ducats.' 'He's married to the king's daughter,' remarks another. The minister and his bodyguards are all light-skinned and fair-haired. Many of those there to offer petitions and seek favor have a darker, olive complexion.

After meeting the minister we voyage on, now to a colder land where we encounter a man laboring in a large shop. He is exhausted by daily work hours that leave him little time to sleep, so we agree to take him with us. But the shopowner catches him leaving, and the man is imprisoned.

We voyage still onward in the TARDIS to a new land where, passing down the road, we see a crew of dark-skinned youths clearing brush all day in the hot sun, their legs shackled and all joined by chains. A light-skinned man watches over them with a weapon in hand.

Where has the TARDIS taken us? The first place we visited was the city of Mecca in the 1500s. The 'delicate' (*raqīq*) man Saffron was a slave in the wealthy, old man's household. He was a *ma'dhun*, meaning a trusted slave who had permission to act as an agent and representative of his master in matters such as business.[39] And he also had an agreement with his master for 'gradual self-purchase,' to buy back his freedom on installments (called a *mukātaba* contract).[40] *Raqiq* was the standard term for slave in Arabic, and epicurean names like Saffron were typical. The younger man being smacked for bad service, who was tied to the household seemingly forever, was the wealthy man's own son. The disparagement his father had heaped on him, and the praise the father had given to Saffron, were paraphrasing a famous Persian verse of poetry: 'One obedient slave is better than three hundred sons. These want their father's death, while that one wishes his lord's long life.'[41]

The second place we visited was the capital of the Ottoman Empire in 1578. The minister was Sokullu Mehmet Pasha (d. 1579, see Figure 3), the grand vizier of the empire during the time of three sultans. At the time of our visit, he had already been one of the empire's richest and most powerful men for almost two decades. He was even married to the sultan's daughter. He owned thousands of slaves. And yet he was also the slave of the sultan. He was a product of the *devshirme* system, by which Christian youths from the Balkans were taken as slaves into the sultan's service, raised as Muslims, and then groomed for high administrative or military service. They occupied the most powerful positions of government for centuries of Ottoman rule. Sokullu Mehmet was born to a wealthy provincial Serbian family in the Balkans. His guards were from the Balkans as well, also *devshirme* slaves of the sultan.[42]

The land where we met the man toiling long hours in a shop was industrial England in 1860. Although the worker was a free man, according to labor laws in England at the time, a worker who failed to show up for work was guilty of stealing from his employer. He could be tried and sentenced as a criminal, and this often occurred.[43] Finally, the last place we visited was rural Arizona in 2004, where the local sheriff was overseeing a chain gang from a juvenile prison.[44]

Setting out on our voyage, we probably had in mind some abstract definitions of slavery, in particular that slavery is owning human beings as property or depriving them of freedom. And we had in our minds a bundle of key features that mark out slavery to us, such as chains, deprivation, racial distinction and violence. Most Westerners today would probably think that the young man being smacked and the chained laborers were slaves, because we associate slavery with physical degradation, harsh labor, chains, violence and racial division. We would probably not assume the 'soft and delicate' man was a slave because he told us he would soon move to another job on his own terms, while we associate slavery with a total loss of agency, presumably for life. We would certainly not presume that the minister was a slave, since he clearly possessed immense wealth and wielded the power over life and death throughout an empire.

As 'sensible people,' then, we did not perform well. We should have been wary. The phrases 'sensible' and 'common sense' are warnings of a certain point of view seeking to impose itself unjustified on other perspectives. These words necessarily imply a particular discourse community and its standards of what is sensible, reasonable, common sense, etc. They are deployed to argue that a claim is necessarily true when it really may only be true for the speaker and like-minded folk.[45] Scholars like Watson hope to skip the question of defining slavery because, the more we scratch the surface of that word and try to define the reality we envision behind it, the more we find that our assumptions and even our words fail us. What we think we mean by slavery means little outside our own Atlantic world experience, and the moment we try to fix what slavery is as a human phenomenon we find a hall of mirrors reflecting our own assumptions back at us.

For us, the state of unfreedom, humans-as-property and degradation are bound together with the word 'slavery,' as is the element of race. But what we encountered on our journey were twin disjuncts. First, we found a disjunct between our abstract definitions of slavery and the bundle of essential features that we use as the basis for analogy when we are deciding if something is 'slavery' as we recognize it: our abstract definition of slavery applied to cases where that bundle was absent. Saffron and the Ottoman grand vizier were both 'unfree' and 'property.' But the features of degradation, powerlessness, permanence and even slaves-as-racially-darker that we associate with slavery were missing. Just as official voices could not accept the Canada and IRS attacks as terrorism even though they fit the abstract definition, Saffron and the grand vizier are not slaves in the way that we *conventionally understand the word.*

Second, we collided with another reality we found in the case of terrorism: our willingness to recognize situations as slavery cannot be separated from the way we view our own history and communities. On our voyage, the bundle of features we recognize as slavery made slaves out of people that few of us would be prepared to call slaves: the English worker and the juvenile prisoners. These aren't slaves, we would react, these are workers and prisoners. Besides, both the US and Britain had abolished slavery long before our visit, so slavery did not exist in those places.

At this point, it should be clear what we were doing when we set off on our journey. We drew on our cultural memory of the Atlantic slave trade and its Western European/Roman legal roots and abstracted certain key features from this: slavery as the absence of freedom, slavery as human-as-property, slavery as degradation and violence, slavery as tied to race.[46] We then assumed that this abstract category of slavery existed 'out there' in the world and could be identified elsewhere. But, as in the case of terrorism, we recognized slavery not on the basis of abstraction but because we saw that bundle of key features that governs our analogical thinking, what looks like slavery *to us.* And we recognized wrong.

Our hypothetical trip in the TARDIS reveals that what we would recognize as slavery is determined by our own cultural memory of what the English word \ˈslā-v(ə-)rē\ means to us. These are images familiar from *Twelve Years A Slave* (2013), *Roots* (1977) and countless other films or media. The images are seared in our mind: Black African men, women and children being seized by ruthless slave traders, torn from their homes and each other, packed like chattel into the holds of stifling slave ships, sold like cattle at auction to white plantation owners, who worked, oppressed, raped and lashed them mercilessly for the rest of their lives. Slavery in our cultural memory is the reduction of a person, against their will, to the status of property, owned by another person who had absolute right over their labor and who deprived them of the natural right to freedom and family. We assume that, like Justice Potter's pornography, we would know slavery when we saw it. But slavery is not a naturally occurring, tangible reality out there in the world. It is a category, like bears and dogs, that we have abstracted and called into existence simply because we assume that what exists within our own communal history exists beyond it as well, just as we assume that cancer or depression or motherhood do.

DEFINING SLAVERY AS STATUS OR A CONDITION

'It is impossible to define the precise degree of subjection which constitutes what is called Slavery[,] the idea of which is different in different countries.' So wrote the pioneering Scottish economic historian, John Millar (d. 1801).[47] Historians and social scientists have been vexed by the problem of defining 'slavery' since the founding of their disciplines in the eighteenth and nineteenth centuries. The reason for this is simple if viewed from our perspective of definition/abstraction and discourse formation: they have been trying to abstract definitions for something they already know, and then they end up conflicted when phenomena they encounter in other times and places either look like slavery but do not fit their abstract definitions or fit their abstract definitions but do not look like slavery. So scholars continue to hone and refine definitions in the hope that everything they see or define as slavery will eventually fit into the slavery-shaped hole in the Western mind.[48]

The result of all this is that historians and social scientists disagree over whether there is some transhistorical phenomenon called 'slavery' at all. Even within the dominant camp that says there is such a thing, there remains intense disagreement over the best definition for slavery. The only agreement seems to be that, if there is such a thing as slavery 'out there' in world history, it is astoundingly diverse. The scholar of Southeast Asia Anthony Reid described how the field of slavery studies faces the reoccurring choice between 'a category with difficult boundaries [and] a category so broad as to be almost meaningless.'[49] Either we use the word 'slavery,' which means something specific to us, or we choose broader terms like servitude, bondage or dependency, which end up netting things we do not think of as falling under the slavery rubric. If we want to find a definition that fits everything we might recognize as slavery, that definition is so vague as to be almost useless. Thus, slavery is 'the forced labor of one group by another,' according to one social science definition.[50] Sometimes these definitions uncover profound insights about the nature of what we think of as slavery. But they would also subsume things we would never call slavery. Ehud Toledano, the leading scholar of slavery in the Ottoman world, writes that slavery is best understood as 'an involuntary relationship of mutual dependence between two quite unequal partners.'[51] This is profound, but it could also describe parent–child relations. Recently the University of Bonn inaugurated a research center that tries to bypass the terminological and paradigmatic problems that have long dogged slavery studies. Its Center for Slavery and Dependency Studies seeks to move beyond the cultural and historical vocabulary of slavery and focus on exploring the spectrum of 'strong asymmetrical dependencies.'[52] This is promising, but it remains to be seen how and if it will deal with strong asymmetrical dependencies like the parent/child relationship that 'we' would not place side by side with slavery.

Moreover, there is immense diversity even among those practices and institutions that scholars have comfortably placed in the slavery column because they were labeled as such in Western history or by traditions comparable to the West (like Islam). As Toledano remarked, it is difficult to treat slavery as one definable phenomenon just within the Ottoman Empire, let alone globally (though he stresses that the varieties of slavery in the Ottoman realm differed in degree not in kind).[53] Another scholar of Ottoman slavery, Nur Sobers-Khan, has observed that slavery in Ottoman Istanbul was so diverse that it hardly makes sense to talk about slavery as a unified phenomenon even in one city, let alone in the whole Mediterranean region.[54]

On the issue of definition, the Western academic study of slavery can be divided into two broad camps. The first, exemplified by scholars like Watson and even more so by the African historian Paul Lovejoy, insists that there is a transhistorical category that we can call slavery and define with reasonable clarity. The second, exemplified by the historian Suzanne Miers (d. 2016), is skeptical of claims about a transhistorical 'slavery' and insists that things we are tempted to stamp with the uniform label of 'slavery' be understood within their own cultural contexts. Trying to find a definition for slavery globally is, to her, 'a fruitless exercise in semantics.'[55]

And yet we continue to use the word 'slavery,' whether in scare quotes or not. This is because one of the features of discourses is that they are almost impossible to escape if one wants to communicate naturally. To speak about politics, violence or security without using the word 'terrorism,' even if to contest its usage, is almost impossible. Similarly, one cannot escape using the word 'slavery' when talking about slavery studies – even if one is contesting its definition or if it exists as a reality out there in the world to begin with.[56]

So, let us set aside for a time the debate over whether slavery exists as a transhistorical category. Let us assume it does. A transhistorical definition of slavery has nonetheless proven very hard to find. Scholars have yet to agree on where to start. In the pre-modern and early modern Western and Islamic traditions, slavery was defined as a legal status, oscillating between slave-as-property and slave-as-unfree. Though many modern scholars continue to focus on these ideas, many historians, operating within a Marxist paradigm, have sought to explain slavery as an economic phenomenon: a slave must be thought of first and foremost as a source of labor, and slavery as a system of labor exploitation. Others, especially scholars of slavery in the Islamic world, have stressed that slavery is often much more of a social phenomenon: slavery is a way of structuring and building relationships. Between these two poles, anthropologists, sociologists and many historians of slavery in various contexts have coalesced around either relationship or condition as the key identifying features of slavery, either slave-as-marginal figure/family-less outsider, or slave-as-object-of-violent-coercion.[57] Historians have also stressed that slavery functions differently depending on its scale and importance in a society or economy. The famous scholar of Classical history, M. I. Finley, noted the difference between slave societies like the American South, where slavery was economically and socially fundamental, and mere societies with slaves, like the Near East.[58]

Let's now examine the two main avenues of thought in defining slavery, the first the idea of slavery as legal status (unfree, property), and the second the idea of slavery as a relationship or condition.

SLAVERY AS UNFREEDOM

We usually think of slavery as something that exists in a dichotomy with freedom. Slaves are people who are not free. If we think of the household we visited in Mecca, however, who was free there? The son in the household was technically free, but he depended on his father for his livelihood and standing and had to obey him or face his anger. If he fled his home to get away, he would be ostracized by all those he knew and loved. The man's slave, Saffron, meanwhile, had time off to earn his own money and would soon be free of his master. What does it mean to be free, and how do we evaluate that?

The notion of slavery as depriving someone of freedom is rooted in the Roman legal tradition and has been hugely influential in both Western and Islamic civilization.[59] As Aristotle mentioned and Justinian's (d. 565) codification of Roman law explained, a free person exists in that natural state 'enjoyed by each one to do as he pleases, unless prevented by force or by law.' A slave, by contrast, is a person 'subjected to the authority of another, contrary to nature.'[60] (It is important to note that by 'contrary to nature' Roman jurists meant that slavery was not the default state of affairs, not that it was morally wrong. We will discuss this at length in Chapter Four.)

In the Quran, the dichotomy of master (*rabb*) and slave (*ʿabd*) is fundamental to the revelation's articulation of the relationship between God and man. Within human society the distinction was replicated in the dichotomous hierarchy of free (*ḥurr*) and slave (*ʿabd, raqīq*). In Islamic civilization, 'free' and 'slave' defined each other through their differences, with free basically meaning 'not slave' and slave meaning 'not free.'[61] In the formative period of the Islamic legal tradition, slavery was not actually defined. Neither did the legal status of freedom (*ḥurriyya*) receive much discussion.[62] It was just assumed that everyone understood the nature of these statuses, which were undeniable realities of economic and social life in the Late Antique Near East.

This dichotomy is deceptive, however. Although slavery here is defined in contrast to freedom, the two are not opposites at all. This results in a tension summed up beautifully by David Graeber. Slaves are people whose freedom to act is limited by other people, i.e., their owners. But within what their owner allows, a slave can do whatever they want. So a slave is free to do whatever they want except what they are not allowed to do. But that is the same as the definition of a free person, whose freedom to act is also limited, in this case by the law. Within the law, they can do what they want. So, freedom and slavery are not dichotomous, they are just two degrees of unfreedom. Slavery is not the opposite of freedom. It is just a more extreme degree of restriction as defined within a specific social and legal system.[63]

But surely there are some restrictions that are universally seen as marking some grave change in status. In an important article addressing efforts to define slavery, Suzanne Miers states that, though what freedom means certainly differs between cultures, 'some forms of curtailment of personal liberties are universally considered to be forms of slavery.'[64] But she does not actually specify what these are (probably because this would be impossible to do). Where exactly, then, do we locate the line between freedom and slavery?

In the Western tradition freedom is much more of a construct than a consistent reality. How we understand freedom is inherited from classical Greece and Rome, where 'free' was the legal category of citizens of a notionally democratic republic. A free person is autonomous, at liberty to do whatever he or she wants unless the law prohibits it. Everyone one else is a slave. But even in Classical times this legal definition of freedom was no more than a 'rhetorical argument,' as one scholar puts it, since in reality few people in the Greek and Roman world were 'free' by this definition. Almost everyone was constrained by powerful social, economic and even legal bonds.[65] Were we to apply this rhetorical definition of freedom globally or transhistorically, the results would not be surprising. Even in theory this notion of freedom only applies in liberal democracies. In autocracies – perhaps a majority of societies in human history – almost no one would be free.[66] Yet freedom in the classical Greco-Roman sense remains an enduring imaginary in the West. As the legal scholar Vaughan Lowe jibes, inverting Rousseau's (d. 1778) famous line about man's natural state of freedom, 'Man is born in chains, but everywhere he thinks himself free.'[67]

What could we think of freedom as meaning beyond this Greco-Roman conception? One way would be to eschew the abstract for a more concrete, if less elegant, understanding. In the formalized discourse of post-eleventh-century Islamic law, the status of free was defined as not being a slave, and slavery was defined not as an abstract notion but as an amalgamation of the specific restrictions that the Shariah placed on a slave. Slavery was 'a legal weakness (*ḍa'f*/*ḍu'f ḥukmī*)' or 'a legal handicap (*'ajz ḥukmī*).'[68] For example, a slave could not bequeath or inherit property (with a few exceptions) or occupy the position of supreme leadership in a Muslim polity.

Another way to think about freedom is to distinguish it from autonomy and the absence of constraint, concepts viewed as virtually synonymous with freedom from the Roman legal tradition all the way to Henry David Thoreau (d. 1862). Building on the tradition of Rousseau and earlier twentieth-century thinkers like Emma Goldman (d. 1940), the Oxford philosopher Isaiah Berlin (d. 1997) distinguished between 'negative freedom,' or the absence of interference in our capacity to act, and 'positive freedom,' which was the extent to which a society enables its members to fulfill themselves.[69]

Since the Enlightenment, the type of freedom that jumps first to mind in the West is Berlin's negative freedom. It is the freedom of the cowboy on the open range and of innumerable lone heroes and anti-heroes in American films and television.[70] Slavery destroys this negative freedom, shackling it with chains. But, as the case of Sokullu Mehmet shows, even when negative freedom has been greatly constrained by slavery, positive freedom can both flourish and be tempting. Sokullu Mehmet was not free in the strict Shariah definition. *Devshirme* slaves like him could be immensely powerful, but they were still slaves according to the law. When one of his predecessors as grand vizier, the powerful Ibrahim Pasha (d. 1536), went to testify in a case that concerned him, the judge refused to accept his testimony because he was a slave.[71] But being a *devshirme* slave massively increased Ibrahim's and Sokullu Mehmet's *positive* freedom, as they accrued wealth, power and prestige that they never would have had if legally free. (It is important to note that both the Islamic and pre-Enlightenment Western understandings of freedom fell somewhere between Berlin's negative and positive freedom. Freedom in these traditions was not envisioned as a total lack of constraint but, rather, the freedom to use reason and divine guidance to fulfill one's purpose as a human seeking virtue and obedience to God.)[72]

We are so used to thinking of freedom as negative freedom that we can forget how this might not always be more desirable than positive freedom. As the sociologist Georg Simmel (d. 1918) observed, to value freedom and autonomy, societies must have structures to protect individuals; freedom and autonomy are only possible *within* institutions and structures.[73] In an influential 1977 chapter theorizing slavery, the anthropologist Igor Kopytoff (d. 2013) and Suzanne Miers point out that in many societies, especially ones in which strong state structures are absent, 'freedom' does not lie in autonomy or the choice to do what one wants but, rather, in belonging to strong, protective but also constraining social structures like the family.[74] This is positive freedom, not autonomy. It is this often crucial gain in positive freedom that could lead temporary slaves to seek permanent enslavement with a household, as took place in Old Testament law.[75] In the Hadramawt valley of Yemen in the 1930s Freya Stark met a young girl who seemed utterly wretched. 'Is she a slave?' she asked. The girl was an orphan, was the reply. Stark was staying in a household lined with slaves and their garrulous children. All of them had a place there. The orphan, Stark was told, 'has nothing.'[76]

Beyond the problem of what the free/slave distinctions mean, societies could lack a clear distinction altogether, consisting instead of multiple tiers of control, subordination and dependence. Were we to travel to the Malay world of Southeast Asia between the fifteenth and nineteenth centuries, we would find that the region's languages had no word even roughly equivalent to the English word 'free' and that there was no single label or category corresponding to 'slave.' Malay legal texts in that period include no less than five different terms that European scholars and colonial administrators at various times have or have not translated as 'slave.'[77]

Nor does freedom always exist on a single plane. Even in societies with clear, theoretical legal distinctions between free and slave, the actual control, autonomy and dependence could be more relational than absolute. The terms 'free' and 'slave' could expand or contract depending on the relationship in question. In the ancient and medieval Mediterranean world (both European and Islamic civilizations), a slave's intense subordination was not absolute. He or she was subordinated to his or her master, not to society as a whole. So Roman and later Byzantine masters used slaves to run their shops and to be the public faces of their businesses, negotiating and arguing with countless 'free' customers and contractors on a daily basis.[78] The slave was not the lowest rung on the ladder in the streets of Rome or Constantinople/Istanbul. If their master was a powerful or wealthy person, the slave enjoyed the status of that connection in public life. The status of the slave depended on the status of his or her master.[79]

SLAVERY AS HUMAN PROPERTY

A common English dictionary definition of a slave is 'someone who is legally owned by another person and is forced to work for that person without pay.'[80] This notion of slavery as reducing human beings to *things* owned by other people has been a major theme in how the concept has been understood in the West.[81] Indeed, it goes all the way back to Plato and Aristotle, the latter defining a slave as 'a living piece of property.'[82] Slavery-as-property achieved salience from the late 1600s onward, and it was this definition that was dominant as the Abolitionist movement gathered steam from the 1780s onward.[83] Slavery-as-property has been cemented into place through the definition of slavery put forth in the 1926 Slavery Convention (reaffirmed in the subsequent 1957 Supplementary Convention): slavery is 'the status or condition of a person over whom any or all of the powers attaching to the right of ownership are exercised . . .'[84] It is also present in the Roman and Islamic traditions. The Quran in one place juxtaposes a person with full capabilities to 'a slave, owned' (Quran 16:75). Indeed, the word 'owned' (*mamlūk*) became one of the primary technical terms for a slave in Islamic civilization, with the earliest Arabic dictionary defining slave (*ʿabd*) as such. For Muslim jurists, becoming the property of someone was understood to be a result of the legal weakness or handicap that defined the slave status.[85]

As with freedom, however, defining slavery through the prism of ownership leaves more questions than answers. As the Finnish sociologist Edward Westermarck (d. 1939) observed, property and ownership are themselves gaping legal abstractions.[86] They are even more fraught than the notion of freedom. What does ownership mean? A person's ownership of something or something's status as property are not static or simple. In the common law tradition property law deals with the rights people have regarding things. Ownership is a 'bundle of rights' that owners enjoy: the rights to use, exclude, destroy and sell off.[87] Sometimes an owner has some of them, often with significant restrictions, and sometimes the owner has them all. I might own land, but others might have an easement (a non-possessory right to use it). Or there might be covenants, conditions and restrictions (CC&R) that limit how I can use my home and the land it occupies. Ownership is complicated and can be contested.[88]

Interestingly, our archetypal image of slavery in Western memory is intimately bound up with the concept of ownership. Chattel slavery, or slavery in which the slave is owned as property, is often the term used to distinguish Atlantic slavery from other forms of slavery historically. In a revealing remark, Miers invokes the way in which human property is understood in Western society: chattel slaves are human property, 'under the complete domination' of the master, she writes, who has power of life and death over them.[89]

This has often been true for slaves. In early Roman law, slaves were conceptualized as people with no rights. Since they were, in theory, prisoners of war who had been spared execution, they were legally dead anyway.[90]

During the period of the Roman Republic (6th–1st centuries BCE), there was no legal constraint on a master's treatment of his slaves. In Ming China (1368–1644 CE), slaves were often referred to as 'not human.' Not only could they not own property, marry or have legitimate children, killing one of them posed no legal problem.[91] Among the Toraja people of Sulewesi (today in Indonesia), someone who had been convicted of a capital crime could have one of his slaves executed instead of himself.[92] A judge in South Carolina in 1847 declared that a slave 'can invoke neither magna carta nor common law'; for the slave the law was whatever the master said.[93]

Yet this evocation of 'property' and 'ownership' in its complete form, in which the full bundle of rights is held by the owner as if we were speaking of someone owning a pencil, often did not apply to chattel slavery. In the Shariah, a legal system in which slaves were considered human property (hence, chattel), it was strictly prohibited for a master to kill or severely physically discipline their slave (unless the master was the only enforcer of law available or, according to some schools of law, the slave had committed a capital or corporal offense).[94] Nor was this the case in Roman law after the legal reforms of the Emperor Hadrian (d. 138 CE). As the number of slaves in the expanding Roman Empire increased, laws were put in place to protect them. Hadrian forbade excessive punishment as well as killing a slave without a legal ruling. The emperors Antoninus Pius (d. 161 CE) and later Constantine (d. 337 CE) made it clear that if a master killed his slave in cold blood or by excessive punishment he was guilty of homicide.[95] And in the legal code of Justinian the master's rights to do violence to his slave were limited to reasonable discipline.[96]

Yet not only were legal realities often quite complicated, so were the social realities behind the laws. Many historians assert that legal restrictions on punishing slaves in the Roman Empire had little impact in reality.[97] In the American South, all thirteen colonies had laws regulating race and slavery, which were occasionally updated. In fact, in North Carolina and Virginia a handful of white slave owners were executed or imprisoned for murdering or cruelly treating their slaves. But this veneer of legal protection in no way represents the legal and lived reality of American slaves. Although many states in the South had slave codes making it a crime to mistreat slaves, mistreatment was understood in relation to the severity of the disobedience or infringement that the master was punishing. Amputating limbs, castration and execution were all allowed as punishments when the alleged crime was severe. And it was the master who evaluated this severity. It was almost impossible for slaves to challenge any treatment in court, since they could not even testify.[98]

Moving beyond these powers of life and death, what would it mean to 'own' a person? Is it a matter of exercising full control over them? If so, we exercise full control over some people we would not readily admit as slaves: our young children. Certainly, our children are not like chairs or pens. We cannot abandon them or seriously physically harm them without legal consequence. But, as was just mentioned, nor could a master do this to their slave in some major *chattel* slave systems. The majority position in Islamic schools of law was that masters could discipline their slaves as they would their children or wives (though some Muslim jurists allowed a degree more of severity).[99] Certainly, Roman laws of slavery from the first promulgation of laws in the Republic until Hadrian's time did allow a master to physically injure or even kill their slave with theoretical legal impunity. But this does not help us much in distinguishing slaves from children in the Roman context. At least in theory, the Roman law principle of *patria potestas* meant that Roman heads of household had the power of life and death over *every* member of their family – free or slave – and could kill them with impunity. Though this was more a legal theory than a practice (and even the theory was eroded by the time of Constantine), it was not uncommon for heads of household to leave unwanted infants to die in the Roman and Byzantine periods.[100]

The overwhelming vagueness of what it means to define slavery as owning people as property is demonstrated by Kopytoff and Miers. If slavery is 'classifying humans as property,' and if the most general definition of property can be no more specific than rights of people regarding things, then we end up defining a slave as 'a person over whom certain (unspecified) rights are exercised.'[101] Who does not fall under that definition?

As Orlando Patterson has pointed out, that we in the global West call relationships to things 'ownership', but do not use that term for relationships with people, has more to do with how we want to project our image of relationships than with the actual degree of control being exercised.[102] Modern Westerners would gasp at the notion of 'owning' their children, but from the Roman through the medieval period in Europe parents could and did sell their children off as slaves to creditors in order to pay debts. This was also common in India into the nineteenth century as well as in Southeast Asia.[103] Moreover, poor parents abandoning unwanted children was a regular source for slave markets in medieval Europe.[104] Yet, in all these cases, these children started off as technically 'free' in the legal sense, not legally owned by anyone.

Scholars of slavery have often preferred to focus on control rather than strictly adhering to the specific idiom of property and ownership. Though the word is drawn etymologically from the Latin root for ownership (*dominium*), scholars like Patterson have chosen the phrase 'domination' as a key element of slavery. But once again we see that a definition does not apply to important historical instances uniformly categorized as slavery. In the medieval Islamic world, it was sometimes the slaves who dominated free people. Even before the Ottomans began their system of imperial slaves, Egypt and Syria were ruled by what historians called the Mamluk (literally, 'slave') state (*circa* 1260–1517). Although they were freed after they finished their military training, the Mamluk Dynasty of Turkic or Caucasian warlords reproduced itself generation after generation by importing new slave soldiers into a ruling military elite that defined itself by its military slave experience.[105] Far from being dominated by anyone, they were their own masters and dominated the whole of the state and society. Patterson argues that slave elites in Islamic civilization were still effectively powerless because their fate still hung on the whim of their masters. But the frequency with which Egyptian Mamluks and Ottoman Janissaries summarily executed their masters when it suited them strongly suggests otherwise.

Moreover, shifting from ownership to domination does not escape the pitfalls of abstraction and ambiguity. Indrani Chaterjee has shown that the final British prohibition of slavery in India in 1843 succeeded in ending the practice not by changing reality on the ground but by artful redescription. Citing the definition of slavery phrased by the influential eighteenth-century British jurist William Blackstone (d. 1780), British officials in India announced that the 'complete domination' of some human beings by others no longer existed in the Raj. Lesser forms of domination (read 'slavery') continued. But they were not technically slavery.[106]

If by 'ownership/property' we mean more limited rights of control and use, then even in modern liberal democracies people own each other in numerous ways all the time because of the relationships and rights they have with and over one another.[107] In the US, wives and husbands have numerous claims on and powers over each other and their labor. Sometimes this is exposed when relationships are forced onto the bitter rocks of litigation, as becomes clear during divorce. For example, in many US states a wealthy husband whose wife has begun divorce proceedings would find himself prohibited from sequestering or even spending *his own* assets, since laws prohibit a spouse from 'dissipating' his or her assets prior to the divorce so that that spouse cannot undermine a court's later equitable distribution of the couple's pool of property.[108] Sometimes ownership over a person is revealed when etiquette is stripped away and raw power relations stand exposed. In English, suddenly describing a relationship between notional, legal equals in the idiom of ownership (e.g. I 'own you'), is to lay bare the real, definitive power differential disguised by our ownership-averse social niceties (as Russell Crowe's corrupt New York mayor tells a private detective he had hired in *Broken City* [2013], 'I chose you because I own you').

In the modern West, speaking of marriage as a relationship of ownership would be repugnant. But this was not always the case. Astoundingly, between 1760 and 1880 – less than a century and a half ago – there were 218 cases of Englishmen holding auctions to sell off their wives, even advertising this in the newspaper.[109] Other societies have openly expressed the marriage relationship in the idiom of ownership, or at least done so in specific circumstances. In early imperial China husbands regularly listed their (free) wives as property in their will, bequeathing them to some friend.[110] As Kopytoff and Miers show, societies in Africa have often had kinship and social arrangements in which individuals in families and clans are essentially bought and sold through institutions such as marriage. Put another way, totally normal family or communal relationships could have features that Europeans would recognize as slavery, namely transacting for people.[111]

Since classifying control as 'ownership' or something/one as 'property' has no necessary link to the degree of control exercised, one can also find the converse situation: there might be people who we would certainly recognize as being slaves and whom the society itself might also consider to be slaves as we understand the word, but who might not be technically classified as property. Slavery existed in imperial China, but it was not conceptualized primarily through ownership. Slaves were not legally 'owned' fully as property for the very technical reason that Chinese law could not categorize people as 'things.'[112] As we will see later, conceptions of 'Modern Slavery' also rest on the premise that slavery can exist without anyone being owned.

Patterson & Natal Alienation

Avoiding the pitfalls of the abstractions of property and freedom, Orlando Patterson has argued that there is one element of domination that is always present as an element of slavery. Patterson proposed a definition of slavery as a global and transhistorical phenomenon, asserting that it always exhibits three features. Slightly altering his order, Patterson argues that slavery always involves 1) perpetual domination ultimately enforced by violence; 2) the denial of honor; and 3) a state of natal alienation. This last feature is 'the loss of ties of birth in both ascending and descending generations,' which precludes making claims of birth or passing them on to one's children and which cuts the slave off from family and community except as allowed by the masters. Slaves inherit no protection or privilege and can pass none on to their children. For Patterson, slavery is thus defined as the 'permanent, violent domination of natally alienated and generally dishonored persons.'[113] The features of perpetual domination enforced by violence and dishonor we will turn to later. For now, let us focus on the feature that falls most clearly under the rubric of property: natal alienation.

In natal alienation, Patterson sees the consistent trait that betrays slavery even when a slave, like Sokullu Mehmet Pasha, is immensely powerful and enjoys high social standing. Whatever their power, Patterson says that elite Ottoman imperial slaves were still slaves according to the Shariah and therefore could neither inherit nor bequeath property. He is technically correct (though we will see that there were some exceptions to this rule): according to the letter of the Shariah in Ottoman lands, even elite slaves could not bequeath their wealth, and it reverted back to the treasury (*bayt al-māl*) upon their death.[114]

But the real application of the law differed from its letter. When an elite imperial slave like Sokullu Mehmet died, what transpired was a form of negotiation between Ottoman state officials and the heirs. Many of these slaves had amassed – and stashed – colossal hordes of cash in any number of unknown locations. Instead of hunting for these assets it was more efficient for the state to negotiate for a portion of it in return for allowing the heirs to receive the remainder without legal problems.[115] So the slave's natal alienation was not an absolute reality. It functioned more as an irregular estate tax than a total deprivation of their right to pass on their property to their heirs. There were also other easy means for circumventing the natal alienation of wealth. Like many wealthy citizens of the Ottoman Empire, imperial slaves could place their wealth in endowments (*waqf*, pl. *awqāf*) and make their descendants the beneficiaries (*circa* 1700, around 20 percent of agricultural land in the empire was *waqf* land).[116]

Furthermore, the children of elite Ottoman imperial slaves retained the privileges of their fathers' proximity to power as well as the status of their mothers. Sokullu Mehmet's wife was the daughter of the sultan, so his sons attained high office. What is more striking is that, in many cases, Ottoman imperial slaves maintained their relationships to their original families in the Christian areas of the Balkans, using their newfound power to elevate their relatives.[117] Sokullu Mehmet appointed his brother as an Orthodox Patriarch in the Balkans, and his cousin later followed him to the office of grand vizier.[118] In the late eighteenth century, the Georgian slave elite in charge of administering the Ottoman province of Egypt maintained close relations to their families back in the Caucasus and even received visits from them.[119] Sometimes exploiting family connections was one of the major purposes of enslavement. Though technically slaves, Christian Europeans captured by the Ottoman naval forces of Algiers in the eighteenth century were often more like hostages. They could send and receive mail from their families and, if their masters were lucky, their families paid ransoms to free them. In the meantime, they could own property, make money (those assigned to elite jobs like 'cofeegi', coffee pourer, might live better than in their home country) and mix freely.[120]

Finally, Patterson's concept of natal alienation fails outright to apply to many instances of what we would otherwise think of as slavery and even to some who considered themselves slaves. Byzantine imperial slaves could own property and bequeath it to their children.[121] The Ottoman agricultural slaves who had settled on imperial lands passed their estates on to their children for generations.[122] In the case of Islamic law, children born of free fathers and slave-concubine mothers were born free. This contradicted the normal rule that slave status was inherited from the mother. In this case, the child effectively inherited their father's freedom, as did their mother when her master died. This was even the case if her child was stillborn. Until then the master could not sell her (according to Sunni law).[123] Far from being natally alienated from her child, its status as the child of a freeman ensured the mother's own freedom.

SLAVERY AS DISTINCTION: THE LOWEST RUNG & MARGINALITY

Perhaps the best argument for the existence of a transhistorical category of slavery – however hard it is to define – is that in almost all societies there has been a category, sometimes more than one, that Western historians, explorers, colonialists or ethnographers have seen fit to translate as 'slave.'

To put it more crudely, no matter where you are, there seems always to be a lowest rung in society. A leading scholar of slavery in West Africa, Paul Lovejoy, has argued that the signal feature of slavery is that, however a society defines freedom or property, etc., the slave is always distinguished from – and below – the free.[124] Other scholars like Moses Finley, Miers and Kopytoff have argued that, if we try to find anything universal about something we are trying to treat as a consistent phenomenon of slavery, it is that those we call slaves are always marginal, either in a society as a whole or in relation to the principally powerful groups within society.[125] Other anthropologists, such as Benveniste and Meillassoux, have suggested that the slave is always an outcast.[126] Whether it is within a vertical hierarchy of higher/lower or a horizontal one of cores and margins, it is this distinction that counts.

This seems a compelling argument, not just to define what we identify as slavery transhistorically but also to justify our creative act of claiming that there is something 'out there' to define in the first place. But this appeal again reveals another projection of our own: the Western-centered historical imagination and its privileging of the 'free/slave' binary. Even in societies with heritages of a binary distinction between 'free' and 'slave,' this was sometimes absorbed or overshadowed by other markers of inequality or marginality. In the case of medieval Scandinavia, free and slave simply ceased to be the most meaningful and consequential socio-economic distinction. Slavery gradually disappeared because it was not as important as other markers of status or relationship.[127] In the Malay world from the 1400s to the early 1900s, there were so many levels of formal and substantive dependence/subordination that European observers were able to impose one single distinction between slave and free only by shoehorning numerous, highly diverse social categories into each one. The tensions this created between anti-slavery colonial administrators in British Malaya and those subjects reliant on bonded laborers (*orang berbutang*) helped spark armed conflict in 1875. The British had wrongly placed these bonded laborers under the heading of 'slavery,' which they were in the process of abolishing, much to the chagrin of landowners who depended on those bonded laborers for work.[128] Gwyn Campbell speaks of 'webs of dependence' as a more apt description of 'slavery' in the Indian Ocean world than the non-slave/slave distinction.[129]

One way to bypass this complexity would be simply to say that, whatever the structure of a particular society, the segment or category that is the lowest or most dishonored will be termed 'slaves.' This is essentially the solution proposed by David B. Davis: in order for the category to apply across human history, slavery can only be defined as extreme social 'debasement.' Whatever the hierarchy, slaves are always at the bottom.[130]

This general approach lies behind what has emerged as a common schema that modern scholars have developed for discussing slavery transhistorically. Since ownership, freedom and exploitation come in shades of gray, we should not talk strictly just about slavery but about a spectrum or a continuum of dependency, coerced labor or subordination. The main categories frequently referred to by historians and social scientists are, from the most to the least severe:[131]

- **Slavery/chattel slavery:** this is the notion we have been discussing so far, of humans as unfree, property, marginal figures or subjects of violent coercion, etc.
- **Debt servitude:** historically, this has been one of the most widespread and common forms of coerced labor. When a person is unable to repay a debt, he or she becomes the slave/dependant of the creditor. This was extremely common in Southeast Asia, constituting most of what Western observers categorized as slavery.[132] It is often distinguished from chattel slavery because this condition was often supposedly temporary and included more protections for the person in question than chattel slaves in Europe and the Atlantic world enjoyed.
- **Bonded labor/indentured servitude:** this is similar to debt servitude and has been very common in history. A person willingly enters into an agreement to exchange their labor and a loss of some freedoms for a fixed period of time in return for some service or up-front payment. This differs from debt servitude because the person willingly surrenders their labor and a degree of freedom.
- **Serfdom:** in Europe, this tradition goes back to ancient Greece but expanded in use in the second century CE. Laborers, usually peasant farmers, were free in the sense that they owned their own clothes, tools, livestock as well as much of the fruits of their labor. They could have families. But they were bound to the land on which they lived or to their landlord wherever he might go.[133] Serfs were not outsiders or uprooted; they lived in their homes

and communities. Serfdom in medieval Europe developed as the status of free peasants, slaves who had been granted rights to homes and use of land, and settled barbarian prisoners of war in the late Roman Empire collapsed into a single class of 'quasi-servitude' not too different from slavery.[134] Serfdom disappeared in most of Western Europe in the century after the Black Death in the mid-1300s, though it continued in the institution of villeinage in England and in parts of France until around 1600. And it persisted into the 1800s in mining areas of Scotland and some German-speaking lands. Serfdom is most associated with Russia, where it came to replace slavery in agriculture and the domestic sphere in the late 1600s and early 1700s.[135]

- **Master/servant relationship:** when serfdom disappeared from Western Europe, it was replaced by the relationship between the laborer and the landowner/employer. Unlike our modern notion of a worker's contract, however, failing to live up to this contract was a criminal offense. Only in the British colonies in North America did a notion of free labor eventually appear in the 1700s, and this did not make its way back to Britain until 1875.[136]

There are three serious problems with this continuum of dependence/servitude/coerced labor model and the definition of slavery that it implies. First of all, applying a name to a category for the most debased individuals in a society might be creating a category where none exists. The bottom of the society might not be a rung at all but merely the lowest section of an undifferentiated whole. For example, we might visit a village in some distant, unknown land and see several individuals who are consistently abused, dishonored, denied autonomy and what seem like the rights enjoyed by others. We could categorize them as the 'slaves' of this society. But they might simply be the poorest individuals there, no different in formal status or standing from other poor people except by degree. Similarly, aliens could visit modern America and perceive that 'white-collar' people were constantly being served by 'blue-collar' slaves for subsistence wages. But this would be either to exaggerate or introduce a category distinction between people 'we' all see as free and equal.

Second, even the categories that exist in a society might not track consistently with our metrics of debasement or dishonor. In India, slaves from upper-caste backgrounds enjoyed higher social standing than lower-caste free folk.[137] Among the Muslim population in Sindh, for example, slaves (recognized as such by the Shariah) indeed had a lower status than free Muslims. But the castes whose duty it was to remove garbage were seen as even lower in status than those slaves.[138]

Third, and most importantly, these categories themselves do not escape the problem of definition that we began with. Like species, they are often constructs caulked onto reality, not objective realities in and of themselves. They are constructs either inherited from Western European tradition or elaborated by social scientists. They are not fixed or hermetically sealed. They bleed into each other, making it very hard to come up with a clear line distinguishing slavery from other forms of coerced labor.

We might be tempted to treat debt servitude as different from slavery. But indebtedness was the principal route into slavery in the ancient Near East and remained so in many other regions for centuries.[139] Moreover, the less permanent nature implied by the title 'debt slave' might be meaningless in practice. In some times and places, debts were regularly so large that paying off the creditor was impossible, and the servitude was permanent. This was even more likely when the labor of debt 'slaves' was counted as the interest on their loan, not as the principal, as in Southeast Asia.[140] The same was true in the fifteenth-century duchy of Muscovy, where there emerged what scholars have termed 'limited service contract slavery.' In this common contract, a person asked someone for a loan for a year, after which they'd have to pay them back. In the meantime, the borrower would work for the lender instead of paying interest. If the borrower could not pay the creditor back after a year, they became their slave. Most often, they became a lifetime slave.[141]

The division between slavery and indentured service can similarly be hard to pin down. Indentured servants from Britain, who made up two-thirds of the immigrants to British North America before 1776, could be sold, worked to exhaustion and beaten for misbehavior. They could not marry and, in Virginia at least, could be mutilated if they tried to escape. In Maryland the punishment was death.[142] Slavery in colonial America was worse, but only in that it was permanent. The debt slavery that emerged in fifteenth-century Muscovy came to replace all forms of slavery in Russia. And yet there was also indentured servitude at the same time, differing from slavery only in that an indentured servant could not be physically harmed by their master.[143]

The dividing line between slavery and serfdom is so blurry as to be virtually useless as a consistent marker.[144] Even the words themselves betray the shifting sands of these categories. The term serf came from the Latin *servus*, meaning slave. Its distinction from slave only appeared when merchants from Italy and other parts of the Mediterranean found a source of profitable human labor in Eastern Europe that was cheaper than the servile peasant population in the West.[145] The word slave in English (*esclave* in French, etc.) comes from the medieval Latin word for this new pool of coerced labor: Slavic peoples, *Sclavus*, who were the population in the Balkans and Eastern Europe from which European slave traders drew their cargo from the seventh up through the thirteenth century.[146]

Serfdom and slavery blended into each other for centuries. Scottish mining serfs often wore collars with the names of their masters on them, for example, something we would probably associate more with slavery.[147] Focusing on freedom-as-autonomy, the French humanist scholar Jean Bodin (d. 1596) and later the Scottish economic historians Adam Smith (d. 1790) and John Millar (d. 1801) considered the villeins of Britain and the serfs of continental Europe to be slaves.[148] According to the French economic historian Pierre Bonnassie, 'liberty' in medieval Southwest Europe basically meant that one could not be beaten or lashed. But slaves were not the only ones who fell below this bar. Serfs, villeins and even servants could be and were beaten as well.[149]

European serfs were often treated and/or categorized as slaves, and just as often those classified as slaves at various times were treated more like European serfs. As early as the 1400s in the Ottoman Empire, people captured in war were sometimes settled to work lands owned by the sultan. Although technically slaves, their condition was closer to serfdom. These slaves formed families that lasted generations and passed down the land they worked to their children. Only if a head of household died without any children would his estate revert back to the imperial treasury. Later on, as Ottoman cities industrialized, factory owners preferred using slave labor because slaves would not leave for seasonal work elsewhere. By agreeing to *mukataba* contracts with these slaves – in which the slaves bought their own freedom by installments – these factory owners were able to maximize the slaves' productivity.[150] They were, in effect, more like wage laborers working for a set term in a master/servant relationship than what we understand as slaves.

SLAVERY AS COERCION & EXPLOITATION UNDER THREAT OF VIOLENCE

In our expedition through history, we could have protested. We could have confronted the police overseeing the juvenile chain gang or the British worker's harsh supervisor and told them that what they were doing was slavery. In both cases, however, those authorities would have replied that, actually, there was no such thing as slavery in their countries because it had been abolished decades or over a century earlier. If we define slavery as a legal status, like humans being owned as property or being unfree, we would have no reply. It has been illegal to own humans as property in some countries for over two hundred years, in most since at least the early twentieth century and in all countries since Mauritania officially abolished slavery (again) in 1981.

This poses a huge problem: if slavery is defined as a legal status or a formal socio-economic category, to end it you simply abolish that status or category. The people previously falling within that status or category can still be treated in exactly the same way as before. This predicament was noted by the abolitionists who had labored so hard to end slavery in the British Empire in the nineteenth century. Having emphasized the barbarity of buying and selling human beings, abolitionists were left with no objection to continued exploitation of the same people they had just freed once it became technically illegal to own them. British abolitionists succeeded in ending the slave trade in the Indian Ocean in the decades after 1830, with the formal end to slavery in India coming in 1843. But then they found that laborers were still being transported to East Africa from India in the same horrid conditions as slaves and with the same high mortality rate. They were just called 'coolies'.[151]

The fact that the substantive realities of slavery continued even after the official institution was banned led abolitionists to move gradually from defining slavery as a formal status to defining it as a set of conditions, akin to moving from slavery as an abstraction to slavery as a bundle of key features. As the twentieth century progressed, this activism succeeded in having new definitions of slavery officially recognized in international treaties and by the new multilateral organizations formed after the First and Second World Wars. The landmark was the definition used by the 1926 Slavery Convention (eventually committed to by one hundred and six countries and expanded in the subsequent 1956 Supplementary Convention): slavery is 'the status or condition of a person over whom any or all of the powers attaching to the right of ownership are exercised . . .'[152] Humans might not be able to be classified as property, but they could still be treated like it. And that treatment was slavery.

In the decades since the 1926 convention, the definition of slavery has expanded to include more and more forms of what are widely viewed as exploitative labor or exploitative relationships, from debt bondage to human trafficking, forced marriages and organ trafficking. In the 1990s this impetus came together in a trend often called 'New Abolitionism', whose representatives have devoted themselves to combatting what is often termed 'New Slavery', 'Modern Slavery', or 'Modern-Day Slavery'. (For the sake of convenience, we will refer to 'New Abolitionists' and 'Modern Slavery'). Their main proponents include classical abolitionist organizations like Anti-Slavery International (founded in 1839) as well as new ones such as the American Anti-Slavery Group (1993), Free the Slaves (2000) and the Walk Free Foundation (2011).

One obstacle confronting modern definitions of slavery is the same one we have encountered before. Tying the definition of slavery to treating someone *like* property leaves you with the same problem as defining slavery as someone actually *being* property: property and ownership are concepts that are so abstract that they can apply accurately to all sorts of relationships or institutions that many would never acknowledge as slavery. Nonetheless, some have insisted that ownership of a human being is still the heart of slavery, even if this is de facto and not de jure ownership, in other words, even if ownership is defined as the *effective* control someone wields over another rather than formal legal ownership.[153] Other legal scholars, like Antony Honoré, have moved from the idiom of property and ownership to defining slavery as a relationship of intense, unresolved subordination.[154]

But the most influential Modern Slavery discourse has been that of New Abolitionists who have shifted their definitions of slavery toward it being a condition of coercion underpinned by the threat or use of violence. As a leading voice of the New Abolitionist movement, Professor Kevin Bales, has phrased it, slavery is 'not being able to walk away.'[155] It is important to note that Bales is not naïve. He and other New Abolitionists adamantly insist that New Slavery is not a metaphor, like someone complaining that their boss is making them work like a slave. It is *actual* slavery.[156] They acknowledge that there are many wage laborers who have little choice in what they do, but they are not slaves.

According to Bales, slavery is a much more intense and controlling phenomenon in which the person in question is exploited ruthlessly. Violence or its immediate threat are omnipresent. For Bales slavery has another essential feature as well: the egregious exploitation of labor. At one point he defines slavery as 'control based on the potential or actual use of violence; a lack of remuneration beyond subsistence; and the appropriation of labor or other qualities of the slave for economic gain.'[157] Bales has elsewhere defined slavery as 'The total control of one person by another for the purpose of economic exploitation . . .,' a situation in which people are 'controlled by violence and denied all of their personal freedom to make money for someone else.'[158] Perhaps revealing the difficulty of defining slavery, Bales has also offered a definition centered on the loss of free will, saying that slavery is 'a state marked by the loss of free will, in which a person is forced through violence or the threat of violence to give up the ability to sell freely his or her own labor power.'[159] The American Anti-Slavery Group has summarized Bales' definitions of slavery succinctly as 'forced labor for no pay under the threat of violence.'[160]

In this focus on coercion rooted in violence, which is either protected by the law (pre-abolition) or ignored by it (post-abolition), the New Abolitionists dovetail with pioneering sociologists like Westermarck. In the early twentieth century he wrote that slavery's chief characteristic was 'the compulsory nature of the slave's relation to his master.'[161] As far back as classical Athens, Xenophon (d. 354 BCE) observed that slavery came about when victors intimidated the defeated so badly that they had to 'accept slavery as an escape from war with the stronger.'[162] This discourse has continued to influence scholars of slavery globally. For example, in her work on slavery in Chinese history, Pamela Crossly offers a succinct definition of slavery in general as the 'physical coercion of labor from individuals who are invisible as legal persons.'[163]

Although the slavery-as-coercion definition has become very influential, the 1926 Slavery Convention's use of ownership still holds great weight. A set of recent national and international court decisions have highlighted the tension between defining 'slavery' as the de facto property-control over a person – in effect, that bundle of traits that 'we' are accustomed to associating with slavery – and defining it in the more abstract language of coercion. Two landmark cases have erected twin poles of how the statutory language of Modern Day slavery should be understood. In the 2005 case Siliadin vs. France, the European Court of Human Rights found that a

Togolese woman who had served as a maid in Paris without receiving payment and with her passport confiscated by her employers could be considered a victim of forced labor. But she was not a slave. Drawing on the 1926 Convention's focus on treatment as property, the Court interpreted slavery in its historical form and not as the more abstract conditions of coercion used by New Abolitionists. The woman's 'employers' did not exercise 'a genuine right of legal ownership over her,' such as was the case with slavery for centuries, which would reduce her 'to the status of an "object".'[164]

In 2008 the Australian High Court planted the opposite pole. In Queen vs. Tang, it moved away from the formal focus on whether a person was property in favor of a functional test. It found that Wei Tang was guilty of possessing slaves because of the de facto condition of the people in question and that, even as understood through the language of the international conventions on slavery, slavery was at heart a matter of the exercise of intensive control and coercive power over a person.[165]

THE PROBLEM WITH MODERN-DAY SLAVERY

In a very important sense, New Abolitionist definitions of slavery avoid many of the pitfalls we have so far encountered in defining slavery or justifying why we are speaking of slavery as a global, transhistorical phenomenon to begin with. By focusing on conditions instead of status or category, their approach makes it irrelevant whether someone is technically free or owned or whether some category translatable as 'slavery' even ever existed in a particular society. All that matters are a person's conditions and how they are treated.

This focus on conditions underpins what is essentially a strong aspirational character of New Abolitionism. The list of practices and economic arrangements subsumed under contemporary definitions of slavery has been steadily growing since the 1956 Supplementary Convention, raising the world community's ethical and legal bar higher and higher. In 2014 the term New Abolitionism even began to be used to refer to the fight to reduce global climate change, with explicit parallels drawn to the Abolitionist movement in America.[166] One Muslim reform activist even invoked the idiom of abolitionism in her call to combat what she perceived as the whole gamut of Islam's regressive beliefs and practices.[167]

Many of these aspirations are laudable and desirable. But the challenges posed by our juvenile chain gang and our British worker remain. Modern definitions of slavery only confirm our inability to be consistent in our application of definitions of slavery, in the present and even more so backward into the past.

Beginning with history, if we were to apply definitions of Modern Slavery to the past, then vast swaths of humanity throughout recorded history who have always been seen as free would be categorized as slaves. Even in Western history, and even in recent centuries, we would find that almost no one was free by New Abolitionist standards.[168] As Julia O'Connell Davidson has aptly pointed out, even the white wife of an eighteenth- or nineteenth-century plantation owner would be classified as a slave today.[169] Coercion and the immediate threat of violence are not historical rarities. Imperial slaves like Sokullu Mehmet Pasha as well as non-elite Ottoman slaves were all kept in line by a coercive system ultimately underpinned by violence. But so were non-slave members of the Ottoman elite (with the exception of the ulama), young madrasa students and any number of other subordinate social groups.[170] In fact, as the seventeenth and eighteenth centuries passed, the abusive practice of seizing the wealth (*müsadere*) of members of the Ottoman elite, which was rooted in and justified by their notional status as slaves, bled into the increasingly large majority of senior administrators and wealthy elites who were not slaves.[171] As Patricia Clark has shown in her examination of domestic slavery in Late Antique North Africa, violence and its threat were the currency of power that undergirded the entirety of the domestic hierarchy, subsuming free and slave alike. Slaves were beaten to keep them in line, but so were wives and children.[172]

Interestingly, the leading scholar of slavery in the Ottoman period, Ehud Toledano, offers an observation that presents the converse challenge to the slavery-as-coercion definition. He argues that, while coercion certainly plays a role at some points in the enslavement/slavery lifecycle, when it comes to the relationship between a slave owner and their slaves 'no amount of coercion can be economically efficient in the long run.' Any slave owner interested in the productive and stable use of his slave must arrive at some understanding with them.[173] Depending on what sort of work is being asked from a slave, a productive outcome is most likely reached through the application of some mixture of coercion, reward and incentive.[174]

Although not engaged in the New Abolitionist discourse, the French anthropologist Claude Meillassoux proposed that slavery can be defined as a mode of exploitation that is uniquely characterized by its means of reproducing itself, namely through political violence or captivity in war.[175] But political violence lay at the heart of almost all complex societies and arguably still does. Moreover, as the tremendous frequency in world history of debt slavery and selling one's children into slavery shows, capturing slaves in war was but one source.

The usefulness of defining slavery as resulting from coercion would seem most obvious in distinguishing slavery from the other types of dependent labor on our spectrum. Indentured servants *chose* to enter into those contracts. Debt slaves originally *chose* to take a loan. Slaves would never *choose* to become slaves, right? But realities are much more complicated. Outside of slavery in the colonial Americas, voluntary slavery was not uncommon at all in world history.[176] In Ming China many impoverished tenants sold themselves into slavery when they could not pay rent.[177] In 1724, the Russian czar abolished slavery and converted all of Russia's slaves into serfs because serfs were offering themselves as slaves to avoid paying taxes; serfs paid taxes, slaves did not.[178] In the Merina state in Madagascar during the eighteenth and nineteenth centuries, many slaves preferred their status to freedom, since free farmers were subject to the backbreaking duty of forced public labor (*fanompoana*). Desperate free farmers sometimes even auctioned their wives off, at which point these free women often fetched less than a skilled female slave of the day.[179] In nineteenth-century China, it was common for women to be sold by their families to wealthier families as wives, concubines or sexually vulnerable servants. But the girls and women involved often consented in order to alleviate their own or their families' poverty.[180]

Ironically, some historical situations both recognized as slavery by the terms of their own societies and normally defined as slavery by Western historians would *not* qualify as slavery by New Abolitionist standards. If we see egregious exploitation of labor as key to defining slavery, then Sokullu Mehmet Pasha was definitely not a slave. He was paid handsomely for his work as grand vizier and accumulated immense wealth. In many contexts in Islamic civilization, slaves earned wages sufficient for them to purchase their freedom on installments. Hence the frequency of *mukataba* contracts. In a study of court documents concerning slaves in the Galata district of greater Istanbul between 1560 and 1572, Nur Sobers-Khan has shown that many slaves were skilled laborers who earned wages sufficient to pay off their *mukataba* contracts, usually set at two to eight years. The towering Suleymaniye Mosque complex in Istanbul was constructed by a nearly equal share of free laborers and slaves, all of whom were paid a daily wage.[181]

More tragic than ironic, Bales has discovered that in some grave ways Modern Slavery is much more severe than what he terms the Old Slavery of the pre-modern world. In Old Slavery, slaves were very often expensive and valuable property. Maintaining them was important for their owners. New Slavery, by contrast, is based on the incredible cheapness and abundance of human labor. Modern Slaves often suffer horrific treatment because they are so cheap, making them, in Bales' words, disposable people.[182]

More controversial than its consistency in the past is the application of the New Abolitionist definition of slavery to contemporary situations. One of the most salient features of how the term Modern Slavery is defined and used is its historical elasticity. In 2015, in the wake of ISIS's eruption onto the world stage, and again in 2017, *The Economist* ran articles on Modern Slavery. The first, 'Modern slavery: Everywhere in (supply) chains' (March 12, 2015), focused on bonded labor in various industries, especially in South and Southeast Asia. The second, a chart entitled 'Modern slavery is disturbingly common' (September 20, 2017), showed statistics such as the means of coercion (the most common three were withheld wages, then threats of violence, then physical violence). Both articles referenced and relied mainly on data provided by the International Labor Organization (ILO), now a branch of the UN. The ILO's 2017 report *Global Estimates of Modern Slavery* employs a definition of slavery drawn from New Abolitionism: 'situations of exploitation that a person cannot refuse or leave because of threats, violence, coercion, deception, and/or abuse of power.' It includes forced labor (such as prison labor), bonded labor, forced marriages and related practices.[183]

This definition of slavery shows how much semantic drift has taken place in the last eight decades. The ILO's landmark 1930 Convention concerning Forced or Compulsory Labour did not use the word slavery at all. It delineated only forced and compulsory labor.[184] Many of the practices that the 1930 Convention counts as forced or compulsory labor are detailed in the 1956 Supplementary Convention against slavery, which actually looks to the 1930 ILO convention at several points in its text. The 1956 Supplementary Convention, the full title of which was *Supplementary Convention on the Abolition of Slavery, the Slave Trade, and Institutions and Practices Similar to Slavery*, explicitly excludes these practices from the slavery rubric. It distinguishes slavery from 'servile status,' which it defines as institutions or practices similar to slavery, such as debt bondage, serfdom, forced marriage (in which a bride is exchanged for some monetary gain), child labor and child marriage.[185] So neither the ILO convention nor the 1956 convention classify debt bondage/bonded labor as slavery. In fact, the 1956 text places it clearly under servile status. Today, however, both the ILO and major media view bonded labor as one of the main forms of slavery.

The semantic field of the term Modern Slavery is expanding primarily because it is a prescriptive, activist term rather than merely a descriptive one. Just as the practice of slavery is an extreme exercise of power by some human beings over others, wielding the language of slavery is a claim to *moral authority* over others. The reason for invoking the word slavery instead of other definitions such as bonded labor or child labor is clear: slavery provokes an emotional reaction that spurs people into action and support for a cause. Speculating why the word 'slavery' is still so widely used despite the trenchant and sometimes vituperative disagreement over its definition among scholars, Suzanne Miers offers a simple answer: 'it gets attention.'[186] From students to rock stars, who wouldn't support ending slavery?

It is the moral power of deploying the term 'slavery' (*qua* Modern Slavery) that results in the most serious problem with both the term and its usage. Since labeling a practice as Modern Slavery is effectively painting a target on it and condemning it morally, the term has emerged as deeply political. This is perhaps the most serious problem with the Modern Slavery label, in that the consistency of its application suffers from the ebb and flow of political currents.

Nowhere is this more visible than in the debate over whether prison labor in the United States qualifies as Modern Slavery. In the United States, there have been concerted efforts by social justice advocates to call attention to the country's vast, unmatched prison population and to argue that the enslavement of African Americans has continued under the guise of detention in the justice system. The critically acclaimed 2016 documentary *13th* raised awareness of the fact that the Thirteenth Amendment to the Constitution, which formally abolished slavery in 1865, exempted those convicted of crimes from the prohibition on 'slavery or involuntary servitude.' Prisoners themselves have taken up this mantle of protest, engaging in strikes over what they call their slavery.[187]

In the late 1990s some in the New Abolitionist movement began acknowledging this, especially in the then novel phenomenon of America's private prisons. In 1999 Daniel Harr wrote passionately that prison labor is analogous to slavery not just in its substance but in its phenomenology.

A 2015 *Atlantic* magazine article, 'American Slavery, Reinvented,' observed about a documentary film shot in a Louisiana prison, 'As the camera zooms out and pans over fields of black bodies bent in work and surveyed by a guard, the picture that emerges is one of slavery.'[188] In a shocking 2008 book, *Slavery by Another Name*, Douglas Blackmon shows how the violently coerced labor of African Americans in the South continued uninterrupted after the Civil War. Laid out in painful detail, Blackmon reveals how at least one hundred thousand (and possibly twice that number) African Americans (mostly men) in the South were arrested on absurd charges like 'vagrancy,' fined sums they could never afford and sold by law enforcement to industrial or agricultural companies. There they were worked without compensation to the point of exhaustion, illness and death, beaten, lashed and finally buried in unmarked graves near their work sites.[189]

Yet this argument about prison labor has not convinced important New Abolitionists.[190] In 2006 Kevin Bales wrote that prisoners held without due process by illegitimate regimes could certainly be reasonably assessed as slaves. Yet '[w]hen an inmate of a British prison is voluntarily enrolled in a work project for which he or she is remunerated, this can hardly be described as slavery.'[191]

There are two clear objections to Bales' argument. The first is straightforward. By the widely accepted definitions of Modern Slavery and according to the established precedent of how New Abolitionists have deployed the term, a large portion at least of American prison labor qualifies per se as Modern Slavery. Both the ILO's 1930 convention and its most recent report categorize as forced labor those prisoners who are 'hired to or placed at the disposal of private individuals, companies or associations.' And the ILO's 2017 report on Modern Slavery specifically classifies this type of forced labor as Modern Slavery.[192] There is no dispute that US prisons have hired out convict labor to for-profit businesses, such as sewing garments for Victoria's Secret, and have been doing so for at least two decades. Moreover, US courts have ruled that prisoners are not covered by labor protection statutes.[193] It is thus undeniable that at least a portion of America's prison-population labor should be categorized as slaves.

The second objection reveals the same sort of problem we have seen with other definitions of slavery: coercion/violence is a concept almost as abstract as freedom and property. As Bales notes, prisoners in the US can *choose* not to work. But slaves have always been able to *choose* not to perform their labors. They just faced punishments – often severe punishments – for this refusal. But then at what point do the consequences of refusal drop below the threshold of counting as 'coercion'? Prisoners in the US who choose not to work are very often punished for this. In some cases, they are placed in solitary confinement (a standard punishment in the US Federal system, where work is required). Considering that solitary confinement is held by many, including the UN, to be a form of torture, that would indisputably qualify as coercion.[194] Prisoners can also lose privileges such as family visitation or access to the canteen.[195] Since prisons in the US generally stop providing food after around 5:30 pm, prisoners unable to access the canteen are left without food for up to fourteen hours. Denying someone the chance to see their family or forcing them into malnutrition are serious punishments that arguably count as coercion just like corporal punishment.

Some articulate critics of New Abolitionism have noted the selective application of Modern Slavery. Here we see the cracks beginning to show in the definition and use of the concept. Like terrorism, it only means what *we* think of when we say it. Prisoners in the West are widely viewed as both enjoying humane treatment and deserving of what discomforts prison involves. That some New Abolitionist activists remain hesitant to classify many American prisoners as slaves most likely reflects the unpopularity of such a claim among powerful interests in US policy-making circles, in which condemning foreign labor practices (particularly those in Muslim countries) as slavery is not controversial at all. Fewer rock stars and students would be as willing to accuse the US government of engaging in ongoing slavery than would condemn the treatment of sex workers in Thailand or construction workers in the Persian Gulf states.

This situation has shifted markedly since the election of Donald Trump. As many in the centrist media and Democratic Party have embraced the anti-Trump 'Resistance,' Leftist activism that was previously considered too radical has become more mainstream. This is evident in media and cultural production. The 2017 summer superhero blockbuster *Thor: Ragnarok* featured Jeff Goldblum as an alien dictator who is a caricature of the Western faux-conscientious corporate politician. When his minister tells him that his 'slaves are revolting,' he tells the minister not to use 'the s-word.' 'Sorry,' the minister responds sardonically, 'the prisoners with jobs are revolting.' The increased currency of branding US prison labor as slavery would have been inconceivable without the increased palatability of what had previously been viewed by the American mainstream as radical activist positions, including protesting police violence against African Americans (publicized as no longer deniable by the Black Lives Matter movement), the case for reparations for slavery (made most prominently by Ta-Nehisi Coates)[196] and the success of the January 2017 Women's March.[197] But as recently as 2018, well into the Anti-Trumpian popularity of Leftist activism and the much increased acknowledgment of Black suffering in the US, even the left-leaning *Guardian* has run headlines like 'Florida prisoners plan Martin Luther King Day strike over "slavery".'[198] Such articles are sympathetic to the prisoners' complaints about their forced labor at gunpoint in tropical heat with meaningless compensation. But slavery is still placed in scare quotes.

SLAVERY & ISLAM – A VERY POLITICAL QUESTION

Just two months before the prisoner strike in Florida, CNN journalists uncovered footage of migrants from sub-Saharan Africa being sold at auction in Libya. International outrage was immediate. Protests jammed the streets of Paris. *Time* ran an online story entitled 'The Libyan Slave Trade Has Shocked the World. Here's What You Should Know.'[199] The CNN story begins with undercover footage of traffickers holding an auction of African migrants. As the auctioneer takes bids, the camera pans over Black African men. As the footage ends, the correspondent comments gravely, 'You are watching the auction of human beings.' The correspondent then attends another auction and is left nearly speechless.

The CNN report, entitled 'People for sale,' is certainly troubling, but not only because of the auction footage. The migrants who had escaped the traffickers were being held in a holding center in Libya, caged and crowded like a prison. They complain to the correspondent about how they were being given 'no food, no water, nothing' and wanted to return to their home countries. Asked about their time with the traffickers, they tell the CNN team how they been beaten, sodomized with sharp objects, forced to work and some even killed. Yet neither the migrants' complaints about their conditions at the center nor the suffering they had endured at the hands of the traffickers elicits any comment from the correspondent. She asks only – and repeatedly – if the migrants had been sold at any point. Yes, one says, giving a brief account. The correspondent ends the report by concluding that CNN's footage had proven that people were being sold and hoping such evidence would help ensure that such scenes 'are returned to the past.' The scenes the correspondent meant are those of the auction. But auctions and being sold were clearly neither the migrants' main concern nor the source of their pain and anger. As they tried to tell the correspondent repeatedly, their treatment at the hands of the traffickers and the conditions at the detention centers were.

Why was the *Guardian* skeptical about the Florida prisoners' cry of slavery? Why was the CNN correspondent obsessed with the auction of human beings to the point of ignoring the accounts of horrific suffering the migrants were desperate to tell? The answer to both questions is the same: because slavery is what *we* think slavery looks like. Slavery is humans-as-property, humans on the auction block. Slavery is not migrants being beaten or attacked. It is not people behind bars, especially not if those people have 'done something wrong.' Slavery is what Westerners find others, especially Muslims, doing. *We* do not do it any more.

Uncovering an Arab/Muslim-run slave trade in North Africa fits into a well-worn Western narrative. Western neurosis over Muslim slavery goes back centuries, particularly over the 'white slave trade.' In the eighteenth century and even the nineteenth, the fear of being captured by Muslim pirates in the Atlantic and western Mediterranean loomed large in the Western European (particularly British) imagination, even sprouting some of the earliest literary productions of what Lila Abu-Lughod has called 'the pornography of Muslim bondage' (see Figure 4).[200] And, indeed, thousands of British and Americans were taken as slaves in such a way. We still see the cultural imprint of this fear in movies like *Never Say Never Again* (1983), where James Bond rescues Kim Basinger from a remarkably out of place Arab slave auction; in Jackie Chan's *Operation Condor* (1991), where the same occurs; and in *Taken* (2008), where Liam Neeson finally rescues his daughter from first (Muslim) Albanian traffickers and finally from the lascivious Arab sheik who had bought her.

We are skeptical, however, of the claims of the prisoners in Florida. After all, *we* don't enslave people. *We* abolished slavery in the nineteenth century. And yet this conviction – that slavery is something that other, backward (mostly Muslim) people do – forms a knot of cognitive dissonance that serves to boost and protect our Western moral standing. It both asserts our superiority over the barbaric other and ensures that we could never be guilty of their barbarism. Western abolitionists in the nineteenth century chose to define slavery as treating human beings as property in part because, if they defined slavery as harsh deprivation or exploitation, their pro-slavery opponents would just point to the factory conditions of industrial England and America and note that 'free' workers were being treated just as badly.[201] But what was implicit and unrecognized – what could not be recognized – in the abolitionists' strategy was the distinct possibility that those industrial workers *were* tantamount to slaves.

Our Western cultural memories are quite selective. During the same era that Europeans and Americans were decrying capture and enslavement by Muslim pirates, the enslavement *by* Europeans *of* Muslims from the Ottoman Empire was booming.[202] Western audiences likely felt no outrage in *The Spy Who Loved Me* (1977) when Bond visits the harem of his Arab sheik friend and is offered one of the women (when in the Orient, says the sheik, 'one should delve deeply into its treasures').[203] From the British tabloids to then private citizen Donald Trump, in 2015 many parroted the claim that Muslims in northern England were luring young white girls to be sex slaves. Some Muslims were doing this, but few media reports stated that the majority of offenders were actually white men.[204]

There is one final problematic aspect of New Abolitionism and Modern Slavery. As has been stated, there can be no objection to urging the global community to end exploitative practices such as human trafficking. As a hortatory device, labeling such things as 'slavery' is no doubt effective. As we saw at the beginning of this chapter, the power of 'slavery' today is the moral power of the word. But as the umbrella of slavery grows wider and raises the bar of moral expectation higher and higher, the suffering of those in the past who were victims of truly dehumanizing treatment is progressively cheapened. New Abolitionism works by taking the colossal payload of moral condemnation that eighteenth- and nineteenth-century abolitionists attached to 'slavery' and directing it at practices that, while pernicious and oppressive, would not have merited the label 'slavery' in past ages.

With a word denoting clear moral evil applied to an ever widening variety of phenomena, what is happening to the currency of condemnation? Even a recent film satirizing capitalism's abuse of labor, *Sorry to Bother You* (2018), acknowledges the absurdity potentially lying ahead on the New Abolitionist trajectory. When the protagonist is accused of helping to sell 'slave labor,' he retorts, 'Man, what the fuck isn't slave labor?!' What happens when large portions of society are not able to tell the difference between Modern Slavery and bad jobs? In early 2018 British police raided a daffodil farm because of concerns that the workers there were slaves. The workers responded by protesting outside the police station denying they were slaves and demanding an apology.[205]

In debates over race in America, the verbal bludgeon of 'slavery' is being stretched to its limit. Seeking to capitalize on the moral status of slavery's victims, White nationalists in the US have claimed that the Irish indentured servants who came to America were slaves. This has enraged Progressive voices, who see this as cheapening the suffering of enslaved Africans.[206] But, according to the operative definitions of slavery in use today, the Irish *were* slaves (since indentured service/bonded labor constitutes the bulk of Modern Slavery). Critics point out that they were not slaves like Africans were slaves in North America.[207] This objection rests on the tacit admission that slavery as New Abolitionists define it today is not the same as slavery was in the past. And, more crucially, that it is nowhere near as bad.

But the New Abolitionist movement is built on the assertion that Modern Slavery is *real* slavery. The crusade against prison labor in the US as slavery by another name is premised on revealing it to be a continuity of that barbarism that Americans thought they had ended with the Civil War. But if it is not accurate to refer to Irish indentured servants as slaves because Modern Slavery is not the same as the *real* slavery back then, if it is much less severe, is it really accurate to call American prison labor slavery? Prison work is certainly not as bad as plantation slavery either. If we shouldn't call the Irish 'slaves' because they weren't really slaves, then why do we call American prison labor 'slavery'?

CONCLUSION: OF COURSE, SLAVERY EXISTS

There is a logical fallacy sometimes called the continuum fallacy or the bald man argument. This is the mistaken argument that just because one cannot provide a concise definition for a thing, that thing is unidentifiable or non-existent. At precisely what point is a man bald? When he has lost a few hairs? A quarter of his hair? Just because we might not be able to agree on exactly when baldness occurs does not mean that we cannot point to a man who has no hair and say he's bald.[208] Similarly, just because we cannot agree on definitions of slavery or terrorism that apply consistently to all those individual cases we consider inside and outside those categories does not mean that some people are not totally deprived of autonomy and forced into coercive labor, or that non-combatants are not killed by non-state actors for some ideological cause. Similarly, just because there is not a real, definite, naturally occurring line separating Canidae and Ursidae from sibling families does not mean that dogs and bears do not exist as groups.

What I hope I have made clear in this chapter, however, is that definitions are crucially important because they are the basic building blocks of the discourses we construct to pretend that categories like slavery, terrorism, dog and bear are objective realities instead of being part of an order we project onto reality. A person with no control over his life and forced to work for another exists whether he is called a slave or not. A child killed in a car bombing dies whether the attack is deemed terrorism or not. But that we choose to call certain situations of control, subordination and coercion 'slavery,' that we link this category intimately with key features like chains, dishonor and violence, and that we condemn this category as evil, are lines drawn of our own making. And they are lines we should be wary of projecting onto foreign spaces, especially when doing so has long served to vilify others and boost our own moral standing.

THE PROPER TERMS FOR SPEAKING ABOUT 'SLAVERY'

How does one speak about a thing when the assumption of its very thingness presents so many problems? Sadly, it cannot be done elegantly. In the chapters that follow we will use several terms to refer to the concept at the center of this book. We'll use the word slavery when the discussion is one that clearly moves within the orbit of the Western understanding of that word and its associated institutions. We'll use 'slavery' when we need to remind ourselves that this concept is a construct that others might challenge. Finally, we'll use the Arabic word '*riqq*' when we are talking about the institution of dependent labor that was recognized and regulated within the Shariah.

2

Slavery in the Shariah

In the end, among all men who fear God, slaves are part of the family in certain ways.

A Muslim slave dealer to a French general in colonial Algeria, 1839[1]

WHAT ISLAM SAYS ABOUT SLAVERY – IDEALS AND REALITY

On the tenth anniversary of 9/11, *The Economist* ran an article with a section entitled 'Messing with the Mind of Islam.'[2] I've often thought how convenient it would be if this 'mind of Islam' could be questioned to find out what the religion said about a particular issue. Many might hope that, on issues as controversial as slavery, perhaps it could even be convinced to change its mind.

To answer any question accurately, one must first define one's terms. For the moral problem of slavery and Islam, we have already dealt with the challenge of defining slavery in general. But what exactly is this Islam whose opinion on slavery we are so eager to know? For decades Western scholars have been wrestling with the question of what Islam or, in fact, any religion actually is. Who defines a religion? Is there one person, a class of individuals or a tradition that has that authority? There is understandable reluctance to essentialize exactly what Islam is. Is it a practice or an idea, or both? If Islam is a practice, then is it the customs of villagers in Bangladesh, where visiting the grave of a holy man might be an important ritual? Or is it the religious understanding of people in Saudi Arabia, whose more austere practice of Islam rejects marking graves and venerating saints? If Islam is an idea, is it lessons told by a mother in Sarajevo to her daughter? Or is it the high religious tradition of the **ulama**, as Muslim cleric-scholars are known, with their tomes of theology, law and mysticism? If so, which ulama, and which tomes?

One approach to the study of religion in general is to view it as a human phenomenon, produced and defined by communities. From this perspective, Islam is whatever Muslims do or say it is. A second approach is that of the ulama, Muslim scholars of their own religion. For them, the true message of Islam is the religion revealed by God to the Prophet Muhammad, then inherited and guarded by generations of ulama ever since. The problem here is, of course, that various schools of thought or sects have long disputed who has accurately preserved this 'true Islam.' We can find a middle ground that both affirms that there is a normative Islam with certain boundaries and characteristics but also acknowledges the role played by human beings in shaping and contesting that revealed message. This third approach views Islam as a *discursive tradition*, an extended conversation between the past and the present that unfolds over time and communicates via a language that evolves but always binds the new and the old. From this perspective, there is not one, essential Islam that can be pointed to without objection. But there is the overlapping constellation of beliefs, norms, texts and practices that Muslims, both ulama and the lay communities with which they remain in dynamic dialogue, have used to argue what Islam is. This is the Islamic tradition.[3] In the discursive tradition of Islam, the touchstones that maintain the coherence of the faith over time and space are the **Quran**, the word of God revealed in Arabic to the Prophet Muhammad, and the person and precedent of that Prophet himself. Muhammad's authoritative precedent is known as the **Sunna**.

Unlike the Quran, which is a relatively small book, set down within a few years of the Prophet's death and memorized word for word by millions of Muslims to this day, the Sunna is not a bounded text or even a text at all. It was an idea embodied and passed on by Muslim scholars in the first two centuries of Islam in several forms. Communal practice, especially as nurtured by the nascent ulama, preserved aspects of rituals and laws alike. The most senior of the Prophet's **Companions**, as the first generation of Muslims was known, tried to apply and embody the values the Prophet had taught them as they encountered new situations. These methods of legal reasoning were passed on to the next generation, then the next as Sunna. Finally, a key form of preserving the Sunna was the corpus of **Hadiths**, or reports about the sayings and actions of the Prophet. These were transmitted and compiled by Muslim scholars primarily during the first four centuries of Islamic history.

The Hadith tradition has presented serious historiographical challenges to the ulama and non-Muslim scholars of Islamic history alike. Unlike the Quran, which (whether one believes it is revelation or not) dates from the mid-seventh century in Hejaz, Hadiths were not written down in any systematic way until around a century after the Prophet's death.[4] Early Muslim scholars realized that swaths of Hadiths were being forged in order to promote various political, sectarian, cultural or legal agendas among the burgeoning Muslim populace of the early Islamic Empire, so different schools of thought developed different methodologies for sifting forgeries from what they concluded were reliably the words of the Prophet.[5] Though the ulama differed in their methods of authentication and conclusions, Hadiths were generally categorized into sound (*ṣaḥīḥ*), acceptably reliable (*ḥasan*), weak (*ḍaʿīf*) and clear forgeries (*mawḍūʿ*).

As the Muslim community spread outward from Arabia in the mid-seventh century, Muslim scholars diverged in how they understood their rituals, theology and law. In part this was because they differed in emphasis in how they conceptualized the Sunna, some favoring a reliance on communal practice, others on sticking to the details of Hadiths, still others on inherited methods of legal reasoning. In part, the ulama differed because of the huge contrasts in local cultures and conditions, as some scholars found themselves pondering right and wrong and what the Quran meant in the mountains of Iran surrounded by Zoroastrians and Buddhists while others did so among Christians in the deserts of North Africa. Collectively, the ulama sought to elaborate the **Shariah**, the idea and ideal of God's law, which offered an answer to every question and a ruling for every possible saying or deed. The results of the ulama's interpretive efforts was known as ***fiqh***, which was the human effort to reflect the ideal of the Shariah.

Differences in methodology and local traditions led to the gelling of different ***madhhabs***, or schools of law, each with its own methodology for interpreting the Quran and Sunna, its own tradition of authoritative teachers and each developing its own body of law. By the 1100s CE Sunni Islam had solidified into four *madhhab*s, each based on the legal heritage of a founding jurist: the Maliki school grew out of the work of the Medinan scholar Malik bin Anas (d. 796), the Hanafi school out of the learned circle of Abu Hanifa (d. 767) in Kufa, the Shafi school was built on the thought of Malik's student Shafiʿi (d. 820) and the smaller Hanbali school on the teachings of Shafiʿi's Baghdadi student Ibn Hanbal (d. 855). In the Shiite tradition, the Ja'fari and Zaydi schools of law eventually formed. The Ibadi school, originating in the early Islamic sect known as Kharijites, and the small, contrarian and bookish Zahiri school are two other recognized *madhhab*s.

In time, some *madhhab*s would come to dominate certain regions of the Dar al-Islam (Abode of Islam), the lands where the Shariah ruled. North Africa and Muslim Iberia were all Maliki, while Southeast Asia became Shafi domain. The Hanafi school would become the favored school of Turks as they established their empires in Anatolia and India. The school of Zaydi Shiism is limited to the mountains of Yemen, while the Ja'fari school of the larger Imami Shiite sect predominates in Iran, southern Iraq and much of Lebanon. Ibadi Islam is found in Oman and southern Algeria, while the Zahiri school has never amounted to more than a collection of scattered intellectuals throughout Islamic history.

The ramification of Islam into different schools of law and theology did not threaten the coherence of Islam as a discursive tradition. It accommodated internal disagreement easily provided its touchstones were respected. Sunni and Shiite Islam have disagreed on core questions of law, theology, politics and history, but they both share essential features such as veneration for the Quran, the Sunna and the Prophet's character.

There is another divergence that concerns us more immediately. There have been countless fruits of Islam's discursive tradition that are entirely 'Islamic' in that they are beliefs or practices that are fully expressed in the vocabulary of that tradition. Muslim mystic poets have sung endlessly about wine, and court litterateurs mused at length about the ecstasy of falling in love with young boys. These were both common expressions of Muslim culture for centuries. But they are not *normative* expressions of Islam. Drinking wine and engaging in homosexual sex are both categorically prohibited by the Shariah.[6]

In taking up the moral problem of slavery in Islam, we are concerned primarily with what the normative voice of Islam, the Shariah, says Muslims should or should not do or believe, and what they must or must not do or believe. In the next chapter we'll take up the question of how slavery was practiced in the vast diversity of the Abode of Islam over the reality of thirteen centuries. But in this chapter we look at the ideal, how the Shariah conceptualized *riqq* in theory. This is essential because, in theory, Muslims committed to following their religion today are not bound by the way that slavery was practiced in tenth-century Baghdad or how slaves were trafficked in eighteenth-century Zanzibar. They are compelled, however, by the message of the Quran, the Sunna and the tradition of the Shariah erected on top of them.

SLAVERY IN THE QURAN & SUNNA

The Quran is not first and foremost a book of law, so it is not surprising that it deals with the legal aspects of slavery in only a few contexts. It permits marriage between free and slave Muslim men and women, and it permits the male owner of a female slave to take her as a *surriyya* (plural *sarārī*) – a female slave whose master has a sexual relationship with her (the term concubine is generally used in Western scholarship, but in this book I will use the term 'slave-concubine') (Quran 2:221, 4:25).* The Quran gives a female slave guilty of a sexual offense half the punishment of a free woman (4:25) and tells owners to accept manumission agreements should slaves propose them (24:33). But by far the most striking mentions of slavery in the Quran come in the many exhortations to free slaves either as a good deed done for the sake of God or as a required expiation for certain sins or crimes. A verse revealed early on in the Prophet's career tells Muslims they have been given the choice of two paths, and that theirs is the hard path of ascent (*'aqaba*). It is to free a slave, to feed the hungry, the orphan, one's kin and strangers (90:12–16).

The Quran also includes slaves among those groups that can receive the Zakat charity tax required from all Muslims. This was widely understood as offering aid to slaves who had *mukataba* agreements in order to help complete the purchase of their freedom (2:177, 9:60).[7] But the verse of the Quran that is seen as the anchor for Islam's conception of slavery is the command:

> Worship God, and ascribe not partners unto Him. And be virtuous towards parents and kinfolk, towards orphans and the indigent, towards the neighbor who is of kin and the neighbor who is not of

* Concubinage, in its original Latin usage and in many other contexts, has been understood as a category of sexual partner that is lower in status than wife but not necessarily a slave. Concubines have often been slave women, but in the Roman world and imperial China they were often free women. In the context of the Shariah and Islamic civilization, concubine is used to translate *surriya* or *jariya*, or a female slave in a sexual relationship with her male owner. See *Corpus Iuris Civilis, Digest*, 32.49.4.

> kin, towards the companion at your side and the traveler, and towards those whom you possess rightfully (i.e., slaves). (4:36)

The Quran sets manumission as an explicit form of expiation for a variety of sins and torts. A Muslim who accidentally kills another person should free a Muslim slave and pay compensation to the victim's family (4:92). A Muslim who breaks their oath should free a slave, or, if unable, feed ten needy people, or, if unable to do that, fast for three days (5:89). A Muslim man who returns to his wife after having made an oath of renunciation (*ẓihār*) must free a slave, or, if unable, feed sixty needy, or, if unable to do that, fast for two months (58:3). We find this course of expiation extended by the Prophet to a Muslim who has had sex with their spouse during the Ramadan fast (or, according to the Hanafi and Maliki schools of law, a Muslim who breaks their fast intentionally in any way).[8]

We find far more material about slaves in the Hadith corpus. Considering the ubiquity of *riqq* in Islamic law, relatively few Hadiths address its legal dimensions, leaving Muslim jurists with the task of basing their laws regarding slavery on narrow scriptural foundations. The Hadith corpus nearly spills over, however, with a plethora of reports exhorting the kind treatment of slaves and describing the tremendous rewards awaiting those who free them. Ranging from well-attested reports considered totally authentic by Muslim scholars and dating from the early Islamic period to reports obviously fabricated centuries after the death of the Prophet, this material could easily fill a modest tome on its own.[9] The pivot for the treatment of slaves and their rights is the widely transmitted Hadith in which the Prophet upbraids one of his Companions for cursing his slave, saying:

> Your slaves are your brothers, whom God has put under your control. Feed them from what you eat, clothe them from what you wear, and do not burden them with work that overwhelms them. If you give them more than they can do, then assist them.[10]

Other respected Hadiths specify that a slave's 'food and clothing are based on what is right by custom (*ma'rūf*),' and still others raise the standard for desired conduct even higher. If your slave brings you food, one Hadith instructs, even if you do not seat him at the table you should still offer him a bite or two.[11] The Prophet never struck a slave, we are told, and he urged his followers not to strike anyone who prayed. He advised his followers that they should forgive slaves seventy times in a day for their mistakes or shortcomings.[12] Slaves that do not please their owners should be sold, other Hadiths state, and owners should 'not inflict pain on the creation of God.'[13] In fact, 'One who is a bad owner [to their slaves] will not enter Heaven,' warns an oft-cited Hadith.[14]

Widely recognized Hadiths drew more explicit limits on the punishments that could be meted out to slaves: 'Whoever beats his slave for something other than a Hadd [i.e., a recognized corporal punishment under the Shariah] and blood flows, the expiation is freeing him,' said the Prophet, as the Abbasid caliph Al-Mansur (d. 775) recalled after he had struck and then freed one of his slaves.[15] Other commonly cited Hadiths prohibit physically mutilating a slave or castrating him ('Whoever mutilates his slave, we'll mutilate him'; 'Whoever castrates his slave, we'll castrate him').[16] A man who murdered his own slave was ordered by the Prophet to be lashed one hundred times, exiled for a year, deprived of his shares of any spoils of war and forced to free another slave.[17]

Sound Hadiths promise the rewards of salvation in the afterlife for those who free their slaves. Freeing a slave liberates all one's limbs from Hellfire, explains one Hadith. 'Any man who frees a Muslim man, [that freed slave] will be his freedom from the Fire. And any woman who frees a Muslim woman, she will be her freedom from the Fire,' promises another.[18] 'One who frees [their slave] upon death is like one who gives away food after having eaten his fill,' the Prophet cautioned those planning to make full use of their slaves while alive and then carry out the virtuous act of manumission only in their last will and testament. Well-known Hadiths encourage freeing slaves in the event of an eclipse or some other natural reminder of God's power.[19]

Another body of Hadiths addresses slaves themselves. Many warn slaves against fleeing their masters or mention the special rewards that await them for their good service. The Prophet states that there are two people who will receive a double reward from God on the Day of Judgment. The first is the slave who fulfilled their duties to both God and their master. The second is the man who had taken his slave woman as a concubine, educated her well, then freed her and taken her as his wife.[20] One Hadith states that the runaway slave has engaged in unbelief (*kufr*) until he returns, though Muslim scholars made clear this meant that such conduct was typical of an unbeliever or ingrate and not that the slave had actually left Islam. Another version states that the runaway slave's prayers will not be accepted until they return to their owner.[21]

The Prophet also sets the precedent that authorities should not only protect slaves from abuses but also that they can force their manumission, with no need to consider the owner's property right. After one brother in a large family struck the family's slave girl in the face, the Prophet obliged them to free her.[22] The Prophet also freed a slave whose master had castrated him in a fit of anger, assuring him that all the Muslims would guarantee he would not be enslaved again.[23]

The conduct of the Prophet's Companions and other early pious exemplars reiterates these themes, sometimes implementing them to an even more dramatic extent. Though the Quranic verse instructing *mukataba* would come to be understood generally as a recommendation, not a requirement, the second caliph, ʿUmar bin al-Khattab (d. 644), forced a rich Companion to accept his slave's desire for a *mukataba* contract.[24] Commenting on a Hadith he was narrating in which the Prophet instructed Muslims to support those dependent on them, the Companion Abu Hurayra (d. 678) added a quick explanation that this included one's children, womenfolk and slaves. The latter two groups could demand to be divorced or sold if they were not being adequately supported, Abu Hurayra opined. Later Muslim jurists all agreed. The most famous judge of Islam's first generation, Shurayh (d. *circa* 695), responded to an objection that he was allowing a slave to testify in court with a curt reminder of mankind's shared standing before God: 'You are all the sons of slave men and women.'[25]

The figure from Islam's ideal early community who would stand out as the archetype for the journey from slave to free Muslim was the Prophet's Companion and first muezzin, Bilal bin Rabah (d. *circa* 640 CE). At least partly of African ancestry, Bilal was born into slavery in Mecca before Muhammad's prophethood and was one of the earliest converts to the new faith. He was tortured mercilessly by his unbelieving master for it. Eventually, Bilal was bought and freed by the man who would become the first successor (caliph) of Muhammad: Abu Bakr (d. 634). Bilal became the Prophet's personal attendant and a respected leader in the Muslim community. When Muhammad and his followers emigrated to Medina, Bilal served as the first muezzin, calling the believers to pray. And when the Prophet's army reconquered his home city of Mecca, Bilal climbed to the top of the Kaaba to deliver the *adhan* there. The caliph ʿUmar would praise Bilal by recalling, 'Abu Bakr was our master (*sayyidunā*) and he freed our master.'[26]

In the early Muslim community, embodying the Prophet's teachings on the good treatment of slaves and emancipation could approach hyperbole.

As caliph, ʿUmar was reported to visit the upper areas of Medina every Saturday to reduce the labor of slaves there who had been overburdened with work.[27] When the caliph went to Mecca on Hajj and the Meccan nobleman Safwan bin Umayya served him a sumptuous feast, ʿUmar chastised his hosts for not allowing their slaves to eat with the guests. 'May God revile a people who favor themselves over their slaves and don't see it fit to eat with them!'[28] The caliph's son, ʿAbdallah Ibn ʿUmar (d. 693) would free any slave of his whom he saw engaging in pious or meritorious actions. When he was warned that these slaves were just performing for him so they could be freed, he replied, 'By God, let us be deceived in favor of him who deceives us by God.'[29] Salman (d. 656), a Persian follower of the Prophet who had come to Medina as a slave but eventually purchased his own freedom, was later appointed as the governor of the former Sasanid capital region of Ctesiphon. One day he was seen kneading dough and was asked why he hadn't left this task to his slave woman. He replied that he had already sent her on an errand and did not want to burden her with another.[30] When the exemplarily pious Umayyad caliph ʿUmar bin ʿAbd al-ʿAzīz (d. 720) came to the throne he refused the pomp and luxuries enjoyed by his less praiseworthy predecessors. Presented with the household's slave women, the caliph spoke with each in turn, asking where she was from and how she had come into slavery. Then he offered each one the choice of returning to her family and homeland. Meanwhile, his own personal slave-concubines wept at his accession, as he told them he could no longer keep them as he would not have enough time to give each the attention she deserved.[31]

The Hadiths mentioned above are all considered either sound or acceptably reliable by Sunni scholarship. But there is an enormous body of Hadiths on kindness to slaves, the merits of manumission and the otherworldly rewards for loyal slaves that Muslim scholars acknowledged to be either unreliable or outright forgeries. In fact, in my opinion there is an unusually large number of such Hadiths on slavery-related topics. Some are simply mixed-up versions of better attested Hadiths.[32] Some are later legal rulings retroactively phrased as Hadiths by some careless scholar.[33] But many, many of them are creative forgeries aimed at conveying more artfully the salvational risks awaiting those who mistreat their slaves and the great rewards due to beneficent masters. In a sizable historical irony, the same Islamic tradition that took immense pride in its commitment to textual authenticity generally allowed the propagation of unreliable Hadiths as long as they were not utterly indefensible forgeries, and provided they touched not on issues of law or theology but on matters of ethics – precisely the case with these Hadiths on slavery.[34]

One such Hadith describes how the Muslim nation will be the greatest in terms of both its orphans and its slaves, but both should be treated as one's children and, 'when your slave prays with you, he is your brother.'[35] 'Woe to the master from the slave, and woe to the slave from the master,' says another.[36] Some questionable Hadiths were more prosaic: 'The slave enjoys three particulars with his master: that the master not rush the slave in his prayers, that he not force him to get up from his meal, and that he provide for him to eat his fill,' or even 'Do not beat your slave women over your [broken] pots, for indeed pots have an appointed time just as people do.'[37] A set of unreliable Hadiths all make the claim that the first people to enter Heaven will be slaves who fulfilled their duty to God and their masters.[38] On the other hand, 'Any slave who dies while a fugitive enters the Hellfire, even if he were martyred in the path of God most high.'[39]

One of the longest 'Hadiths' ever, a colossal ninth-century forgery purporting to be the Prophet's last sermon in Medina, includes numerous exhortations involving slaves. For example, whoever offers a particularly rude dismissal to a slave, God will do the same to them on the Day of Judgment and will cast them into Hellfire. Not only will freeing a slave be a Muslim's ransom from Hell, 'indeed all the rest of the treasures of the Throne will be raised up for him before God.' This über-forgery even uses the rewards promised for manumission as an alluring unit of currency to exhort Muslims toward other good deeds. For example, the 'Hadith' explains that, whoever guides a blind person to the mosque or his home, 'God writes [as a reward the equivalent of] the freeing of one slave for each time that person raises and puts down his foot as he walks.'[40] In another forgery, when a woman asks for instructions on the best deeds to perform, the Prophet tells her, 'Chant the glory of God (*sabbiḥī*), for one hundred mentions of the glory of God is the equal of freeing one hundred slaves.'[41]

Finally, one disputed Hadith provides a powerful endorsement for the social standing of children born of slave-concubines. It is reported that the Prophet said that his son Ibrahim, who was born of his Egyptian slave-concubine Mariya, would have been a prophet had he not died in childhood. He even promises that, had Ibrahim lived, none of his mother's Coptic countrymen would be enslaved.[42] The reliability of this Hadith was contested among Sunni scholars because it seemed to contradict a fundamental tenet of Islamic dogma, namely the finality of Muhammad's prophethood. But the incredible esteem it offered to a child born of a slave-concubine was reflected in the Shariah. Mariya and Ibrahim would be the buckler for slave-concubines and their children. When the caliph Al-Mansur insulted the pious Medinan rebel Muhammad the Pure Soul (d. 762) because his mother was a slave, he replied by invoking the image of Mariya and Ibrahim.[43]

INHERITING THE NEAR EAST – ROMAN, JEWISH AND NEAR EASTERN LAWS VERSUS ISLAM

The Roman Near East that the Muslim conquerors encountered was a devasted place. Plagues in the mid-500s CE and wars in the early 600s had decimated the population of the eastern Mediterranean. The Western Roman Empire had already fragmented under Germanic invasions and migrations. Amid this turmoil and impoverishment, the scale of slavery in the Western Roman realm had decreased as the entire society and economy collapsed into relative primitiveness. In the eastern Mediterranean, however, a widespread system of domestic household slavery remained in place and ended up bridging the advent of Islam.[44]

Few events in human history have been total ruptures with what preceded them. The revelation of Islam is no exception. In fact, a boast of continuity is one of the religion's prominent features. The Quran conceived of itself as the final iteration of previous revelations and stamped select Arabian traditions like the Hajj as authoritative for Muslims. The Quran, Hadiths and eventually the Shariah also frequently acknowledged custom (*'urf*) as a shaper of law.

Western scholars have debated furiously for more than a century over the extent to which Islamic law either innovated new content or mimicked existing legal traditions and, if so, which ones. One school of thought, led by the Hungarian scholar Ignaz Goldziher (d. 1921), argued that Muslim jurists imported their rulings wholesale from Roman law. The late Patricia Crone (d. 2015) insisted that the Shariah patterned itself after Roman provincial law as it had been adopted into and transmitted through Jewish law. Joseph Schacht (d. 1969) concluded that the origins of Islamic law lay in the entirety of the Near East's diverse legal heritage. Finally, some scholars have seen Islamic law's origins more in pre-Islamic Arabian custom than anywhere else.[45]

Muslims' own history of their sacred law views it as novel not because it denies continuities with pre-Islamic traditions but because it reveres the Shariah as wisdom granted by God, not a human legacy inherited or cheaply imitated by man. This view embraced an element of continuity, since the Shariah cast itself as a continuity of the past – 'fasting has been prescribed for you as it was for those who came before you', states the Quran (2:185). And it accommodated and validated unobjectionable customs, such as what conditions are understood to be part of a sale or what determines a slave's food and clothing. As a result, in its foundations of rules and ritual the Shariah would necessarily be bound intimately to the world in which it emerged. And in its later elaboration and practice it would always be influenced by the regions into which it spread.

Slavery was one area of law in which there was tremendous continuity between the Shariah and its pre-Islamic predecessors. In great part this is because, as has long been noted, Islam did *not inaugurate* a novel regime of slavery. The Quran did not define or explain slavery. It referenced it as an unquestioned and familiar fact of life. As Muslim jurists developed their law relating to *riqq*, they were greatly influenced by the existing traditions of servitude and dependent labor in the Late Antique Near East. We can think of this influence occurring in two ways. The first was Islamic scripture, whether the Quran or the Hadiths, affirming rules or concepts that were already part of some existing slavery system, essentially stamping them with Islam's approval. The second was existing understandings of slavery influencing Muslim jurists both in their interpretation of scriptural evidence and in their addressing questions on which the scriptural evidence was totally silent, as when they resorted to analogy (*qiyās*) or equitable reasoning (*istiḥsān*).

One major point on which Islamic law seems to have hitched itself to the caravan of continuity with no scriptural instruction is in tracing a person's slave/free status through their mother. This had been noted by Roman jurists for centuries as being the common law of all nations (*ius gentium*), at least as Romans understood the world.[46] There does not seem to be any evidence in the Quran or the Hadith corpus that slave status should be transmitted through the mother. In fact, as Shafiʿi recognized, this rule breaks with the pattern that both lineage (*nasab*) and religion are patrilineal, following the father.[47] It was left to later Muslim scholars to make sense of this. Ibn Taymiyya (d. 1328) notes in a tangential comment during a discussion on crop ownership that 'the dominant factor in ownership of animals comes from the mother's side.' Hence Muslims follow the mother in freedom or slavery, he observes.[48] Another Hanbali scholar of the fourteenth century, Ibn Rajab (d. 1392), reasons that the child born of a Muslim slave woman is still a slave because the child is part of her and thus a continuation of her slavery.[49] Of course, Islamic law broke with this pattern in one of its major innovations in slavery law, namely that the child born of a free man and his slave-concubine was free, legitimate and of the same social standing as children born of a free wife.

If following the mother's status in slavery seems to have been adopted from the Near Eastern milieu without any scriptural basis, in many other instances the Quran and Hadiths affirmed established traditions in Near Eastern law. Legal relationships such as *mukataba*, the patronage relationship (*walā'*) that persists between a former master and their freed slave, the limited rights slaves had to amass property, the role of the state in protecting abused slaves and, indeed, the concept of slavery itself are all continuities of pre-Islamic practices and institutions.[50]

In one exemplary case, Prophetic Hadiths follow the same trajectory as Eastern Roman law and particularly Jewish law from the late Second Temple period. Roman and Jewish law allowed co-owning a slave. But in classical Roman law, if one of the owners manumitted his share of the slave, this had no effect – the slave was still totally enslaved. Roman law in Egypt, however, seemed to allow for partially freed slaves. How would this work? Rabbinic law permitted it through two different approaches. The Bet Hillel school held that the slave worked for his remaining master whatever portion of the week he was still enslaved. The Bet Shammai school, by contrast, required a slave freed by one owner to work extra to earn enough money to pay off his remaining owners and fully free himself.[51]

Though not mentioned in the Quran, the partial ownership of a slave and how that complicates manumission is the subject of numerous Hadiths. They offer solutions along lines similar to the Jewish schools but nonetheless differ on important points. In one Hadith, the Prophet says that if someone manumits his share of a slave then, if he is well off, he *must* pay the other owner for his share, resulting in the full manumission of the slave. A second Hadith says that if the part-owner/manumitter cannot afford to pay off the other owner then the slave is only partially freed. Still another Hadith splits into two contrasting narrations. In one, the Prophet explains that, if the owner/manumitter does not have enough money, then he has to save up to pay the other owner, provided this is not too burdensome. In the second narration, the slave has to work extra to pay off the remaining owner (Muslim Hadith scholars debated whether this second narration was really the Prophet's words or merely a comment made by a later narrator of the Hadith).[52] In another, less well-known Hadith, the Prophet says that the slave freed by one of his owners is freed in totality because 'God has no partner,' though in one narration of this Hadith the Prophet obliges the manumitting partner to compensate the other owner.[53]

Ultimately, three of the four Sunni schools concluded that, if the part-owner who had freed his share of the slave can afford it, he *must* pay the other owners to complete the manumission, even if he does it in installments. Otherwise, the slave works one portion of the time for himself and the rest for his remaining owner. Only the Hanafi school holds that the slave must work extra, above his normal duties, to earn money and pay the remaining owner so that his manumission can be complete.[54] The Shariah thus followed Jewish law in the notion of requiring the slave to pay off their remaining owner. But it differed in that it required the part-owner of a slave who acts on the urge to manumit his share to pay off the other owners as well, presumably to maximize the Shariah's aim of emancipation.

Another fascinating difference comes in how the pre-Islamic Near Eastern traditions and Islam phrased and incentivized the humane treatment of slaves. In the Greco-Roman philosophic tradition, the motive was maximizing productivity. In Islam it was maximizing reward in the afterlife. Certainly, for Stoic philosophers like Epictetus (d. 135 CE), who was himself a former slave, there was a strong ethic of empathy – one should treat slaves as one would like to be treated oneself.[55] But even the Stoic-inclined philosopher Philo of Alexandria (d. 50 CE) saw the main incentive for the humane treatment of slaves as maximizing their master's benefit. Roman and Jewish sources from the first centuries CE promote mild treatment of slaves because it improves their productivity, obedience and service. Hence Philo called for owners to provide their slaves with ample food, drink, clothes and time to relax. Owners should promote slaves having families and hold out the hope of manumission. Slaves would thus be much better servants and, more importantly, have longer productive lifespans.[56]

Islamic and Christian teachings emphasized brotherhood with slaves (Ephesians 6:9). But the main point of emphasis in the most prominent Late Antique Christian exhortations on treating slaves mildly, the many homilies of John Chrysostom (d. 407), is that treating slaves cruelly injures the master's own soul and is socially disgraceful.[57] In the Islamic tradition, as seen in the Hadiths noted above and in numerous surviving documents, the main incentive to be a beneficent owner was fear for one's fate in the life to come.[58]

Treatment of slaves in criminal matters is another break in continuity. As Kyle Harper points out, Roman society was violent because it was a slave society in which violence was seen as essential for affirming that society's hierarchy of domination. Laws restricting extreme savagery and punishing masters for killing slaves (in theory) appeared in the second century CE, but Roman treatment of slaves still seems to have been atrocious. Lashing was the most common means of discipline, along with confinement, shackling, display in wooden stocks and public shaming by nudity. Masters also withheld food. Even in Roman Egypt, where the treatment of slaves seems to have been milder than in the West, the Roman rule that slaves were tortured as a routine part of giving testimony in court still applied.[59]

The Shariah differed dramatically. Infliction of pain on any suspect prior to conviction was highly contested, and, in any case, whether the subject was slave or free made no difference.[60] Whereas John Chrysostom felt that excessive lashing by masters was what exceeded thirty blows, this was well above most of the punishments for crimes meted out in the Shariah.[61] As we'll discuss below, slaves generally received half the punishments set for free Muslims in the Quran and Sunna. For the discretionary punishments (*taʿzīr*) handed down by judges for offenses with no set punishment, the Shafi school set a limit of twenty lashes for slaves (forty for free), the Hanafis thirty-nine for free and slaves, and the Hanbalis ten for both, with a few exceptions. The Maliki school set no limit on discretionary punishment.[62]

An even more dramatic break comes in compensation payments for injuries or death. In what must certainly be one of the most productive instances of analogical reasoning (*qiyās*) in Islamic intellectual history, the Quranic command that female slaves who commit sexual offenses receive half the punishment of free women became the basis for innumerable other legal rulings. Not only was this extended by analogy to male slaves and to most of the other Hudud crimes (i.e., crimes in which God or the Prophet set a specific punishment), it yielded offspring in totally unrelated areas of law.[63] In all the Sunni schools of law but the Maliki, male slaves could only marry up to two wives – half of the limit of four that the Quran set for (presumably) free men. The waiting period for slave wives whose husbands had died or who had divorced them was half the periods that the Quran set for (presumably) free women (2:228, 234; 65:4). In the Hanafi and Shafi schools, if a man married both a free woman and a slave woman, then the free wife was due twice as much time and attention as the slave wife. Only the Maliki school disregarded the extension of this one-half analogy to matters of marriage and family, considering the original Quranic ruling on slave women receiving half punishments to be totally unrelated to other areas of law.[64]

This notion of the slave as half a free person in terms of both key punishments and privileges seems to be novel to Islam. Jewish law does not feature reduced or half-punishments for slaves. The Hammurabi Code and Old Hittite Law only mention reduced fines for lower social orders.[65] Jonathan Brockopp suggests an antecedent in Roman law: the original Roman Republic's laws of the Twelve Tables state that if one breaks the bone of a slave one pays only half of what one would pay for a free person.[66] Upon examination, however, this seems unrelated to the Islamic tradition.

First of all, the Twelve Tables date from the mid-fifth century BCE and had long been superseded in Roman legal history. Second, compensation for injury is one of the few legal issues on which the half principle does *not* apply in the Shariah. The Quran sets the principle of paying compensation (*diya*) to the family of someone slain, and a lengthy Hadith of the Prophet sets the value of the life of free men and women as well as the value of a number of specific body parts and injury types.[67] A man's life, for example, is compensated by one hundred camels or one thousand gold pieces. Destroying an eye or a hand requires paying half of that. In the case of a slave, however, Muslim jurists concluded that the compensation due his owner was the slave's value (see later in this chapter). For non-fatal injuries done to slaves, according to almost all schools of law, the compensation due was simply the set fraction for that injury in the case of a free person multiplied by the slave's value. For example, since damaging an eye requires paying half the *diya*, someone who had destroyed the eye of a slave would pay the owner half the slave's value. If the injury was not among those listed in the Hadith, then compensation was however much the slave's value was reduced by the injury.[68]

Islam also took a new direction on the issue of slave concubinage, reversing a trend in the Near East and embracing the practice fully. In Antiquity both Jewish and Roman law allowed a man to have sex with his own slave women, though the offspring would be slaves and illegitimate. Rabbis continued to hold this view into the Late Antique period, though there seems to have been a degree of spiritual disdain for it. Marriage between a free person and slave was still impermissible, though rabbis were not averse to recognizing such a matrimony by resorting to legal ruses like the husband freeing the wife by marrying her.[69] The institution of concubinage with a non-slave woman (*pilegesh*) seems to have disappeared from Jewish practice well before the advent of Islam.[70] Centuries of Christian concern over Roman and Near Eastern sexual liberties had led Christian authorities in the Eastern Empire to funnel the variety of standard sexual relationships involving slave and free, wife and concubine, all into the institution of monogamous wedlock.[71] Despite these top-down efforts, polygyny, including a man having sex with his slave women, seems to have continued among the Christians of Syria, Iraq and Persia into the Islamic period.[72] But this was certainly not what the Church, the Roman state or the law wanted.

Islam headed in the opposite direction on matters of sex. With both polygamy and sex with slave women permitted by the Quran and Prophetic precedent, the early Muslim conquerors pushed both practices to what seem like their logistical maximums. The Quran set the limit on wives at four at any one time (4:3). There was no limit on the number of slave-concubines a man could have, and he could have them at the same time as he had free wives. This was unlike Roman concubinage, which was an alternative to marriage and could not occur along side it. Though in terms of marriage serial monogamy was always much more common than polygamy in Islamic civilization, some Muslims, among them some of Islam's early pious exemplars, were serial polygamists with enormous numbers of slave-concubines. The Prophet's grandson Hasan (d. 670) is reported to have married around seventy women (no more than four at a time) and had more than three hundred slave-concubines.[73]

ISLAM'S REFORM OF SLAVERY

So strong are the continuities with Near Eastern traditions of slavery that we could easily overlook the significant and even revolutionary breaks made by Islam. The text of the Quran itself brought several ruptures with the past. First, it brought unprecedented incentives to free slaves: 1) the use of alms to help emancipate slaves and aid freed ones; 2) requiring freeing slaves as an expiation for certain sins or crimes; 3) and the encouragement of *mukataba*.[74] The Sunna of the Prophet brought more breaks with the status quo, particularly in the practice of concubinage. From the earliest years of Islam, the children born of slave-concubines received exactly the same legal status and social standing as children born of free wives. This deviated from every existing tradition in the Near East. In addition, the Shariah uniformly prohibited sex with one's *mukataba* slave women.[75]

Perhaps the most dramatic change brought by Islam was the foreclosure of all means of enslavement except capture during war (note: enslavement means making an otherwise free person a slave. This differs from simply acquiring more slaves). The routes into enslavement in the Late Antique Near East included birth to a slave mother, capture in war, kidnapping, selling or giving oneself into slavery (self-dedition), selling one's children or kin, enslavement for debt, raising abandoned children as slaves or enslavement as punishment for a crime.[76] These were all longstanding features in Near Eastern life and law, permitted to one extent or another by all the major legal regimes and religions present in the region prior to Islam.

With the exception of enslaving captives, each of these means of enslavement was prohibited by the Shariah as it emerged in its mature form after the 800s CE. Though the Quran does not address these issues explicitly or comprehensively, the Prophet's warning that selling a free man as a slave would earn God's enmity on the Day of Judgment seems to have had quite an impact.[77] The first century and a half after the death of the Prophet were characterized by a surprising diversity in legal and theological opinions, as Muslims with various incomplete bodies of Hadiths and differing new cultural surroundings settled down after the tidal wave of Islam's conquests. But even in this period of flux laws regarding the sources of slavery diverged little from the more standardized Muslim legal discourse that was channelled into order by figures like Malik, Abu Hanifa and Shafiʿi in the late 700s CE. There is evidence that some early scholars allowed a form of debt bondage, but otherwise the Prophet's command that free people not be enslaved seems to have been well understood.[78]

Of course, as we will discuss below, means of enslavement are not the same as the sources for acquiring slaves. The only people that Muslims were allowed to *enslave* were non-Muslim prisoners of war or captives. But they could purchase non-Muslim *slaves* from outside the lands of Islam with the assumption that their enslavement had been legitimate.[79] It was by purchase, not capture, that most slaves entered Islamic civilization. Another source of slaves, especially in the first two centuries of

Islam, was receiving slaves as part of the tribute paid by states or communities under Muslim suzerainty.[80]

BASIC PRINCIPLES OF *RIQQ* IN THE SHARIAH

The foundational principle of slavery in the Shariah is that the natural, default state of humans is freedom.[81] This is not some romantic claim back-projected onto history. It was a continuation of an important principle in Roman law. For Muslim jurists, it was as certain as a dictate from God.[82] Ibn al-Mundhir (d. 930), an early Muslim scholar who devoted several works to issues on which Muslims had come to a consensus or to what extent they disagreed, wrote that 'God most high created Adam and fortified him (*ḥaṣṣanahu*) against anyone owning him, and the same with Eve (*Ḥawā'*). And all people come from those two.' 'So, all the children of Adam are free,' Ibn al-Mundhir added, and the only people who can be enslaved are those non-Muslims whom Muslims captured.[83]

It has been observed that in the Semitic tradition there had long been unease with enslaving members of one's own 'nation,' with a tendency to lighten the yoke for those who were enslaved.[84] Though the Torah allowed Jews to take other Jews as debt slaves, they received better treatment than their gentile counterparts.[85] In one sense, Islam took this to a new extreme, but in another it broke with it completely. There was no doubt or disagreement in the Shariah that no one belonging to the *umma* of Muhammad could be enslaved.[86] Even when enslaved by non-Muslims, Muslim jurists considered this condition to be legally meaningless.[87] But slaves who converted to Islam or who were born Muslim to Muslim slave parents were slaves in the same sense as non-Muslim slaves. Their legal status differed from non-Muslim slaves in the same ways that free Muslims differed from free non-Muslims.[88] Unenslavability extended to non-Muslims living under Muslim rule. There was agreement that these *dhimmis* could not be enslaved even if they rebelled against the Muslim government. Even if enemies from outside the Abode of Islam captured *dhimmis* living under Muslim rule and took them as slaves, they were not legally owned according to the Shariah.[89]

The second major principle of slavery in the Shariah is that slaves were property – 'owned,' as the Quran referred to them (16:75). They could be bought, sold, rented or lent out, and inherited. With the exception of the Maliki school of law and some opinions in the Hanbali school, they could not own property because they themselves were property. Only in rare cases could they bequeath or inherit. In books of Islamic law, chapters or discussions on the treatment of slaves were often followed by those on the treatment of animals.[90] In some cases, in fact, laws on slavery were the basis of analogy for knowing how to treat livestock. One cannot load an animal with more than it can bear, for example, because this is analogous to the command not to overburden a slave. This analogy also lies behind the ruler's or state's obligation to force derelict owners to take proper care of their animals.[91]

Much more dramatic was a third main feature of Islamic law on slavery: its powerful impulse toward emancipation, best phrased in the legal maxim that 'The Lawgiver (i.e., God and the Prophet) looks expectantly towards freedom.'[92] The notion that freedom was the natural state of human beings was shared with Roman law. In the case of Islamic law, however, this presumption of freedom combined with the clear mandate for emancipation found in the Quran and Muslim practice to make tipping a slave into the category of freeperson extremely easy.

One way in which this manifested itself was in the licenses (*rukhṣa*, pl. *rukhaṣ*) or exceptions that Muslim jurists carved out for manumission from general rules of contract or declarations. For example, though across Islamic schools of law there was great reticence to allow conditional sales or contracts, in the Shafi and Hanbali schools selling a slave on the condition that they be freed was permitted. As the Hanbali scholar Ibn Taymiyya explained, this broke with legal form on this issue but was allowed because of God's desire for freedom.[93] A declaration of manumission that was coerced or made while drunk was valid in the Hanafi school, as it was when joking and even without the person having intended it in the Shafi and Hanbali schools. This was based on the Prophet having said that there are three things on which jest and seriousness were alike: marriage, divorce and manumission.[94] If one co-owner of a slave freed their part, then in the Hanafi and Hanbali schools the slave would be fully freed. There was just a question of who would bear the cost of compensating the other owner.[95]

Rulings like these could lead to bizarre situations, some of which were hypotheticals discussed by jurists and some of which actually arose. Ibn Hanbal stated that, in theory, if a man runs into a woman on the street and tells her 'Move aside, good lady (literally, free woman),' and she turns out to be his slave, she is freed.[96] It was agreed that, if an owner says to his slave 'You're my son,' the slave is automatically freed because of a Hadith that no one can own a relative.[97] Many jurists exempted cases in which the slave was older than the owner, since parenthood would be impossible, but Abu Hanifa still applied the ruling.[98] In a fatwa from the Shafi school, if an owner tells their slave 'You're free once you've finished this task (i.e., you're done with work for the day),' this means the slave has been manumitted in the eyes of the law regardless of what the owner intended.[99] During a time of civil strife in Andalusia in the late ninth century, many free Muslims were illegally taken as slaves by warring parties. One slave woman went to the court in Cordoba and protested that this had happened to her. She was declared free. But a few days later she returned and said she had lied. The judge was perplexed and sought the opinions of other jurists, many of whom replied that she had to remain free because once her original complaint had been accepted, neither she nor anyone else had the right to give themselves up as a slave.[100] Several decades later another judge in Cordoba, Ibn Zarb (d. 991), heard the case of an 'ignorant woman' who had called her female slave 'My *mawla* (*mawlātī*),' meaning 'my former slave,' at which point the slave woman claimed she was free. The owner protested that she had thought what she said meant 'my slave (*mamlūkatī*).' But after hearing advice from another leading jurist, the judge affirmed the woman's freedom.[101]

If the scriptural exhortation to emancipate slaves blossomed into absurdity in mature Islamic law and practice, the Prophet's instructions on the humane treatment of slaves and that they be dealt with as 'brothers' was tempered by the logic of hierarchy in the Shariah. Another major principle was therefore that, in the eyes of the law, slaves were generally not the equals of free people. The most common definition for *riqq* in Islamic legal works was that it was a legal handicap, weakness or deficiency that dropped individuals below the level of free counterparts in specific areas such as the capacity to own property or give witness in court. Maintenance of this hierarchy became a reoccurring theme in laws involving *riqq*. While kind treatment was recommended and loved by God, the Shariah only *required* slaves' basic needs and rights be tended to. So the Hadith stating that slaves' clothes and food were due to them according to what was customary was agreed upon as a requirement. But the Hadith urging owners to feed slaves and clothe them from their own food and clothes was only a recommendation.[102] As a famous fifteenth-century Egyptian scholar wrote, this Hadith must be understood as calling for charitable beneficence (*muwāsā*), not parity in every respect (*musāwā min kull jiha*). In fact, he added, an owner who seeks to meet the Prophet's standard for exceptionally good treatment of his slaves must not do so in a way that would favor the slave over his own free children.[103]

Similarly, while the Quran ordered that 'those among your slaves who seek an agreement [for *mukataba*], make an agreement if you know there to be good in them . . .', only early Muslims from the Kharijite sect, some Hanbali scholars and the minority literalist school of the Zahiriyya understood this as a requirement for owners. The vast majority of Muslim scholars saw it only as a recommendation. It was rightly pointed out that the verse left it up to the master to determine if the slave was suitable for freedom. But the main reason that the verse could not be read as an obligation was that it gave the slave effective power over his master. If the slave asked for *mukataba*, they would get it.[104] The Quran had allowed free Muslims to marry Muslim slaves, but according to the majority position in the Shariah a man should only marry a slave woman if he was unable to afford a free wife. In the Hanafi school, for example, one could marry a free woman after one already had a slave wife. But one could not marry a slave woman when one already had a free wife, since this would be insulting to her standing.[105]

A fourth and final major feature of the *riqq* system was the role of the Muslim state as its conceptual tent pole. The Prophet's precedent had laid out the role of the ruler or state as the guarantor of slaves' proper treatment. And it was the Muslim state that received and processed enslaved captives of war. As we will see when we discuss arguments for the abolition of slavery in Islam, later Muslim scholars responded to European calls to end slavery by insisting that *riqq* was already moribund: slaves could only be generated by capture in war, and this no longer happened. Of course, this response completely missed the mark because capture in war was not how slaves had mainly been acquired in Islamic civilization. They had been bought from small-scale slave dealers. John Hunwick sees this insistence on conceptualizing slaves as captives in war, a notion rooted in the Quran (47:4), as the ulama willfully overlooking the reality of *riqq* on a civilization-wide scale.[106] But I think this conceptualization is more accurately understood as reflecting the stubborn, state-centric framework that undergirded the *riqq* system even when it was obscured by the mundaneness and ubiquity of commerce in slaves. The famous incident in which Saladin (d. 1193) ordered that the daughter of a Frankish woman (who had come to his court pleading that Muslims had enslaved her child) be found and returned, is justly read as testimony to the ruler's chivalry. But neither Saladin nor any medieval Muslim ruler had any compunction about enslaving captives. Perhaps

Saladin was moved by this particular woman's grief. Or one could read this story as the state-centric nature of *riqq* asserting itself. The daughter had not been captured in war. The Frankish woman had described how 'Muslim thieves' had come into the tent by night and taken her child.[107]

The lingering, often counterintuitive, primacy that Muslim jurists reserved for the state in *riqq* is best understood by viewing slave ownership and trade within the Islamic polity as akin to a secondary market. The status of *riqq* was created and retained by the Muslim state, notionally through its conquests and capture of prisoners. The state then parceled out and allowed the use and exchange of slaves. This is evident even in the early days of the Islamic conquests, when the principle was established that sex with a captive woman was prohibited until the spoils of war had been processed and distributed. During the caliphate of ʿUmar, a warrior who had sex with a woman he had captured but before the spoils had been accounted for was deemed guilty of rape even though he had received permission from his immediate commander.[108] As Hanafi scholars made clear, the servile status of the slave was not possessed by their owner. It belonged to God's law (*ḥaqq al-sharʿ*) and by that fact to the Muslim state (*ḥaqq al-ʿāmma*). The slave's owner only enjoyed the ownership rights that came with the slave. This was a derivative function of the state's enslavement of that person, which Muslim jurists termed a 'right of God.' *Riqq* was a 'right of God' because only God could take away a person's inborn freedom. This contrasted with a 'right of man,' which Muslim jurists understood as people's rights to property, contracts and physical inviolability. A person could sell off their own property because this was a right of man. But a free person could not make themselves a slave even if they wanted to because it would 'undermine a right of God.'[109] And *riqq* was also the right of the state because enslavement happened through conquest and the ruler's acquisition and subsequent distribution of the spoils of war.[110] As a result, when a Muslim bought a slave from the slave market in Cairo, for example, they were not buying the slave status itself. They were buying the property right (*māliyya*) of the slave.[111]

The gravity of this legal framework is visible in a thread of legal discussion within the Shafi school of law that spanned some five centuries, produced numerous fatwas and at least one book. It centered on the legality of owning slaves who had not had the *khums* (one-fifth) tax paid on them. Based on a Quranic command, the *khums* was a one-fifth share taken out of the spoils of war for 'God, and for the Messenger, and for those near of kin, the orphans, the needy and the wayfarer' (Quran 8:41). The remaining four fifths went to the conquering soldiers. The Shafi and Hanbali schools concluded that, after the death of the Prophet, the portion of the *khums* due to him should go to the best interests of the Muslims, while the Hanafi school divided it among the other groups mentioned in the verse. The Maliki school left it up to the Muslim ruler to do as he saw fit with the *khums* based on the common good.

Abu Muhammad Juwayni (d. 1047) would later be overshadowed by his more famous son, but in his time and for many centuries afterward he was esteemed as a supremely pious and learned scholar of Shafi law from the Persian city of Nishapur. In a book on pious caution (*wara'*), Juwayni stated that it was best to avoid buying slave girls who had been taken via raiding into non-Muslim territory since the proper procedures for taking in and distributing spoils were regularly ignored. This opinion was recalled later by another pillar of the Shafi school, the Egyptian judge and senior jurist Taqi al-Din Subki (d. 1355). Subki fields a question from Aleppo about whether slave girls brought from India, Turkic lands, Byzantine Anatolia and beyond can be purchased licitly from slave dealers if those slaves were gotten in raids and if the buyer is unsure if the *khums* tax had been paid on them. An earlier Shafi scholar had said that the division of the spoils of war is entirely up to the Muslim ruler, so there is no need to worry about *khums* tax having been paid if the ruler approved of this sort of buying and selling.[112] But Imam Nawawi (d. 1277) and other scholars had disagreed and proved that in the Shafi school the *khums* tax must be paid on all spoils. As a result, if a slave girl has been taken by means that require the *khums* to be paid, then owning her without that having been done is not valid. She could only be legally bought in the market and owned if she had originally been brought into the Abode of Islam via the ownership of either a soldier in the raiding party or one of the people eligible to receive the *khums* (or their agent).

This left Subki to answer the question of what the means are of acquiring slaves that would require *khums*. Captives got in open war or in a raid done with the Muslim ruler's permission require this. There was debate about a raid done without the ruler's permission (which Subki notes is disliked according to the great majority of scholars). Subki concludes, however, that the body of law in the Shafi school is so insistent that any property taken from unbelievers outside of the Abode of Islam requires payment of the *khums* tax that the path of pious caution would be to avoid buying any slave girl who might have been seized or stolen by raiders.

Years later, Subki was asked again about the *khums* issue along with a related question about the possibility that slave girls might originally be Muslims who had been enslaved illegally. Should acquiring a slave-concubine these days be considered forbidden (*ḥarām*) out of precaution? Subki's overall solution for those interested in the path of pious caution is that a judge oversee the purchase of the slave and hold the *khums* in reserve, should one of its theoretical claimants appear. For those just interested in knowing if acquiring such a slave girl was permissible or not, Subki replies that if the slave girl protested that she was Muslim, she should not be bought. But otherwise it is acceptable to rely on the ownership (*yad*) of the slave dealer and the assumption that the means by which the slave came into that person's possession was legitimate and that the *khums* had been paid.[113]

Incredibly, this issue was still exercising concern among Shafi scholars two hundred years later, when the Ottoman prince (and convert to Shafiism from his native Hanafi school) Shehzade Korkud (d. 1513) wrote a sizable book on the topic. He is even more skeptical than Subki, concluding that many of the slaves being bought and sold in his time were not actually legally ownable. In the case of a slave girl, this meant that sex with her was not permissible. Korkud had even consulted the senior Shafi jurist of his day, the Cairean Shaykh al-Islam Zakariyya Ansari (d. 1520), who replied that if a slave girl says she had been acquired and brought into the lands of Islam by means subject to *khums*, then she is not licit to anyone.[114]

The important role of the Muslim ruler in the *riqq* system could have more concrete and practical manifestations as well. Foremost of these was the role of the ruler and Shariah judges in the oversight of how slaves were treated. Pre-modern states did not have the means or resources to police the private lives of their citizens, especially since slaves were their owners' property. But slaves seem to have complained frequently to Shariah courts, and judges responded to them.[115] One example from thirteenth-century Damascus reveals the types of discussion that could take place in such situations. When a singing woman had bought a slave girl and then forced her to engage in 'corrupt conduct,' probably prostitution, scholars debated whether the owner should be forced to sell the slave or simply be prohibited from that conduct. Ibn al-Salah (d. 1245), a leading Shafi jurist, gave the fatwa that she should be sold on the basis of an earlier ruling in the school that an owner, if he forced his slave to do work he could not bear, was forced to sell him. Similarly, scholars addressed the question of a male owner who was found to be forcing his male slave into sex. The ruling was that the slave could be sold by the authorities.[116]

THE AMBIGUITIES OF SLAVERY IN THE SHARIAH

As has been noted by numerous scholars of slavery in world history, slavery is an inherently ambiguous condition. Slaves are very often classified as property, but they are very clearly also human beings. In the Shariah this ambiguity meant that on particular issues of law major legal principles could clash as the subject oscillated between these statuses or jurists' perspective shifted from, for example, viewing slaves as humans in an unusual situation to property in an unusual form. So, while it was agreed in all but the Maliki school of law that slaves could not generally own property, Ibn Qudama (d. 1223) argued that in his Hanbali school of law a slave could own property legitimately if their master allowed it. This was because, the prolific Damascene scholar argued, the slave was a living human being and thus enjoyed the natural capacity to own things.[117] While it was agreed that a male slave owner could look at his female slave totally nude even if he had not started a sexual relationship with her (she was his property), a Hadith of the Prophet stated that if the owner married the slave woman off to someone then he could no longer look at her private area, namely between her navel and her knees. She was still his slave, but she had gone from being his totally uncovered property to being the wife of another man as well.[118]

If a prisoner captured in battle claimed that he was actually a Muslim and thus unenslavable, it was agreed that he required direct evidence (*bayyina*) to prove his claim because it contradicted the circumstances of his capture (why would a Muslim be fighting against Muslims?). In the Hanbali school, the evidentiary threshold was the one used for cases involving property or contracts, namely one witness and an oath from the plaintiff. In the Shafi school, it was the one used in cases of injuries or crimes, namely the testimony of two upstanding witnesses, since this question dealt with the status and fate of a human being.[119]

Finally, in the Shafi school the property nature of a slave could even become the basis for thinking about the legal rights of a free person. For Shafi scholars, the process for assessing the compensation payment due when a person had caused someone else an injury not specified in the Hadiths was to imagine the victim was a slave and ask how much the injury would have detracted from their value. Turning the normal assumption on its head, here Shafi jurists acknowledged that – since this was a question of the monetary value of a human body – the best way to address it was to treat even a free person as property.[120]

Similarly, there was a reoccurring tension between, on the one hand, the hierarchy that placed slave below free and, on the other, the equality of human beings or of all Muslims. This was evident in the issue of an owner murdering their own slave. A well-known Hadith of the Prophet warned, 'Whoever kills his slave, we kill him.' But no school of law acted on this. In part this was because there were doubts about the authenticity of the Hadith.[121] But the main reason that all the Sunni schools of law except the Hanafi rejected executing a free Muslim for murdering *any* slave was the Quranic verse on retaliatory punishment, which read 'a free person for free person, a slave for slave . . .' (Quran 2:178). This was seen as superseding the Quran's egalitarian declaration of 'a life for a life' (5:45). The Hanafi school, however, understood the free-for-free, slave-for-slave verse as meaning it did not matter what one's tribe or ethnicity was, and that all free people were of equal standing in terms of the value of their lives, etc. The principle of 'a life for a life' was still supreme. But if murdering a slave could lead to a free person's execution according to the Hanafi school, even that school did not allow a master to be executed for murdering *his own* slave. Here the longstanding hierarchical logic of the Shariah tradition trumped the other evidence: a person could not be killed for destroying their own property, since they would ultimately be the person compensated.[122] It is important to note that an owner who killed his slave was still punished for the crime, but not by death. Highlighting the tension present in this issue, the famous exegete Qurtubi (d. 1273) rejected all this reasoning and even broke with his own Maliki school, insisting that a master could be executed for murdering his own slave. This is what the Prophet had clearly said, insisted Qurtubi, and enough master scholars of Hadith had authenticated that report to make it binding.[123]

If homicide was accidental or, in the case of murder, if the victim's family chose not to have the murderer executed, then the Shariah mandated payment of compensation to the family. All schools of law agreed that the compensation payment (*diya*) for killing a slave was not the amount that the Prophet had set for men or women but, rather, the slave's market value. The main position of the Hanafi school, however, did not allow this amount to go above the value of a free person's life.[124] The hierarchy of free over slave could not be violated. In the Shafi school, however, the payment due was whatever the slave's value was regardless of whether it exceeded the *diya* of a free person. The slave was property, after all, that had to be replaced.[125]

This ambiguity showed itself in many other cases as well. Though in most schools a slave-wife received only half the time and attention that her free co-wife did, in the Maliki school they both received equal time because both were equal in their marriage contract.[126] Though there was agreement that a Muslim could take as many slave-concubines as he wanted, there was also consensus that he could not have two sisters as concubines at the same time. They were property, but they were also women who clearly fell under the Quranic command that men must not marry sisters at the same time (4:23). A man could own two sisters, but he could only have a sexual relationship with one of them.[127] The Maliki and Hanbali schools did not allow slave men to lead Friday congregational prayers, since they were analogous to women and children in that Friday prayers were not required for them; their presence was not counted toward the minimum number of people needed for the Friday prayer to be held. Shafiʿi and Abu Hanifa did allow male slaves to lead the Friday prayer, however, because they are men whose Friday prayer is valid if their masters allowed them to attend.[128] Finally, in the Hanbali school it was decided that, when taking enemy prisoners as slaves, not only could mothers and their children not be separated but also fathers as well. Scholars reached this conclusion by analogy to a Hadith in which the Prophet told a young, free man that he could not volunteer to fight in jihad unless he had his parents' blessing. The fact that both parents are mentioned means that fathers are also harmed by separation from their children. On this point Hanbali scholars again treated slaves as just as human as free Muslims, rather than as property.[129]

RIQQ & RIGHTS IN THE SHARIAH

What are the Shariah's conceptions of the rights of slaves? In this section we look at the majority position of Muslim jurists on the primary rights of religious practice, movement, social and contractual personhood, family relations, property, physical integrity and treatment. As in almost all points of law in the Shariah, Muslim jurists and schools of law very often differed, making it difficult or impossible to make categorical statements about what 'the Shariah says.' In what follows I therefore present the majority positions, noting minority opinions when they promise some benefit for discussing the moral challenge of slavery in Islam. I have mostly avoided listing the positions of specific schools of law because the distribution of opinions often crosses school boundaries, particularly when a school's position changes over time.

Religious Practice

In terms of religious practice, Muslim slaves had the right to perform their required prayers but were not required to attend the Friday communal prayer, pay Zakat or perform Hajj. Slaves could attend Friday prayer if their master allowed it, and a preponderance of jurists even allowed slaves to lead the Friday prayer. Slaves could lead daily congregational prayers due to Hadiths stating that slaves did so during the time of the Companions.[130] A Muslim master cannot force their non-Muslim slave to convert to Islam, and one cannot prevent a *dhimmi* slave from performing their religious obligations or from drinking wine. In twelfth-century Seville, 'My Christian slave girl bought it' was even an excuse employed in court by Muslims caught with wine in their possession.[131]

Freedom of Movement

In terms of the right to free movement, this was under the control of the master unless the slave had an agreement to buy back their freedom over a period of time (*mukātaba*) in which case they could not be prevented from relevant travel.[132]

Social and Political Roles

In terms of other roles in social and political life, slaves could not be the leader (imam, caliph) of the Muslim *umma* or of a state because of their legal incapacity to own property and because this would be the ultimate subversion of the free/slave hierarchy.[133] Slaves could serve in lesser leadership positions due to Prophetic Hadith ordering obedience to commanders 'even if he is an Ethiopian slave.'[134] Only the Hanbali school, some Hanafis and the Zahiri Ibn Hazm (d. 1064) allowed slaves to serve as witnesses in court, but the reasoning of the Hanbali Ibn Qudama is instructive: being a slave has no link to uprightness (*'adāla*), virtue (*muruwwa*), piety or knowledge, so slavery has no impact on functions based on these qualifications.[135] Slaves can engage in contracts and agreements if permitted by their master, and slaves can even make binding offers of protection for non-Muslims travelling in Muslim lands.[136] Slaves could and did take free people to court for violating contracts or similar arrangements, as in one case in Istanbul in which a Christian slave sued a free Muslim over a cattle deal and won.[137]

Marriage and Family Life

In terms of marriage and family relations, slave mothers could not be separated from their young children, with the Hanbali school holding that separating any family members to the level of uncles/aunts is prohibited and Hanafis deeming it strongly discouraged (all due to numerous Hadiths on this).[138] The Hanbali, Shafi and often the Hanafi schools did not allow a master to force a male slave to marry or divorce against his will, since this was a fundamental right of man that did not change with slavery.[139] A master could not prevent a slave woman who was married from being with her husband at night, and a married slave woman was off limits for her owner physically as well as in terms of what he could see of her body.[140] A master was required to arrange a marriage for a male or female slave who expresses a desire for a partner (or, in the case of a female slave, a master could make her his slave-concubine).[141] There was agreement that male slaves needed their masters' permission to marry, though in the Maliki school this only meant that a master whose slave had married without his agreement could annul the slave's marriage if he chose. The marriage was otherwise valid.[142]

The right of a slave to personal privacy was complicated: they were both property to be examined for purchase and people with private parts as acknowledged by the Shariah. More modest manuals on the proper conduct for buying and selling slaves required buyers to respect the slave's *'awra* (nudity, private parts). In such books we find the guideline that a male buyer could have the women of his household look at a potential slave woman, but he could not see her unclothed himself.[143] It seems to have been routinely accepted, however, for buyers at slave markets to press on the buttocks and breasts of potential purchases. Ibn 'Umar is reported to have pressed on the buttocks, breasts and stomachs of slave girls he was considering buying. The early Kufan scholar Sha'bi (d. *circa* 725) said that a buyer could look at everything but her vagina (*farj*).[144] Contracts for the sale of slave women in Egypt from the 800s and 900s frequently include boilerplate language indemnifying the buyer against defects in a slave woman's genitals – which strongly suggests they were not examined.[145]

The issue of sex with female slaves is a probably the most troubling aspect of *riqq* for modern minds. It crystalizes the moral problem of slavery like nothing else. And yet it was not questioned in the ancient Near East and the Mediterranean even in the early Christian centuries.[146] According to the Quran, both marriage and ownership (in the case of a female slave and her male master) were relationships in which sex was licit (Quran 23:5–6). Within these relationships, consent for sexual relations was assumed or irrelevant. In marriage the relationship itself entailed ongoing consent for sex, and with a female slave it was not needed (assuming the slave girl was solely owned by one man and not married; in both cases she was off limits). Kecia Ali has observed that there is no evidence for any requirement for consent for sex from slave women in books of Islamic law from the eighth to the tenth centuries.[147]

In this regard, slave women had a status similar to underage daughters. Both could be married off by their fathers without their consent (since their consent had no legal bearing).[148] The marriage contract is different from the consummation, which could only occur when daughters had reached appropriate maturity as determined by reasonable standards in a community.[149] Kecia Ali has written about how slavery and 'femaleness' often resembled one another as handicaps in the letter of Islamic law.[150] And the historian Ehud Toledano insightfully observes that the lack of choice faced by female slaves taken as slave-concubines by their owners did not differ much from the lot of brides headed into marriages arranged by their families, either in medieval Islamic civilization or Western Europe.[151]

The Shariah offered protection to both wives and slave-concubines, but it came not under the rubric of consent but that of harm. By definition, the crime of rape (i.e., forced *zina*) could not occur within a licit relationship.[152] But transgressive harm could still be done by the man. Wives and concubines could complain to local judges if they were being abused or if his demands for sex were excessive (we'll discuss the issue of concubinage and consent in depth in the concluding chapter of this book). The Hanbali scholar Buhūtī (d. 1641) even says that if a master forced a slave woman unable to bear intercourse to have sex and injured her, she would be freed as a result.[153]

Right to Property

The slave's right to property was a complex issue in Islamic law, since the main proof texts seemed to resist the principles that jurists felt were entailed by the status of slavery. Most clearly, the Quran urges masters to agree to *mukataba* contracts if their slave seeks one. The fact that the slave would be amassing money to pay the installments suggests some ownership rights.[154] The Prophet also said in a Hadith agreed upon as sound that, when selling a slave, 'The slave's property/wealth belongs to the seller.' This affirms the notion of a slave owning property, but it also clearly states that this property will be kept by the master if he sells the slave off. This latter point led the majority of jurists to conclude a principle that slaves cannot own property or, at the very least, 'The presumption is that the wealth of the slave belongs to the master.'[155] Since the master owns both the slave and the slave's production (*manfaʿa*), this majority school of thought held that it makes no sense that the slave could have his or her own property.

In the Maliki school however, as well as in one opinion in the Shafi and Hanbali schools, slaves had qualified property ownership provided their master affirmed it. In the Maliki school, male slaves could actually own their own slave-concubines.[156] One ambassador of the West African ruler Muhammad Bello (d. 1837) was an elderly slave woman who herself owned almost forty slaves.[157] Ibn Qudama states that, if the master gives his slave something, then it is the slave's property, since a slave is a human being and has the same basic capacity to own as a free person.[158] The influential but erratic Andalusian jurist Ibn Hazm, an advocate of the extreme minority Zahiri school, insisted on slaves' absolute right to own property because there is no scriptural evidence that would entail otherwise.[159]

There was consensus that slaves could neither inherit nor bequeath, though in the Hanbali school a *mukatab* slave could bequeath to their heirs if the slave had enough property to have purchased their own freedom at the time of their death.[160] In addition, one opinion in the Hanbali and Shafi schools was that a slave who had been partly freed (i.e., by one of his owners in a shared ownership situation) could bequeath and inherit on a prorated basis.[161]

Rights to Life and Physical Protection

In terms of the right to life and physical integrity, it was prohibited to kill or seriously injure one's slave. In the Hanafi school of law, killing someone else's slave was even punishable by death. Any severe punishment or treatment that left lasting scars was grounds for forced manumission, and in the Ottoman period (the period for which we have the best records) slaves continually approached courts on these grounds.[162] Castrating slaves was prohibited.[163] A master could discipline their slave verbally or physically, but the majority position was that this could not exceed what a husband/father could do to his wife or child. Other jurists allowed harsher punishment due to an inference from the Hadith, 'Would one of you hit his wife like a slave and then sleep with her at the end of the day?' The Shafi jurist Khattabi (d. 996), however, objects that this Hadith is a rhetorical condemnation of striking one's wife and in no way amounts to any permission to beat slaves.[164]

In terms of treatment, Hadiths made it clear that slaves could not be overworked, but what constituted a normal workload was based on customary understandings of workload in that society. They must be fed, clothed and housed according to established local conventions of humane treatment, on the basis of a Hadith stating that 'The slave is owed his food and his clothing according to what is right in custom (*ma'rūf*) . . .'[165] Masters had to provide slaves with dress comparable to those of a similar station in that society, but their clothing had to be appropriate to the weather and could not be limited merely to covering the slave's nudity (*'awra*).[166] And a master could not require a slave to work for money if the master was then going to take those earnings from them. Such an exchange had to come as part of a *mukataba* agreement.[167] If a slave became sick, crippled or old, the master still had to provide for them because that responsibility stemmed from ownership, not from the slave's work.[168]

SUMMARY: LAW AND ETHICS

As the Shariah conceptualized *riqq*, slave men and women had rights that were comparable to other dependent segments of society, such as minor children or wives (except wives had full capacity to own property and engage in contracts, etc.). Slaves had the right to unencumbered conjugal relationships, the right to religious observances and limited rights to property. In terms of physical integrity and protection from abuse and exploitation, their position was similar to that of wives and minor children, including the owner's obligation to care for slaves unable to work.

One of the results of the systematic hierarchy of the free over slaves in the Shariah was that many of the norms regulating the relationship between master and slave fell under the legal category of recommendation (*nadb*) or discouragement (*karāha*) instead of required (*wājib*) or prohibited (*ḥarām*). These were still legal rulings of the Shariah – in fact, most of the myriad points of law in the Shariah tradition fell into the recommended or discouraged categories. But recommendation and discouragement lack the firmness that many today would expect as protection and the guarantees of rights. Ironically, a less rigid conceptualization of religious norms in Islam has proven attractive in recent years, as concerns crescendo around Islamic 'extremism' and states seek to promote 'moderate' Islam. Many Muslim intellectuals and ulama interested in reform have stressed that Islamic thought should focus on ethics rather than law. Though the Shariah historically encompassed both, today ethics is associated more with broad moral guidelines and priorities than legal hard dos and don'ts.[169]

While it does not break with the Shariah in how it addresses the issues of slaves and slavery, the Islamic ethical tradition (*akhlāq*) provides interesting insights. Islamic ethics built on the existing traditions of Greco-Roman moral philosophy as well as the Persian and Indian heritages of political guidance. Brilliant Muslim intellectuals like Ibn al-Muqaffaʿ (d. 756), Miskawayh (d. 1030) and Mawardi (d. 1058) combined these traditions with Shariah sensibilities and Islamic narratives. *Akhlaq* centered on the classical principles of moderation, the virtue of the Golden Mean, and with each participant in state and society playing their proper role. Establishing and maintaining this balance was the duty of rulers, viziers, fathers, husbands and masters.

As exemplified by widely studied works such as Miskawayh's *Refinement of Ethics* (*Tahdhīb al-akhlāq*), the *ʿAdudiyya* of ʿAdud al-Din Iji (d. 1355) and its commentaries, Islamic ethical teachings on slavery stressed compassionate and just treatment of slaves and servants. Because of its inherent power imbalance, the relationship between master and slave must be governed by justice, with each party receiving their rights. Otherwise resentment and anger will spoil the relationship and make it ineffective or unmanageable.[170] Masters should express concern for each slave's wellbeing and talents while also applying appropriate discipline when they err or disobey. Compassion toward slaves is essential, since the best service is that rendered out of love and shared interest, not out of fear. But appropriate discipline is crucial for maintaining work ethic and boundaries. These ethical works draw on the same Hadiths we discussed, exhorting Muslims to care for their slaves with kindness and to remember that both slave and master are ultimately slaves of God.

Books of ethics remind us that the strict lines and prohibitions of the Shariah were outer boundaries and that virtue should keep slave owners' conduct well within them. In a work on ethics, the Ottoman scholar Tashkoprizade (d. 1561) reminds his audience that slaves receive half the punishment of free Muslims for the Hudud crimes and that slave owners should observe this principle in any disciplining or punishment of their slaves. Moreover, any harsh disciplining or any beating that leaves a mark (*ḍarb mubarriḥ*) contravenes virtue (*muruwwa, futuwwa*) 'and, indeed, the rules of the Sacred Law.'[171]

One late medieval commentator, Kaziruni, introduces a psychological aspect to managing one's slaves not seen in the legal writings focused on in this chapter. There are three types of slave, Kaziruni writes. The first is the slave who is actually, by their nature, free (*ḥurr bi'l-ṭab'*). This slave the master should raise up and treat like his own children. The second is one who is a slave by nature, meaning that they can be dealt with like a beast of burden. The third type of slave is a slave to desire (*'abd bi'l-shahwa*), which means they can be directed and controlled by appealing to their strong appetites and desires.[172]

Whether with the legal rulings of the Shariah or the norms of Islamic ethics, how slaves were treated and how *riqq* functioned were matters regulated first and foremost within households and the informal spaces of public life. Unless a slave complained to a court or community leader, the policing of these norms was left up to families, communities and slaves' owners. Understanding the theory of *riqq* and its ideal application in the Shariah are crucial for tackling the moral problem of slavery in Islam. But *riqq* was more than anything a reality, and we must come to terms with its practice in Islamic civilization.

3

Slavery in Islamic Civilization

When hardship comes, I cry out to a lord,
By whom all hardship is repulsed, all harm stripped away.
I hope for a master who fails not his slave,
Holder of majesty and blessings, creation and command.

Poem by the Sufi Ahmad bin Rawh (d. *circa* 910 CE)[1]

WHAT IS ISLAMIC CIVILIZATION?

Several years ago I remember listening to a famous travel writer speak on the radio about his 'journeys into Islam.' Is Islam a place you can visit? It might as well be. In his famous clash of civilizations thesis, Samuel Huntington's map of the world reserved a sizable chunk for Islamic civilization. Among academics and foreign policy boffins alike it is normal to speak about the Islamic or Muslim world. But what exactly makes that world we speak of 'Muslim' or 'Islamic'? Is everyone there Muslim? Is everything they do dictated or even influenced by Islam? In the last chapter we looked at how the high religious tradition of Islamic law and ethics conceptualized and regulated *riqq*. But what about the reality of *riqq* as it was practiced by the Muslims who supposedly lived according to that high religious tradition? What about slavery in that Islam?

In the last chapter we also touched on the problem of essentialization; if you talk about Islam, you need to define what Islam you're speaking about. In recent years, even many in the less scholarly, policy-making class have proposed the term 'Muslim-majority countries' instead of the Muslim world. They have realized the precariousness of grouping an incapacitatingly diverse 1.5 billion-strong collection of peoples, their cultures and histories, into one block. Yet, if for no other reason than convenience, the lure remains strong to speak of 'Islam' as an area on the map or about 'the Muslim world.' Can this be justified? Does this polyglot really have anything common unifying it?

I think it does. When the rulers of local states in both Malaysia and Nigeria are called 'sultans,' and when Eid is the biggest public holiday in Kuala Lumpur and Kano, there is something important linking these places and their inhabitants. Whether visiting Marrakesh or Mombasa, Belgrade or Bombay, we find at least one common element of real importance: kindred slices of a shared history. It is the history of a vibrant civilization that was and perhaps still is, the Dar al-Islam.

Defining Islamic civilization is easier than defining slavery, but the result is still blurry at its edges. Perhaps this is inevitable when one generalizes over immense expanses and epochs. A useful definition of Islamic civilization is that network of peoples, states, cultures and societies bound together by the institutions of the Shariah and the infrastructure, symbols and sentiments that were developed roughly between the death of the Prophet Muhammad and the thirteenth century. During this period, in a cradle that spanned the belt of arid land, mountains and rolling grassy hills between the Nile and the Oxus Rivers, these institutions and the vision of ritual, law and ethics known as the Shariah that pervaded them all grew into their mature form. Institutions like the *madrasa*, *waqf* (pious endowment) and Sufi lodge formed. They created the stable structure of societies joined by a common identification with the *umma* (the global community of Muslims) and ruled over by sultans who derived legitimacy from upholding the order of God in the name of the figurehead caliph at its pinnacle. From the twelfth to the seventeenth century, expansion of the area under the control of Muslim states or impacted by Muslim trade resulted in the export of this civilizational framework into Central Asia, India, the Sahel region and the Indian Ocean world from the coast of East Africa to Southeast Asia.[2]

IS THERE 'ISLAMIC SLAVERY'?

In every aspect of human life, the Abode of Islam was and remains a teeming sea of diversity. Its experiences are too numerous and varied to encompass. One can only catch glimpses and perhaps sense stark contrasts. Here is a sample of lived moments of slavery in Islamic civilization:

A slave dealer in Basra in the early 700s eager to sell off a 'lazy' slave. A distraught man in Takedda (modern Niger) in the 1350s begging the man to whom he had sold his slave girl to give her back.[3]

A slave woman in Egypt in the late 600s freed by legal decree after her mistress had cut off her nose. A woman in Egypt just a few years later giving her property as an endowment for a slave girl she had freed.[4]

A Black slave in twelfth-century Yemen standing by his master during years on the run, handsomely rewarded when his master became governor. A Persian slave near Merv in the 1800s who escaped on his Uzbek master's fastest horse and slew the lady of the house when she tried to stop him.[5]

A Muslim nobleman in sixteenth-century India receiving high praise for merely giving his slaves the day off on Sunday. A Muslim slave owner in early nineteenth-century Cape Town being said to 'forfeit [his] title to be considered Mahometan' because he would not let his Muslim slave eat at the family table.[6]

A slave in Cordoba in the early 800s arranging (successfully) to have respected citizens falsely testify that his deceased master had freed him, given him his daughter in marriage and left him a sizable inheritance. A Black eunuch in *fin de siècle* Alexandria earnestly trying to shield his young charge from prying eyes on her first trip to a department store.[7]

The slave of an old woman in Edirne becoming one of the best-known Ottoman poets of the early 1500s. A well-educated English slave in Algiers, his accounting skills more valuable than any ransom, despairing in a 1646 letter home that 'my breeding is my undoing.'[8]

The Ottoman Sultan's Black eunuchs, honored with retirement in the Haram of Mecca, having their hands kissed in the streets of the holy city. Noble Minangkabau women of Sumatra taken as concubines by the Sultan of Johor in the mid 1700s in an unforgivable act of humiliation.[9]

These are just snapshots of civilizational experience across thirteen centuries. We have already seen the challenges of defining slavery transhistorically, and we have recognized the assumptions and claims we make in doing so. The lands and eras traversed in the handful of examples given above raise the same question again. Are the relationships depicted really instances of one, unified phenomenon called 'slavery'? Are these experiences comparable or even part of the same conversation? Was the 'slavery' that was practiced in Islamic civilization 'Islamic slavery'? Was it even one kind of 'slavery' at all?

Three factors have led many Western scholars to speak, whether out of ignorance or expertise, of 'Islamic slavery.' The first is the correct notion that the Shariah strongly influenced Muslims' practice as slave owners and slaves wherever and whenever those Muslims were. The second is the perceived inseparability of Islam and enslavement in Western culture. This perception is compounded at the popular level by association of this enslavement with the telltale desert landscapes and flowing garb of Saharan Africa and the Middle East. Third is the longstanding habit of equating the Islamic world with what is today called the Middle East and North Africa, treating Muslim and Arab/Middle Eastern as synonymous.[10] Since, as we will see, there was indeed much internal consistency in the practices of slavery in that region, eliding this as 'Islamic slavery' and ignoring the rest of Islamic civilization has been all too easy.

Just as scholars have wriggled in discomfort at 'the Muslim world' and 'Islamic civilization,' some historians have challenged the framing of 'Islamic slavery.' They point out that it sometimes takes the 'slavery' done by particular Muslims in one region or era and essentializes it as 'Islamic.' So the slave trade in the nineteenth-century Sahara is 'Islamic slavery,' not slavery done by Muslims in a particular time, place and environment. And sometimes this framing presents us with 'slavery' in which Muslims are involved but rips it out of the economic and cultural contexts that are essential for understanding it in that particular case. So the labor, trade and political economy of the nineteenth-century Indian Ocean world, with its extensive European colonial involvement, is 'Islamic slavery,' not slavery in that complex, multicultural Indian Ocean network. Critics further object that often what is being discussed when people talk about 'Islamic slavery' or 'the Muslim slave trade' are really the slave trade*s* from trans-Saharan and eastern Africa to the Mediterranean, Red Sea and Indian Ocean. These were distinct trade systems that were compound, spanned cultures and oceans, fed different markets and involved much more than just Muslims and Islam. The gross simplification of reducing this all to 'Islamic slavery' makes 'Muslim' into 'Arab' and treats all of this as alien to the 'real' Africa. Yet there is nothing more specifically 'Islamic' about it than there was something markedly Christian about the European slave trade in the Atlantic.[11]

THE SHARIAH & ISLAMIC SLAVERY

This criticism of framing things as 'Islamic slavery' offers an important correction, but it obscures two important points. First, the ubiquitous religious edifice of the Shariah *did* play an important role in shaping how people who identified as Muslim thought of and practiced what they understood as *riqq*. No scare quotes appear around the slaves mentioned in the examples from Islamic civilization because each and every person mentioned in them was a *raqiq*. If brought before a Muslim judge in Tangier or Delhi, each of those individuals would be instantaneously recognized as a slave according to the Shariah. Regardless of whether or not we agree that slavery is one transhistorical reality at a global level, wherever there was the Shariah there was *riqq*.

Of course, there are always ambiguities. Whether the perspective we take is that of modern historians invoking 'Islamic civilization' to help organize the past or that of medieval Muslims imagining a shared Abode of Islam, this was a world that could blur in and out of focus even in its core regions. And it blended with neighboring cultures and systems at its extremities. Nonetheless, there were features of *riqq* – of slavery in Islamic civilization – that were close to consistent. Across the stretch of arid land from the Sahel to the fringes of north India (what one might call the classic slavery zone) there was a clear bifurcation corresponding to free and slave in the vocabulary of both Roman law and the Shariah. Even in areas where this bifurcation faded into complex hierarchies or webs of dependent relationships, like in India or Southeast Asia, among Muslims there was, to my knowledge, always a category called or translating *'abd/raqiq*.[12]

This Islamic slavery shared certain features. These included classifying the children born of concubines as freeborn and the frequency of manumission (though this last feature seems less prominent in Southeast Asia. This was perhaps due to the prevalence of debt slavery there, since debt slaves could redeem themselves). Slaves generally had to come from outside the

Abode of Islam. And race was 'minimized,' as Paul Lovejoy describes it, in relation to servile status. These were all features directly promoted by the Shariah.[13]

The Shariah was, of course, not in any way the only factor shaping the practice of slavery in this world or even the most significant one. Local or regional cultures and institutions played important roles. The practice of slavery and the slave trade among the Tuareg of North Africa were shaped more by the matrilineal character of Tuareg society and the harshness of its environment than by the rules of the Shariah.[14] Muslims could completely ignore direct commands from the Quran, as in the case of slave owners in Aden in the 1200s who rented out their slave girls as prostitutes.[15] The law of the Malay Muslim state of Melaka in the fifteenth century broke with the established tradition of Islamic law when it stated that a man could be made a slave if he had committed certain crimes, been fined an amount of money he could not afford to pay or had fallen into debt (though this latter situation resulted in a servile status less permanent than the Shariah category of *abdi*).[16] Criminals pardoned by the sultan could also become his slaves.[17] While the Shariah rarely allowed slaves to inherit, the property of farm slaves in the Kano Emirate in Hausaland was mostly inherited by their children, as were the farms of imperial slaves settled to work Ottoman lands.[18] The Shariah uniformly prohibited castrating human beings, but this was nonetheless sometimes done by unscrupulous Muslim slave raiders. It was also carried out at times by Muslim rulers eager to avoid the high cost of importing eunuchs (many who underwent the surgery died), as in the case of the emir of Bagirmi in the nineteenth century.[19] The Shariah clearly prohibited enslaving non-Muslim subjects living under a Muslim ruler (*dhimmīs*). But they were also occasionally enslaved, as Muslim slave raiders did with Christians in Nubia who had been granted *dhimmi* status in the Mamluk Empire in 1276 CE or, indeed, with ISIS's 2014 enslavement of Yazidis in Iraq.[20]

Muslims Enslaving Muslims

Some Muslims even broke the clear and categorical rule that no Muslim could be enslaved.[21] Sometimes this was done with the justification that those enslaved were actually not Muslims at all. Such was the case of the Ottoman enslavement of the extremist Shiite followers of the Safavid Shah Isma'il (d. 1524). The Ottoman Shaykhs al-Islam Ibn Kamal (d. 1534), Abu

Su'ud Efendi (d. 1574), 'Abdallah Efendi (d. 1743) and the Ottoman scholar Nuh Hanafi (d. 1660) declared his followers unbelievers (*kuffār*). The men could be killed as apostates or, according to one opinion, return to the fold of Islam as free Muslims. Their women and children could be enslaved, though Abu Su'ud exempted any children over five or six who pronounced the Muslim testimony of faith. The Ottoman forces exceeded the fatwas, it seems, since they often took the men as slaves as well.[22]

Of course, the Safavid forces very arguably were not Muslims, since they believed their Shah was God incarnate on earth.[23] But, as we will see below, many of the arguments proffered by these senior Ottoman scholars applied to orthodox Imami Shiites as well. Much more dubious was the claim proffered by the armies of the twelfth-century Almohad revivalist movement in the Islamic West when they took the women of Marrakesh as slaves upon conquering the city. They did so because the Almohads rejected as unbelievers any Muslims who did not embrace the absurdly narrow creed of their founder, Ibn Tumart (d. 1130).[24]

Sometimes enslaving other Muslims was done without any pretense for respecting the rules of the Shariah. In the early twentieth century many slave women in Fez were still brought from Berber areas in the country. This was occurring hundreds of years after Islam had permeated Morocco and despite the sultan appointing an inspector in the Fez slave market to prevent this.[25] In Kano in the nineteenth century Muslims fought and enslaved other Muslims with abandon, recalled one former slave without a hint of irony.[26] Deceitful guides or nomad bandits preying on Muslims performing the Hajj became a salient abuse in the late nineteenth and early twentieth centuries, in particular the abduction of pilgrims from Africa, Baluchistan and Southeast Asia.[27] Brazenly enslaving Muslims from Somalia and Yemen, and even within Arabia, seems to have been particularly common in the same period.[28] Sometimes Muslims enslaved other Muslims out of gross ignorance of the Shariah. This may have been the case with the inaptly named Sunni 'Ali (d. 1492). This ruler of Songhay simply did not care about enslaving Muslims, but he also did not know how to pray.[29]

Perhaps the most egregious and long-running case of Muslims enslaving Muslims was the extensive enslavement of Shiite Persians by Sunni Turkmen nomads and semi-sedentary Sunni Uzbek tribes, who raided extensively into the adjacent Persian province of Khurasan from the mid-1700s to the early 1900s. We should note, however, that this practice attracted significant criticism as soon as it began in the 1520s, when warfare between Uzbek tribes and the Shiite Safavid Empire heated up. A Safavid court chronicler from the early 1600s registered the moral shock felt at the enemy stooping to this new low.[30] Mulla ʿAli Qari (d. 1606), a senior Hanafi (i.e., Sunni) scholar of Mecca who originally hailed from Herat, addressed the issue repeatedly in a lengthy polemic against Shiism. Qari's own teacher had been killed in Herat by the Safavid invaders, and he was no lover of Shiism. He condemned numerous aspects of it as falling outside the bounds of Islam. But he stressed that this did not mean that all Shiites were unbelievers, and he noted the immense communal strife and violence that had resulted from this sectarian escalation. He also specifically condemned the Uzbek enslavement of Shiite women and children as repugnant sectarian chauvinism that flew in the face of the caution that the Prophet had taught regarding declaring other Muslims unbelievers. Even more outrageous, added Qari, these attackers often made no distinction between the Shiite and non-Shiite inhabitants of Khurasan. As a result, many of these Uzbeks were themselves in grave danger of lapsing into unbelief for their decision that it was licit to have sex with illegally enslaved women. Nor was Qari alone in this. He was a moderate, he noted, compared to some other Hanafi scholars who had actually declared the Uzbek enslavers themselves to be unbelievers for permitting what God had clearly forbidden.[31] Over two centuries later, the observant British explorer Alexander Burnes (d. 1841) heard that Persian rulers had also communicated their Shariah objections. But the Turkmens were unmoved.[32]

Did the Sunni enslavers of Persian Shiites have any justification? Uzbek and Turkmen oral tradition held that one of their scholars in the sixteenth century, a Shams al-Din Muhammad Herati, had issued a fatwa allowing the enslavement of Safavid followers.[33] Burnes reports that the justification came when Uzbek ulama visited Persia and heard the first three caliphs being cursed. They decreed that Shiites were unbelievers who should be fought and could be enslaved. Other fatwas allowed this jihad so that the unbelieving Shiites could be forcibly converted to Sunnism.[34]

Here there is a major contradiction in the flimsy Shariah arguments being proffered. Non-Muslims who are enslaved cannot be forcefully converted to Islam. Turkmens and Uzbeks generally acknowledged this and allowed their Christian slaves to practice their religion unmolested. Converting Shiites to Sunnism through capture could be allowed if they were categorized as heretics, since heretical Muslims can be fought and brought back into the fold under the laws of rebellion (*bughāt*). But these are clearly Muslims and hence cannot be enslaved. This was not the case with apostates. Muslim groups who have been declared apostates (as was the case with the Persian Shiites) must be fought and killed – at least their menfolk must be. If they repent and re-embrace Islam, then Muslim scholarly opinion was divided on whether this can be accepted. But either they were killed or returned to Islam as full Muslims. Slavery was not an option.

All this was clear from the fatwas of the Ottoman Shaykhs al-Islam, who only allowed the enslavement of Safavid Shiite women and children if they allowed enslaving any Shiites at all. One exception – and the one notionally valid justification for enslaving male Shiites – came from a fatwa of the Ottoman Shaykh al-Islam ʿAbdallah Efendi in the 1720s. If the Ottomans' Persian foes were not categorized as apostates but, rather, simply as infidels who had never been Muslims to begin with, he implied, then they were no different from any other unbelievers whom Muslim armies encountered outside the Abode of Islam: their men, women and children could be enslaved. But this does not seem to have been the reasoning of Uzbek and Turkmen slavers. Many seemed to lack the patience for such cogitation. Jeff Eden's ongoing research shows that, though it was uncommon in comparison with the trade in Shiite slaves, Turkmens also enslaved other Sunnis, either because they simply did not care or sometimes because they tortured them into declaring themselves Shiites.[35]

THE CLASSIC SLAVERY ZONE

The second important fact obscured by challenging too vigorously the notion of an 'Islamic slavery' is that there were definitive, common features of slavery in the region stretching from North Africa through the eastern Mediterranean, through to Iran and into northern India.[36] This fact predated Islam and survived the establishment of the faith. As Lovejoy points out, Islam inherited the existing patterns and traditions of slavery that were relatively consistent across this area. Slaves were used more for domestic service than for large-scale agricultural production, for example. Within this greater region, the Near East had its own stubborn mixture of Roman and Semitic patterns of slavery, many of which persisted after Islam came to dominate there.[37] It may be coincidence, but almost two millennia after Cicero (d. 43 BCE) gave a speech mentioning that slaves in Rome expected to be freed within six years if they worked hard, Ottoman slaves still expected to be manumitted after seven to ten years.[38]

CONSUMING PEOPLE & 'ASCENDING MISCEGENATION'

From the Islamic conquests of the 630s to the early 1900s, Islamic civilization essentially inhaled masses of humanity. Though we can do little more than estimate, available data suggest that over fourteen centuries, from Morocco to Southeast Asia, tens of millions of people were sucked as slaves into the Dar al-Islam.[39] The slave population in Islamic civilization generally had a very low rate of natural reproduction, as opposed to slavery in the Roman Empire or the United States.[40] In part this was due to disease and in part because, at least in some times and places, slaves did not have many children. In nineteenth-century Egypt, for example, though most slaves married, around 70 percent of the freed Black slaves left no progeny. This may be because they did not start families until relatively late in life, after they were freed.[41]

The greatest cause, however, was probably the high rate of emancipation. As John Hunwick observed, this meritorious aspect of the Shariah was a 'two-edged sword.' As slaves were manumitted, new slaves had to be brought in to meet labor demands.[42] Mansa Musa (d. 1337), the fabulously wealthy ruler of Mali, was renowned for his piety. A chronicler of Timbuktu wrote that 'One of the signs of his righteousness is that he manumitted a person every day.' But he also bought and owned thousands of slaves – his wife (one of them?) alone had five hundred slave women – and Mali's wealth in part came from the slave trade north.[43] Some scholars have estimated, very roughly, that the average service life of slaves in Islamic civilization was around seven years (this is an enormous generalization). This means that every year about 15 percent of the slave work force had to be replaced.[44]

The high rate of emancipation and the fact that children born to concubines were free resulted in what the late Ali Mazrui called the pattern of 'ascending miscegenation' in the Islamic world.[45] Many, if not most, of the slaves sucked into Islamic civilization converted to Islam. Many, if not most, of them were emancipated after a period of years. Those women who had children with their free masters, as well as the great swaths of manumitted Muslim slaves, were all succeeded by free Muslim descendants. To stretch the biologic metaphor, many, perhaps most, of those inhaled into the body of Islam were not cordoned off in a slave class or cast out after use. They were mixed with and exhaled into the free Muslim population. This process was rendered more dramatic by the inordinately large percentage of the slaves brought in who were female, at least via the important routes from across the Sahara. Twice as many female slaves as men came via this trade (the opposite of the male-heavy Atlantic slave trade).[46] Visiting the Tihama coast of Yemen in 1763, Carsten Niebuhr was approached by a wealthy old merchant who had gone through over eighty slave-concubines in his day, marrying them off or freeing them all. He sought medicinal aid from the Danish scholar so he could pleasure two new ones he had just bought.[47]

The constructive power of this incorporative process is most evident in the phenomenon of the *mawali* in the early Islamic period.[48] *Mawali* (*mawālī*, plural of *mawlā*) was the term that Arabs in the pre-Islamic Hejaz used to refer both to non-Arabs integrated into their society's tribal structure as well as to freed slaves, who would also be incorporated into formal relationships with their former masters. The term *mawla* was thus ambiguous; a *mawla* could be a freed slave or just an associated person from outside the local tribe. According to Daniel Pipes, about one-tenth of the Prophet's Companions were *mawali*. Of them, about five-sixths were freed slaves, meaning that around eight percent of the Companions were freed slaves. The early Islamic conquests resulted in both a massive number of captive, non-Arab slaves and newly conquered populations of non-Arabs interested in converting to Islam. The *mawla* relationship become the vehicle by which both groups became free, or Muslim, or both.[49]

With the conquest of the Persian Empire and the Byzantine lands of the Middle East by a small Muslim elite, the integration of the *mawali* resulted in what Chase Robinson describes as 'absorbing enormous volumes of cultural capital – especially Late Antique learning.'[50] Many of the *mawali* were not just freed slaves who became Muslim. They quickly formed the bulk of Islam's nascent scholarly and administrative elite. As Zuhri (d. 742), a major early Muslim scholar of Arab descent, remarked in his old age, the days of the Arabs had gone. 'Knowledge has been taken over by the *mawali*,' explained Zuhri, naming leading scholars like Hasan Basri (d. 728) and Ibn Sirin (d. 728), who were sons of freed slave fathers (being the child of a free father and a slave mother was inconsequential). ʿIkrima (d. 723–4), probably a Berber, Nafiʿ (d. 736) and Makhul (d. 731), both probably Persians, were all also freed slaves who were among the foremost scholars of their generation.[51] One of Zuhri's most illustrious students, Muhammad Ibn Ishaq (d. 767), a leading jurist and Hadith transmitter as well as the author of the earliest full biography of the Prophet, was the grandson of a freed slave. A generation later, Ibn al-Mubarak (d. 797) would emerge as a chief scholar of his generation and a pillar of Sunni Islam. His mother was a Persian from Khwarazm on the Aral Sea, and his father was a slave of Turkic origin. Ibn Jinni (d. 1002) was a premier Arabic grammarian and lexicographer; his father was a Byzantine slave.[52] The famous geographer and literary scholar Yaqut Hamawi (d. 1229) was also originally a Byzantine Greek enslaved as a child and educated in Baghdad by his master, for whom he worked until he was freed at the age of thirty.[53]

Countless scholars of lesser renown were also freed slaves or the children of freed slaves. One Muslim saint in tenth-century Egypt was the locus of such compelling miracles that his Christian slave girl, previously annoyed at an ascetism that often left her collaterally hungry, finally embraced Islam and became a devoted teacher of the Quran, Hadith and Islamic law. She was seen years later giving lessons in the mosque of Hims in Syria.[54] In the 1300s the traveler Ibn Battuta noted that the judge of Aden was the son of a slave.[55] Maymun Ghulam Fakhkhar (d. 1407) lived his whole life in slavery in Fez and wrote several short books on Islamic law and other topics.[56]

A second, dramatic episode of ascending miscegenation is the story of the 'children of the people (*awlād al-nās*),' as the offspring of the ruling class were known in the Mamluk Empire, which ruled Egypt, Syria and the Hejaz from 1260 to 1517 CE. Membership in the Mamluk military elite was theoretically only open to those who had been brought as slaves in childhood from the Turkic steppes, the Caucasus, or occasionally other places. Some of their sons won well-paid positions in Mamluk military units, and a few managed to succeed their fathers as sultan. The most spectacular example of this was the long reign(s) of Sultan Al-Nasir Muhammad (d. 1341), who inherited the throne from his father and in turn passed it on to his son. But the vast majority of the *awlad al-nas* formed a cascade of well-heeled spawn overflowing from the Mamluk elite down into the native-born society below. Many of them either found work in the civilian administration, lived off comfortable sinecures set up by their powerful patriarchs or flourished in business. Some would emerge as leading ulama in the Mamluk period, such as the jurist-Hadith scholars Zarkashi (d. 1392), ʿAla'i (d. 1359), ʿAyni (d. 1451) and the historian Safadi (d. 1363).[57]

SLAVE POPULATIONS

Slaves ended up constituting appreciable portions of the population in Islamic civilization, though this differed widely and seems to have been most concentrated in urban areas. A census carried out by the Umayyad caliph ʿAbd al-Rahman III (r. 912–961) in the mid-tenth century showed a maximum of 13,750 'Slavic' slaves in the capital of Cordoba, with 'Slavic' meaning any non-Black slave from Europe, North Africa or Central Asia.[58] This would mean that slaves made up between 3 and 14 percent of the population as a whole, based on best estimates of Cordoba's population at the time.[59] Lovejoy estimates that between a quarter and a half of the population of the nineteenth-century Sokoto Caliphate were slaves, though Bruce Hall has shown how the data on which such estimates are based probably inflate the number.[60] For most of the nineteenth century the slave population of Cairo was between 12,000 and 15,000.[61] Assuming an average population of 300,000, this would make slaves between four and five percent of the city's inhabitants.[62] Indeed, at the end of the nineteenth century slaves made up around five percent of the population of the Ottoman Empire as a whole.[63] An 1868 census in Tehran, capital of Qajar Persia, reported that 12 percent of the city's population was African slaves or domestic servants (who might also be slaves).[64]

In Muslim Southeast Asia and East Africa, slaves seem to have made up a much larger portion of the population. A variety of dependent laborers categorized as 'slaves' by Europeans constituted the majority of the population of Dutch Makassar and Batavia in the seventeenth and eighteenth centuries.[65] Nineteenth-century Mombasa may well have had the highest percentage of slaves. One European observer estimated in 1848 that three-quarters of the population of its surrounding villages were slaves.[66] In the mid-1800s, when clove export was at its peak, the slave population in and around the town of Zanzibar (estimated at 60–100,000) was comparable to and perhaps more than the entire population of the town itself (roughly estimated at 60–70,000) in the same period.[67]

ROUTES OF THE MUSLIM SLAVE TRADE

Slavery in Arabia on the eve of Islam was widespread, but the number of slaves was relatively small. Slaves were mostly taken by raiding, debt, the sale of children, kidnapping or punishment for crimes. Of a sample of slaves in the Prophet's community, the majority were Arab, about one-third were Africans (probably from Ethiopia), and there were also Byzantines (i.e., Christians from the lands north of the Hejaz), Copts and Persians, all procured through an economy of capture and sale. As was normal in the Near East and beyond, female slaves were sexually available to their male owners.[68]

As Majied Robinson has shown, the number of concubines taken by Muslims jumped dramatically with the early Islamic conquests.[69] This suggests a similar leap in the number of slaves taken more generally. One of the first public buildings erected in the new Muslim garrison city of Fustat (later Cairo) was a slave market.[70] According to the doctrines of the Shariah as they were ironed out in subsequent decades, the inhabitants of areas conquered by force (*ʿanwatan*, as opposed to by negotiated settlement, *ṣulḥan*) could be taken as slaves.[71] But this seems not to have generally occurred, since the new Muslim ruling class was interested in little more than establishing political control and collecting taxes from a productive agricultural population. They wanted hard-working farmers paying taxes, not slaves torn out of a disrupted economy.[72] There are reports that the caliph ʿUmar bin al-Khattab (d. 644) even prohibited Muslims from buying the slaves owned by their non-Muslim subjects.[73]

Writings by Christian and Zoroastrian clergy in the early decades of Muslim rule certainly recall the Islamic conquests as a cataclysmic trauma, with the Muslim invaders allegedly taking large numbers of captives, stripping women from their husbands and children from their families.[74] An Umayyad-era correspondence from the Byzantine emperor includes a scathing criticism of what he sees as Muslims' inexcusable licentiousness, including their habit of indulging in concubinage.[75] These descriptions, however, should not be relied upon as unbiased accounts of reality, since such material often served polemical purposes like vilifying the new faith.[76] Yet Christian writers like Athanasius of Sinai in the late 600s CE do mention moving episodes they themselves witnessed, like a Christian slave accompanying his Muslim master on a visit to Mount Sinai and pleading with a Christian holy man there to save him from 'this oppression.'[77]

Slaves continued to be taken as the conquests petered out in the mid-eighth century and were replaced by seasonal raiding into the non-Muslims lands of Central Asia and the Caucusus, along the Byzantine frontier in Syria, across the sea into Italy and nearby Mediterranean islands, and from

Muslim Iberia into the Christian areas to the north. Slave raiding would be very active in various times and places, such as in Ottoman raids across the Austrian frontier in the 1600s.[78] And it would continue in places like the Sahara and Southeast Asia until the twentieth century (even in the twenty-first century in the Sahara).

But after the end of the early Islamic conquests the main source of slaves became importing them from non-Muslim lands (see Figure 1). The Nile/Oxus heartland of Islamic civilization was an irresistible magnet for this trade. In the early medieval period, the markets of the Islamic world paid up to four times more than those in Europe for a European slave.[79] The average price of a Turkic slave fit for military service in Egypt in 1400 CE was between fifty and seventy gold coins, but it could go as high as two thousand. In the large Ottoman cities of the late fifteenth century, the average price for a slave was between twenty-five and fifty gold pieces.[80] Historians have observed how the Islamic heartland of the Mediterranean Middle East had a 'voracious appetite' for human labor, in particular after an instance of the bubonic plague in 750 CE cut down the indigenous labor force.[81] Like the European colonies in the Americas in later centuries, Islamic civilization truly 'consumed' masses of human beings.[82]

In the course of the fourteen-century-long history of Islamic civilization, slaves would be drawn from three main population pools: the Slavs of Eastern Europe, the Turkic peoples of the Russian and Central Asian steppes and the Black African population of the Sahel and east Africa.[83] The slave trade route that would burgeon early in Islamic history and would arguably play the most influential role in Islamic civilization was one importing slaves from among the Turkic and Caucasian peoples on the steppes of Russia, from north of the Caspian Sea eastward to the lower Syr Darya River. It would furnish the slave markets of Samarqand, Ferghana, Baghdad and Cairo. The route fed different markets with different types of slaves at different times and it flourished from the eighth century all the way until the early nineteenth, when Circassian women from the Caucusus were still sought after for the harems of the Ottoman elites in Istanbul and Cairo.

Hordes of Islamic coins show that during the ninth century the flow of money and slaves circulated between Baghdad and the southern Volga River region. In the tenth century, it was between the Samanid province of Khurasan and Transoxiana at one end and the great Volga River commercial center of Bulgar on the other.[84] At least in the 800–900s CE, most slaves coming into the Nile/Oxus heartland via Muslim merchants moved along what Marek Jankowiak calls small, 'capillary trade networks.' These merchants bought slaves at distant, multi-ethnic trade entrepôts outside the Abode of Islam, like Bulgar, where Muslim merchants were foreign visitors among many others.[85] From there slaves were brought to the slave market of Urgench in the Samanid realm or down through the Caucasus to the market of Derbent on the west coast of the Caspian Sea, and from there to Baghdad.[86]

From the thirteenth to the sixteenth centuries, the constant need to provide young Turkic and Circassian slaves for the powerful Mamluk Empire emphasized the trade route from Cairo to Tabriz. The famous Karimi Muslim merchants would either purchase slaves at the emporium of Tabriz or head further north into 'the lands of the Tatars' to bring slaves back.[87] After the conquest of Constantinople by wayward Crusaders in 1204, Genoese merchants set up slave trading posts on the northern coast of the Black Sea to bring Slavic, Caucasian and Turkic slaves to Muslim markets. When the Ottomans conquered Constantinople in 1453, they took over control of the Black Sea slave trade (ironically forcing Europeans to turn to Africa for slaves).[88] From the mid-1400s to the mid-1700s the Black Sea slave trade would boom under the control of the Crimean Tatars, close allies of the Ottomans who would serve as avid procurers of slaves for the markets of Istanbul, raiding into Russian territory and the Caucasus to acquire their inventory.[89]

A second major route drew in slaves extracted from the Slavic peoples of Eastern Europe and took place at the hands of European Christian merchants, primarily Italians. They acquired slaves from the Balkans and Eastern Europe, either by raiding or by purchasing them at slave markets on the River Danube. Italian merchants then transported these slaves via the trade centers of Venice and Genoa, selling them across the Mediterranean in Alexandria or transporting them onward to Baghdad. This trade flourished from the ninth to the twelfth centuries, when the Black Sea trade eclipsed it and by which time most of the Slavic populations had converted to Christianity, which placed them theoretically off limits to Italian slavers.[90]

Muslim Spain and North Africa also inhaled large numbers of slaves via a route from the Rhine River in France and Eastern Europe, from the 700s through the 1000s. In the hands of Frankish, Italian and Jewish Radanite merchants, slaves were drawn first from outlying Frankish lands and later from the Slavs beyond the River Danube. From there they were brought to Lyon, then eventually to Narbonne for sale to Muslims in Spain or even for transport to Egypt and the Red Sea port of Jeddah.[91]

The largest number of slaves brought into the Islamic world almost certainly came from Africa. These included Berbers from the Sahara, Black Africans (called *Sūd*) from the Sahel and the forest zones just to its south, Ethiopians and Somalis (called *Ḥabash*), and Black Africans from the coastal interior of the central east African coast (called *Zanj*). One route, which operated prior to Islam and saw its most intensive activity from the late seventeenth century through the late nineteenth, was bringing slaves by sea from the east African coast and interior north to Aden and Jeddah, through the Persian Gulf to Persia, or east to India.[92] Similarly, slaves from the Horn of Africa were brought via the port of Zayla in Somalia through the strait of the Bab al-Mandab to the commercial center of Zabid on the Red Sea coast of Yemen.[93] East African ports like Mombasa became major centers of the slave trade in the nineteenth century.[94]

The most dramatic and well-documented route of the slave trade into Islamic civilization was the network of caravan trails connecting the north African centers of Marrakesh, Benghazi, Tunis and Cairo to the Sahel region that stretched from modern-day Senegal all the way to Sudan. With its main entrepôts at Gadames and Zawilah in the deserts of modern-day Libya, the slave trade along these routes became highly active from the 800s CE onward. Early on it was in the hands of Berber merchants, who worked with Jewish partners. Later on, Tuareg and Arab merchants took over. This route survived the legal abolition of slavery in Tunis in the 1840s, thriving for several more decades. Benghazi provided slaves to Istanbul even into the 1920s. Over twelve and a half centuries, between six and seven million Black Africans were transported as slaves across the Sahara.[95] Another route led from the lands east of Lake Chad into modern-day Sudan and Ethiopia. From there slaves were taken north up the Nile to Cairo and the Mediterranean world. Though this route had been active since the eleventh century, it saw particularly intensified activity in the seventeenth through the nineteenth centuries.[96]

Although in no way reciprocal in terms of the volume of trade, some trade routes were two-way. Reports from the 1300s suggest that at least some wealthy Sahelian African Muslims had Arab slave girls from places like Damascus.[97] The Indian Ocean saw some commerce move in the opposite direction too during the medieval period, selling Indian slaves through the Red Sea. Women in particular were brought from the Indian port of Goa to Aden, and from there sold on to the Hejaz and Egypt.[98]

India was also the source for a lesser known but still substantial slave trade: a steady flow of dozens and perhaps hundreds of thousands of Hindu slaves north into the Turkic states of Muslim Central Asia. This began when Turkic warlords started raiding into India in the 1000s and continued as the Delhi sultanate and later the Mughal Empire established Muslim rule in northern India. Their expansions further south yielded huge numbers of enslaved Indian captives. Slaves were also sometimes demanded as part of tax revenue from subordinate Hindu lords, and desperately poor Indian subjects also sold their children into slavery. Many of these slaves were traded north into Central Asia, a trade which continued into the nineteenth century.[99]

Of course, some regions within the Islamic world also had complex internal slave trades. This seems to be the case in nineteenth-century Central Asia and in particular in Southeast Asia, where the slave trade was more internal than aimed at export to other Muslim lands.[100] To help monopolize the spice production in their Southeast Asian colonies in the seventeenth century, the Dutch East India Company imported a huge number of slaves from East Africa, Madagascar, Bengal and other parts of Southeast Asia to work their plantations.[101]

Muslims were not the only religious group involved in the commerce of slaves in Islamic civilization. In the early medieval period the Radanite Jews had a trade network that stretched from France to North Africa, Egypt, the Red Sea and even beyond. Both Muslims and Christians in the Horn of Africa engaged in the slave trade there.[102] In 1838 a Scottish explorer encountered a boatload of slave girls being brought up the Nile from Kordofan in the Sudan and was shocked to find that their purveyor was a Greek Christian.[103] Since the Shariah prohibited Muslims from castrating human beings, the production of eunuchs became a niche activity for Christians both inside and outside the Dar al-Islam. In the early medieval period, first Verdun and then Venice were important locations for castrating youths (though various treaties with the Carolingians technically prohibited this), as was Armenia and in later centuries Ethiopia and Bagirmi in the central Sahel.[104] A French physician in the late nineteenth century described how castrating slaves brought up the Nile from the Sudan was the monopoly of Coptic priests in the village of Zawiyat al-Dayr in upper Egypt.[105]

BLACKNESS AND SLAVERY IN ISLAMIC CIVILIZATION

As we discussed briefly in the introduction, racial discrimination and racial stereotypes have long existed in Islamic civilization and among Muslims. Chief among these is the conception of Blackness as a deficiency and its association with slavery, as we still see with the habit in some parts of the Arab world of referring to Black people as slaves (*ʿabīd*).

Riqq was often racialized in Islamic civilization. Blackness was just one aspect of this. Unlike North America, where slavery and Blackness were synonymous, to the exclusion of other racial categories, slavery in Islamic civilization was racialized in numerous directions and with both negative and positive valences. Different words for slave connoted race in different ways at different times. Mentioning the word *mamluk* in fourteenth-century Cairo would suggest a powerful Kipchak Turkic member of the ruling military class. Two centuries earlier a *mamluk* would have been a Black African slave soldier serving in the Fatimid army. Saying *kul* in sixteenth-century Istanbul would bring to mind a light-skinned elite slave of the Ottoman sultan, like the Serbian Sokullu Mehmet Pasha. In Isfahan *ghulam* would mean an Armenian imperial slave of the Safavid shah. *Jariya* (female slave) in nineteenth-century Istanbul would probably mean a blonde Circassian woman, but across the Mediterranean in Cairo or Mecca it could also mean an Ethiopian or Greek.* Eight centuries earlier in North Africa, *jariya* would probably have meant a Berber woman, while a Persian of the day would have pictured a Turkic, Indian or Slavic woman.[106]

Numerous scholars of Islamic history and slavery more broadly have pointed out the association of Blackness and slavery in Islamic civilization as well as the use of Blackness to justify enslavement.[107] As Chouki El Hamel notes, Ibn Butlan (d. 1066), a Christian physician who wrote a guide to buying slaves, does indeed describe Nubian women as submissive and obedient to their masters, 'as if they were created for slavery.' But these words come just after his praise for them as pious, chaste, goodly and ethical. And this all forms part of a taxonomy of slave women from various

* According to the Dutch Orientalist Snouck Hurgronje (d. 1936), who visited the holy city, Meccan men were particularly taken by dark African and Ethiopian women. Visiting Paris in the 1820s, a Muslim scholar bemoans how the French see no beauty in Blackness, while Arabs have 'two directions in love'; Hurgronje, *Mekka in the Latter Part of the Nineteenth Century*, 106–9; Rifʿat al-Tahtawi, *An Imam in Paris*, 180.

ethnicities, each one listed with its strengths and weaknesses. It is not Blackness that Ibn Butlan associates with slavery but Nubianness; three other groups that both modern Americans and the Arab-Islamic tradition would categorize as Black Africans are not styled as natural slaves by Ibn Butlan.[108] His contemporary, the humanist scholar Miskawayh (d. 1030), notes that the virtue of loyalty in slaves is most prominent in Ethiopians and Nubians . . . and Greeks.[109]

Sadly, anti-Black racism has long been present in Islamic civilization, even planting itself retroactively in Prophetic soil.[110] One Hadith attributed to the Prophet (considered forged by leading Hadith scholars) states, 'The Black African, he steals when hungry and fornicates when sated.' Many such reports treated Black African and slave as coterminous. Though such ersatz scripture probably originated from the sayings of lay folk, some circulated among the ulama as well. One story describes the great early scholar Shafiʿi teaching in a mosque. When he sees a man come in looking around among the servants and slaves sleeping in the mosque, Shafiʿi sends one of his students to ask the man if he was looking for a one-eyed, Black slave. If so, Shafiʿi tells him, he will find the slave in jail. And, indeed, that was where he was. Asked how he predicted this, Shafiʿi explains he deduced it using the Prophet's wisdom: either the slave had been arrested for stealing or detained for fornication.[111]

Yet there is no indication that the story about Shafiʿi is historically reliable, and evidence strongly suggests that leading Muslim scholars considered it apocryphal.[112] There is a strong, perhaps dominant, strain among Muslim Hadith scholars of acute skepticism toward such overtly racist material. The Damascus scholar Ibn al-Qayyim (d. 1351) categorized the supposed Hadith Shafiʿi cited as a manifest forgery. He listed it along with a whole series of Hadiths denigrating Black Africans and African slaves. These are betrayed as forgeries, Ibn al-Qayyim explained, by their racist content.[113]

Muslim scholarly opposition to anti-Black racism can be seen most clearly in the reaction of influential ulama to the notorious myth of the Curse of Ham. This story originates in the Bible (Gen. 9:21–29), which tells how Noah became drunk and lay nude in his tent. Noah's son Ham saw his father naked and did not act to cover him but instead told his brothers, who covered his nudity. When Noah awoke and learned what had happened he pronounced, 'Cursed be [Ham's son] Canaan, the lowest of slaves shall he be to his brothers.' El Hamel shows how the Talmudic tradition built on this biblical story and eventually propagated a version of the Ham myth that added an element of Blackness to the abasement of Ham's descendants as well. In his book-length study on the Curse of Ham, however, David Goldenberg argues the association of Ham with Blackness is first found in a fourth-century Syriac Christian text. Goldenberg further argues that the Blackness and slavery versions of the Curse myth were fused into a compound narrative in the first century of the Islamic period.[114]

Though scholars like El Hamel demonstrate how the Ham myth influenced and reinforced stereotypes about Blackness and Africans in the Islamic Middle East, they do not give enough credit to the critical response of numerous prominent ulama, both to the versions that center on Blackness and those that include the curse of slavery.[115] Muslim historians and litterateurs related the Curse of Ham material from the biblical tradition as part of their review of human history. In general, Muslim historians and exegetes drew liberally on the Bible and other bodies of Jewish and Christian lore to flesh out the stories alluded to in the Quran and to fill in the history of eras before Islam. There were Hadiths from the Prophet on such things, but they did not suffice for reconstructing human history, since they lacked the biblical tradition's comprehensive detail. Mas'udi (d. 956), one of the earliest Muslim historians to note the Curse of Ham, contrasts this biblical material with authoritative reports coming from Muslim authorities, noting some discrepancies.[116]

Muslim scholars recognized that relying on biblical lore was a fraught enterprise, since they were certain that much of the biblical material (really para-biblical material) they had found was not preserved revelation. Rather, it had been altered to obscure the timeless message of God to His prophets.[117] What was authentic content that could be still used, however, and what had been adulterated? Material that clearly contradicted explicit teachings in the Quran and the Sunna could be dismissed, but the situation was ambiguous with stories that either seemed unproblematic or only clashed with established Islamic teachings if understood from a particular point of view.[118] Muslim scholars could and did disagree on where an item of biblical lore fell on this spectrum. Some might have no qualms about repeating the story of David and Bathsheba, while others would condemn this as a baseless attack on the moral infallibility of prophets.[119] And they disagreed on the Curse of Ham.

When Mas'udi and earlier the Sunni Ibn Qutayba (d. 889) present the Curse of Ham story, the curse-of-slavery element is cited directly from the biblical tradition.[120] The only version they cite from a Muslim source is the one mentioning Blackness, which is reported from the early Muslim storyteller Wahb bin Munabbih (d. 732). But Wahb himself drew a large portion of his writings from biblical lore, such as the story of David and Bathsheba.[121] Another curse-of-Blackness version of the story appears in the *Mustadrak* of the Sunni Hadith scholar Hakim (d. 1014), attributed to the Companion Ibn Mas'ud. But Hakim's Hadith collection was severely criticized by later scholars for its uncritical acceptance of dubious material, and this report in general was dismissed as weak.[122]

Biblical lore also lay at the root of most Muslim transmissions of the curse of slavery version. In his history of Egypt, Ibn 'Abd al-Hakam (d. 871) includes a report from the Companion Ibn 'Abbas that mentions Noah condemning Ham's sons to be slaves of his brother Sham when Ham did not answer his call.[123] This is a Companion of the Prophet passing on exegetical material from the Biblical tradition, however, not information traced back to the Prophet himself. In his famous *History*, Tabari (d. 923) draws only on Muslim sources in presenting this episode. He includes two reports of the slavery-curse version from the earlier historian Ibn Ishaq. But Ibn Ishaq was roundly criticized for centuries for drawing uncritically on biblical material like that from Wahb.[124] Tabari includes another report on the slavery curse from the respected Successor Sa'ib bin Malik Thaqafi (d. early 700s). Sa'ib cites no authority, however. What he reports is his own opinion, not the authoritative legacy of the Prophet or even of his Companions.[125] Moreover, we should not assume that Tabari believed this report was true. Inclusion of reports in his *History* in no way meant that Tabari approved of or believed them.[126]

Real criticism of the Curse of Ham myth begins with the Baghdad jurist, chronicler and Hadith scholar Ibn al-Jawzi (d. 1201), who makes quick work of it. 'As for what is reported that Noah's nudity was uncovered and he [Ham] did not cover him and thus turned black, this is something that is not established as reliable or sound.'[127] Three centuries later Suyuti (d. 1505) explains that Ibn al-Jawzi's refutation applied to the curse of slavery element as well, since the wording that Ibn al-Jawzi had referenced comes from the curse-of-slavery version of the Ham story. Suyuti concludes that the most reliable source and received truth about the origins of humans' color is the Hadith that God created Adam from a handful of multi-colored earth.[128] The famous historian Ibn Khaldun (d. 1406) notes that the story in the Bible makes no mention of Blackness, only the curse of slavery, and that these are all 'fables of storytellers (*khurrafāt al-quṣṣāṣ*).' Skin color, he explains, is the product of environment.[129]

The notion that the nation of 'Blacks' had been rightfully condemned to slavery by a prophetic patriarch was simply inaccurate to scholars like Ibn al-Jawzi and Suyuti. They wrote works listing the virtues and historical accomplishments of Black Africans to contest the association of Blackness with both baseness and slavery. This was similarly the aim of the famous litterateur Jahiz (d. 868) in his *Pride of the Blacks over the Whites* (*Kitāb Fakhr al-sūdān 'alā al-bayḍān*) and most likely the aim of a similar, lost work by Ibn al-Marzuban (d. 919).[130] Ibn al-Jawzi prefaces his book on the virtues of Black Africans by explaining that he composed it to comfort Black Africans by reminding them that 'what matters is piety (*iḥsān*), not beautiful visages.'[131]

Does this mean that Black is not beautiful in Ibn al-Jawzi's opinion? Yes, and it is undeniable that this and many other expressions of Arab-Islamic thought associate Blackness with ugliness (see Appendix 1 – A Slave Saint of Basra). But for scholars like Ibn al-Jawzi this was a *conventional, aesthetic judgment,* not a moral one or an assessment of inherent human value.[132] The same prominent Sunni scholar who affirmed the longstanding position that saying the Prophet was Black was an act of unbelief (*kufr*) also affirmed the longstanding rule that any supposed Hadith denigrating 'Ethiopians or Blacks' was by definition a forgery. This was not a contradiction. This scholar explained that calling the Prophet Black was only problematic if it was meant as an insult. This is how it would be understood among peoples like the Arabs, he explained, who prized light skin and saw darkness as base and ugly. Among some African peoples, he added, darker complexions were considered more beautiful, so calling the Prophet Black in those contexts would not be considered demeaning.[133]

This might seem like a tortured defense of a tradition denigrating Blackness, but dismissing it as such ignores the enormous effort that a number of the most famous scholars in Islamic history put into disassociating Blackness from slavery and contemptibility. Ibn al-Jawzi was not engaged in some pathetic attempt to deflect accusations of racism. He, Suyuti and others compiled multiple books running to hundreds of pages and dedicated to proving that Blackness had often been the color of spiritual nobility and accomplishment. The books compiled by Jahiz, Ibn al-Jawzi and Suyuti consist mainly of inspiring biographies of leaders, saints and scholars from Islamic times and before who were Black. These were exemplars for all, not slaves to others.

Of course, racism dies hard even among the educated clerisy. The story of Shafiʿi identifying the Black slave was cited as an example of his perceptiveness in several books. Commenting on Ibn al-Marzuban's book on the virtues of Black Africans, one seventeenth-century Ottoman bibliophile dismissed it as coming from the same author who had penned *Favoring Dogs over Many of those Who Wear Clothing* (i.e., humans).[134] Slaves were sometimes lumped in with other perennial subalterns in male-produced urban culture. Another saying (probably falsely) attributed to Shafiʿi dictates that 'There are three who will insult you even if you honor them: women, slaves, and farmers.'[135]

THE ROLES AND EXPERIENCES OF SLAVES IN ISLAMIC CIVILIZATION

Islamic civilization included all the dizzying diversity one would expect of a constellation joining together herders in West Africa with ulama in Belgrade and merchants in Aceh. *Riqq* saturated this world. There was hardly an area of law, culture or economy that did not see the interaction of slaves and the free and thus raise the question of what their relationships, rights and obligations should be. To provide an exhaustive catalog of slavery in Islamic civilization would overwhelm both reader and author, but offering simplistic generalizations would be misleading. As we've seen, there are some general features of slavery in Islamic civilization, or at least of *riqq* as it was practiced, and we must remember that they always existed alongside exceptions, whether those were betrayals of an ideal or simply inevitable variations in a wide world.

Taking as an example the area of West Africa spanning modern Mali and northern Nigeria over a period of three centuries, even within one region of the Islamic world the diversity of slavery can be surprising. In the Songhay Empire (centered at Timbuktu) in the 1500s, slaves were ubiquitous. They could be found as concubines even among the non-elite, as workers toiling in salt mines, as objects of sale to be traded north to the Mediterranean, as singers and musicians, as eunuchs guarding the harems of nobles, as a major part of the ruler's elite cavalry unit, as agricultural workers or, according to Leo Africanus (d. *circa* 1550), the sole agents of buying and selling in Timbuktu's vegetable market.[136]

Even in a sphere as restricted as small-scale farming, the practice of slavery varied widely. Bambara-speaking Maraka Muslims in the late 1700s used large numbers of slaves for farming, while their non-Muslim Bambara neighbors worked the fields themselves with fewer slaves to help.[137] Nor was small-scale farming the only type of agricultural work that slaves experienced. With the formation of the powerful Sokoto Caliphate, there emerged the new phenomenon of large, slave-worked plantations owned by merchants or nobles. There between twenty and a thousand slaves worked either tilling the owner's land to the beat of a drum, weaving cotton or working as slave families farming their own land but providing occasional labor to their master.[138]

Slaves enjoyed markedly different treatment even within a relatively narrow geographic area. Hausa slave families working on farms for their masters in the Kano Emirate were basically self-supporting households with their own land to work and time to work it. They provided occasional labor to their owners. The owners' ability to sell off family members was highly restricted by public opinion, *mukataba* was common and freed slaves owed their former masters no patronage duty (*bara*). In the neighboring Zariah Emirate, however, even freed slaves of the Fulani elite remained a type of unfree person, paying rent to their or even their ancestors' former owner.[139]

Rather than attempting some regional or chronological survey of slavery in Islamic history, it may be more efficient to explore some of the most salient roles that slaves played in Islamic civilization and the most common aspects of their experiences. It may also be a more intimate glance into the millions of lives they lived.

THE SLAVE AS UPROOTED PERSON AND COMMODITY

Even in the idealized vision of *riqq* in the Shariah, slaves were before all else uprooted people. They had been made prisoner on the battlefield, taken as booty in conquered territory or, more frequently, either captured in some raid or sold by their kin in a distant land. Though they could pass through the hands of slave traders from multiple nations and serve any number of owners before reaching Muslim hands, slaves' journey began when they were reduced to chattel, almost always against their will.

We find almost no echo of the voices of the slaves brought into premodern Islamic civilization. But the recorded recollections of slaves from the nineteenth and twentieth centuries are chilling. Most of these were set down on paper by European observers, many of whom considered slavery an Oriental barbarism and were often predisposed to enhance portrayals of Muslim cruelty. There is little evidence, however, that the overall description they provide was inaccurate.[140] An Austrian merchant recalls his experience accompanying the Ottoman-Egyptian army on a slave expedition in 1838 into the Kordofan region west of Khartoum in modern-day Sudan. One village they raided surrendered without a fight, being accustomed to annual tributes exacted in slaves. The inhabitants of another fled into the mountains before the party arrived, and their homes were burned in their absence. A third village tried to repulse the attackers, and when they were finally overwhelmed less than half of the population was still alive. Many had killed themselves to avoid enslavement.[141] The memories of an aged ex-slave named Griga in French Algeria, recounted to a French author in 1945, describe his capture by Tuareg raiders when he was fourteen in what is today southern Niger. The attack was vicious, and in all twenty young men and twice the number of women were taken, along with children. Several old women had their throats cut then and there, probably because they promised little profit. We must be cautious, however, not to lapse into the lazy narrative that slavery was a curse brought by heartless Muslims from the north. In the course of Griga's description, he exposes that his village chief owned slaves as well.[142]

Recollections of the march to the slave markets of Cairo or Gadames are equally filled with cruelty and reminiscent of descriptions of the Atlantic Middle Passage. Young and old were yoked together at the neck and beaten when they lagged behind. Mothers were forced to carry their young children, and anyone whose illness or exhaustion made keeping them less profitable than leaving them to die or killing them met an immediate fate.[143] In the trans-Saharan slave trade of the early modern period, the protections available to slaves in the markets and homes of Muslim cities seem often to have been absent. The German physician Gustav Nachtigal was even-handed in his description of slavery in his travels in the Sahel during the 1870s. He acknowledged the good treatment of slaves when he saw it. But he recalls that, between capture and arriving at the market for sale, slaves 'did not enjoy even the theoretical protection of the law.' The Shariah seemed not to come into effect 'until the slaves were brought into safe Muslim territory: while still on the road they were simply booty.'[144] Of course, not all traffic was so brutal. A 1761 Danish expedition found itself traveling by sea from Istanbul to Alexandria lodged beneath a cabin of slave women destined for the Cairo market. They were secluded from the other passengers but managed to giggle loudly, converse with the Danish passengers through the windows and exchange curiosities.[145]

The lot of slaves did not necessarily improve when they were manumitted. Griga looked back bitterly on his life in the years after his master had freed him; he was impoverished and indebted, working a small plot of land right beside his former fellow slaves but with none of the support they received.[146] A British ethnographer's description of the conditions of Black slaves in Istanbul in the 1860s describes them as overworked, sold from owner to owner and beaten. Though some were freed by kind masters and set up in life, he claims that most were freed and left to beg in the streets.[147] Hurgronje's description of freed slaves in Mecca around the same time is very different. Household slaves were usually freed around the age of twenty, and there was 'hardly an office or position that is unattainable to such freedmen.'[148] Considering the vast diversity of experiences had by slaves in the expanse of the Abode of Islam, from tender affection and feelings of belonging to dehumanization and isolation, from slaves trying to make the best of their situations to dissimulating to please their masters, the contrasting testimony of Griga and the British traveler Charles Doughty (d. 1926) are instructive. Doughty writes of slaves in the Hejaz in the 1880s:

> In those Africans there is no resentment that they have been made slaves – they are often captives of their own wars – even though cruel men-stealers rent them from their parentage. The patrons who paid their price have adopted them into their households, the males are circumcised and – that which enfranchises their souls, even in the long passion of home-sickness – God has visited them in their mishap; they can say, '*it was His grace*,' since they be thereby entered into the saving religion.[149]

Griga would disagree. The slaves he knew were harassed by their masters and fellow slaves alike until they embraced Islam. At least one prominent West African Muslim scholar of the day encouraged this.[150] 'Nevertheless,' Griga adds, 'all of us, deep in our hearts, clung to our ancestral customs, though most of the Negroes, to make themselves look better, aped their masters and exaggerated everything.'[151] How can we know, peering back into the recesses of human experiences long passed, whether what Doughty or Griga described was more common? The lives lived by millions of slaves in Islamic civilization no doubt lie somewhere in between.

THE SLAVE AS DOMESTIC LABOR . . . EVEN TRUSTED MEMBER OF A HOUSEHOLD

Though generalizations made at the level of a civilization admit so great a range of exceptions that their value is questionable, in general the majority of slaves in Islamic civilization worked as domestic servants of one sort or another, from cooking to cleaning to running errands to manning businesses, leading caravans, singing and/or dancing.[152] Sometimes they could have niche specializations. Slaves in fourteenth-century Fez were the masters of surgery in the city.[153] More than just being basic laborers, slaves could be used to generate profit. In Istanbul, records from the sixteenth century show that slaves skilled in carpentry, rope-making, ship-repair and other trades were given *mukataba* contracts and rented out as walking investments by their owners.[154]

For much of Islamic history we can only catch glimpses of the dynamics of slaves' lives in the homes of their owners or in nearby slave quarters. Much like the 'mammies' of the American South, slave women who tended to children could become beloved members of the family. Huda Sha'rawi (d. 1947), the famous Egyptian feminist, recalled fondly her childhood in a wealthy Egyptian home in which loyal slaves raised her with love and were appreciated in return. Sa'id Agha, the chief Black eunuch who ran the household and carefully protected the honor of his charges, would remain an important part of Sha'rawi's household even into her adulthood when she worked as an activist.[155] In the early twentieth century, the Sudanese Muslim scholar Mahmud Muhammad Taha (d. 1985) recalls that he was raised by a slave woman named Al-Rabb Biyjud (The Lord is Beneficent), who stayed with his family even after slavery was abolished. She was devoted to him and his siblings, and he called her 'my mother.' She continued to live with Taha until her death in the 1970s. He himself buried her.[156]

Many slaves were bought as children so that their owner's household would be the only home they knew, and they would be more likely to be loyal. The Swiss traveler Jean Burckhardt (d. 1817) described how the slaves brought north for sale in Egypt in the early 1800s were mostly under fifteen years old, since people did not trust slaves brought up in another household.[157] Abu Nasr Gharnati (d. 1170), a remarkable Muslim traveler and author, wrote that while in the land of the Bulgars on the Volga River he had bought a fifteen-year-old slave girl who was 'as beautiful as the moon, with black hair and eyes, and skin as white as camphor.' He needed her to cook, sew and embroider. Interestingly, her family apparently lived nearby. He also bought an eight-year-old Greek slave girl:

> One day I bought for half a dinar two jars full of honeycomb with its wax and I said to her: 'I want you to purify this honey and extract the wax.' Then I went out and sat on a bench at the door of the house, where people were gathered. After sitting with them for a while, I went back into the house and saw five disks of wax as pure as gold and two jars full of liquid honey that seemed like rose water . . . She had a child, but it died. I freed her and gave her the name Maryam.[158]

Some slaves became closer to their owners than even the owners' friends, family or associates. Under the Shariah, a slave who was formally recognized as a trusted agent of their master was called a *ma'dhun* and could engage in transactions and contracts on behalf of them. As proof in a theological treatise he was writing, a scholar in early tenth-century Nishapur invokes something 'we might witness' in daily life. He gives the example of a wealthy man giving two of his slaves one hundred thousand silver coins each to invest, hoping to make a profit.[159] Sometimes such *ma'dhun* slaves could become like adopted sons. The Mamluk commander Sudun, nephew of the powerful Mamluk sultan Barquq, had a slave named Urgun who eventually became his major domo, secretary and even his son-in-law.[160]

According to the Shariah, slaves who were disobedient, made mistakes or fled could be physically disciplined. And they certainly were. In late nineteenth-century Kano there was a special house for holding slaves who had been sent there for punishment. There slaves were 'usually beaten until they defecate[d],' recalled one slave, though he noted troublesome slaves were usually just sold.[161] In Damascus Ibn Battuta came across a pious endowment (*waqf*) devoted solely to providing slaves who had broken earthenware vessels with comparable replacements so they could avoid punishment.[162] Yet there are interesting examples of masters demonstrating exemplary conduct by not punishing their slaves. Ibn Harbawayh (d. 922), the chief judge of Egypt, had a slave girl who 'went crazy on him,' in the words of a chronicler, and demanded to be sold.[163] Ibn Qudama, the Hanbali scholar who has been quoted so many times in this book, had a slave girl who treated him with shocking disrespect. Muslim biographers noted how his character showed in his refusal even to reprimand her.[164] One pious scholar in eighth-century Mecca freed a female slave out of gratitude that God had spared his home from flooding. His good conduct seems to have been rewarded: one of his male slaves who had absconded and prospered in India returned to him with enough profits to pay his master's debts. In Rumi's (d. 1273) *Masnavi*, a pious merchant bound for India promises each of his male and female slaves to bring them back whatever gift each desired.[165]

With domestic slaves in every area of life, the consistent deployment of violent coercion would be both exhausting and ultimately dangerous. Staying in the Duʿan valley in Hadramawt in the 1930s, Freya Stark witnessed a day-long strike by the slave woman of the family who was hosting her. The woman refused to leave her room until the head of the family talked to her and arranged for the return of her daughter, who had been sold to a nearby village. He agreed, and 'the slave woman reappeared in our family circle,' Stark concluded, 'her little eyes smiling as before . . .'[166] Toledano's observation is apt here: the constant threat of violence is unsustainable. Productive life requires some form of agreement. With slaves moving about in every area of a household, quarter, town and city, keeping them happy and invested in their relationships seems the only alternative to constant fear.

SLAVE AS SEXUAL PARTNER

Among the distinguishing features of slavery in Islamic civilization were the ubiquity of slave-concubinage (at least among the elite), the fact that it could occur legally alongside marriage to free women, and the free status of the children that slave-concubines bore. The circumstances of a concubine depended greatly on the status of her owner. And, of course, much depended on the owner's character. Two senior scholars of Baghdad in the ninth century were disgusted when visiting the home of another scholar to hear his transmission of Malik's works. When a beautiful slave girl came into the room, the host told them that he had made love to her from behind. The slave girl was greatly embarrassed, and the scholars refused to eat or drink in the house, let alone transmit knowledge from their host.[167] Relationships could take on dynamics familiar to us today. One tenth-century Abbasid notable gave up on his dream of moving to a livelier part of Baghdad because his slave-concubine preferred living near the palace. Ibn Hazm never got over the death of his first love, a slave girl.[168]

Concubines in the homes and palaces of the elite could rise to the pinnacle of wealth and power. This phenomenon was most visible in the Abbasid and Ottoman periods. Almost all Abbasid caliphs and Ottoman sultans were born of slave-concubines, whether of Greek, Persian, Balkan, Black African or other origin.[169] Khayzuran (d. 789), of either Yemeni or Berber origin, became the powerful concubine of the Abbasid caliph Al-Mahdi (d. 785). It would be two of her sons who would succeed their father as the caliphs Al-Hadi (d. 786) and Al-Rashid (d. 809), not the sons of his free wife.[170] During the time of the Seljuq Turks' reign over Iraq and Iran, the slave-concubine Khatun Safariyya (d. 1121) bore the Seljuq sultan Malik Shah (d. 1092) his successor, Sanjar (d. 1157). She also used her authority to send for her mother and family to come and join her after having not seen them for forty years.[171]

The acme of political power achieved by slave-concubines came in the seventeenth-century Ottoman Empire, a period that chroniclers sometimes referred to as the 'sultanate of women.' In that time the position of 'mother of the sultan' (*valide sultan*) could be the key to domination of the state, especially in the case of ambitious and capable slave-concubines like Kösem Sultan (d. 1651), a Greek woman who wielded authority over her weak sons during their reigns. Gülnush (d. 1715), another powerful *valide sultan*, was of noble Venetian ancestry and endowed a charming mosque and madrasa complex overlooking the Istanbul neighborhood of Uskudar. It was not just the slave-concubines of rulers who could attain authority in their households. The mother of Huda Sha'rawi was a Circassian slave-concubine who remembered the trauma of her childhood enslavement but who had also risen to become the matriarch in an elite Egyptian family.[172]

During the Abbasid period, the homes of elites in cities like Baghdad copied the harem arrangements of the caliph's palace. These upper-class families were sprawling mixtures of free wives and slave-concubines, with a plethora of male and female slaves tending to the home.[173] Elite concubines had high expectations of how they should be treated and considered themselves of equal standing to free women.[174] One aspect of this was the wealth and respect they could accrue. The famous early philologist and poet Asma'i (d. 828) was invited to the court of Harun Al-Rashid in Raqqa to evaluate the learning of two slave girls he had been given, and who appeared immensely knowledgeable about the arts and sciences. Asma'i posed them a series of challenging questions about literature and language, and they answered all superbly, composing extemporaneous poetry. The caliph was so pleased that he sent Asma'i back to Baghdad with one hundred silver coins. Departing the palace, the scholar encountered a servant and a slave girl awaiting him. The girl told Asmaʿi that she was the slave girl (*jāriya*) of one of the two slaves he had examined, and that the caliph had given her mistress so huge an amount of money as a reward for her sophistication that she was giving Asmaʿi his share – one thousand gold coins.[175]

We also have evidence of elite slave-concubines exercising significant control over their reproductive fortunes. Athl, who would one day give birth to the Spanish Umayyad ruler Al-Mundhir (d. 888), was a Berber slave girl who once belonged to the ruler at the time but refused to have sex with him when he approached her. This only made him desire her more. He finally struck her, which sent her into a rage that subsided only when he manumitted her.[176] Asmaʿi, who seems to have had numerous noteworthy interactions with female slaves, once visited a friend who asked him if he had a slave-concubine or if he was married. He replied that he had only a slave girl for mundane service. The friend then offered Asmaʿi a beautiful and refined slave girl as a gift to be his concubine. Before Asmaʿi could reply, the girl rushed into the room they were sitting in and began protesting vigorously that she would not be stuck with someone as old and ugly as their guest. The mortified host offered Asmaʿi a gift of one thousand gold coins instead.[177]

The privileges enjoyed by elite concubines should not obscure the fact that females who became concubines began as slaves and often remained so. They were purchased property. Despite the objections of some Muslim scholars like Shayzari (d. 1193–4), it seems to have been routine in Islamic civilization for buyers at slave markets to press on the buttocks and breasts of potential *jariya*s. Sometimes buyers even examined the genitals of male or female slaves, though papyri of sale contracts from the 800s and 900s frequently include boiler-plate language suggesting they were not.[178] Ultimately, slave women were sexually vulnerable and at the mercy of their masters. In 1863 Ottoman officials manumitted a pregnant slave woman who had come to them seeking refuge after both her owner and his brother had had sex with her, and then quarreled over paternity before trying to beat her into miscarrying.[179] Yet we should remember that, in reality, free wives often had little more choice in matters of sex or protection from abuse than slave-concubines.[180] Both slaves and wives had the same recourse to courts or members of the community. Unlike wives, however, slaves were almost by definition cut off from support networks other than their owners.

Given the fact of slavery, becoming a concubine was not necessarily a bad development for a female slave. If she gave birth to a child or even miscarried, not only was her child freed but she was too, upon her master's death. Her master could not sell her, and her child had the same legal standing as a child born of a free marriage. Ibn Hanbal was asked about a case in which a slave girl's owners wanted to sell her to a man but only on the condition that he take her as his concubine as opposed to a domestic service (*khidma*) slave (this was permitted).[181] Describing the slave markets of Kuka on Lake Chad, Nachtigal writes that the young girls being sold there seemed much happier than the other slaves. For if they became a slave-concubine in a house of even moderate means they could become authorities there, cared for well and immune to sale if they bore a child.[182] For wealthy or powerful men, slave-concubines were often prized possessions who constituted a great part of his honor. The trope of disgracing such a man by publicly insulting his slave-concubines was not uncommon.[183]

In the nineteenth century, E. W. Lane (d. 1876), whose wife in Egypt had been a slave woman herself, describes how slave women in the harems of the wealthy had mixed fortunes. Some bore scions and lived in luxury. Others had to endure the caresses of unappealing owners. In middle-class homes, however, they were better off. If a slave-concubine and her master had a pleasant relationship, then her situation was better than that of a free wife. Wives could be divorced with ease and left with nothing; slave women who had become pregnant by their masters could not be sold and would be freed upon their death. If they did not produce children, they were generally eventually freed and married off to someone respectable with a sizable dowry.[184] Court documents show that in nineteenth-century Cairo slave-concubines often received more inheritance (via bequest) from their lords than if they had been free wives.[185] Describing concubinage in Mecca, Hurgronje says that a respected man would never sell off a *jariya* after having had sex with her, even if she was not pregnant. And only a scoundrel would deny the paternity of a child so he could sell the mother.[186] Hurgronje describes how concubines were usually happier being kept by their master as opposed to being freed to marry someone else because, as a wife, they could easily be divorced.[187]

The tension around sexual relations with slave women, the challenges to hierarchy this could cause for free wives, and the possibility that a man could either have sex with his female slave or free her and take her as a wife formed a tight and complex knot. All the schools of Islamic law either prohibited or cautioned against a free man marrying the slave woman of another man when he could marry a free one or purchase his own concubine. One tenth-century pietistic manual quotes a saying that 'The stupidest person is the free man who marries a slave girl, and the smartest is the slave who marries a free woman. Part of the second one is freed, while part of the first one is enslaved [i.e., his children belong to his wife's owner].'[188] But marriages between a free person and a slave seemed to happen despite the leanings of the written law. In 1332 the Mamluk sultan appointed a Hanbali judge in Damascus because the population needed the Hanbali school's flexibility on, among things, male slaves marrying free women.[189]

These tensions can be seen in the Hadiths that were forged and deployed to argue for various behaviors. One Hadith, which Muslims scholars admitted was grossly unreliable, quotes the Prophet telling Muslims to 'Take slave women as concubines, for indeed their wombs are blessed.'[190] Another admitted forgery quoted the Prophet 'saying' that whoever wants to meet God in a pure state should marry only free women.[191] The Egyptian polymath Suyuti closes his treatise on the virtues of Black Africans with a chapter on 'The Virtue of marrying slave-concubines and cautioning against not aiding in a slave's chasteness.' Consisting of nothing more than a list of Hadiths with few comments, the chapter includes the baseless Hadith praising the wombs of concubines as well as other respected Hadiths praising the merits of freeing one's concubines and then taking them as wives. It then presents an extremely rare and unreliable Hadith, which warns, 'Whoever takes [for sex] from amongst his slaves other than those he marries, and then she fornicates, her sins will be upon him too.' This suggests an awareness that men were having sex with their slave girls haphazardly, neither offering them regular attention nor marrying them off so that they could have a more regular relationship. Suyuti, who mourned his own concubine when she died while pregnant with his child, ends his book with the Hadith in which the Prophet reminds Muslims, as his last testament, to take care of their prayers and their slaves.[192]

SLAVE AS SAINT, SCHOLAR OR POET

Since *riqq* permeated Muslim societies, slaves could appear in almost any role, including those widely admired. Whether elite concubines or anonymous domestics, slaves could rise to the level of noted scholar or litterateur, pious exemplar or even saint (*walī*). We already saw how many early Muslim scholars were either freed slaves or their descendants. During the Abbasid period in the ninth and tenth centuries slaves provided the material for not only a new breed of poet but a new literary hero (or heroine).[193] Among slave courtesans of elite Abbasid society and the caliphal court, some emerged as famous and sought-after 'singing girls' (*qiyān*), renowned for their beauty, charm, performances of song and instrument as well as for their composition of poetry. One of the most famous was ʿArib (d. 890), who thrived as a lutist, singer and poet in the courts of five caliphs.[194] As slaves, these singing girls had usually led challenging lives and overcame prodigious obstacles to rise to their positions. They relied on little more than their wit, artistic talents, their ability to entice powerful men and cunning in surviving the machinations of court life. As poetesses and protagonists in the epics spun around them, these singing girls were commemorated in works like Abu al-Faraj Isfahani's (d. 967) *Female Slave Poets* (*Imā' al-shawāʿir*).[195]

The Abbasid era also saw powerful slave-concubines emerge as admired exemplars of religious devotion. Shaghib (d. 933), the *umm walad* of the Abbasid caliph Al-Muʿtadid and mother of his successor Al-Muqtadir, had originally been a Byzantine slave. But she used the wealth and power she accrued as the caliph's consort and then the caliph's mother to support pious causes. Her lands produced a revenue of one hundred thousand gold dinars a year, much of which Shaghib spent on maintaining the infrastructure needed for Hajj and on caring for pilgrims. When her son was killed and the throne usurped by Al-Muʿtadid's son from another concubine, the new caliph tortured Shaghib to death to make her hand over her property. She was commemorated by chroniclers as a pious martyr to the cruel turnings of dynastic politics.[196]

Toward the end of his biographical dictionary of Sufi saints, the Hadith scholar Abu Nuʿaym Isbahani (d. 1038) includes a subtly marked out section on slave saints. He explains, 'And among servants [i.e., slaves] there are saints whose truth God has hidden from the eyes, and whose names and ancestries He has wiped away from fame and memory.' In doing this, God had 'made them a protection for the inhabitants of the realms, and by their calling upon Him ruin is warded off.'[197] After he and all the other leading scholars of eighth-century Basra had prayed for God to end a disastrous draught – to no effect – the famous preacher Malik bin Dinar (d. *circa* 745) saw an unknown Black slave bring down torrents of rain after invoking God quietly and alone in a small mosque. Recognizing a saint beloved to God when he saw one, Malik bin Dinar and another well-known scholar purchased the slave, who wondered why they would want him so much in their service. No, they replied, 'we bought you so that *we* can serve *you* ourselves, gladly.'[198]

An important theme in Sufism which was coming together in the 1000s and would later prove fundamental to how Muslim scholars and even sultans understood the governance of the earth and the cosmos was the notion of an 'inner' (*bāṭin*) caliphate, the axis on which the world turned. It is the perennial, hidden counterpart of the crass worldly authority of the 'outer' (*ẓāhir*) caliphate. And it is the true repository of power.[199] At the center of this spiritual hierarchy was the Axis of the Age (*quṭb al-zamān*), the person around whom creation spins. Around the Axis, placed anonymously throughout the world, are other lofty saints called the *Abdal* (literally, substitutes). It is both fitting and poetic that, as Abu Nuʿaym implies, this cosmic radial spreads out in the world among the ranks of the most materially disempowered. As one Hadith notes, 'The *Abdal* are from among the *mawali*.'[200]

SLAVE AS ELITE ADMINISTRATOR & COURTESAN

The Near Eastern and Roman worlds had long known slaves in positions of power, whether as confidants, managers in the households of the wealthy or officials in the courts of the Caesars and shahs. This was not a manufactured phenomenon. It was the natural product of social systems in which slaves accompanied free masters at every level, including the highest levels, of a hierarchy. This was akin to the role of non-commissioned officers in many Western militaries, acting as adjutants to generals even at the senior ranks. Elite slaves laced the structures and organs of power in most Muslim dynasties from the Abbasids to the Ottoman Empire, from the Muslim dynasties of the medieval Deccan in India to Safavid Persia and the Sokoto Caliphate in West Africa.

There are early reports that the caliph ʿUmar bin al-Khattab wanted to appoint his Christian slave as a senior administrator in the young Muslim state, but the slave refused to embrace Islam. The caliph knew he could not compel him to and did not want to put a non-Muslim in charge of Muslim affairs.[201] The use of slaves in administration seems really to have begun under the Abbasid caliph Harun Al-Rashid, who gave prominent positions to eunuch slaves.[202] The number of slaves in the Abbasid palace in the ninth and tenth centuries was enormous. The palace of Al-Muqtadir (r. 908–932) reportedly had eleven thousand male slaves, of which seven thousand were Black and four thousand Slavic. It also had four thousand free and slave women as well as thousands more domestic servants.[203] Many of the male slaves were likely eunuchs.[204]

One of the most prominent positions for a slave in the imperial palace was held by slave women: that of stewardess (*qahramāna*), who could be charged with anything from running errands to serving as a female major domo for her mistress within the caliphal palace or even for the palace as a whole. Prominent *qahramana*s served as an interface between the palace, the bureaucracy and the outside world. Judicial affairs were also often also entrusted to them. The *qahramana* Zaydan was responsible for detaining high-level political prisoners and was also the guardian of the state jewels. In 918 CE the *qahramana* Thumal famously was placed in charge of one of the appeals courts in the Rasafa palace of Al-Muqtadir.[205] One moving and lengthy story tells how the *qahramana* of Al-Muqtadir's famous mother, the concubine Shaghib, fell in love with a merchant and schemed to marry him. To do so she had to marshal all her cunning in order to win both her mistress's and the caliph's approval. This unnamed *qahramana* had her own coterie of slave girls and possessed enormous wealth – the caliph gave her fifty thousand gold coins as a wedding gift alone. Her husband would later recount how they had flourished happily for years, living 'the life of caliphs.'[206]

More often in Islamic history it was male slaves who achieved positions of power. After 1590 the Safavid Shah ʿAbbas (d. 1629) appointed Armenian slaves as governors of important provinces, replacing unreliable Turkic tribal leaders.[207] Malik ʿAmbar (d. 1626, see Figure 2) was an Ethiopian slave brought to serve the Nizam Shahi court in the Indian city of Ahmadnagar in the Deccan. He served as a senior military commander, and, when the dynasty fell into turmoil after its capital was captured by the Mughals, Malik ʿAmbar rallied its forces and managed to elevate a new member of the dynasty to the throne. Supported by other Ethiopian slave soldiers and administrators, Malik ʿAmbar remained the power behind the throne for the rest of his life.[208] Recalling his visit to Gujarat in 1839, the Indian traveler Lutfullah met three slave or former slave governors of cities in that region alone.[209] The importance of slaves in state administration and rule was clear in the extreme west of Islamic civilization as well. In both the period prior to the Sokoto Caliphate in Hausaland and in the Caliphate slaves often held senior positions in the military and administration.[210] Slaves occupied high administrative offices until the formal abolition of slavery in the Muslim world. In the early twentieth century, the grand vizier of the Omani Sultan Faisal bin Turki (d. 1913) was his slave Sulayman bin Suwaylim.[211]

The pinnacle of the slave administrator was certainly the Ottoman Empire of the sixteenth and seventeenth centuries, when *devshirme* slaves like Sokullu Mehmet Pasha held the reins of power as the state's senior administrators. The *devshirme* (literally, gathering in) system originated in the late 1300s as a way to recruit slave soldiers (see below) from captives the Ottomans had taken during their conquests in the Balkans. The idea of culling boys or men from captives or conquered populations seems to have had its roots in the *khums* tax (Ottoman, *pençik*), and by 1438 there is evidence that boys were being taken from the Christian *dhimmi* communities in the Balkans.

Enslaving *dhimmi*s was, of course, against the Shariah. A number of explanations have been offered by historians as to why the Ottomans felt doing this was acceptable, from sheer necessity (an excuse advanced by one leading Ottoman intellectual), to the notion that the Ottomans still considered the Balkans to be outside the Abode of Islam, to an interesting but far-fetched theory that they were acting on the Shafi ruling that Christians were only qualified to receive *dhimmi* protection if their ancestors had converted to Christianity *before* Muhammad's mission.[212] Hakan Erdem offers the most convincing explanation: one of the options that the Shariah allowed for conquering Muslim states was to enslave captured peoples. This was rarely done, but those communities whom the Ottomans conquered by force were 'theoretically' still enslavable even long after their conquest. This explains why *dhimmi* communities whom the Ottomans had absorbed via peace settlements were exempted from the *devshirme* while the populations of areas conquered pure and simple were subjected to the tax.[213]

The *devshirme* functioned by Ottoman officials visiting Christian villages in the Balkans and Anatolia every three to four years and taking a certain number of young boys between the ages of ten to around eighteen back to Istanbul as slaves. A child was taken from one in every forty households, with only sons exempted. Greeks, Serbs and Albanians were the main ethnic groups that the *devshirme* drew from. The boys were circumcised, given Muslim names and raised as Muslims. They were educated in the

Quran, Islamic law, Arabic and Turkish. Those who showed particular intellectual acumen were educated further in the Sultan's palaces in the 'Inner School (Enderun Mektebi),' founded by Murad II (d. 1451), which officially functioned until 1909.[214] Those being groomed for high administrative positions became the Sultan's personal slaves, serving him in his private chambers. By that point they were often totally invested in the Sultan's welfare. Devoted service promised immense reward. Rüstem Pasha (d. 1561), the powerful vizier of Sulayman the Magnificent, came from a family of Christian swineherds in Bosnia. 'Gathered in' by the *devshirme*, he excelled in his studies and rose to become a private page of the Sultan. When the Sultan dropped something accidentally from a window and the other pages ran down the stairs to retrieve it, Rüstem distinguished himself – he threw himself from the window.[215] Those *devshirme* recruits not selected for further education were sent to live with Turkic families to learn Turco-Muslim ways. Then they moved to the barracks for training as 'Slaves of the Porte' (*kapıkulu*) in the military, police or even in the elite Janissary corps (see below). The last known *devshirme* occurred in 1751, though it had already become sporadic in the 1600s.[216]

SLAVE AS SOLDIER – WHEN SOLDIERS OFTEN RULED

The case of Malik ʿAmbar illustrates the porous boundary between the roles of slave-as-senior-administrator and slave as, effectively, the ruler. It also shows how lines blurred between these roles and another one that emerged as a feature unique to Islamic civilization and crucially important: the slave soldier. There is no one, convincing explanation for why the large-scale reliance on slave soldiers emerged as a particular feature of the Dar al-Islam.[217] Some scholars like Patricia Crone and Daniel Pipes have proposed that the Muslim polities of the Umayyad and Abbasid eras simply lacked the Islamic legitimacy of the first decades of idealized, pious rule under the Rightly Guided caliphs. As a result, the pious Muslim elite withdrew from the political field when the ideals of an Islamic state were not met. In the vacuum that followed, imported slave soldiers dominated the political sphere.[218] David Ayalon suggested that the Abbasids turned to slave soldiers because they lacked the manpower to fulfill Islam's mission of conquest.[219] Robert Irwin offered a more multifaceted explanation: the slave soldier phenomenon was generated by the complex factors of the Near East's urbanized society,

Islamic laws on slavery and the demographic presence of a large population of Turkic warriors on the northern frontier of the Dar al-Islam, with their uniquely effective techniques of mounted archery.[220]

Though some slave soldiers were used by the Umayyads in the Second Civil War (680–692), their first notable use was by the Aghlabid dynasty in North Africa and in Umayyad Spain in the early 800s CE.[221] The first real build-up of a sizable regiment of slave soldiers, however, occurred at the behest of the Abbasid caliph Al-Muʿtasim (r. 833–842). Even when still just a prince, Al-Muʿtasim began amassing a bodyguard of Turkic soldiers, which the caliph's Samanid allies in Khurasan procured for him from Central Asia. When he succeeded to the caliphate, Al-Muʿtasim brought in even more Turkic soldiers, to the point that their behavior proved so disruptive in Baghdad that in 836 CE the caliph had a new capital built at Samarra to house them. Eventually their number grew to between ten and fifteen thousand. Some of these Turkic soldiers hailed from the Khazar areas north of the Caucasus and others were from the Khwarazm region near the Aral Sea. Some were no doubt Muslims already when they were brought to Iraq, but others converted upon arrival. What made these warriors so formidable was their ability to fire their arrows quickly and accurately in any direction while mounted on their horses.[222]

It is not clear how many of these Turkic soldiers were actually ever slaves and, if they were, for how long. Many were certainly bought as slaves from Central Asia or the Volga region but were most likely freed upon arrival in the caliphs' service. Some were already Muslim and thus free. Contemporaneous sources refer to them not as *mamluk* but as *mawali* or *ghilman*, ambiguous terms that could mean 'slave' or a former slave who had been freed. They were also paid salaries and even provided with slave girls as spouses in their military capital of Samarra.[223] As Matthew Gordon has pointed out, whatever their origins or status, the Turkic military units had their own culture of politics, which would shape rule in Abbasid Baghdad for the next century.[224] After the caliph Al-Mutawakkil (d. 861) was assassinated by his Turkic Praetorian, the Turkic military elite would be the real power in the Abbasid capital for the next eighty years.

The system put in place by the Abbasids replicated itself in some provinces. The son of one of the caliph's Turkic slave soldiers, Ahmad Ibn Tulun (d. 884), became the ruler of Egypt under the Abbasids and independent in all but name. He created his own slave military units by importing slaves from the Sudan and Byzantine lands. This remained a trend in Egypt. Black

African slave soldiers grew into the bulwark of the Fatimid dynasty, which ruled Egypt and parts of Syria and the Hejaz in the tenth through the twelfth centuries.[225] After the Abbasids in Baghdad had fallen under the domination of, first, their Turkic Praetorian, then the Buyid family from Iran and then later the Seljuq Turkic dynasty, slave soldiers once again helped shift the balance of power. Turkic slave soldiers were a mainstay of the Seljuq armies.[226] When the Abbasid caliph Al-Muqtafi (r. 1136–60) succeeded in regaining a degree of autonomy for the Abbasid dynasty in Baghdad by pushing back against Seljuq suzerainty, he did so by building up a corps of Armenian and Byzantine slave soldiers.[227]

In polities in which 'slaves' were senior administrators, or in which the military was the ultimate depository of power and consisted of 'slaves,' it is not surprising that slaves could wield effective political authority. 'Slaves' could thus be rulers. But we must bracket the term 'slave' here in bold scare quotes, as we will soon see. 'Slave rule' was neither the norm nor normatively acceptable under the Shariah. Sometimes it resulted from situations of exceptional instability, as in the case of Mujahid (r. 1014–1044/5). This slave of the Umayyad dynasty in Spain had been placed in charge of administering the province of Dénia and the Balearic Islands. When the Umayyad dynasty and state collapsed in 1009, however, he continued on as the independent ruler there. In other cases, slaves ruled under the pretense of being a regent, as in the famous case of Kafur (d. 968) in Egypt. This Nubian eunuch was a successful military commander of the Ikhshidi dynasty, which had emerged from the household of a Turkic soldier affirmed in that position by the Abbasid caliph. Kafur was placed in charge of the education of the dynasty's young princes, a position from which he first ruled for two decades from behind the throne and then openly as the official regent.

But the most famous and enduring case of 'slave rule' was the Mamluk Dynasty, which ruled Egypt, Syria and the Hejaz from around 1260 until the Ottoman conquest in 1517. In the 1240s, the last effective ruler of the Ayyubid state in Egypt increased the by then standard use of imported Turkic slave cavalry to an unprecedented level. In particular, he purchased around one thousand Kipchak Turkic youths and housed them in a barracks on an island in the Nile to be trained as his military elite. Known as the Bahri (River) Mamluks, they were the bodyguard of the sultan and proved their mettle by aiding in the defeat of the Crusaders at the Battle of Mansoura in 1249. A decade later, the death of the Ayyubid sultan, ceaseless crises, dynastic infighting and finally a glorious defeat of the Mongol armies in

1260 left the Bahri Mamluks in charge and their leader, Al-Zahir Baybars, as sultan. Bahri rule would continue until 1390, with Mamluk commanders within the unit climbing the ranks, jockeying for power, amassing their own households of slave soldiers, seizing power and then trying (sometimes successfully) to pass power to their sons. In 1390, a Mamluk named Barquq took control with his cadre of Circassian slave soldiers and established the Burji dynasty.[228]

Though the practice and institutions of the Mamluk system changed over time, there were several general features. Senior Mamluk commanders would maintain, train and build their own households by importing young slaves either from the Turkic steppes or from the Circassian tribes in the Caucusus. Mamluks had other origins as well, including Mongols and even Europeans, but these never approached the two main sources in importance. As a whole, this motley collection would end up manning posts from crack cavalry units to lowly night watchman. The import of slaves to serve in the Royal Mamluk unit was overseen by the official Mamluk Trader (*tājir al-mamālīk*), but otherwise the trade was in the hands of private merchants. Once in Cairo, the young charges bought by senior commanders or sultans were housed in barracks under the oversight of eunuchs, with each floor constituting a military unit. They were given Muslim names, and teachers were brought in to educate the boys in Arabic, the Quran, Hadith and Islamic law (in later years some Mamluks were purchased as adults and not educated at all). Most importantly, they underwent years of rigorous military instruction. This extended and intensive period of training instilled the two most important loyalty relationships in the Mamluk system. The first was that between the new Mamluks and their master (*ustādh*).[229] The second was that of *khushdashiyya*, the *esprit de corps* of each unit and their loyalty and connection to one another. Upon graduation, each Mamluk was given arms and a horse. Most importantly, especially after the mid-1300s, he was manumitted and given a certificate to prove it. Officials were scrupulous that the purchase and eventual manumission of the Mamluks were done properly and documented.[230]

So, the main myth surrounding the Mamluk Dynasty was that it was ruled by slaves. It was most certainly not. It was ruled by *former* slaves. Senior Mamluk emirs certainly had slaves from a variety of origins in their retinue, but they were eager for all to know they were no longer slaves themselves.[231] However that may be, the consistent core of the Mamluk state system was a military elite whose binding identity and ethos of solidarity was their servile origin in distant lands and their collective training as military slaves. They were scrupulously freed after their training for the same reason that Kafur ruled as a regent and not as sultan: *because slaves cannot be rulers according to the Shariah.* The Mamluk Empire is the name others used to refer to the state. It referred to itself as 'The State of the Turks' or 'The State of the Circassians.' A famous story underscores this. One of the most revered scholars of Egypt and Syria during Bahri Mamluk ascendance was ʿIzz al-Din Ibn ʿAbd al-Salam (d. 1262). Legend has it that when the ulama and elite of Cairo were gathered to give their oaths of allegiance (*bayʿa*) to Al-Zahir Baybars, Ibn ʿAbd al-Salam objected. 'I recognize you as the slave (*mamlūk*) of so-and-so,' he shouted and refused to offer his oath until Baybars had proven that he had been manumitted.[233] This story reveals much about Mamluk rule, the role of the ulama in Islamic civilization and the conception of *riqq* in the Shariah. The sultan is forced to satisfy the demand of the scholar, the ostensible true guardian of Islam. The slave cannot rule over the free. And, of course, this was either an act of theatre to indulge ulama anxieties or perhaps a tale made up by ulama to reassure themselves that they were still in charge!

The Mamluk system was not limited to the eastern Mediterranean. In 1206 CE in northern India, a Turkic *mamluk* general named Qutb al-Din Aybak (d. 1210–11) rose to replace his master upon his death. Aybak was a slave of the Ghurid dynasty, which had expanded its control from the mountains of modern-day Afghanistan to the Ganges plain. In what became the first Muslim dynasty to build its capital at Delhi, Aybak presided over a slave-soldier system that lasted into the 1260s and was similar to the Mamluk state in Egypt. Its elite were Turkic *mamluks* who served as the state's chief administrators and generals. Like Egypt, the Indian Mamluk Dynasty was not a 'slave dynasty.' Only the first two main rulers were ever slaves. According to Ibn Battuta, Aybak had to officially prove his manumission in the presence of judges and jurists before he could formally rule. The rest of the dynasty consisted of the free descendants of Aybak and his successor or members of their coteries who seized control. The elite of the Delhi Sultanate also included freeborn Persians, Afghans and indigenous Indian Muslims, all of whom played crucial roles in the state. Overall, historians do not know which of the Delhi Mamluk rulers were freed slaves or just people who rose up within and upheld a system based on the idiom of military slavery.[233]

Slave soldiers would continue to play a major role in armies in Islamic civilization into the early modern period. The Ottoman Janissaries were the burly slave counterparts of the cerebral slave graduates of the Enderun Mektebi. For centuries they were the feared shock troops of the formidable Ottoman army, and later they formed the stout and immovable centerpiece of the Ottoman business and social establishment. In India, Malik ʿAmbar was hardly alone. From the fifteenth to the seventeenth centuries significant numbers of Ethiopian slaves were imported to serve as soldiers in the Indian Muslim kingdoms of the Deccan plateau, where they became the ruling class in the princely states of Bijapur and Ahmadnagar. This feature distinguished those polities from the powerful Mughal realm to the north, which was nearly alone among major Muslim states of the era in not employing large numbers of slave soldiers.[234] Far to the west, the main founder of the Alawid dynasty of Morocco, Mawlay Ismaʿil (d. 1727), formed an enormous elite regiment out of Black African slaves, making them swear an oath to the Prophet's Sunna on a copy of *Sahih al-Bukhari* and dubbing the unit 'The Slaves of Bukhari (*ʿabīd al-Bukhārī*; we'll dwell on this controversy in depth in Chapter Five).'[235] Slave eunuchs made up a large part of the Songhay ruler Askia Muhammad's (d. 1538) cavalry.[236] Even in the twentieth century, the bodyguard of the founding king of Saudi Arabia, ʿAbd al-ʿAziz Ibn Saud (d. 1953), were mainly Black slaves. One trusted slave stood behind him in all court meetings, armed with a sword and rifle. He never left the king's presence and watched over him even as the king prayed.[237] In the Hadramawt valley of Yemen in the 1930s, Freya Stark was protected by slave soldiers throughout her journey and visited one city whose governor was a slave.[238]

SLAVE AS REBEL

There is no way even to estimate such an immeasurable statistic, but it seems likely that a large percentage of slaves in Islamic civilization would rather not have been enslaved. Indeed, during the disruption caused by British and French colonial conquests in West Africa, there are estimates that between 20 and 40 percent of slaves fled their masters.[239] Given their number and ubiquity, however, surprisingly few slaves in Islamic civilization turned to violence to liberate themselves. Legal manuals and scattered court records strongly suggest that many slaves ran away, whether in a fit of anger, in an impromptu effort to avoid imminent punishment, or to try and escape slavery entirely.[240] But because vast plantations, with their large-scale 'gang slavery,' were much less common in Islamic civilization than in parts of the Roman world or later in the Americas, conditions in the towns and cities of the Muslim world made it much harder for slaves to gather and coordinate a rebellion. Most slavery in Islamic civilization was domestic. Some slaves were elite administrators or courtesans, some were soldiers and some were integrated well enough into families or communities that they preferred their life as it was to the unknown. Whatever the case, most slaves in the Muslim world were scattered like atoms in small, medium or large households in towns or cities. Joining forces to rebel or flee en masse would have been challenging.

There were a few notable slave rebellions in Islamic history. Several took place in southern Iraq in the early Islamic period. A small uprising in 689–90 CE was easily put down, as was a larger one in 694. But what would live on in history as the largest and most daunting slave rebellion lasted fifteen years, from 869 to 883 CE and plunged Iraq and the lands around the headwaters of the Persian Gulf into chaos. This was the famous Zanj rebellion, named after the main group of slaves who rebelled and who had been brought from parts of eastern Africa. The Zanj rebellion was more than a revolt. It was the formation of a small state under the rule of the man who had incited and organized the movement, ʿAli bin Muhammad, known as 'Sahib al-Zanj' (roughly, the 'Man of the Zanj').

ʿAli bin Muhammad was allegedly Persian and allegedly had Shiite leanings, but anything even remotely certain about him has been lost to history. His story was told by those who ultimately vanquished him and his rebellion. The Zanj slaves had been put to work on the alluvial plains of southern Iraq clearing the nitrous topsoil in the prohibitive summer heat. When ʿAli bin Muhammad went from town to town recruiting them as followers, he promised them that they could reduce those who had been their masters to slaves themselves. He commiserated with them over how they had been mistreated, paraphrasing the Hadith in which the Prophet warned owners not to overburden their slaves in his invectives against their masters. They had, he preached, 'done to the slaves what God had prohibited.'[241]

The rebel slaves and others who joined them under ʿAli bin Muhammad seized the city of Basra, then Abbadan, Ahwaz and Wasit. They set up their capital at a city they dubbed Al-Mukhtara (The Chosen) on the Tigris, where ʿAli bin Muhammad ruled as the messianic figure of the Mahdi and perhaps, though the coins they minted bearing the title are ambiguous, the caliphal 'Commander of the Faithful.' Ironically, no Zanj are known to have been in senior positions of authority in the mini-state, which had its own slaves. Later historians claimed the followers of ʿAli bin Muhammad practiced communal property and took noble women of the Prophet's family as concubines.[242]

There were a few other slave rebellions in Islamic civilization. In the early twentieth century one occurred in Sokoto, where large, slave-worked plantations did exist.[243] But other instances in which slaves joined forces and employed violence seem to have been more born of overall breakdowns in law and order than they were misfunctions of a slave system. In Mamluk Egypt slave gangs would occasionally loot and form bandit groups, but they were just one type of gang among others wreaking havoc at those times.[244]

4

The Slavery Conundrum

> It did not occur to our minds at all, as Arabs, that we would live to see the day, and one in the twenty-first century, when we would see a living embodiment of the slave trade in our countries and our lands, at the hands of those claiming to belong to this ancient nation, to the magnanimous Islamic faith, which was the first to battle this shameful phenomenon.[1]
>
> ʿAbd al-Bari ʿAtwan, editor-in-chief, *Rai al-Youm*

So wrote ʿAbd al-Bari ʿAtwan, one of the most conscientious mainstream Arab journalists, in November 2017 after CNN broke the story of the slave trafficking in Libya. But surely ʿAtwan should not have been *that* surprised. In Mauritania, very much an Arab and Islamic country, slavery was only formally abolished in 1981, and it continues informally to this day.

Arab-Muslim intellectuals are not the only ones to have been confronted recently by what they thought were moral specters vanquished long ago. In August 2017, a rally dubbed Unite the Right was organized in Charlottesville, Virginia, with the stated goal of preventing the removal of a statue of Robert E. Lee from a public park. Lee was the general who led the army of the slavery-committed South during the American Civil War. Seemingly half of all major roads in Virginia (and the *Dukes of Hazard*'s car) are named after him. Charlottesville is the site of the University of Virginia, founded by Thomas Jefferson, an architect of the American republic and author of the famous statement that 'All men are created equal' and endowed with the 'inalienable right' to liberty. He also owned slaves and fathered children with them.

During the march in Charlottesville, violent clashes between those defending the statue and liberal protesters calling for its removal reminded

Americans that both the wounds of the Civil War and the questions that sparked it remain quite open. Attending a pro-Trump rally in the conservative state of Alabama just a few weeks after the clashes, a reporter was challenged by a triumphant Trump supporter, who demanded, 'Show me the place in the Bible where slavery is condemned!'[2] During the presidential campaign, polling found that 13 percent of Trump supporters disapproved of Abraham Lincoln's order freeing the slaves during the Civil War.[3]

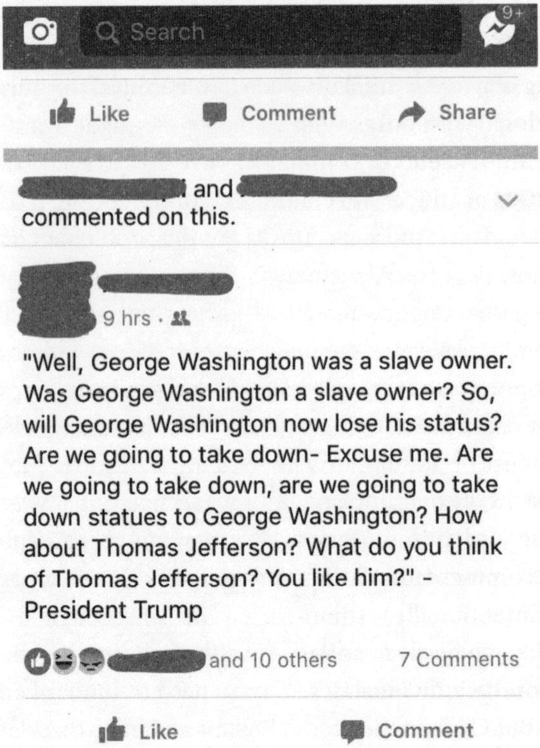

The above Facebook comment was made in August 2017 by a thoughtful and observant young Muslim working in Washington, DC. It quotes President Trump's comments on the conflict over the Robert E. Lee statue. It does not do so approvingly. Indeed, this young Muslim is mocking the President's words with the contempt that so many in the US feel toward Trump in particular and towards Conservatives in general. It is all the more ironic, then, that the President is making an important point. And it is precisely in that point – and in the liberal dismissal of it – that the heart of the slavery conundrum lies for both Muslims and Americans. For, with the proper adjustments, Trump's words would apply equally to the Prophet Muhammad.

This chapter will feature a number of screenshots or citations from social media, but not as a gimmick. This book overall and this chapter in particular take up a gravely troubling subject, one that remains pertinent to both the global Muslim and global Western public square. Sharing (anonymized) snapshots of our public and semi-public discussions on the issue of slavery is the best means I know to show just how pervasive the cognitive dissonance surrounding the issue remains.

Discussing slavery is difficult not only because the subject provokes strong emotional responses. As ʿAtwan's outrage, President Trump's remarks and the Facebook comment above all reveal, it also bends our minds into knots of ethical and communal contradiction. It does so because of the *moral problem* it presents. This is not the problem of whether slavery is wrong or not. *Pace* the Alabaman Trump supporter, that point has been settled in the global public square by Muslims and non-Muslims alike. The moral problem of slavery is the question of *what kind of wrong* slavery is. And, more importantly, it is a question of what the moral wrongness of slavery means for communities and traditions that see their pasts as authoritative in some sense or another, that look to those pasts for guidance.

On August 15, as the protests and debates over what was happening in Charlottesville roiled the waters of American public life, Fox News' conservative commentator Tucker Carlson took up the topic in a way that (perhaps unintentionally) summed up its unreconciled tensions. He explained, 'Now, to be clear, as if it's necessary, slavery is evil. If you believe in the rights of the individual, it's actually hard to think of anything worse than slavery.' But Carlson then reminded his audience that slavery had been the norm in human history until the 1800s. 'Plato owned slaves,' he explained, 'so did Muhammed, peace be upon him.'[4] Slavery is evil, Carlson was saying. But he wanted to know if we were really going to topple all the figures of America's founding pantheon because of this. President Trump had set forth the predicament with a succinctness only he could muster: 'George Washington was a slave owner . . . are we going to take down statues to [sic] George Washington?'[5]

Nor was what happened in Charlottesville the only recent controversy to highlight the moral problem of slavery. Two months earlier, debate had swirled around the *Atlantic Monthly* article 'My Family's Slave,' written by the late Alex Tizon, a Pulitzer-winning, Filipino American journalist.[6] The article told the story of how Tizon's Filipino family had a 'slave' (I place the word in scare quotes here because it is precisely what we mean by slave that is at issue). She was known as Lola. They had brought her to America with them, and she had served them for decades.

Response to the article was not surprising. Some, including many Filipinos, argued that the term 'slavery' was misleading in the article because it brought to mind American plantation slavery. This Filipino 'slavery', they argued, was not comparable at all.[7] Some argued that in the Filipino case 'slaves' often became 'part of the family.' Some even asserted that 'slavery' like that of Lola's made economic and even moral sense in the context of the Philippines' poverty and underdevelopment.[8]

Other readers, by contrast, responded with outrage at what they saw as the casual treatment of or apology for a clear moral evil.[9] They insisted that every member of the author's family, as Lola's masters, was guilty of a heinous crime. Some voiced further outrage at those defending the author, accusing them of being apologists for slavery and comparing their arguments to those used by defenders of slavery in the Antebellum South.[10]

NO SQUARING THE CIRCLE: THE AMERICAN/ ISLAMIC SLAVERY CONUNDRUM

In ʿAtwan's op-ed, Trump's remarks, Carlson's wordbox and the outrage around the *Atlantic* article lies the crux of this chapter. I have termed it the **Slavery Conundrum**. The events around Charlottesville concern an American version of this, but the Islamic Slavery Conundrum is its sibling. The Slavery Conundrum is, quite simply, that people are trying to do the cognitively impossible – to affirm a triad of axioms that cannot all be held coherently at the same time. Here I lay them out with some explanation. An expanded discussion will follow:

Axiom 1: Slavery is an intrinsic and gross moral evil. Nazism can be joked about, but even Black comedians joke about slavery at their own peril.[11] As Tucker Carlson said, 'it's actually hard to think of anything worse than slavery.' Depriving people of their freedom, their relationship and turning them into property to be exploited is unconscionable. It doesn't matter how you dress it up or what apologies you offer for it, slavery is Just. Plain.Wrong. It was wrong two thousand years ago, and it is wrong today.

As expressed by the mortified principal of a Texas school where a teacher had asked students to list the pros and cons of slavery, 'To be clear, there is no debate about slavery. It is immoral and a crime against humanity.'[12] This is not an intellectual point of debate. It is felt at a visceral level and with profound moral certainty.

Axiom 2: Slavery is slavery. As we saw scholars like Watson and Lovejoy assert in Chapter One, there is an objective reality 'out there' called slavery, which can be located and labeled across history and geographical expanse. We can thus talk about slavery in ancient Greece, slavery in medieval China and slavery in the American South and be having one, unified ethical conversation. Some historians like Suzanne Miers might argue either that there is not one coherent phenomenon called 'slavery,' or that 'slavery' is so different from place to place and time to time that one really cannot talk about it as one phenomenon with any brevity. But that opinion is of no consequence. According to this axiom, slavery is slavery. Period.

Axiom 3: Our past has moral authority over us. In the climactic final courtroom scene in the moving film *Amistad* (1997), the aged former president John Quincy Adams makes a case against slavery before the US Supreme Court. Seeking to fulfill the ideal of the universal right to inalienable liberty put forth in the Declaration of Independence, he literally turns to the statues of the Founding Fathers and seeks 'the wisdom and strength they fathered and inspired.' He lists their names in turn: Thomas Jefferson, George Washington and his own father John Adams.[13] This final axiom recognizes that we, like Adams in the film, belong to traditions and communities that draw moral guidance from figures and texts in our pasts. Our pasts thus both offer us inspiration and have some degree of moral or even legal claim on us. To some extent or another, figures in our past were better and wiser than we are, and we turn to them again and again for guidance. We might hear flaws or imperfections in these voices from the past, but they cannot be evil. Otherwise why would we heed them?

I refer to these three items as axioms because no mainstream voice in the American public square can challenge any of them without significant consequence. If you argue that American slavery wasn't always that bad, you are considered a right-wing extremist.[14] If you argue that slavery in other parts of the world was not or is not as severe as American slavery was, then, as reaction to the Tizon article shows, you are branded an apologist for slavery. Finally, the pantheon of American exemplars cannot be easily attacked. President Trump's mention of taking down statues of George

Washington was a *reductio ad absurdum* argument: removing Washington from the nation's pantheon would be as politically unthinkable as it would be toponymically exhausting. As the contrarian comedian and commentator Bill Maher Tweeted, removing everything pro-slavery would mean removing the Washington Monument. On the other hand, Maher, an avowed atheist, notes approvingly we would also have to dispense with the Bible.[15]

These axioms form a conundrum because they cannot each be denied, but neither can they all be true. If slavery (i.e., everything we call 'slavery' in the past or present) is an intrinsic and gross moral evil, then anyone who affirmed or practiced it is guilty of a grievous moral offense and is an unfit source for moral or legal guidance today.

The Slavery Conundrum was on full display in the wake of Charlottesville. Or, more properly, flimsy attempts to resolve its contradictions or at least gloss over them were on full display. President Trump could not resolve the contradiction. He could only point out the cost of its logical conclusion: if you condemn the moral authority of all those who allowed slavery, you lose the Founding Fathers (implied: that is not acceptable). Carlson and various other pundits tried to square the circle by fudging the first axiom and subtly minimizing the moral evil of slavery. On his show *Real Time*, Bill Maher chided that the comparison of Washington and Lee was nonsense because, in the idiom of software, 'For Washington slavery was a bug, for Lee it was a feature.'[16] *Vox*'s Matthew Yglesias offered a slightly wordier version of the same argument: slavery was only part of Washington's or Jefferson's legacy, while it was the entirety of someone like Lee's.[17] *The Economist* used a bait and switch tactic. It argued that it was fallacious to compare Washington and Lee by turning the Civil War focus from slavery to the South's secessionist aim: Washington and Jefferson had fought to found the Union, the author wrote, while Lee had taken up arms against it.[18] Perhaps the author hoped the reader would not notice that the issue at hand was slavery and not preserving the Union.

The problem, however, is that slavery cannot be both an intrinsic and profound moral evil (as Carlson said, 'It's hard to think of anything worse than slavery') and also just a 'moral taint' (as he labeled it just seconds later). If slavery is a profound moral wrong across space and time, then it cannot merely be 'a bug' or 'part of someone's legacy.' It would be a fatal bug, and it would obliterate their entire moral legacy and authority, especially if the figure in question was not just a philosopher or statesman but a prophet or an embodiment of divine perfection. Emphasizing how fixed this sentiment is, the wildly popular TV programme *Game of Thrones* has explored the moral gray areas of incest, murder and almost every other crime imaginable. But even the genuinely awful people of Westeros all know that slavery is beyond the pale and outlawed it millennia ago.[19]

Our modern public ethics in the West are rooted in the principles of equality, autonomy and freedom. Slavery is a fundamental infringement on all three. How could a figure who viewed them with such contempt be part of a modern conversation about ethics, morality or justice? In Western democracies today, would we allow a person who believed slavery was acceptable or who owned slaves to rise to a position of even medium moral, political or communal authority? No, because we expect even children to know that slavery is evil.

Before proceeding further, we must recognize up front two major differences between the Islamic Slavery Conundrum and the American one, one in favor of the Islamic and one in its disfavor. First, American slavery is inexorably bound up with the issue of race in America, both in the horrendous racial justifications used to defend American slavery and in the fundamental way that slavery shaped what race still means in America today. As we have already discussed, slavery in Islamic civilization was associated with various races in different contexts. But race was never a *definitive* or even consistent element of slavery across Islamic civilization; saying 'slave' did not consistently connote any particular race or phenotype. More importantly, at the level of normative theory, race had no role in *riqq* as conceptualized in the Shariah.[20] The Prophet had been clear: no race is superior to any other except by faith in God.[21] No Muslim *should* harbor racist ideas or associate race with slavery, and in this chapter it is the normative *should* that concerns us.

Second, the authority that we are dealing with in American history is that of the tradition of Enlightenment liberalism and its articulation by the Founding Fathers. It is ultimately human authority, and it is thus inevitably flawed. In the case of the Islamic tradition, the authority we are dealing with is – according to Muslims – that of God and His final prophet, Muhammad. As we will discuss at length later on, this authority cannot sanction moral evil. This difference has great consequences for how American and Islamic thought can conceive of moral failings at their foundings.

Now, let us examine each of the axioms in the Slavery Conundrum in the hopes of finding some way to resolve the moral problem it presents.

SLAVERY IS EVIL

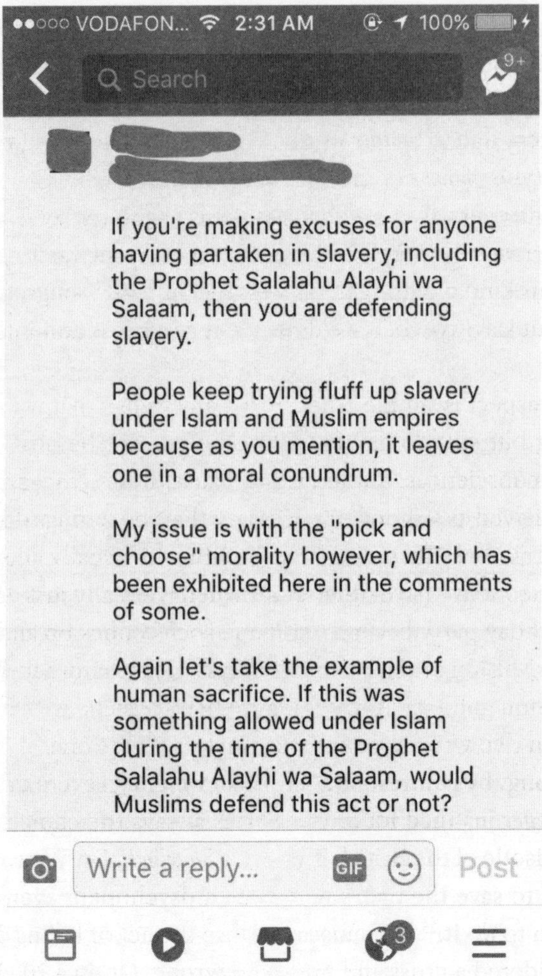

The above Facebook comment comes from a sincere and thoughtful young Muslim man, and it helps illustrate the first axiom – that slavery is an intrinsic and gross moral evil. The analogy that occurs to him is that of human sacrifice. It is totally indefensible in any place and at any time. As the leading historian of slavery in the West, David Brion Davis, wrote, by the late 1700s for many, slavery had become 'a symbol of the ultimate injustice.'[22] The abolitionists' emphaticalness on the profound moral evil of slavery was not just an expression of their passion. It also served a clear strategy. Abolitionists had to insist so strenuously that slavery was sinful and evil in and of itself because many American defenders of slavery were very willing to take steps to improve the conditions of slaves provided that the abolitionists acknowledged that such mitigated, regulated slavery was acceptable.[23] To eliminate slavery, its evil had to be something beyond the bounds of the political negotiations that had left the US with slave-owning states to begin with. The evil of slavery had to be *intrinsic* because otherwise there was the possibility of some type of slavery that was acceptable.

It is not controversial to say that slavery is absolutely evil, the ultimate injustice or intrinsically morally wrong. But what do such statements mean? Where does this kind of wrong fit on the spectrum of wrongs, and what are we saying about slavery when we describe it as a gross and intrinsic moral wrong?

The 'gross' aspect is simple. There are many things that we all acknowledge as wrong but still do anyway. This is often not because we are bad people or lack consciences. Rather, it is because these wrongs are means to ends that are viewed as so good or necessary that the wrongs done are justified. We might all agree that lying is wrong. But we usually allow white lies like telling someone we have other plans when we really just don't want to go to their birthday party because we value social cohesion and tranquility (as the famous Muslim scholar Ghazali notes, 'How many a lie is permitted for some common good').[24] And sometimes we are faced with an inevitable choice between two wrongs, so we take the less severe one.

A gross wrong, by contrast, is a wrong so weighty, severe or reprehensible that it is *never* justified for any end. It is always the choice you cannot make. In an episode of the British TV series *Sherlock*, Dr. Watson refuses to execute a man to save the man's wife from a psychopath even though the man wants him to do it.[25] He refuses because the act of killing an innocent person is considered a gross and profound wrong. Or, in a 2006 episode of the new sci-fi classic *Battlestar Galactica*, Admiral Adama refuses to commit genocide against the Cylons even though this would safeguard all of humanity from likely destruction.[26] He refuses because genocide is a monstrous moral evil no matter what ends it secures.

What about the qualifier 'intrinsic'? When it comes to understanding what 'intrinsic' means in discussions of morality, we have to remember that things can be wrong in two ways. To put it differently, the wrongness in things can be of two natures. Something can be wrong *intrinsically*, or per se, which means that its moral wrongness or evil is present in and of the thing itself, no matter when, where or what the consequences are. This is often referred to in ethics as a *deontological* wrong. We could argue that murder and genocide are intrinsically morally wrong, and many would argue that torture is intrinsically morally wrong too. Or things can be wrong by consequence, i.e., because of what they lead to. This is sometimes referred to as a *teleological* or *consequentialist* wrong. Depriving someone of food is wrong because it leads to their suffering and eventual starvation. But it could be right if the consequence being sought is good, like depriving a child of food for a time so that they can take medicine.

There have generally been two main routes by which humans have arrived at the conclusion that something is intrinsically morally wrong. The first is by divine command – the divinity deems something right or wrong. Humans can be made aware of such a command through various means, the most prominent one being prophets receiving commands through revelation. Worshipping a god other than the one God and committing adultery are both thus intrinsic wrongs established by God in the Bible and the Quran. For St. Augustine (d. 430), lying was intrinsically wrong because it placed one's soul in mortal jeopardy, and it was prohibited no matter what.[27]

The second route is via the use of reason, especially through what is known as natural law reasoning. This is a philosophical-legal tradition that holds that humans can use reason to arrive objectively at some understanding of a higher law that transcends custom and personal whim. Natural law reasoning has taken various forms. For some, like Plato (d. 347 BCE) and the Greco-Roman Stoic philosophers, it emerges from a belief that there is some divine reality beyond, behind or within our world, and that our human reason can either connect with or reflect it. For others, like Ghazali (d. 1111) and the Roman jurist Ulpian (d. *circa* 220 CE), it has come from the belief that we can use our reason to reflect on our nature as a species and come to conclusions about what is basically necessary, beneficial or harmful for us. We can label these things good or bad at a basic level, if not at a moral one then at least at a material one.[28]

This second register is a very low-level reasoning about human nature at a species level, concluding that what is good for humans is that which brings benefit and happiness, and what detracts from these is bad. Using it we might conclude that murder is wrong. We might observe that humans have an instinctive understanding that fairness and equity are right and that unfairness and inequity are wrong. Indeed, even some monkeys seem to know this.[29] We might note that all human cultures condemn immediate family incest, as Muslim theologians noticed animals do as well.[30] By contrast, the first register of natural law reasoning, associated with Plato, the Stoics and medieval Christian scholastics, reaches to more abstract levels of what goods humans aspire to and what is required or prohibited for them to achieve those goods. Thus, Stoic philosophers concluded that theft is wrong because all humans have an equal right to their own property.

Another ethical philosophy that uses reason to identify the intrinsic moral nature of things is Kant's (d. 1804) deontological ethics. This system seeks to eschew the physical and natural realm and to proceed from a pure realm of disembodied reason. It demands that each human being be dealt with 'as an end and never solely as a means' and that one should act according to rules that a rational person would accept as universal laws.[31]

Kantian ethics seem like a natural tool for condemning slavery as an intrinsic wrong, but slavery is far too material and particular for this ethical system to apply in such a way. The morality of slavery would depend on how the reasoner defined it. If the reasoner's society enslaved children from some primitive island and sincerely argued that this was not exploiting them as property but, rather, rescuing them from savagery and giving them the chance to live in a safe and enlightened environment, enslaving these people would not mean ignoring them as ends in themselves (not coincidentally, both Christian and Muslim justifications of slavery often used this argument). Using Kantian deontological ethics, one could argue that slavery was *sometimes* moral. Indeed, Kant himself approved of enslaving Africans and Native Americans based on a theory of racial superiority not too removed from the above hypothetical.[32] Slavery is thus not necessarily intrinsically wrong according to this system. It would only be intrinsically wrong if it was *rationally* intrinsically wrong, in other words, if something inherent in it prohibited the human agent from acting according to the moral law. But, as we will see, Kant followed the Stoics and the main strand of Western and Islamic philosophy in viewing freedom and moral agency as internal matters of will mostly insulated from physical constraints.[33]

Of course, there are numerous other philosophies of ethics that use reason to identify right and wrong. Utilitarianism seeks to maximize the greatest good for the greatest number of people. Virtue ethics looks at how cultivating certain virtues can facilitate happiness and excellence. These philosophies could and have been used to argue for both the rightness and wrongness of slavery.[34] But they do not deal with the intrinsic moral nature of actions. Utilitarianism relies on consequentialist reasoning that could allow for the enslavement of some people if it increased the overall happiness of more people. These theories *could* both allow slavery as ethically acceptable. Because I've posited that today it is axiomatic that slavery is intrinsically wrong (try arguing at a cocktail party that slavery is *sometimes* OK), we will not engage with Utilitarian or virtue ethics in this chapter.

In our daily lives, most of the moral wrongs we encounter belong to the category of consequentialist wrongs. Indeed, much of what we deem right and wrong in our everyday interactions is right or wrong because it is the first link in a chain of consequences that we believe eventually lead to intrinsic wrongs, like those discussed above.

Many mundane moral wrongs have no intrinsic moral value. Shouting at someone is not an intrinsic moral wrong, since what is shouting, harsh or a rude tone in one society might be totally normal in another. Neither does driving on the left-hand side of the road in the US have any inherent moral status. In these cases, what is wrong is acting in a way considered harmful or a violation of agreed social norms. Violating customary morals might not be intrinsically wrong, but many instances of custom (what is customarily right or wrong) are instances of social contracts or understandings of equitable conduct in relationships. And one could certainly argue that violating agreements (even implied ones) or acting inequitably are intrinsic wrongs.

Moreover, committing customary wrongs like driving on the wrong side of the road very likely also lead to types of real harm, which could be an intrinsic wrong or at the very least be wrong in that it leads to the denial or reduction of an intrinsic good. Finally, driving on the left-hand side of the road in the US is also illegal. While the law has no necessary overlap with intrinsic right (we all know of unjust laws), harming the rule of law and the social good it accomplishes would be an undesirable consequence. Plato gives us a paradigmatic example of this when he describes Socrates deciding not to accept help escaping his impending execution, itself an unjust ruling, because doing so would damage the rule of law so essential to harmonious life in Athens.[35]

Sometimes the consequentialist reasoning that has led us to declare something morally wrong is so compelling that we treat that thing as effectively wrong in and of itself. Some conversations around intolerance and hatred thus see these two things as so guaranteed to lead to agreed-upon wrongs, such as violence or baseless discrimination, that they should be combatted *like* intrinsic wrongs. When someone says 'That's so intolerant,' we in the global West seldom require them to explain why such intolerance is seen as likely to lead to some undesirable end. It has effectively become an intrinsic wrong for many people.

So far, we have been talking about how wrongness attaches to something. An equally important question is what is the nature of morality itself. Returning to the dichotomy between Realism and Nominalism discussed in Chapter One, does moral value have its own, objective existence? Or is it merely a description we give to certain configurations of acts? Put differently, would morality exist if we were not here to talk about it? For modern materialists, or those who believe that the only existence is this physical world we see, feel and observe around us, morality is a category we have come up with to rate our acts according to judgments we have developed either through custom or through reasoning about the harms we want to avoid and the goods we want to pursue. We can think of this as morality with a lower case 'm'. By contrast, for those who believe in divine command or the higher register of natural law reasoning, morality has a real existence on its own plane, like a reality parallel to our material world and reflected in it. It is the Good of Plato or the Reason of the Stoics. And it is the will of God, either as imbued in the actions done in His creation or sent down as divine commands and prohibitions.[36] All this we can think of as Morality with a capital 'M'.

The Intrinsic Wrongs of Slavery

Why has slavery been seen to be an intrinsic moral wrong? This conclusion has mainly been reached through natural law reasoning (not divine command, awkwardly, see below) and on the basis of three related themes: 1) the fundamental equality of humans; 2) the fundamental right of freedom; and 3) the wrongness of treating humans as property.

The intrinsic moral evil of slavery stems from the very fact of one or more of these states: ownership, domination and/or unfreedom. But there is also an argument by consequence lying close by. Some argue that these three features are also consequentialist wrongs because they are steep and slippery slopes to unacceptable exploitation, suffering and the deprivation of rights. In fact, they are such slippery slopes that they are *effectively* intrinsic wrongs by this fact alone. This we will have to look at later. For now, let us examine each intrinsic wrong of slavery in more depth:

Intrinsic Wrong #1: Slavery as fundamental inequality. The earliest objections to slavery (even if they were anonymous, inchoate and ignored) came from a notion that all humans were fundamentally equal and that slavery subverted this.[37] The idea of human equality was located in the natural law reasoning of the Stoic school of philosophy in classical Greece and Rome. Stoics held that the world was permeated by a Divine Fire, which was Reason itself (Greek, *orthos logos*; Latin, *recta ratio*), to which all nature conformed and to which our actions should conform if we want to be happy. As Cicero (d. 43 BCE) wrote, Stoics seek as much as possible to live according to nature.[38] Each human being has their equal share of this Divine Fire, so humans are all spiritually equal with the same basic duties toward one another.[39] The Stoic idea of all human beings as autonomous equals resurfaced in the seventeenth- and eighteenth-century revival of Stoic thought as well as among skeptics like John Locke, who saw freedom and equality as both part of the blank slate of basic human nature and also as God-given rights.[40]

Intrinsic Wrong #2: Freedom vs. domination. Out of the idea that all humans are equal comes the linked notion that all humans should be free to choose their actions and beliefs, at least to the extent allowed by law. Since Roman times there has been a widespread belief in Western and Islamic thought that freedom is the default status and natural state of human beings. In the Enlightenment, thinkers like Locke, Montesquieu (d. 1755) and Rousseau moved beyond the assertion that freedom was the just man's natural state to the tenet that this was a fundamental and inalienable right.[41] It was infringed upon when one human being came to exercise unacceptable domination over another. Absolute domination is a wrong in and of itself, and it has also been understood as a sure path to exploitation.

Intrinsic Wrong #3: Humans as property. As one author summarizes, the principal moral wrong of slavery is that it allows and involves 'human beings owning other human beings as property.'[42] The human-as-property notion is perhaps the most commonly decried feature associated with slavery. Indeed, it has been fundamental to definitions of slavery in the Western and Islamic traditions (though not necessarily elsewhere) up to the present.[43] Aristotle acknowledges the profound ethical questions raised by one person holding another as property, since one is exploiting the other as if they were a tool.[44] Being property is problematic because it seems to deny a human being basic rights such as equality and autonomy. And it also suggests the real possibility of mistreatment and cruelty.

Like domination, in this sense the wrong of slavery-as-human-property is not just intrinsic. It might also be the case that one person being the property of another is so likely to lead to abuse, exploitation and a deprivation of rights that slavery-as-human-property is actually a consequentialist wrong as well. But this consequence is so closely associated with the status of property that it is treated as an intrinsic wrong.

Religions and Slavery

Note the absence of any reference to divine command as a source for the intrinsic moral wrongness of slavery. This is because, quite simply, all major religious traditions either permitted, condoned or endorsed slavery. This was true through the eighteenth century for some and well into the twentieth century for others.

Starting from east to west, Jonathan Silk writes about Buddhism that 'there is almost no indication in any premodern Buddhist source, scriptural or documentary, of opposition to, or reluctance to participate in, institutions of slavery.'[45] In the case of Hinduism, it is difficult to speak about slavery strictly within the parameters of religion because of how closely intertwined Indian religions are with the specific political, social and economic history of India. Isolating slavery as an issue is also complicated because Indian religious tradition was permeated with divinely sanctioned, stratified social hierarchies of power (i.e., the caste system).[46] Several complex systems of slavery were features of social and economic life in India from the Vedic period (*circa* 1500–500 BCE) onward. In the first few centuries BCE and CE, in India slavery 'was a fairly general institution in use among high and low alike.'[47]

As Isaac Mendelsohn observed about the religions and philosophies of the ancient Near East, including the Old Testament, 'nowhere in the vast religious literature of the Sumero-Accadian world is a protest raised against the institution of slavery, nor is there anywhere an expression of the mildest sympathy for the victims of this system.'[48] Specifically in the Abrahamic tradition, the Torah allowed the Israelites to enslave non-Jews in war or to buy them from traders, and to take their women as slave-concubines. Israelites could become debt slaves of other Israelites as well, though the Torah does not allow them to be treated like non-Jewish slaves (Jewish debt slaves could only be kept for a maximum of seven years).[49]

Freedom/non-slavery was simply not a moral imperative in the pre-Enlightenment Jewish tradition. This is all too clear in what the rabbinic tradition describes as the Noahide laws, namely those injunctions reiterated to Noah after the Flood as the basic moral foundations for rebuilding humanity. According to seminal Jewish thinkers like Maimonides (d. 1204), they are universal and incumbent on every human being, Jewish or gentile. They are, indeed, the main criteria by which the uprightness of a non-Jewish person can be established. The Noahide laws are seven: 1) the duty to establish courts of law so that justice can be done; 2) the prohibition of blasphemy; 3) the prohibition of idolatry; 4) the prohibition of sexual license (in particular incest, adultery, homosexuality and bestiality); 5) the prohibition of homicide (including abortion); 6) the prohibition of robbery; and 7) the prohibition of eating limbs torn from a living animal.[50] Here we immediately see that freedom/non-enslavement does not appear among these injunctions. In fact, David Novak observes that, contrary to film depictions, in the Bible the Israelites had to be dragged out of enslavement in Egypt 'kicking and screaming' to their freedom.[51]

Turning to Christianity, in the New Testament Jesus never condemns slavery and even assumes the master/slave relationship to be an unremarkable reality of life.[52] The Apostles included slave owners, and Paul instructed slaves to 'be submissive to their masters' and to obey them 'as you would Christ' (more on this later).[53] Augustine and Isidore of Seville (d. 636) explained and justified slavery as the result of original sin or personal sin. To explain how a seemingly righteous Christian could be the slave of a godless pagan, they drew on the Stoic tradition that, for the pious, the legal and material condition of slavery was meaningless. The only true enslavement was being a slave to one's passions or sins, and the faithful were all free in Christ.[54]

At some points in medieval Europe, the Catholic Church was a leading slave owner.[55] Though there is ample evidence that the Catholic Church criticized or condemned the excesses of slavery in the Americas and aspects of the Atlantic slave trade, Cardinal Avery Dulles (d. 2008) wrote in 2005 that the Catholic Church had 'never made an absolute condemnation of slavery as such . . .' Nor had Pope John Paul specifically asserted that slavery was an 'intrinsic evil,' as some have claimed. Other Catholic thinkers disagree strongly with Dulles' conclusions, but the evidence he marshals about the Church's historical positions on slavery seems uncontested.[56] The Protestant reformer John Calvin (d. 1564) was supportive of ending slavery in Europe but not on any deeply moral grounds. He noted that the New Testament did not forbid or condemn it.[57] In the seventeenth century, when the Protestant Quakers began advocating the abolition of slavery as a moral and spiritual evil they were the only Christian sect to hold anything near that position.[58]

And, of course, slavery was affirmed by Islam's scriptures. Though the Quran encourages the manumission of slaves and their good treatment, and the Prophet Muhammad required Muslims to treat their slaves well, neither the holy book nor the Prophet's teachings condemned slavery per se or banned it. The Prophet owned a total of fifteen male slaves, all of whom he eventually freed.[59] He also had two concubines, Mariya and Rayhana.[60] The first was a Coptic Christian from Egypt who was sent to the Prophet as a gift by the patriarch of Alexandria. Although Mariya was legally assured her freedom when she gave birth to the Prophet's child, pre-modern Muslim historians uniformly referred to her as the Prophet's slave-concubine (*jāriya, surriyya, umm walad,* etc.), not his wife (see Appendix 4 – Was Māriya the Wife or the Concubine of the Prophet?). There are conflicting reports on the status of Rayhana, who was originally from a Jewish tribe. Either the Prophet slept with her as his slave woman or freed her and married her. Both Mariya and Rayhana converted to Islam soon after coming into the Prophet's possession.[61]

Minimizing the Unminimizable or Historicizing the Unhistoricizable

In the global West, not all gross transhistorical wrongs are damning. In general, historians often criticize what they refer to as anachronistic judgments, or judging the people of one age by the standards of another. They argue that this privileges the present (a notion called presentism) and prevents real understanding of why people in the past acted the way they did.[62] In general, both Western historians and Western public discourse have abided well by this guideline.[63] We understand that times change. Wagner's (d. 1883) Ring cycle still plays in Western opera houses despite his anti-Semitism. Music and racial views are not necessarily related, it is said. American law school professors continue to lavish praise on the superb legal mind and lucid writing of Justice Oliver Wendell Holmes (d. 1932). Indeed, we name elementary schools after him. All this despite the fact that he was a eugenicist who wrote, in a Supreme Court decision in support of forced sterilization of 'mental defectives,' that 'three generations of imbeciles are enough.'[64]

Slavery proves a rare exception to this rule against anachronistic judgment, a fact that forms a major part of the Slavery Conundrum. Even when writing about times in which slavery was widespread and considered unremarkable or about thinkers for whom the naturalness of slavery was obvious, modern historians often feel the need to make their objection to the institution known. In his 1812 edition of Gibbon's (d. 1794) monumental work of history, *The Decline and Fall of the Roman Empire*, a French scholar performs his outrage at the author's matter-of-fact description of Roman slavery and goes on at length about his 'blamable indifference' to their suffering (elsewhere Gibbon calls the slave trade 'abominable').[65] One scholar of Aristotle speaks of the 'justifiable outrage' we feel at the Philosopher's discussion of those who are 'natural slaves.' The great Alasdair MacIntyre calls his defense of slavery 'indefensible.'[66] Another calls this aspect of Aristotle 'an embarrassment,' while yet another contemporary scholar dismisses Aristotle's conclusion about natural slavery as an obvious product of his cultural bias, devoting a whole footnote to pleading that this is clear beyond the need for evidence.[67] Even in a casual conversation, suggesting that we not judge the past by present standards or judge some cultures by the standards of others will usually lead to an accusation of moral relativism, an accusation then hammered home with the irrefutable nail of 'Well, then would slavery be OK?' No one can rebut that argument, since everyone knows that slavery is slavery, and slavery is objectively wrong throughout time and space.

SLAVERY IS SLAVERY: THE PROBLEM OF LABELING 'SLAVERY' WITH ONE MORAL JUDGMENT

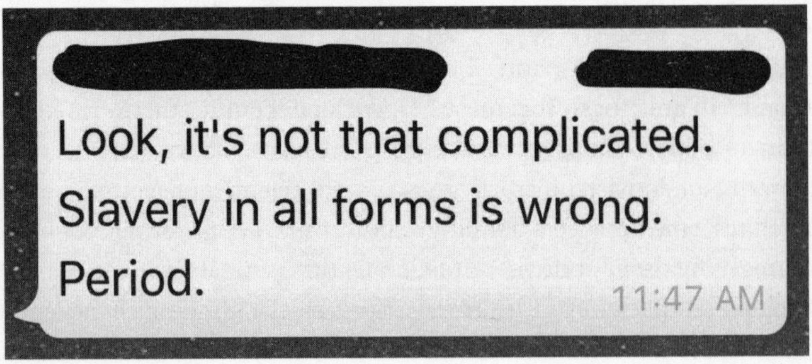
[redacted] [redacted]
Look, it's not that complicated.
Slavery in all forms is wrong.
Period.
11:47 AM

The above message was sent to a discussion group of young Muslim professionals in the wake of a public debate within the Muslim community on slavery. It sums up most concisely the second axiom of the Slavery

Conundrum. This axiom was also on display in the commotion surrounding the Tizon article, 'My Family's Slave.' When some people defended the author and his family by explaining that 'slavery in the Philippines is not like slavery in the Americas; slaves in the Philippines are like part of the family,' they were savaged for defending slavery. Implicit in the minds of their critics was that there is one consistent, operative definition of slavery and that, per axiom one, it is a gross and intrinsic moral wrong. As the Sudanese scholar Yusuf Fadl Hasan once stated in response to the common observation that slavery in the Arab world was less voluminous and brutal than the Atlantic slave trade, 'Slavery is slavery and cannot be beautified by cosmetics.'[68]

There is indeed a substantial block of opinion in slavery studies that there is a transhistorical phenomenon called slavery that can be accurately defined. But even scholars who espouse this position would recognize that this phenomenon has been incredibly varied. In the case of the Tizon article, once a specialist weighed in on the online discussion there was little objection that could be made against him. Vincente Rafael, a professor of Southeast Asian history from the University of Washington, brought the controversy around the article down from the plane of rhetoric to empirical reality by stating the obvious: '"slavery" is not the same everywhere at all times.'[69] This is so well established in scholarship on slavery that when I wrote in an online essay that 'ownership, freedom and exploitation come in shades of gray' and that forced labor and involuntary servitude exist on a spectrum, one scholar of Indian Ocean slavery commented that this was 'an absolutely uncontroversial statement . . .' In fact, it was 'really a quite banal one.'[70]

But why is public discourse on slavery at such odds with scholarship on the topic? In great part, this results from the difficulties that still remain in defining exactly what 'slavery' is in the first place. As we saw at length in Chapter One, activists, historians and social scientists have all been hard pressed to come up with a definition for slavery that fits everything we are used to calling slavery but does not include things we are not accustomed to placing under that label.[71] The most well-received definitions have centered on the themes of freedom, ownership and the controlling threat of coercive violence. One of the reasons that 'slavery is slavery' is such a dominant idea is that these three themes are often construed as binaries. Either one is free or not, either one is property or not. As a result, slavery is (inaccurately) construed in the public mind as the binary opposite of freedom, homogeneous and monochrome. Slavery is slavery because the only other option is not-slavery. As we have seen and will see further, this is very much *not* the case.

A second reason grows out of the dynamic of debate between abolitionists and supporters of slavery in America and the British Empire in the nineteenth century. Defenders of slavery used the difficulty of defining the term as the opening salvo of their arguments, often followed by trying to draw a distinction between 'good' and 'bad' slavery.[72] Many defenders of slavery in the colonial Americas or slave systems in British India argued that the slavery *they* were supporting was benevolent, not the immoral 'absolute or pure slavery' of the Roman emperors.[73] This argument convinced some abolitionists to accept a delay in banning slavery in British India and the empire's east Asian territories for decades.[74] The window that it seemed to create for protecting slave systems led many advocates of abolition to adopt an uncompromising 'slavery is slavery' position.[75] In light of this history, we must be cautious about what uses are made of the distinctions drawn within the broader category of 'slavery.' They can be used to defend unacceptable exploitation, so skepticism is warranted.

The problem that the axiom 'Slavery is slavery' presents for any kind of detailed moral thinking, however, is clear: if we insist that 'slavery is slavery' and label all slavery as a gross and intrinsic moral wrong, then we are applying the same level of moral condemnation to an institution that included both some of history's wealthiest, most powerful individuals (like the Ottoman grand viziers) and its most desperate and oppressed. This is very crude moral reasoning, which only works if one views the category of 'slavery' itself as the complete locus of moral evil. As we shall show below, this does not work well.

The Moral Wrongness of Slavery as Unfreedom

As we saw in Chapter One, one of the enduring understandings of slavery in the Western and Islamic worlds is depriving someone of freedom. This is rooted originally in the Roman legal tradition and has been extremely influential in both Western and Islamic civilization. Justinian's codification of Roman law stated that people are either free or a slave. A free person exists in that natural state 'enjoyed by each one to do as he pleases, unless prevented by force or by law.' A slave, on the other hand, is a person 'subjected to the authority of another, contrary to nature.'[76]

As we have discussed at length, however, this binary is deceptive. Slavery is not the opposite of freedom. It is just less freedom than what 'free' people enjoy. Freedom is not the absence of constraints on autonomy. It is just less constraint than 'slaves' endure. The line between 'free' and 'slave' is effectively an arbitrary one drawn by the legal and cultural traditions of a society.

This raises real challenges for the axiom that slavery is a gross and intrinsic moral evil. If slavery is an evil because (in this case) slavery is making someone unfree, then at what point does unfreedom merit this qualification of moral evil? As David Graeber points out, if freedom is natural (read, right), but at the same time 'freedom and slavery are just matters of degree, then, logically, would not *all* restrictions on freedom be to some degree unnatural' (read, wrong)?[77] Clearly this cannot be the case, or all societies would be inherently evil in their totality, since all societies restrict their members' freedoms to some extent or another.

But then when does restriction move from the normal to the realm of morally wrong? And what would we say about situations we categorized as 'slavery' in which the restrictions on freedom did not reach that point? Would that 'slavery' be acceptable or still be wrong? As we have already seen, at various points in history people categorized as slaves could own property, earn a living, have a family, bequeath and inherit property and enjoy legal protection against mistreatment from their owners. The status of many slaves in the Ottoman Empire in the eighteenth and nineteenth centuries, for example, did not differ much from their contemporaries working as free wage laborers in Britain. These slaves certainly lacked some of the rights and advantages of free people in Ottoman society, but swaths of people categorized as free in the past and present have also lacked these advantages. Where exactly, then, do we locate the intrinsic wrongness of slavery?

Here we should pause to reflect on a common trope in historical moralizing on slavery. Condemnations of slavery often cite that Roman law recognized that it was 'contrary to nature,' which modern readers gloss as 'morally wrong.' But Roman jurists did not mean that at all. They simply meant that slavery was not the default state of affairs. People were ordinarily born free, which was the natural human condition. But they could be enslaved rightly and legally. Slavery was morally acceptable to Roman jurists because it was affirmed by the *ius gentium*, the common law of nations that Romans imagined all peoples shared. Although the Roman legal notion of the law of nations has sometimes been conflated with international law, for major Roman jurists it was actually tantamount to natural law. The influential jurist Gaius (d. *circa* 180 CE) called the *ius gentium* 'that law which natural reason has established among all human beings,' in other words, natural law.[78] Because Roman jurists thought of natural law on a spectrum between a basic, low-register species reasoning at one end, and a more elaborate notion of shared human morals and conventions on the other, innate freedom and slavery were both considered totally 'natural' in Roman legal thinking.[79] Pointing out the ambiguity of the term 'natural' in relation to right and wrong in the Roman context, the great Robert Cover remarked that for Romans, 'The law of nature was not meant to be a mandate for Spartacus.'[80]

The Moral Wrongness of Slavery as Owning Human Property

As we discussed in Chapter One, there is perhaps no definition of slavery more common in both the Western (particularly post-1700s) and Islamic traditions than that slavery is owning a human being as property. The very phrase turns stomachs and consciences today. But we also demonstrated that, like freedom, ownership and property are concepts that are so abstract that they can mean virtually anything. 'Owning a person' does not necessarily mean anything more than 'having some unspecified right over that person.' As Patterson observes with great insight, describing a relationship as ownership is really a choice of idiom rather than an objective reflection of a degree of control. In many societies, basic social and family relationships like marriage and apprenticeship can be formed, marked and expressed using a transactional idiom that we in the West would perceive as buying and selling people. But this merely reflects our accumulated social preferences. It says nothing about the actual nature or quality of the relationships at stake. Take marriage as an example. What one society terms a relationship of partnership and another a religious sacrament, still another society might define in the idiom of ownership.[81] The actual features of the relationship could be the same across all three societies. Is a relationship morally acceptable in the first two cases but indefensible in the third? Should we declare a relationship to be an intrinsic, gross moral wrong simply because it is phrased in the idiom of ownership when its actual nature might be no different from relationships we consider normal?

The bizarre way in which the complexity of relationship, love and ownership can comingle confusedly is evident in the liminal case of pets.

We own our pets. We are their 'masters.'[82] And we can even destroy them if we see fit. In the US, all states and the Federal government prohibit to some extent or another cruelty to animals. Yet killing them is generally allowed. Every US state has some prohibition on killing domestic animals, but these are almost always limited to killings that are 'unnecessary,'[83] 'cruel,'[84] 'unjustifiable,'[85] 'malicious,'[86] that cause severe or needless suffering,[87] or in which the animal belongs to someone else[88] (i.e., the person killing it does not have the legal privilege to do so).[89] Maine allows you to shoot your cat or dog if you are an adult and do so in a way that minimizes suffering and danger to others. In the state of Washington, economic distress is an affirmative defense against a charge of animal cruelty in the second degree (i.e., killing one's animal in a way that does not cause unnecessary suffering).[90] So you can kill your dog if you feel you're too poor to pay for its food anymore. Whether on their own or with the help of a veterinarian, Americans can kill their pets because they are their property.

Yet few would imagine that this relationship of ownership, and indeed our legal power of life and death over our animals, means that having pets is morally wrong. We have immense affection and loyalty for our pets (and vice versa). Cinemagoers know that killing someone's dog can move even a seasoned gunfighter to tears (see the film *Open Range*, 2003), lead to vendetta mayhem (see *John Wick*, 2014) and that men will die to defend their dogs (see *White Fang*, 1991). A Facebook video entitled 'Humans Reunited with Dogs' is difficult to view without at least a few tears.[91] Jerry Seinfeld once observed that aliens viewing Earth from space and seeing one species collecting the feces of another would conclude that dogs ruled humans.[92]

One might object that owning human beings is qualitatively different from owning a dog. But strict animal rights activists respond that this distinction is arbitrary and amounts to nothing more than 'speciesism.' Why should humans have any more or less rights than other animals, especially mammals? Some more radical animal rights activists who call for the 'abolition' of animal ownership use that language explicitly because both the status of owning them as property and exploiting their labor are comparable to slavery.[93]

So the question is clear: if ownership is so vague as to have any number of potential meanings and manifestations, many of which are equal or even identical to relationships we consider totally normal, where does the moral evil of slavery-as-owning-human-property begin?

The Moral Wrongness of Slavery as Inequality

The first argument we noted for an intrinsic evil in slavery was that it involved fundamental inequality among human beings. Here a keen observer might suggest that focusing on slavery and its definition is barking up the wrong tree. If inequality itself is an evil, then slavery is simply the most extreme example of the real moral wrong at hand, namely relationships of inequality and power asymmetry. Aren't these the roots of exploitation?

This observation is packed with more insight than it seems at first. A leading scholar of slavery in Africa, Paul Lovejoy, has argued that the signal feature of slavery is that, however a society defines freedom or property, etc., the slave is always distinguished from – and below – the free.[94] It is this distinction that matters. Yet the distinction between slave and free is but one possible marker of inequality. It became just one of many, and perhaps not even the most dramatic, in medieval Scandinavia, much of Africa and the Indian Ocean world. In such cases, the free/slave distinction loses much of its importance and moral sting.[95] One of the obstacles that those raising the alarm over Modern Slavery have faced is that, in today's world, the features they argue define Modern Slavery sometimes do not stand out starkly in a global political and economic system replete with gradations of freedoms and rights. Citizenship and documented legal status are just two of the *legal* ways that some people are denied the freedoms and rights enjoyed by others for no reason other than the accident of birth.

Debating the rightness or wrongness of inequality is a worthy discussion, but it is one that strikes at a question much more fundamental than that of slavery: is inequality in human societies wrong? Or is it only *inequity* that is wrong (i.e., individuals not getting what they deserve or have earned, as opposed to each person getting an equal share)? Is the good of individuals and a community best served by accepting as natural and right certain hierarchies and relationships of limited domination and exploitation? Or should humans seek to remove these features from our societies altogether?

Here we are faced with the dichotomy best summarized in the disagreement between radical calls for equality by many French revolutionaries and the archetypal Conservatism of Edmund Burke (d. 1797), the British statesman who criticized them. Burke believed that society was built on and out of families, traditions, the relationships of authority between the different levels of society and the respect for property. These are all locations of inherent inequality. As Burke wrote in response to the revolution in France, 'men all have equal rights, but not to equal things.' Nor do they have equal rights to the same 'share of power, authority, and direction . . .' People should enjoy liberty and certainly not be oppressed or treated unacceptably, but trying to remove all hierarchies of power and all degrees of exploitation was both unnatural and anarchic.[96]

Before Burke, another passionate advocate of liberty, John Locke, had nonetheless acknowledged that men *generally* have natural – read morally defensible – domination over women due to their being stronger, and parents have natural domination over their children (at least for a time).[97] As P. A. Brunt observed about pre-modern societies in general, the aesthetic ideals and philosophical, scientific and religious pursuits called for by 'civilization' were always premised on the existence of a leisure elite who could engage in such study and were supported by the exploited labor of their social lessers.[98]

In contrast to Burke, the most radical French revolutionaries held that existing hierarchies and inequalities could and should be swept away. The new state and society should enforce equality, not equity, since notions of certain individuals 'deserving' their inherited wealth, power or status had no natural basis and could thus be eliminated in a giant leap into a bold new world.[99]

Reasonable people have disagreed and will continue to disagree on the correct understanding of equality versus equity. But that is a debate between contrasting political and social philosophies. It is not the topic of this book. For our purposes, the question is, if there is some degree of inequality and exploitation allowed in society, when does that degree reach the point of gross, intrinsic moral wrong? Societies disagree on the answer. So where is the moral evil of slavery located?

The Moral Wrongness of Slavery as the Threat of Violence

Finally, perhaps the most compelling definition for slavery has been offered most concisely by New Abolitionists. According to this definition, the essential feature of slavery is violence or its threat, the condition of coercion that leaves one 'not able to walk away.' The American Anti-Slavery Group has summarized discourse around the New Abolitionist definition of slavery well. Slavery is 'forced labor for no pay under the threat of violence.'[100]

Again, we are confronted with a question. If we take this notion of violence (essential for coercion) as the key to identifying slavery, how close and how impending does its threat have to be for the moral censure of slavery to apply? Debt was the main route into some form of servile labor or another from the ancient Near East and Roman Empire to early modern Southeast Asia. People became slaves because they could not repay their debts, and their creditors had coercive power over them. But this coercive element is also present in debt that has not resulted in slavery. As far back as Aristotle there has been an understanding that the threat of violence *always* looms over the debtor-lender relationship.[101] Societies that have condemned slavery as morally evil still allow debt and often usury. At what point does the threat of violence lying behind such relationships make them grossly morally wrong?

As citizens of modern states we all live under the shadow of violence from the organs of those states – it is the claim of monopoly on violence that defines the modern state – though that violence or its threat often seem far off for many of us. For others, it is not far off at all, as has been amply demonstrated by the experience of African American men at the hands of the US justice system and, more recently, the stunning number of instances in which police have shot or killed unarmed African Americans for negligible causes. As has been illustrated by scholars like Michelle Alexander, African Americans moved from slavery to formal freedom, and then eventually to formal equal rights. But the very real and immediate threat of violence, whether at the hands of slave owners, lynch mobs or law enforcement, has remained a constant feature. Thus, again, we find ourselves dealing with a spectrum. Where on this spectrum of violence or the threat of violence does the intrinsic and gross moral evil of slavery appear?

The Bald Man Fallacy and the Wrongness of Slavery

There are two serious problems with attaching the judgment that slavery is a gross, intrinsic moral wrong to the formal legal categories of un-freedom and humans-as-property, or to the presence of violent coercion. First, these concepts are tremendously abstract, so it is not clear precisely at which point the moral judgment should take effect. Second, how these categories and concepts are understood and when their labels are applied are the products of specific cultural traditions and therefore hugely inconsistent. This severely undermines the universal moral claim being made, namely that slavery is *always* wrong. Freedom and property are either spectrums or abstractions on and in which people whom we definitely do not label as 'slaves' have lived and still live to this day. And few would be willing to categorize all these situations in the past or these situations in the present as gross, intrinsic moral wrongs. Assuredly, we might not like to find ourselves in some of America's more subordinated or compelled socio-economic stations. But we would be hard pressed to call the existence of those stations an intrinsic, gross moral wrong.

As we saw in our effort to define slavery, we must be wary of the Bald Man Fallacy. Just because we cannot fix exactly where or why the intrinsic moral wrongness of slavery begins, that does not mean we cannot point to a situation of horrific exploitation and say 'That's intrinsically evil.' But if we cannot state clearly exactly what slavery is, and where and when precisely it becomes intrinsically wrong, then we must consider how much utility there is in thinking in terms of the corresponding binaries of free and slave, acceptable and intrinsically evil.

It may be more accurate to conceive of a spectrum of freedom, rights, exploitation and coercion. In his influential essay on slavery as a transhistorical category, Moses Finley proposed a spectrum between 'absolute freedom to exercise all rights' and 'absolute rightlessness.'[102] We could imagine that there is a point on that spectrum at which a reasonable person would say, 'This is a truly undesirable condition and these conditions are morally repugnant,' and it is at that point that the intrinsic, gross moral wrong of slavery appears. But the problem is that reasonable people disagree on where that point is and what those conditions are. Many in the West would say that being classified as property or unfree would alone suffice as morally repugnant. But, as we'll see with the two testimonies from slaves (pages 174–5), at least some reasonable people disagree with that. It would be less contentious to forget looking for a firm boundary of slavery and its moral evil and just independently evaluate the ethical or moral status of any point on our spectrum.

Moving away from concise legal categories like 'unfree' or 'property' to a spectrum of conditions, rights or treatment would force us to be more morally nuanced in our judgments. But it would also significantly dull the edges of our moral declarations. We lose the moral force of the slavery label. But such labels also do violence to accurately describing moral reality. The usefulness of formal categories is precisely that they are formal categories. Everything that falls within them is 'slavery,' and everything outside is not. But if we decide that at some point on a spectrum we've reached slavery, it is not clear how much morally worse that condition is from that of those only slightly better off. The difference between a poor but still 'free' Indian construction worker in the Persian Gulf and a 'modern slave' Indian construction worker in the Persian Gulf is the difference between 1) an Indian construction worker who has accepted a multi-year contract to work under grueling conditions for very low pay, surrendered his passport and agreed to live with numerous restrictions on his movement, with these rules enforced by company security services; and 2) someone who fits exactly the same description but who receives slightly lower wages and whose employer's guards are slightly crueler. Not to diminish the plight of either of these workers, but this is analogous to the difference between a restaurant that barely passes health inspection and one that barely fails. Are we really comfortable with the first but not the second?

One could also move the argument away from slavery-as-intrinsic-moral-wrong altogether toward a consequentialist argument of 'Statuses like humans-as-property, humans-as-unfree are so likely to lead to unacceptable treatment that that they are *effectively* intrinsic wrongs.' In saying this, however, one is shifting the argument about slavery's moral wrongness away from the intrinsic to the consequential. If slavery is a moral wrong not because of what it is in and of itself but, rather, because of what it very often has led to, then the first axiom of the Slavery Conundrum has vanished. Slavery is no longer an intrinsic, gross moral wrong. It is just very bad policy.

When Slavery is 'Not that Bad': The Problem with Conditions vs. Formal Categories

Now, to be very clear, in what follows I am *not* arguing that slavery in Muslim societies was benevolent or pleasant. As we have already seen, Islamic civilization was too vast to make such a generalization. I am simply offering two (unedited) reports for the purpose of understanding the nature of the moral problem of slavery.

The following was sent to me by an American Muslim scholar who was studying in Mauritania in 2005 and had the following conversation with a slave there:

> I basically asked him why there didn't seem to be a drive amongst a number of slaves in the desert villages to seek freedom, especially considering the various attempts the authorities in Nouakchott (the

capital) had made to inspect out there. Some of the things mentioned in the response were:

> – What exactly am I to do with this freedom? I'm part of a tribe that takes care of my shelter and food. Do I have to do that by myself? Do I have to worry about zakat and taxes?
> – My kids can study with the teachers if they wish. Many of our children are *fuqahā'* (legal scholars) and *ḥuffāẓ* (people who have memorized the Quran).
> – I take care of the livestock, get water from the well and sometimes takes trips to sell meat or buy rice. I keep my prayers, and I don't cheat anyone. I don't have much, but I'll be light when I meet my Lord. What else do I want?
>
> Admittedly, the slaves I saw lived under very pious, just masters. I'm sure the situation was different for others, but these men and women were certainly not yearning for freedom.

And the following was reported by Tanya Cariina Newbury-Smith, a British anthropologist working in Saudi Arabia:

> Once I saw one young girl run in to the room where I was talking with a fairly high-ranking prince, just casually. She raced in to hug and kiss him on the forehead, interrupted us, and he asked her how school was that day. She explained her homework to him and he said he'd help her later when I left. I asked him, when she left, who was this girl who was as black as a Nubian slave? He replied that it was the daughter of his 'servant' Muhammad. I was surprised, and the prince laughed and said, my god do you actually think we don't treat them like family? They *are* family. This is Islam: they are treated with love and gentility. He was later getting much mileage from our dinner guests, at my expense. They all understood: the West cannot get out of the notion of Western 'slavery' and project it to other cultures. Indeed, this family lived better than I did by far, affording a new Mercedes for [Muhammad's] sons every year. I asked Muhammad if he'd ever leave and return to Sudan. On pain of death, he would never leave, Muhammad said. He will stay with the prince for life.[103]

These are just two contemporary testimonies of an observation that was common among Western commentators on slavery in the Ottoman Empire, Muslim India and on African slavery from the sixteenth to the twentieth centuries: that under the Shariah slaves were treated humanely, much better than slaves owned by Western Europeans, and perhaps better than the indigent in Western lands (some Muslim travelers among Europeans had the opposite impression and were shocked by Western slavery).[104] What these reports point out is that, if you move the cause of moral condemnation from formal categories of 'slave' to a set of deplorable conditions, then it becomes very possible that some situations of people falling under our usual, formal category of 'slave' might be significantly better than those defined deplorable conditions. In fact, in some instances, individuals or groups might prefer living in the formal status of slavery over what they had experienced or felt they were likely to experience as free people. In such cases, what grounds would there be for declaring those situations of 'slavery' to be intrinsically morally wrong?

One could object that how an enslaved person felt about their situation does not necessarily reflect its moral rightness or wrongness. This could well be an instance of what philosophers and social scientists refer to as adaptive preference, a concept used in rational choice theory and often found in feminist work. In brief, adaptive preference is the idea that people in unpleasant or oppressive relationships or situations essentially cope with these by deciding that things are not so bad or that they do not need them to be any better. An abused wife can thus cope with living with her husband by internalizing the idea that she doesn't deserve any better or that this is as good as it gets. She might even *choose* to remain with him because of this.[105] Viewed from the perspective of adaptive preference, victims of oppressive circumstances can essentially surrender important portions of their autonomy.[106]

Critics of how the concept of adaptive preference is used, however, point out that an abused wife or, in our case, a slave might actually be seizing and expressing their autonomy in a profound but unexpected way in choosing to embrace or even remain in their situation. Though potentially valid, some scholars have pointed out that viewing adaptive preference as an act of reclaiming agency by the oppressed might only further cement the power of the oppressor.[107] A better response to the adaptive preference objection is that a recourse to adaptive preference or the similar theory of false consciousness militates against the fundamentals of applied liberalism and democracy, namely that individuals are able and entitled to decide what they want. If slavery studies often involve the imposition of Western structures onto non-Western society and history, then such an imposition surely reaches new heights if we discount the subjective judgment of non-Western peoples about their own conditions.

Do Some People Deserve to be Enslaved? Or, is Freedom a Human Right?

Perhaps the aspect of slavery that is most troubling to many is something that has not been mentioned so far. Most people would agree that there are certain circumstances in which people can be deprived of their freedom; for example, if they commit a crime. Many in the US (but certainly not all) find no ethical problem in those prisoners' labor being exploited. And many people (not I) would accept that a prisoner could be tortured to extract information in the proverbial 'ticking time bomb' scenario. But in each of these cases the person deprived or subjected to this treatment has at least notionally committed some wrong for which they *deserve* what is happening to them.

In the US context we are accustomed to talking about slavery as a subject of immense moral condemnation and as bound intimately to insidious conceptions of racial superiority. We forget that, in the Roman, Near Eastern and Germanic heritages of Western Europe, slavery was not a racial or moral issue at all (though from the seventh century onward there were concerted efforts by the Church to end the enslavement of Christians).[108] Unlike the race-based slavery of the Americas, where there was at least an attempt (as repulsive and baseless as it was) to justify slavery by arguments of racial superiority/inferiority, for most of human history slavery has not been explained by any reference to phenotype.[109]

As has been observed about slavery in the ancient Near East and the Roman Empire alike, slavery was a 'misfortune' that could befall anyone. 'Slaves are human beings too,' says Trimalchio in a satire by Petronius (d. 66 CE). It is just that 'luck's been against them.'[110] Aristotle, Cicero and other moral philosophers could talk all they wanted about the just, 'natural slavery' of those unable to govern themselves, and Church Fathers could speak about how slavery resulted from sin. But they all knew that these categories did not map onto reality at all. Anyone, moral pillar or cad, Roman or barbarian, Christian or pagan, was one financial disaster or pirate raid away from being a slave.[111] Even if we could assign some blame to a person for falling into debt or being captured by an enemy, what about a child born to slave parents and thus born into that condition through no evident fault of its own?

The randomness of enslavement caused discomfort for Muslim jurists as they tried to theorize slavery as conceptualized by Islamic law. The default, natural state of human beings is freedom, they agreed. So how could the enslavement of people who had committed no crime, or the birth of a child into slavery, be explained? What basis was there for them being moved out of man's default condition? A tendentious explanation, which seems to have been accepted without contest by the mid-eleventh century, was put forth in what became the standard Shariah definition of slavery, namely 'A legal weakness/handicap caused by unbelief.'[112] Because in the Shariah only non-Muslims living outside the Abode of Islam could be legally enslaved, Muslim scholars proposed that slavery was a punishment for their unbelief. As one thirteenth-century Muslim scholar put it, when an unbeliever had disdained becoming a slave of God, God made that person a slave of God's slave.[113] This status did not end if a slave embraced Islam. They remained a slave, which Muslim scholars explained as being earthly discomfort stemming from the vestiges of unbelief. This was nonetheless superior to suffering in the afterlife.[114]

But this explanation is extremely flimsy. First of all, as the Prophet explained to a recent convert eager for his past sins to be forgiven, 'Islam wipes away what came before it,' by which Muslim scholars understood the sins of unbelief and disobeying God.[115] Second, the same schools of thought that formulated this etiology for slavery also held that people outside the lands of Islam who had either no knowledge or grossly inaccurate information about Islam were not held accountable by God for not embracing it.[116] So if people alien to the message of Islam would not be punished by God on the Day of Judgment for not being Muslim, why would the same people have to be punished by God in their earthly life for not being Muslim? The only answer offered by Muslim legal theorists, in this case by the Hanafi jurist ʿAbd al-ʿAziz Bukhari (d. 1330), was that the legal status of slavery continued for a slave who converted to Islam or whose descendants had been born Muslim because this was just the ruling of God's law. That person's ongoing slave status was 'established as a rule of the Sacred Law (*sharʿ*) . . . without the meaning of it being a punishment [for unbelief] being maintained.' In this way it was like the land tax (*kharāj*) levied on the conquered lands of non-Muslims. When a Muslim bought this land, he continued to pay that tax.[117]

The Shariah, like Roman law, saw freedom as the default status of human beings and their natural state. An unidentified child found abandoned was assumed to be free. And the Shariah tradition reiterated again and again that God the Lawgiver 'looks expectantly towards freedom,' as was made most clear by the Quran's and the Hadith's repeated commands and encouragements to free slaves. But for Muslim jurists, freedom was not the non-derogable human right it is today, like the Shariah and modern human right not to be mutilated or not to be killed without just cause (see Appendix 5 – Was Freedom a Human Right in the Shariah?). Just as in Roman law, one could lose one's status as a free person if one was legally enslaved. In the Shariah, this occurred when a non-Muslim from outside the Abode of Islam was captured or when a slave woman gave birth to a child whose father was someone other than her owner.[118] Once someone or their ancestor had been legally enslaved, even if that person became Muslim or if their child was born Muslim, they remained slaves. This was because the property right (*milk*) of their owner trumped both the original, natural state of freedom into which humans are otherwise born and also the fact that the legal cause of the person's enslavement – their unbelief – had been rendered moot by their Islam.[119]

While Muslim jurists could not consistently theorize the reason for this loss of freedom, there are insights to be gained from a phenomenology of the jurists' lexicon, in particular the legal concept of *musiba*. A solid translation for the 'misfortune' mentioned by the modern scholars above, a *musiba* is a misfortune that befalls someone and can deprive them of a legal right or cause them suffering but which was either not caused by a wrong or which cannot be compensated for. Slavery was precisely such a phenomenon. Like bankruptcy or disease, slavery was just something bad that happened to someone as part of God's grand and unfathomable plan. As one former slave in Kano (now in northern Nigeria) recalled when asked if slaves liked their lot, 'Everyone disliked being a slave, but anyone who had the means usually purchased a slave.' He explained that everyone dislikes 'doing things, especially tedious tasks, by himself.'[120]

Of course, slavery is not a natural phenomenon. People enslave people. But that does not mean that people have always ideally *chosen* to enslave people, making this moral choice in a vacuum. People are subject to economic forces that often make choices for them. Our oldest records about slavery, from the ancient Near East, suggest that it started as a means of dealing with enemy captives in war.[121] This was the main type of slavery present in Arabia at the time of the Prophet. Long before the early modern period, when states emerged with the resources to handle masses of prisoners of war, absorbing captives into the population as slaves either to work or to be ransomed back to their families was a useful mechanism. In Babylonia and the world of the Old Testament, however, the single greatest reason for enslavement was debt or poverty, including the indigent selling themselves or their kin into slavery to improve their lot. This phenomenon was common from Western Europe to Southeast Asia for centuries.[122]

Slavery was a choice made, sometimes by the powerful and sometimes by the vulnerable, because it was the preferred solution to the material, economic challenges at hand. This is how we explain three British Enlightenment thinkers, each a vocal advocate of the natural right to liberty, separately proposing that the problem of widespread and severe poverty in eighteenth-century Britain be dealt with by enslaving the poor to save them from ruin. Liberty was of tremendous importance to these philosophers, but it could not be enjoyed by all people all the time. They concluded that, in the case of the very poor in their society, it had to be sacrificed to stabilize what they saw as the bottom rung of that society (ironically, their description of this restricted form of slavery was similar to *riqq* in Islamic law).[123]

Returning to the Shariah, a clear question arises: if slavery was just an unpleasant fact of life – perhaps akin to occupying the poorest rung on the socio-economic ladder – why do the Quran and Sunna call Muslims so consistently to free their slaves? Why did the Prophet, according to one Hadith, mutter over and over as he lay on his deathbed, 'Prayer, prayer, and fear God regarding those whom you possess rightfully'?[124] If slavery was just the lowest rung on the ladder – and there is always a lowest rung – why worry about it or try to move people out of it?

The answer is, of course, that simply because the Shariah did not see *riqq* as an intrinsic, grave moral wrong does not mean that it was seen as desirable. Muslim scholars acknowledged that *riqq* inflicted harm (*ḍarar*) on the slave, not least of which was the serious restriction on the slave's freedom of choice.[125] As Ibn Rushd (d. 1126, the famous jurist grandfather of the celebrated jurist and philosopher of the same name) noted, freeing slaves removed 'the harm (*ḍarar*) of slavery' from them and allowed them full freedom.[126] This harm occurred because slavery deprived humans of autonomy, full legal personhood, and the right to control and benefit from their own labor. In a revealing passage, one of the medieval Islamic world's most prolific jurists, the Hanbali Ibn Qudama (d. 1223), writes that the Prophet had encouraged manumitting slaves because:

> . . . it entails freeing a human being, inviolable, from the harm of slavery, [giving] him ownership of himself and the fruits of his labor (*manāfi'ihi*), making complete his legal standing, and enabling him to act regarding his own person and in labors according to what he chooses.[127]

Poverty is a useful comparison. It seems to exist everywhere and could befall anyone, but that does not mean we shouldn't try to alleviate it. Yet neither was slavery the worst fate according to the Shariah.[128] Slavery was an unfortunate and unhappy condition that it was best to remove people from if doing so would benefit them.

This last condition is essential to note. A crucial difference between the Shariah's conception of slavery and the modern Western one is that moving people from the category of slave to free was not the ultimate good according to the Shariah. It was not, for example, more important than providing non-Muslims with an environment in which they could learn about Islam and be encouraged to convert. Nor was it more important, as some Muslims explained to abolitionists in the nineteenth century, than saving Africans from alleged savagery.[129] And freedom was certainly not more important than ensuring that vulnerable and incapable slaves were cared for. So the Quran's exhortation that masters agree to *mukataba* contracts if their slaves proposed them closes with the conditional clause 'if you see good in them' (Quran 24:33). This 'good' was most commonly understood as the slaves having the capacity to earn a living once they were freed.[130] The Maliki school prohibited owners from freeing their slaves if they would be worse off free, for example, if they were in serious debt.[131] Ibn Qudama wrote that, 'What is recommended is manumitting those who are religious and have the capacity to earn a living and would thus benefit from manumission.' Otherwise, he explained, freed slaves would be burdens on others. In addition, if the owner felt that it was likely that the freed slave would return to non-Muslim lands (*dār al-ḥarb*), apostatize from Islam or do some other harm, then it was disliked (*makrūh*) to free the person. And if any of these was very probable (*ghalabat al-ẓann*) then it was prohibited (*ḥarām*).[132]

THE PAST AS MORAL AUTHORITY: CAN WE PART WITH THE PAST?

In the wake of the Charlottesville protests, Xavier Burgin, an African American writer/director and social media commentator, offered one solution to what I have been calling the Slavery Conundrum. In a tweet he imagined a brief exchange between 'racists' and 'Black People.' The racists ask if not honoring Jefferson means that Americans should stop praising George Washington too, since he also owned slaves. 'Yes,' reply the Black people. The racists are left speechless by a logical answer to what they assumed was a rhetorical question.[133] The message here is clear: there is a way out of the Slavery Conundrum, namely to let go of the notion that our Founding Fathers have any moral claim on us. If slavery is evil, and George Washington owned slaves, then why not just call a shovel a spade and throw George Washington's legacy where it belongs, onto the refuse heap of history?

That would be sound reasoning. But the refuse heap would be immense. It would, in fact, contain almost the entirety of mankind's philosophical, legal and religious heritage. The architects of every major philosophical and religious tradition either endorsed slavery, condoned it or, at the very least, saw it as morally tolerable. We have already discussed how many of the world's great religions viewed slavery. In the Greco-Roman philosophical tradition, Plato saw the proper ordering of adults and children, different professions and classes, 'slave and free,' each playing their proper role, as essential for a just state. Not only did he consider slavery natural and right, his proposed laws for the treatment of slaves were often harsher than practices in Athens in his day.[134] His student Aristotle stated that it was wrong to enslave people by violence without the correct supervision of the law. Slavery was both permissible and just, however, if those enslaved were people who were unable to properly govern themselves. These were 'natural slaves,' and in this case slavery was beneficial to both the slaves and the masters.[135] Some modern scholars of natural law have argued that Aristotle's natural slave and natural master were more theoretical archetypes than something he envisioned as a social reality.[136] But Aristotle's framing became such an essential means of justifying slavery across numerous schools of philosophy for centuries that the point he originally intended is practically irrelevant.[137]

The Natural Law Tradition and Slavery

The tradition of natural law reasoning built on Classical pillars like Aristotle and followed in the Classical conclusion that slavery was both natural and morally inoffensive. Even when they began exhibiting more moral skepticism about the practice, natural law discussions of slavery in the Enlightenment generally reserved the acceptability of enslaving captives in war, people from societies that seemed to ignore proper law or 'naturally slavelike' populations (see Appendix 2 – Enlightenment Thinkers on Slavery).[138] Meanwhile, the Enlightenment's most uncompromising arguments for the moral wrongness of slavery, such as that advanced by Rousseau, may have been based on a belief in the natural freedom of man, but they mocked the natural law tradition, in particular its justifications for enslaving captives.[139]

In the modern period, philosophers and ethicists who have sought to revive the natural law tradition have found again and again that slavery is its Achilles heel and undisguisable shame. If the authority of natural law rests on the claim that reasonable and thoughtful people aware of human nature should all come to certain shared moral realizations, then what does it tell us that over a millennium and a half of the best practitioners of this reasoning all concluded that slavery was morally acceptable?[140] Some modern advocates of natural law have tried to write off this colossal error as a flawed application of their method. But if its founders and greatest articulators got something so enormously wrong, why should we have any confidence in the conclusions of modern practitioners?[141]

This is on full display in the engagements of one of the world's most prominent natural law advocates, Alasdair MacIntyre. Although a disciple of Aristotle, MacIntyre argues fervently that the Teacher had erred grievously in his musings on 'natural slavery.' MacIntyre insists that, on the basis of Aristotle's own ethics of virtue, in which right and wrong are determined by how an act promotes or prevents the attainment of established virtues and goods, slavery cannot be allowed. For slaves cannot secure the full range of human virtues.[142] But the problem is that MacIntyre's rescue of Aristotelian natural law reasoning depends on accepting not only Aristotle's virtue ethics, but MacIntyre's understanding of them. Countless other philosophers like Plato, the Stoics and theistic philosophers like Augustine or the entirety of the Islamic tradition have not considered freedom to be essential to living a fully virtuous, righteous or pious life.

Other modern scholars have tried to resuscitate natural law reasoning by abandoning the higher register and hewing to a minimalist vision closer to species reasoning. Though a critic of this tradition, H. L. A. Hart (d. 1992) proposed a famous 'minimum content' for natural law. This Hart conservatively defined not as a set of basic rights but, rather, as a set of undeniable conditions needed for humans trying to live together. Human nature necessitates food, clothing and shelter. Overall, human communities thus need systems of 'mutual forbearance and compromise' that use coercive means to ensure our basic physical security and property. Hart's 'minimum content' seems as close to universal as one can imagine. But freedom or non-slavery appears nowhere in it.[143]

Other scholars of natural law have been less austere, following in the footsteps of Thomas Aquinas (d. 1274). They acknowledge and accept the natural law tradition's defense of slavery, but they insist on Aquinas' distinction between servile status that does not reach the level of intrinsic wrong and the total domination and degradation that they argue does. The French Catholic philosopher Jacques Maritain (d. 1973) wrote that people have the natural right to full personal liberty, answerable only to 'God and the laws of the city.' But the realities of human society and economy have thus far stymied this ideal, which will only be fully realized with the coming of the Kingdom of God. Though technology and law bring us closer to this utopia, historically it has not been intrinsically wrong to force people into servility provided it was not 'slavery in its absolute form, in which the body and life of the slave as well as his primordial goods, like the freedom to marry, are at the mercy of the master.' This is 'absolutely contrary' to foundational natural rights, writes Maritain.[144] Based on the arguments of Aquinas, the basic natural rights that could not be removed by the unnatural state of slavery were the 'primordial goods,' such as a right to family. Eighteenth- and nineteenth-century Catholic natural law scholars stated that slave owners could not treat slaves cruelly or overburden them, deprive them of adequate food or clothing, separate husband and wife or a mother from her young children.[145]

Some contemporary Catholic scholars have explained that the slavery that has been allowed by the Church was always limited to 'just title servitude,' which excludes the severe depravations of plantation slavery in the Americas but includes lesser forms of servile labor. It includes arrangements or institutions that, though controversial or unacceptable today, were not so even in the recent past: servitude for prisoners of war, criminals and those who offered themselves willingly.[146]

Critics of Slavery and the Call for Abolition

So ubiquitous was the pre-modern philosophical acceptance of slavery that the only Classical schools that did not see slavery as natural in some way or as a normal outcome of social hierarchy were the Sophists and the Skeptics. But this was not because they were morally ahead of their time. They did not think slavery was necessarily wrong, just that it was not *naturally right*. This was because they denied any universal, natural morality and believed that right and wrong were simply determined by local culture.[147] This may have been the position that Aristotle was rebutting when he advanced his natural slavery argument. He notes that some people argued that slavery was not natural but, rather, was based on nothing more than the stronger forcing the weaker into submission.[148]

Although it has been argued that the Stoics opposed slavery, their position was more complicated.[149] Stoics affirmed the spiritual equality of all human beings, i.e., their equality in terms of their rights and duties as ethical beings before divinely infused Nature. And they taught that this equality should inform how humans treat one another. The great Stoic teacher Epictetus (d. 135 CE) was himself a former slave. He wrote passionately that 'You avoid slavery; take care that others are not your slaves,' and that 'vice has no communion with virtue, nor freedom with slavery.'[150] But many Stoics also affirmed the social hierarchy of the better over the worse, the qualified over the unqualified, the naturally governing over the naturally governed. This was as natural and desirable as reason governing the emotions and appetites, the latter by force if necessary. So, like Aristotle's natural slavery, enslaving anyone not unable to govern themselves was not unjust.[151] This corollary was perhaps not an organic expression of Stoic sentiment. But combined with the Stoics' influential assertion that true slavery was a matter not of external constraint but of one's internal bearing, it enabled them to reconcile themselves to the ineluctable reality of slavery in their day. Slavery became simply the most extreme case for applying the Stoic principle that satisfaction and peace came with mastering one's perspective on events outside one's control.

Stoic belief stood out against other ancient worldviews in its universalism. It diverged from Christian/Muslim views in its lack of a confessional or theological anchor for justifying slavery when it did occur. There was no unenslavable in-group and enslavable other. But its deference to social and political institutions meant that Stoicism did not present a moral or theological objection to slavery per se. Slavery might not be naturally right, but it was socially normal.

Simply put, denying the validity of slavery in the ancient Mediterranean would have been like condemning the idea of private property in modern America. For the Hellenized Jewish philosopher of Alexandria, Philo (d. 50 CE), who was deeply influenced by Stoicism, slavery was a necessity due to 'the vast number of circumstances' in life that requires slaves' labor. Aristotle could only imagine dispensing with slaves if looms powered themselves.[152]

If slavery was a fact of life, Stoics like Epictetus and Philo turned to stressing that it had no real meaning for the philosophically self-aware. *Real* slavery was not a matter of one's formal legal status, they stressed over and over. If one truly understood the nature of virtue – that it was a matter of how one reacted to what one could not control – then whether one was legally a slave or not was unimportant. Real slavery was to be controlled by one's desires or fears, and true freedom came in mastering one's internal self. Philo even penned a treatise entitled *Every Good Man is Free*. 'No man is free who is not master of himself,' wrote Epictetus in turn.[153] Christian thinkers like Augustine had to resort to the same argument to handle the fact that some Christians who were enslaved were much less sinful than their non-Christian masters.[154] Centuries later, the concepts of moral freedom and moral slavery as enslavement to passions were important to Kant.[155] And, of course, this theme was prominent in the Sufi tradition, in which poetic axioms like 'The free man is a slave as long as he desires, and the slave is free as long as he is content' were common.[156]

There were rare – extremely rare – voices who criticized slavery *qua* slavery in the pre-Enlightenment world. But before identifying them, it is crucial to recognize that condemnation of slavery per se is often wrongly inferred from other sorts of critique. Condemnation of slavery in and of itself should not be confused with sympathy for slaves when they were mistreated, as we see in Diodorus' (*fl.* first century BCE) explanation that the slave rebellions that racked Sicily in the late second century BCE resulted from the awful abuse of the slaves. Whether the rebellion of Spartacus or the Zanj slaves in Abbasid Iraq, the aim of pre-modern slave uprisings was escaping specific conditions, not fighting against slavery per se. Both Spartacus and the Zanj rebels enslaved some of those they defeated.[157]

Nor should we confuse condemnation of slavery per se with criticisms of slavery's excesses or with objections over who could or could not justly be enslaved. The famous advocate for the rights of Native Americans, the

Dominican friar Bartolomé de las Casas (d. 1566), spent decades decrying their horrific and unjustifiable treatment as the Conquistadors dragooned them into slave labor. But one of his solutions was to replace indigenous labor with African slaves imported from his native Spain. This was because the slavery he was familiar with in Spanish regions like Castile was a much more regulated and humane system of labor than the ruthless exploitation of Native Americans. When de las Casas succeeded in his efforts, however, he saw that the African slaves brought to the Americas were treated awfully too, so at the end of his life he regretted his support for enslaving anyone. But de las Casas' discourse is all about the extreme brutality of how slaves were treated, not the inherent evil of slavery itself.[158] De las Casas engaged in a famous debate with the Spanish philosopher Sepúlveda (d. 1573) over whether the population of the Americas could be justly enslaved, which hinged on Aristotle's concept of natural slavery. De las Casas did not disagree with the natural slavery argument as presented by Sepúlveda. He just did not think it applied to Native Americans, whom he felt were far too capable to qualify as natural slaves.[159] Other early pioneers of human rights often cited as critics of slavery *qua* slavery, such as Hugo Grotius (d. 1645) and Locke, still remained within the Roman law framework that saw enslaving those captured in war as legitimate.[160]

We should also be wary of vague or ambiguous claims about condemnations of slavery per se. There are conflicting reports that the mysterious Jewish sect of the Essenes repudiated slavery because it diminished virtue among slaves and masters, but these reports are contested and inconclusive.[161] Ilaria Ramelli has made a learned argument that this ascetic group, as well as another sect of Jewish ascetics called the Therapeutae, rejected or morally disapproved of slavery per se for reasons of social justice. But their disapproval or disuse of slavery was not because they felt it was immoral to own humans as property or because slavery constituted a morally unacceptable degree of control. Rather, it was because they considered owning property altogether to be impure (in the case of the Essenes), they believed that any accumulation of wealth was unjust because it deprived others of their needs and because their extreme humility made them radical egalitarians.[162] Similarly, the Cappadocian bishop and saint, Gregory of Nazianzus (d. *circa* 389 CE), called on people to give up their slaves. But he called on them to give up *all* their possessions.[163] Implicit in our modern discussion of the moral condemnation of slavery is the assumption that slavery is morally reprehensible even in a society that cherishes the right of property, that cheers the amassing of wealth and that accepts inequality in status. A moral objection to slavery cannot just be a function of an ascetic rejection of property, wealth and status. We in the global West would *all* be immoral in the eyes of the Essenes or Gregory of Nazianzus.

One of the lone voices raised against slavery *qua* slavery was a close family friend and follower of Gregory, the early Christian theologian Gregory of Nyssa (d. 394 CE). This Church Father of Cappadocia wrote a passionate plea against enslaving humans, since every human being was equally an image of God and thus priceless, and only God could own such an item.[164] The Neapolitan humanist poet and prose essayist Gioviano Pontano (d. 1503) was a pioneer when he penned an essay on obedience in which he devoted a short section to slavery (*De Servitute*). He repeats the uncontroversial fact of Roman law that slavery is not the natural state of man, but his language carries a moral barb absent in earlier ages. Slavery may be ancient and universal, but it 'opposes natural freedom (*naturali repugnat libertati*).' He reviews how some barbarous peoples are natural victims of slavery, but he ends his discussion by calling slavery a wrong or offense (*iniuria*) to the human race. He acknowledges its legitimacy in the *ius gentium*, but his wording implies that this is a wrong facilitated by flawed convention rather than a morally innocuous phenomenon approved of by natural law.[165] The French polymath Jean Bodin (d. 1596) was exceptional in stating that slavery (which he conflated with serfdom, since the two institutions had blended) was an affront to religion and reason alike. It was obviously harmful to both slaves and masters, whom it pushed to inhuman cruelty, and was thus not natural at all.[166]

Only in the late 1600s and early 1700s did the solitary voices of Gregory of Nyssa, Pontano and Jean Bodin find any echo. The first stirrings of what emerged as the Abolitionist movement were found among the Quakers in the American colony of Pennsylvania. In 1693 George Keith (d. 1716) published a short tract warning Quakers of the moral and spiritual evils of slavery, stressing that Christ had come to free all mankind and that slavery violated the Golden Rule.[167]

Around the same time, the immorality of slavery found expression among Christian philosophers as well, such as Locke. The notion that humans had an *inalienable* right to liberty and that slavery was intrinsically immoral because it violated this right took shape only in the 1700s. Montesquieu's rejection of the classical natural law arguments for slavery in his *Spirit of the Laws* molded Blackstone's (d. 1780) condemnation of slavery as 'repugnant to reason and the principles of natural law' in his über-influential manual of law, which became the textbook of every British and American jurist from the 1770s onward (of course, both Locke and Montesquieu excused slavery in some contexts).[168] French philosophes like Voltaire (d. 1778) and the authors of Diderot's (d. 1784) *Encyclopedia* mounted harsh invectives against American slavery and the Atlantic slave trade, with one writing, 'If a commerce of this kind can be justified by a moral principle, then there is no crime, however atrocious, that cannot become legitimate.'[169]

So how do we explain this moral awakening? Did a few pious Quakers in Pennsylvania, a handful of philosophers in Britain and France all simply wake up around 1700 and realize that slavery was wrong? The greatest minds and souls of history had all missed this, and these few pioneers finally got it right?

Basically, yes, according to the most prevalent and popular view (which we can term the **Moral Awakening view**). Although nineteenth- and early twentieth-century historians of the Abolitionist movement framed it as the gradual victory of right over wrong, this view is really a narrative of absolute *moral progress*. It is not as if, at the time of Aristotle or Jesus, a minority of philosophers and sages believed slavery was wrong and it just took almost two thousand years to convince others. Until the late 1600s effectively *no one* thought slavery was wrong, let alone one of the ultimate injustices.[170] As Auguste Comte (d. 1857), architect of the Progressive ideology, observed, we feel 'righteous horror' at slavery today because of humanity's 'moral progression.'[171]

Indeed, it was a new narrative of progress that provided the framework for the abolitionist argument. A belief that history was progressing in a positive direction was unknown prior to the Renaissance in Europe. The classical Greco-Roman view was that history was cyclical, and the Abrahamic view was that it was headed downhill after the preeminent moment of contact with the Logos (in Christ or the Quran). It was the influential thinkers of the eighteenth-century Scottish Enlightenment (among whose luminaries are names like David Hume and Adam Smith) who articulated a secular notion of human history as a linear progress of economic development, political refinement and concomitant social progress, from the primal to the increasingly civilized.[172] As we shall see, for the Christian argument for abolition to take hold, it also had to adopt this narrative of moral progress.

By contrast, what is often called the **Economic Explanation** for the emergence of abolitionism sees the end of slavery as the product of economic and technological changes. We can find the roots of this explanation in the Scottish Enlightenment as well. It was not some moral awakening that had led to the disappearance of slavery in Europe, wrote the Scottish historian and economist John Millar (d. 1801), but socio-economic change.[173] The Economic Explanation gained much support from historians and sociologists in the twentieth century. They have pointed out that it is no coincidence that Jean Bodin was one of the first to condemn slavery as immoral; just prior to his time slavery had disappeared in France due to economic reasons.[174] Nor was it mere coincidence that, in the grand sweep of human life and history, it was in the first areas to experience the massive increase in wealth and urbanization of the early Industrial Revolution that the moral condemnation of slavery was first expressed in any meaningful way and where it first gained traction. Britain's rate of economic growth in the eighteenth century was astounding, and, as Howard Temperley has noted, the relative increase in wealth and population in Britain's North American colonies was unmatched in the world. Finally, it is no coincidence that Britain and the northern US states had achieved this growth without any significant reliance on slave labor.[175] In the mid-1700s a new generation of liberal economists like Adam Smith (d. 1790) advanced what would soon become both economic orthodoxy and key to later consumer capitalism: that free workers paid wages would be more productive than unpaid slaves and that their participation in the economy would drive growth.[176]

Since the mid-twentieth century, historians in the West have debated furiously whether abolition was the result of an ideological or material spark. In my opinion, this is a case in which *post hoc ergo propter hoc* (after this, therefore because of this) reasoning is simply too compelling. A major ubiquitous and previously unquestioned component of humanity's economy of labor came under fierce and convincing moral attack during precisely the era in which the introduction of new technologies of agriculture, the use of fossil fuels and the resulting steel-based technologies enabled societies to break from their millennia-old reliance on human and animal labor. These developments cannot be unrelated. It simply strains credulity to argue that it was some moral realization as opposed to the unprecedented material changes that drove them, and that the end of slavery did not come, as Aristotle had predicted, when looms powered themselves.

Historians have gone back and forth over the exact link between the emergence of capitalism as a regional and global economic system and the abolition of slavery. But there is little doubt that the end of slavery must be explained at least in part by the formation of the modern economic system: slavery as a globally protected legal system was phased out because it no longer served the economic interests of the powerful.[177]

Temperley convincingly argues that the Moral Awakening and Economic Explanations are both correct in part. But they must be understood as a feedback loop, in which economic change created social circumstances in which slavery could realistically be condemned and which amplified a perception of progress, which then further drove the abolitionist mission. The inhabitants of nineteenth-century Britain and the northern US experienced an increase in wealth, technology, knowledge and power that created a compelling sense that they were riding a wave of progress in every sense of the word.[178] Capitalism led them to think about the present and future as things they could bend to their moral and material interests, and, as Thomas Haskell wrote, abolitionism 'reflected the needs and values' of an emerging capitalist system.[179] The Scottish Enlightenment vision of history as a process of growth and refinement provided a framework for Quaker abolitionists and French philosophes alike to express an idea of history as spiritual and moral progress.[180] Equally important, the fact that slavery had become economically obsolete in Britain and the northern US meant that they could afford to imagine it as morally evil. The spread of abolitionist conviction and the rapid steps taken to end the slave trade further fueled this narrative of progress. As Davis describes, for nineteenth-century liberals abolition was not just proof of some limited moral maturation. It was proof of 'the transcendent purpose of history.'[181]

Another factor worth noting was the utter brutality of plantation slavery in the Americas and the Atlantic slave trade. This shocked early figures like de las Casas, who were otherwise indifferent to slavery, into opposition. And over a century later it still grabbed the attention of Enlightenment thinkers, whose criticisms of slavery often turned on the unique inhumanity of the Atlantic slave system and the absurdities of its racial justifications.[182]

Whatever the case, the call to label slavery a moral evil and abolish it arose and first succeeded in the places and times when it was, perhaps for the first time in history, actually economically feasible to so. That is not a coincidence. Nor is it a coincidence that, though laws against slavery often certainly reduced the practice, in many places abolition-in-name only became *actual* abolition – in the sense of an end to intense relationships of dependent labor – when socio-economic change had rendered slave labor unimportant.[183] As Temperley describes, for all of human history until the late 1700s, 'slavery was accepted with that fatalism which men commonly reserve for aspects of nature which, whether they are celebrated or deplored, have to be borne. To argue against slavery was to argue against the facts of life.'[184]

The Consequences of Moral Progress

If humanity made a great leap of progress in the 1800s with its moral awakening about slavery, then what moral use is our heritage prior to that realization, when humanity was apparently asleep to this grave and ubiquitous wrong? Why should people pay any heed to philosophers or prophets who had not only not recognized slavery's moral evil or condemned it, but who had often defended and justified it?

As can be expected, there were profound potential theological consequences for the Moral Awakening narrative. We can see it in a debate between the abolitionist (and Founding Father) Benjamin Rush (d. 1813) and an American plantation owner. If slavery was a gross and intrinsic moral wrong, asked the owner, why had Jesus not condemned it? The abolitionist response to this was that Jesus had not banned slavery because, if he had, he would have antagonized too many people or caused civil strife. The plantation owner countered by accusing Rush either of being wrong or of being blasphemous, since if Jesus had known slavery was morally evil but had not spoken out against it then that would mean that the son of God had lacked the courage of his convictions.[185] As slave owners wrote in their petition to the Virginia legislature in 1785 opposing a law supporting manumission, 'Christ, while on earth and giving instructions for things necessary for salvation, did not forbid [slavery] . . .'[186] Responding to abolitionist Christians' claim that Jesus had not condemned slavery because of the potential backlash, the Princeton theologian Charles Hodge (d. 1878) noted that the same danger still hung over the horizon in his own day.[187] It caused the Civil War.

Considering the problems that the text of the Old and New Testaments posed to the Moral Awakening narrative, it makes sense that the Christian drive for abolition first appeared among Quakers. More than any other

Christian denomination, Quakers believed that the true message of Christ was not contained in the pages of the New Testament (which many early Quakers believed was not entirely textually authentic anyway)[188] but in the Inward Light of guidance that God cast into the hearts of the faithful. More importantly, Quakers believed in 'progressive revelation,' namely that God could speak to latter-day people with the same authority as in biblical times and communicate new knowledge about His will to them.[189]

Put simply, Quakers were not limited to the Bible to know the mission of Christ. The Bible was imperfect, and true guidance lay outside its pages. It was not until well into the nineteenth century – a full century and a half after the first Quaker anti-slavery tracts – that the idea that the Bible was not the inerrant and eternal word of God became widely accepted among mainline Protestants in Britain and the US.[190] It seems possible that this increased belief in a historicized scripture was a prerequisite for many Christians to accept the moral evil of slavery.

Pioneered by the Quakers, the overall Christian argument for abolition was that, regardless of what Jesus or Paul said or did not say about slavery, Christ had been sent to liberate all mankind. He was like the epicenter of a wave of divine emancipation, which future generations of Christians would amplify and carry forward, combatting injustice and oppression, until God finally revealed His full glory with the coming of His kingdom. Jesus had washed the feet of his companions, like a slave, and in coming to mankind he took 'the form of a slave' (Philippians 2:5–8) to free all of mankind by urging all to serve.[191] This vision of moral and spiritual progress reconciled Christianity's biblical tradition with the abolitionist mission. The slavery practiced by the Israelites in the Old Testament was abrogated by the new covenant of Christ, and Jesus had not been an absolute moral law but, rather, a moving and ever-advancing moral standard.

This might be compelling, but it raised serious challenges for Christian theologians who realized that both scripture and the Church rested much of their authority on the unchanging constancy of their moral teachings. How could such a radical change in morality be justified? Some theologians justified this as the Church coming to understand an idea that was always latent within scripture. For more liberal Catholic theologians, slavery remains the prime example of how it can take centuries for the Church to finally realize the true teachings of the New Testament. Others have argued that the Church's moral doctrine is like an organic being, growing and maturing, with its later and more developed understandings expressing the same nucleus of truths that had always been there but in a more sophisticated way.[192] In recent decades, Protestant theologians have seen slavery as exemplary of the need for what is termed trajectory hermeneutics, a reading of scripture in which the sacred text plants the seeds of themes whose trajectories the later community is charged with following.[193]

But this Christian liberation take on the Moral Awakening narrative still does not resolve the Slavery Conundrum. It only distracts our attention from it. The core issue has never been explaining moral progress. It is explaining how God ever endorsed something absolutely morally wrong to begin with. As Christian opponents of abolitionism pointed out, **if slavery was a deep and intrinsic moral wrong, then God would never have allowed it *even in the Old Testament*.**[194] To use a different example, would God have allowed cannibalism or human sacrifice in the Old Testament? In response to this objection, radical abolitionists like William Lloyd Garrison (d. 1879) said that if one had to choose between condemning slavery as an intrinsic and absolute evil or believing in the Bible's inerrancy, that was too bad for the Bible.[195] More moderate abolitionist churchmen like Horace Bushnell (d. 1876) had to violate the slavery-is-slavery axiom by conceding that the slavery allowed for the Jews in the Old Testament was not 'of such a nature' that it would be impossible for God to allow it at some points in history. This was in contrast to slavery in the Americas, which moderate abolitionists argued was a 'monstrous aberration.'[196]

As a result, if abolitionists committed to the moral and textual integrity of the Bible wanted to insist on the gross, intrinsic evil of the Atlantic slave trade, they had to admit that Old Testament slavery was not as serious or that it was not slavery at all. They had to concede that either not everything that had generally been referred to as slavery in history was actually slavery, or that not everything that fell under their broad, historic category of slavery was intrinsically evil, since God would never have commanded or allowed such a thing for anyone, anywhere, even in the Old Testament. The Christian liberation take on the Moral Awakening explanation thus violates either axiom one or two of our Slavery Conundrum. This could not be resolved as long as Christians believed that the Old and New Testaments were reliable records of God's communications with humanity.

Some late nineteenth-century Christian theologians took this step. They dealt with the theological consequences of the moral change around slavery by drifting away from scripture's truth claims – adopting what was, in effect, a less caustic phrasing of Garrison's challenge. After the Civil War and the abolition of slavery in the US, American Christian theologians had to make sense of how their scripture had been used in defense of an institution that was no longer socially acceptable to defend. This took place as the Bible's truth claims were facing two even more penetrating threats. Darwin's writings provided critics of religion and the Church with an enormous bludgeon, and advances in the historical critical method meant that even theologians and clerics were increasingly amenable to seriously questioning the Bible's textual integrity. Against this backdrop, American Protestant theologians developed a 'New Theology' in which God's truth was progressively manifested not through historical scripture but through mankind's ongoing march toward truth in history.[197]

This New Theology hinted at a way out of the Slavery Conundrum: sacrificing the axiom of the authority of the past. The texts of the Bible were not timeless records of God's revealed will. They were locked in history and expressions of it, and their truth was limited to what their original audiences could bear. Latter-day Christians did not have to account for the details and laws these texts included because they were not really records of God's will in the first place. If God reveals His truth not in literal revelation but in our ongoing march forward, then our past has no more authority over us than does the path behind us. This violates, or at least seriously weakens, the third axiom of our Slavery Conundrum. Our past may be no more than a nostalgic companion. As Comte described, humanity is evolving toward perfection. It now venerates itself, and we pay homage to our past only to remind ourselves of the path that took us to these new heights.[198]

Muslim Efforts to Salvage the Past

In the next chapter we will look at the rich literature on Islamic arguments for the abolition of slavery. Ironically, prohibiting *riqq* in the Shariah would be – and has been – very straightforward. It is both possible and quite simple. The problem is that, in the many discussions I have had about slavery with Muslims and non-Muslims alike, prohibiting slavery is not good enough. It does not suffice to say that slavery is not allowed by the Shariah today. One must *morally* condemn slavery as a gross and intrinsic moral evil across space and time. Again, the real issue is the *moral* problem of slavery. In other words, our Slavery Conundrum.

Muslims find themselves faced with the same problem that confronted Christian abolitionists of the eighteenth and nineteenth centuries. We Muslims feel deeply that slavery is a profound moral evil and must always have been, and that this applies to everything called 'slavery,' namely whenever a person was not free or was someone else's property. But if we say this then we are saying that not only did Islamic law allow a profound moral evil, but that it was allowed in the very revelation of God in the Quran. What is more, we are saying that the Prophet of God himself committed this profound moral evil. All evidence makes it clear that he accepted at least two slave-concubines. We could deny these reports, but the permissibility of slavery and concubinage is undeniable in the Quran itself, a historically intact scripture and Islam's ultimate bedrock.

In a public debate on this issue, one Muslim repeatedly demanded that I condemn slavery not just today, but across history and in all time periods. I asked him first to answer a version of the Slavery Conundrum. Which of the following was the case: was the historical record wrong about the Prophet owning slaves? Or is the moral wrongness of slavery something relatively new in human history? Or did the Prophet Muhammad commit a grave moral wrong? The man refused to answer in public, saying he would only discuss this in private.

He was quite wise (if stunningly hypocritical) to avoid answering, for there was no way out of this conundrum that allowed adhering to Islam as it has generally been understood for fourteen centuries while also remaining a modern citizen in good moral standing. If one does not deny at least one of our first two axioms (i.e., slavery was always evil; all slavery is slavery), then one must do one of three things. The first is utterly unconvincing. The second and third entail denial of fundamental pillars of the Islamic creed.

1) The first option would be to totally overhaul the manner in which the Quran and the Prophet's life are read and understood. Of course, this would involve denying reports that the Prophet had slaves, allowed others to have them and the unbroken scholarly tradition that has confirmed the overall reliability of this corpus of material. But the Quran still makes ample and explicit reference to slavery and slave-concubinage.

   This Quranic problem could be solved by engaging in a dramatic re-reading of the sacred text in virtual isolation from the Hadith corpus and the accepted body of Islamic legal interpretation, both of which contain prodigious material on the permissibility of *riqq*. This was the approach taken by the influential if controversial Indian

Islamic modernist Sir Syed Ahmed Khan (d. 1898). In Khan's Urdu-language writings on slavery from the early 1870s, he preached that the Quran categorically prohibited slavery, which he argued contravened God's will and human nature. To construct his case, Khan had to draw his evidence almost exclusively from the Quran, while cherry-picking select historical reports of the Prophet's life and essentially ignoring the Islamic tradition built on it.

The main pillar of Khan's argument is that the Quran only permitted the slavery *ongoing* at the time of its revelation; it never condoned enslavement or new slavery in the future. Khan considered all the Quranic verses allowing the enslavement of prisoners of war or mentioning slaves to be abrogated by Quran 47:4, which gives Muslims the option of freeing or ransoming prisoners but not of keeping them as slaves. Khan condemns slave-concubinage even more firmly, noting that all the verses mentioning 'those whom you possessed rightfully' appear in the past tense. They thus offer no mandate for 'future slavery.' In the case of Mariya, interestingly, Khan breaks with his strategy of ignoring historical reports about the Prophet's life or dismissing them as apocryphal. He admits that, according to Arab custom, Mariya was 'under the control (*taṣarruf*)' of the Prophet, but this in no way sanctioned continued slavery.[199]

Khan's argument seems very tendentious, however. Beyond its dismissal of Islam's oceanic historical, legal and exegetical heritage, it rests on the unproven assumption that all the Quran's pronouncements about slaves and slavery, such as its rules on *mukataba*, freeing slaves as expiation for sins, etc., are superseded by one verse (47:4). And even if, as Khan argued, the Quran saw slavery as something that should only exist in the past tense, it does not furnish the *moral condemnation* that modern audiences seem to demand. The holy book neither articulated slavery's moral wrongness nor required Muslims to immediately wash their hands of this repugnant practice. Like the New Testament, the Quran saw slavery as a worldly reality so uncontroversial that it could be used as the basis of an unrelated parable (Quran 16:71, 75). It seems impossible to read the Quran in a way that does not at least condone the continuation of existing slave and concubinage relationships. Trying to force more out of a reading is no more convincing than mid-nineteenth-century Christian theologians claiming that the Old Testament never endorsed slavery, that what had been read as 'slave' in the Bible was really 'servant,' and that someone being 'bought' in the Bible really meant them being paid in advance for their services.[200]

2) A second option for addressing this scriptural problem would be to follow the secular path of biblical scholarship and deny that Islam's scripture represents a direct and untouched revelation from God, professing instead that it is a text produced by humans in history. Many scholars of the Bible have concluded that the Old Testament verses describing and calling for the Israelites to massacre the men, women, children and even the suckling infants of their enemies were shaped by the political ideology of the later kingdom of Israel and were not reflective of God's true teachings.[201] In the context of one such order to kill innocents, Martin Buber (d. 1965) simply concluded that the prophet Samuel had 'misunderstood God.'[202] As Susan Niditch writes, many modern religious scholars 'are simply incapable of seeing their God as one who demands and receives humans in exchange for victory.'[203] But denying that the Quran is the literal word of God or concluding that 'Muhammad misunderstood God' takes one out of the fold of Islam, at least as Islam has always been understood.

3) The third option would be to affirm the standard understandings of the Prophet's life and the Quran's overall content on slavery but simply to concede that these two sources were wrong on the moral problem of slavery. According to the consensus of Muslim scholars across fourteen centuries, however, stating that the Prophet had committed a grave sin (*kabīra*) or unambiguously belittling his moral judgment would be unbelief (*kufr*) that removed someone from Islam.[204] An early twentieth-century Egyptian mufti known for liberal leanings, who was trying to be as understanding as possible to Westernized Egyptian intellectuals who rejected many Hadiths, nonetheless could not avoid concluding that someone who knowingly considers himself above (*mustakhiff*) the notion of the Sunna is an unbeliever.[205] The influential late Hanafi scholar Ibn ʿAbidin (d. 1836) even

> affirmed an earlier ruling that, if you say that the actual act of having a concubine is morally repugnant (*qabīḥ*), there is real danger that you have committed *kufr*.[206] According to Islamic theology, not only is the Prophet protected from committing major sins, he is protected from any actions that are prohibited (*ḥarām*) by God. According to the majority of the Sunni schools, he is even shielded from lapsing into acts that fall into the less severe legal category of disliked (*makrūh*).[207]

Some Muslims have argued that the Prophet was not morally perfect and that, in fact, our belief that he was is a form of *shirk*, the grave sin of associating partners with God. According to the entirety of the Islamic tradition, however, the Prophet's moral infallibility and unmatched moral excellence in no way clash with his mortality and humanness. As the famous Shafi scholar of Cairo, Zarkashi (d. 1394), wrote, the most beautiful verse of the famous *Burda* poem composed in praise of the Prophet was:

> The most that can be said of him is that he was a man,
> And that he is the best of all God's creation.[208]

There has been much debate among Muslim scholars over whether prophets can commit minor sins (*ṣaghā'ir*), oversights, or factual errors. But none of these apply to the question of slavery, since the belief today is that slavery is not simply an error of judgment but history's lengthiest and most brutal crime.

Indeed, attributing the gross, intrinsic moral wrong of slavery to the Prophet comes along with an equally consequential corollary: presumably he would not have *knowingly* committed such a wrong. So he was not even aware of the nature of the wrong he was committing. This would be a dramatic assertion indeed. It would, in effect, overturn Islamic theology and moral epistemology entirely. The foundation of Islamic doctrine and law rests on the premise that the Prophet's authoritative precedent (Sunna), to some degree or another provided the context, application and explanation of God's message in the Quran. The Quran is read through the Sunna of the Prophet. To say that we post-abolition humans passed through a moral awakening that made us more morally aware than those who preceded the nineteenth century would be to render the guidance of the Quran and the Prophet morally obsolete.

Recently, one Muslim scholar of slavery in Islamic civilization offered the argument that we are not more morally mature or advanced than the Prophet. It is simply a matter of our moral horizons having moved beyond those of people in previous epochs. We live in a time when what we can morally envision is different from what could be morally envisioned during the Prophet's time. There are two problems with this argument. First, the isolated voice of Gregory of Nyssa in fourth-century Anatolia shows that it was possible for a man of God to condemn slavery from both a theological and philosophical standpoint in the Late Antique Near East. That moral horizon was certainly visible to him. According to this scholar's proposal, the Prophet Muhammad not only had more restricted moral horizons than we do, he had more restricted moral horizons than Gregory of Nyssa! Second, I think this appeal to metaphor is a euphemism. As with the flaw in the Christian explanations for changes in the Church's moral doctrine, the problem here is not reconciling our moral progress with our religious heritage. The problem is not justifying that slavery is wrong *now*. The problem is that our Slavery Conundrum leaves us with the undeniable fact that God and His prophets allowed and practiced something that we say **was as profoundly wrong in those prophetic days as it is now.**

This becomes immediately clear if we imagine the following thought experiment: suppose that a Muslim today was able to travel back to Medina during the time of the Prophet and arrived there the day after he had been given Mariya, the Coptic slave girl, as his concubine. What would this Muslim say to the Prophet? 'What you're doing is a profound moral evil, O Messenger of God'? That is not a conceivable statement for a Muslim to make and remain Muslim. But that's what a Muslim feels today, is it not? So what does that mean? This is the question we will turn to in our last chapter.

5

Abolishing Slavery in Islam

> ... There, under whip and chain and sun, he lived out his youth and his young manhood dreaming the death of slavery two thousand years before it finally would die.
>
> *Spartacus* (1960)

> Kubrick was not given control of the script, which he felt was full of easy moralizing.
>
> *Rolling Stone* interview with Stanley Kubrick, director of *Spartacus* (1987)[1]

Debonair and wielding a pen that cut with the sharp, anti-colonial insights of Fanon's *Wretched of the Earth* and soothed with the Persian ink of the Shiite tradition, Ali Shariati (d. 1977) was one of the most compelling Muslim writers of the twentieth century. The colonized, the Third World, Muslims, Iranians, they were all the Quran's 'weak and oppressed of the earth' (8:26). Islam had come to free them. The Prophet had smashed the false idols, all the false idols, that bind minds and bodies. He had come down from the cave of Hira, Shariati wrote, to 'declare war against the capitalists and the slave dealers of Mecca.'[2] A decade before the Shah had Shariati assassinated, the Egyptian author Sayyid Qutb (d. 1966) had been executed for his influential manifesto *Milestones*. Nationalism, communism, capitalism, these were all graven images, Qutb had taught. Islam had come to free men from being slaves to one another (*'ibādat al-'ibād*) by calling them to be slaves to God alone.[3]

Shariati and Qutb were Islamists – they believed that Islam held the key to political mobilization against imperial powers – and during their lives and since their deaths they have attracted fierce criticism from Muslims and non-Muslims alike. Many have accused them of disguising foreign political ideologies in Islamic garb and insinuating them into Muslim minds. But their portrayal of Islam as at heart a liberating message can hardly be dismissed as a modern re-reading or imposition. The Quran refers over and over to human beings as 'the slaves of God (*'ibād Allāh*),' continuing the tradition of Semitic cultures and the Bible by fusing the idioms of slavery and worship.[4] The image that the Prophet uses to describe someone who abandons the worship of God alone in favor of some lesser power (*shirk*) is that of a runaway slave, a slave who has turned away from their true Lord.[5] One of Qutb's favorite stories is of the encounter between a Muslim emissary and the leader of the Persian army on the eve of the Muslim conquest of Persia. Why had they come?, the Persian general asks. The emissary answers, 'God has sent us to bring whomever wishes from the servitude (*'ibāda*) of men to the servitude of God alone.'[6] Another vignette from the early days of Islam tells how the caliph 'Umar (d. 644) rebuked the Muslim governor of Egypt for letting his son unjustly lash a subject; 'Since when have you made slaves of people when their mothers gave birth to them free?'[7]

But if Islam is a call for the slaves of God to remember to whom their worship and service are truly due, its scripture treats the enslavement of man by man as an unremarkable reality. Not only does the Quran seem very clearly to permit slavery, the power and status imbalance between masters and slaves is assumed to be so mundane that the holy book uses it as the basis for parables to make unrelated points (see Quran 16:71, 75). 'Umar's above rebuke is widely quoted by Muslims stressing Islam's antagonism toward slavery. But the caliph uttered it not in the context of actual enslavement but when the son of a leading Muslim arrogantly whipped a man who had beaten him in a race. 'Umar had no compunction about enslaving prisoners captured in conquest, nor did the later tradition of Islamic law.

So there was a palpable tension at the very foundation of the faith between Islam as the absolute servitude of man to God alone and the servitude of other men to Muslims. Contrary to what we would expect today, this tension over slavery was theological more than moral. If the power of God over man is so overwhelming, why aren't the asymmetries of power between human beings dwarfed into insignificance? The Prophet upbraided a Muslim for striking his slave by warning that 'God has far more power over you than you have over him.'[8] Medieval Muslim scholars winced at a report of the Companion Salman Farisi, who had come to Medina as a slave before

Muhammad's prophethood, telling how he 'had been handed off from lord to lord almost ten times (*min rabb ilā rabb*)' before he was finally freed.[9] The Prophet had later made it clear that slaves should not call their masters 'my lord,' nor should their masters call them 'my slave (*ʿabdī*).' 'For indeed,' the Prophet explained, 'you all are slaves, and the lord is God most high.'[10] The earliest known Arabic dictionary, from the mid-eighth century, makes a point of beginning the entry on slave (*ʿabd*) by affirming that, 'Free or slave (*raqīq*), all are the slaves of God.'[11] This tension reared its head from time to time throughout Islamic civilization. When the Ottoman sultan Mehmet IV (d. 1693) began referring to the Janissaries too comfortably as 'my slaves,' they reminded him that they were the slaves of God alone.[12]

Before delving deeper, we should take care about the terms we use. *Emancipation* and *abolition* are not the same thing, and we must be conscious of which term we use and when. Emancipation means freeing a slave or slaves. It is roughly synonymous with *manumission*, though manumission is often used to mean the slave's owner freeing them, while emancipation could also be done by a state. *Abolition* is understood as the ending of slavery as a legal status and institution altogether.

IS ABOLITION INDIGENOUS TO ISLAM OR NOT?

In the animated movie *Bilal* (2015), the birth of Islam is portrayed as a struggle for liberation and equality against the structures of slavery and racism.[13] Why then, when British diplomats in mid-nineteenth-century Egypt, Morocco and Iran pushed for the abolition of slavery in those realms, did the royal courts and ulama repeatedly respond that they could not forbid what God and His Prophet had allowed?[14] Why, when reports came to the Hejaz in 1855 that the Ottoman sultan would ban the slave trade, did a leading cleric there issue a fatwa declaring this a violation of the Shariah and condemning the Ottomans as heretics?[15]

In light of such responses, it is no surprise that William Muir (d. 1905), an East India Company officer and leading British scholar of Islam, swore that as long as Muslims believed in the Quran, slavery would 'flow from the faith, in all ages and in every country.'[16] Snouck Hurgronje (d. 1936), an influential Dutch Orientalist and colonial official, observed that Islam 'allows, nay orders' Muslims to enslave their enemies.[17] The inseparability of slavery and Islam as a religion has been reiterated by many more recent

Western scholars, including leading scholars of Islam in Africa.[18] Even some Muslims have admitted that abolition is foreign to Islam. Amina Wadud, an African American feminist Muslim scholar, is openly skeptical that the Islamic tradition would ever have contributed significantly to the moral or theological impetus behind what was ultimately the European-led project of abolition. Abdullahi An-Na'im, a Sudanese Muslim reformist teaching at Emory University, observes that the Shariah lacks any 'internal mechanism' by which slavery could be ended for good.[19] Others are less certain. As one of the leading scholars on slavery in Islamic civilization, William Clarence-Smith, has noted, Muslim discourse on the moral problem of slavery was indeed prompted by the challenge of European abolitionism. But it drew substantially on the pre-modern Islamic legal tradition and those theological tensions surrounding slavery that were evident from the very origins of Islam.[20]

So, is slavery in the DNA of Islam? Or is the faith a force of liberation, whose emancipatory gene was just suppressed by the material forces of history and the failings of Muslims? Did Muslims, or could Islamic thought, ever innovate an indigenous call to abolish slavery? These have been incredibly loaded questions since the mid-nineteenth century, when slavery in Islam and the Islamic world became a major humanitarian cause for European abolitionists and a polemical weapon for European colonialism and Christian missionaries alike.[21]

The great moral challenge of slavery in Islam unfolded in the shadow of Europe's political domination of Muslim lands. As a result, discussion around slavery and abolition among Muslims could never take place insulated from the overwhelming forces of European colonialism and Western cultural imperialism, which climaxed alongside and in many ways through the debate over Islam and slavery (that colonial powers found abolition too destabilizing to enforce in many areas is left out of this discussion).[22] For many Muslims, the Western cry about the evils of slavery has thus always been a proxy for condemning Islam itself. How does a Muslim defend the goodness of their religion in such a context, especially when what started as European moral condemnations of slavery quickly became a global sentiment felt by all in our modern world and questioned only by pariahs?

The major responses of Muslims to the challenge of slavery and abolition can be traced back to three epicenters. In Ottoman North Africa in the 1840s, Muslim scholars and statesmen turned a centuries-old Islamic legal discourse on the illegality of enslaving Black Muslims into a justification for ending slavery altogether. In the 1870s in British India another, more radical approach emerged that denied that slavery had ever had any moral or legal basis in Islam. At the same time, Muslim intellectuals who had come from India and the Ottoman world to study in Western Europe responded to abolitionist criticism of Islam by arguing that their scripture and legal tradition had intended to stamp out slavery as soon as it was possible. They were followed by a cadre of Muslim scholars and political activists in the Ottoman Mediterranean. The Tunisian reformist scholar Muhammad Bayram Khamis (d. 1889) settled in Cairo and rearticulated the North African arguments for abolition in a more sophisticated form. There the activist intellectual circle of Muhammad ʿAbduh (d. 1905) and Rashid Rida (d. 1935) wove the various strands of Islamic anti-slavery arguments together, bolstered them with more technical arguments from the Shariah heritage and packaged them for an Arabic-speaking public. Finally, more conservative Muslim scholars from the Middle East to South Asia justified abandoning slavery not out of any moral conviction but because it served Muslim communal and political interests.

ISLAM AS EMANCIPATORY FORCE – AN ALTERNATIVE HISTORY

We already saw that a few Islamic modernists, like Sir Syed Ahmed Khan (d. 1898), were willing to make radical breaks from the accepted reading of the Quran, the narrative of the Prophet's life and the consensus of the Muslim legal tradition by arguing that the Quran had actually prohibited slavery. But this claim did not convince many prominent Muslim intellectuals, as it required ignoring the established readings of the text as well as the manifest evidence of Islamic history from the life of the Prophet onward.

From the late 1800s to the present day, one of the most influential basic arguments advanced by Muslims wrestling with the moral problem of slavery has been the claim that Islam had always aimed at abolishing slavery but that the Quran and the Prophet could not order this directly.[23] According to this argument, slavery was so entrenched in the socio-economic life of Arabia and beyond that immediate abolition would have proven disastrous for both the Prophet's mission and social stability. The same argument had been made by British and American abolitionists as far back as the late 1700s when they were asked why Jesus had not condemned slavery.[24]

Christian discourse very likely exerted an influence here, since the Muslim intellectuals who developed this argument were well acquainted with the history and internal dynamics of Christian abolitionism. In fact, they were usually addressing their arguments at Western critics of Muslim slavery. Rashid Rida even used the American Civil War as a warning for what could happen when slavery was abolished before the society and economy were prepared for it.[25]

Perhaps the first Muslim to advance this delayed abolition argument was a contemporary of Khan, Syed Ameer Ali (d. 1928), who was in London studying law at the same time that Khan visited the city in the early 1870s. Ali, a Shiite Muslim who mixed in abolitionist circles in London and would later go on to serve as a judge on the Bengal High Court, engaged with Khan's writings on slavery but felt his claims were too far-fetched. Ali concluded that God had not prohibited slavery in the Quran, but the rules that Islam put in place and its encouragement of manumission were meant to result in its rapid extinction. Any allowance of slavery in Islam was meant to be temporary, Ali argued, though Muslims had failed to appreciate this. The time had finally come, Ali urged, for Muslims to reclaim their faith's message of liberation and human equality by fighting to end slavery everywhere.[26]

A second early articulator of this approach to the challenge of slavery was also a student studying in Europe, the Egyptian Ahmad Shafiq (d. 1940). This young member of the Ottoman elite and soon-to-be statesman had been in Paris when he heard an invective against Muslim slavery preached by a leading French churchman and abolitionist. In a rebuttal he published in French in 1891, Shafiq wrote that the Prophet was 'an incomparable diplomat.' Instead of directly taking on the powerful interests of his slaveholding surroundings, Muhammad followed the indirect route to the same objective. His teachings ameliorated slaves' conditions, restricted the means of enslavement and strongly encouraged manumission.[27]

Shafiq became friends with Rashid Rida in Cairo, where Rida was mentoring another young Egyptian educated in Cairo's new, European-style medical college.[28] Muhammad Tawfiq Sidqi (d. 1920) makes an argument similar to Ali's and Shafiq's in a 1905 article written for Rida's influential reformist journal, *Al-Manar* (The Lighthouse). Sidqi reiterates Ali's and Shafiq's points about how Islam had substantially restricted the pathways into slavery and required humane treatment of slaves. Although he does not explicitly claim that Islam would have ended slavery if it were possible, he

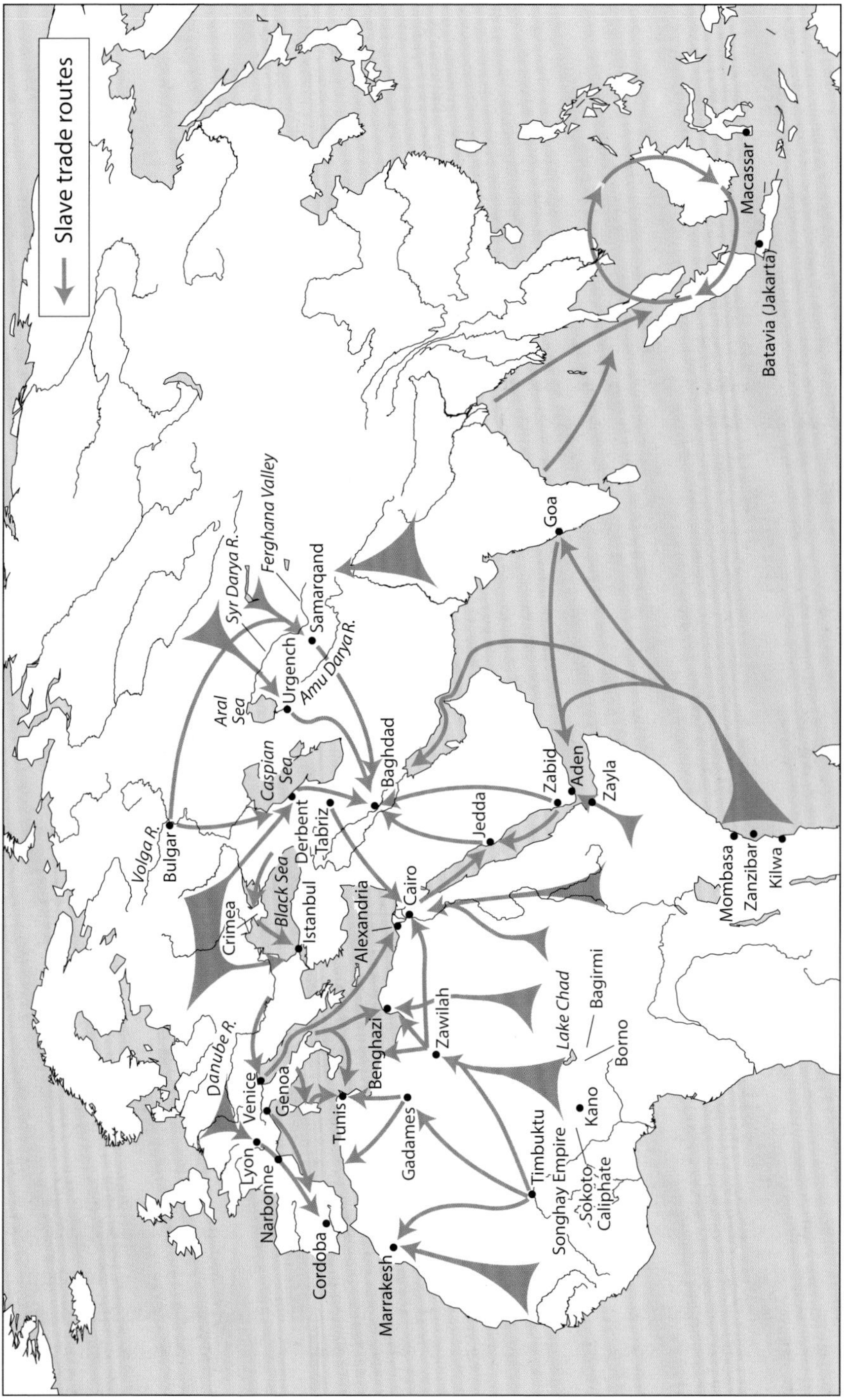

FIGURE 1.

Slave trade into Islamic civilization from the eighth to the early twentieth centuries.

FIGURE 2.

Early seventeenth-century portrait of an African courtier, probably Malik ʿAmbar, from the Deccan (photograph © 2019 Museum of Fine Arts, Boston).

FIGURE 3.
The grand vizier Sokullu Mehmet Pasha (seated) holding court after the conquest of Szigetvár in Hungary in 1566. From Faridun Ahmad Beg's *Nuzhat al-akhbar dar safar-i Sigitwar* (*circa* 1568, image courtesy of the Topkapi Palace Museum).

FIGURE 4.
The Slave Market by Eduard Ansen-Hofmann (German, d. 1904). The slave trade in the Muslim Mediterranean was a favorite theme in the Orientalist genre of painting, which flourished in the nineteenth century. The 'White slave trade,' especially the possession of European women by swarthy Muslim men, featured prominently and had an obvious voyeuristic element (image courtesy of the Knohl Collection).

takes another fascinating abolitionist tack. He recognizes that abolition was a 'great accomplishment' for which Europeans deserved credit. But, if anything, it was Islam that should have brought slavery to an end. Europeans had only come to abolition after centuries of plying the grotesque Atlantic slave trade. And, despite the claims of missionaries, Christianity had served far longer as a defender of slavery than an inspiration for ending it. Ultimately, Sidqi contends, it was not moral advancement or spiritual enlightenment that drove Europeans to abolition. It was merely the technological, economic and scientific advancement of their civilization. Considering the Quran's and the Prophet's repeated injunctions to treat slaves well and to free them, Sidqi concludes, had Muslims kept apace of European development they would no doubt have beaten them to the abolition punch.[29] In 1911 another Egyptian author went so far as to claim that Islam had actually inspired abolitionism in Europe.[30] Rida added that, had Muslims followed the trajectory laid out in the Quran, the precedent of the Prophet and the first four Rightly Guided (*rāshidūn*) caliphs, slavery would have become extinct in Islam within the faith's first century.[31]

Whatever God intended, however, the simple fact is that Islam did not bring slavery to an end. If anything, Islamic civilization fashioned the institution of *riqq* into a social and political model for managing relationships of power and loyalty that was unique in scale and pervasiveness. Regardless of this, some modern Muslim scholars have maintained that Islamic civilization does have an indigenous anti-slavery tradition. They point to the same emancipatory strain that Shariati and Qutb discerned in the Quran, the Prophet's sayings and the Islamic legal tradition and which surfaced again and again in Islamic history. Though they do not deny the history of slavery that was, they highlight this emancipatory strain and with it trace the arc of an alternative history of liberation.

One of the most extensive expressions of this alternative history comes in the writings of the Senegalese Muslim cleric Musa Kamara (d. 1945), who bridged the tradition of Islamic learning in the Senegal River valley and the Francophone culture of colonial West Africa.[32] At the center of Kamara's legacy were histories he penned of the ulama movements in West Africa and the place of Black Africans and slavery in Islam. Like many earlier Muslim scholars, Kamara refutes the Curse of Ham at length, drawing both on medieval Muslim historians who had detailed its unreliability as well as on modern discoveries about humanity's origins. He gives examples of how many prominent early Muslim saints and scholars had been Black, and how many others had been freed slaves. Kamara adds that the Prophet had freed all his slaves before his death and was so insistent in urging others to free their slaves that 'some would say he was forcing them.' He recounts the numerous Hadiths praising manumission and the many situations in which the Shariah requires Muslims to free their slaves. So praiseworthy was freeing a slave, in fact, that it was called for even in the face of deception. Kamara recounts the story of Ibn ʿUmar (Kamara mistakes him for his father) freeing any slave of his whom he saw engaging in pious or meritorious actions, even if they were only doing so to be freed ('By God, let us be deceived in favor of him who deceives us with God'). Kamara ends by praising the French colonial power for abolishing slavery, noting that the French treasured liberty and did not think any person could own another. But he also locates this in his own, Islamic tradition: 'Perhaps this was [Muhammad's] desire, may God bless him and grant him peace.'[33]

The most eloquent contemporary advocate of what he calls 'an emancipatory thread' in Islamic history is the University of California professor Rudolph (Bilāl) Ware, whose book *The Walking Qur'an* documents the history of a state founded by Muslim clerics in the Senegambia region (roughly modern Senegal, Gambia, Mali, Mauritania and Guinea) in the latter half of the 1700s and how it intersected with the forces of Islamic spirituality and the Atlantic slave trade. The leaders of the Imamate of Fuuta Tooro, Sulayman Baal (d. 1776) and his successor ʿAbd al-Qadir Kan (d. 1807), began a rebellion against the existing states in the region after they witnessed the capture of Muslims for eventual sale to European slave traders. This was unacceptable to them because, according to the Shariah, Muslims cannot be legally enslaved by anyone.

To this Ware adds the strong West African tradition of Muslims memorizing the Quran as children, such that the holy book is fused with their being and they become, literally, walking Qurans. Seeing 'the Book in chains' led Baal and his followers to try and eliminate the enslavement of any Muslims in the region. Anyone who could repeat a phrase from the Quran or even muster a garbled version of the Muslim testimony of faith was manumitted. Several treaties between the Fuuta Toora imamate and European slave-trading powers pledged that Muslims would not be purchased for export. An early nineteenth-century scholar in the region went so far as to issue a fatwa prohibiting selling any slave to a Muslim trader the seller thought might sell them on to Europeans. Ultimately, however,

European powers simply aided rival local potentates with the money and weapons needed to overthrow the imamate.[34]

Ware holds out Baal's and Kan's movement as distinguished proof of Islam's emancipatory credentials. When, in 1787, the Society for the Abolition of the Slave Trade was formed in London, Ware notes, Baal and Kan had already abolished slavery in their realm. In 1789 a leading British abolitionist held up Kan as a role model for European rulers. Nor were Baal and Kan aberrations. They emerged out of an existing Islamic scholarly tradition in Senegambia that had already begun restricting Muslim participation in the Atlantic slave trade during the previous century. Muslims did not learn abolition from Europeans, Ware argues. It was 'these African Muslims who showed them how it was done.'[35] Ware stresses that, far from being reluctant late-comers to abolition, 'Africans abolished the European slave trade dozens if not hundreds of times.' It was the persistence of the European demand for slaves that revived it whenever Muslims tried to stamp it out (we should note, however, the demand for slaves from the Ottoman Mediterranean as well).[36]

This idea that West African Muslims were fulfilling Islam's liberatory mission also imbued the small but fascinating Sufi revivalist movement in West Africa begun by Shaykh Yacouba Sylla (d. 1988), a Muslim scholar and Sufi master who hailed from the border region between Senegal and Mauritania. Yacouba preached against the highly stratified order of his society, in which slaves, ex-slaves and their descendants occupied the lower rungs, as well as against luxury and the economic hurdles to a pious life, such as the high cost of marriage. His followers came mainly from Mauritania's Soninke minority, and many were either ex-slaves or of slave ancestry. Yacouba taught them that slavery was an experience of redemptive suffering. When his followers greeted each other, they would use the Soninke word *komaxu,* meaning slave, which both affirmed a common sense of belonging to their movement and also reminded them that all humans are no more than slaves of God. Ultimately, Yacouba taught his disciples that their movement was a step toward fulfilling the social revolution started by the Prophet Muhammad when the Muslims freed Bilal.[37]

In recent years, many Muslim scholars (and some sympathetic non-Muslims) have reached farther back in time for evidence of Islam's emancipatory impulse. A favorite example is Ahmad Baba (d. 1627), a prominent Maliki jurist of the great West African scholarly and commercial center of Timbuktu. Baba devoted an entire treatise to discussing the prohibition on enslaving Muslims, how the pious should avoid purchasing slaves if they might be Muslim, the ethics of properly treating slaves, rebutting the Curse of Ham myth and, most importantly, designating which ethnic groups and areas in West Africa had become Muslims and which remained animist.[38]

A second, less famous example is that of ʿAbd al-Salam bin Hamdun Jassus (d. 1709), an accomplished Muslim jurist of Fez. The powerful ruler of Morocco, Mawlay Ismaʿil (d. 1727), decided to increase the strength of his army by enslaving all those Black Africans who had previously been slaves or whose ancestors had been (collectively known as *ḥarāṭīn*, plural of *ḥarṭana*) and forming them into regiments. Numerous prominent Muslim scholars vociferously condemned this policy as blatantly violating one of the clearest rules of the Shariah. Indeed, enslaving a free Muslim was enumerated as one of the most serious sins in Islam.[39] Jassus appeared before Mawlay Ismaʿil to protest the policy and was immediately thrown in prison. After being released on the condition that he remain silent on the re-enslavement, Jassus wrote a stern and well-documented legal opinion concluding that what his ruler was doing was 'tantamount to total rejection of the Holy Law.' Moreover, Mawlay Ismaʿil was associating the Shariah with a practice so vile that 'the Holy Law will forever remain an object of ridicule.' As a consequence, Jassus was re-imprisoned, tortured and then executed.[40] Jassus suffered the worst, but he was not alone among the Muslim scholars of Mawlay Ismaʿil's realm who combatted his policy. Numerous others were harassed or fled into the mountains.[41]

Similar events occurred on other frontiers of the Dar al-Islam. In Herat in the early 1300s, a Muslim judge had to intervene repeatedly with the hordes of Turkic warriors based near the city. They would raid down into the Indus Valley, bringing back booty and captives to sell or keep as slaves. When Muslim Indian women were caught up in these raids, the judge would arrange for their release. When he forced a Turkic warlord to part with a Muslim woman he had taken as a slave-concubine and was particularly fond of, the judge paid with his life.[42] Over a century later, Herat's most famous Sufi poet, Mulla Jami (d. 1492), was still receiving petitions to intervene with warlords for the same reason.[43] In the late eighteenth century, a revivalist Sufi order in the Minangkabau area of Sumatra also took up the cause of curtailing rampant and indiscriminate enslavement. Preventing the seizure of free people and the selling of relatives was understood by the Muslim scholars who led this effort, such as Tuanku Nan Tuo (d. 1830), as a pillar of truly establishing Islam among the people.[44]

We already saw how, from the 1000s through the 1500s CE, there was a strong concern expressed among Shafi jurists from Persia to Egypt over the propriety of buying slaves brought into Islamic lands under dubious circumstances. The first issue was that slaves were being acquired illegally, through unsanctioned raids, sale by their families, or that they were actually Muslim. The second was that ownership of them was invalid, since slaves acquired by various types of raiding were not being channelled through the state as spoils of war, with the proper distribution and taxes paid. Much as Ahmad Baba advised those thinking of buying slaves about whose status there was doubt to err on the side of caution, leading Shafi scholars and even some Central Asian Hanafis during this period suggested that Muslims concerned with avoiding sin should not purchase any such slaves, especially not as concubines with whom they would possibly be having illicit sex.[45]

A similar tradition of anxiety over practices of enslavement that violated the Shariah can be found in India's Islamic tradition. A stubbornly enduring phenomenon in Indian history, as well as other regions of the pre-modern period, was the practice of parents selling their children into servitude.[46] Though many Indian parents – Muslims and Hindus – who did this only did so in times of famine, when they were unable to feed their families, it was also not uncommon for parents who sold their children to have less noble aims in mind.[47]

Selling one's children was generally rejected as baseless by the Hanafi school of law, which predominated in India, and it was a social problem that both Indian ulama and Indian Muslim rulers tried to prevent. But there was a long-running temptation to concede to the child-sale custom, especially in times of scarcity, when the practice seems to have been uncontrollable. In the mid-1500s, a jurist compiled a comprehensive manual of Hanafi law for Ibrahim ʿAdil Shah (d. 1558), ruler of the princely state of Bijapur on the western edge of India's Deccan plateau. This book, which came to be known as the *Fatawa Ibrahim Shahi*, included the ruling that parents could sell their children into slavery when impelled by hunger.[48] This provoked a reoccurring controversy. The north Indian scholar and historian, ʿAbd al-Qadir Badayuni (d. 1596), recounts disapprovingly how one of the leading jurists of his day, Mubarak Naguri (d. 1593), had issued fatwas permitting child sale on the authority of the *Fatawa Ibrahim Shahi*, despite the book contravening the established position of the Hanafi school.[49] Perhaps in an effort to find a lasting solution, the Mughal Emperor at the time, Akbar

(d. 1605), issued a decree that parents who had been forced by hunger to sell their children could buy them back when their situation improved.[50]

The controversy over selling children resurfaced in the early years of direct British administration over north-east India in the 1780s–90s and would remain an issue of grave humanitarian concern. It deeply troubled two successive governors general of the East India Company, so much so that they undertook initiatives (unsuccessfully) to end slavery in India because they knew that only such drastic action could prevent the sale of children. Queried in 1808 by East India Company legal officials about what Islamic law said on the matter, Muslim jurists replied that no one could enter into slavery by sale but, rather, only by some form of capture by Muslims in non-Muslim lands. And children could not be sold into slavery even in times of famine.[51]

ABOLISHING SLAVERY . . . FOR WHOM? CONCENTRIC CIRCLES OF ABOLITION

The response of the Muslim jurists to British concerns over slavery in India is perhaps the earliest instance of Muslims trying to 'spin' the issue of slavery in Islam for a Western audience.[52] At least some British officials were convinced. One reported (inaccurately) that slavery was almost extinct among Muslims in India, since slaves could only be made by capturing non-Muslims in non-Muslim territory.[53] Mollifying British anxiety over the slave trade clearly played a part in the Muslim jurists' answer, since they omitted that many slaves in Islamic lands had not been made slaves by capture at Muslim hands. They were already slaves, bought from slave dealers who had either captured them or bought them from some other, non-Muslim dealer, whose ownership of their goods was presumed to be legitimate.[54]

Another Muslim scholar who had worked with the East India Company, ʿAbd al-Qadir Khani (d. 1848), provides a fascinating inflection point in Muslim discourse about slavery, transitioning from the Muslim thread of emancipation as expressed in Islamic legal thought to absolute abolition, from specific concern for certain violations of the Shariah laws on *riqq* to more general moral qualms about slavery per se. Writing after the Company's 1843 edict denying the legal status of slavery, Khani recounts with outrage how even in the 1820s some ulama had still insisted on citing the *Fatawa Ibrahim Shahi* to legitimize people selling their children. He grouped this practice along with selling slave-concubines who had given birth to their owner's children (also against the Shariah) as great injustices (*sitam*) that had contributed to Muslims losing control of India to the British in the first place. From there, however, in what is admittedly very vague prose, Khani seems to pivot his criticism toward a larger 'evil custom' that had been almost totally extirpated by the British in India and other lands.[55] Though he does not account for what he means by this or the consequences of such a judgment, his language suggests he meant the institution of slavery.

These cases of Shafi and Indian Hanafi concerns remain relatively obscure. Cases like Ahmad Baba, however, are frequently held up as indigenous examples of Muslims opposing slavery and seeking to abolish it. Ware states repeatedly that Baal and Kan 'abolished slavery' in their Senegambian realm. In an online debate among Western professors of Islam and Islamic history, one Muslim professor from Europe cited Ahmad Baba as a premodern Muslim who prohibited slavery.

But is any of this accurate? The Imamate of Fuuta Tooro did effectively end slavery in Senegambia for a time, but only the enslavement of Muslims. Jassus and Ahmad Baba did emphasize over and over that Muslims cannot be enslaved. But they had no compunction about enslaving non-Muslims. In fact, in one sense Baba was even less 'progressive' on this question than what had been the main position of his Maliki school of law. The general Maliki rule had been that, if a person who had been enslaved claimed they were actually a Muslim and thus unenslavable, their claim enjoyed the presumption of truth. The burden of proof lay on the slave trader to disprove them. Ahmad Baba, by contrast, states that he would not believe the enslaved person's claim unless they could provide some direct evidence (*bayyina*) as proof.[56] This would become the principal position of the school after Baba, though the opposing one survived as well.[57]

Yet none of these scholars had any moral objection to slavery *qua* slavery. In fact, one could even object that their failure to see the moral evil inherent in enslaving *any* person was compounded by what was in effect their indulgence of religious discrimination.[58] This judgment is tempting. Indeed, it seems inevitable given modern sentiments. But it is wrong. Faulting figures like Baba and Jassus for not grasping that slavery is absolutely and categorically wrong for all people is to stumble into the trap of presentism. We assume that the only categories that have true meaning are those that have meaning for us, now. And we forget that in time our choices for where meaningful lines should be drawn might well seem as benighted and capricious as those of Baba and Jassus seem today.

Just as the concept of 'slavery' turns into quicksand upon examination, so the concept of 'abolition' also proves much more complex than expected. Indeed, just as our understanding of what 'slavery' is and how we should judge it are projections of the specific history of the Atlantic West, so the word 'abolition' is much less a clear ideal than a peculiar product of recent Western history.[59] Despite what we've seen about the unsustainability of the Moral Awakening Narrative for abolition, there remains a stubborn belief among many Western scholars and non-scholars alike that the ember of abolition was always present as a moral virtue in the Western European character, slowly burning its way through medieval accretion. This is because the narrative of the West awakening to slavery's evil and then dragging the Orient, Africa and everything else that was not the West into the light by means of inspiration and force has been crucial to the formation of Western identity.[60]

Modern Muslim scholars might plausibly be accused of constructing a new narrative of Islam-as-abolitionist force, but generations of Western intellectuals constructed a similar, multi-layered narrative of how slavery ended in and then was ended by the Christian West. Westerners proud of abolition might crow that Muslims would never have considered ending slavery, much less felt compelled to do so, without morally driven Western political pressure. But if a tradition can only prove itself worthy through an unprompted moral awakening, then neither can the West claim credit. Without the epochal economic and technological changes of early industrialization and the emergence of a capitalist system, Western societies would not have accepted abandoning slavery.[61]

We have already seen how the Moral Awakening narrative, despite its flimsiness, is bound up inseparably with a belief in a modern and progressive world led by the moral vanguard of the West. There is a similar myth spun around Christianity. The thesis that Christianity ameliorated the condition of slaves in the Roman world remained (or remains) gospel for generations of Western historians and Sunday school teachers alike despite having been disproven repeatedly since the mid-twentieth century.[62] Moreover, from the Carolingian period onward, throughout the Middle Ages in Western Europe, any bans on enslavement that did exist were bans on enslaving or selling off Christians. Sometimes Christian here only meant those who followed the Pope in Rome.[63]

Narratives about freedom from slavery helped shape the national narratives of Western Europe. Beginning in 1571, the kings of France declared on principle that 'There are no slaves in France,' a slogan that echoed in Britain after Lord Mansfield ruled in 1772 that slavery was unnatural and unconscionable in England. The idea that all Frenchmen or all Englishmen were free and that their lands were abodes of freedom was integral to the construction of French and British political identity. Of course, equally essential – and ironic – to those realms' material success was their titanic exploitation of slave labor in their colonies well into the 1800s.[64]

The end of slavery is the natal miracle of European civilization. No less a figure than the seminal French historian Marc Bloch (d. 1944) called the disappearance of slavery in Western Europe 'one of the most profound' transformations ever. Nineteenth-century humanist historians saw it as the inevitable convergence of the West's Classical (read Stoic) and Christian character. European Marxist historians saw it as a crucial, materially determined step in Europe's preset economic journey.[65] Among European historians of all stripes, the idea that indigenous slavery 'ended' in Western Europe at some point in the early Middle Ages became axiomatic.[66]

But, just like the cases of Ahmad Baba and Jassus, this story relies on a specific understanding of what slavery was and who was a slave. Susan Mosher Stuard has shown how much the truism about slavery ending in Europe rests on an image of 'slavery' as men working in the fields. Even after the end of such agricultural/male slavery, women were still domestic slaves working in homes on Europe's Mediterranean coast through the end of the fifteenth century. Forcing us to confront further our assumptions about what exactly the 'slavery' was that ended, David Wyatt observes that, if we acknowledge the clear link between female enslavement and sexual exploitation, then the enslavement of women – through sex trafficking – has lasted up until today.[67] In fact, the New Abolitionist movement as a whole, with its ongoing campaigns against bonded labor, human trafficking and prison labor, could be understood as an attempt to unfetter what has long been a relatively parochial Western view of what 'slavery' can be.

We fault Muslim scholars for only fighting to protect Muslims from slavery while defending the enslavement of non-Muslims because such discrimination seems hard to fathom. When a Muslim slave-raid commander in the 1830s in present-day Algeria found that a soldier had accidentally captured a Muslim on the raid, he viewed this as a profound moral affront. 'He is your brother in religion,' the leader shouted. 'Like you, he recognizes only one God.'[68] One miracle of a Muslim saint from Morocco was that, when he had been enslaved by Europeans and placed on their slave ship, the ship would not move. Though his captors tried to free him, he refused to leave until all the Muslims on the ship were released.[69] How could these people be so blind, we ask? How could they not see that freedom is a *human* right that belongs to *all* human beings?

But perhaps we too are blind in our time. Why should the right not to have one's labor exploited and one's basic rights curtailed be limited to one particular species, namely *homo sapiens*? Don't other primates and other mammals suffer as well when worked too hard, caged or separated from their families? Strict animal rights proponents have consciously adopted the language of abolitionism because they view the detention of animals for labor, entertainment or food as no different from slavery (worse in the case of eating meat). Why is non-human life and suffering worth less than that of humans? According to these activists, drawing such a line of distinction between species is entirely arbitrary. It is tempting to respond that humans have a uniquely advanced consciousness of their own pain and mortality. But strict animal rights advocates respond that this is inconsistent. Why, if our rights are functions of our awareness or understanding, are special rights not then given to brilliant professors and denied to obtuse factory workers or the seriously developmentally disabled? We could respond that it's because they are all human beings. But why does that distinction matter more or less than any other?[70]

Such animal rights arguments seem laughable. Many might find it hard not to chuckle at a recent PETA alert about an enslaved horse. Of course human beings are different from animals, we interject. To this, strict animal rights activists respond that this is mere *speciesism*.[71] This word might also prompt chortling. Yet so did neologisms like Native American and African American when they were introduced by their advocates. The term ableism (discrimination or prejudice against individuals with disabilities) is laughed at in many circles today, but for many others it represents as noxious a form of discrimination as racism. Just as the principle that race, religion and gender should not be valid categories for denying rights has been predominately accepted only in the last century, so depriving a living creature of its rights because of its species might well be disparaged in coming decades. Should that day arrive, those thousands of generations of humans who enslaved their fellow mammals may well be looked at with the same moral condescension we feel for Aristotle's natural slavery or the European enslavement of Africans. We read stories of slave raids in past centuries with horror, and it makes no sense to us how humans could be so depraved as to commit such crimes. But it is entirely possible that future generations will be equally shocked by the moral hypocrisy of law enforcement in our day using enslaved dogs to help track down human traffickers.

By bringing up these examples I am not arguing that, because meanings change over time, our modern sentiments about slavery somehow mean less. I am saying that, because meanings change over time, things that mean nothing to us today nonetheless meant a great deal to others in the past . . . and may well do so in the future.

'THE LAWGIVER LOOKS EXPECTANTLY TOWARDS FREEDOM' – ABOLITION AS AN AIM OF THE SHARIAH

Moving outward in concentric circles of moral conviction, from the claim that the Quran itself ended slavery, past the notion that God would have ordered it so were it feasible, we come to a third Muslim response to the challenge of slavery and abolition. It holds that emancipating slaves – and by extension ending the practice of slavery – is one of the aims (*maqāṣid*) of the Shariah. At first this might seem indistinguishable from the previous position. In both cases God has always wanted Muslims to end slavery but did not order this explicitly in His revelation. The previous position, however, assumes that something went wrong. Muslims *should have* ended slavery long ago, but Islamic civilization went off the rails and ended up erecting a massive slavery edifice.[72] The position that ending slavery was one of the aims of the Shariah shares the assumption that God had some good reason for not ordering the immediate elimination of slavery. But it does not insist that the presence of slavery for centuries in Muslim society and its moral acceptance in Islamic law were errors. More importantly, the practice of *riqq*, at least as a theoretical ideal, was not morally wrong prior to the nineteenth-century age of abolition. All Muslim responses to the moral challenge of slavery emphasize that the Shariah greatly restricted the means of enslavement, required slaves be treated humanely and strongly encouraged freeing them. But these elements are particularly vital for the abolition-as-an-aim-of-the-Shariah position, since it essentially defends the moral acceptability of *riqq* in the pre-modern age.[73]

Also unlike the previous responses we have seen, this one does not bypass fourteen centuries of Islamic thought to make its argument directly from the Quran or the Prophetic precedent. Instead, it expresses itself in the language and tradition of those fourteen centuries of Shariah jurisprudence. As such, its central pivot is the well-established legal maxim, which can be dated back to some of Islam's earliest surviving texts, that 'The Lawgiver looks expectantly towards freedom.'[74]

Rida was perhaps the first to utilize the technical term 'aim of the Shariah' in this argument, but the idea was present in Ahmad Bey's 1846 edict abolishing slavery in Tunis (see pages 228–9). And it was explicitly clear in the writings and teachings of Rida's mentor, Muhammad ʿAbduh, who along with India's Sir Syed Ahmed Khan made up the two epicenters of Islamic modernist thought.[75] Perhaps the most explicit advocate of this approach has been the Tunisian state mufti Muhammad Tahir Ibn ʿAshur (d. 1973), who wrote in his influential work *The Aims of the Shariah* that 'one of the most important aims of [the Shariah] is ending slavery and making freedom the general condition.'[76]

DOUBLING DOWN – PROGRESSIVE ISLAM & THE AXIOMATIC EVIL OF SLAVERY

In the wake of 9/11, a movement coalesced among some Muslim intellectuals in the West that embodied many of the concerns of Islamic modernists like Ahmed Khan and ʿAbduh but which brought them into the twenty-first century. According to its proponents, Progressive Islam seeks to understand the faith as a force for liberation that affirms social justice, human rights, religious equality and – an issue of particular emphasis – gender equality, the latter now embracing many LGBTQ rights.[77] Obviously, for Progressive Islam the moral abhorrence of slavery in any and all forms is undisputable.

Unlike earlier Islamic modernists, Progressive Muslim scholars generally do not try to argue that notions like the prohibition of slavery were clear in the text of the Quran. Rather, their approach is akin to the trajectory hermeneutics of liberal Protestantism and Catholicism. The Quran and Sunna may lay down instructions about marriage between men and women and condemn same-sex relations. But, according to leading Progressive Muslim scholars, what we should glean from these texts today is not the historical particulars of the Sodom and Gomorrah story but that God endorses consensual and nurturing relationships, even between same-sex partners.[78]

This Progressive Muslim method of interpretation has its roots in the highly influential work of the Pakistani scholar Fazlur Rahman (d. 1988), who was forced out of his country and eventually settled down as a professor of Islamic history at the University of Chicago.[79] Rahman argued that the laws laid down by the Quran and Sunna should not be simply taken at face value, since these sources were revealed in a specific historical context. Rather, we must understand what ethical or moral objectives those laws aimed at accomplishing and then ask what rules Muslims should follow to pursue those same objectives in our context today.[80] Of course, the conflict arises when the way we think we should live out the Quran's ethical imperatives today directly contradicts the holy book's specific commands, as in the case of the Quran ruling that a daughter inherits half the amount of a son (4:5). While Muslim jurists had always understood this as a rule valid for all time, Rahman read it not as final but as a step toward a more just system of inheritance rights given the patriarchal economy of seventh-century Arabia. Today, in an economy so dramatically changed, we should adjust that rule to further promote the same aim.[81]

Addressing the question of slavery in particular, some avowedly Progressive Muslims have stuck closely to Rahman's method. A proudly professed Progressive Muslim, the Bosnian Muslim professor Adis Duderija (pronounced Judayriya) assumes the moral repugnance of slavery as a given. The Quran accepted and dealt with it because it was part of the context in which the book was revealed. The repeated exhortations to free slaves and to assure their humane treatment, however, convinces Duderija that 'the moral trajectory' of the Quran and Sunna should lead modern Muslims to conclude that eradicating slavery is what God has always wanted.[82]

Another prominent Progressive Muslim intellectual, Professor Kecia Ali, takes an approach similar to the abolition-as-aim-of-the-Shariah. While the basic foundations of the Shariah provide the minimum floor of legal duties that Muslims must fulfill, God's law calls Muslims to a higher ethical standard. As changes in economy and society have made practices like slavery unnecessary, she writes, Muslims are better able to pursue God's aim of justice by relegating slavery to the past. What distinguishes Ali's response from others who claimed that abolition was an aim of the Shariah is that those ulama consciously chose to phrase their claim in the vocabulary of Islamic jurisprudence, which would never sound any note of dissonance between the Quranic text and the expectations of justice. In her suggestion that Muslims embrace abolition, Ali's tone differs slightly but significantly, suggesting that Islam's true ethos is to be found above and beyond the text of its revelation. The ethical imperative of prohibiting slavery 'suggests that the Quranic text itself requires Muslims sometimes to depart from its literal provisions in order to establish justice.'[83]

Although he does not fit entirely into the category of Progressive Muslim, the reformist Iranian theologian Ayatollah Mohsen Kadivar provides one of the most comprehensive treatments of the moral challenge of slavery and Islam in the modern world. Indeed, his relatively short piece on the subject manages to draw on every approach dealt with in this chapter except the radical Quranic abolitionism of Ahmed Khan. Kadivar acknowledges that the exhortation to manumit slaves and to treat them well in the Quran and Sunna certainly lays the groundwork for concluding that slavery was not meant to be a permanent institution in Islam. But rather than relying on such vague, aspirational thinking, Kadivar turns to the method of Islamic juristic reasoning known as abrogation by reason (*naskh ʿaqlī*) to provide the ultimate justification for concluding that slavery is no longer permissible according to Islam.[84]

Abrogation has long been a well-established interpretive concept in Islamic thought, providing an 'indication for the duration of a ruling' found in the text of the Quran or Hadith.[85] Though abrogation has generally denoted an instance of a chronologically later Quranic verse or Hadith replacing the ruling of an earlier one, it could also occur when scholars concluded through an examination of context that a ruling from scripture had lost its applicability. Abrogation by reason involves determining, on the one hand, the original context and purpose of a law laid down in the Quran or Hadith, and, on the other, whether that ruling applies or achieves the intended results in a later context. Though not mentioned by Kadivar, one example would be that the normal requirement that a Muslim wash their feet as part of preparing for prayer no longer applies if they lose their feet in an accident.[86]

The similarity between Fazlur Rahman's method of reading scripture and abrogation by reason should not escape the reader. Both look at the purpose of a scriptural rule and ask whether that purpose is still being fulfilled. What separates a scholar like Kadivar from Rahman, however, is that Kadivar does not break with pre-modern Islamic thought by historicizing the rulings of the Quran and Hadith almost across the board. He acknowledges that the presumption in divine rulings is that they are meant for all times, and in order to prove that they should no longer apply after a certain point one needs some kind of clear evidence (*dalīl*). Whereas this clear evidence has generally been understood by ulama as material from the Quran, Hadiths, or some unquestionable principle of reason, with slavery Kadivar sees it in the revolution in human values that has occurred since the Enlightenment. This has led us to understand that slavery contradicts the value of human dignity inherent in Quranic verses like 'Indeed We have honored the children of Adam' (17:70).[87] What places Kadivar alongside Progressive Muslims like Duderija and Kecia Ali on the question of slavery is that for all of them it is the modern, Western-articulated concept of human rights that provides the determinative evidence that slavery is wrong and that Islamic law must be reinterpreted to remove any basis for it.

Although more of a twentieth-century Western liberal than a Progressive, Abdullahi An-Na'im proposes a similar solution. Moral problems like the acceptance of slavery in the Shariah should be overcome by realizing that the intended trajectory of the Shariah was always for humans to one day transcend it and adopt the perspective of modern human rights discourse.[88]

A Short Timeline of Abolition & the Muslim World[89]

c. 1787	Imamate of Fuuta Toro prohibits European traders from trading in Muslim slaves
1789	British East India Company prohibits import, export and the internal slave trade in India, with only moderate effect
1803	Denmark abolishes slave trade
1807	British Abolition Act prohibits slave trade for British subjects
1812	Slave trade banned in Delhi region; slavery disappears within twenty years there
1815	At Congress of Vienna, France, Britain, Russia, Prussia, Austria and Spain condemn slave trade as 'repugnant to the principles of humanity and universal morality'
1818	Dutch ban slave trade in Dutch Southeast Asia, French ban slave trade, both at British behest and both to little effect

1833	British Emancipation Bill abolishes slavery in the empire (with compensation) except in India and East Asian possessions as well as in later African 'protectorate' colonies
1839	Imam of Masqat in Oman and Trucial states of the Persian Gulf agree to British request to limit African slave trade
1843	Slavery 'abolished' in British India when courts cease recognizing slave status; actual slavery continues
1845	Imam of Masqat agrees to bring no more slaves from his African territory
1846	Ahmad Bey of Tunis abolishes slavery there
1847	Ottoman Sultan issues decree banning African slave trade from East Africa while insisting this is not the abolition of slavery in the Ottoman realm; Ottoman Sultan closes the Istanbul slave market
1848	France abolishes slavery in its colonies but not its protectorates
1848	Shah of Persia bans African slave trade in the Gulf at British request
1851–2	Russian Empire issues abolition decrees in some of its conquered Kazakh territories, reissued repeatedly as late as 1869
1854	Ottomans ban Georgian and Circassian slave trade, but it continues to supply elite harems through the end of the Empire
1854–5	Khedive Sa'id of Egypt issues ban on public slave markets and importing slaves from Sudan, with little effect
1857	Ottomans reissue general prohibition on African slave trade, specifically exempting Hejaz
1860	Dutch prohibit owning slaves for Dutch and Chinese subjects in areas of Southeast Asia under direct Dutch control (a minority of areas); implementation takes decades
1861	Russian Empire implements abolition of the economically defunct but massive institution of serfdom, roughly 40 percent of the population, by far the largest-scale emancipation

1862	In British India it becomes a legal offense to own slaves
1865	Egypt grants European consuls the right to take in and free slaves who seek refuge
1865	US makes slavery illegal
1877	Anglo-Egyptian convention to suppress African slave trade bans all import, export and internal trade, with limited effect
1880	Anglo-Ottoman convention to suppress African slave trade grants British officials the rights to search and seize ships
1895	New Anglo-Egyptian convention bans all types of slave trade, including White slave trade, with severe punishment for those involved; slavery gradually ends in Egypt as supply cut off, economy and social norms change
1889–90	Brussels Conference sees Congress of Vienna states plus Persia and Zanzibar condemn slavery and slave trade
1897	Sultan of Zanzibar abolishes slave status
1898	American conquest of Philippines brings slave raiding in Southeast Asia to an end
1898–1900	French shut down slave markets in Niger valley
1900	British abolish slave status in Nigeria
1907	Abolition of slavery on Kenya coast
1915	Slavery abolished in all of British Malaya (Malaysia)
1922	Morocco bans internal slave trade
1923	Egyptian constitution states that all Egyptian citizens are free
1924	Turkish Republic bans slavery
1929	Shah abolishes slavery in Persia
1952	Qatar abolishes slavery (with compensation)
1956	Morocco bans slavery
1962–3	Saudi Arabia prohibits slavery (with compensation)
1970	Oman fully bans slavery
1980–81	Mauritania becomes last country to abolish slavery (abolition decrees already issued in 1905 and 1961)

PROHIBITED BY THE RULER BUT NOT BY GOD: THE CRUCIAL MATTER OF *TAQYID AL-MUBAH*

The idea that the eventual emancipation of all slaves and the abolition of slavery are aims of the Sacred Law poses an important question. How would this total emancipation of slaves or the abolition of slavery actually take place? This could be achieved organically – Islam's strong encouragement of manumission combined with the changes brought by the modern economy would lead to the extinction of slavery in Muslim societies. As we've seen, this did in fact lead gradually to a lasting cessation of slavery in many locations. In the end, however, the complete abolition of legal slavery in the Muslim world occurred just as it did elsewhere: via top-down orders from the government.

But how was this justified? Hadn't numerous Muslim rulers, advised by a whole corps of ulama, told European officials in the nineteenth century that no Muslim could prohibit what God and His Prophet had allowed? The Quran had instructed believers, 'Do not prohibit (*tuḥarrimū*) those goodly things that God has made licit for you' (Quran 5:87), and when the Prophet renounced relations with one of his womenfolk God revealed the verse, 'O prophet, why do you prohibit what God has made licit for you?' (Quran 66:1).

Though these verses have generally been read as warning Muslims not to venture into monastic asceticism or deny themselves lawful pleasures, some leading Muslim scholars have seen in them a broader affirmation of the Shariah's timelessness. The influential exegete Zamakhshari (d. 1144) concludes that Muslims must not prohibit what God has made permissible (*ḥalāl*) because doing so is to claim more knowledge than God. The Creator allowed things for some wisdom or good (*maṣlaḥa*) known to Him, explains Zamakhshari, even though it might be unknown to mankind. The seminal theologian Fakhr al-Din Razi (d. 1210) was more emphatic: to declare *haram* what God had made *halal* was to lapse into unbelief (*kufr*).[90] The most explicit expression of this principle comes from the Shiite tradition. Imam Jaʿfar Sadiq (d. 765) told his students, 'The permissible of Muhammad is permissible forever, until the Day of Resurrection, and the prohibited [of Muhammad] is prohibited forever, until the Day of Resurrection . . .'[91]

In the Shariah, it is only the Lawgiver (*shāriʿ*), understood as God and by extension His Messenger, who have the authority to prohibit. Muslim jurists, 'the heirs of the prophets,' inherited this power so that the substance of God's revealed law could be discovered and applied after the end of revelation, in new times and as new questions emerged. The ulama have the authority to declare things *haram* if they are convinced that the established sources of God's law – the Quran, the Prophet's Sunna, the practice of the early Muslim community and the accepted traditions of legal reasoning built on them – call for such a ruling. But to arrogate to themselves the authority to declare forbidden what had clearly been allowed by God and the Prophet was to exceed this mandate. We see this as early as the mid-700s CE in Egypt. When a group from one Arab tribe protested before the judge Ruʿayni (d. 771) that a man had married one of their women and that they wanted the marriage annulled, the judge responded that he would not prohibit what God had allowed. If the woman's guardian (*walī*) had agreed, then the marriage stood. The men appealed the case to the governor, who ordered the judge to annul the marriage. He once again refused.[92]

The concepts of prohibited (*ḥarām*) and permissible (*ḥalāl*) that we are discussing here, however, should not be understood in a mundane, secular sense. These are rulings of the Sacred Law. Razi is careful to note that one can choose to desist from doing something without declaring it *haram*. And in some situations the principles of ambiguity and caution can render the licit illicit. If a stolen item is mixed up with legitimate property, for example, so that one cannot distinguish one from the other, they all become *haram* for the owner. In this case, what is making the permissible *haram* is not a person raising his flawed fiat to the level of divine command. It is the Shariah principles of caution applied to a situation of ambiguity.[93]

The right to legislate by interpreting God's law belongs to the ulama as the articulators of Islamic law and as the judges who applied it. But part of the obligation to know and apply the Shariah has fallen on Muslim political authorities as well. It is ultimately political authorities who hold the coercive power to compel people to obey the judge's rulings, and Muslim jurists have always granted political authorities jurisdiction in matters such as taxation, law and order, basic administrative law and diplomacy. What the famous jurist Qarafi (d. 1285) termed 'administrative acts' (*taṣarruf al-imām*) were legally binding.[94] Gradually, the ruler's authority was even allowed to enter the functioning of *fiqh*, the details of law as derived by the ulama, as well. By the 1300s it had become accepted that, regardless of what school of law a judge followed, the ruler could legitimately require him to rule according to whichever school of law the ruler specified.[95] By the 1600s in the Ottoman Empire, it was not uncommon for the state's official school of law, the Hanafi, to reference sultanic edicts in its main lawbooks.[96] Within this acknowledged purview of state legal authority lay the power to administratively restrict. Not to declare something *haram* in the eyes of God, but illegal according to the state.

What this meant was that, by the 1300s, a concept later referred to as restricting the permissible (*taqyīd al-mubāḥ*) had coalesced in Islamic legal thought. In short, it held that a Muslim ruler (or state) could restrict what was otherwise permissible if this had some basis in the objectives of the Shariah, such as promoting some common good.[97] In a region in which one school of law predominated, this might mean applying the school's more restrictive ruling. For example, the Ottoman judiciary dropped the Hanafi school's main ruling that a bride does not need her guardian's permission to marry in favor of the opinion requiring it, citing dealing with 'the corruption of the age' as justification.[98] In a more legally diverse region, it might mean a ruler drawing a more restrictive ruling from one school of law as opposed to another, as with Mamluk rulers preferring Maliki judges' more severe verdicts in cases of religious troublemakers accused of heresy.[99] Finally, it could involve the ruler introducing an administrative rule where no clear one had existed at all, as with the seventeenth-century Ottoman order setting a fifteen-year statute of limitations for legal claims regarding benefits received from endowments or restricting the rights of cultivators to leave their land and move elsewhere.[100]

Although the corpus of the Shariah was so vast and diverse that some basis from some school of law or Muslim authority could usually be found as a precedent for an instance of restricting the permissible, in theory a Muslim ruler could create a restriction out of whole cloth. This was comparatively rare, but one such example was prohibiting judges from marrying off underage girls (i.e., those who had not reached puberty) without their guardian's permission, when normally a judge could stand in as the bride's guardian.[101] Another was the practice in Marrakesh of judges assigning a socially senior guarantor to a husband who had been accused of beating his wife. Normally the couple would just be placed under observation by a trusted neighbor or, if the husband were found guilty, he would owe his wife compensation and/or the marriage would be dissolved. This additional requirement of the guarantor aimed at holding a further threat over the husband's head: his fear of disgracing his patron if he reoffended.[102]

Such decisions by rulers were by no means uncontested, and the power of 'restricting the permissible' was precarious. Not only was the distinction between *haram* and illegal easily obscured, but this power also presented a slippery slope toward political abuse.[103] Perhaps the first scholar to take up the validity of the concept at any length, ʿAbd al-Ghani Nabulusi (d. 1731) of Damascus, did so with mixed feelings. He dealt with it in the course of his comments on the Ottoman sultan Murat IV's ban on smoking and coffee houses. In one of his books, Nabulusi reacted fiercely to rulers prohibiting something when God had not done so directly in scripture and if there were no solid grounds for Muslim scholars declaring it prohibited (*ḥarām*) or disliked (*makrūh*). Nabulusi does, however, leave a window open for the ruler if the restriction does not emanate from his own opinion or desires but rather furthers the 'command of God.' In a second, far shorter treatise written a year later, Nabulusi explicitly acknowledges this exception; a ruler may restrict (*taqyīd al-mubāḥ*) something agreed on as otherwise permissible if doing so promotes the common good of Muslims by bringing some benefit or preventing some harm.[104]

Restricting the permissible expanded into a more robust and oft-invoked principle in the late nineteenth and early twentieth centuries, in part due to controversial issues like slavery and polygamy. Muhammad Bayram Khamis and later ʿAbduh pointed to the ruler's right to restrict the permissible as a key tool needed to abolish slavery. Rida had concurred that Muslim rulers should prohibit (*manʿuhu*) slavery if they felt that was in the best interests of Muslims.[105] The Tunisian master Maliki scholar Ibn ʿAshur, who as a young man had met and admired ʿAbduh, invoked this authority when asked if a Muslim government could ban polygamy. 'The ruler can prohibit (*yamnaʿa*) the people from doing this permitted act,' he replied, 'due to the existence of some harm in it. And Islamic history is full of examples showing this . . .' It was also cited – again, on the question of slavery – by the most famous Hanafi scholar in Pakistan today, Muhammad Taqi Usmani.[106]

IF YOU CAN'T DO IT RIGHT, YOU CAN'T DO IT AT ALL – PROHIBITING *RIQQ* POORLY DONE

In January 1846, Ahmad Bey (r. 1835–55), the Ottoman governor of Tunis (essentially modern Tunisia), ordered the emancipation of all slaves in the territory and declared that, from that time on, all people born in Tunis would be born free. He offered no compensation to the slave owners. Ahmad Bey's motivations have long been debated by scholars. On the one hand, he seems to have been genuinely concerned about the poor treatment of slaves brought into and through Tunis from Sub-Saharan Africa (his own mother had been a slave woman captured in Sardinia). As had been clear since the time of Ahmad Baba in the seventeenth century, the slave trade into the Mediterranean from south of the Sahara had resulted in the improper enslavement of many Black African Muslims.

On the other hand, Ahmad Bey also had political interests. Ottoman Tunis was a semi-autonomous province with significant control of its own affairs. But in the decades prior to the 1846 decree the Ottoman central government had begun encroaching more and more on Tunis' affairs as part of its efforts to centralize the empire. Moreover, in 1830 the French had occupied neighboring Algiers (essentially modern Algeria). In the face of impending domination by Istanbul or Paris, Ahmad Bey sought to improve relations with Great Britain. And the British government, as represented by its consul in Tunis, was concerned with ending the slave trade and, if possible, slavery itself. When the British consul approached Ahmad Bey in 1841 and asked him to take measures against the slave trade, the governor shocked him by responding immediately that he would end slavery in Tunis altogether. He quickly prohibited any slave trade activity and closed down the slave market. With the importation of slaves banned, he ended slavery entirely several years later with his 1846 emancipation decree. This was affirmed by both the senior mufti of the Hanafi school (the official school of the Ottoman state) and the Maliki one, which predominated among the inhabitants of the province.[107]

The text of the decree was as follows (formatting mine):

> To proceed: it has been established beyond all doubt that most of the people in our state in this time are not properly exercising ownership (*milkiyya*) over Black African slaves (*sūdān*), who have no power or means themselves, since, according to discussions among the scholars, the basis of their ownership has not been established. This is particularly the case since the faith [of Islam] dawned in the [Sahel] region some time ago.
>
> So where are those who own their brothers in the legitimate legal manner that the Lord of Messengers (Muhammad) taught to us in his final lesson, at the end of his time in this world and the beginning of his time in the next, that among the principles of his Sacred Law is aspiring to freedom and obliging the slave's owner to manumit him on the basis of harms [done to him]?

> Thus our concern that kindness be done for those poor [enslaved] people in this their earthly life, and also for their owners in their afterlife, in our current condition, entails that we prohibit people from this permitted (*mubāḥ*) but disagreed-on practice [i.e., slavery]. This is out of our worry that [the slave holders] might fall into something agreed upon by consensus and study as forbidden, namely their harming their brothers whom God put in their care.[108] And in this we also have common political interests, among them the [slaves] fleeing to the sanctuaries of officials outside their nation [i.e., European consulates].
>
> So, we have assigned official notaries to the Sufi lodge (*zāwiya*) of Sidi Muhriz of the Bakriyya, and of Sidi Mansur to record [documentary] proof of our ruling on manumission for any [slave] who comes seeking aid against his owner, which should be presented to us for us to seal. And you all, may God guard you, if a slave should come to you all seeking aid against his master, or if you should hear of some instance of a slave being owned, send the slave to us. And beware of his owner seeking out means against him, for your sanctuary is being sought for emancipation (*fakk raqabatihi*) by those whose proper ownership is most probably not valid. And we would not rule in favor of the [slave owner] claiming that it was [valid] in this current age. And avoiding what is permitted out of fear of falling into the realm of the forbidden is part of the Sacred Law, especially since this factor has now been added to by what the common good (*maṣlaḥa*) demands. So people must be directed to this end. And God guides to what is straightest and gives good tidings of great reward to those believers who do good deeds. And peace.[109]

Many of the themes we've seen already appear in Ahmad Bey's decree, which is the earliest such local abolition decree in the Muslim world: the references to the Prophet's commands that slaves are 'your brothers, whom God has put under your care', that an owner should free a slave he had harmed and the Prophet's repeated urging on his deathbed that Muslims care for their slaves. Again, we see the problem of Black African Muslims being enslaved contrary to the Shariah. We find again the maxim that the Lawgiver 'looks expectantly towards freedom.' Finally, the notion reappears that *riqq* was permissible but not required. It was thus proscribable by the ruler, especially when some common good could be achieved in doing this.

The thread running throughout the decree, however, is subtler but nonetheless extremely important. It was highlighted almost two decades later in 1863, when one of Ahmad Bey's successors as governor, Husayn Pasha (d. 1890), wrote to the American consul in Tunis discussing how slavery had ended there and urging Americans to follow suit. In his letter, Husayn notes several times that it was the Shariah itself that obliged the government of Tunis to prohibit slavery. The Sacred Law had strict conditions for *riqq*, including the proper care of slaves and that Muslims under no conditions be enslaved.[110] As Ahmad Bey's edict had stated, not only had many slaves in Tunis been enslaved illegally by the traders who had brought them there, their owners were also treating them cruelly and thus violating the Shariah's conditions. As with Razi's example of stolen goods mixed in with legally owned ones, when it became clear that the people of Tunis were systematically failing to meet these conditions, the only solution was to end the practice of slavery in Tunis altogether.

A full exposition of the Tunis edict came from Muhammad Bayram Khamis (d. 1889), the nephew of the Hanafi mufti who had affirmed it. This scion of an elite political and scholarly family in Tunis had received the finest education in the Islamic sciences and excelled as a teacher in Tunis' storied Zaytuna Madrasa, as a prolific author and a high-level state administrator. Though he would fit squarely into the reformist camp of later figures like ʿAbduh and Rida, Bayram was devoted to the preservation of the Shariah and Muslims' political independence.[111] And he understood that the two were linked. As French colonial designs closed in on Tunis in the late 1870s, Bayram left his homeland for exile. Eventually he settled in Cairo, where he died just as ʿAbduh and Rida were gaining influence.

Bayram was worried that Ahmad Bey's edict was being dismissed as nothing but a justification for appeasing European powers. In the early 1880s he penned a short treatise entitled *The Proper Study on the Question of Slavery* (*al-Taḥqīq fī mas'alat al-raqīq*), which he intended to prove that the edict was entirely in accord with the Shariah and that it was the religious duty of Muslims to enforce abolition.[112] This was all the more necessary, he admitted, since Europeans had been using Islam's fundamental acceptance of slavery to attack the faith.[113]

Among its other arguments, *The Proper Study* lays out how the principle of caution invoked by Ahmad Bey clearly entailed that the two main sources of slaves of the day, Circassians and Black Africans, should be off-bounds to the slave trade. Either these populations lived under the rule of colonial powers with whom Muslim states like the Ottomans had treaties (more below), were selling their children or relatives into slavery out of desperation or included large numbers of Muslims who were being illegally enslaved. Each of these situations meant that these people were not legally enslavable according to the Shariah. Yes, there were people who had been legitimately enslaved or who were born slaves, Bayram admitted. But these were far too few in number to explain the burgeoning slave markets of North Africa and the Hejaz. Moreover, Black African slaves were regularly treated with cruelty that fell afoul of the Shariah's standards. Since the slave trade and slavery as it existed were frequently violating Shariah norms, Muslim rulers were right to ban them in order to prevent such wrongs from occurring. By their administrative decree, 'the permissible becomes prohibited.'[114]

Ahmad Bey's response to the challenge of slavery and abolition was one of the earliest we know of. But *The Proper Study* is its full exposition. It is the urtext of Islamic abolition, outlining most of the Shariah arguments drawn on by ʿAbduh, Rida and others in subsequent decades. Though they do not cite Bayram, we know that ʿAbduh was in contact with him and that both he and Rida respected Bayram a great deal and considered him a fellow traveler.[115] Their writings echo the Tunis argument. ʿAbduh stated that a key element of the Shariah's conception of slavery is that the caliph can order all slaves freed if he concludes that the legal status or treatment of slaves in Muslim lands is not correct (*ghayr ṣaḥīḥa*).[116]

The notion that *riqq* was valid under the Shariah but only if the Sacred Law's conditions were met – and that they are not or cannot be met in the present time – has been invoked numerous times in the century and a half since Ahmad Bey's edict. It provided the justification for the Ottoman sultan's shuttering the Istanbul slavery market in 1847 and was implied in his defense of restrictions on the African slave trade in the 1850s.[117] It was the primary justification for King Faysal's 1962 decree prohibiting slavery in Saudi Arabia. 'It is well known that slavery in the present era,' Faysal's edict reads, 'falls short of many of the legal conditions that Islam required for the permissibility of slavery.'[118] And in the mid-twentieth century in Zanzibar, the scholar Saʿid bin ʿAli insisted that the slavery practiced there had never been the *riqq* allowed by the Shariah. The Indonesian exegete Hamka (d. 1981) suggested the same for slave-concubinage during the Dutch period.[119]

Oddly, the failings identified by Baba and Ahmad Bey persisted much longer in Iran and raised public calls for abolition to a much higher volume there. From the 1870s through the first decades of the twentieth century, Qajar Persia saw the emergence of popular outrage against slavery, including among traditionalist Muslim clerics. This was not due to some moral awakening. It came, rather, from a spike in the enslavement of free Muslims both by Turkmen nomads raiding into the country's weakly protected north-east and also by Iranian slave traders seizing Baluchis in the south-east.[120] The first situation was due to the weakness of the Qajar state and its inability to secure its borders. The second, ironically, was due to the stubborn demand for slaves pushing dealers to seek new internal sources after the Persian government acceded to British demands to end the seaborn slave trade.

One of the Iranians enslaved by Turkmen raiders in the late 1800s was a master of the Niʿmatallahi Gunabadi Sufi order.[121] In 1914 his nephew Nur ʿAli Shah (d. 1918) would write the most extensive Persian treatise on the Islamic argument for abolition. One of the clearest articulations of the argument that *riqq* cannot be allowed because it is not done properly came from his grandson, the Iranian cleric and Sufi master Sultan Husayn Tabandeh (d. 1992), who penned a commentary on the Universal Declaration of Human Rights in 1966.[122] As we will see, this line of argument also undergirds the next approach to answering the question of how Muslims in the modern world should address slavery's place in Islam.

SAME SHARIAH, DIFFERENT CONDITIONS – THE OBSOLESCENCE OR UNFAVORABILITY OF SLAVERY

In March 1882, Muhammad ʿAbduh wrote a letter to an English friend who moved in the circles of the British elite. He confirmed Wilfred Blunt's (d. 1922) impression that slavery in Islam had only ever been allowed in legitimate religious warfare by Muslims against infidels, but not against non-Muslims who were allies or who had peace treaties with the Muslim state. Blunt reproduced ʿAbduh's letter. It reads in part, 'Hence the Mohammadan religion not only does not oppose abolishing slavery as it is in modern time [sic], but radically condemns its continuance.' ʿAbduh adds that, in just a few days' time, the Shaykh al-Azhar would issue a fatwa stating that abolishing slavery is in accordance with Quran, Islamic tradition and the Sacred

Law.[123] About a month earlier Blunt had posted a letter to the Anti-Slavery Society in London. He claimed that no less than the Shaykh al-Azhar himself, Muhammad Inbabi (d. 1896), had affirmed that the Quran had only allowed enslaving prisoners taken in war against idolaters. It was not an expression of God's prospective will but merely a reliance on existing custom in Arabia at the time. Since there were no longer legitimate wars taking place, the slaves taken in the Sub-Saharan slave raids that so horrified European readers were actually totally illegitimate according to the Shariah and the slaves taken in them legally free. Egypt's powerful Minister of War at the time, in effect the ruler in Cairo after triumphing (briefly) in a revolt against Egypt's monarch, had even told Blunt that he would shortly ban slavery in Egypt.[124]

But no fatwa and no abolition decree were forthcoming. Within a few months of ʿAbduh's letter to Blunt, British forces had crushed the army of the Minister of War, ʿUrabi Pasha, and returned the king to power. ʿUrabi and ʿAbduh were arrested and sent into exile. Inbabi was dismissed from his position and replaced by a senior scholar more loyal to the Egyptian king.

The idea that slavery as permitted in the Quran and the Islamic legal tradition was valid but only in certain conditions was one of the earliest responses to the moral challenge of slavery. We already saw it deployed by Muslim scholars in British India in the early 1800s. Though perhaps not the most influential among the Muslim laity, in my opinion this argument remains one of the most convincing as measured by the historical standards of the Islamic legal tradition. It runs as an important theme throughout Shafiq's treatise on slavery, appears in Bayram's work and it was taken up by the traditional Maliki scholar, historian and litterateur Ahmad Nasiri (d. 1897) in his multi-volume history of Morocco.

Nasiri addresses the question of slavery in the same context that Ahmad Baba and Jassus had: the illegal (in Islamic terms) enslavement of Black African Muslims. Nasiri made sure to reiterate the same points that had been stressed by those earlier scholars: whole ethnic groups of Black Africans had been pious Muslims for centuries, and the Shariah's presumption of freedom combined with the questionable conduct of slave traders meant that the buying and selling of Black 'slaves' was highly suspect. He echoes Baba in recommending that pious caution should lead Muslims to avoid purchasing slaves in such ambiguous circumstances. In fact, he argues, the Islamic legal principle of 'blocking the means' (*sadd al-dharāʾiʿ*), which held that otherwise permissible acts that most probably led to prohibited results should themselves be prohibited, should really foreclose any purchase of slaves at all. Nasiri adds a final point to drive home his argument: the justification for slavery as sanctioned by the Quran and practiced by the Prophet, namely dealing with prisoners taken in holy war aimed at 'elevating the word of God,' was absent (*mafqūd*) in modern times.[125]

This argument that Islam only allowed the enslavement of people when they were taken as prisoners in a just and legitimate war waged by a Muslim ruler was repeated numerous times by ʿAbduh's chief acolyte, Rashid Rida. As he explained, this argument came with an important corollary, which had earlier been articulated by another of Rida's teachers, the Lebanese traditionalist Shaykh Husayn Jisr (d. 1909): Islam had only ever allowed slavery because it was a military necessity given the conventions of warfare in the world into which the religion was born. More crucially, Rida continued, recent history had provided a second premise for the argument: religiously legitimate wars no longer existed, and many areas lacked legitimate Muslim rulers who could declare them to begin with.[126] As a result, enslavement was no longer permissible in any way. Later prolific Muslim jurists like the Egyptian Muhammad Abu Zahra (d. 1974) and the Syrian Wahba Zuhayli (d. 2015) as well as the Islamist intellectual Muḥammad Qutb (d. 2014, brother of Sayyid Qutb) disseminated the argument Rida had articulated in their influential publications.[127]

Rida also implied a second line of reasoning. Since enslaving one's defeated enemies was the norm in the seventh century, the Quran had allowed slavery because it was simply employing the same tactic that the Muslims' enemies used against them.[128] As Abu Zahra phrased it several decades later, Islam had allowed slavery as a 'law of reciprocity' (*al-muʿāmala bi'l-mithl*). If the enemies of Islam ceased taking Muslims as slaves, Muslims could forgo enslaving their foes as well.[129]

A third line of argument is similar but hinges less on the absence of the initial factor justifying slavery and more on its unfavorability as a policy. The germs of this approach came first in Sir Syed Ahmed Khan's English-language writings on slavery and were developed more fully by Bayram and Rida.[130] Since that time, it has been relied on by numerous conservative Muslim scholars addressing the question of slavery. It is based squarely in the Quranic verses on warfare. The holy book had given the Prophet four options to deal with prisoners captured in battle: 1) free them, 2) keep them as slaves, 3) ransom them back to their kin, or 4) execute them.[131] Executing prisoners was based on Quranic commands such as the warning that the Prophet should not take prisoners until he had greatly reduced the power of his enemy (Quran 8:67) and established reports that the Prophet had executed some leading figures among those captured after the conquest of Mecca.[132] Enslaving prisoners, ransoming them or simply freeing them were all justified by the Quran and the Sunna. The holy book commanded that, after defeating the enemy, 'make fast their bonds, and thereafter either grace or ransom until war lay down its burdens' (Quran 47:4). The Prophet took as slaves some folk from the defeated tribes of Hawazin (and ransomed others) and Banu Qurayza, and this practice was continued under his successors.[133]

The Islamic schools of law did not stray far from these scriptural indications, though from the time of the Companions onward there was a strong trend that considered executing prisoners to have been an allowance limited to the early, weak stages of the Prophet's community and to have been abrogated by Quran 47:4. The Shafi, Hanbali, Imami Shiite and Zaydi schools all allowed the Muslim authority to choose one of the four options based on what best serves the interests (*maṣlaḥa*) of the Muslims, provided that the soldiers agree that the choice means forgoing their compensation from the spoils of war. The Maliki school was even more flexible, allowing the ruler to free prisoners without any concern for who had rights to the spoils. The most restrictive school was the Hanafi. Its main position limited the Muslim ruler to executing the prisoners or keeping them either as slaves or as free subjects under Muslim rule. Allowing them to leave and fight another day, with or without ransom, was not permitted. Crucial to all schools of law, however, was that whatever policy was chosen, the choice lay in the hands of the Muslim political authority and should promote the best interest of Muslims.[134] Rida summarized this well in a 1910 article. *Riqq* originated with prisoners of war, and forgoing it was within the authority of the ruler. So Muslim rulers in the present day should prohibit slavery if they felt that was in Islam's best interests.[135]

What was in the best interest of Muslims in the modern period? In his 1891 booklet, Shafiq had noted that killing or enslaving captives taken in war was part of the laws of war in the world into which Islam came. But, Shafiq added, this was no longer the case. International laws and conventions now governed how prisoners of war were dealt with.[136] Rida picked up on the same note three decades later when he argued that slavery had been too deeply entrenched in Late Antique warfare and society to be banned outright by the Quran. Enslaving people had to be ended by international agreements in which the whole system was changed. This had occurred in the modern period, Rida added in 1922, and the Ottoman state (which had survived the First World War and would exist for another ten months) had now agreed to these international accords as well.[137] The late Syrian cleric Muhammad Sa'id Ramadan Buti (d. 2013) developed this point further in a 1969 book. He argued that the choice of how to deal with prisoners clearly placed legislation and policy around slavery within the discretion of the state, which selected the policy that best promoted the interest (*maṣlaḥa*) of the community in any particular context. In some circumstances, such as those in the twentieth century, Buti added, Muslim states might find themselves among other states signing accords or treaties on how to handle prisoners of war. In this case, Muslim states can follow such agreements.[138]

Completing his uncle's monumental commentary on *Sahih Muslim* over nearly two decades (it was finished in 1994), Mufti Taqi Usmani devoted several pages to the problem of slavery in which he ultimately followed in Rida's and Buti's footsteps while answering questions they had left unaddressed. Almost all states in the world, he wrote, had signed conventions banning the enslavement of prisoners of war. But did the Shariah allow Muslim rulers to sign on? Although Usmani acknowledged that this was a novel question in Islamic legal thought, he considered it permissible. *Riqq* was not required by the Shariah. It was permissible (*mubāḥ*) as one of the four options available to the Muslim state in dealing with prisoners. 'And it seems evident,' he added, 'from the rulings on the virtues of manumission and other such things that emancipating is more beloved to the Islamic Shariah.'[139] The well-known Egyptian scholar, long resident in Qatar, Yusuf Qaradawi affirms Usmani's conclusion. In his 2009 *Jurisprudence of Warfare* (*Fiqh al-jihād*), Qaradawi argues fervently that abiding by the international agreements and rules of warfare is clearly in the best interests of Muslims and Islam.[140]

This argument has been widely deployed in recent decades, especially by Muslim scholars from more conservative environments. Asked about the permissibility of slavery today in light of ISIS's crimes, the Saudi scholar 'Abd al-'Aziz Fawzan replied that the issue hinges on what the Muslim ruler (*imām*) decides to do with prisoners of war on the basis of pursuing the common good (*maṣlaḥa*). And, in this case, it is that there is no slavery today.[141] This argument is even more robust in the Imami Shiite tradition, which only allows offensive jihad to be declared by the Hidden Imam.[142]

Until his apocalyptic return, this leaves only the possibility of defensive jihad.

The Imami Shiite tradition features one element that I have not seen anywhere in Sunni responses to the challenge of slavery and abolition. In 1847, when the Qajar Shah began facing pressure from British representatives to curb or end the slave trade into Iran, he asked a number of leading Shiite clergy within his realm and in the shrine city of Najaf in southern Iraq if this would be permissible. While the Najafi scholars tended to reiterate that no ruler could prohibit what God and the Prophet had allowed, some of the Iranian clerics replied that, though slavery itself could not be banned, the slave trade could. Their main evidence for this was a Hadith of the Prophet well known in Shiite sources but non-existent in Sunni ones in which the Prophet states, 'The worst of people is the one who sells people.' This had generally been understood as meaning the sale of free people, which would match similar condemnations in Sunni Hadith collections.[143] But the unrestricted wording of this Hadith made it ideal for providing a Prophetic mandate for prohibiting the slave trade.

From the response of the Muslim ulama to the East India Company in 1808 to Ahmed Khan's writings in the 1870s, Bayram's *Proper Study*, ʿAbduh's 1882 letter and Shafiq's 1891 treatise onward, whichever approach Muslim clerics or intellectuals have taken to the question of slavery, they have almost always stressed that Islam restricted the pathways into slavery to one: capture by Muslim armies in war.[144] Combined with either the 'Today there are no legitimate wars or Muslim rulers who can declare them' or the 'Muslim political authorities have chosen that enslaving prisoners is not best' arguments, this would close off completely the flow of slaves.

There is a bait and switch in this war-based approach, however. Abu Zahra had proclaimed that Islam would welcome a time when slavery was prohibited.[145] But this is a reactive acceptance of abolition, not a proactive push for it. Committing not to enslave prisoners of war is not the same as abolishing slavery. Prisoners of war had been *one* source of slaves in Islamic civilization, but at least since the era of the early Islamic conquests they had not been the *main* source, namely purchase from non-Muslim slave traders inside or outside Muslim lands.[146] As Taqi al-Din Subki (d. 1355) wrote, it was absolutely permissible for a Muslim to buy a non-Muslim slave who had been enslaved in non-Muslim lands and then brought to Muslim lands by a dealer.[147] Historically, there were certainly restrictions on matters like buying children from their non-Muslim parents outside the Dar al-Islam.

But the pragmatic mainstream of Islamic legal thought generally presumed that goods being sold in such settings were legitimate and deferred to practices of enslavement among non-Muslims communities. As a result, Muslim jurists tended to assume that a slave being offered to a Muslim merchant in a city like Bulgar or the Sahel could be legitimately purchased.[148] And even ʿAbduh admitted that, along with capture in jihad, being born of slave parents was a second source of slavery in Islam.[149] Muslim rulers deciding not to enslave prisoners of war would only mean an end to slavery if other countries had already eliminated the global slave trade and if all existing slaves were emancipated. Writing four years after the landmark 1926 convention on ending slavery and the slave trade, Rida still had to acknowledge that, even with no legitimate wars or prisoners to enslave, there might still be inherited slaves in some Muslim societies.[150]

SLAVERY: A MOOT POINT & BAD PR

If Muslim rulers could sign treaties on the treatment of prisoners of war and restrict the slave trade due to abuses, could they move on to banning slavery itself? This had been the core of Ahmad Bey's edict, and both Bayram and Rida had proposed that, since *riqq* was not required in Islam, Muslim rulers should ban it if they felt this promoted the common good (*maṣlaḥa*).[151] If all schools of law agreed that rulers could determine how to deal with prisoners, how could any Muslim scholar object to a ruler issuing an administrative ban on *riqq*?

One crucial difference is that the ruler's discretion on the matter of prisoners is Quranically mandated. Any decision banning slavery, by contrast, could be (and, as we have seen, was) rejected by many Muslim scholars as trying to prohibit what God had allowed.[152] Restricting the permissible (*taqyīd al-mubāḥ*) requires there to be some common good promoted in doing so. If we held that emancipating slaves on as great a scale as possible was an aim of the Shariah, then this would present no obstacle at all – employing the state's right to restrict the permissible would be proactively advancing God's will.

Yet not all Muslim scholars have been convinced by the aim-of-the-Shariah argument. In part this is because the attainment of freedom only attracted attention as 'one of the most important aims of the Shariah,' as Ibn ʿAshur called it, around the dawn of the twentieth century. Emancipation had certainly always been encouraged in Islam. But this theme, often cited in recent times as evidence for a strong indigenous mandate for abolition in Islam, only rose to such prominence in response to European abolitionist pressure. The aim of freedom receives only minor mention, for example, in the *Muwafaqat* of Shatibi (d. 1388). This Andalusian scholar's work anchors the modern *Maqasidi* school of thought in Islamic law, which invokes the aims of the Shariah as a means to adapt Islamic law organically to modern needs. Shatibi divides the aims of the Shariah into three broad categories. Necessities (*ḍarūriyyāt*) are those essentials whose attainment is also one of Islam's ultimate objectives, such as the protection of life and property. Needs (*ḥājiyyāt*) are those things the Shariah intended so they can remove hardship in life and help maintain order in society, like commerce and transport. Finally, comforts (*taḥsīniyyāt*) are those things that are not essential for society or the functioning of the law but which bring ease. Shatibi only lists freeing slaves (*ʿitq*) in the comforts category (I will respond to this below).[153]

Some Muslim scholars are thus uncomfortable acknowledging any compelling moral good in abolishing slavery, perhaps because they see this as validating Western-based moral sentiments in the place of the Shariah, which never deemed slavery to be morally noxious. Such scholars tend to be either very conservative themselves or to be speaking in conservative settings, like Saudi Arabia. Yet they have still supported an administrative prohibition on slavery, justifying it not through any appeal to moral value but by citing the legitimacy of administrative fiat provided it is done so for some *maslaha* (common good). This *maslaha* need not be particularly inspiring. It might be no more than abstract judgment about promoting social good or preventing abuse, and at worst it could be a cynical calculation of political benefit. During the attempted genocide of Bosnian Muslims in the 1990s, students asked the influential Saudi scholar Ibn ʿUthaymin (d. 2001) if Muslim soldiers could take captured Serbian or Croatian women as slave-concubines. He answered that they could not, but not because slavery was prohibited or morally wrong. It was because of what were sure to be seriously negative political repercussions and the awful PR such conduct would create.[154]

This brings us to our last response to the moral challenge of slavery and abolition, the one that lies furthest away from our original core of moral conviction about the wrongness of slavery. It is a completely reactive recognition that slavery no longer exists as a legal reality in the world and thus that discussing its place in Islam is moot. This is how Muhammad

Abu Zahra responded to a questioner in the 1960s asking about the permissibility of slavery.[155] The former Grand Mufti of Egypt, Ali Gomaa, implies this when he writes that slavery is an example of the disappearance of the locus of a ruling (*dhahāb maḥall al-ḥukm*). Just as a person losing an arm renders the Shariah rulings on how they should wash their hand to prepare for prayer irrelevant, so also all questions regarding slavery are irrelevant in a world that has abolished it.[156] Similarly, the conservative Mauritanian shaykh Muhammad Hasan Dadaw answers a question from a TV host about charges that slavery still exists in his country by repeating that slavery had been outlawed by the government for decades.[157] And when the senior Saudi cleric Salih Fawzan was asked whether people can bring slaves into the Kingdom, he replied, 'We know of no legal slavery (*al-riqq al-shar'ī*),' and importing any slaves into the county would be forbidden because 'they banned (*mana'ū*) [slavery] a long time ago.'[158]

DEFENDING SLAVERY IN ISLAM

More than any other, the theme that has unified Muslim writings on slavery since the nineteenth century has been the claim that slavery as ordained by the Shariah is far more humane and conscientious than that practiced in other civilizations, especially in the Americas. These notes are by now familiar: Islam greatly restricted the sources of slavery, strongly encouraged manumission and granted slaves so many rights and protections that calling them 'slaves' as the word is understood in the West is misleading.[159]

This basic defense was the foundation of arguments even from Muslims who believed that the Quran actually ended slavery or that God intended Muslims to do so as soon as it was feasible. Ahmed Khan meditated at length in his English-language writings on the mildness of the Prophet's slavery, 'if slavery it can be called at all.'[160] 'The truth is that the institution of slavery is a mere name in Islam,' wrote Muhammad Iqbal (d. 1938), a later luminary of Islamic thought in South Asia.[161]

Beyond just providing the first stages of a response, highlighting the humaneness of *riqq* has constituted near the totality of the arguments made by Muslim scholars who unapologetically defend *riqq*, such as Rida's teacher Husayn Jisr, the Egyptian statesman and historian 'Ali Pasha Mubarak (d. 1893), the Ottoman judge Yusuf Nabhani (d. 1932), and later Qaradawi and

Usmani.[162] Those who criticized Islam for not ending slavery, Usmani wrote, did not realize that it had removed slavery's essence (*ḥaqīqat*).[163]

One of the most unapologetic defenses of *riqq*, even in the late twentieth century, comes from the conservative Salafi scholar Muhammad Nasir al-Din Albani (d. 1999). Asked if Islam had intended slavery to be eliminated over time, Albani replies by asking where anyone could have got that idea. Quite the opposite, he explains, the Shariah has given Muslims 'rulings valid until the end of time that assume slavery,' such as the Quranic commands that those who break oaths or commit manslaughter free a slave as expiation. Asked about joining in with multilateral conventions against slavery such as those sponsored by the UN, Albani scoffs. All these Muslim rulers who hardly follow their own religion, he muses, but they all want to follow the UN! At any rate, he asks, why should Muslims follow unbelievers? Their legacy of slavery is the opposite of Islam's. Through slavery non-Muslims sought 'insolence and corruption in the land,' he claims, 'while Muslims aim at the opposite of that.' The Shariah seeks the best interest of slaves in this life and the next, as is clear from the Prophet's precedent and the rulings of the Sacred Law. As for the deep pangs of conscience that modern Muslims feel about *riqq* in the Shariah, Albani laments that 'Western thought armies had attacked the minds of Muslims and, at the very least, weakened their faith in some of their laws.'[164]

The most vociferous defense of slavery in Islam, however, is certainly that offered by the South Asian Islamist intellectual and founder of the influential Jamaat-e Islami movement, Abul A'la Maududi (d. 1979). Addressing the question of women's dress and seclusion (*purda*) in Islam in a 1935 book, Maududi frames the issue within the power dynamic between Western colonizers and the colonized Muslim mind. In the nineteenth century Muslims had become mentally enslaved to the colonial West, adopting its norms and modes of living. They then dutifully found fault with and decried whatever aspects of Islam and Islamic tradition their Western masters disliked, from jihad to slavery. No doubt with figures like Sir Syed Ahmed Khan in mind, Maududi lambasted those Muslims who, upon being told that slavery was morally wrong, denied that it had ever had any valid place in Islam. Those who criticized slavery in Islam failed to realize that, like polygamy and other aspects of the Shariah, it had to be looked at as part of a larger system.[165] Presumably Maududi meant that within the Shariah system slavery was humane and actually aimed at benefiting the slave, as he wrote in a much later work on Islam and human rights. And benefit they did, he added. Many of those enslaved in Islamic civilization later went on to become leading scholars and even rulers.[166]

In this later work, written in 1977, Maududi touched on the same themes we have seen in almost all modern Muslim discussions of slavery: that masters had to treat their slaves kindly, that manumission was strongly encouraged and that enslavement could only befall non-Muslim prisoners captured in jihad. The aged Maududi's views on slavery seemed to have softened, however. Though he never approached more radical modernists like Khan, he turned his very capable mind to exploring new avenues in responding to the slavery challenge. He proposes that those prisoners taken in jihad were only meant to be kept as slaves if their governments or families did not ransom them back. He suggests that this Islamic rule actually anticipated the nineteenth and twentieth-century conventions on dealing with prisoners of war, which Maududi accurately points out were not followed in any way by states like the Soviet Union in its treatment of prisoners taken during the Second World War.

Maududi also introduces the novel idea that the Prophet's numerous warnings against Muslims enslaving free people were never technically restricted by the qualifier that those free people be Muslim, as had been understood by the ulama. By this argument, that prohibition which had so moved scholars like Ahmad Baba could in theory be applied to the free followers of any religion.[167] Forbidding enslaving any free person would accomplish what earlier writers like Shafiq, Rida and Muhammad Qutb had been aiming at, namely delegitimizing the type of Muslim slave raiding in Africa that so outraged Europeans and that continues to flare up from time to time even today.[168]

We've seen that intellectuals like Shafiq, ʿAbduh and Kamara acknowledged the West's immense moral accomplishment in leading the struggle for abolition. But some Muslim thinkers combine a defense of *riqq* with what they see as revealing the superficiality or cynicism of the West's abolitionist triumph. ʿAbdallah Nasih ʿUlwan (d. 1987) was a Syrian Muslim scholar and activist who had strong links to the Muslim Brotherhood and eventually taught at mosques and secondary schools in Aleppo. In his book *The System of Slavery in Islam*, he offered the standard evidence for the humaneness and morality of *riqq*. But he also devoted a chapter to the continued presence of exploitative labor and racial oppression around the globe, including in Western countries. Slavery, he concludes, had been abolished in name alone.[169] Muhammad Qutb, a leading intellectual in Arab Islamist circles after his brother Sayyid's execution, came to the same conclusion in his popular book *Matters of Confusion about Islam*. 'Let us not be deceived by names,' he urges. Islam was forthright, he explains. It acknowledged *riqq* and regulated it. The West, however, exploits labor while claiming to have liberated it.[170]

ʿUlwan's and Muhammad Qutb's observations overreach at times. Apartheid was morally repugnant and oppressive, but it was not slavery by another name. Yet they presciently align with New Abolitionism and the crusade against Modern Slavery. Like some New Abolitionists, these Islamists raise the question of whether the climate of moral triumph and self-congratulation that followed the erasure of legal slavery can function to distract us from and conceal persistent forms of serious exploitation.

The Iranian cleric ʿAllama Tabataba'i (d. 1981), one of the leading lights of Shiite scholarship in the twentieth century, makes a more forceful point. He judges Western criticism of slavery in Muslim lands to be at best hypocritical and at worst a scheme to justify colonialism. For him, it is plainly an error to conflate what he deems the humane institution of *riqq* with Western slavery. It is even worse, he argues, for the West to direct the world's moral outrage toward Muslim slavery while massacring and displacing countless thousands from Algeria to India. 'The decision of abolition,' Tabataba'i concludes, 'was nothing but a political game.'[171]

Where do the responses we've traced leave Muslims today? What does 'Islam say' about slavery now? Are there areas of consensus about the illegality of slavery and its moral repugnance? If so, how do we explain the arguments used by ISIS for its revival. It is to these questions that we turn next.

6

The Prophet & ISIS: Evaluating Muslim Abolition

> With Major Lawrence, mercy is a passion. With me, it is merely good manners. You may judge which motive is the more reliable.
>
> Prince Faisal, *Lawrence of Arabia* (1962)

DO MUSLIM APPROACHES TO ABOLITION PASS MORAL MUSTER?

In the previous chapter we traced Muslim responses to the challenge of slavery throughout the encounter with the West from the early nineteenth century to the present day. They fall along a moral spectrum, from a deep moral outrage at the idea that slavery could even be associated with Islam to indifference and, of course, to a defense of *riqq* as humane and morally innocuous.

Are any of these responses correct or convincing? The answer depends on our moral and epistemological worldview. One answer would be that a successful Muslim response to the challenge of slavery and abolition would be one that employs the tools and methods of Islam's pre-modern intellectual tradition without twisting them into internal incoherence or selectively manipulating them. This is, I suppose, the dream of academics.

A more realistic answer would be that Muslim responses to the challenge of slavery work or don't work depending on whether they give the audience what it needs. In the case of Islamic thought in the modern world in general, and with painfully controversial questions like slavery in particular, the 'success' of a Muslim argument is often judged by whether it meets one of two pre-selected ideological litmus tests. Those who believe religion should be reformed to some extent or another to meet modern (read Western?) expectations are only satisfied by a Muslim argument that does this. By contrast, those who feel that modernity or globalized Western culture are hegemonies to be fought or temptations to be resisted are unlikely to approve of an answer that even unintentionally placates those hegemonies.

These two camps clash over issues from women's rights to the acceptable use of violence. But those are issues contested even in Western societies and among non-Muslims. The belief that slavery is an absolute moral barbarism, on the other hand, seems nearly ubiquitous, at least in the global public square. As a result, only the most conservative Muslim scholars, by which I mean those who consciously resist rooting their moral worldview in anything other than the pre-modern Islamic tradition, offer any resistance to the idea that, somehow, Islam embraces abolition.

In my own experience from traveling widely and discussing this issue, lay Muslims generally draw on the stock answers that *riqq* was mild and humane or that Islam sought to end slavery. Pushing a conversation further often leaves people tense or upset. Many are shocked and confused when they hear that the Prophet had a slave-concubine. The film *Bilal* is not unusual; Islamic Sunday schools in the West often teach young Muslims that Islam ended slavery. Only the most conservative Muslims, whether laity or scholars, unapologetically accept that Islam allowed slavery without adding that the faith envisioned its eventual abolition.[1]

But this moral discomfort is a recent development. Even in the anti-slavery strain we find in the Hadiths and early Islamic history, slavery is problematic because of the *theological* tension it causes (how can a human 'slave of God' be a lord or slave of another human?), not because of moral or humanitarian reasons. The emancipatory arc running through figures like Ahmad Baba and ʿAbd al-Qadir Kan rages against the enslavement of Muslims, not against slavery itself.

Moral revulsion over slavery *qua* slavery seems only to have arisen in Muslim societies after prolonged and intensive exposure to European abolitionism. It is no surprise that it first seems to have appeared in Muslim discourse in British India, where Muslims had longest been under British rule and where Muslim jurists (maulavis, or law officers) had been serving side by side with British judges in Shariah courts as early as 1769. One such official, ʿAbd al-Qadir Khani, praised British efforts to stamp out the 'evil custom (*rasm-i bad*)' of slavery in India as far back as the 1820s.[2] We have already seen Sir Syed Ahmed Khan's revulsion at slavery. But Sir Syed received a knighthood from his colonial empress. And his contemporary anglophone Indian author Syed Ameer Ali, who described slavery as bearing 'from its outset the curse of inherent injustice,' received an English legal education, served in the highest ranks of Britain's colonial judiciary in India and eventually retired in England.[3] For all their considerable merits, these two men personified the absorption of modern Western sensibilities.

In the Ottoman realm, Toledano has shown that, when British diplomats first approached Ottoman statesmen about the moral necessity of ending the slave trade in 1840, the initial reactions were bemusement or dismissal. Indeed, from Algeria to Bukhara to Zanzibar, some of the earliest Muslim responses to European criticism of *riqq* were that European workers and peasants still suffered degradations that made *riqq* look appealing and disgust at how European men fathered children with servants or slaves and then denied paternity.[4] As the British ambassador to Istanbul wrote in his report after broaching the issue, the Turks 'are far from thinking our wisdom or our morality greater than their own.' Toledano convincingly argues that, for many in the Ottoman political and cultural elite, there was sincere incomprehension over why Europeans conflated the elite, urban slavery of Ottoman metropolises with the horrors of American plantations. But these privileged Ottomans were ignoring the brutality of the slave trade that supplied Istanbul. By the 1870s and 1880s reform-minded Ottoman administrators like Midhat Pasha (d. 1884) and the governor of Jeddah were decrying the cruelties of the slave trade from North Africa and the Red Sea. But these elite critics did not touch on slavery itself. Meanwhile, Ottoman playwrights and novelists – pioneers in new genres outside the traditional elite – began expressing the conflict they felt over the cruelties often involved in an institution that both permeated Ottoman society and drew its legitimacy from Islam.[5] Also after the 1870s, in Qajar Persia the network of constitutionalist reformists like Malkum Khan (d. 1908) also began decrying slavery because it violated what they saw as the universal rights that would undergird the constitutional regime which they were advocating.[6] It was these reformist networks that produced and consumed the Islamic arguments for abolition. But their objections were phrased as decrials of the abuse of *riqq* or the slave trade, not as condemnations of slavery itself.

Since Muslim discourse around the moral problem of slavery *qua* slavery unfolded in conversation with European powers and often under their direct or indirect control, it is not always easy to know if the sentiments expressed were sincere or merely efforts to curry favor. The Ottoman sultan Abdul Majid's (d. 1861) confession to a British diplomat in 1851 that 'It is shameful and barbarous practice for rational beings to buy and sell their fellow creatures' might be an example of an early convert to the anti-slavery cause. But it is far from clear that he was being sincere.[7] When Blunt wrote in 1882 that in Egypt's reformist circles it is 'a first principle' that slavery is morally repugnant (kabahat, [i.e., *qabāḥa*]) and needs to be abolished globally, we cannot know if he was accurately reporting the genuine sentiments of people like ʿAbduh.[8] Discussions around slavery were and remain riddled with ambiguities. Were these Egyptians speaking about the slave trade, all kinds of slavery, slavery in the Americas, *riqq* when it failed to meet the standards of the Shariah or *riqq* per se?[9]

How do the various Muslim responses to the problem of slavery fare when measured against the modern axioms of the Slavery Conundrum, 1) that slavery is an intrinsic and gross moral evil, and 2) that 'all slavery is slavery'? In answering this, we'll proceed from the most morally committed position to the least. In the case of the axiom that 'all slavery is slavery,' no mainstream Muslim response would pass the test. With the exception of avowedly Progressive Muslim intellectuals writing in recent years, all Muslim responses to the moral problem of slavery have included the element of explaining that slavery in the Quran and the Prophet's life or in Islamic civilization was in theory, and even in general practice, milder and less morally problematic than plantation slavery in the Americas. This tack is even taken by the few scholars, like Sir Syed Ahmed Khan, who argued that the Quran actually prohibited slavery and that Islam deemed it to be evil and contrary to the laws of nature.

Moving to the axiom that slavery is a gross and intrinsic moral evil, the position that the Quran actually did prohibit slavery is the most adamant expression that slavery is a profound moral wrong that God could not command. Of course, like the various abolitionist Christian attempts to square the intrinsic moral evil of slavery with scripture that at least at some point allowed it, this approach leaves telltale loose ends. Even Syed Ahmed Khan acknowledges that the Quran condoned the *existing* slave relationships in the Prophet's community. If slavery is a gross and intrinsic moral wrong that God could never affirm, how could He expressly allow even those relationships that already existed to continue?

The approach that holds that God wanted to end slavery with the revelation of the Quran, but it was too entrenched in a wider social and economic system to do so without causing prohibitive resentment or harm, should be familiar to us. It raises the same question as abolitionist Christian claims that Jesus had wanted to abolish slavery but couldn't. Viewed from within

Christianity and Islam, neither Jesus nor the revelation of the Quran were particularly non-confrontational. Jesus overturned the tables of the money-lenders in the Temple for turning his Father's house into 'a den of thieves' (Matthew 21:12–13). The Prophet Muhammad smashed the idols around the Kaaba and had those in neighboring cultic sites destroyed. If Islam prohibited alcohol, put an uncompromising end to idolatry and extirpated polytheism from Arabia during the time of the Prophet, why could it not have put an end to slavery as well? Rida responded to this question by arguing that slavery was far more tightly woven into human societies than these other ills; it would never have been abandoned simply because Islam prohibited it.[10] But even if this were the case, why did God or the Prophet not simply explain to Muslims in no uncertain terms that slavery was morally wrong and should be ended as soon as possible?[11]

The answer to this comes with the response that what Islam brought was not a clear condemnation of slavery but, rather, a consistent and gradual push toward emancipation. In other words, that emancipating slaves was always an aim of the Shariah and that abolishing slavery thus constitutes its laudable culmination. But, again, if slavery is a gross and intrinsic wrong, how could God *ever* have condoned it, even temporarily? And why did God and the Prophet not make it *explicitly* clear that Islam called for eliminating slavery as an institution? Neither the response that God wanted to end slavery but couldn't, nor that doing so was an eventual aim of His religion, can explain why God condoned and at times commanded a gross, intrinsic evil without condemning it as such.

The abolition-as-aim-of-the-Shariah response has been so appealing because it has allowed relatively conservative ulama like Ibn ʿAshur to embrace European-led abolition as the fulfillment of an authentically Islamic aim without condemning the Quran, the Prophet or the thirteen centuries of Islamic thought and practice that followed. But because this response sees ending slavery as morally laudable rather than morally necessary, it fails the test of condemning slavery as a gross and intrinsic moral evil in all times and places.

The Progressive Muslim responses to the challenge of slavery suffer from a similar problem. Because they are built on a model of moral progress, they can only offer justifications for Muslims embracing a *new* understanding of their religion based on changing circumstances or changed morality. They cannot explain how something absolutely evil could have been endorsed by God *in the past*. The only way around this is the route eventually taken by liberal Christianity, namely to eventually conclude that one's scripture was never the flawless vessel of divine guidance that had been previously thought. In Islam, however, this leaves one outside the fold of the religion.

One attempt to compensate for this has been to argue from within the language of the Shariah that Islam's acceptance of slavery never amounted to moral approval. This was pioneered by Rida when he wrote that, far from being required or even recommended in and of itself (*li-dhātihi*), slavery in Islam was only allowed out of necessity (*ḍarūra*) because of how widespread it was at the time of Islam's coming.[12] Two consummate modern ulama, Abu Zahra and later Zuhayli, rephrased and advanced this claim. Abu Zahra claimed that *riqq* was the most hated thing to God and the Prophet and asserted that there was no clear text in the Quran stating its permissibility (*ibāḥa*). Zuhayli seconded him, adding that neither was there any clear text from the Prophet's Sunna.[13]

As suggested by his prominence in the previous chapter, Rida was a giant of modern Islamic thought and activism. But his activist agenda sometimes led him to misrepresent evidence from the Islamic heritage and at times even to manipulate it disingenuously.[14] Abu Zahra and Zuhayli, on the other hand, were both pillars of rigorous scholarship. Yet what all three were arguing here does not differ much from Sir Syed Ahmed's more radical claims. By stating that there is no explicit evidence that God or the Prophet *permitted* slavery but instead that it was indulged without choice out of complete necessity, these three orthodox Sunni ulama were essentially proposing that Islam never actually allowed slavery, at least not *morally*.

Though much less provocative than Sir Syed Ahmed's strident writings, this assertion nevertheless met resistance. Zuhayli's prominent Syrian peer, Buti, stated frankly that it was nonsense. The Quran's repeated commands that Muslims manumit slaves either as expiation for sins or as good deeds, and the countless Hadiths to the same effect, are nothing if not evidence that owning slaves was legitimate (*mashrūʿ*) according to the Shariah.[15] Mufti Taqi Usmani offers a comprehensive response to the claim of Khan and other South Asian Islamic modernists that any condoning of slavery in the Quran was abrogated (*mansūkh*) by the verse that Khan calls the Verse of Freedom (47:4), which states that prisoners of war should either be ransomed or released. All evidence, Usmani argues, suggests that verses mentioning 'those whom you possess rightfully (*mā malakat aymānukum*)' like Quran 4:24 and 33:50 were revealed *after* the Verse of Freedom. They could not have been replaced by its ruling. Along with the manifest practice of slavery by the Prophet, the precedent of the early Muslim community, and in the entirety of the Shariah since then, this leaves no doubt that slavery *was* permitted in Islam.[16]

But is Buti's and Usmani's argument really iron-clad? As some ingenious modern Christian theologians have proposed in the case of what has always been seen as Paul's condoning slavery in the Bible, perhaps advice and regulations regarding slavery were never an endorsement. Perhaps these were just instructions on how to deal piously with an immoral reality.[17] Perhaps the Quran's and the Prophet's innumerable commands to manumit slaves and care for them were similarly no more than instructions on how to live as ethically as possible in a world in which slavery was an omnipresent reality. What this means is that, even if slavery was long accepted in the Shariah, slavery was nonetheless *always* morally wrong.

Reflecting on this question, the analogy of warfare and violence seems apt. The Quran at times allowed and at times commanded violence, while condemning its excesses and recognizing that it is often the hated and unpalatable alternative to strife, injustice and dishonoring God (Quran 2:190–93, 217; 22:39–40). But the violence that the Quran permitted and commanded was clearly morally acceptable to God. *Riqq* seems comparable. *Riqq* was not unqualified slavery. It was slavery as restricted and conditioned by the Quran and Sunna. *Riqq* may well have been an inescapable reality, and violating its rules was a dire transgression, but how does one argue that *riqq* done properly was not morally acceptable to God? Moreover, rules that the Quran and the Prophet laid down for *riqq* in the burgeoning Muslim polity of Medina were not the epistles or the subversive sermons of the powerless, as were the writings of the New Testament. Islam came to end the Age of Ignorance, and even in the Prophet's own lifetime its temporal success was manifest.

But let us return to the familiar question: if slavery is a gross and intrinsic moral evil, how could God have allowed it and condoned His servants engaging in it even if it was a fact of life? This presents us with a profound choice. Buti, Usmani, and indeed almost the entirety of the Islamic interpretive tradition have all understood Islam's founding scriptures as deeming slavery permissible – and thus at least morally passable – provided it met certain ethical standards. Khan, Rida, etc., meanwhile, claimed that slavery was always morally wrong in God's eyes, and His scriptures only tolerated slavery as long as it was materially inescapable.

Which position is correct? Deciding means choosing between two fundamentally different readings of Islamic scripture and law. In my opinion, to do so we must look at the epistemological and moral commitments guiding our selection. The overwhelming majority of scriptural evidence and interpretation in the Islamic tradition favors the Quran permitting slavery. There is no Muslim voice prior to the nineteenth century stating that *riqq qua riqq* is morally wrong. The choice that slavery was never morally permitted, by contrast, lacks any significant support from the pre-modern Islamic tradition. Moreover, its main force comes from the abolitionist impulse that originated not only outside of Islam but also outside of humanity's longstanding moral traditions, in the relatively recent economic and technological revolutions brought by industrialization and capitalism. Even the notion that advancing freedom was an aim of the Shariah, though certainly part of Islam from the beginning, was not considered a *major* aim of Shariah prior to the modern period. More importantly, it never led anyone to call the morality of *riqq* into question.

In other words, the assertion that Islam always deemed slavery a moral wrong and only tolerated it when it was unavoidable originates in the modern sentiment that slavery is an intrinsic evil, and this sentiment in turn provides that assertion's only significant support. But I am writing this book because it is precisely this modern belief in slavery's intrinsic evil that Islam's scriptural endorsement of *riqq* challenges. So does a Muslim's moral framework come from the morality produced by the emergence of the modern West or from Islam's own pre-modern scriptural tradition?

The writings of Fazlur Rahman afford an excellent example of this choice and force us to examine our assumptions. Responding to conservative ulama who were arguing that slavery should not be abolished because it would deprive Muslims of the chance to perform the immense good deed of freeing slaves, Rahman's reaction is understandable. He excoriates this position, stating that '[this] sort of reasoning that would retain slavery is, of course, seldom employed by any intelligent and morally sensitive Muslim.'[18] For Rahman, it is simply inconceivable that Muslims could choose such a minor advantage over eliminating an obvious moral evil that the Quran clearly had long ago set them on a trajectory to abolish. I imagine few modern readers would disagree.

Rahman's dismissal of his opponents' argument, however, reveals how conditioned his stance is by modern priorities, which view ameliorating worldly conditions like slavery as far more important than securing salvation in the afterlife. His reasoning would have been foreign to his own predecessors in Muslim scholarly circles just a century earlier. In 1709 Shaykh Jassus had written that one of the reasons against enslaving free Muslims was that it 'closed the door of manumission,' since manumitting someone who was never legally a slave had no basis and brought no divine reward.[19] This was not said in jest, and we can hardly accuse Jassus of stupidity or moral obtuseness. He wrote this in the fatwa that sealed his death warrant and led to his family's worldly ruin. Here then was at least one learned Muslim scholar who would have seen some real moral and spiritual benefit in retaining *legal* slavery in the Shariah. Why are his moral sentiments worth less than Rahman's in our estimation? It is only the hegemony of modern values that determines this (values that, at present, grant all humans the right to freedom but not our nearest relatives). And it is precisely the question of whether those modern values should overrule the values and laws embedded in scriptural traditions that lies at the root of the crisis addressed in this book.

Returning to evaluating the Muslim responses against the criteria of the Slavery Conundrum, our last group of responses held that slavery was allowed in Islam, but only if 1) it was done properly, 2) if the conditions under which it was allowed still applied, or 3) if Muslim states deemed it in the best interest of the Muslim community. The glaring problem with all these answers is that they do not provide any moral condemnation of slavery per se. According to them, slavery is not morally wrong in all times and places. It is only wrong if it's done badly, in inappropriate circumstances or if it happens to clash with communal interests as determined by a Muslim government. This raises a final, alarming question: if slavery is acceptable in certain circumstances, could it be allowable under the Shariah at some point in the future?

A CONSENSUS ON ABOLITION

In the last two decades a novel approach to the challenge of slavery has also appeared: that there is a consensus (*ijmāʿ*) of Muslim scholars that slavery is no longer permitted. Interestingly, the earliest instance I have found of this claim comes from an African American Muslim scholar of American law, Bernard Freamon. In a 1998 article, Freamon points to over a century of accumulated pro-emancipation Muslim opinion and suggests that 'there is now a consensus among Muslim jurists, and indeed among the *'ulamā'*, that slavery is *ḥarām* (forbidden).'[20] This argument has been repeated frequently in recent years, especially since the rise of ISIS.

And a powerful argument it seems to be. In fact, consensus is the ultimate proof in the Sunni intellectual tradition. Unlike the scriptures of the Quran and the Hadith, which are read and yield interpretations, consensus locks one particular interpretation into authoritative place. When Qadi Abu Yusuf (d. 798), one of the founding figures of the Hanafi school and the first chief judge the Abbasid Caliphate, lay gravely ill, it is reported that he recanted every opinion he had ever held except 'what was in the Book of God and what the Muslims had come to consensus on.'[21] Consensus is, as a saying in the Azhar Mosque has it, 'The firm pillar on which the religion rests.'

But as with many powerful tools, *ijma'* has very often been wielded irresponsibly. It is such an authoritative seal that since the early period of Islam Muslim scholars have been tempted to claim it even when it clearly does not exist. Hence the formative early scholar Shafi'i (d. 820) and his student Ibn Hanbal (d. 855) both expressed deep skepticism not about the authority of *ijma'* or its validity but, rather, about how frequently and falsely it was being invoked. It could only realistically be claimed, pointed out Shafi'i and numerous scholars since his time, on basic points of law and dogma, such as the five daily prayers and the finality of Muhammad's prophethood, on which all Muslim scholars actually did all agree.[22]

Does the claim of *ijma'* on the prohibition of slavery stand up? It is certainly true that slavery has been prohibited by the laws of all majority-Muslim countries. But this is a statement of legal fact, not of interpretive agreement. Moreover, 'slavery is illegal' is a statement of *administrative* legal fact. Saying there is a consensus that slavery is prohibited today is like saying 'All US states have speed limits on highways of between 60 and 85 mph.' This statement is accurate, but it has no necessary link to value or morality. 'All Muslim scholars agree that slavery is illegal' reflects the laws in their lands. It does not mean that 'slavery is *haram*' is a legitimate interpretation of the Quran, Sunna and Islam's legal tradition, let alone the sole valid one. Whether within government, as with Muhammad Bayram, or outside it, as in the case of 'Abd al-Rahman Kawakibi (d. 1902), many of the ulama who facilitated and approved of laws ending slavery in Muslim states did so because they believed this was within the purview of the executive authority to restrict the permissible. It was not necessarily because they believed that *riqq*, which God and the Prophet had allowed, was *haram* in God's eyes.

Some Muslim scholars have been careful in how they word claims of consensus. The Syrian scholar Muhammad Yaqoubi, employing the consensus argument in his rebuttal of ISIS, notes that all Muslim scholars have agreed on 'slavery's nullification (*ibṭālihi*) and its non-permissibility.'[23] The claim of consensus on the illegality of slavery, however, is generally phrased in the language of religious prohibition, not administrative proscription.[24] Bayram's *Proper Study on the Question of Slavery* was an effort to convince Muslims to obey government bans on the slave trade and slavery not with the cynical selectiveness with which they might heed speed limits but, rather, with religious conviction. It was obligatory, he writes, for all Muslims to obey these bans 'in secret and in the open, and to know that owning [a slave] is invalid (*fāsid*).' A Muslim ruler has the right to prohibit the permitted if it promotes some common good, and Muslims are required to obey their ruler. This is what the Shariah teaches, Bayram concludes, and 'disobeying the Sacred Law (*sharʿ*) is truly *haram*.'[25] But Bayram's argument is a house of cards in this regard. Its dimension of religious obligation rests on the religious obligation to obey the law of the land, not some profound moral teaching. Its religious component is no more moral than was Socrates' refusal to break the laws of Athens when offered the chance to escape the city and his unjust sentence.

If we did accept 'There is consensus that slavery is prohibited' as a statement of religious interpretation, would it hold water? From what we have seen, it does not seem likely. Muslim legal theorists have disagreed throughout the centuries over precisely what the requirements of *ijmaʿ* are – can there be dissenting voices, and if so, how many? – but there is little doubt that the disagreement of a number of major, widely and well-regarded ulama would undermine it. As we will see, leading contemporary scholars such as Buti, Qaradawi and Usmani do not consider *riqq* to be inherently wrong such that it should be branded *haram* under the Shariah. For them, *riqq* is a legitimate component of the Islamic legal and institutional heritage that was legitimately employed in the past and could well be used in the future.

COULD SLAVERY IN ISLAM EVER BE UNABOLISHED?

If modern discourse around slavery insists on morally condemning it rather than just prohibiting it, the reason why is clear. Laws, administrative restrictions and policies can all be dropped if priorities or public sentiment changes. It is felt that only by deeply rooting something in people's consciences and anchoring those moral commitments to something perceived as absolute can such fickleness be avoided. In the secularized West of the post-war era, this has been done through the gradual enshrinement of human rights, one of the most basic of which is the fundamental right not to be enslaved.

All countries, including all Muslim countries, have banned slavery. But what guarantee do our different Muslim responses offer that slavery could not be made legal again in the future? Two responses chart trajectories totally hostile to the reintroduction of legal slavery: that slavery was a moral wrong prohibited by the Quran, and that it was a moral wrong that God intended to be prohibited as soon as possible. None of the other responses, however, can offer the same commitment. This is because, unlike the prior responses, they are articulated from the historical mainstream of the Islamic legal tradition, which viewed *riqq* as morally acceptable and a valid tool of statecraft. They cannot condemn the past of the Shariah as morally errant. This endows these responses with a strong Islamic legitimacy. But it also prevents them from foreclosing out of hand any use of elements of that Shariah corpus in the future.

For example, those responses that tie an end to slavery to the disappearance of its supposed causes and justifications, namely legitimate jihad and the captives it yields, cannot promise that Muslims would not be allowed to enslave prisoners if such wars again appeared. Some more conservative ulama admit as much. In 1987–8 Saudi Arabia's Permanent Council for Academic Research and Fatwa (*al-Lajna al-Dā'ima li'l-Buḥūth al-ʿIlmiyya wa'l-Iftā'*) published that, if there were legitimate wars (*ḥurūb sharʿiyya*) today, then non-Muslim prisoners could be taken as slaves if the Muslim ruler judged it appropriate.[26] Although he does not explicitly address a reintroduction of slavery, Qaradawi defends engaging in *riqq* if it promotes the 'highest good (*al-maṣlaḥa al-ʿulyā*)' of the Muslim community.[27]

This question is dealt with in most depth by Buti, who was a respected Shafi jurist and scholar known for his ties to the Syrian government. Despite his establishment leanings, however, Buti sees the very unfashionability of the Shariah's rules on *riqq* as proof of Islamic law's suitability for all places and all times.[28] Though Muslim states may have legitimately judged that prohibiting slavery and signing international conventions against it best promote the interests of Islam and Muslims today, the situation could change. Muslims might one day find themselves fighting the same sort of wars they fought in the past, in which prisoners had to be dealt with by means other than those used today. In such cases, Muslims will be glad to have the tool of *riqq* available to them. Buti likens *riqq* to an emetic or poison that doctors use: they are not pleasant, but sometimes they are what works best.[29]

An insightful assessment of the aims-of-the-Shariah and the changing-context/*maslaha* approaches to the slavery question comes from the secular liberal Abdullahi An-Na'im. He offers what he feels is an admission: no response to the slavery challenge that presents itself as a continuity of the Shariah's historical tradition can ban slavery *permanently*. For him, the solution rests in realizing that the Shariah is not Islam. While the Shariah might not be able to absolutely condemn slavery, Islam's original ethos can. This can only be realized, An-Na'im proposes, by transcending the aims-of-the-Shariah line of thinking and realizing that cutting loose from the historical continuity of the Shariah and adopting the perspective of modern human rights discourse is what Islam and its legal tradition intended all along.[30]

ABOLITION VS. ISIS

With the dramatic and terrifying emergence of ISIS in 2014, the question of open, avowed slavery reappearing ceased to be academic. ISIS took slaves from the populations it conquered in Iraq and Syria, in particular from non-Muslim minority communities such as the Yazidis.[31] Global outrage flamed as news of this spread, in particular news of Yazidi women and girls being taken as slave-concubines.[32]

ISIS was utterly unapologetic. Not only were its leaders confident that they were acting according to the Shariah, but they also claimed that reinstituting slavery was part of restoring rule by God's law and promoting a more virtuous society than that in the West.[33] Muslim condemnation of ISIS as either completely misguided, heretical or even as having exited the fold of Islam has been so uniform that virtually the only Muslim scholars who support ISIS's acts work for ISIS. But Muslim scholars around the world were stunned by ISIS's revival of slavery. Many were left speechless.

The most comprehensive response came from Muhammad Yaqoubi. Writing in exile from Syria's civil war, he took up the question of *riqq*. Muslims scholars in the modern period had come to the consensus that enslavement was illegal, he pointed out, and Muslim states had signed treaties to this effect. No Muslim could violate these agreements unless their enemies did so first. Moreover, whatever the actual religious status of the Yazidis, Yaqoubi continued, Muslim states had treated them as a protected religious minority.[34] We find a section addressing ISIS enslavement in another response, the 'Open Letter to Baghdadi' written to ISIS's leader, which was organized anonymously by figures in the Jordanian royal court and then signed onto by over 125 Muslim scholars, preachers and organizations. 'One of Islam's aims, which no one among the ulama denies,' the letter argues, 'is extirpating slavery.' In addition, the entire world community and all Muslims have agreed that slavery is prohibited.[35]

In 2014, ISIS's newly formed Council of Research and Fatwa (*Dīwān al-Buḥūth wa'l-Iftā'*) published a short booklet explaining the rulings on enslaving prisoners of war and the proper treatment of slaves under the Shariah. The chief issue of contention that arises in the book is the question of whether one can have sex with female slaves if they come from religious communities other than Christians and Jews, such as Yazidis. Here ISIS breaks with what it admits is the vast majority position of Muslim scholars, namely that doing so is prohibited. But ISIS cites early scholars like the Successor Sa'id bin Musayyab (d. 713) and the prominent later scholars Ibn Taymiyya and Ibn Qayyim al-Jawziyya as allowing it based on a Hadith in which the Prophet allowed Muslim soldiers to have sex with female prisoners taken from the Hawazin tribe. This tribe was polytheist Arabs, the booklet states, and there is neither indication that those prisoners had converted to Islam after their capture nor had there been enough time for them to do so.[36]

What is remarkable is that ISIS's booklet does not respond to any of the very predictable Muslim arguments that slavery has been prohibited, which either had or would soon be directed at the group. In fact, the booklet takes the permissibility of slavery in Islam as axiomatic, stating that only some 'Modernist' Muslims deny it.[37] One could imagine that the reasoning of the ISIS scholars was fairly clear-cut. As Kecia Ali has pointed out, if enslaving prisoners was only allowed in legitimate jihad, then what could be more 'legitimate' than defending Sunni Muslim lands from the military aggression of Western unbelievers and polytheists (as ISIS labeled Shiite Muslims and the Iraqi government)? If the decision to enslave prisoners of war is the prerogative of a Muslim government, ISIS not only claimed to be a legitimate Islamic state, it claimed to be *the only* legitimate Islamic state, ruled by the new caliph of the Muslims.[38]

As for the argument that Muslim states had signed treaties and accords committing not to engage in slavery, these were meaningless to ISIS and the Jihadi-Salafi strain of modern Islamic movements from which ISIS emerged. Groups like Al-Qaeda and the main ideologues of Jihadi-Salafism, such as Abu Muhammad Maqdisi, had long argued that the entire nation-state world order is a Western regime that divides up the *umma* along meaningless lines. Supposedly Muslim rulers were mere stooges of this order, who did not carry out that most basic duty of a Muslim state: to implement the law of God.[39] So who cared about the treaties and conventions signed by the governments of other supposedly Muslim countries, agreed to as they were under Western coercion and justified by 'Modernist' or 'moderate' Muslim scholars? Addressed to an audience like ISIS, most of the criticisms launched by Yaqoubi and the 'Open Letter to Baghdadi' simply fall flat.

What is clear here is how much the various responses offered by Muslim scholars to the problem of slavery depend, on the one hand, on a regnant international legal and moral consensus on the repugnance of slavery, and on the other on the assumed legitimacy of Muslim governments existing within that international system. Intellectuals like Sir Syed Ahmed Khan were declared unbelievers in their own time by some mainstream Muslim scholars for their condemnation of *riqq*, and their arguments that the Quran actually prohibited slavery would appear worse than nonsense to ultra-radicals like ISIS.[40] The notion that God wanted to end slavery but could not do so right away, and the argument that doing so was always an aim of the Shariah similarly clearly depend on an abolitionist backdrop. They require a compelling and enveloping moral conviction that even *within Islam* slavery was always inherently bad and that the historical justifications Muslim scholars have offered for it are either less compelling or irrelevant. None of the other Muslim responses get off the ground without the assumption that the age of jihad has ended, and that it had been ended by legitimate Muslim authorities who can now choose how to deal with prisoners, sign treaties and ultimately legally restrict what had been allowed under the Shariah for well over a millennium.

Skeptics of Muslim responses to the moral challenge of slavery might point to the ISIS phenomenon and conclude that it confirms what Western scholars had been saying for over a century – that slavery is part of Islam's DNA – and that all the anti-slavery essays and treatises written by Muslim scholars and intellectuals amount to nothing more than a cosmetic cover-up of this reality.[41] In the end, those skeptics might say, ISIS can point to the Quran, the Prophet's precedent, and the undeniable consensus of centuries of Islamic scholarship to justify enslaving non-Muslims. Many such skeptics would argue that the only protection against an ISIS phenomenon reappearing is for Muslims to finally transcend the historical tradition of the Shariah and embrace a vision of morality and law grounded firmly and completely in human rights. Only by leaving behind the idea that anyone can acceptably enslave any other human being and affirming that immunity to enslavement is a fundamental right of all human beings can horrors such as ISIS be averted. As long as Muslims retain a substantial or even a romantic attachment to the Shariah, they will be too susceptible to relapsing into pre-modern barbarism.

This line of thinking is incorrect, in my opinion. It fails to recognize two flawed assumptions. And it overlooks two facts, one that non-Muslim audiences might understandably be unaware of, and the other so glaring and tragic that they should know it by now.

The first flawed assumption is that, because the push for the abolition of slavery as a global institution did not emerge indigenously in Muslim thought, Muslim condemnation of slavery since the late nineteenth century is somehow insincere. But worldwide Muslim horror at ISIS's revival of slavery was real. As Muslim scholars of slavery's legal and social history such as Ingrid Mattson, Bernard Freamon, Bilal Ware and Nathaniel Mathews have written, abolition has become as sincere a passion in many Muslim societies as it was in Western ones. As Mathews describes, the moral agenda of abolition, both in the 'Old Abolitionist' sense of ending formal slavery and the New Abolitionist struggle against contemporary modes of exploitative labor, have fused with the call for emancipation so evidently indigenous to the Quran and Shariah tradition.[42]

The second flawed assumption is that human rights inherently have some claim over people that is somehow more powerful than other value systems. Like all regimes of law, human rights are only theoretical unless they are committed to and upheld by states and societies.[43] Subscribing to a regime of human rights does not in any way guarantee against the re-emergence of practices like slavery or the rape of civilians by militias or armies. Human rights only have power if there is widespread commitment to upholding and enforcing them. For all the moral majesty seen emanating from the human rights halo, human rights discourse has only been an influential force in international conflicts and politics since the 1970s.[44] And even since then, basic human rights have been regularly and egregiously violated by states seen as the leading pillars of the liberal, human-rights and rules-based order. Moreover, recent years have seen populist leaders emerge in states previously thought to be confirmed members of that order who publicly mock human rights. The Philippines president, Rodrigo Duterte, for example, said in 2016 that he doesn't 'give a shit' about human rights.[45]

This is not to trivialize the international regime of human rights or to relativize it. I am merely stating two points. First, that the narrative that humanity has entered a new era in which a transcendent ideal of human rights has helped banish many barbaric abuses to the past ignores that those abuses often still occur, either in the same form as before or under thin legal disguise.[46] And, second, that it is not the notional existence of an international regime of human rights that protects us against abuses but, rather, a real and practical commitment to upholding that order. What matters is not the shape or form of a generally acceptable regime of law. What matters is a commitment to enforcing it. From this perspective, it does not matter whether we ban slavery through an appeal to human rights or through the agreement of Muslim nations to forgo *riqq*. Only the commitment to upholding these agreements matters. If that commitment fails, there is nothing stopping human rights abuses like a return of slavery from occurring unopposed.

The fact unknown to many in the West is that ISIS is not merely the latest or most successful iteration of Muslim violent extremist organizations. ISIS represents a departure in kind from the groups that came before it, such as Al-Qaeda. For all the great volume and amplitude of horror and outrage that ISIS has generated in the Western media, the enormity of the danger that ISIS presents has rarely been appreciated. ISIS did not just break with the political consensus among Muslim scholars and states that slavery was illegal. It did not just dismiss the political legitimacy of other Muslim states and the Muslim scholars whose opinions buttressed those states' policies. ISIS essentially denied the very existence of any Islamic right or argument outside of its own vision. It held that any Muslim who did not set out to move to the caliphate was guilty of ideological idolatry (*shirk*), since they had chosen nationalism over Islam.[47] All Muslim scholars who criticized or opposed ISIS's claim to legitimacy or the legality of its actions were deemed apostates (*murtaddūn*) whose blood was licit.[48] Shiite Muslims were polytheists (*mushrikūn*) and denied the very claim of ever having been Muslims and killed on the spot. The fact that even earlier states like the Ottoman Empire* had not only not enslaved Yazidis but freed them when they were wrongly taken means nothing to ISIS because it does not deem any other Muslim state to be truly Islamic.[49] Not only does ISIS declare its enemies to be unbelievers worthy of death, but an influential strain within the movement has warned that anyone who does not do this is themself an unbeliever worthy of death.[50]

Al-Qaeda is moderate in comparison.[51] Though its leaders have judged Muslim regimes from Saudi Arabia to Pakistan to be false claimants to the mantle of Islam, the group does not declare ulama who oppose it or support those regimes to be unbelievers. They are merely 'misguided' or stooges of tyrants.

The claim that ISIS has simply revealed that Islam's slaving DNA lies just beneath a civilized patina assumes that all the scholarly discussion we saw in the previous chapter and all the abolitionist policies enacted by Muslim states are nothing but part of a cosmetic cover-up.

But that confuses the grotesque and egregious exception with the rule. Not even Al-Qaeda revived slavery in those areas of Yemen or Afghanistan that it has at times controlled. Using the analogy of human rights and a rules-based world order, ISIS would not be a country that was openly skeptical about human rights or that engaged in human rights abuses. It would be a country that rejected that entire order so fundamentally that any state and anyone who upheld or defended it would lose all their rights, including the right to life. Albani might defend *riqq* unapologetically, but he steadfastly defended the political legitimacy of even the most impious Muslim rulers and the treaties they signed as well as the faith of those scholars who supported them.[52] Shaykh Muhammad Hasan Dadaw is one of the most outspoken critics of the Gulf Arab autocracies and their pro-Western policies, and he would never concede that *riqq* as outlined in the Shariah was morally wrong. Yet he unflinchingly stands by the decision of the

* It is important to note that the Ottoman state also engaged in occasional campaigns of violent persecution against the Yazidi community, as in 1892; Emanuela C. Del Re, 'The Yazidi and the Islamic State,' 275–77.

government of his native Mauritania to ban slavery and calls on those who continue to practice it to cease. Some Mauritanian scholars, like the late Hasan Wald Binyamin (d. 2017), have called the ban on slavery illegal. But they do not condemn the Mauritanian state as illegitimate.[53]

In short, the emergence of a polity that completely rejected all received Muslim scholarly opinion, even the basic rights and obligations of other states, is just as far-fetched and jarring as the emergence of a polity that completely dismissed the entire notion of human rights. ISIS is horrifically outrageous, and its revival of slavery is shocking. But its crimes are not specifically 'Islamic.' ISIS cast off all the norms and agreements of Muslim states and societies. This is comparable to a non-Muslim polity dismissing human rights and reviving slavery. That the former actually occurred in the case of ISIS while the latter seems inconceivable is due to the second, and final, glaring fact.

This fact pertains more to the emergence of ISIS than it does directly to slavery, but considering it is nonetheless crucial. In the wake of ISIS's debut on Western TV screens, there was extended debate in the Western media about whether 'ISIS was truly Islamic or not.' In other words, was ISIS the true face of Islam finally showing itself? What these discussions consistently omitted was that the proximate cause of ISIS in Iraq was not the presence of Islam, which had first come to Iraq in the 630s CE. It was the 2003 US-led invasion of Iraq, which utterly destroyed that country's government, institutions, infrastructure and economy and led to the emergence of the Jamaʿat al-Tawhid wa'l-Jihad, ISIS's forerunner. Prior to the 2003 invasion, there was no Sunni Jihadi activity in the Iraq of Saddam Hussein. And the cost of the invasion has been chilling. At the low end of estimates, in 2013 the NGO Iraq Body Count reported that there had been 122,000 Iraqi civilians killed in violence since 2003.[54] A higher estimate from 2015, by Physicians for Social Responsibility, was that around one million Iraqis had died since the invasion.[55] A more recent (2018) study by The Watson Institute at Brown University has tallied between 182,000 and 205,000 direct civilian deaths.[56]

To convey a sense of how debilitating such trauma has been for Iraqis, if the United States had undergone bloodshed at that scale, the result would be between one million and 8.3 million dead American civilians. If the murder of around three thousand American civilians on 9/11 caused a national trauma that led to an upheaval in American conceptions of law and civil liberties, not to mention the bloody and ongoing 'War on Terror,' what would have happened to Americans' love of peace, freedom and justice if a conflict had left millions of their number dead? With this in mind, skeptics should consider that the revival of slavery in Iraq under ISIS was not the result of Islam's supposed latent slavery DNA. Along with numerous other brutalities, it occurred because Iraq had been completely destroyed as a polity and community and subjected to a level of violence, disruption and civilian death that is literally impossible for people in the West to imagine.

THIS AUTHOR'S OPINION

In one Hadith, the Prophet tells how Gabriel came to him and admonished him about caring for slaves, 'until I thought that he would set a period of time that, when they reached it, they would all be freed.'[57] It is manifestly clear that emancipating as many slaves as possible was always an aim of the Shariah. The Quran introduced to the world the requirement of manumitting slaves to expiate certain crimes and sins. The teachings of the Prophet and the precedent of the early Muslim community leave no doubt that, from the outset, Muslims took the Quran's exhortation to 'free a neck' to the level of obsession, with frequent disregard for their own wealth. There is simply no interpretation of Islam's scripture or early history that does not yield this conclusion. Even assuming that much of the history of the Prophet's career and the early Islamic conquests was concocted after the fact by Muslims sometime during Islam's first two centuries, that would simply confirm that those early Muslims understood their religion and their Prophet as veritable turbines of emancipation. Even those Hadiths that Muslim scholars admitted were egregious forgeries fabricated centuries after the Prophet's time reveal that even in those latter days Muslims were still expressing an obsessive will to emancipate, even at their civilization's acme, when Islam's alleged 'slaving DNA' was at its most dominant.

Nothing illustrates this better than the rulings of the Islamic schools of law on issues relating to manumission. So frequent and so blatant is their disregard for the Shariah's usual concerns for property rights, the importance of intention in contracts and formal consistency that one can only conclude that its architects took the divine call to free God's slaves to a level that did not verge on the absurd.[58] It passed well into the realm of the absurd. And it was propagated to an extent that makes the abolitionist crusade of the nineteenth century seem reserved.

It is all the more remarkable that this obsession with emancipation did not hinge on the zeal of a network of awakened activists. It was programmatically baked into the Shariah's internal logic and functioning, reaffirmed and applied ceaselessly for over a millennium. If the Shariah tradition did not elevate maximizing freedom to a *main* aim of the Shariah until the twentieth century, and if Islamic civilization did not universalize its drive to emancipate or call for ending slavery as an institution, it was because none of this was or had ever been conceivable anywhere to anyone. No slaveholding society in human history had abolished slavery prior to the early modern period, when it started becoming economically possible and even advantageous for societies to do so.[59]

Why did no real indigenous abolitionist movement emerge in Islamic civilization? Why did no consciousness of the moral evil of slavery *qua* slavery arise among its slaves? A possible explanation was the high rate of slaves, ex-slaves and the children of slaves assimilating into their slave-owning Muslim societies. In general, the majority of slaves in Islamic civilization were women. They tended to become more integrated into households than male slaves, especially through intimate relations with their masters. The children born of these relations were free Muslim citizens. This ascending miscegenation resulted in a blending of phenotypes; one could not tell someone's slave or free status from their appearance. Moreover, manumission was very common. As a result, a Black man in Cairo, Fez or Mecca, for example, could be a slave. But it was as likely that he was a free, former slave in good social standing. And he could just as easily be the freeborn son of a wealthy father and a Black slave-concubine mother. In North America, by contrast, slaves and ex-slaves were marked by race and kept permanently below the free and enfranchised White population.[60]

Muhammad Tawfiq Sidqi was certainly right about one thing. There was nothing in Europe's moral or religious heritage that made abolition expectable or inevitable. This came only with technological and economic revolution. But as one of the earliest surviving texts in Islamic history states, 'God wishes freedom.'[61] Abolition is the best means to make that wish a universal reality. If doing so is within our means, Islam can give no reason this should not be done.[62]

7

Concubines and Consent: Can We Solve the Moral Problem of Slavery?

> That which they call freedom and which they crave is what we call justice and equity . . .
>
> The Egyptian Rif'at Tahtawi on France, *circa* 1830[1]

One of the first books I read on Islam was the translation of a popular modern biography of Muhammad written by an Arab intellectual in the 1930s. It refers to Mariya as the Prophet's wife. Years later, after I had learned Arabic and was writing my own biography of the Prophet, I realized that the Arabic original calls her a slave-concubine (*surriyya*).[2] I was not surprised by this 'creative' translation. In the late 1990s I had attended a class for frequently asked questions about Islam at a mosque in the Washington, DC area. An attendee asked the imam teaching the class about Mariya, and I remember his response vividly because of his visible discomfort. 'Mariya was . . . free,' he replied. I've heard the same answer many times since. Just in the last year two senior Muslim scholars in the US have told me that 'there is an opinion' or 'there is a report' that Mariya was the Prophet's wife, not his slave.

The problem with this explanation is that it lacks any support whatsoever. It is a denial of history, not an interpretation of it. Aside from modern Muslim authors, there is simply *no evidence* that Mariya was *not* a slave woman of the Prophet who bore him a son.[3] I certainly sympathize with Muslim scholars or imams who tell audiences that the Prophet married her. They understand very clearly the crisis of faith that can be triggered by the problem of slavery and that it feeds ammunition to the powerful Islamophobia industry. And they know that for many Muslims in the West and even for some in the Muslim world it is simply unthinkable – it cannot be thought – that the Prophet had sex with a slave woman.[4]

Earlier I proposed the thought experiment of traveling back in time to Medina during the time of the Prophet and meeting him the day after he had received Mariya as a gift from the patriarch of Alexandria. What do we say to him? Do we tell the Messenger of God that he is engaging in an egregious moral wrong? If we politely asked him to explain why having a slave-concubine was acceptable, could we ever be convinced by his response? The simple fact is that the figure who Muslims are taught is their moral exemplar and the infallible medium of God's revelation did something that we know with every moral fiber of our beings to be profoundly wrong. How could this possibly be resolved by any means other than denying it could ever have happened?

SPECIES OF MORAL CHANGE

To unravel this conundrum, we must return to the question of what lies within and behind our statement that something is morally wrong. A thing can be morally wrong because there is some intrinsic wrong in and of that thing itself. Or it can be wrong because it leads to a consequence we deem morally wrong. Or it can be both. The ontological nature of moral wrongness can also differ depending on our worldview. Moral value can have its own real existence 'out there' in the world and independent of our perceptions or opinions, either because there exists some external moral reality that our minds apprehend when we make a moral judgment, or because what we call moral value is fused into our nature as human beings, and our minds can recognize this. This is universal Morality with a capital 'M', found in divine command, Platonic realism, natural law reasoning and some theories behind human rights. Or moral value can lie in our perceptions and evaluations of actions or ideas. It does not exist outside our discursive communities. It is brought into existence by us. This is morality with a lower case 'm', found in customary or culturally specific notions of right and wrong.

It is simple to explain why perceptions of (lower case) moral wrong change over time or between communities, even if that wrong is seen as intrinsic by people in some time and place. This moral wrong can be particular to some communities and thus relative to others. In some cultures, shouting between family members in a household is normal. In others it is 'wrong' and 'uncivilized.' Bosnian Muslims pleading a case before a judge in New Zealand in 1909 refused his order to remove their fezzes in the courtroom because doing so would be disgraceful. A century later, Muslims can wear religious headwear in New Zealand courts while someone wearing a fez in Sarajevo would be stared at.[5]

It is much more difficult to explain how universal, ontologically real (upper case) Moral Wrong could change over time, or even how our perceptions of it could change. If Moral Value has some real existence separate from our perception or within our natures, it should not be subject to change, at least not if we assume that nature is unchanging. Of course, there is the possibility that our perceptions or realizations of this Moral Value could change if our awareness or capacity to understand improved. This raises the perennial debate over whether human civilization has been on a trajectory of progress or simply repeating the same crimes and missteps in different garb. I am not in a position to resolve this meta-dispute, but in the sub-debate over whether human morality has progressed the question of slavery features prominently. The abolition of slavery stands as the one great proof of human moral progress. Prior to the late 1600s almost no one in human history considered slavery an intrinsic, gross moral wrong. Now almost everyone does. Even those curmudgeonly skeptics who deny progress, assert that abolition was an illusion and that slavery has continued unabated 'under different names' still have to admit that mankind's moral *awareness* has progressed.[6]

The question of how abolition came about and its relationship to moral realization are central to the question under discussion here. It is useful to recall the two narratives for explaining how the abolition of slavery took place in the early modern period: the Moral Awakening and the Economic Explanation narratives. Each is associated with a corresponding view on the nature of moral value. The Moral Awakening narrative generally casts slavery as a gross and intrinsic (upper case) Moral Wrong that was as evil three thousand years ago as it is today. After centuries of not perceiving this, humanity awoke to this fact in the Enlightenment. The Economic Explanation holds that the severe (lower case) moral evil of slavery is not ontologically real. For millennia human societies did not consider slavery to be a gross, intrinsic moral wrong but, rather, an undesirable condition that was part of human social and economic reality. It was no more morally wrong than disease, poverty or war. Only when it became economically realistic to abolish slavery (and the slavery immediately in question happened to be uniquely brutal), and only when social and economic change had made it possible to envision such moral progress, did societies declare slavery a gross and repugnant moral evil.

Looked at with an eye for discerning species of moral value, the Moral Awakening narrative unravels on its own internal contradiction. Humanity *did* dramatically and, in terms of the grand scope of history, suddenly 'awaken' to the nature of slavery. But such an awakening entails that what was realized could not have been a gross, intrinsic and universal Moral Wrong because such a Wrong would *always* have been present. The only way mankind could have 'awakened' to it is if we attained some new capacity for moral perception. Yet the only real evidence of such a new capacity having been gained is the alleged moral awakening of abolition . . . which is precisely the issue of contention at hand. Certainly, average IQs have risen in the last century with improved diet, and education and literacy have become geometrically more widespread. But those gains all took place *after* the age of abolition.[7] There is no evidence that mankind's thought leaders post-1700 were any more intelligent or capable than those prior.

The Moral Awakening narrative asks us to accept that children today know with conviction a moral fact that eluded Aristotle, Buddha, Moses, Jesus, Muhammad, John Locke, Augustine, etc. Aside from being a patently preposterous claim, we've already seen that we today are not more capable of profound moral insights than those individuals. We simply weigh and prioritize matters differently. Pre-modern Muslim scholars were not oblivious to the harms and even the moral pitfalls of *riqq*. They simply did not consider them to be significant in all cases. Islamic thought always recognized that *riqq* caused harm by denying people their natural rights to make their own decisions and control their own labor – hence the virtue of emancipation. But, according to the ulama, these wrongs were outweighed by the property rights of owners and even the potential benefit to the enslaved. According to Muslim scholars, *riqq* only rose to the level of gross wrong when people were improperly enslaved or when slaves were mistreated.

Looked at transhistorically, phenomena that we call 'slavery' have been the locus of intrinsic Wrongs (upper case) that are universal and widely viewed as ontologically real, such as the harms of exploitation and the fact of baseless inequality. And 'slavery' has also constituted a *gross* moral wrong (lower case) that has only existed in our cultures since the early modern period, namely unfreedom or treating humans as property. But the intrinsic

Moral Wrong that is ontologically real and universal is not gross, and the gross moral wrong we perceive in slavery today is not ontologically real or universal. There was a Wrong inherent in historical institutions like *riqq* and slavery in Western Europe, but until relatively recently it was not sufficiently weighty for anyone to condemn these institutions. For almost three centuries, many have perceived a gross and intrinsic evil in slavery. But this is not a universal Moral Wrong that has existed throughout time and space. It is only one that has existed since the early modern period.

So, whether we define it as a person being unfree or property, the mere fact of a person being a 'slave' is not a gross, intrinsic moral evil at all points in history. There may well be degrees of domination and exploitation that are themselves intrinsically evil, whether we determine this through a minimalist natural law reasoning like that of Jacques Maritain or by divine command as in the Shariah. But the types of servitude or dependent labor that do not descend to those levels are not absolute moral wrongs per se.[8] None of this means that we should not seek to end less serious forms of exploitation or alleviate suffering that might result from instances of dependent labor. But we cannot condemn as intrinsically morally evil *all* those various institutions and relationships in humanity's past or present that we have labeled at one time or another as 'slavery.'

Looking back on human history, the solution to the Slavery Conundrum is simple: not everything in history that we've termed 'slavery' was intrinsically, grossly morally wrong. When discussing 'slavery' transhistorically, we cannot adequately define the phenomenon we are condemning nor what about it precisely would make it evil. When we try to pin these down, we end up condemning institutions or relationships in the past and present that many do not feel merit this brand. The mind-knotting, bile-churning difficulty of saying 'Not all things we call slavery were intrinsically and profoundly wrong' is the product of a paradox we have created for ourselves. The Slavery Conundrum was always an illusion of our own making: we back ourselves into condemning our past as morally reprehensible because we lump a massive variety of human engagements and relationships under one uniform heading, and then we declare everything under that heading evil. So we condemn the very pasts we still prize and venerate. Clinging to this paradox is inaccurate and unfair to both those generations who came before us and to our relationship with them. Moreover, our Western designation of 'slavery' is a projection of our own cultural memory. It remains eminently political, serving to distinguish the 'us' of the West from the 'them' of the Muslim other. As it is deployed today, the label of slavery vilifies some and passes over the offenses of others, validates the suffering of some and ignores that of others.

MORAL DISGUST AT SLAVERY TODAY

But if the gross and intrinsic evil of slavery is only a wrong with lower case 'w', then we face a stark conclusion: the certainty we feel about the absolute moral wrongness of slavery is not reflective of some moral reality that holds true across space and time (Morality with a capital 'M'). But what then does it reflect?

It is useful here to return to the most sophisticated contemporary Muslim discussion of the moral problem of slavery, that written by the Iranian scholar Mohsen Kadivar. Kadivar argues that modern Muslims are justified in prohibiting *riqq* because the revolutionary change in human mentality over the past few centuries has revealed that slavery violates the Quran's affirmation of human dignity. This change in attitude among mankind is obvious. The challenge is how to render it admissible as evidence in Islamic rule-making. Kadivar turns to the capacity of human reason to identify universal moral right and wrong (*taḥsīn va taqbīḥ-i ʿaqlī*), which was a feature of Muslim rationalist theology and remains part of Imami Shiite law and theology today. According to this school of theology, it is this rational faculty that has recognized the true offense that slavery commits against human dignity. Its finding reflects God's moral truth in the world and is thus compelling for Muslims.

In an important article, however, the American Muslim scholar Dr. Sherman Jackson discusses how reliance on such moral realist reasoning today suffers from the same weakness it did a millennium ago.[9] If there is a moral reality 'out there' in the world, and if human reason is capable of grasping it, then why do some people think slavery is right and others that slavery is wrong? Why did essentially everyone in 500 CE think slavery was morally acceptable while essentially all their descendants in the year 2018 consider it inherently barbaric? These questions could only be answered if you held an evolutionary view of human moral reasoning. This would mean, however, that we had capacities for moral understanding that Moses, Jesus and Muhammad lacked. We would have no need for their guidance, and our attachment to their moral and spiritual legacies would be little more than nostalgia, like adults looking fondly at their childhood scribblings.

If it is not the faculty of human reason operating as a mirror for transhistorical moral truths that has led us to our passionate rejection of slavery in the modern period, then what is it? The answer is that it is more localized and contextualized moral reasoning rooted in how modern societies have prioritized various goods and bads, valued the construct of equality over that of hierarchy and favored the categories of both humanity and nation-state identity over religious confession. In the Islamic legal tradition, such contextual and communally specific moral reasoning is termed *ʿurf*, which means both 'custom' in its arational sense (Americans wear outdoor shoes in the house even though it is clearly disgusting), as well as customary morality in its reasoned sense (husbands should share in household work because both men and women are equal in terms of their rights to professional ambition and success).

To many it may seem demeaning to boil our deeply felt moral condemnation of slavery down to nothing more than 'custom.' But this reaction betrays two unusual, modern tendencies. We trivialize custom as mundane, and we conflate what we 'feel' to be wrong with absolute Moral Wrong identified as such either by some perceived grasp of mankind's true nature or by indisputable reason.

The response to this objection is simple, though it might be unsatisfying to many. Simply put, depth of feeling does not equal a true reflection of a universal moral reality. And custom is far more powerful than determining what type of gifts we give at weddings. Americans presented with a plate of dog meat would probably vomit out of an indissoluble mixture of moral disgust and sheer revulsion. But in many parts of China dog meat has been 'a minor but regular part of the diet' for over two millennia.[10] This is custom pure and simple. Modern Western moral thinking has become so centered on viewing morality as ascertainable by employing universal rights, maxims of liberal ethics and Kantian deontological reasoning that we easily overlook the immense role of custom. Why is eating a dog any different from eating a lamb? Writing at times when claims of universal reason were at bay, leading minds remind us of custom's power. Noting the stunning diversity of customs between Greece and India, Herodotus (d. *circa* 420 BCE) invoked a verse of the poet Pindar (d. *circa* 438 BCE): 'Custom is king of all.' Montaigne (d. 1592) observed that 'we seem to have no other criterion of truth and reason than the type and kind of opinions and customs current in the land where we live.' Less than a century later his countryman Blaise Pascal (d. 1662) wrote that, aside from what God has commanded or condemned, all claims of justice are merely grounded in custom.[11]

None of this is meant to delegitimize our customary notions of right or wrong or to undermine culturally specific moral reasoning. As I was writing this book, many Americans found themselves both shocked and primally outraged that Roy Moore, a Republican candidate for the US Senate, had relationships with underage teenagers when he was a grown man. Of course, what Roy Moore did was morally wrong. But it was morally wrong because it violated our present-day American notions of when a person is mature enough to enter into a sexual relationship, what the proper age range is for a couple and how all this fits into the systems of goods that we value in our society, such as education, independence, career choice and our understanding of emotional maturity.

Yet these are all just *our* customs, *our* choices. They are very important to us, but they are not unchanging reality itself. History leaves us in no doubt about that. St. Augustine, whom many in the West would acknowledge as a pillar of religious thought, was engaged to a ten-year old girl when he was over thirty (the marriage was supposed to be two years later), and this was uncontroversial.[12] Even categories and moral principles that seem axiomatic to us today are only recent developments. In the US, that marriage should be between equals, that children are not suited to marry, that childhood is marked off by age and not physical maturity and that people under that age are not appropriate objects of sexual interest are all convictions that emerged only in the mid- to late nineteenth century, first in industrial areas and later in the American South.[13] The reasons that marriage to children remained morally acceptable much longer in the South than in more developed regions also apply to areas in the world where child marriage remains common and socially acceptable today, such as the Sahel, Yemen and Afghanistan, and they include: a dearth of state institutions, such as schools, that cultivate awareness of age by grouping populations into age cohorts; limited medical care; and low life expectancy.[14]

Just thinking about such things disgusts many people today. But, again, we must remember that even the physical reaction of disgust, which we naturally assume indicates that some deeply unnatural moral wrong is being done, is almost always culturally conditioned. Our feelings of disgust rarely reflect some unchanging moral or even biological reality (one such rare exception appears to be immediate-family incest). Disgust is culturally conditioned to warn us or drive us away from things our communities have determined to be bad or dangerous.[15] In situations in which socio-economic and technological change have been dramatic and rapid, as with slavery and marriage age, it is worth considering whether the physical revulsion that so many today feel toward these acts may be structural devices designed to rapidly cement novel norms in society. Whether slavery or child marriage, the things that trigger the fiercest moral disgust in American society today were morally acceptable and relatively common just decades before they were widely condemned. So disgust *does* often reflect our profoundest moral values. But these are not necessarily or even regularly *universal* moral values. Indeed, they might not have even been *our* values for very long.

This is not some extended effort to undermine the modern condemnation of slavery by deconstructing it. Quite the opposite, I argue that Muslims' moral disgust at slavery is both expectable and laudable. It is expectable because many Muslims are products of the same social forces that have shaped modern views on slavery overall. It is laudable because the abolition of *riqq* and 'slavery' more generally promotes an important aim of the Shariah, namely maximizing emancipation. For Muslims, *riqq* was not an obligatory practice or even recommended. It was one form of an economic reality that existed in some shape in every civilization. As contemporary Muslim scholars of slavery have written, the desire to end slavery and protect people from its misfortune have become sincere moral priorities for Muslims. This rejection of slavery and the horror that so many Muslims felt at ISIS's revival of it are deeply felt.

As I said at the beginning of this book, almost no one questions that slavery is wrong today. It is morally wrong in the following ways, some of them applicable only to Muslims and some to all people. Most simply, slavery is wrong because it is illegal, since all countries have signed international agreements banning it. This is well within the rights of a Muslim ruler or state to do. There are certainly unjust laws, but respect for the rule of law is a moral imperative, as Plato pointed out and as the Quran commands – 'Obey God, and obey the messenger, and those in authority amongst you' (4:59). And the Quran commands the believers to 'fulfill your contracts' (5:1).

Slavery is also morally wrong for Muslims today not in the sense of being an intrinsic, universal moral wrong in all times and places but in the sense of violating our existing standards of right conduct and propriety, our *ʿurf*. Slavery is not Morally Wrong, i.e., the statement 'slavery is wrong' does not reflect an eternal moral reality outside and above human custom (what

Jackson calls 'an independently, ontologically instantiated moral plane'). But slavery is morally wrong because what Muslim communities determine to be suitable or unsuitable, fair or unfair, right or wrong has real moral and legal weight within the Shariah and Islamic ethics provided it does not violate the Shariah's outer bounds. As the Companion Ibn Mas'ud said, within the boundaries set by God's law, 'What the Muslims see as good is good according to God. What the Muslims see as bad is bad according to God.'[16]

Muslims can choose, and have chosen, to eliminate *riqq* as a legal phenomenon. The Prophet would most likely be very pleased with that. But *riqq* is not grossly and intrinsically wrong. Slavery is morally wrong because it has become customary to consider it morally wrong. We feel moral disgust at its very mention, but that disgust does not reflect some intrinsic, eternal moral reality. In effect, the fact that what ISIS has done is morally wrong does not mean that what the Prophet did was morally wrong too. We are not more morally mature or more aware of eternal moral truths than our ancestors. We just have a more refined *'urf* (custom). Similarly, some of the senior Companions of the Prophet routinely reacted to what they perceived as affronts to the Prophet's honor by offering to chop off the offender's head (the Prophet invariably refused).[17] This seems like fanatical violence to modern Western audiences, Western Muslims included. But performing such hyperbolic responses was part of the *'urf* of Arabia in the era. Few observant Muslims would claim to be better Muslims or to have a keener understanding of Islam's teachings than the Prophet's closest Companions. And, indeed, we are not more morally or spiritually mature. It is just that our *'urf* is more refined and delicate than theirs.

This increased refinement is not as indicative of moral progress as it is of economic and technological progress, the result of massive economic, social and political change. Inhabitants of the urban West today can shower daily and prevent foul bodily odors that were ubiquitous just a few decades ago. And now we disparage those who do not observe this hygiene as backwards or barbaric. But at root this has been a material, not a moral change. The ever-insightful Freya Stark observed that the Muslims she encountered in early twentieth-century Arabia lived in a world embattled by disease and poverty, a world they could not control. They could only hope to assuage the effects of disease or slavery by trying to mitigate them with charity and kindness. In her native West, by contrast, technology and development had allowed societies to eliminate many of these 'causes of sorrow.' Western and

'Eastern' perspectives on slavery, she concluded, stemmed from disparate capacities to exercise control over the world.[18]

CONCLUSION & CRISIS: CONCUBINAGE AND CONSENT

It is unusual to end a book not with a summary or conclusion but with a discussion of new subject matter. But slavery is no ordinary topic. No issue distills more intensely the conflict between pre-modern and modern moral sensibilities. If slavery is the crucible of this moral dilemma, then sex slavery is its most concentrated admixture. To slavery's affront to dignity and equality it adds the transgression of sexual autonomy and consent.

Before plunging into this moral crevasse, however, a concluding review of my argument about the moral problem of slavery is in order. Of course, a number of compelling arguments exist for the moral evil of *riqq* and other relationships generally categorized as 'slavery,' either in our current time or transhistorically. I would not deny that. What I have tried to do is to point out the theological and communal consequences of many current public and even scholarly discussions around the morality of 'slavery' as well as some inconsistencies within them.

As a Muslim myself, it is specifically the phenomenon of *riqq* that concerns me. I cannot condemn it as grossly, intrinsically immoral across space and time. To do so would be to condemn the Quran, the Prophet Muhammad and God's law as morally compromised. I have no qualms about condemning all forms of what is conventionally termed 'slavery' today, because such condemnation helps fulfill an aim of the Shariah and accords with the valid current norms and priorities of Muslims and non-Muslims alike. I feel no inadequacy in my religion's late arrival to the abolitionist front, because that effort was not the result of one group of people, one culture or one religion enjoying some unique moral insight or achieving a moral awakening before others. It resulted from economic, social and technological change that triggered revolutions in moral reasoning sooner in some places than in others. The moral reasoning of abolition is no less indigenous to Islam than it is to any other religion or philosophy. In fact, it is arguably more innate in that religion whose revelation and prophet called undeniably, forcefully and in novel ways to the earthly emancipation of all human beings.

I view the institution of *riqq* in the Shariah similarly to the way conservative Catholic natural law philosophers have viewed slavery in Church doctrine. *Riqq* as ideally defined in the Shariah was not the utter domination that natural law philosophers like Aquinas or Maritain saw as intrinsically evil. It did not transgress the moral boundary into what Maritain called slavery's 'absolute form,' in which 'the body and life of the slave, as well as their primordial goods, like the freedom to marry, were at the mercy of their master.'[19] In *riqq* in theory if not in all practice, slave men and women had rights that were comparable to other dependent segments of society in the Shariah, such as minor children and wives (except wives had full capacity to own property and engage in contracts, etc.): slaves had the right to unencumbered conjugal relationships; the right to religious observances; limited rights to property; and in terms of physical integrity and protection from abuse and exploitation, their position was similar to that of wives and minor children, including the owner's obligation to care for slaves unable to work.[20] In their legal capacity to own property and their protections from physical harm, it is worth noting that the *raqiq* was comparable if not better off than British and American women through the late nineteenth century.[21]

Consent and Concubines

Even if the reader is willing to accept the above features of *riqq* as falling within the realm of the morally tolerable, the master's right to have sex with his female slaves is simply too discordant with modern sensibilities. Even among medieval Jewish and Christian communities, for whom slavery was uncontroversial, the Muslim practice of slave-concubinage was outrageous (and alluring).[22] Perhaps even more than with slavery itself, the moral chasm between Islamic slave-concubinage and our modern morality seems too vast to bridge. We cannot countenance such transgression of a person's autonomy. And yet, like slavery more generally, that female slaves should be sexually available to their male masters looms throughout wide expanses of the human past as normal and morally unproblematic.[23] 'The obligation to provide sexual labor was a critical feature of enslavement for women . . .' notes Elizabeth Elbourne, 'in almost every society in which slavery existed.'[24] The patriarch of the Abrahamic tradition had a concubine (Hagar), as did the seal of its prophets. The right of a master to have sex with his female slaves in certain circumstances was totally normal in societies from the ancient Near East and the Roman Empire in the early centuries of Christianity to medieval and even early modern China, to name just a few epochs.[25]

The best way to understand why there is such dissonance between sexual morality in many Westernized societies today, particularly the US, and moralities that viewed 'sex slavery' as unremarkable even a century ago is to recognize how unusually prominent and exclusive consent is in our morality and law today. This illustrates, first, how rare it will be to find moral systems elsewhere in history that are comparable to ours today, and, second, how precarious our construct of consent really is.

Here I will focus on our contemporary American society, where consent is an idea loaded with immense moral and legal importance. Even moderate examination, however, reveals its fragility. This is due to three points of weakness. First, our near-exclusive focus on consent as the *sine qua non*, perhaps to the exclusion of other criteria, for morally acceptable relations means ignoring other indicators of right and wrong, benefit and harm.[26] Second, the lines we draw for who can validly do consent have the odd combination of being both arbitrary and morally absolute. And third, a fragmented moral culture means we default onto legal lines for moral judgment.

Before looking into this we should recall why we think consent is important to begin with. In one sense, increasingly prominent in recent decades, consent safeguards the abstract value of each individual's autonomy. This is not the primary importance of consent, however. Autonomy is not everything to us, as the question of suicide reveals. We are not Roman Stoics, for whom suicide was the ultimate act of autonomous choice.[27] Most countries (and all but a few US states) still prohibit physician-assisted suicide out of fear that people will be pressured or even forced to end their lives and also because choosing to kill oneself is still seen by many in the post-Christian West as inherently sinful. 'He asked me to kill him' is not an affirmative defense against homicide.[28] Going back to John Locke and John Stuart Mill (d. 1873), consent is mainly important because individuals have the right to choose their own actions and, crucially, *decide what is best for themselves.* When it comes to sexual relationships, we believe that individuals know what is good for themselves, so their consent is what makes a relationship morally and legally acceptable. This liberal principle has only been reinforced in recent decades, as secularization, increased cultural diversity and movements for women's and LGBTQ rights have fractured dominant cultures of consensus on social values.

But here are some real problems. First, though the increasing focus on legal consent over the last few decades has aimed at transcending cultural debates over who should be having sex with whom and how, both law and morality still place brackets on consent that both reveal surviving cultural biases and are often arbitrary. There is still agreement that there are some people who are not able to make decisions about what is best for themselves. The most obvious group is children, whose parents decide what they should eat, whom they meet, what they believe and what happens to their bodies. As parents, it is our notion of what is good that defines what is good for our children. But because autonomy and the capacity to consent that it affords function to fill in for social guideposts that are seen by many as regressive or fragmented, we lack the social consensus on how to judge when a person attains such a capacity. As a result, we default to legal demarcations. The ability to consent thus appears one day when a child turns eighteen. Suddenly, they have the capacity to consent and decide what is best for themselves. This is, of course, totally arbitrary and was acknowledged as such as far back as Blackstone in the eighteenth century.[29] There is nothing about a certain birthday that conveys some deep capacity to understand. Even if cognitive studies demonstrated that around the age of eighteen children's brains achieve some new plateau of capability, this no doubt appears in some children younger than eighteen and may never appear in some people far older.[30] It may even be mistaken to talk about such a capacity as anything constant; even with adults, the capacity to consent changes depending on the circumstances or emotional conditions.[31]

My point here is not to deny that advancing in age from childhood to adulthood generally brings more capacity to make good decisions. Of course it does. My point is that this process takes place at different times for different people, so drawing a line at a certain age for everyone is arbitrary and in no way serves to protect the goods we value. Individuals mature at different times, so only a case-by-case evaluation would reflect accurately when a person was able to make good decisions.[32]

This results in a conundrum: we give consent (and the capacity to do it) incredible power to stamp acts or relationships as morally and legally passable, yet we attach consent (and its capacity) to an arbitrary moment in someone's life that has no link to their actual capacity to know what is beneficial. What is more, we bestow upon consent the power to make things morally and legally acceptable even though we know that there are people who regularly consent to situations that we agree are incredibly destructive for themselves and others. Yet if we point out this incredible tension, we skate close to the edge of thinkable thought in our society.

The second problem is that consent does not adequately address all our moral concerns. Despite the power of social liberalism in global Western mores, vestigial taboos and moral red lines persist.[33] Neither the law nor majority sensibilities allow people to consent to their own killing. Polygamy is still reviled in the West even between consenting adults, and consent is largely viewed as irrelevant as a defense of bestiality. More pertinently, placing the whole burden of legal and moral approval on arbitrary legal lines of consent means ignoring widely accepted senses of harm and benefit.[34]

These problems become clear in the following hypothetical: let us suppose that reasonable adults in the US can look at a relationship and see that it is healthy, rewarding, nurturing and happy. We know what we think makes up such a relationship, and we have a good sense what its external signs are. We see a couple, a male and female, sitting in a restaurant next to us and, after observing them for a good amount of time, conclude that they have just such a relationship. Now imagine that suddenly we learn that the woman is really a fifteen-year-old girl and the man is twenty-five. Now this is not only illegal, it has become morally repulsive. And yet all that has changed is the ages. By contrast, if there are two fifty-year-olds engaged in a sexual relationship that is emotionally, spiritually and even physically devastating to both of them, this is morally tolerable (and legal) in our society. We look away and don't judge. They are consenting adults.

So the factors that we all know are morally meaningful – the nature of a relationship, the impact it has on those involved – actually mean nothing for our socio-moral approval. The factor that is in and of itself meaningless – age – means everything. Like an alchemical spell, age-based consent transmutes sex from immoral and illegal into something legal and morally passable. Yet this capacity just appears in a person, one day, on a certain birthday. Its absence prior to that makes someone a sex offender. Its presence a day later makes sex unobjectionable. We imagine that consent works because people can decide what is best for themselves. But it is obvious that many people have *no idea* what is right or wrong for themselves, whether they are fifteen or fifty. And it is obvious that consent does not guarantee that the emotional and material goods we value in relationships are being pursued. Joseph Fischel puts it eloquently:

> . . . consent is flimsy. It cannot do all the work of sexual adjudication assigned for it by law or by the social. Sex that is regretted, unpleasant, or even harmful occurs in legally consensual relations. And some

of the sex that occurs in legally nonconsensual relations, between minors or between adults and minors, is formative, transformative, good, great, OK, or non-momentous.[35]

Consent is thus both absolutely all-important in our late modern sexual morality and also mercurial, even a fiction we conjure to fill the gap previously played by custom, family guidance and family approval. Even more ironic is that in every US state couples can marry under eighteen (usually as young as sixteen) with their parents' or a judge's consent.[36] Twenty-seven states have no minimum age in such situations.[37] These facts are controversial, as much recent reporting on child marriages in the US demonstrates.[38] But they remain facts nonetheless.

Allowing the marriage of minors in the US with parental consent introduces a third, real problem: where exactly is the dividing line between the autonomy of the individual – the idea of what he or she thinks is best – and the influence and priorities of those whom that individual loves and values? Imagine this situation: an American parent assents to their fifteen-year-old daughter getting married to her twenty-five-year-old boyfriend. In this case, a minor, who cannot consent according to our moral and legal conventions, is able to marry because her guardian believes she is making a decision that is good for her. But what if this parent, the person who has been making decisions on what is best for their daughter for fifteen years, *suggests* to her that marrying a certain man would be good for her. And the daughter agrees. That would be legally acceptable in American society, too.

This becomes even more complicated when we move outside what we imagine to be Western liberal society, either in space or backwards in time, before mass urbanization and the fracturing of societies into disintegrating nuclear families. Let's continue with the case of the hypothetical American parent and daughter, except now the parent is not American but a farmer in rural Yemen. This father decides to marry his daughter to his neighbor's son because they are part of the same clan, whose integrity is essential for all their lives and feelings of community. His daughter does not know or particularly like the boy, but she so honors her father and so trusts him to do what is best for their entire family, herself included, that she agrees to the marriage. Is that an instance of consent? How is it different from the previous hypotheticals?

We imagine consent as reflecting the choice of an autonomous individual, a free mind in a free and unencumbered body, in a liberal, secular democracy. Judith Butler draws attention to how our language of consent 'encodes a fantasy of the liberal subject.'[39] As Lila Abu-Lughod writes in the case of young brides in rural Yemen, this 'fantasy of autonomy' just does not function in the same way in a society in which family solidarity, clan interests and parental wishes mean a tremendous amount to individuals.[40] What does it mean to 'consent' to a marriage if what your family wants you to do means more to you than what you yourself desire, not because you're oppressed but because you truly trust and value them? Even Kevin Bales, a leading articulator of New Abolitionism, acknowledges the challenges of combatting 'unfree marriage,' which the 1956 convention added to the list of slavery-like practices. Bales admits that identifying exactly what constitutes an 'unfree marriage' proves quite difficult because it hinges on an incredibly fluid and ambiguous concept, namely consent, and on outsiders determining 'the location of consent within cultural boundaries.'[41] In nineteenth-century China, for example, it was common for women to be sold by their families to wealthier families as wives, concubines or sexually vulnerable servants. But the girls and women involved often consented in order to alleviate their own or their families' poverty.[42]

What does any of this have to do with slavery and concubinage in Islam? In one sense, nothing. However inchoate or problematic our American conception of consent might be, it is nonetheless the undeniable foundation of what Americans deem not just morally acceptable sexual relationships but also what is morally acceptable sex *within* existing relationships. In the legal conception of the Shariah, by contrast, consent plays no formal role within a licit sexual relationship or in initiating some relationships to begin with (it is worth remembering that only in the 1970s did US states begin acknowledging that it was possible for a husband to rape his wife).[43] As noted earlier, marriage and a male's ownership of a female slave were the two relationships in which sex could licitly occur according to the Shariah. In marriage, the consent of the wife to sex was assumed by virtue of the marriage contract itself.[44] In the case of a slave-concubine, consent was irrelevant because of the master's ownership of the woman in question. As Kecia Ali has noted, there is no evidence for any requirement for consent from slave women in books of Islamic law in the formative centuries of Islamic law.[45] Books of Islamic law and marital ethics are full of exhortations for husbands to engage in foreplay and stress the wife's right to orgasm. But such books also foreground Hadiths and laws obliging wives to meet their husbands' sexual needs without contest.[46]

Consent was important in the Shariah's conception of sexual relationships. It just was not as important as it is in post-1970s, global Western morality. It did not come from an assumed, universal and equal autonomy. According to the Shariah, children did not have autonomy; their parents made decisions about their best interests. And reduced autonomy was part of the 'legal handicap' that defined *riqq*. This was not a denial of autonomy. Non-Muslim slaves could not be forcibly converted to Islam, for example, or denied their religious rights. But it was a greatly diminished autonomy. In the Shariah, consent was crucial if you belonged to a class of individuals whose consent mattered: free women and men who were adults (even male slaves could not be married off against their will according to the Hanbali and Shafi'i schools, and this extended to slaves with *mukataba* arrangements in the Hanafi school).[47] Consent did not matter for minors. And it did not matter for female slaves, who could be married off by their master or whose master could have a sexual relationship with them if he wanted (provided the woman was not married or under a contract to buy her own freedom).

Slavery, *riqq* included, is illegal and should remain so. On the level of moral hypotheticals, however, even if we as late-modern Westerners conceded the moral acceptability of some tailored version of *riqq* in its ideal and idealized form, it seems impossible to reconcile our ethics with the sexual exploitation of slave women that *riqq* allowed. Yet realizing that our global Western, particularly American, emphasis on consent is peculiarly intense reveals a mitigating element and suggests several points for potential reconciliation between Islamic law and late-modern Western norms.

First, if we were to envision the range of the role played by consent in the history of human sexual morality, contemporary American public norms would be an outlier from the median point, and not entirely on the basis of good reasoning. Critics could point to any number of absurdities created by our supercharged notion of consent. And even if we try to think of consent in a more modest and broadly applicable way, it is hard to pin down what consent is in societies less individualistic than our own. None of this justifies today the Shariah right of a master to sex with his female slave, but realizing our own idiosyncrasy may make societies in the past – even the recent past – that allowed slave-concubinage less incomprehensible.

I want to preface the second point by reiterating that I am not advocating the revival of *riqq*; this is an exercise in moral reasoning within a religio-legal tradition. Dismissing out of hand Shariah norms around sex within marriage and with slave-concubines because they ignore consent distracts us from an element of Shariah reasoning that does effectively the same moral and legal work. Just because Muslim wives or slave-concubines could not make moral or legal claims on the basis of consent does not mean they were left with no defense against sexual treatment that was abusive, harmful or excessive. But they found this by complaining to family or to a court about **harm** (*ḍarar*), not about sex that occurred without consent.[48] The following graphic example decided by a Maliki judge named Abu Tahir Dhuhli (d. 979) in Egypt is illustrative:

> A woman brought [a complaint] to [the judge] that her husband had a hairy penis and that she could not bear it. So he ruled that she not prevent him [from having sex with her] on the days that he used depilatory syrup (*yatanawwaru*). Then he said to him [i.e., the husband]: Use the depilatory syrup every day if you like.[49]

Another Maliki judge, Ibn Manzur (d. 1349), was asked about a case in which a woman complained that her husband was taking too long to have sex and would not even climax, causing her, in her words, 'great harm that she was unable to bear.' Ibn Manzur was unconvinced and advised the woman to grin and bear it. But he also offered to arrange a separation from her husband. In the early twentieth century, the traditionalist Moroccan jurist Wazzani (d. 1923) commented that the Maliki school allowed a man to have sex with his partner up to either four or eight times within twenty-four hours. If the wife complained about the size of the man's penis, this should be looked into, with the option either of the judge ordering anything from using lubricant to a judicial separation of the couple upon her request.[50]

A modern audience might not be pleased with these rulings, but they reveal a crucial feature of Islamic legal reasoning on the limits of permissible sex: even within a relationship in which consent was assumed or irrelevant, men could be prevented from exercising their notional right to sex if it caused the woman harm. This had long been acknowledged as applying in the opposite direction. Shafiʿi himself, in a ruling followed dutifully by the major figures of his school, did not *require* a husband to have sex with his wife or slave-concubine because, 'as for sex, it is a locus of pleasure and no one should be compelled to do it.'[51]

What constitutes harm (*ḍarar*) in the Shariah is determined by custom and local norms. From the perspective of Islamic law, matters such as the expected conduct of husbands and wives fall within the boundaries of *'urf*. Within the outer limits of the Shariah, the moral and legal restrictions and liabilities on such matters are set by what a particular culture deems normative. Ibn Qudama explains that, beyond the husband's and wife's basic obligations to one another, both should do what is expected based on custom 'because this is the custom (*'āda*), and the situation will not go well unless it accords with [that custom], neither will their life find any order.'[52] Ibn Taymiyya explains that marital relations and duties, including the frequency and mechanics of sex, are determined by *'urf* (provided the act is not forbidden per se, like anal sex) and that what causes harm is not allowed (on the basis of Quran 2:228).[53] Other matters determined by custom and its conception of harm include the age at which women were considered able to have sex. Consummation of marriage was not allowed if the woman was 'not of the age at which those like her have sex.'[54]

Such rules could very easily be translated in terms of what we would understand as consent. Hurgronje tells of a rich Meccan friend who could have had any woman he wanted from his ample harem, but he broke down in tears before the Dutchman because one Black African slave woman with whom he was infatuated would not *agree* to have sex with him. Legally speaking, she had no right to say no. But, Hurgronje observes, 'here with decent people the principle holds good: all can be got by force except one thing.'[55]

The culturally determined no-harm rule for appropriate conduct within relationships offers an obvious solution to the incompatibility of the Shariah's black-letter law and modern norms on consent. If, within relationships where consent is formally assumed or formally irrelevant, sex cannot be allowed if it causes harm, and if harm is determined by custom and culture, then in a culture that condemns 'non-consensual' sex as gravely injurious per se, shouldn't non-consensual sex be prohibited entirely due to the substantial harm involved? One might object that such a rule might result in a husband/master never being able to have sex if his wife/slave never consented. This would defeat a core purpose of the relationship for him. This is true, but this would also be the case if sex caused the woman in question some other type of harm, like unbearable physical pain. Marriage or ownership of a female slave does not mean one has an undeniable right to sexual access. If there is some prohibitory harm that makes sex impossible, then the husband could have the marriage annulled (*faskh*) or sell his slave-concubine. He could do the same if she refused to consent.

DISBELIEF IS UNPRODUCTIVE

In many conversations with Muslims and non-Muslims who have asked me about the problem of the Shariah's lack of concern for consent within marriage and in slave-concubinage, I have raised this possibility of the harm concept bridging the moral divide. In almost all those interactions I can recall, my interlocutors responded with an admixture of horror and confusion. Just as they could never condone a moral or legal system that did not have consent as its foundation, they could not believe they were speaking to someone who would take such a system seriously enough to bother with reconciliation.

My response to this remains: shouldn't we take all major human legal and ethical traditions seriously, and what message are we sending to their adherents when we refuse to do so? If we object to them, what is the more effective mechanism to promote change, disgusted disbelief or constructive engagement? Do we really think that all cultures in every time and place should be just like the modern West or the US? If there are common values shared by humanity (I believe there are), is it really so odd to think that one culture might phrase them in terms different from another? Doesn't it behoove us to overcome differences through translation?

In many ways, this dynamic of moral disbelief reflects the overall point I have tried to make in this book regarding our engagement with the concept of slavery. The mission to promote justice and rightful contentment in the world is a mission that Muslims share with the rest of humanity. Enabling as many individuals as possible to pursue truth and social benefit helps fulfill this mission. Just as we live in a time when mankind overall enjoys unprecedented worldly comforts, so we have been able to mitigate the subservience of some humans to others. Yet it would be self-righteous and dangerous to think that we inhabit a moral sphere that has risen completely above the benighted strata of even our recent past. Those relationships and ideas that we profess ourselves too mature to fathom were commonplace for our parents, our grandparents, our presidents, our philosophers and our prophets. We still speak their language, employ their principles, seek guidance in their exempla and worship their gods. We value 'freedom,' 'consent,' 'kindness,' 'justice' and 'equality' because they elaborated these ideas – slave owners and slaves though they were. How we value and prioritize these goods has changed with our advances in economy and technology, but to pretend that we have transcended our past is naïve. It either leaves us in cultural and cognitive dissonance, harshly denouncing a heritage we still venerate. Or it deludes the wealthy and comfortable of the globe today into the fiction that all the darkness is in our past, letting us exploit and oppress while we forget 'that one may smile, and smile, and be a villain.'[56]

Appendix 1

A Slave Saint of Basra

The following report comes from the Ornament of the Saints *(*Ḥilyat al-awliyāʾ*, 10:173–4) of the Shāfiʿī jurist, Hadith scholar and Sufi Abū Nuʿaym al-Iṣbahānī (d. 1038* CE*). The figures mentioned in the beginning of the story were all leading ascetics, scholars or transmitters of Hadiths in Basra during the first half of the 700s* CE*. ʿAṭāʾ al-Sulaymī (d.* circa *760) was a pious scholar and well-known Sufi of Basra. Muḥammad bin Wāsiʿ (d. 740-1* CE*) was a scholar and Hadith transmitter. Ḥassān bin Abī Sinān was a prominent merchant of Basra who turned to pious asceticism. The Ḥabīb mentioned could be Habib bin al-Shahīd (d. 762–3), a leading scholar in Basra whose Hadith narrations appear in the main Sunni Hadith collections. He might also be Ḥabīb al-ʿAjamī (d.* circa *770s), a disciple of the Sufi pivot al-Ḥasan al-Baṣrī (d. 728* CE*) and known for his piety and miracles, or Ḥabīb bin Abī Qarība, another ascetic from Basra. ʿUtba al-Ghulām was another well-known pious ascetic of the city. The most famous figures mentioned in the story are Thābit al-Bunānī (d.* circa *744), Yaḥyā al-Bakkāʾ (d. 747–8), Ṣāliḥ al-Murrī (d. 788–9), Ayyūb al-Sakhtiyānī (d. 748–9) and the narrator himself, the famous ascetic and scholar Mālik bin Dīnār (d. 744–5). Abū Nuʿaym received this report from one Abū al-Azhar Ḍamra b. Ḥamza al-Maqdisī, and this is the only report from this source in the* Ḥilya*. For more on Basra's divine love tradition, see Laury Silvers, '"God Loves Me": The Theological Content and Context of Early Pious and Sufi Women's Sayings on Love,'* Journal for Islamic Studies *30 (2010): 33-59.*

Mālik bin Dīnār said: Rain was withheld from us in Basra, so we went out one day to perform the prayer for rain. But we saw no trace of it being answered. So I went out with ʿAṭāʾ al-Sulaymī, Thābit al-Bunānī, Yaḥyā al-Bakkāʾ, Muḥammad bin Wāsiʿ, Abū Muḥammad (Ayyūb?) al-Sakhtiyānī, Ḥabīb Abū Muḥammad al-Fārisī, Ḥassān bin Abī Sinān, ʿUtba al-Ghulām and Ṣāliḥ al-Murrī until we reached a prayer area (*muṣallā*) in Basra. Then the youths came out of their schools and we all prayed for rain but saw no trace of any response. It reached midday and the people left, but I stayed with Thābit al-Bunānī in the prayer area. When night had fallen there appeared a black man with a handsome face, skinny legs and a big belly, wearing two wraps made of wool. I estimated everything on him at two dirhams. He went to the water and wiped himself off then approached the mihrab and prayed two cycles, his bowing and prostrating each of the same, short duration. Then he raised his eyes to the heavens and said, 'My Master, how long will You deny Your slaves what decreases You nothing? Has what You have run out? Or have the treasuries of Your power run dry? O my Master, I beg of You by Your love for me, quench our thirst with Your rains this very moment.'

Mālik bin Dīnār continued: No sooner had he finished speaking than clouds filled the sky and it came down on us as if from the mouths of water jugs. And we hadn't walked out of the prayer area before the water had reached our knees. Thābit and I stood there in awe of the black man. Then he left, so we followed him. I addressed him, saying, 'O black man, are you not ashamed of what you said?' He replied, 'And what did I say?' I said to him, 'You said, ". . . by Your love for me." How do you know that He loves you?' He replied, 'Turn away from matters that you know nothing of, you who should concentrate on yourself. Where was I when He favored me with [belief in] divine unicity (*tawḥīd*) and knowledge of Him. Do you think He did that out of anything but love for me in His proportion and my love for Him in mine?' Then he turned and walked away. I said to him, 'God be good to you, please accompany us!' He answered, 'I'm a slave carrying out a command of my young owner.' So we started to follow him at a distance until he entered the house of a slave dealer. By that time half the night had passed. And how long the second half was for us!

When we awoke [in the morning] we went to the slave dealer and said, 'Do you have a male slave you can sell us to serve us?' 'Yes,' he said, 'I have one hundred male slaves just for that.' So he started bringing them out for us one by one, with me saying, 'No, not that one' for each one, until he had shown us ninety slaves. He said, 'I don't have any others besides these.' But then when we were setting out to leave I walked into a ruined room behind the house and there was the black man, sleeping. It was siesta time. I said, 'It's him, by the Lord of the Kaaba!' I went over to the slave dealer and said to him, 'Sell me that black slave.' He said, 'O Abū Yaḥyā (Mālik's nickname), that slave is bad news and difficult. At night he doesn't want to do anything but weep and during the day nothing but prayer and sleep.' 'That's why I want him,' I said. So the dealer called for the slave and he appeared, sleepy. The dealer told me, 'Take him for whatever you want to pay, but on the condition that I'm not liable for any of his faults.' So I bought him for twenty dinars, taking responsibility for whatever faults he had. But I asked, 'What's his name?' 'Maymūn,' the dealer answered. Then I took him by the hand to return to my house.

While we were walking the slave asked me, 'My young master, why did you buy me, when I'm no good at serving any creature (*al-makhlūqīn*)?' I said to him, 'My love, we bought you so that *we* can serve *you* ourselves, gladly.' 'Why is that?' he inquired. 'Aren't you our friend from yesterday in the mosque?' I responded. 'You two saw that?' he asked back. 'I'm the one who raised the objection to you [afterward],' I told him. So he started walking until he reached a mosque. He went in, prepared himself and then prayed two cycles. Then he raised his eyes to the heavens and said, 'O my God and Master, a secret that was between me and You, You revealed it to creatures (*makhlūqīn*) and embarrassed me with it. So how can life seem good to me now that other than You has found out what was between me and You? I implore You, take my soul now this instant.' Then he knelt in prayer. I went up to him and waited a bit, but he did not raise his head. I shook him and found that he was dead. I straightened out his arms and legs and saw his face was smiling. The blackness had been lifted off, and his face had become like the moon.

Then suddenly there was a young man who came in the door and said, 'May peace and the blessings of God be upon you. May God increase our reward for our brother. Here is a burial cloth, wrap him in it.' And he handed me two pieces of cloth the likes of which I'd never seen and then left. So, we buried him in them. Mālik concluded: And his grave is still sought out today for supplications for rain and by people praying for needs.

Appendix 2

Enlightenment Thinkers on Slavery

The treatment of the slavery question by eighteenth-century Enlightenment thinkers is complex. Late eighteenth-century philosophers like the French nobleman Condorcet (d. 1794) were among the fiercest attackers of the slave trade and slavery. They saw the Atlantic slave trade of their era as, in the words of Condorcet, 'a slavery more barbarous, more productive of crimes against nature' than anything in the ancient world. Yet slavery was a vexed issue, in part because during the 1600s and much of the 1700s the economic systems of France and Britain profited greatly from slavery, in part because many of those who opposed slavery nonetheless had dismissive views toward Black Africans, and in part because colonial slavery was also royal policy in France, so criticizing it could result in prison. Finally, the enmity that thinkers like Voltaire (d. 1778) showed to slavery could be as much a product of their contempt for the Church, which supported slavery, as it was part of their conviction in liberty.

In addition, the racial aspect of slavery was tied to the emerging fields of science and discovery of the day. Particularly in the early 1700s, discussions of race could not be separated from the greater discourse of scientific exploration and its debate over whether all the hominids encountered on the voyages of discovery were actually human beings or not. This greatly complicated the issue of whether there was one human nature or one consistent, natural law. There was a strong sense among thinkers of the early 1700s that slavery was unnatural *for Europeans* or Christians but not necessarily for others. Locke (d. 1704) argued that slavery was against natural law because people had a natural right to choose their own actions. But he followed Roman law in allowing people to enslave those who had attacked them or threatened the rights of others. Based on this, he specifically approved of enslaving sub-Saharan Africans, since he felt they lived in a chaotic state of nature, attacking one another with no regard for rights.

Another pillar of Western liberalism and ideas of freedom, Montesquieu (d. 1755), had views that are equally hard to pin down. He states in his famous *Spirit of the Laws* that slavery is against natural law, since all people are equal and born free (his book was a landmark in its use of natural law to condemn slavery). At other points in the book, however, he endorses Aristotle's natural slavery. But he limits it to those more tropical regions where, he claims, the climate makes people both lazy and emotional. There slavery might be necessary for states to function. In such despotic regions, slavery is 'more tolerable' anyway, since the people there already live in 'political slavery,' and slavery in those regions is 'mild' and more akin to a 'reciprocal' agreement entered into willingly by slave and master. Claudine Hunting argues that Montesquieu's ambiguity on the question of slavery was designed to protect him from punishment for his anti-slavery views. But Kant (d. 1804) voiced a more problematic view: he supported using Black Africans and Native Americans as slave labor because he considered them naturally lazy and unproductive if left to themselves.

Sources Cited: Condorcet, 'On Slavery. Rules for the Society of the Friends of Negroes (1788),' in *Condorcet: Political Writings*, 150; idem, *Outlines of an historical view of the progress of the human mind*, 166; Dorinda Outram, *The Enlightenment*, 68–71; Jennifer Welchman, 'Locke on Slavery and Inalienable Rights,' 67-81; Montesquieu, *Esprit des lois*, 1:443–49, 469–78 (see books 14:ii, 15:i, and 15:v–vi, 15:x); Russell Jameson, *Montesquieu et l'esclavage*, 321–30; Claudine Hunting, 'The Philosophes and Black Slavery,' 405–18, especially 417; Pauline Kleingeld, 'Kant's Second Thoughts on Race,' 573–92; and Margaret Watkins, ' "Slaves among Us": The Climate and Character of Eighteenth-Century Philosophical Discussions of Slavery.'

Appendix 3

Did the 1926 Muslim World Congress Condemn Slavery?

Several publications from noted scholars of slavery in Islamic history have referred to the 1926 World Islamic Congress adopting a resolution condemning slavery. William Gervase Clarence-Smith writes in a 2004 chapter, for example, that, 'In 1926, a World Islamic Congress in Mecca allegedly adopted a resolution condemning slavery, and the sixth World Islamic Congress, held in Mogadishu in 1964, affirmed that "Islam condemns the enslavement of men by men."' He cites as his source Murray Gordon's *Slavery in the Arab World*, which in turn cites Norman Anderson's *Law Reform in the Muslim World* (1976). But there is nothing remotely related to slavery on that page of Anderson's book, and the conference declaration information appears nowhere in the volume.

As far as I can tell, slavery was brought up only once at the 1926 Muslim World Congress (*Mu'tamar al-'Ālam al-Islāmī*), held in Mecca. Martin Kramer concurs in the endnotes of his *Islam Assembled*. It was raised, at British urging according to British reports, by Sayed Mohammed Kefayatullah, President of the Association of Indian Ulama, during the sixteenth session of the conference (July 3, 1926). According to a report about the session digested from Arabic press, Kefayatullah asked (I translate from the French):

> The Congress, considering that the Prophet cursed him who sells a man and profits from his price, and that in principle a Muslim must never be reduced to slavery, and that the slaves of both sexes that are being trafficked in the Hejaz are Muslims, whether they were free but taken by force, or whether one could suppose they were of free origins, [we propose that] the Congress should designate a commission, composed of individuals familiar with the situation of *de facto* and *de jure* slavery, in order to undertake a detailed inquest and

> submit a report to the government of the Hejaz, in hope of ceasing, in conformity with the provisions of the Shariah, the commerce of slaves, out of regard for Islamic liberty and in order to prevent any slavery taking place contrary to the rules of the Shariah.

The digest of the day's agenda adds: 'The executive commission of the Congress affirms this and proposes that the government of the Hejaz take steps to prevent any slavery in the Hejaz that contradicts the Shariah. The assembly adopts this.'

It seems that the 1926 congress only expressed concern over *riqq* being carried out in a way that violated the Shariah by enslaving Muslims. I have been unable to find any information on the alleged 1964 congress held in Mogadishu.

Sources Cited: Clarence-Smith, 'Islam and the abolition of the slave trade and slavery in the Indian Ocean,' 138; Murray Gordon, *Slavery in the Arab World*, 47; Norman Anderson, *Law Reform in the Muslim World*, 186; Martin Kramer, *Islam Assembled*, 216; Achille Sékaly, 'Le Congrès du Monde Musulman à la Mecque: annexe n. 24: seizième séance,' *Revue du Monde Musulman* 64 (1926): 201 (issue available here http://visualiseur.bnf.fr/CadresFenetre?O=NUMM-103857&I=29&M=tdm).

Appendix 4

Was Māriya the Wife or Concubine of the Prophet?

The intense moral crisis that the Prophet having a slave-concubine can precipitate for modern Muslims, and the pattern of contemporary Muslim scholars recasting Māriya as a free wife, have already been noted in brief by scholars like Kecia Ali and received a solid and insightful treatment by Aysha Hidayatullah. In her article on Māriya's portrayal in a broad selection of Muslim historical and biographical sources, Hidayatullah records how Māriya has been referred to. Several modern and contemporary authors, such as Amira Sonbol, refer to her as a wife or marriage partner. All the sources that Hidayatullah consults from the premodern period (and many from the modern), however, use the word *jāriya*, *umm walad*, *milk al-yamīn*, *surriyya* or other phrases that unambiguously mean slave-concubine or female slave. It seems that only in recent decades has Māriya been portrayed as a wife rather than as a slave-concubine.

Some Muslim intellectuals and activists have developed lengthy arguments insisting that the Prophet freed and married Māriya. As Hidayatullah notes, one plank of this argument has been to point to the mainstay chronicles of al-Ṭabarī (d. 923) and Ibn Kathīr (d. 1374), both of which list Māriya along with the wives of the Prophet. But listing slave-concubines, especially one who bore the Prophet a son, along with his wives is not surprising and does not suggest anything in particular.

A scholar named Kaleef Karim offers perhaps the most comprehensive argument. His main evidence is that the term *jāriya* was often used to mean girl and not necessarily slave girl. This is certainly true, but numerous authoritative reports refer to Māriya as *surriyya* (slave-concubine) or *umm walad* (slave mother of the master's child), which are unambiguous in their meaning. Karim presents numerous other quotations from classical sources that ostensibly refer to Māriya as a wife, but upon consulting the original sources, the sections of text are either not there or are liberal translations from Arabic into English that interpolate the wife aspect.

Karim does provide one compelling piece of evidence. He brings a report from the *Mustadrak*, a Hadith collection compiled by al-Ḥākim al-Naysābūrī (d. 1014), in which Muṣʿab bin ʿAbdallāh al-Zubayrī states that 'Then the Messenger of God married Māriya . . . (*thumma tazawwaja rasūl Allāh [s] Māriya bint Shamʿūn . . .*).' Muṣʿab bin ʿAbdallāh al-Zubayrī of Baghdad (d. 851) was a decently regarded Hadith transmitter but was more widely known as a scholar of genealogy (*nasab*) who compiled the respected *Genealogy of Quraysh* (*Kitāb Nasab Quraysh*). He lived two centuries after the Prophet, which certainly in no way disqualifies his statement. But al-Zubayrī provides no chain of transmission to an earlier source for his information; the statement appears as his own. Meanwhile, four other reports in the *Mustadrak*, including some with full chains of transmission back to the Companions, all refer to Māriya as *jāriya/umm walad*. For example, al-Zuhrī (d. 742) reports that 'The Messenger of God (s) took Māriya the Copt as a concubine, and she bore him Ibrāhīm (*istasarra rasūl Allāh [s] Māriya al-Qibṭiyya fa-waladat lahu Ibrāhīm*).'

This evidence, however, merely confirms the received opinion, namely that Māriya was the Prophet's slave-concubine. It does not counter al-Zubayrī's report. His choice of wording, however, should not be given too much weight. *Tazawwaja* does mean 'he took as a wife,' but just a few reports later, and by the same chain of transmission from al-Zubayrī to al-Ḥākim, the compiler of the book, al-Zubayrī states, 'It has reached me that Māriya, the *umm walad* of the Prophet, may God's peace and blessings be upon him, passed away in the year 17 [AH]. The Commander of the Faithful ʿUmar b. al-Khaṭṭāb prayed over her, and she was buried in the Baqīʿ [Cemetery in Medina].' This suggests that al-Zubayrī himself thought that Māriya was a slave-concubine and was merely using the phrase *tazawwaja* in a loose sense of 'took her as one of his women.' This would not be the only time that *tazawwaja* has been used ambiguously to mean marry or have sex with a female slave, as Ann McDougall has shown. That al-Zubayrī considered Māriya to be a slave-concubine of the Prophet is further supported by the fact that, in his book on the genealogy of the Prophet's tribe, he says that Māriya was 'given' to the Prophet by the Muqawqis (the Melkite patriarch of Alexandria).

It is possible that al-Zubayrī meant that the Prophet received Māriya as a gift and *then* freed and married her, hence his wording '*Then* the Messenger of God married Māriya . . .' i.e., then after being given her he married her, etc. But then she would not be his *umm walad*, as al-Zubayrī referred to her.

She would be referred to as his wife. It seems more likely that al-Zubayrī, who often showed the chronology of events like marriages and children born by introducing each sentence with 'Then (*thumma*)', meant nothing more by 'Then' than a transition in his list of the Prophet's womenfolk or in his recounting the events of the Prophet's life. His report with the *tazawwaja* phrasing appears in isolation in the *Mustadrak* and does not appear in his *Kitāb Nasab Quraysh*, so we do not know its context.

Lastly, this entire point may well be moot. The published editions of the *Mustadrak* with the *tazawwaja* wording (i.e., the Hyderabad edition, which is reproduced by the Dār a-Kutub al-ʿIlmiyya and the Dār al-Ḥaramayn printings), seem to include a manuscript copyist error in the relevant sentence. A more recent critical edition by Dār al-Taʾṣīl, which relies on four additional manuscripts not used in the Hyderabad edition, renders the above sentence as '*thumma waladat li-rasūl Allāh Māriya* . . . (Then Māriya bore a child to the Messenger of God . . .).' This is also the conclusion of two other recent critical editions of the *Mustadrak* done by Dār al-Maymān and Dār al-Minhāj al-Qawīm.

Another piece of evidence offered by those arguing today that Māriya was the Prophet's wife is that, in one Hadith in *Ṣaḥīḥ Muslim*, the Prophet counsels Muslims to do good toward Egyptians because that nation will enjoy protection under Muslim rule (*dhimma*) and that they possess *ṣihr*, or an in-law relationship. Proponents infer that the Prophet would not have used this word if Māriya had merely been his slave-concubine. It befits a wife. But this is only one narration of this Hadith, and not the main one listed in *Ṣaḥīḥ Muslim*. The main narration says 'they have *dhimma* and *raḥim* (womb),' meaning that Copts come from the same womb as the Arabs. In fact, the narrations of this Hadith that include the wording *ṣihr* only have it as a parenthetical insertion by one of the narrators of the Hadith: '. . . or he said *dhimma* and *ṣihr*.' Commentators like al-Nawawī (d. 1277) understood this Hadith to be a reference to the idea that Hagar, Abraham's concubine, was from Egypt. He does note that the alternate wording of *ṣihr* would be a reference here to Māriya, but this does not mean he believed this meant that she was the Prophet's wife, particularly since al-Nawawī explicitly calls her the Prophet's slave-concubine (*tasarrāhā*) in another of his works. In addition, a report in the ninth-century history *Futūḥ Miṣr* notes that ʿUmar, the *mawlā* of Ghufra, commented about the *ṣihr* wording that it was because 'The Messenger, may God's peace and blessings be upon him, took a slave-concubine (*tasarrara*) from among them'.

In summary, the only evidence that Māriya was the wife of the Prophet as opposed to his slave-concubine is both extremely rare and unreliable, or it is ambiguous. The evidence explicitly identifying her as his slave-concubine is overwhelming. Another question further narrows the likelihood that Māriya was a wife. Why would early Muslims propagate the idea that she was a slave-concubine if she was not? Why would they offer no resistance as this idea became the exclusive position among biographers, historians and jurists? What agenda would this be serving? Elizabeth Urban has shown how contenders for the caliphate or rule who were the children of slave-concubines invoked the personas of Hagar and Māriya when their parentage was used to insult them. But it hardly seems likely that a historical consensus could be manufactured by a few, scattered claimants in a few dynastic conflicts.

A fascinating theory came from Kaj Öhrnberg, who presented a revisionist historical explanation. A Syriac Christian chronicle from *circa* 670 CE states that the Sassanid Persian shah had two wives, one named Shīrīn (a Persian) and one named Maria (a Byzantine). Three centuries later, the Persian epic of the *Shāhnāme* by Firdawsī (d. 1020) tells of the Byzantine emperor betrothing his daughter Maria to the shah. Since Hagar came from Egypt, and since the standard reports about Māriya being given to the Prophet by the patriarch of Egypt mention that her sister Sīrīn/Shīrīn was given along with her, Öhrnberg proposed that Muslims combined personages and narratives in an act of historical 'transposition'. Just as the Persian shah married a Christian named Maria and a Persian named Shīrīn, the Prophet received two girls named Māriya and Sīrīn/Shīrīn. Just as Hagar the slave woman came from Egypt and bore Abraham (Ibrāhīm) a son and prophetic heir, so Māriya the slave woman came from Egypt and bore Muhammad Ibrāhīm (Abraham), who, according to a disputed Hadith, would have succeeded Muhammad as prophet had he lived beyond childhood. So Māriya 'had to be' a slave woman because she had to correspond to Hagar.

This is a truly engaging theory, but it suffers from two flaws. The first is the flaw of all revisionist histories of early Islam: it requires us to believe in complex conspiracies of collective fabrication in a period in which Muslims were literally fighting civil wars over, among other things, the very claims of religious, legal and cultural identity that were supposedly being forged with such miraculous unanimity. Second, it may well be that some parties *were* trying to replicate the story of a legendary ruler and his wives. But it may have been the patriarch of Egypt who picked the names Māriya and Sīrīn/Shīrīn for the two slave girls he sent in order to placate the Prophet and flatter him with the allusion to imperial tradition. That seems much more likely than that the Muslim community, spread as it was across the entire Near East, North Africa and Iran, and mired in three civil wars in its first century and a half, agreed to invent the Māriya-as-slave-concubine story.

Sources Cited: Aysha Hidayatullah, 'Māriyya the Copt: gender, sex and heritage in the legacy of Muhammad's *umm walad*,' 226; Kecia Ali, *Sexual Ethics and Islam*, 57–58; idem, *The Lives of Muhammad*, 132, 186; Kaleef K. Karim, 'The Prophet Muhammad's Wife Mariyah,' https://discover-the-truth.com/2016/07/14/prophet-muhammeds-wife-mariyah-maria/; al-Ḥākim al-Naysābūrī, *al-Mustadrak* (Hyderabad), 4:38–40; ibid. (Dār al-Ta'ṣīl), 7:73; E. Ann McDougall, '"To Marry One's Slave is as Easy as Eating a Meal",' 140–66; al-Zubayrī, *Kitāb Nasab Quraysh*, 21; *Ṣaḥīḥ Muslim*: *kitāb faḍā'il al-ṣaḥāba, bāb waṣiyyat al-nabī (ṣ) bi-ahl miṣr*; al-Nawawī, *Sharḥ Ṣaḥīḥ Muslim*, 15/16:331; idem, *Tahdhīb al-asmā' wa'l-lughāt*, 2:805; ʿAbd al-Raḥmān Ibn ʿAbd al-Ḥakam, *Futūḥ Miṣr*, 14; Elizabeth Urban, 'Hagar and Mariya: Early Islamic Models of Slave Motherhood,' 225; Kaj Öhrnberg, '*Māriya al-qibṭiyya* Unveiled,' 297–303; *Sunan Ibn Mājah*: *kitāb al-janā'iz, bāb mā jā'a fī al-ṣalāt ʿalā ibn rasūl Allāh (s) wa dhikr wafātihi*. See also http://www.ahlalhdeeth.com/vb/archive/index.php/t-9632.html. Thanks to my friend and colleague Muntasir Zaman, who identified the scribal error in some of the *Mustadrak* printings.

Appendix 5

Was Freedom a Human Right in the Shariah?

The Cairo Declaration of Human Rights in Islam (1990) was developed and adopted by the Organization of Islamic Cooperation (OIC) as a counterpart to the Universal Declaration of Human Rights. Article 11 a) of the Cairo Declaration states, 'Human beings are born free, and no one has the right to enslave, humiliate, oppress or exploit them, and there can be no subjugation but to Allah the Almighty.' Even after consulting with scholars of human rights who have studied the Cairo Declaration, I have not been able to find any information on how its contents were developed or justified on the basis of the Shariah tradition. Was freedom historically seen as a human right in Islam?

The Islamic legal tradition seems to have been an early developer of 'human rights.' From at least the late 700s CE Muslim jurists were referring to *ḥuqūq al-ʿibād* (the rights of God's slaves, i.e., humans) or *ḥuqūq ādamiyya* (Adamic rights, i.e., human rights) to mean rights possessed by all people, whether Muslim or not. Muslim jurists abstracted these from their scripture and legal discourse to form a framework of basic claims of property, contract and security. They included general notions of a right to property, physical integrity and some sort of due process. These concepts were not theorized clearly by early jurists. Rather, they found expression as explanations for concrete rulings derived from proof texts in *fiqh*.

In the eleventh century, this discourse of *ḥuqūq al-ʿibād/ādamiyya* converged with the limited natural law reasoning that was occurring among legal theorists, particularly in discussions around the objectives of the Shariah. The Ashʿarī legal theorist al-Juwaynī (d. 1085) proposed that the prohibitions of the Shariah function to preserve bodily integrity (*dam*), chastity (*furūj*), and property (*amwāl*), a concept that his student al-Ghazālī (d. 1111) developed into the famous Five Universals (*uṣūl*) that constitute the aims of the Shariah (*maqāṣid al-sharʿ*): protecting the integrity of life (*nafs*), reason (*ʿaql*), religion (*dīn*), lineage/paternity (*nasl*) and property (*māl*). The Islamic 'human rights' of physical inviolability and property can be seen as counterparts or perhaps as forerunners of these aims.

Muslim jurists distinguished the 'human rights' from 'the rights of God (*ḥuqūq Allāh*).' This latter group formed the counterpart to crimes and aspects of public law in the civil and common law legal traditions. They subsumed several categories or aspects. First, the 'rights of God' included the Hudud crimes. Second, as noted by Baber Johansen, they included the claims of the state and community on individuals in matters of public order, which made offenses like murder or assault 'public' crimes. Here the phrases 'the right of God' and 'public right (*ḥaqq ʿāmma*)' were synonymous.

Finally, 'the rights of God' included *riqq* because freedom was a right of God. This is because, according to the Shariah, 1) humans are born free and cannot be enslaved except by legal means; 2) what makes a human being enslavable is their *kufr*, and the ultimate right of God, as stated by the Prophet, is to be worshipped exclusively; 3) enslavement is carried out by the Muslim state and thus falls under the rubric of the 'rights of God' *qua* public law; and 4) in the case of a slave woman, her slave status permits a licit potential sexual relationship with her male owner, thus entering into the realm of relevancy to the Hudud crime of fornication (*zinā*).

The 'right of God' element of slavery is most visible in laws on emancipation (*ʿitq*). The Ottoman scholar Shaykhzāde (d. 1544) thus describes how one component of the Quranically ordained compensation for accidental homicide (Quran 4:92), namely freeing a slave, cannot be waived by the victim's kin. They can refuse to take the compensation payment (*diya*) from the guilty party, which is their right, but the expiation of freeing a slave cannot be waived because it is a right due to God (*ḥaqq Allāh*).

If freedom was a right of God, was it also a human right in the Shariah? In other words, was it like the rights to physical inviolability and property that the Shariah acknowledged all humans had regardless of religion? Freedom does appear as a right (*ḥaqq*) along with physical inviolability and property in the work of a subset of medieval Ḥanafī legal theorists. They proposed this as a corollary to their unusual claim that all humans were born in a state of receptiveness and what Murteza Bedir has called 'potential obligation' to the responsibility and trust that God had placed on mankind, not because they were presented with revelation but by dint of their being human. To be capable of such potential obligation, argued the

Ḥanafī jurist al-Dabūsī (d. 1039), humans must be born with 'the right of bodily inviolability, freedom and the capacity to own (*ḥaqq al-ʿiṣma wa'l-ḥurriyya wa'l-mālikiyya*).'

Today, some Muslim scholars point to al-Dabūsī's text as evidence that the Shariah envisions a human right of freedom. This is misleading, however. It builds a faulty assumption on the shared term 'right' (*ḥaqq*). Unlike the modern human rights assertion that no one can ever be legally enslaved, the right of freedom for these Ḥanafī scholars was not a non-derogable right as it is enshrined in the Universal Declaration of Human Rights or the 1966 International Covenant on Civil and Political Rights, Article 8.1. Scholars like al-Dabūsī saw freedom as the necessary natural state of humans. But that was not very different from the maxim agreed upon by all Muslim scholars that 'The default state of human beings is freedom.' That natural state could be legally altered, however. Al-Dabūsī acknowledges that the three rights of physical inviolability, capacity to own and freedom are present in the human species as a whole but can be absent from individuals. Just as life and property could be taken from a person for just cause, Muslim jurists held that freedom could be lost when someone was legally enslaved. In the pre-modern Shariah, non-Muslim/non-*dhimmī* captives in war and non-Muslims from outside of Muslim lands purchased from slave traders were presumed to be legally enslaved. Even after a slave converted to Islam, or when a Muslim slave woman had a child (not with her owner), such that the child was born Muslim, the property right of their owner was seen to supersede the natural human state of freedom even when the notional cause for its loss – unbelief – was not applicable.

Sources Cited: Anver Emon, '*Ḥuqūq Allāh* and *Ḥuqūq al-ʿIbād*: A Legal Heuristic for a Natural Rights Regime,' 325–91; Miriam Hoexter, '*Ḥuqūq Allāh* and *Ḥuqūq al-ʿIbād* as Reflected in the *Waqf* Institution,' 133–56; al-Muzanī, *Mukhtaṣar*, ed. ʿAbd al-Qādir Shāhīn (Beirut: Dār al-Kutub al-ʿIlmiyya, 1998), 133; ʿAbd al-Malik al-Juwaynī, *al-Burhān fī uṣūl al-fiqh*, 2:747; al-Ghazālī, *al-Mustaṣfā*, 174, 179; Baber Johansen, 'Secular and religious elements in Hanafite law,' 300–301; *Ṣaḥīḥ al-Bukhārī: kitāb al-jihād wa'l-siyar, bāb ism al-fars wa'l-ḥimār*; Muḥyī al-Dīn Shaykhzāde, *Ḥāshiyat Muḥyī al-Dīn Shaykhzāde ʿalā Tafsīr al-Bayḍāwī*, 3:384; Abū Zayd al-Dabūsī, *Taqwīm al-adilla*, 1:417–18 (thanks to Arnold Yasin Mol for these last two citations); ʿAbd al-ʿAzīz al-Bukhārī, *Kashf al-asrār*, 4:399.

For the *ḥaqq Allāh* element of *ʿitq*, see: Ibn al-Mundhir, *Kitāb al-Awsaṭ*, 11:428; al-Nawawī, *al-Majmūʿ*, 16:515; al-Wazzānī, *al-Miʿyār*, 10:333; al-Marghīnānī, *al-Hidāya*, 3:431. For the *ḥaqq Allāh* element of a slave woman's sexual status, see al-Ṭarābulusī, *Muʿīn al-ḥukkām*, 168 (citing Abū Ḥanīfa); Osswald, *Sklavenhandel und Sklavenleben*, 30 (discussed by the Mālikī scholar al-Dasūqī [d. 1815]).

Appendix 6

Enslavement of Apostate Muslims or Muslims Declared to be Unbelievers

In general and in theory, the main principles in Sunni law on apostasy and excommunication (*takfīr*) did not provide a very robust rubric for enslavement. In effect, whether or not Sunnis could enslave members of a sect or community that Sunni authorities considered apostate (*murtadd*) and/or *ab initio* non-Muslim (*kāfir*), despite that group self-identifying as Muslim, depended mainly on whether that group lay outside or inside the borders of the Sunni state in question. Those within the borders were almost always immune from enslavement, while those outside were at times seen as legitimate targets.*

The tenth-century Muʿtazilite scholar al-Kaʿbī (d. 931) stated that, as long as a heretical group was considered part of the Muslim religion (*milla*), neither they nor their children could be enslaved. The main Sunni position was tied to the *jizya* tax, which was levied on non-Muslim minorities allowed to live under Muslim ruler. According to this criterion, one group were those religions or communities eligible to pay the *jizya* (i.e., all major groups, including Hindus and Yazidis). If inside the Abode of Islam, they were protected *dhimmīs*. If outside the Abode of Islam, they were unbelievers who could be enslaved. A second group consisted of those deemed ineligible to pay the *jizya*. Like the first group, if encountered outside the Abode of Islam, they could be fought and enslaved. Unlike the first group, if they were found within the Abode of Islam, they should be asked to repent and fought if they refused to embrace Islam.

This second category included 'Muslim' sects whose beliefs put them outside the pale of Islam, like the Safavid Shiite followers and the Qarmatian movement of the ninth and tenth centuries. Such groups were considered apostates, who must either repent or be killed. Enslavement was not an

* Ibn Qudāma, *al-Mughnī*, 10:93.

option for their men, and it was rarely an option for their women (see below). It was seen by most Sunni scholars as acceptable to enslave the young children of apostates, since they were presumed to be non-Muslims like their parents, but their minority meant that they had not committed the crime of apostasy. Thus, the caliph ʿAlī enslaved the children of the tribe of Nājiya, which had apostatized during the Ridda Wars. A major opinion in the Ḥanbalī school did not allow enslaving the young children of apostates, since their birth into Islam had elevated them above that.*

The question of Sunni views on Imāmī Shiites requires close attention in light of the enslavement of Persian Shiite Muslims by Sunni Turkmens and Uzbeks. This discourse is complicated because, though Sunni writers often specify that they are passing judgment on a discrete category they call Rāfiḍīs (i.e., Imāmī Shiites), their judgments as to whether the subjects in question were Muslim or not often focus on specific actions or beliefs that have not been consistent features of Imāmī Shiism, such as cursing Abū Bakr and ʿUmar. This cursing has been encouraged by some Shiite ulama at various times and discouraged by some at others, with popular practice often ignoring ulama opinion altogether.† Just as often, however, Sunni rulings on the status of Imāmī Shiites are found in general books on creed or works dealing with the larger issue of *takfīr*. But these rulings are derived from aforementioned discussions on rulings on specific actions or beliefs. Such general books often assume that tenets and practices like cursing the first two caliphs are synonymous with Shiism.

Since the list of Shiite practices or beliefs that Sunni authors target generally subsumes at least some items that are consistent features of Imāmī Shiite belief (such as the rejection of the legitimacy of the first two caliphs), or were found in Imāmī Shiism as it was elaborated or practiced in some region and at some point in the post-medieval world, I will treat the Sunni discussions summarized below as applicable to Imāmī Shiism overall unless

* Abū al-Qāsim al-Kaʿbī al-Balkhī, *Kitāb al-Maqālāt*, 379; ʿAbd al-Qāhir al-Baghdādī, *Kitāb Uṣūl al-dīn*, 292–93, 322–32; Mullā Hüsrev, *Durar al-ḥukkām*, 1:301; Yaḥyā b. Ādam, *Kitāb al-Kharāj*, 69; Abū Yaʿlā Ibn al-Farrāʾ, *Kitāb al-Muʿtamad*, 273; Ibn Qudāma, *al-Mughnī*, 10:93–94.

† Al-Ṭabāṭabāʾī al-Ḥakīm insists that the core Imāmī position is not to do *takfīr* of any of the Prophet's Companions, though he acknowledges that it is difficult to answer for the breadth of Shiite belief and practice on this issue. He defends cursing Companions as something they did to each other; Muḥammad Saʿīd al-Ṭabāṭabāʾī, *Fī riḥāb al-ʿaqīda*, 1:39–40, 153–55. See Etan Kohlberg, 'The Attitude of the Imāmī Shīʿīs to the Companions of the Prophet,' 32–46, 206–27.

otherwise specified. It is important to note that Sunni fatwas on the status of Imāmī Shiites have been consistently shaped by the political contexts in which they were written.*

The most frequently and vigorously articulated position in pre-modern and much modern Sunni law is that Imāmī Shiites are unbelievers (*kuffār*), mostly because of their rejection of the legitimacy of the caliphate of the first three successors of the Prophet as well as the Shiite custom of cursing the first two caliphs. Scholars advocating this position have often even insisted that anyone who doubts that Shiites are unbelievers is also an unbeliever. The most explicit exposition of this harsh, first position came from the Ottoman Ḥanafī scholar Nūḥ al-Ḥanafī (d. 1660), who wrote that Shiites should be fought and killed either as a Hadd punishment for rebellion and spreading corruption in the land or as the punishment for apostasy. Their repentance could not be accepted. Their women could be enslaved because, in a position unique to the Ḥanafī school, a female apostate could be enslaved if she entered the Dār al-Ḥarb. Their children could also be enslaved, since they followed their mothers in the matter of slavery. Finally, any Imāmī Shiites who remained must be treated like polytheists (*mushrikūn*), meaning they could not be allowed to remain within the Muslim realm or pay the *jizya*.† Decades later this opinion was substantially replicated by the Ottoman Shaykh al-Islam ʿAbdallāh Efendī (d. 1743) during another round of wars between the Ottomans and Safavids: Persian Shiites were apostates who must be killed unless they reverted to Islam, and their women and children could be enslaved. ʿAbdallāh Efendī introduced a more dangerous element as well. If one categorized Shiites not as apostates from Islam but simply as unbelievers who had never been Muslims to begin with, then Shiite lands conquered by a (Sunni) Muslim army were like any unbelieving population – they could all be enslaved.‡

With the Kizilbash Shiite followers of the Safavid Shah Ismāʿīl (d. 1524), the case was exacerbated greatly by the antinomian tendencies of the early

* See, for example, Amalia Levanoni, '*Takfīr* in Egypt and Syria during the Mamlūk Period,' 155–88; Guido Steinberg, 'Jihadi-Salafism and Shi'is: Remarks about the Intellectual Roots of anti-Shi'ism,' 107–25.

† Cited from a book copied by ʿAbdallāh Efendī and cited by Ibn ʿĀbidīn, *Kitāb al-ʿUqūd al-durriyya fī tanqīḥ al-Fatāwā al-ḥāmidiyya*, 1:102–3. Nūḥ's fatwa is found in a manuscript *majmūʿa*, entitled 'Risāla fī wujūb muqātalat al-rawāfiḍ wa jawāz qatlihim,' 4b–7a.

‡ Yanishehirli ʿAbdallāh Efendī, *Behcetül'l-Fetâvâ*, 189–92.

Safavids and their extremist belief that the Shah was God incarnate on earth. For Ottomans like Shaykhs al-Islam Ibn Kamāl (d. 1534) and Abū Su'ūd (d. 1574), this clearly pushed the Safavid movement into the territory of unbelief. They concluded that they were apostates, the land they controlled was Dār al-Ḥarb, and their women and children could be enslaved (though Abū Su'ūd exempted any children over five or six years old who pronounced the Muslim testimony of faith). Their men could either revert to Islam or be killed.*

A second Sunni position on Shiites, which seems to be less salient in Sunni writings but which has historically been more widely followed in practice, considers Shiites to be mere heretics (*mubtadi'a, zanādiqa, ḍāllīn*) as opposed to unbelievers. Ibn Taymiyya (d. 1328) articulated this clearly when he explained that Imāmī Shiites were Muslims/believers both inwardly and outwardly, though he considered their scholars to be hypocrites and heretics (*munāfiqūn, zanādiqa*). Al-Ghazālī (d. 1111) explained that denying the caliphates of the first three rulers did not violate any core principles (*uṣūl al-dīn*) of the religion and was seconded by the great theologian al-Taftāzānī (d. 1390). Ibn Abī al-'Izz al-Ḥanafī (d. 1390) cautioned against declaring Shiites unbelievers, and Mullā 'Alī al-Qāri' (d. 1606) warned against overgeneralization and severity in this. Ibn 'Ābidīn (d. 1836) only applied the unbeliever label to those Shiites who held extremist beliefs like Gabriel having erred in giving the revelation to Muhammad instead of 'Alī or accusing Aisha of fornication.† Opinions in the Shāfi'ī school on declaring Shiites unbelievers have been split.‡

Despite episodes of sectarian violence, it is this more lenient opinion that has characterized the general treatment of Shiites by Sunni Muslim

* Ertuğrul Düzdağ, *Ebussuud Efendi Fetvaları*, 138-139; Muḥammad al-Kawākibī, *al-Fawā'id al-samiyya*, 2:396; *al-Fatāwā al-Hindiyya*, 2:264; Ibn Kamāl Pāsha, *Majmū' rasā'il al-'allāma Ibn Kamāl Bāsha*, 5:457-461. See also Vladimir Minorsky, *Medieval Iran and Its Neighbors*, Chapter 8: 'The Poetry of Shah Ismā'īl'.

† Ibn Taymiyya, *Minhāj al-sunna*, 2:452–53; Denise Aigle, 'The Mongol Invasion of Bilād al-Shām by Ghāzān Khān and Ibn Taymīya's Three "Anti-Mongol" Fatwas,' 99; al-Ghazālī, *al-Iqtiṣād fī al-i'tiqād*, 122; Ibn Abī al-'Izz, *Sharḥ al-'Aqīda al-Ṭaḥāwiyya*, 320–24; Sa'd al-Dīn al-Taftāzānī, *Sharḥ al-Arba'īn al-Nawawiyya*, 60; idem, *Sharḥ al-'Aqā'id al-Nasafiyya*, 1:206; Ibn 'Ābidīn, *Ḥāshiyat Ibn 'Ābidīn*, 4:237, 5:11; Mullā 'Alī al-Qāri', *Majmū'*, 6:348 ff., 361–63, 371, 381, 419–25 (from his treatises *Shamm al-'awāriḍ fī dhamm al-rawāfiḍ* and *Sulālat al-risāla fī dhamm al-rawāfiḍ min ahl al-ḍalāla*).

‡ Taqī al-Dīn al-Subkī, *Fatāwā*, 2:577–94; Ibn Ḥajar al-Haytamī, *al-I'lām bi-qawāṭi' al-islām*, 17; Lutz Wiederhold, 'Blasphemy against the Prophet and His Companions,' 39–70.

jurists, rulers and communities. Moreover, regardless of whether Shiites are unbelievers or not, the general rule and practice among Sunni Muslims has been that even minority groups that are considered unbelievers or apostates are left alone provided they do not spread their beliefs or disrupt order, as exemplified by the Sunni treatment of Kharijite groups on the fringes of Sunni lands. The Ottoman Shaykh al-Islam Abū Su'ūd Efendī even stated that the Kizilbash Shiite followers of the Safavid Shah, if they dwelt peacefully and quietly in Ottoman lands, should be left alone.* Interestingly, Mullā 'Alī al-Qāri' studied with the son of an imam in Herat who was killed by the Safavids but still drew attention to what he saw as an unacceptably excessive anti-Shiite sentiment among the Uzbeks in particular, and how this had led to an escalation of persecution between them and the Safavids. He even directly contradicted the senior Ottoman ulama of his own Ḥanafī school by declaring that the Safavid realm of Khurasan was not Dār al-Ḥarb, since some of its Shiite inhabitants might only be heretics, not unbelievers, and there was no guarantee at all that Sunni inhabitants there would not also be enslaved or killed.†

In practice, the enslavement of self-identifying Muslims by fundamentalist Muslim movements has tended to meet with outrage. On the Red Sea coast of Yemen, a fanatic named 'Alī bin Mahdī (d. 1159) adopted the view that anyone who sinned or disagreed with his religious views was an apostate, and their women and children could be enslaved. This was considered outrageous. In the early 1800s, the Sokoto Caliphate revivalist movement expanded based on the claim that many of its neighboring 'Muslim' states were actually non-Muslim and had to be brought back into the fold. Its founding figures, however, stated that, while it was licit to make war on deviant and apostate Muslims, they could not be enslaved. In the 1880s, when a leading Muslim scholar in Senegal issued a fatwa allowing his ruler to enslave a defeated opponent's followers and their families on the flimsy grounds that their leader was a heretic, it remained an issue of controversy for decades. The enslavement of Persian Shiite Muslims by Sunni Uzbeks and Turkmens was similarly objected to by some Sunni Muslim scholars.‡

* Ibn Qudāma, *al-Mughnī*, 10:58–60; al-Nawawī, *Sharḥ Ṣaḥīḥ Muslim*, 7/8:175–77; Ibn Ḥajar, *Fatḥ al-Bārī*, 12:353; al-Kawākibī, *al-Fawā'id al-samiyya*, 2:396.

† Al-Qāri', *Majmū'*, 6:358, 362–63.

‡ A. Bivar, 'The *Wathīqat Ahl al-Sūdān*,' 240–41; Ware, *The Walking Qur'an*, 158–60; Najm al-Dīn 'Umāra al-Yamanī, *al-Mustafīd fī akhbār Ṣan'ā' wa Zabīd*, 236; Mullā 'Alī al-Qāri', *Majmū' rasā'il*, 6:357–63, 371, 381.

Select Bibliography

This bibliography is limited to the sources cited in the endnotes of this book. It makes no distinction between primary and secondary sources. 'Al-' is omitted from the first letter of listed Arabic names unless it is part of how a contemporary author specifies their name. I have not listed some Classical or canonical sources like Rousseau's *On the Social Contract*, instead citing them by standard conventions for those texts and pointing out in the endnotes if a particular translation was relied on.

ʿAbd al-Jabbār al-Asadabādhī. *Al-Mughnī fī abwāb al-tawḥīd wa'l-ʿadl*. Ed. Ibrāhīm Madkūr et al., 15 vols. Cairo: al-Mu'assasa al-Miṣriyya, 1960–69

ʿAbdallāh b. Aḥmad Ibn Ḥanbal. *Masā'il al-imām Aḥmad Ibn Ḥanbal riwāyat ibnihi*. Ed. Zuhayr al-Shāwīsh. Beirut: al-Maktab al-Islāmī, 1981

ʿAbdallāh Efendī, Yenishehirli. *Behcetü'l-Fetâvâ*. Ed. Süleyman Kaya et al. Istanbul: Klasik, 2011

ʿAbduh, Muḥammad. *Al-Aʿmāl al-kāmila*. Ed. Muḥammad ʿImāra. 6 vols. Cairo: Dār al-Shurūq, 1993

Abou El Fadl, Khaled. 'Cultivating Human Rights: Islamic Law and the Humanist Imperative.' In *Law and Tradition in Islamic Thought*, ed. Michael Cook et al. New York: Palgrave Macmillan, 2013

—. *The War on Terror*. Oxford: Oxford University Press, 2009

Abu-Lughod, Lila. 'Authorizing Moral Crusades to Save Muslim Women.' Farhat Ziadeh Annual Lecture. Seattle: University of Washington, 2012

—. *Do Muslim Women Need Saving?* Cambridge, MA: Harvard University Press, 2013

Abū Suʿūd Efendī. *Tafsīr Abī Suʿūd*. 9 vols in 5. Beirut: Dār Iḥyā' al-Turāth al-ʿArabī, n.d.

Abu Taleb, Mirza. *Westward Bound*. Trans. Charles Stewart. New Delhi: Oxford University Press, 2005

Abū Zahra, Muḥammad. *Fatāwā*. Ed. Muḥammad ʿUthmān Shabīr. Damascus: Dār al-Qalam, 2006

—. 'Introduction: On the Practice of Slavery in Islam.' In *Sharḥ al-Siyar al-kabīr*, by Muḥammad Ḥasan al-Shaybānī and Muḥammad b. Aḥmad al-Sarakhsī, ed. M. Abū Zahra and Muṣṭafā Zayd, 1:78–84. Cairo: Cairo University Press, 1958

Adelman, Jeremy. *Sovereignty and Revolution in the Iberian Atlantic*. Princeton: Princeton University Press, 2006

Aford, Terry. *A Prince among Slaves: The True Story of an African Prince Sold into Slavery in the American South*. Oxford: Oxford University Press, 2007

Ahmed, Shahab. *What is Islam?: The Importance of Being Islamic*. Princeton: Princeton University Press, 2016

Aigle, Denise. 'The Mongol Invasion of Bilād al-Shām by Ghāzān Khān and Ibn Taymīya's Three "Anti-Mongol" Fatwas.' *Mamlūk Studies Review* 11, n. 2 (2007): 89–120

ʿAjlūnī, Ismāʿīl. *Kashf al-khafā ʿammā ishtahara min al-aḥādīth ʿalā alsinat al-nās*. Ed. Aḥmad al-Qalāsh. 2 vols. Cairo: Maktabat Dār al-Turāth, 1997

Akgündüz, Ahmed. *Ottoman Harem*. Rotterdam: IUR Press, 2015

Al-Attas, Syed Naquib. *Prolegomena to the Metaphysics of Islam*. Johor: Universiti Teknologi Malaysia Press, 2014

Albānī, Muḥammad Nāṣir al-Dīn. *Ḍaʿīf Sunan Abī Dāwūd*. Kuwait: Mu'assasat Gharrās, 2002

—. *Ḍaʿīf Sunan Ibn Mājah*. Riyadh: Maktabat al-Maʿārif, 1997

—. *Fatāwā al-shaykh al-Albānī*. Ed. ʿUkāsha ʿAbd al-Mannān al-Ṭayyibī. Cairo: Maktabat al-Turāth al-Islāmī, 1994

—. *Irwā' al-ghalīl fī takhrīj ḥadīth Manār al-sabīl*. Ed. Muḥammad Zuhayr al-Shāwīsh. 9 vols. Beirut: al-Maktab al-Islāmī, 1979

—. *Silsilat al-aḥādīth al-ḍaʿīfa wa'l-mawḍūʿa*. 14 vols. 2nd edn. Riyadh: Maktabat al-Maʿārif, 2000–2005

—. *Silsilat al-aḥādīth al-ṣaḥīḥa*. 7 vols. Riyadh: Maktabat al-Maʿārif, 1995–2002

Ali, Abdullah Hamid. 'The "Negro" in Afro-Arabian Muslim Consciousness.' PhD dissertation, Graduate Theological Union, 2016

ʿĀlī, Gelibolulu Muṣṭafā. *Siyaset Sanatı: Nushatü's Selâtîn*. Ed. Faris Çerçi. Istanbul: Büyüyen Ay, 2015

Ali, Kecia. 'Concubinage and Consent.' *International Journal of Middle East Studies* 49, n. 1 (2017): 148–52

—. *The Lives of Muhammad*. Cambridge, MA: Harvard University Press, 2014

—. *Marriage and Slavery in Early Islam*. Cambridge, MA: Harvard University Press, 2010

—. *Sexual Ethics and Islam*. 2nd edn. London: Oneworld, 2016

—. 'Slavery and Sexual Ethics in Islam.' In *Beyond Slavery: Overcoming its Religious and Sexual Legacies*, ed. Bernadette J. Brooten and Jacqueline Hazelton, 107–24. New York: Palgrave Macmillan, 2010

Ali, Mohamed M. Yunis. *Medieval Islamic Pragmatics: Sunni Legal Theorists' Model of Communication*. Richmond, UK: Curzon, 2000

Ali, Syed Ameer. *A Critical Examination of the Life and Teachings of Mohammed*. London: Williams and Norgate, 1873

Allain, Jean, ed. *The Legal Understanding of Slavery: From the Historical to the Contemporary*. London: Oxford University Press, 2012

—. 'R v Tang: Clarifying the Definition of 'Slavery' in International Law.' *Melbourne Journal of International Law* 10, n. 1 (2009): 246–57

—. and Robin Hickey. 'Property and the definition of slavery.' *International & Comparative Law Quarterly* 61 n., 4 (2012): 915–38

Alpers, Edward A. *The Indian Ocean in World History*. Oxford: Oxford University Press, 2014

Alwani, Taha Jabir. *Shaykh Taha Jabir al-Alwani on Issues in Contemporary Islamic Thought*. Herndon, VA: International Institute of Islamic Thought, 2005

Amitai, Reuven. 'Continuity and Change in the Mongol Army of the Ilkhanate.' In *The Mongols' Middle East*, ed. Bruno De Nicola and Charles Melville, 38–54. Leiden: Brill, 2016

Andalusī, Muḥammad b. Sirāj. *Fatāwā Qāḍī al-Jamā'a*. Ed. Muḥammad Abū al-Ajfān. Beirut: Dār Ibn Ḥazm, 2006

Andaya, Leonard Y. *The Kingdom of Johor 1641–1728*. Kuala Lumpur: Oxford University Press, 1975

Anderson, Norman. *Law Reform in the Muslim World*. London: Athlone Press, 1976

An-Na'im, Abdullahi. *Towards an Islamic Reformation*. Syracuse: Syracuse University Press, 1990

Anjum, Ovamir. 'Islam as a Discursive Tradition: Talal Asad and His Interlocutors.' *Comparative Studies of South Asia, Africa and the Middle East* 27, n. 3 (2007): 656–72

—. *Politics, Law and Community in Islamic Thought*. Cambridge: Cambridge University Press, 2012

Ansari, Mohammad Azhar. *European Travellers under the Mughals 1580–1627*. Delhi: Idarah-i Adabiyat-i Delli, 1975

Anscombe, G. E. M. 'Modern Moral Philosophy.' *Journal of the Royal Institute of Philosophy* 33, n. 124 (1958): 1–19

'Aqqād, 'Abbās Maḥmūd. 'Mas'alat al-riqq fī al-Islām.' *Minbar al-Islām* 18, n. 9 (1961): 17–19

Arendt, Hanna. *On Revolution*. London: Penguin Books, 1990; reprint of Viking Press, 1963

Argument of John Quincy Adams, before the Supreme Court of the United States, in the case of the United States, appellants, vs. Cinque, and others, Africans, captured in the schooner Amistad... New York: S.W. Benedict, 1841

Aristotle. *Metaphysics*. Cited by convention.

—. *Politics*. Cited by convention.

Asad, Muhammad, trans. *The Message of the Qur'ān*. Gibraltar: Dar al-Andalus, 1980

Atçıl, Abdurrahman. 'The Safavid Threat and Juristic Authority in the Ottoman Empire during the 16th Century.' *International Journal of Middle East Studies* 49, n. 2 (2017): 295–314

Atçıl, Muhammet Zahit. 'State and Government in the Mid Sixteenth-Century Ottoman Empire: The Grand Vizierates of Rüstem Pasha (1544–1561).' PhD dissertation, University of Chicago, 2015

Aṭfayyish, Muḥammad Yūsuf. *Sharḥ Kitāb al-Nīl wa Shifā' al-'alīl*. 17 vols. Jeddah: Maktabat al-Irshād, n.d.

Augustine. 'Lying (*De Mendacio*).' In *The Fathers of the Church* 16. Trans. Sister Mary Sarah Muldowney. New York: Fathers of the Church, 1952

Awlaki, Anwar. 'The Ruling on Dispossessing the Disbelievers wealth [sic] in Dar al-Harb.' *Inspire* 4 (2011): 55–60

Ayalon, David. *L'Esclavage du Mamelouk*. Jerusalem: Israel Oriental Society, 1951

—. 'Preliminary Remarks on the *Mamlūk* Military Institution in Islam.' In *The Mamluk Military Society*, 44–58. London: Variorum, 1979

Aydoğdu, Nergiz. 'Makyavelist Düşüncenin Türkiye'ye Girişi: Onsekizinci Yüzyıl Osmanlı Siyaset Felsefi.' PhD dissertation, Marmara University, 2008

'Aynī, Badr al-Dīn Maḥmūd. *Al-Ramz sharḥ al-Kanz*. MS. 906. Maktabat Wizārat al-Awqāf al-Kuwaytiyya

Ayoub, Samy. '"The Sulṭān says": State Authority in the Late Ḥanafī Tradition.' *Islamic Law and Society* 23, n. 3 (2016): 239–78

Azam, Hina. *Sexual Violation in Islamic Law*. Cambridge: Cambridge University Press, 2015

Bābā, Aḥmad al-Tunbuktī. *Mi'rāj al-Ṣu'ūd: Ahmad Baba's Replies on Slavery*. Ed. and trans. John Hunwick and Fatima Harrak. Rabat: Institute of African Studies, 2000

Babaie, Sussan et al. *Slaves of the Shah: New Elites of Safavid Iran*. London: I. B. Tauris, 2004

Bābartī, Akmal al-Dīn Muḥammad b. Muḥammad. *Al-'Ināya sharḥ al-Hidāya*. 10 vols. Beirut: Dār al-Fikr, n.d.

Bacharach, Jere L. 'African Military Slaves in the Medieval Middle East: The Cases of Iraq (869–955) and Egypt (868–1171).' *International Journal of Middle East Studies* 13, n. 4 (1981): 471–95

Bachrach, Bernard S. *Early Medieval Jewish Policy in Western Europe*. Minneapolis: University of Minnesota Press, 1977

Badā'ūnī, 'Abd al-Qādir. *Muntakhab al-tavārīkh*. [Lucknow]: Nawal Kishore, 1868 (Persian original)

—. *Muntakhabu-t-Tawārīkh*. Trans. W. H. Lowe. 3 vols. Delhi: Renaissance Publishing, 1986

Baer, Gabriel. *Studies in the Social History of Modern Egypt*. Chicago: University of Chicago Press, 1969

Baghdādī, 'Abd al-Qāhir. *Kitāb Uṣūl al-dīn*. Istanbul: Maṭba'at al-Dawla, 1927

Baghdādī, al-Khaṭīb. *Al-Jāmi' li-akhlāq al-rāwī wa ādāb al-sāmi'*. Ed. Maḥmūd Ṭaḥḥān. 2 vols. Riyadh: Maktabat al-Ma'ārif, 1983

—. *Tārīkh Baghdād*. Ed. Muṣṭafā 'Abd al-Qādir 'Aṭā. 14 vols. Beirut: Dār al-Kutub al-'Ilmiyya, 1997

Balādhurī, Aḥmad b. Yaḥyā. *Futūḥ al-buldān*. Ed. 'Abdallāh Anīs al-Ṭabbā'. Beirut: Mu'assasat al-Ma'ārif, 1987

Baldwin, Barry. 'Two Aspects of the Spartacus Slave Revolt.' *The Classical Journal* 62, n. 7 (1967): 289–94

Bales, Kevin. *Disposable People: New Slavery in the Global Economy*. Berkeley: University of California Press, 2012

—. *Understanding Global Slavery*. Berkeley: University of California Press, 2005

Ba'lī, 'Abd al-Raḥmān b. 'Abdallāh. *Kashf al-mukhaddarāt wa riyāḍ al-muzhirāt li-sharḥ Akhṣar al-mukhtaṣarāt*. Ed. Muḥammad Nāṣir al-'Ujaymī. 2 vols. Beirut: Dār al-Bashā'ir al-Islāmiyya, 2002

Balkhī, Abū al-Qāsim al-Ka'bī. *Kitāb al-Maqālāt*. Ed. Hüseyin Hansu. Istanbul: Kuramer, 2018

Barcia, Manuel. *West African Warfare in Bahia and Cuba*. Oxford: Oxford University Press, 2014

Batran, Aziz Abdalla. 'The 'Ulama of Fas, Mulay Isma'il, and the Issue of the Haratin of Fas.' In *Slaves and Slavery in Muslim West Africa* – Volume II, ed. J. R. Willis, 1–15. London: Frank Cass, 1985

Bayhaqī, Abū Bakr Aḥmad. *Al-Sunan al-kubrā*. Ed. Muḥammad 'Abd al-Qādir 'Aṭā. 11 vols. Beirut: Dār al-Kutub al-'Ilmiyya, 1999

—. *Manāqib al-Shāfi'ī*. Ed. Al-Sayyid Aḥmad Ṣaqr. 2 vols. Cairo: Dār al-Turāth, 1970

—. *Shu'ab al-īmān*. Ed. Muḥammad Sa'īd Zaghlūl. 7 vols. Beirut: Dār al-Kutub al-'Ilmiyya, 1990

Bayram al-Khāmis, Muḥammad. 'Al-Taḥqīq fī mas'alat al-raqīq.' Parts 1 and 2. *Al-Muqtaṭaf* 15, n. 8 (1891): 505–13; 15, n. 9 (1891): 577–84

—*Ṣafwat al-i'tibār bi-mustawda' al-amṣār wa'l-aqṭār*. Ed. 'Alī al-Ṭāhir al-Shanūfī et al. 2nd edn. Tunis: al-Majma' al-Tūnisī li'l-'Ulūm wa'l-Ādāb, 2000

Bender, Thomas, ed. *The Antislavery Debate*. Berkeley: University of California Press, 1992

Bergelson, Vera. 'Consent to Harm.' In *The Ethics of Consent*, ed. Franklin G. Miller and Alan Wertheimer, 163–92. Oxford: Oxford University Press, 2010

Berlin, Ira. *Many Thousands Gone: The First Two Centuries of Slavery in North America*. Cambridge, MA: Belknap Press, 1998

Berlin, Isaiah. *Isaiah Berlin: The Proper Study of Mankind*. New York: Farrar, Straus and Giroux, 1998

Berquist, Emily. 'Early Anti-Slavery Sentiment in the Spanish Atlantic World.' *Slavery & Abolition* 31, n. 2 (2010): 181–205

Bivar, A. D. H. 'The *Wathīqat Ahl al-Sūdān*: A Manifesto of the Fulani *Jihād*.' *Journal of African History* 11, n. 2 (1961): 235–43

Blackmon, Douglas. *Slavery by Another Name: The Re-enslavement of Black People in America from the Civil War to World War II*. New York: Doubleday, 2008

Blecher, Joel. *Said the Prophet of God: Hadith Commentary across a Millennium*. Oakland: University of California Press, 2018

Blunt, Wilfrid Scawen. *Future of Islam*. Dublin: Nonsuch, 2007, originally published 1882

—. *Secret History of the English Occupation of Egypt; Being a Personal Narrative of Events*. New York, A. A. Knopf, 1922

—. 'Slavery in Egypt.' *Anti-Slavery Reporter* 2, n. 4 (April 1882): 91–92

Boahen, A. Adu. *Britain, the Sahara, and the Western Sudan 1788–1861*. Oxford: Clarendon, 1964

Le Bon, Gustave. *La Civilisation des Arabes*. Paris: Librairie de Fermin-Didot, 1884

Bonnassie, Pierre. *From Slavery to Feudalism in South-Western Europe*. Cambridge: Cambridge University Press, 1991

Boomgaard, Peter. 'Human Capital, Slavery and Low Rates of Economic and Population Growth in Indonesia, 1600–1910.' *Slavery & Abolition* 24, n. 2 (2003): 83–96

Botte, Roger. *Esclavages et Abolitions en Terres d'Islam*. [Paris]: André Versaille, 2010

Boyar, Ebru and Kate Fleet. *A Social History of Ottoman Istanbul*. Cambridge: Cambridge University Press, 2010

Brace, Laura. *The Politics of Slavery*. Edinburgh: Edinburgh University Press, 2018

Bradley, K. R. *Slaves and Masters in the Roman Empire: A Study in Social Control*. Brussels: Latomus Revue d'Études Latines, 1984

Brady, Robert. 'The Role of Las Casas in the Emergence of Negro Slavery in the New World.' *Revista de Historia de América* 61–2 (1966): 43–55

Bray, Julia. 'Men, women and slaves in Abbasid society.' In *Gender in the Early Medieval World: East and West, 300–900*, ed. Leslie Brubaker and Julia M. H. Smith, 121–46. Cambridge: Cambridge University Pres, 2004

Broad, Jacqueline. 'Mary Astell on Marriage and Lockean Slavery.' *History of Political Thought* 35, n. 4 (2014): 717–38

Brockopp, Jonathan. *Early Mālikī Law: Ibn ʿAbd al-Ḥakam and his Major Compendium of Jurisprudence*. Leiden: Brill, 2000

—. 'Islamic Origins and Incidental Normativity.' *Journal of the American Academy of Religion* 84, n. 1 (2016): 28–43

Brooke, Christopher. *Philosophic Pride: Stoicism and Political Thought from Lipsius to Rousseau*. Princeton: Princeton University Press, 2012

Brooke, Rosalind and Christopher. *Popular Religion in the Middle Ages.* New York: Barnes and Noble, 1984

Brown, Jonathan A. C. 'Even if It's Not True It's True: Using Unreliable Hadiths in Sunni Islam.' *Islamic Law and Society* 18 (2011): 1–52

—. *Hadith: Muhammad's Legacy in the Medieval and Modern World.* 2nd edn. London: Oneworld, 2017

—. 'Is the Devil in the Details?: Tension between Minimalism and Comprehensiveness in the Shariah.' *Journal of Religious Ethics* 39, n. 3 (2011): 458–72

—. *Misquoting Muhammad.* London: Oneworld, 2014

—. 'Scripture, Legal Interpretation and Social Praxis in the Islamic Tradition: The Cases of Polygamy and Slavery.' In *Religious Minorities in Christian, Jewish and Muslim Law (5th–15th Centuries),* ed. Nora Berend et al., 99–113. Turnhout: Brepols, 2017

Brown, Kenneth. 'Profile of a Nineteenth-Century Moroccan Scholar.' In *Scholars, Saints and Sufis,* ed. Nikki Keddie, 127–48. Los Angeles: University of California Press, 1972

Brulin, Rémi. 'Le discours américain sur le terrorisme: Constitution, evolution et contextes d'enonciation (1972–1992).' PhD dissertation, Université de la Sorbonne Nouvelle, 2011

Brunt, P. A. *Studies in Greek History and Thought.* Oxford: Clarendon Press, 1993

Buber, Martin. 'Autobiographical Fragments.' In *The Philosophy of Martin Buber,* ed. Paul Arthur Schlipp and Maurice Friedman. London: Cambridge University Press, 1967

Buckland, W. W. *The Roman Law of Slavery.* New York: AMS, 1969, reprint of Cambridge University Press, 1908

Buhūtī, Manṣūr b. Yūnus. *Kashshāf al-qināʿ ʿan matn al-Iqnāʿ.* 6 vols. Beirut: ʿĀlam al-Kutub, 1983

—. *Al-Rawḍ al-murbiʿ.* Ed. Bashīr Muḥammad ʿUyūn. Damascus: Maktabat Dār al-Bayān, 1999

Bukhārī, ʿAlāʾ al-Dīn ʿAbd al-ʿAzīz. *Kashf al-asrār ʿan Uṣūl Fakhr al-Islām al-Bazdawī.* Ed. ʿAbdallāh Maḥmūd ʿUmar. 4 vols. Beirut: Dār al-Kutub al-ʿIlmiyya, 1997

Bukhārī, Muḥammad b. Ismāʿīl. *Ṣaḥīḥ al-Bukhārī.* Cited to standard editions.

—. *Al-Tārīkh al-kabīr.* Ed. Muṣṭafā ʿAbd al-Qādir ʿAṭā. 9 vols. Beirut: Dār al-Kutub al-ʿIlmiyya, 2001

Burak, Guy. 'Faith, law and empire in the age of Ottoman "Confessionalization" (fifteenth–seventeenth centuries): the case of "renewal of faith".' *Mediterranean Historical Review* 28, n. 1 (2013): 1–23

Burke, Edmund. *Reflections on the Revolution in France.* Ed. Thomas H. D. Mahoney. Indianapolis: Bobbs-Merrill, 1955

Burnes, Alexander. *Travels into Bokhara.* 3 vols. London: John Murray, 1834

De Busbecq, Ogier. *Turkish Letters.* Trans. E. S. Forster. London: Eland, 2001

Bush, Michael L., ed. *Serfdom and Slavery: Studies in Legal Bondage.* New York: Longman, 1996

Būṭī, Muḥammad Saʿīd Ramaḍān. *Hādhihi mushkilātuhum.* Damascus: Dār al-Fikr, [1994]

—. *Min al-fikar wa'l-qalb.* Rev. edn. Damascus: Dār al-Faqīh, [1997], originally published 1969

Butler, Judith. 'Sexual Consent: Some Thoughts on Psychoanalysis and Law.' *Columbia Journal of Gender and Law* 21, n. 2 (2011): 405–29

Cairns, John W. 'The Definition of Slavery in Eighteenth-Century Thinking.' In *The Legal Understanding of Slavery*, ed. Jean Allain, 61–84. London: Oxford University Press, 2012

Campbell, Gwyn, ed. *Abolition and its Aftermath in Indian Ocean Africa and Asia.* London: Routledge, 2005

—, et al. 'Introduction: Resisting bondage in the Indian Ocean world.' In *Resisting Bondage in Indian Ocean Africa and Asia,* ed. Campbell et al., 1–9. London: Routledge, 2006

—. 'Introduction: Slavery and other forms of Unfree Labour in the Indian Ocean World.' *Slavery & Abolition* 24, n. 2 (2003): ix–xxxii

—, ed. *The Structure of Slavery in Indian Ocean Africa and Asia.* Portland: Frank Cass, 2004

—. 'Unfree labour and the significance of abolition in Madagascar, c. 1825–97.' In *Abolition and its Aftermath in Indian Ocean Africa and Asia,* ed. Gwyn Campbell, 66–82. London: Routledge, 2005

— and Elizabeth Elbourne, ed. *Sex, Power and Slavery.* Athens, OH: Ohio University Press, 2014

Caner, Daniel F. *History and Hagiography from the Late Antique Sinai.* Liverpool: Liverpool University Press, 2010

Caplan, Lionel. 'Power and Status in South Asian Slavery.' In *Asian and African Systems of Slavery*, ed. James L. Watson, 169–94. Oxford: Basil Blackwell, 1980

Carey, Daniel. *Locke, Shaftesbury, and Hutcheson.* Cambridge: Cambridge University Press, 2006

Casewell, Fuad Matthew. *The Slave Girls of Baghdad: The Qiyān in the Early Abbasid Era.* London: I. B. Tauris, 2011

Cevdet, Ahmet Pasha. *Tezâkir: 1–12.* Ed. Cavid Baysun. Ankara: Türk Tarih Kurumu Basımevi, 1953

Chatterjee, Indrani. 'Abolition by denial: The South Asian Example.' In *Abolition and its Aftermath in Indian Ocean Africa and Asia,* ed. Gwyn Campbell, 150–68. London: Routledge, 2005.

—. *Gender, Slavery and Law in Colonial India.* New Delhi: Oxford University Press, 1999

— and Richard Eaton, ed. *Slavery & South Asian History.* Bloomington: Indiana University Press, 2006

Chattopadhyay, Amal Kumar. *Slavery in the Bengal Presidency 1772–1843.* London: Golden Eagle Publishing House, 1977

Chebel, Malek. *L'Esclavage en Terre d'Islam.* [Paris]: Fayard, 2007

Chelebī, Kātib. *Kashf al-ẓunūn.* Ed. Muḥammad ʿAbd al-Qādir ʿAṭā. 7 vols. Beirut: Dār al-Kutub al-ʿIlmiyya, 2008

Christman, John. 'Analyzing Freedom from the Shadows of Slavery.' *Journal of Global Slavery* 2 (2017): 162–84

Cicero, Marcus Tullius. *On the Commonwealth.* Trans. George Holland Sabine and Stanley Barney Smith. Indianapolis: Bobbs-Merrill, 1976

—. *On Duties III.* In *Selected Works,* trans. Michael Grant. London: Penguin Books, 1971

Clarence-Smith, William Gervase. 'Islam and the abolition of the slave trade in the Indian Ocean.' In *Abolition and its Aftermath in Indian Ocean Africa and Asia,* ed. Gwyn Campbell, 137–49. London: Routledge, 2005.

—. *Islam and the Abolition of Slavery.* Oxford: Oxford University Press, 2006

— and David Eltis. 'White Servitude.' In *The Cambridge World History of Slavery,* Volume 3: *AD 1420–1804,* ed. David Eltis and Stanley Engerman, 132–59. Cambridge: Cambridge University Press, 2011

Clark, Lorenne M. G. 'Women and John Locke; Or, Who Owns the Apples in the Garden of Eden?' *Canadian Journal of Philosophy* 7, n. 4 (1977): 699–724

Clark, Patricia. 'Women, Slaves, and the Hierarchies of Domestic Violence: The Family of St. Augustine.' In *Women and Slaves in Greco-Roman Culture*, ed. Sandra Joshel and Sheila Murnaghan, 109–29. London: Routledge, 1998

Cobb, Thomas R. R. *An Inquiry into the Law of Negro Slavery*. Philadelphia: T. & J. W. Johnson; Savannah: W. Thorne Williams, 1858

Colley, Linda. *Captives*. New York: Pantheon Books, 2002

Comte, Auguste. *General View of Positivism*. New York: Robert Speller, 1957

Condorcet, Nicolas de Caritat. *Condorcet: Political Writings*. Ed. Steven Lukes and Nadia Urbinati. Cambridge: Cambridge University Press, 2012

—. *Outlines of an historical view of the progress of the human mind*. Philadelphia: M. Carey, 1796

Cook, Michael. *Ancient Religions, Modern Politics: The Islamic Case in Comparative Perspective*. Princeton: Princeton University Press, 2015

Cooper, Frederick. 'Islam and Cultural Hegemony: The Ideology of Slaveowners on the East African Coast.' In *The Ideology of Slavery in Africa*, ed. Paul E. Lovejoy, 271–308. Beverly Hills: Sage, 1982

Cover, Robert M. *Justice Accused*. Hew Haven: Yale University Press, 1975

Cox, Oliver J. W. 'Frederick, the Prince of Wales, and the First Performance of "Rule Britannia!"' *The Historical Journal* 56, n. 4 (2013): 931–54

Crecelius, Daniel and Gotcha Djaparidze. 'Relations of the Georgian Mamluks of Egypt with Their Homeland in the Last Decades of the Eighteenth Century.' *Journal of the Social and Economic History of the Orient* 45, no. 3 (2002): 320–41

Crone, Patricia. '"Even an Ethiopian Slave": The Transformation of a Sunni Tradition.' *Bulletin of the School of Oriental and African Studies* 57 (1994): 59–67.

—. *Roman, Provincial and Islamic Law*. Cambridge: Cambridge University Press, 1987

—. *Slaves on Horses: The Evolution of the Islamic Polity*. Cambridge: Cambridge University Press, 1980

Crossley, Pamela Kyle. 'Slavery in Early Modern China.' In *The Cambridge World History of Slavery*, Volume 3: *AD 1420–1804*, ed. David Eltis and Stanley Engerman, 186–214. Cambridge: Cambridge University Press, 2011

Cruft, Rowan, Liao, S. Matthew and Massimo Renzo, ed. *Philosophical Foundations of Human Rights*. Oxford: Oxford University Press, 2015

Culbertson, Laura. 'Slaves and Households in the Near East.' In *Slaves and Households in the Near East*, ed. Laura Culbertson, 1–20. Chicago: Oriental Institute, 2011

Dabūsī, Abū Zayd. *Taqwīm al-adilla*. Beirut: Dār al-Kutub al-ʿIlmiyya, 2001

Daddi Addoun, Yacine. 'Slavery and Abolition in Ibāḍī Theology: The Thought, the Un-Thought, the Unthinkable.' In *Ibadi Theology: Rereading Sources and Scholarly Works*, ed. Ersilia Francesca, 233–42. Hildesheim: Georg Olms, 2015

Daumas, G. E. *Le Grant Désert*. Paris: Librairie Michel Lévy Frères, 1856

Dawīsh, Aḥmad ʿAbd al-Razzāq, ed. *Fatāwā al-lajna al-dā'ima li'l-buḥūth al-ʿilmiyya wa'l-iftā'*. 5th edn. Vol. 16. Riyadh: Dār al-Mu'ayyad, 2004

Davidson, Julia O'Connell. *Modern Slavery: The Margins of Freedom*. New York: Palgrave Macmillan, 2015

Davies, Wendy. 'On servile status in the early Middle Ages.' In *Serfdom and Slavery*, ed. Michael Bush, 225–46. New York: Longman, 1996

Davis, David Brion. *Challenging the Boundaries of Slavery*. Cambridge, MA: Harvard University Press, 2003

—. *The Problem of Slavery in the Age of Revolution*, 1770–1823. Revised ed. New York: Oxford University Press, 1999
—. *The Problem of Slavery in Western Culture*. Ithaca: Cornell University Press, 1966
—. *Slavery and Human Progress*. Oxford: Oxford University Press, 1984
Del Re, Emanuela C. 'The Yazidi and the Islamic State, or the Effects of a Middle East without Minorities on Europe.' *Politics and Religion* 9, n. 2 (2015): 269–93
Dhahabī, Shams al-Dīn Muḥammad. *Manāqib al-Imām Abū Ḥanīfa*. Ed. Muḥammad Zāhid al-Kawtharī. Cairo: Lajnat Iḥyā' al-Ma'ārif al-Nu'māniyya, 1947
—. *Mīzān al-i'tidāl fī naqd al-rijāl*. Ed. 'Alī Muḥammad al-Bijāwī. 4 vols. Beirut: Dār al-Ma'rifa, n.d., reprint of 'Īsā al-Bābī al-Ḥalabī, 1963-4
—. *Siyar a'lām al-nubalā'*. Ed. Shu'ayb al-Arnā'ūṭ et al. 3rd edn. 25 vols. Beirut: Mu'assasat al-Risāla, 1992–98
Diakho, Muhammad. *L'Esclavage en Islâm*. Beirut: Albouraq, 2004
The Digest of Justinian, Volume 1, 1–39. Trans. Alan Watson. Philadelphia: University of Pennsylvania Press, 1998
Dihlawī, 'Ālim b. al-'Alā' Farīd al-Dīn. *Al-Fatāwā al-Tātārkhāniyya*. Ed. Shabīr Aḥmad Qāsim. 20 vols. Deoband: Maktabat Zakariyyā, 2014
Dihlawī, Shāh Walī Allāh. *Ḥujjat Allāh al-bāligha*. Ed. Sayyid Aḥmad Balanpūrī. 2 vols. Deoband: Maktabat Ḥijāz, 2010
Diodorus Siculus. *Diodorus of Sicily*. Cambridge, MA: Harvard University Press, 1933
Diop, Abdoul Malal. 'Le vie et l'oeuvre de Cheikh Moussa Kamara de Ganguel (1864–1945).' PhD dissertation, Univérsité Cheikh Anta Diop de Dakar, 2014
Diouf, Sylviane A. *Servants of Allah: African Muslims Enslaved in the Americas*. New York: New York University Press, 1998
Ḍirār b. 'Amr. *Kitāb al-Taḥrīsh*. Ed. Hüseyin Hansu and Mehmet Keskin. Istanbul: Dār al-Irshād, 2014
Donner, Fred. *The Early Islamic Conquests*. Princeton: Princeton University Press, 1981
O'Donovan, Joan Lockwood. 'The Theological Economics of Medieval Usury Theory.' In *Bonds of Imperfection: Christian Politics, Past and Present*, ed. Joan Lockwood and Oliver O'Donovan, 97–120. Grand Rapids, MI: William B. Eerdmans Publishing, 2004
Drescher, Seymour. *Econocide: British Slavery in the Era of Abolition*. 2nd edn. Chapel Hill, NC: University of North Carolina Press, 2010
—. 'The Shocking Birth of British Abolitionism.' *Slavery & Abolition* 33, n. 4 (2012): 571–93
Dubler, César E. *Abū Ḥāmid El Granadino y su Relación de Viaje por Tierras Eurasiáticas*. Madrid: Imprenta y Editorial Maestre, 1953
Duderija, Adis. 'A Case Study of Patriarchy and Slavery: The Hermeneutical Importance of Qur'ānic Assumptions in the Development of a Values-Based and Purposive Oriented Qur'ān-sunna Hermeneutic.' *Hawwa* 11 (2013): 58–87
—. *The Imperatives of Progressive Islam*. London: Routledge, 2017
Düzdağ, Ertuğrul. *Ebussuud Efendi Fetvaları*. Istanbul: Kapı, 2012
Dyer, Christopher. 'Memories of freedom: attitudes towards serfdom in England, 1200–1350.' In *Serfdom and Slavery*, ed. Michael Bush, 277–95. New York: Longman, 1996
Dyer, Justin Buckley. *Natural Law and the Antislavery Constitutional Tradition*. Cambridge: Cambridge University Press, 2012
Eaton, Richard. 'The Rise and Fall of Military Slavery in the Deccan.' In *Slavery & South Asian History*, ed. Indrani Chatterjee and Richard Eaton, 115–35. Bloomington: Indiana University Press, 2006

Eden, Jeff. 'Beyond the Bazaars: Geographies of the slave trade in Central Asia.' *Modern Asian Studies* 51, n. 4 (2017): 919–55

—. *Slavery and Empire in Central Asia*. Cambridge: Cambridge University Press, 2018

Elbourne, Elizabeth. 'Introduction: Key Themes and Perspectives.' In *Sex, Power and Slavery*, ed. Gwyn Campbell and Elizabeth Elbourne, 1–42. Athens, OH: Ohio University Press, 2014

El Cheikh, Nadia Maria. 'The Qahramâna in the Abbasid Court: Position and Functions.' *Studia Islamica* 97 (2003): 41–55

—. 'Revisiting the Abbasid Harems.' *Journal of Middle East Women's Studies* 1, n. 3 (2005): 1–19

El Hamel, Chouki. *Black Morocco: A History of Slavery, Race, and Islam*. Cambridge: Cambridge University Press, 2013

—. ' "Race," Slavery and Islam in Maghribi Mediterranean Thought: The Question of the Haratin in Morocco.' *Journal of North African Studies* 7, n. 3 (2002): 29–52

El Shamsy Ahmed and Aron Zysow. 'Al-Buwayṭī's Abridgement of al-Shāfiʿī's *Risāla*: Edition and Translation.' *Islamic Law and Society* 19 (2012): 327–55

Eltis, David. *Economic Growth and the Ending of the Transatlantic Slave Trade*. New York: Oxford University Press, 1987

— and Stanley Engerman, ed. *The Cambridge World History of Slavery*, Volume 3: *AD 1420–1804*. Cambridge: Cambridge University Press, 2011

— and Stanley Engerman. 'Dependence, Servility, and Coerced Labor in Time and Space.' In *The Cambridge World History of Slavery*, Volume 3: *AD 1420–1804*, ed. David Eltis and Stanley Engerman, 1–22. Cambridge: Cambridge University Press, 2011

Emecen, Feridun M. 'Osmanlı Hanedanına Alternatif Arayışlar Üzerine Bazı Örnekler ve Mülahazalar.' In *Osmanlı klasik çağında hanedan, devlet ve toplum*. [Istanbul]: Timaş Yayınları, 2011

Emon, Anver. '*Ḥuqūq Allāh* and *Ḥuqūq al-ʿIbād*: A Legal Heuristic for a Natural Rights Regime.' *Islamic Law and Society* 13, no. 3 (2006): 325–91

—. *Islamic Natural Law Theory*. Oxford: Oxford University Press, 2010

Empey, Heather J. 'The Mothers of the Caliph's Sons: Women as Spoils of War during the Early Almohad Period.' In *Concubines and Courtesans*, ed. Matthew S. Gordon and Kathryn A. Hain, 143–62. New York: Oxford University Press, 2017

Encyclopaedia of Islam, 2nd edn. Ed. P. Bearman, Th. Bianquis, C.E. Bosworth, E. van Donzel, W.P. Heinrichs. Leiden: Brill, 2012

Engerman, Stanley. 'Slavery at Different Times and Places.' *American Historical Review* 105, n. 2 (2000): 480–84

—. 'Slavery, serfdom and other forms of coerced labour: similarities and differences.' In *Serfdom and Slavery*, ed. M. L. Bush, 18–41. New York: Longman, 1996

Ennaji, Mohammed. *Slavery, the State, and Islam*. Cambridge: Cambridge University Press, 2013

Epictetus. 'Fragments.' Published in *Enchiridion*. Trans. George Long. Mineola, NY: n.p., 2004

Erdem, Y. Hakan. *Slavery in the Ottoman Empire and its Demise, 1800–1909*. New York: St. Martin's Press, 1996

Erlich, Reese. 'Prison Labor: Workin' for the Man.' *Covert Action Quarterly* (Fall 1995), available at http://people.umass.edu/kastor/private/prison-labor.html

Esack, Farid. *On Being a Muslim: Finding a Religious Path in the World Today*. Oxford: Oneworld, 1999

Eton, W. *A Survey of the Turkish Empire*. 2nd edn. London: T. Cadell & W. Davies, 1799

Evliyā' Efendī. *Narrative of Travels in Europe, Asia and Africa in the Seventeenth Century*. Trans. Joseph von Hammer. 2 vols. London: Oriental Translation Fund, 1846–1850

Fasawī, Ya'qūb b. Sufyān. *Kitāb al-Ma'rifa wa'l-tārīkh*. Ed. Akram Ḍiyā' al-'Umarī. 4 vols. Medina: Maktabat al-Dār, 1990

Fāsī, 'Allāl. *Maqāṣid al-sharī'a al-islāmiyya wa makārimuhā*. 5th and revised edn. Beirut: Dār al-Gharb al-Islāmī, 1993

Fatāwā al-Hindiyya. 6 vols. Beirut: Dār al-Fikr, n.d., reprint of Cairo: Maṭba'a al-Amīriyya, 1893

Fay, Mary Ann, ed. *Slavery in the Islamic World: Its Characteristics and Commonality*. New York: Palgrave, 2019

Fede, Andrew T. *Homicide Justified: The Legality of Killing Slaves in the United States and the Atlantic World*. Athens, GA: University of Georgia Press, 2017

Fenoaltea, Stefano. 'Slavery and Supervision in Comparative Perspective: A Model.' *Journal of Economic History* 44, n. 3 (1984): 635–68

Field, Daniel. *The End of Serfdom: Nobility and Bureaucracy in Russia, 1855–1861*. Cambridge, MA: Harvard University Press, 1976

Finley, Moses. 'Slavery.' In *The International Encyclopedia of the Social Sciences*, ed. David L. Sills, 14:307–13. [New York]: Macmillan Company, 1968

Fischel, Joseph J. *Sex and Harm in the Age of Consent*. Minneapolis: University of Minnesota Press, 2016

Fisher, Allan G. B., and Humphrey J. Fisher. *Slavery and Muslim Society in Africa*. London: C. Hurst & Company, 1970

Fisher, Humphrey J. 'Review: Of Slaves, and Souls of Men.' *Journal of African History* 28, n. 1 (1987): 141–49 (a review of *Slaves and Slavery in Muslim Africa*, ed. J. R. Willis).

—. *Slavery in the History of Muslim Black Africa*. New York: New York University Press, 2001

Fisher, Samuel. 'Rusticus ad Academicos (The Rustic's Alarm to the Rabbis).' In *The Testimony of the Truth Exalted*. n.p.: n.p., 1679

Forman, David. 'Kant on Moral Freedom and Moral Slavery.' *Kantian Review* 17, n. 1 (2012): 1–32

Foucault, Michel. 'The Order of Discourse.' In *Untying the Text: A Post-Structuralist Reader*, ed. Robert Young, trans. Ian McLeod. Boston: Routledge, 1981

Frampton, Travis. *Spinoza and the Rise of Historical Criticism of the Bible*. New York: T&T Clark, 2006

Francione, Gary L. 'The Abolition of Animal Exploitation.' In *The Animal Rights Debate: Abolition or Regulation?*, ed. Gary Francione and Robert Garner, 1–102. New York: Columbia University Press, 2010

Freamon, Bernard. 'Slavery, Freedom, and the Doctrine of Consensus in Islamic Jurisprudence.' *Harvard Human Rights Journal* 11 (Spring 1998): 1–64

—. 'Straight, No Chaser: Slavery, Abolition, and the Modern Muslim Mind.' In *Indian Ocean Slavery in the Age of Abolition*, ed. Robert Harms et al., 61–80. New Haven: Yale University Press, 2013

Friedman, Lawrence M. *A History of American Law*. 2nd edn. New York: Simon & Schuster, 1985

Frost, J. William. 'Why Quakers and Slavery? Why Not More Quakers?' In *Quakers and Abolition*, ed. Brycchan Carey and Geoffrey Plank, 29–42. Urbana, IL: University of Illinois Press, 2014

Fynn-Paul, Jeffrey. 'Empire, Monotheism and Slavery in the Greater Mediterranean Region from Antiquity to the Early Modern Era.' *Past & Present* 205 (2009): 3–40

Fyzee, Asaf A. A. *Cases in the Muhammadan Law of India, Pakistan and Bangladesh*. Ed. Tahir Mahmood. 2nd edn. New Delhi: Oxford University Press, 2005

Galenson, David. 'The Rise and Fall of Indentured Servitude in the Americas: An Economic Analysis.' *Journal of Economic History* 44, no. 1 (1984): 1–26

Garcin, Jean-Claude. 'The regime of the Circassian Mamlūks.' In *The Cambridge History of Egypt*, ed. Carl F. Petry, 290–317. Cambridge: Cambridge University Press, 1998

Gel, Mehmet. 'Kanûnî Devrinde "Müftî" ile Rumeli Kazaskeri Arasında Bir "Hüccet-i Şer'iyye" İhtilafı Yahut Kemalpaşazâde-Fenârîzâde Hesaplaşması.' *Osmanlı Araştımarları* 42 (2013): 53–91

Gervais-Courtellemont, Jules. *Mon Voyage à la Mecque*. 4th edn. Paris: Librairie Hachette, 1897

Ghamidi, Javed Ahmed. *Islam: A Comprehensive Introduction*. Trans. Shehzad Saleem. 2nd edn. Lahore: Al-Mawrid, 2014

Ghazal, Amal. 'Debating Slavery and Abolition in the Arab Middle East.' In *Slavery, Islam and the Diaspora*, ed. Behnaz A. Mirzai, Ismael Musa Montana and Paul Lovejoy, 139–54. Trenton: Africa World Press, 2009

Ghazālī, Abū Ḥāmid. *The Fatāwā of al-Ghazzālī*. Ed. Mustafa Mahmoud Abu-Sway. Kuala Lumpur: International Institute of Islamic Thought, 1996

—. *Al-Iqtiṣād fī al-iʿtiqād*. Cairo: Maṭbaʿat Muṣṭafā al-Bābī al-Ḥalabī, 1966

—. *Miʿyār al-ʿilm*. Cairo: Maṭbaʿat al-ʿArabiyya, n.d.

—. *Al-Mustaṣfā*. Ed. Muḥammad ʿAbd al-Salām ʿAbd al-Shāfī. Beirut: Dār al-Kutub al-ʿIlmiyya, 1992

—. *On the Boundaries of Theological Tolerance in Islam: Abū Ḥāmid al-Ghazālī's* Fayṣal al-Tafriqa. Trans. Sherman A. Jackson. London: Oxford University Press, 2002

Ghazālī, Muḥammad (unknown author). '*Hidāyat al-murīd fī taqlīb al-ʿabīd*.' In *Nawādir al-makhṭūṭāt*, ed. ʿAbd al-Salām Hārūn, 1:391–410. 2 vols. Cairo: Muṣṭafā al-Bābī al-Ḥalabī, n.d.

Ghazzālī, Muḥammad (d. 1996). *Fiqh al-sunna*. 4th edn. Cairo: Dār al-Shurūq, 2008

Ghumārī, ʿAbd al-ʿAzīz. *Mā yajūzu wa mā lā yajūzu fī al-ḥayāt al-zawjiyya*. Ed. Muḥammad ʿAbdallāh al-Shaʿʿār. Amman: Dār al-Fatḥ, 2009

Ghumārī, ʿAbdallāh. *Afḍal maqūl fī manāqib afḍal rasūl*. Cairo: Maktabat al-Qāhira, 2005

—. *Al-Khawāṭir al-dīniyya*. 2 vols in 1. Cairo: Maktabat al-Qāhira, 2004

—. *Al-Rasāʾil al-ghumāriyya*. Ed. Kamāl Yūsuf al-Ḥūt. [Cairo]: Dār al-Janān, 1991

Ghumārī, Aḥmad. *Al-Burhān al-jalī fī intisāb al-ṣūfiyya ilā ʿAlī*. Ed. Aḥmad Muḥammad Mursī. Cairo: Maktabat al-Qāhira, n.d.

—. *Masālik al-dilāla ʿalā masāʾil matn al-Risāla*. 3rd edn. Cairo: Maktabat al-Qāhira, 1995

—. *Al-Mudāwī li-ʿilal al-Jāmiʿ al-ṣaghīr wa sharḥay al-Munāwī*. 6 vols. Cairo: Dār al-Kutub, 1996

Gibbon, Edward. *The History of the Decline and Fall of the Roman Empire*. 4 vols. New York: Harper & Brothers, 1836

Gilli-Elewy, Hend. 'On the Provenance of Slaves in Mecca during the Time of the Prophet Muhammad.' *International Journal of Middle East Studies* 49, n. 1 (2017): 164–68

Ghoshal, U. N. 'On a Recent Estimate of the Social and Political System of the Maurya Empire.' *Annals of the Bhandarkar Oriental Research Institute* 40, no. 1 (1959): 63–69

—. *Studies in Indian History and Culture*. Bombay: Orient Longmans, 1965

Glancy, Jennifer A. 'The Sexual Use of Slaves: A Response to Kyle Harper on Jewish and Christian *Porneia*.' *Journal of Biblical Literature* 134, n. 1 (2015): 215–29

—. *Slavery as Moral Problem in the Early Church and Today*. Minneapolis: Fortress Press, 2011

Glassman, Jonathon. *War of Words, War of Stones: Racial Thought and Violence in Colonial Zanzibar*. Bloomington: Indiana University Press, 2011

Goitein, S. D. *Jews and Arabs*. Revised edn. New York: Schocken Books, 1974

—. 'The Sexual Mores of the Common People.' In *Society and the Sexes in Medieval Islam*, edn. Afaf Lutfi al-Sayyid-Marsot, 43–62. Malibu: Undena, 1979

—. 'Slaves and Slavegirls in the Cairo Geniza Records.' *Arabica* 9, n. 1 (1962): 1–20

Goldman, Emma. *Red Emma Speaks*. Ed. Alix Kates Shulman. 3rd edn. Atlantic Highlands, NJ: Humanities Press, 1996

Gomaa, Ali (ʿAlī Jumʿa). *Al-Bayān li-mā yashghalu al-adhhān*. Cairo: al-Muqaṭṭam, 2005

Gómez-Lobo, Alfonso. *The Foundations of Socratic Ethics*. Cambridge: Hackett, 1994

Goodman, R. David. 'Demystifying "Islamic Slavery": Using Legal Practices to Reconstruct the End of Slavery in Fes, Morocco.' *History in Africa* 39 (2012): 143–74

Gordon, Matthew S. 'Abbasid Courtesans and the Question of Social Mobility.' In *Concubines and Courtesans*, see entry below

—. *The Breaking of a Thousand Swords*. Albany: SUNY Press, 2001

— and Kathryn A. Hain. *Concubines and Courtesans: Women and Slavery in Islamic History*. New York: Oxford University Press, 2017

Gordon, Murray. *Slavery in the Arab World*. New York: New Amsterdam Books, 1989

Graeber, David. *Debt: The First 5,000 Years*. New York: Melvillhouse, 2011

Gray, John. *The Silence of Animals: On Progress and Other Myths*. London: Allen Lane, 2013

Green, Arnold H. *The Tunisian Ulama 1873–1915*. Leiden: E. J. Brill, 1978

Grey, Cam. 'Slavery in the Late Roman World.' In *The Cambridge World History of Slavery*, Volume 1: *The Ancient Mediterranean World*, ed. Keith Bradley and Paul Cartledge, 482–509. Cambridge: Cambridge University Press, 2011

Grotius, Hugo. *Commentary on the Law of Prize and Booty*. Ed. Martine Julia van Ittersum. Indianapolis: Liberty Fund, 2006

Grubbs, Judith Evans. *Law and Family in Late Antiquity*. Oxford: Clarendon, 1995

Gullick, John M. 'Debt Bondage in Malaya.' In *Slavery: A Comparative Perspective*, ed. Robin Winks, 51–58. New York: New York University Press, 1972

Haarmann, Ulrich. 'Joseph's Law – the careers and activities of Mamluk descendants before the Ottoman conquest of Egypt.' In *The Mamluks in Egyptian Politics and Society*, ed. Thomas Philipp and Ulrich Haarmann, 55–84. Cambridge: Cambridge University Press, 1998

—. 'The Sons of Mamluks as Fief-holders in Late Medieval Egypt.' In *Land Tenure and Social Transformation in the Middle East*, ed. Tarif Khalidi, 141–68. Beirut: American University of Beirut Press, 1984

Hadler, Jeffrey. *Muslims and Matriarchs: Cultural Resilience in Indonesia through Jihad and Colonialism*. Ithaca, NY: Cornell University Press, 2008

Hair, P. E. H. 'Slavery and Liberty: The Case of the Scottish Colliers.' *Slavery & Abolition* 21, n. 3 (2000): 136–51

Hall, Bruce. *A History of Race in Muslim West Africa, 1600–1960*. Cambridge: Cambridge University Press, 2011

—. 'How Slaves Used Islam: The Letters of Enslaved Muslim Commercial Agents in the Nineteenth-Century Niger Bend and Central Sahara.' *Journal of African History* 52 (2011): 279–97

Hall, Stuart George, ed. *Gregory of Nyssa: Homilies on Ecclesiastes*. Berlin: Walter de Gruyter, 1993

Hanioglu, M. Sukru. *A Brief History of the Late Ottoman Empire*. Princeton: Princeton University Press, 2008

Hanke, Lewis. *Aristotle and the American Indians*. Bloomington: University of Indiana Press, 1959

Hanretta, Sean. *Islam and Social Change in French West Africa*. Cambridge: Cambridge University Press, 2009

Hansen, Thorkild. *Arabia Felix*. New York: Harper & Row, 1964

Haqqani, Shehnaz. 'Islamic Tradition, Change, and Feminism: The Gendered Non-Negotiable.' Phd dissertation, University of Texas at Austin, 2018

Harper, Kyle. *From Shame to Sin: The Christian Transformation of Sexual Morality in Late Antiquity*. Cambridge, MA: Harvard University Press, 2013

—. *Slavery in the Late Roman World, AD 275–425*. Cambridge: Cambridge University Press, 2011

Harr, Daniel. 'The New Slavery Movement.' *Social Policy* (Summer 1999): 28–32

Harris, Sam and Maajid Nawaz. *Islam and the Future of Tolerance*. Cambridge, MA: Harvard University Press, 2015

Harrison, Christopher. *France and Islam in West Africa, 1860–1960*. Cambridge: Cambridge University Press, 1988

Hart, H. L. A. *The Concept of Law*. 2nd edn. New York: Oxford University Press, 1994, original edition published 1961

Hartman, Saidiya. *Scenes of Subjection: Terror, Slavery and Self-Making in Nineteenth-Century America*. Oxford: Oxford University Press, 2007

Hasan, Mushirul, ed. *Seamless Boundaries: Luftullah's Narrative beyond East and West*. New Delhi: Oxford University Press, 2007

Hasan, Yusuf Fadl. 'Historical Roots of Afro-Arab Relations.' In *The Arabs & Africa*, ed. Khair El-Din Haseeb, 27–43. London: Croon Helm, 1985

Hassan, Riffat. 'On Human Rights and the Qur'anic Perspective.' *Journal of Ecumenical Studies* 19, n. 3 (1982): 51–65

Hattox, Ralph. *Coffee and Coffeehouses*. Seattle: University of Washington Press, 1985

Van der Haven, Elisabeth C. 'The Bey, the mufti and the scattered pearls: Shari'a and political leadership in Tunisia's Age of Reform – 1800–1864.' PhD dissertation, Leiden University, 2006

Haykal, Muḥammad Ḥusayn. *The Life of Muhammad*. Trans. Isma'il Ragi al-Faruqi. n.p.: American Trust Publications, 2005, originally printed 1976

Heath, Malcolm. 'Aristotle on Natural Slavery.' *Phronesis* 53 (2008): 243–70

Heller, Henry. 'Bodin on Slavery and Primitive Accumulation.' *Sixteenth Century Journal* 25, n. 1 (1994): 53–65

Hellie, Richard. 'Russian Slavery and Serfdom, 1450–1804.' In *The Cambridge World History of Slavery*, Volume 3: *AD 1420–1804*, ed. David Eltis and Stanley Engerman, 275–95. Cambridge: Cambridge University Press, 2011

Herz, Rachel. *That's Disgusting: Unraveling the Mysteries of Repulsion*. New York: WW Norton, 2012

Hezser, Catherine. *Jewish Slavery in Antiquity*. Oxford: Oxford University Press, 2005

Hickey, Robin. 'Seeking to Understand the Definition of Slavery.' In *The Legal Understanding of Slavery*, ed. Jean Allain, 220–41. London: Oxford University Press, 2012

Hidayatullah, Aysha. 'Māriyya the Copt: gender, sex and heritage in the legacy of Muhammad's *umm walad*.' *Islam and Christian-Muslim Relations* 21, n. 3 (2010): 221–43

Hill, Polly. 'Comparative West African Farm Slavery Systems.' In *Slaves and Slavery in Muslim Africa II*, ed. John Ralph Willis, 33–50. London: Frank Cass, 1985

Hilliard, Constance. '*Zuhur al-Basatin* and *Ta'rikh al-Turubbe*: Some Legal and Ethical Aspects of Slavery in the Sudan as Seen in the Works of Shaykh Musa Kamara.' In *Slaves and Slavery in Muslim Africa I*, ed. J. R. Willis, 160–81. London: Frank Cass, 1985

Hiskett, Mervyn. *The Sword of Truth: The Life and Times of the Shehu Usuman dan Fodio*. 2nd edn. Evanston, IL: Northwestern University Press, 1994

Hobbs, T. R. *A Time for War: A Study of Warfare in the Old Testament*. Wilmington: Michael Glazier, 1989

Hodgson, Marshall. *The Venture of Islam*. 3 vols. Chicago: University of Chicago Press, 1974

Hoexter, Miriam. '*Ḥuqūq Allāh* and *Ḥuqūq al-ʿIbād* as Reflected in the *Waqf* Institution.' *Jerusalem Studies in Arabic and Islam* 19 (1995): 133–56

Hogendorn, Jan S. 'The Location of the "Manufacture" of Eunuchs.' In *Slave Elites in the Middle East and Africa*, ed. Miua Toru and John Edward Philips, 41–68. London: Kegan Paul, 2000

Honoré, Antony M. 'The Nature of Slavery.' In *The Legal Understanding of Slavery*, ed. Jean Allain, 9–16. London: Oxford University Press, 2012

—. 'Ownership.' In *Oxford Essays in Jurisprudence*, ed. A. G. Guest, 107–47. London: Oxford University Press, 1961

Hoyland, Robert. *Seeing Islam as Others Saw It*. Princeton: Darwin Press, 1997

Howard-Hassman, Rhoda E. 'Reparations for the Slave Trade: Rhetoric, Law, History and Political Realities.' *Canadian Journal of African Studies* 41, n. 3 (2007): 427–54

Hudūd al-ʿĀlam: The Regions of the World. Trans. V. Minorsky. Karachi: Indus Publications, 1980

Humphreys, R. Stephen. 'Egypt in the World System of the Later Middle Ages.' In *The Cambridge History of Egypt*, ed. Carl F. Petry, 446–61. Cambridge: Cambridge University Press, 1998

Hunt, Peter. *Ancient Greek and Roman Slavery*. Hoboken, NJ: Wiley Blackwell, 2018

Hunwick, John. 'Falkeiana III: The *Kitāb al-Tarsīl*, an Anonymous Manual of Epistolatory and Notary Style.' *Sudanic Africa* 5 (1994): 179–84

—. 'Islamic Law and Polemics over Race and Slavery.' In *Slavery in the Islamic Middle East*, ed. Shaun Marmon, 43–68. Princeton: Markus Wiener, 1999

—. 'Notes on Slavery in the Songhay Empire.' In *Slaves and Slavery in Muslim Africa* II, ed. J. R. Willis, 16–32. London: Frank Cass, 1985

—. *Sharīʿa in Songhay: The Replies of al-Maghīlī to the Questions of Askia al-Ḥājj Muḥammad*. London: Oxford University Press, 1985

— and Eve Troutt Powell. *The African Diaspora in the Mediterranean Lands of Islam*. Princeton: Markus Wiener, 2002

Hunting, Claudine. 'The Philosophes and Black Slavery: 1748–1765.' *Journal of the History of Ideas* 39, n. 3 (1978): 405–18

Hurgronje, C. Snouck. *Mekka in the Latter Part of the Nineteenth Century*. Leiden: Brill, 2014

Hussin, Nordin. 'Trading Networks of Malay Merchants and Traders in the Straits of Melaka from 1780 to 1830.' *Asian Journal of Social Science* 40 (2012): 51–82

Ibn ʿAbd al-Ḥakam, ʿAbd al-Raḥmān. *Futūḥ Miṣr wa akhbāruhā*. Ed. Muḥammad Ṣubayḥ. Beirut: Dār al-Fikr, 1996

Ibn ʿAbd al-Ḥakam, ʿAbdallāh. *Sīrat ʿUmar b. ʿAbd al-ʿAzīz*. Ed. Aḥmad ʿUbayd. Cairo: Maktabat Wahba, n.d.

Ibn Abī al-ʿIzz al-Ḥanafī, ʿAlī b. ʿAlī. *Sharḥ al-ʿAqīda al-Ṭaḥāwiyya*. Ed. Muḥammad Nāṣir al-Dīn al-Albānī. Amman: al-Dār al-Islāmī, 1998

—. *Al-Tanbīh ʿalā mushkilāt al-Hidāya*. Ed. ʿAbd al-Ḥakīm Muḥammad Shākir and Anwar Ṣāliḥ Abū Zayd. 6 vols. Riyadh: Maktabat al-Rushd, 2003

Ibn Abī al-Wafā', Muḥyī al-Dīn ʿAbd al-Qādir. *Al-Jawāhir al-muḍiyya fī ṭabaqāt al-ḥanafiyya*. Ed. ʿAbd al-Fattāḥ Muḥammad al-Ḥuluw. 5 vols. Giza: Mu'assasat al-Risāla, 1978–1988

Ibn Abī Ḍiyāf, Aḥmad. *Itḥāf ahl al-zamān bi-akhbār mulūk tūnis wa ʿahd al-amān*. 8 vols. Tunis: al-Dār al-ʿArabiyya li'l-Kitāb, 2001

Ibn ʿĀbidīn, Muḥammad Amīn. *Ḥāshiyat Ibn ʿĀbidīn*. 8 vols. Beirut: Dār al-Fikr, 2000

—. *Kitāb al-ʿUqūd al-durriyya fī tanqīḥ al-Fatāwā al-Ḥāmidiyya*. 2 vols. Beirut: Dār al-Maʿrifa, n.d.

Ibn al-ʿArabī, Abū Bakr. *ʿĀriḍat al-aḥwadhī bi-sharḥ Ṣaḥīḥ al-Tirmidhī*. 13 vols. Beirut: Dār al-Kutub al-ʿIlmiyya, 2008 (reprint of Cairo edition)

Ibn ʿAsākir, ʿAlī b. Ḥasan. *Tārīkh madīnat Dimashq*. Ed. ʿUmar ʿAmrawī. 80 vols. Beirut: Dār al-Fikr, 1995-1997

Ibn ʿĀshūr, Muḥammad Ṭāhir. *Fatāwā al-shaykh al-imām Muḥammad Ṭāhir Ibn ʿĀshūr*. Ed. Muḥammad Ibrāhīm Bū Zughayba. Tunis: Markaz Jumʿat al-Mājid, 2004

—. *Maqāṣid al-sharīʿa al-islāmiyya*. Tunis: al-Sharika al-Tūnisiyya li'l-Tawzīʿ, 1978

—. *Uṣūl al-niẓām al-ijtimāʿī fī al-islām*. 2nd edn. Tunis: al-Sharikat al-Tūnisiyya li'l-Tawzīʿ, 1985

Ibn Baṭṭāl, ʿAlī b. Khalaf. *Sharḥ Ṣaḥīḥ al-Bukhārī*. Ed. Yāsir Ibrāhīm. 10 vols. Riyadh: Maktabat Ibn Rushd, 2003

Ibn Baṭṭūṭa, Muḥammad b. ʿAbdallāh. *Ibn Battuta in Black Africa*. Ed. and trans. Said Hamdun and Noël King. London: Rex Collings, 1975

—. *The Travels of Ibn Battuta*. Trans. H. A. R. Gibb. 3 vols. New Delhi: Munshiram Manoharlal, 2004

Ibn Buṭlān, al-Mukhtār b. al-Ḥasan. 'Risāla jāmiʿa li-funūn nāfiʿa fī shirā al-raqīq wa taqlīb al-ʿabīd.' In *Nawādir al-makhṭūṭāt*. Ed. ʿAbd al-Salām Hārūn. 2 vols., 1:351–89. Cairo: Muṣṭafā al-Bābī al-Ḥalabī, n.d.

Ibn Ḍuwayyān, Ibrāhīm. *Manār al-sabīl fī sharḥ al-Dalīl*. Ed. Zuhayr al-Shāwīsh. 7th edn. 2 vols. Damascus: al-Maktab al-Islāmī, 1989

Ibn al-Farrā, al-Qāḍī Abū Yaʿlā. *Kitāb al-Muʿtamad fī uṣūl al-dīn*. Ed. Wadi Z. Haddad. Beirut: Dar al-Machreq, 1986

Ibn Ḥajar al-ʿAsqalānī. *Fatḥ al-Bārī sharḥ Ṣaḥīḥ al-Bukhārī*. Ed. ʿAbd al-ʿAzīz Bin Bāz and Muḥammad Fu'ād ʿAbd al-Bāqī. 16 vols. Beirut: Dār al-Kutub al-ʿIlmiyya, 1997

—. *Lisān al-mīzān*. 7 vols. Beirut: Dār al-Fikr, n.d.

—. *Rafʿ al-iṣr ʿan quḍāt miṣr*. Ed. ʿAlī Muḥammad ʿUmar. Cairo: Maktabat al-Khānjī, 1988

—. *Talkhīṣ al-ḥabīr*. Ed. Ḥasan ʿAbbās Quṭb. 4 vols. [Cairo]: Mu'assasat Qurṭuba, 1995

Ibn Ḥajar al-Haytamī, Aḥmad. *Al-Fatāwā al-ḥadīthiyya*. Ed. Muḥammad ʿAbd al-Raḥmān al-Marʿashlī. Beirut: Dār Iḥyā' al-Turāth al-ʿArabī, 1998

—. *Al-Fatāwā al-kubrā al-fiqhiyya*. 4 vols. Cairo: ʿAbd al-Ḥamīd Aḥmad Ḥanafī, 1938

—. *Al-Iʿlām bi-qawāṭiʿ al-Islām*. Cairo: al-Maṭbaʿa al-Wahbiyya, 1876

—. *Al-ʿUmda fī sharḥ al-Burda*. Ed. Bassām Muḥammad Bārūd. Abu Dhabi: Dār al-Faqīh, 2005

—. *Al-Zawājir ʿan iqtirāf al-kabāʾir*. Ed. ʿImād Zakī al-Bārūdī. 2 vols. Cairo: al-Maktaba al-Tawfīqiyya, 2003

Ibn Ḥanbal, Aḥmad. *Musnad*. Cited to Maymaniyya printing

Ibn Ḥazm, ʿAlī b. Aḥmad. *Al-Muḥallā fī al-āthār*. 11 vols. Cairo: Dār al-Ṭibāʿa al-Munīriyya, 1933

Ibn Ḥibbān al-Bustī. *Kitāb al-Majrūḥīn*. Ed. Ḥamdī ʿAbd al-Majīd al-Salafī. 2 vols. Riyadh: Dār al-Ṣumayʿī, 2000

Ibn Hubayra, Yaḥyā b. Muḥammad. *Ikhtilāf aʾimmat al-ʿulamāʾ*. Ed. al-Sayyid Yūsuf Aḥmad. 2 vols. Beirut: Dār al-Kutub al-ʿIlmiyya, 2002

Ibn al-Humām, Kamāl al-Dīn. *Fatḥ al-qadīr*. 10 vols. Beirut: Dār al-Fikr, n.d.

Ibn al-Jawzī, ʿAbd al-Raḥmān. *Al-Muntaẓam fī tārīkh al-mulūk waʾl-umam*. Ed. Muḥammad ʿAbd al-Qādir ʿAṭā and Muṣṭafā ʿAbd al-Qādir ʿAṭā. 18 vols. Beirut: Dār al-Kutub al-ʿIlmiyya, 1992

—. *Tanwīr al-ghabash fī faḍl al-sūdān waʾl-ḥabash*. Ed. Marzūq ʿAlī Ibrāhīm. Riyadh: Dār al-Sharīf, 1998

Ibn Kamāl Pāsha, Aḥmad b. Sulaymān. *Majmūʿ rasāʾil al-ʿallāma Ibn Kamāl Bāsha*. Ed. Ḥamza al-Bakrī et al. 8 vols. Istanbul: Dār al-Lubāb, 2018

—. *Rasāʾil Ibn Kamāl*. Ed. Ahmet Cevdet. Istanbul: Asetane, n.d., orginally published Istanbul: Iqdam, 1899

Ibn Kathīr, Ismāʿīl. *Al-Bidāya waʾl-nihāya*. 15 vols. Beirut: Maktabat al-Maʿārif, 1990

—. *Musnad al-Fārūq*. Ed. Imām ʿAlī Imām. 3 vols. Fayyoum: Dār al-Falāḥ, 2010

Ibn Khaldūn. *Tārīkh Ibn Khaldūn*. Ed. Khalīl Shahāda and Suhayl Zakkār. 8 vols. Beirut: Dār al-Fikr, 1988

Ibn Mujāwir, Muḥammad b. Masʿūd. *A Traveller in Thirteenth-Century Arabia: Ibn al-Mujāwir's Tārīkh al-Mustabṣir*. Trans. G. Rex Smith. London: Hakluyt Society, 2008

Ibn al-Mulaqqin, ʿUmar b. ʿAlī. *Mukhtaṣar al-Mustadrak liʾl-ḥāfiẓ al-Dhahabī*. Ed. Saʿd ʿAbdallāh Āl Ḥumayyid and ʿAbdallāh Ḥamad al-Luḥaydān. 8 vols. Riyadh: Dār al-ʿĀṣima, 1991

Ibn al-Mundhir, Abū Bakr. *Kitāb al-Awsaṭ min al-sunan waʾl-ijmāʿ waʾl-ikhtilāf*. Ed. Khālid Ibrāhīm al-Sayyid. 11 vols. Fayyoum: Dār al-Falāḥ, 2009

Ibn Nujaym, Zayn al-Dīn Ibrāhīm. *Al-Baḥr al-rāʾiq sharḥ Kanz al-daqāʾiq*. 2nd edn. 8 vols. Beirut: Dār al-Kitāb al-Islāmī, n.d.

Ibn Qayyim al-Jawziyya, Muḥammad b. Abī Bakr. *Al-Manār al-munīf fī al-ṣaḥīḥ waʾl-ḍaʿīf*. Ed. ʿAbd al-Fattāḥ Abū Ghudda. Beirut: Maktab al-Maṭbūʿāt al-Islāmiyya, 2004

—. *Al-Ṭuruq al-ḥukmiyya fī al-siyāsa al-sharʿiyya*. Ed. Nāyif Aḥmad al-Ḥamad. Riyadh: Dār ʿĀlam al-Fawāʾid, n.d.

—. *Zād al-maʿād fī hady khayr al-ʿibād*. Ed. Shuʿayb and ʿAbd al-Qādir al-Arnāʾūṭ. 3rd ed. 6 vols. Beirut: Muʾassasat al-Risāla, 1998

Ibn Qudama, Muwaffaq al-Dīn al-Maqdisī. *Al-Mughnī*. Ed. ʿAbdallāh al-Turkī and ʿAbd al-Fattāḥ al-Ḥuluw. 12 vols. Cairo: Hujr, 1986

Ibn Qutayba, ʿAbdallāh b. Muslim. *Al-Maʿārif*. Ed. Tharwat ʿUkāsha. 4th edn. Cairo: Dār al-Maʿārif, 1981

Ibn Rajab al-Ḥanbalī, ʿAbd al-Raḥmān. *Al-Qawāʿid*. Beirut: Dār al-Fikr, n.d.

Ibn Rushd al-Jadd, Muḥammad b. Aḥmad. *Masāʾil Abī al-Walīd Ibn Rushd al-Jadd*. Ed. Muḥammad al-Ḥabīb al-Tijkānī. 2 vols. Beirut: Dār al-Jīl, 1993

Ibn Saʿd, Muḥammad. *Al-Ṭabaqāt al-kubrā*. Ed. ʿAlī Muḥammad ʿUmar. Cairo: Maktabat al-Khānjī, 2001

Ibn Sāʿī, Tāj al-Dīn ʿAlī. *Consorts of the Caliphs: Women and the Court of Baghdad*. Ed. Shawkat M. Toorawa. New York: New York University Press, 2015

Ibn Sallāb al-Ibāḍī. *Kitāb fīhi badʾ al-islām wa sharāʾiʿ al-dīn*. Ed. Werner Schwartz and Sālim bin Yaʿqūb. Wiesbaden: Franz Steiner Verlag, 1986

Ibn Sallām, Abū ʿUbayd al-Qāsim. *Kitāb al-Amwāl*. Ed. Khalīl Muḥammad Harrās. Beirut: Dār al-Fikr, n.d.

Ibn Shaddād, Yūsuf b. Rāfiʿ. *Al-Nawādir al-sulṭāniyya waʾl-maḥāsin al-Yūsufiyya*. Ed. Jamāl al-Dīn al-Shayyāl. 2nd edn. Cairo: Maktabat al-Khānjī, 1994

Ibn Taymiyya, Taqī al-Dīn. *Al-Fatāwā al-kubrā*. Ed. Aḥmad ʿAbd al-Qādir ʿAṭā and Muṣṭafā ʿAbd al-Qādir ʿAṭā. 6 vols. Beirut: Dār al-Kutub al-ʿIlmiyya, 1987

—. *Ibn Taymiyya against the Greek Logicians*. Trans. Wael Hallaq. Oxford: Clarendon Press, 1993

—. *Majmūʿat al-fatāwā*. Ed. Sayyid Ḥusayn al-ʿAffānī and Khayrī Saʿīd. 35 vols. Cairo: al-Maktaba al-Tawfīqiyya, n.d.

—. *Minhāj al-sunna al-nabawiyya*. Ed. Muḥammad Rashād Sālim. 9 vols. Riyadh: Jāmiʿat al-Imām Muḥammad b. Suʿūd, 1986

—. *Al-Qawāʿid al-nūrāniyya*. Ed. Aḥmad Muḥammad al-Khalīl. Dammam: Dār Ibn al-Jawzī, 2002

Inalcık, Halil. *An Economic and Social History of the Ottoman Empire*, Volume One: *1300–1600*. Cambridge: Cambridge University Press, 1994

Ingram, John Kells. *A History of Slavery and Serfdom*. London: A. & C. Black, 1895

Iqbal, Muhammad. 'Islam as a Moral and Political Ideal – I.' *Hindustan Review* 20, n. 120 (July 1909): 29–38

Ireland, Ralph R. 'Auguste Comte's Views on Slavery.' *Journal of Negro Education* 20, n. 4 (1951): 558–61

Irons, Charles. *The Origins of Proslavery Christianity*. Chapel Hill, NC: University of North Carolina Press, 2008

Irwin, Robert. *The Middle East in the Middle Ages: The Early Mamluk Sultanate, 1250–1382*. Carbondale: Southern Illinois University Press, 1986

Iṣṭakhrī, Abū Isḥāq Ibrāhīm. *Masālik al-mamālik*. Beirut: Dār Ṣādir, 1990, reprint of M. J. de Goeje's 1927 Brill edition

Istanbūlī, Ismāʿīl Mufīd. *Şerhuʾl-Ahlâkiʾl-Adudiyye*. Ed. Selime Çınar and Eşref Altaş. Istanbul: Türkiye Yazma Eserler Kurumu Başkanlığı, 2014

ʿIyāḍ b. Mūsā, Qāḍī. *Kitāb al-Shifā bi-taʿrīf ḥuqūq al-muṣṭafā*. Beirut: Dār Ibn Ḥazm, 2000

—. *Tartīb al-madārik wa taqrīb al-masālik*. Ed. Muḥammad Sharīf. 5 vols. Rabat: Wizārat al-Awqāf waʾl-Shuʾūn al-Islāmiyya, n.d.

Jackson, Peter. *The Delhi Sultanate*. Cambridge: Cambridge University Press, 1999

—. 'The *Mamlūk* Institution in Early Muslim India.' *Journal of the Royal Asiatic Society of Great Britain and Ireland* 2 (1990): 340–58

Jackson, Sherman. 'The Alchemy of Domination? Some Ashʿarite Responses to Muʿtazilite Ethics.' *International Journal of Middle East Studies* 31 (1999): 185–201

—. *Islam and the Problem of Black Suffering*. Oxford: Oxford University Press, 2009

Jacobsen, Anders-Christian. 'Allegorical Interpretation of Geography in Origen's Homilies on the Book of Joshua.' *Religion & Theology* 17 (2010): 289–301

Jalāl al-Dīn Faqīh al-Ṣaghīr (Sjech Djilâl Eddîn). *Verhaal van den Aanvang der Padri-Onlusten op Sumatra*. Ed. J. J. de Hollander. Leiden: Brill, 1857

Jameson, Russell. *Montesquieu et l'esclavage*. Paris: Hachette, 1911

Jāmī, ʿAbd al-Raḥmān. *Nāmehā va Monšaʾāt-e Jāmī*. Ed. ʿEṣām al-Dīn Urunbāyef and Asrār Raḥmānof. Tehran: Āyene-ye Mirāth, 1999

Jankowiak, Marek. 'What Does the Slave Trade in the Saqaliba Tell us about Early Islamic Slavery?' *International Journal of Middle East Studies* 49, n. 1 (2017): 169–72

Jasper, Margaret C. *Animal Rights Law*. 2nd edn. Dobbs Ferry, NY: Oceana Publications, 2002

Jaṣṣāṣ, Abū Bakr Aḥmad. *Aḥkām al-Qurʾān*. 3 vols. Beirut: Dār al-Kitāb al-ʿArabī, n.d., reprint of Istanbul: Maṭbaʿat al-Awqāf al-Islāmiyya, 1917

—. *Sharḥ Mukhtaṣar al-Ṭaḥāwī*. Ed. ʿIṣmat Allāh ʿInāyat Allāḥ et al. Beirut: Dār al-Bashāʾir al-Islāmiyya, 2010

Jāwī, Muḥammad Nawawī. *Qūt al-ḥabīb al-gharīb*. Cairo: Maṭbaʿat Muṣṭafā al-Bābī al-Ḥalabī, 1938

Jeffery, Arthur. 'Ghevond's Text of the Correspondence between ʿUmar II and Leo III.' *Harvard Theological Review* 37, n. 4 (1944): 269–332

Jeppe, Shamil. 'Leadership and Loyalties: The Imams of Nineteenth Century [sic] Colonial Cape Town, South Africa.' *Journal of Religion in Africa* 26, n. 2 (1996): 139–62

Jisr, Ḥusayn. *Al-Risāla al-ḥamīdiyya*. Ed. Muḥammad al-Muʿtaṣim bi'llāh al-Baghdādī. Tripoli, Lebanon: Dār al-Īmān, 1998

Johan, Khasnor. 'The Undang-Undang Melaka: Reflections on Malay Society in Fifteenth-Century Malacca.' *Journal of the Malaysian Branch of the Royal Asiatic Society* 72, n. 2 (1999): 131–50

Johansen, Baber. 'Secular and religious elements in Hanafite law.' In *Islam et Politique au Maghreb*, ed. E. Gellner et J. C. Vatiṇ. Aix: CRESM, 1979

—. 'Vérité et torture: *ius commune* et droit musalman entre le xe et le xiiie siècle.' In *De La Violance*, ed. Françoise Héritier, 125–68. Paris: Odile Jacob, 2005

Johnson, Walter. 'On Agency.' *Journal of Social History* 37, n. 1 (2003): 113–24

Jones, Jeremy and Nicholas Ridout. *A History of Modern Oman*. Cambridge: Cambridge University Press, 2015

Jones, John Richter. *Slavery Sanctioned by the Bible*. Philadelphia: J. B. Lippincott & Co., 1861

Josephus, Flavius. *Antiquities of the Jews*. Cited by convention

Juwaynī, Imām al-Ḥaramayn ʿAbd al-Malik. *Al-Burhān fī uṣūl al-fiqh*. Ed. ʿAbd al-ʿAẓīm al-Dīb. 2 vols. Cairo: Dār al-Anṣār, 1980

—. *Nihāyat al-maṭlab*. Ed. ʿAbd al-ʿAẓīm Maḥmūd al-Dīb. 20 vols. Jeddah: Dār al-Minhāj, 2007

Kapteijns, Lidwien. 'Ethiopia and the Horn of Africa.' In *The History of Islam in Africa*, ed. Nehemia Levtzion and Randall L. Pouwels, 227–50. Athens, OH: Ohio University Press, 2000

Karčić, Fikret. *Kroz prizmu historije*. Sarajevo: Centar za Napredne Studije, 2017

Karras, Ruth. *Slavery and Society in Medieval Scandinavia*. New Haven: Yale University Press, 1988

Kashmīrī, Muḥammad Anwar Shāh. *Majmūʿat rasāʾil al-Kashmīrī*. Karachi: al-Majlis al-ʿIlmī, 2015

Kaʿt, Maḥmūd Tunbuktī. *Tārīkh al-Fattāsh*. Ed. Ādam Bambā. Damascus: Muʾassasat al-Risāla, 2014

Kattānī, Muḥammad b. Jaʿfar. *Salwat al-anfās wa muḥādathat al-akyās mimman uqbira min al-ʿulamāʾ wa'l-ṣulaḥāʾ bi-Fās*. Ed. ʿAbdallāh al-Kāmil al-Kattānī et al. 3 vols. Casablanca: Dār al-Thaqāfa, 2004

Kawākibī, ʿAbd al-Raḥmān. 'Tijārat al-raqīq wa aḥkāmuhu fī al-islām.' *Al-Manār* 8, n. 22 (1905): 854–61

Kawākibī, Muḥammad b. Ḥasan. *Al-Fawā'id al-samiyya sharḥ al-Fawā'id al-saniyya*. 2 vols. Cairo: al-Maṭbaʿa al-Amīriyya, 1905

Kawtharī, Muḥammad Zāhid. *Maqālāt al-Kawtharī*. Cairo: Dār al-Salām, 2008

Kāzirūnī, ʿAlā' al-Dīn. *Şerhu'l-Ahlâki'l-Adudiyye*. Ed. Ömer Türker et al. Istanbul: Türkiye Yazma Eserler Kurumu Başkanlığı, 2014

Keith, George. 'An Exhortation & Caution to Friends concerning Buying or Keeping of Negroes.' In *The Pennsylvania Magazine of History and Biography*, 13:265–70. Philadelphia: The Historical Society of Pennsylvania, 1889. This reproduces Moore, George H. *The First Printed Protests against Slavery in America* (n.p.: Lennox Library, 1889)

Kelley, Brendan; Whiteley, Andrew and David Tallmon. 'The Arctic Melting Pot.' *Nature* 468 (December 2010): 891

Kelly, Duncan. *The Propriety of Liberty*. Princeton: Princeton University Press, 2011

Kelly, Henry Ansgar. '"Rule of Thumb" and the Folklaw of the Husband's Stick.' *Journal of Legal Education* 44, n. 3 (1994): 341–65

Kennedy, A. G. 'Cnut's law code of 1018.' *Anglo-Saxon England* 11 (1983): 57–81

Kennedy, Hugh. *The Armies of the Caliphs*. Hoboken, NJ: Taylor and Francis, 2013

Khalīl b. Aḥmad. *Kitāb al-ʿAyn*. Ed. ʿAbd al-Ḥamīd al-Hindāwī. Beirut: Dār al-Kutub al-ʿIlmiyya, 2003

Khalīl b. Isḥāq. *Mukhtaṣar Khalīl*. Ed. Aḥmad Naṣr. Beirut: Dār al-Fikr, n.d.

Khalīlī, Khalīl b. ʿAbdallāh. *Al-Irshād fī maʿrifat ʿulamā' al-ḥadīth*. Ed. ʿĀmir Aḥmad Ḥaydar. Mecca: Dār al-Fikr, 1993

Khan, Sir Syed Ahmed. *Ibtāl ghulāmī/Tabriyat al-Islām ʿan shayn al-ama wa'l-ghulām*. n.p.: Maṭbaʿa-i Mufīd, 1893

—. *A Series of Essays on the Life of Mohammed*. Delhi: Idarah-i Adabiyat-i Delli, 1981, first published 1870

Khānī, ʿAbd al-Qādir. *ʿWaqā'iʿ-i Khānī*. Ms. 32/79, Aligarh University Library, Habibganj Collection

Khaṭṭābī, Abū Sulaymān Ḥamd. *Maʿālim al-sunan*. 3rd edn. 4 vols. Beirut: al-Maktaba al-ʿIlmiyya, 1981

Khoury, Raif George. *Modern Arab Thought: Channels of the French Revolution to the Arab East*. Trans. Iḥsān ʿAbbās, ed. Charles Issawi, 152–57. Princeton: Kingston Press, 1983

—. *Wahb b. Munabbih*. 2 vols. Wiesbaden: Otto Harrossowitz, 1972

Kindī, Muḥammad b. Yūsuf. *Kitāb al-Wulāt wa Kitāb al-Quḍāt*. Ed. Rhuvon Guest. Beirut: al-Ābā, 1908 and Leiden: Brill, 1912

Klausen, Jimmy Casas. *Fugitive Rousseau: Slavery, Primitivism, and Political Freedom*. New York: Fordham University Press, 2014

Klein, Martin, ed. *Breaking the Chains: Slavery, Bondage, and Emancipation in Modern Africa and Asia*. Madison: University of Wisconsin Press, 1993

—. 'The emancipation of slaves in the Indian Ocean.' In *Abolition and its Aftermath in Indian Ocean Africa and Asia*, ed. Gwyn Campbell, 199–218. London: Routledge, 2005

Kleingeld, Pauline. 'Kant's Second Thoughts on Race.' *The Philosophical Quarterly* 57, n. 229 (2007): 573–92

Knoch, Stefan. *Sklavenfürsorge im Römischen Reich*. Hildesheim: Georg Olms Verlag, 2005

Kohlberg, Etan. 'The Attitude of the Imāmī Shīʿīs to the Companions of the Prophet.' PhD dissertation, University of Oxford, 1971

Kolchin, Peter. 'Review Essay: Putting New World Slavery in Perspective.' *Slavery & Abolition* 28, n. 2 (2007): 277–88

—. 'Some controversial questions concerning the nineteenth-century emancipation from slavery and serfdom.' In *Serfdom and Slavery: Studies in Legal Bondage*, ed. M. L. Bush. New York: Longman, 1996

Kopytoff, Igor. 'Commentary One [on Lovejoy's Indigenous African Slavery].' In *Roots and Branches*, ed. Michael Craton, 62–76. New York: Pergamon Press, 1979

—. 'Cultural Context of African Abolition.' In *The End of Slavery in Africa*, ed. Suzanne Miers and Richard Roberts, 485–503. Madison: University of Wisconsin Press, 1988

— and Suzanne Miers. 'African "Slavery" as an Institution of Marginality.' In *Slavery in Africa*, ed. Miers and Kopytoff, 8–84. Madison: University of Wisconsin Press, 1977

Korkud, Shehzade Muhammad. *Islâm'da Ganimet ve Cariyelik / Ḥall ishkāl al-afkār fī ḥall amwāl al-kuffār*. Istanbul: İsar, 2013

Kramer, Martin. *Islam Assembled: The Advent of the Muslim Congresses*. New York: Columbia University Press, 1986

Krause, Harry D. and David P. Meyer. *Family Law*. 5th edn. St. Paul: Thomson West, 2007

Küçüktiryaki, Ahmed Yasin. 'Sadreddin Efendi'nin Hukuk-ı Aile Kararnamesine İlişkin Görüşlerinin Değerlendirilmesi.' MA thesis, Gazi Üniversitesi, 2009

Kugle, Scott Siraj al-Haqq. *Homosexuality in Islam*. Oxford: Oneworld, 2010

Kulaynī, Muḥammad b. Yaʿqūb. *Uṣūl al-Kāfī*. Ed. ʿAlī Akbar Ghafārī. Tehran: Dār al-Kutub al-Islāmiyya, 1987

Kumar, Dharma. 'Colonialism, Bondage, and Caste in British India.' In *Breaking the Chains*, ed. Martin Klein, 112–30. Madison: University of Wisconsin Press, 1993

Kunt, Metin. 'Ethnic-Regional (*Cins*) Solidarity in the Seventeenth-Century Ottoman Establishment.' *International Journal of Middle East Studies* 5, no. 3 (1974): 233–39

Laknawī, ʿAbd al-Ḥayy al-Farangī Maḥallī. *Majmūʿat rasāʾil al-Laknawī*. 2nd edn. 6 vols. Karachi: Idārat al-Qur'ān wa'l-ʿUlūm al-Islāmiyya, 2008

Lane, Edward W. *Manners and Customs of the Modern Egyptians*. New York: Cosimo, 2005

Lapidus, Ira. *Muslim Cities in the Later Middle Ages*. Cambridge: Cambridge University Press, 1984

Lassner, Jacob. *The Topography of Baghdad in the Early Middle Ages*. Detroit: Wayne State University Press, 1970

Leavitt, Gregory. 'Taylor vs. Westermarck: Explaining the Incest Taboo.' *Sociology Mind* 3, n. 1 (2013): 45–51

Lee, Anthony A. 'Africans in the Palace: The Testimony of Taj al-Saltana Qajar from the Royal Harem in Iran.' In *Slavery in the Islamic World*, ed. Mary Ann Fay, 101–23. New York: Palgrave, 2019

Lenski, Noel. 'Captivity and Slavery among the Saracens in Late Antiquity (*Ca*. 250–630 CE).' *AnTard* 19 (2011): 237–66

Levanoni, Amalia. '*Takfīr* in Egypt and Syria during the Mamlūk Period.' In *Accusations of Unbelief in Islam*, ed. Camilla Adang, Hassan Ansari, Maribel Fierro and Sabine Schmidtke, 155–88. Leiden: Brill, 2015

Levi, Scott C. 'Hindus Beyond the Hindu Kush: Indians in the Central Asian Slave Trade.' *Journal of the Royal Asiatic Society* 12, n. 3 (2002): 277–88

Levtzion, Nehemiah. 'Islam in the Bilad al-Sudan to 1800.' In *The History of Islam in Africa*, ed. Nehemia Levtzion and Randall L. Pouwels, 63–92. Athens, OH: Ohio University Press, 2000

Lewis, Bernard. *Race and Slavery in the Middle East*. Oxford: Oxford University Press, 1990

Lewis, David M. 'Orlando Patterson, Property, and Ancient Slavery: The Definitional Problem Revisited.' In *On Human Bondage: After* Slavery and Social Death, 31–54. [New York]: Wiley-Blackwell, 2016

Liaw, Yock Fang. *Undang-Undang Melaka: The Laws of Melaka*. The Hague: Martinu Nijhoff, 1976

Lombard, Maurice. *The Golden Age of Islam*. Trans. Joan Spencer. Princeton: Markus Wiener, 2009, original French edition published 1971

López, Carolina. 'The British Presence in the Malay World.' *Sari* 19 (2001): 3–33

Lott, Emmeline. *The English Governess in Egypt: Harem Life in Egypt and Constantinople*. London: Richard Bentley, 1867

Lovejoy, Paul E. 'Concubinage and the Status of Female Slaves in Early Colonial Nigeria.' *Journal of African History* 29, n. 2 (1988): 245–66

—. 'Plantations in the Economy of the Sokoto Caliphate.' *Journal of African History* 19, n. 3 (1978): 341–68

—. 'Slavery in the context of ideology.' In *The Ideology of Slavery in Africa*, ed. Paul E. Lovejoy, 11-38. Beverly Hills, CA: Sage, 1981

—. 'Slavery in the Sokoto Caliphate.' In *The Ideology of Slavery in Africa*, ed. Paul E. Lovejoy, 201-243. Beverly Hills, CA: Sage, 1981

—. *Transformations in Slavery: A History of Slavery in Africa*. 2nd edn. Cambridge: Cambridge University Press, 2000

Lowe, Vaughan. *International Law: A Very Short Introduction*. Oxford: Oxford University Press, 2015

Lowenthal, David. *The Past is a Foreign Country*. Cambridge: Cambridge University Press, 1985

Lunde, Paul and Caroline Stone, trans. and ed. *Ibn Fadlān and the Land of Darkness: Arab Travellers in the Far North*. London: Penguin Books, 2012

Lydon, Ghislaine. 'Slavery, Exchange and Islamic Law: A Glimpse from the Archives of Mali and Mauritania.' *African Economic History* 33 (2005): 117–48

Mabbett, I. W. 'Some Remarks on the Present State of Knowledge about Slavery in Angkor.' In *Slavery, Bondage and Dependency in Southeast Asia*, ed. Anthony Reid, 44–63. New York: St. Martin's Press, 1983

Mabon, Simon. 'Locating Terrorism Studies.' In *Terrorism and Political Violence*, ed. Caroline Kennedy-Pipe et al., 5–17. London: Sage, 2015

MacIntyre, Alasdair. *After Virtue*. 3rd edn. Notre Dame, IN: University of Notre Dame Press, 2007

—. *Are There Any Natural Rights?* Brunswick, Main: Bowdoin College, 1983

—. *Ethics in the Conflicts of Modernity: An Essay on Desire, Practical Reasoning, and Narrative*. Cambridge: Cambridge University Press, 2016

—. *Whose Justice? Which Rationality?* Notre Dame, IN: Notre Dame University Press, 1988

Mackenzie, Robin and John Watts. 'Capacity to consent to sex reframed: IM, TZ (no 2), the need for an evidence-based model of sexual decision-making and socio-sexual competence.' *International Journal of Law and Psychiatry* 40 (2015): 50–59

Macnaghten, W. H. *Principles and Precedents of Moohummudan Law*. Calcutta: Church Mission Press, 1825

Maḥmaṣānī, Ṣubḥī. *Arkān ḥuqūq al-insān: baḥth muqārin*. Beirut: Dār al-ʿIlm li'l-Malāyīn, 1979

Major, Andrea. *Slavery, Abolitionism and Empire in India, 1772–1843*. Liverpool: Liverpool University Press, 2012

Makkī, Abū Ṭālib Muḥammad. *Qūt al-qulūb*. 2 vols in 1. Cairo: Maṭbaʿat al-Anwār al-Muḥammadiyya, 1985

Mālikī, Muḥammad ʿAlī. *Qurrat al-ʿayn bi-fatāwā ʿulamāʾ al-Ḥaramayn*. Cairo: Maṭbaʿat Muṣṭafā Muḥammad, 1937

Mallet, James. 'A species definition for the Modern Synthesis.' *Trends in Ecology & Evolution* 10, n. 7 (1995): 294–99

Manji, Irshad. *Allah, Liberty and Love: The Courage to Reconcile Faith and Freedom*. New York: Free Press, 2011

March, Andrew. *Islam and Liberal Citizenship*. Oxford: Oxford University Press, 2009

Marghīnānī, Burhān al-Dīn ʿAlī b. Abī Bakr. *Al-Hidāya sharḥ al-Bidāya*. 8 vols. Karachi: Idārat al-Qur'ān wa'l-ʿUlūm al-Islāmiyya, 1996

Maritain, Jacques. *Les droits de l'homme et la loi naturelle*. Paris: Paul Hartmann, 1943

Marmon, Shaun. 'Domestic Slavery in the Mamluk Empire: A Preliminary Sketch. In *Slavery in the Islamic Middle East*, ed. Shaun Marmon, 1–23. Princeton: Markus Wiener, 1999

Marṣafī, Ḥusayn Aḥmad. *Ru'ya fī taḥdīth al-fikr al-miṣrī* (with text of the *Risālat al-kalim al-thamān*). Ed. Aḥmad Zakariyyā' al-Shalq. Cairo: al-Hay'a al-Miṣriyya al-ʿĀmma li'l-Kutub, 1984

Marshall, John. *John Marshall in India*. Ed. Shafaat Ahmad Khan. London: Oxford University Press, 1927

Martin, B. G. 'Ahmad Rasim Pasha and the Suppression of the Fazzan Slave Trade, 1881–1879.' In *Slaves and Slavery in Muslim Africa*, Volume II, ed. John Ralph Willis, 51–82. London: Frank Cass, 1985

Marwazī, Muḥammad b. Naṣr. *Ikhtilāf al-fuqahā'*. Ed. Muḥammad Ṭāhir Ḥalīm. Riyadh: Aḍwā' al-Salaf, 2000

Masʿūdī, ʿAlī b. al-Ḥusayn. *Murūj al-dhahab*. Ed. Kamāl Ḥasan Marʿī. 4 vols. Beirut: al-Maktaba al-ʿAṣriyya, 2005

Matheson, V. and M. B. Hooker. 'Slavery in the Malay Texts: Categories of Dependency and Compensation.' In *Slavery, Bondage and Dependency in Southeast Asia*, ed. Anthony Reid and Jennifer Brewster, 182–208. New York: St. Martin's Press, 1983

Mathews, Nathaniel. 'The "Fused Horizon" of Abolitionism and Islam: Historicism, the Quran and the Global History of Abolition.' *Journal of Global Slavery*, forthcoming, 2019

—. 'Slavery, Abolition and the Moral Horizon of the Prophet Muhammad: A Response to Jonathan Brown.' Unpublished paper, available on academia.edu

Mattson, Ingrid. 'A Believing Slave is Better than an Unbeliever: Status and Community in Early Islamic Society and Law.' PhD dissertation, University of Chicago, 1999

Maududi, Abul A'la. *Human Rights in Islam*. 2nd edn. Lahore: Islamic Publications, 1995

—. *Purdah and the Status of Women in Islam*. Trans. Al-Ash'ari. Lahore: Islamic Publication, [1972]

Māwardī, Abū al-Ḥasan. *Al-Ḥāwī al-kabīr*. Ed. ʿAlī Muḥammad Muʿawwaḍ and ʿĀdil Aḥmad ʿAbd al-Mawjūd. 19 vols. Beirut: Dār al-Kutub al-ʿIlmiyya, 1999

—. *The Ordinances of Government*. Trans. Wafaa H. Wahba. Reading, UK: Garnet, 1996

Mawṣilī, Abū Yaʿlā Aḥmad. *Al-Musnad*. 16 vols. Damascus: Dār al-Ma'mūn, 1986

Mawṣilī, ʿUmar b. Badr. *Al-Mughnī ʿan al-ḥifẓ wa'l-kitāb*. Ed. Muḥammad al-Khaḍir Ḥusayn. Cairo: al-Dār al-Ḥusayniyya, 1994

Mayer, Ann E. *Islam and Human Rights*. 2nd edn. Boulder: Westview Press, 1995, originally published 1991
McDougall, E. Ann. 'Discourse and Distortion: Critical Reflections on Studying the Saharan Slave Trade.' *Revue Française d'Histoire d'Outre-mers* 89, n. 336–7 (2002): 195–227
—. '"To Marry One's Slave is as Easy as Eating a Meal": The Dynamics of Carnal Relations within Saharan Slavery.' In *Sex, Power and Slavery*, ed. Gwyn Campbell and Elizabeth Elbourne, 141–66. Athens, OH: Ohio University Press, 2014
—. '"What is Islamic about Slavery in Muslim Societies": Cooper, Concubinage and Contemporary Legacies of "Islamic Slavery" in North, West and East Africa.' In *Slavery in the Islamic World*, ed. Mary Ann Fay, 7–36. New York: Palgrave, 2019
McKee, Sally. 'Slavery.' In *The Oxford Handbook of Women and Gender in Medieval Europe*, ed. Judith M. Bennett and Ruth Mazo Karras, 281–94. Oxford: Oxford University Press, 2013
McKeown, Niall. *The Invention of Ancient Slavery?* London: Duckworth, 2007
Meillassoux, Claude. *The Anthropology of Slavery*. Trans. Alide Dasnois. Chicago: University of Chicago Press, 1981
Meinardus, Otto. 'The Upper Egyptian Practice of the Making of Eunuchs in the XIII and XIX Century.' *Zeitschrift für Ethnologie* 94, n. 1 (1969): 47–58
Mendelsohn, Isaac. *Slavery in the Ancient Near East*. New York: Oxford University Press, 1949
Miers, Suzanne. *Britain and the Ending of the Slave Trade*. New York: African Publishing, 1975
—. 'Slavery: A Question of Definition.' *Slavery & Abolition* 24, n. 2 (2003): 1–16
—. 'Slavery and the slave trade in Saudi Arabia and the Arab states on the Persian Gulf, 1921–63.' In *Abolition and its Aftermath in Indian Ocean Africa and Asia*, ed. Gwyn Campbell, 120–36. London: Routledge, 2005
— and Igor Kopytoff, ed. *Slavery in Africa*. Madison: University of Wisconsin Press, 1977
— and Richard Roberts, ed. *The End of Slavery in Africa*. Madison: University of Wisconsin Press, 1988
Miller, Joseph C. *The Problem of Slavery as History*. New Haven: Yale University Press, 2012
Millingen, Frederick. 'On the Negro Slaves in Turkey.' *Journal of the Anthropological Society of London* 8 (1870–71): lxxxv–xcvi
Mirza, Younus. 'Ishmael as Abraham's Sacrifice: Ibn Taymiyya and Ibn Kathīr on the Intended Victim.' *Islam and Muslim Christian-Relations* 24, n. 3 (2013): 277–98
—. 'Remembering the *Umm Walad*: Ibn Kathir's Treatise on the Sale of the Concubine.' In *Concubines and Courtesans*, ed. Matthew S. Gordon and Kathryn A. Hain, 297–323. New York: Oxford University Press, 2017
Mirzai, Behnaz A. 'The 1848 abolitionist *farmān*: a step towards ending the slave trade in Iran.' In *Abolition and its Aftermath in Indian Ocean Africa and Asia*, ed. Gwyn Campbell, 94–102. London: Routledge, 2005
—. *A History of Slavery and Emancipation in Iran, 1800–1929*. Austin: University of Texas Press, 2017
Miskawayh, Aḥmad b. Muḥammad. *Tahdhīb al-akhlāq*. Ed. 'Imād al-Hilālī. Beirut: Manshūrāt al-Jamal, 2011
Mitter, Ulrike. 'Unconditional manumission of slaves in early Islamic law: a *ḥadīth* analysis.' *Der Islam* 78 (2002): 35–72

Moin, A. Azfar. *The Millennial Sovereign: Sacred Kingship and Sainthood in Islam*. New York: Columbia University Press, 2012
Montana, Ismael M. *The Abolition of Slavery in Ottoman Tunisia*. Gainesville, FL: University of Florida Press, 2013
Montesquieu, Charles. *L'Esprit des lois*. Ed. Laurent Versini. 2 vols. Paris: Gallimard, 1995
—. *Persian Letters*. Trans. C. J. Betts. New York: Penguin Books, 1993
Morgan, Kenneth. *Slavery and Servitude in Colonial North America*. New York: New York University Press, 2001
Morrison, Alexander. 'Twin imperial disasters: the invasions of Khiva and Afghanistan in the Russian and British official mind, 1839–1842.' *Modern Asian Studies* 48, n. 1 (2013): 253–300
Morrow, Glenn R. *Plato's Law of Slavery in its Relation to Greek Law*. New York: Arno Press, 1976
Mottahedeh, Roy. *Loyalty and Leadership in an Early Islamic Society*. Princeton: Princeton University Press, 1980
Moyn, Samuel. 'The 1970s as a Turning Point in Human Rights History.' In *The Breakthrough: Human Rights in the 1970s*, ed. Jan Eckel and Samuel Moyn. Philadelphia: University of Pennsylvania Press, 2014
Mu'ayyad-zāde, ʿAbd al-Raḥmān Efendī. 'Risāla.' MS Bağdat Vehbi 2052, Süleymaniye Library, 129b-152a
Mubārak ʿAlī Bāshā. *ʿAlam al-dīn*. 4 vols. Alexandria: Maṭbaʿat al-Jazīra, 1882
Muir, William. *The Life of Mahomet*. 4 vols. London: Smith, Elder and Co., 1861
Mullā Hüsrev, Mehmet b. Farāmurz. *Durar al-ḥukkām sharḥ ghurar al-aḥkām*. 2 vols. Istanbul: Fazilat, n.d; reprint of Amīriyya print, n.d.
Mundy, Martha and Richard Saumarez Smith. *Governing Property, Making the Modern State: Law, Administration and Production in Ottoman Syria*. London: I. B. Tauris, 2007
Musallam, Basim. 'The Ordering of Muslim Societies.' In *The Cambridge Illustrated History of the Islamic World*, ed. Francis Robinson, 164–98. Cambridge: Cambridge University Press, 1998
Muṭīʿī, Muḥammad Bakhīt. *Majmūʿat rasā'il al-ʿallāma Muḥammad Bakhīt al-Muṭīʿī*. Cairo: Maktabat al-Qāhira, 1932
Myrne, Pernilla. 'A *Jariya*'s Prospects in Abbasid Baghdad.' In *Concubines and Courtesans*, ed. Matthew S. Gordon and Kathryn A. Hain, 52–74. New York: Oxford University Press, 2017
Nābulusī, ʿAbd al-Ghanī. *Al-Ḥadīqa al-nadiya sharḥ al-Ṭarīqa al-muḥammadiyya*. 2 vols. Istanbul: Asetane, n.d., reprint of Istanbul: Maṭbaʿa ʿĀmira, 1878
—. *Al-Ṣulḥ bayn al-ikhwān fī ḥukm ibāḥat al-dukhān*. Ed. Muḥammad Adīb al-Jādir. Damascus: Dār Nīnawī, 2015
Najmabadi, Afsaneh. *The Story of the Daughters of Quchan*. Syracuse: Syracuse University Press, 1998
Nāṣirī, Aḥmad al-Salāwī. *Kitāb al-Istiqṣā li-akhbār duwal al-maghrib al-aqṣā*. Ed. Jaʿfar and Muḥammad al-Nāṣirī. 9 vols. Casablanca: Dār al-Kitāb, 1955
Nawawī, Muḥyī al-Dīn. *Al-Majmūʿ*. Ed. Muḥammad Najīb al-Muṭīʿī. Jeddah: Maktabat al-Irshād, n.d.
—. *Rawḍat al-ṭālibīn wa ʿumdat al-muftīyyin*. Ed. Zuhayr al-Shāwīsh. 12 vols. Beirut: al-Maktab al-Islāmī, 1991
—. *Sharḥ Ṣaḥīḥ Muslim*. 15 vols. Beirut: Dār al-Qalam, 1987

—. *Tahdhīb al-asmā' wa'l-lughāt*. Ed. ʿAbduh ʿAlī Kūshak. 4 vols. Manama: Waqf Maktabat Niẓām al-Yaʿqūbī, 2013

Naysābūrī, al-Ḥākim. *Al-Mustadrak*. Hyderabad: Dā'irat al-Maʿārif al-ʿUthmāniyya, n.d.

Neumann, Christoph K. 'Whom did Ahmet Cevdet represent?' In *Late Ottoman Society*, ed. Elisabeth Özdalga, 117–35. London: Routledge, 2005

Newman, Cardinal John Henry. *An Essay on the Development of Christian Doctrine*. 6th edn. Notre Dame, IN: University of Notre Dame Press, 1989, originally published 1845

Niditch, Susan. *War in the Hebrew Bible: A Study in the Ethics of Violence*. Oxford: Oxford University Press, 2015

Nieboer, H. J. *Slavery as an Industrial System*. 2nd edn. The Hague: Nijhoff, 1910

Nifterik, Gustaaf van. 'Hugo Grotius on "Slavery".' *Grotiana* 22/23 (2002/2003): 233–44

Niẓam al-Mulk. *Siyāsat-nāma*. Ed. Sayyed ʿAbd al-Ḥalīm Khalkhālī. Tehran: Mu'assasa-yi Khurshīd, 1932

Noonan, John T., Jr. 'Development in Moral Doctrine.' *Theological Studies* 54 (1993): 662–77

Noonan, Thomas S. 'Fluctuations in Islamic Trade with Eastern Europe during the Viking Age.' *Harvard Ukrainian Studies* 16, n. 3–4 (1992): 237–59

Norberg, Johan. *Progress: Ten Reasons to Look forward to the Future*. London: Oneworld, 2017

Northrup, Linda. 'The Baḥrī Mamlūk sultanate, 1250–1390.' In *The Cambridge History of Egypt*, ed. Carl F. Petry, 242–89. Cambridge: Cambridge University Press, 1998

Novak, David. *In Defense of Religious Liberty*. Wilmington: ISI Books, 2009

—. 'Natural Law and Judaism.' In *Natural Law: A Jewish, Christian, and Islamic Trialogue*, 4–44. London: Oxford University Press, 2014

Novo, Marta García. 'La doctrina mālikí sobre esclavitud y el Miʿrāŷ de Aḥmad Bābā.' *Espacio, Tiempo y Forma* 23, n. 3 (2010): 75–95

Nubāhī, Abū al-Ḥasan ʿAlī. *Tārīkh quḍāt al-andalus*. Ed. Maryam Qāsim Ṭawīl. Beirut: Dār al-Kutub al-ʿIlmiyya, 1995

Nūḥ b. Muṣṭafā al-Rūmī al-Ḥanafī. 'Risāla fī wujūb muqātalat al-rawāfiḍ wa jawāz qatlihim.' In MS 21523 (*majmūʿ*), Cairo, Egyptian National Library, 4b–7a

Ochsenwald, William. 'Muslim-European Conflict in the Hijaz: The Slave Controversy, 1840-1895.' *Middle Eastern Studies* 16, n. 1 (1990): 115–26

Öhrnberg, Kaj. '*Māriya al-qibṭiyya* Unveiled.' *Studia Orientalia* 55, n. 14 (1984): 297–303

'On Slavery in the East.' *Asiatic Journal* 136, n. 4 (April 1827): 445–53

Origen. *Homilies on Joshua*. Ed. Cynthia White. Trans. Barbara J. Bruce. Washington, DC: Catholic University of America Press, 2002

—. *Origen*. Ed. and trans. Rowan Greer. New York: Paulist Press, 1979

Oshatz, Molly. 'The Problem of Moral Progress: The Slavery Debates and the Development of Liberal Protestantism in the United States.' *Modern Intellectual History* 5, n. 2 (2008): 225–50

Osswald, Rainer. *Das Islamische Sklavenrecht*. Würzburg: Ergon, 2017

—. *Sklavenhandel und Sklavenleben zwischen Senegal und Atlas*. Würzburg: Ergon, 2016

Outram, Dorinda. *The Enlightenment*. Cambridge: Cambridge University Press, 2005

Panzer, Joel S. *The Popes and Slavery*. New York: Alba House, 1996

Parrott, Justin. 'The Golden Rule in Islam: The Ethics of Reciprocity in Islamic Traditions.' PhD dissertation, University of Wales, 2018

Parvez, Ghulam Ahmad. *Islam: A Challenge to Religion*. Lahore: Tolu-e Islam Trust, 1968

Pascal, Blaise. *Pensées*. Trans. A. J. Krailsheimer. London: Penguin Books, 1995, original published 1966

Patterson, Orlando. *Slavery and Social Death*. Cambridge, MA: Harvard University Press, 1982

Peabody, Sue. *There Are No Slaves in France: The Political Culture of Race and Slavery in the Ancien Régime*. Oxford: Oxford University Press, 1996

Pelteret, David A. E. *Slavery in Early Medieval England*. Woodbridge, UK: Boydell Press, 1995

Penn, Michael Philip. *When Christians First Met Muslims*. Oakland: Univerity of California Press, 2015

Peters, Ruud. 'Islamic Law and Human Rights: a contribution to an ongoing debate.' *Islam and Christian-Muslim Relations* 10, n. 1 (1999): 5–14

Petronius. *Satyricon*. Trans. J. P. Sullivan. New York: Penguin Books, 1977

Phillips, William D., Jr. *Slavery in Medieval and Early Modern Iberia*. Philadelphia: University of Pennsylvania Press, 2014

Philo of Alexandria. 'De Specialibus Legibus.' In *Philo*, trans. F. H. Colson et al. Cambridge, MA: Harvard University Press, 1958–1962

Pierce, Leslie. *Morality Tales: Law and Gender in the Ottoman Court of Aintab*. Berkeley: University of California Press, 2003

Pipes, Daniel. 'Mawlas: Freed Slaves and Converts in Early Islam.' *Slavery & Abolition* 1, n. 2 (1980): 132–77

Pollock, Frederick. *An Essay on Possession in the Common Law*. Oxford: Clarendon Press, 1888

Popovic, Alexandre. *The Revolt of African Slaves in Iraq in the 3rd/9th Century*. Trans. Léon King. Princeton: Markus Wiener, 1999

Powell, Avril A. 'Indian Muslim Modernists and the Issue of Slavery in Islam.' In *Slavery & South Asian History*, ed. Richard Eaton and Indrani Chatterjee, 262–86. Bloomington: Indiana University Press, 2006

Powell, Eve Troutt. *A Different Shade of Colonialism: Egypt, Great Britain, and the Mastery of the Sudan*. Berkeley: University of California Press, 2003

—. *Tell This in My Memory: Stories of Enslavement from Egypt, Sudan and the Ottoman Empire*. Stanford: Stanford University Press, 2012

De la Puente, Cristina. 'The Ethnic Origins of Female Slaves in al-Andalus.' In *Concubines and Courtesans*, ed. Matthew S. Gordon and Kathryn A. Hain, 124–42. New York: Oxford University Press, 2017

Pulleyblank, E. G. 'The Origins and Nature of Chattel Slavery in China.' *Journal of the Social and Economic History of the Orient* 1, n. 2 (1958): 185–220

Qāḍī, Muḥammad Mukhtār. 'Bayn al-Sharīʿa al-islāmiyya wa'l-qānūn al-rūmānī: niẓām al-riqq.' *Al-Azhar* 39, n. 4 (1967): 365–71

Qāḍī-zāde Efendi, Shams al-Dīn. *Natā'ij al-afkār*. Ed. ʿAbd al-Razzāq Ghālib al-Mahdī. Beirut: Dār al-Kutub al-ʿIlmiyya, 2003

Qaffāl al-kabīr al-Shāshī, Muḥammad b. ʿAlī. *Maḥāsin al-sharīʿa*. Ed. Muḥammad ʿAlī Samak. Beirut: Dār al-Kutub al-ʿIlmiyya, 2007

Qaraḍāwī, Yūsuf. *Fiqh al-jihād*. 2 vols. Cairo: Maktabat Wahba, [2009]

Qarāfī, Aḥmad b. Idrīs. *Al-Furūq*. Ed. Khalīl Manṣūr. Beirut: Dār al-Kutub al-ʿIlmiyya, 1998

Qarāfī, Shihāb al-Dīn Aḥmad. *Al-Dhakhīra*. Ed. Muḥammad Bū Khubza. 14 vols. Beirut: Dār al-Gharb al-Islāmī, 1994

Qāri', Mullā ʿAlī. *Al-Asrār al-marfūʿa fī al-akhbār al-mawḍūʿa*. Ed. Muḥammad Luṭfī al-Ṣabbāgh. 2nd edn. Beirut: al-Maktab al-Islāmī, 1986

—. *Majmuʿ rasā'il al-ʿallāmā al-Mullā ʿAlī al-Qāri'*. Ed. Māhir Adīb Ḥabbūsh et al. 8 vols. Istanbul: Dār al-Lubāb, 2016

—*Sharḥ al-Shifā'*, printed on the margins of Aḥmad Shihāb al-Dīn al-Khifājī, *Nasīm al-riyāḍ fī sharḥ Shifā' al-Qāḍī ʿIyāḍ*. 4 vols. [Beirut]: Dār al-Kitāb al-ʿArabī, reprint of Cairo: al-Maṭbaʿa al-Azhariyya, 1909

Qudūrī, Aḥmad b. Muḥammad. *The Mukhtaṣar*. Trans. Ṭāhir Maḥmood Kiānī. London: Ta-Ha Publishers, 2010

Quirk, Joel. 'The Anti-Slavery Project: Linking the Historical and Contemporary.' *Human Rights Quarterly* 28, n. 3 (2006): 565–98

Qurṭubī, Muḥammad b. Aḥmad. *Al-Jāmiʿ li-aḥkām al-Qur'ān*. Ed. Muḥammad Ibrāhīm al-Ḥifnāwī and Maḥmūd Ḥamīd ʿUthmān. 20 vols. Cairo: Dār al-Ḥadīth, 1994

Quṭb, Muḥammad. *Shubuhāt ḥawl al-Islām*. 21st edn. Cairo: Dār al-Shurūq, 1992

Qutb, Sayyid. *Milestones*. Trans. Saheeh International. Ed. A. B. El-Mehri. Birmingham: Maktaba, 2006

Rabbat, Nasser. 'The Changing Concept of the *Mamlūk* in the Mamluk Sultanate in Egypt and Syria.' In *Slave Elites in the Middle East and Africa*, ed. Miura Toru and John Edward Philips, 81–98. London: Kegan Paul, 2000

Rāġib, Yūsuf. *Actes de vente d'esclaves et d'animaux d'Égypte médiévale*: Vol. 1. Cairo: Institut français d'archéologie orientale, 2002

Rahman, Fazlur. *Islam and Modernity*. Chicago: University of Chicago Press, 1982

—. 'Status of Women in the Qur'an.' In *Women and Revolution in Iran*, ed. Guity Nashat, 37–54. Boulder: Westview Press, 1983

Ramelli, Ilaria E. *Social Justice and the Legitimacy of Slavery: The Role of Philosophical Asceticism from Ancient Judaism to Late Antiquity*. Oxford: Oxford University Press, 2016

Ramis-Barceló, Rafael. 'Alasdair MacIntyre on Natural Law.' In *The Threads of Natural Law*, ed. Francisco Joséa Contreras, 191–210. London: Springer, 2013

Ransmeier, Johanna. 'Ambiguities in the Sale of Women at the End of the Qing Dynasty.' In *Sex, Power and Slavery*, ed. Gwyn Campbell and Elizabeth Elbourne, 319-344. Athens, OH: Ohio University Press, 2014

Rapoport, Yossef. 'Royal Justice and Religious Law: *Siyāsah* and Shariʿah under the Mamluks.' *Mamlūk Studies Review* 16 (2012): 71–102

Raymer, A.T. 'Slavery – The Graeco-Roman Defense.' *Greece & Rome* 10, n. 2 (1940): 17–21

Rāzī, Fakhr al-Dīn. *Al-Maḥṣūl fī uṣūl al-fiqh*. Ed. Ṭāhā Jābir al-ʿAlwānī. 6 vols. Beirut: Mu'assasat al-Risāla, 1992

—. *Tafsīr al-Fakhr al-Rāzī*. 32 vols. Beirut: Dār al-Fikr, 1981

Reid, Anthony, and Jennifer Brewster, ed. *Slavery, Bondage and Dependency in Southeast Asia*. New York: St. Martin's Press, 1983

Reinhart, A. Kevin. 'Islamic Law as Islamic Ethics.' *Journal of Religious Ethics* 11, n. 2 (1983): 186–203

Richardson, Kristina. 'Singing Slave Girls (*Qiyan*) in the 'Abbasid Court in the Ninth and Tenth Centuries.' In *Children in Slavery through the Ages*, ed. Suzanne Miers and Joseph C. Miller, 105–18. Athens, OH: Ohio University Press, 2009

Riḍā, Muḥammad Rashīd. 'As'ila min Bārīs.' *Al-Manār* 13, n. 10 (1910): 742–48

—. 'Ḥukm ʿabīd ḥaḍramawt.' *Al-Manār* 31, n. 3 (1930): 189–90

—. 'Al-Raqīq al-abyaḍ wa'l-aswad.' *Al-Manār* 20, n. 1 (1917): 19–22

—. 'Su'āl ʿan al-istirqāq al-maʿhūd fī hādhā al-zamān.' *Al-Manar* 23, n. 1 (1922): 31–33
Roberts, David. *Sketches in Egypt and Nubia*. Aalsmeer: Pulchri Press, [1980]
Robinson, Chase. *Islamic Historiography*. Cambridge: Cambridge University Press, 2003
—. 'Slavery in the Conquest Period.' *International Journal of Middle East Studies* 49, n. 1 (2017): 158–63
Robinson, David. 'Un historien et anthropologue sénégalais: Shaikh Musa Kamara.' *Cahiers d'Études africaines* 109, n. 28:1 (1988): 89–116.
Robinson, Majied. 'Prosopographical Approaches to the Nasab Tradition: A Study of Marriage and Concubinage in the Tribe of Muḥammad, 500-750 CE.' PhD dissertation, University of Edinburgh, 2013
—. 'Statistical Approaches to the Rise of Concubinage in Islam.' In *Concubines and Courtesans*, ed. Matthew S. Gordon and Kathryn A. Hain, 11–26. Oxford: Oxford University Press, 2017
Robinson, Richard. *Definition*. Oxford: Clarendon Press, 1954
Rodney, Walter. *West Africa and the Atlantic Slave Trade*. Nairobi: Historical Association of Tanzania, 1967
Rosenfeld, Sophia. *Common Sense: A Political History*. Cambridge, MA: Harvard University Press, 2011
Rosenthal, Franz. 'Fiction and Reality: Sources for the Role of Sex in Medieval Muslim Society.' In *Society and the Sexes in Medieval Islam*, ed. by Afaf Lutfi al-Sayyid-Marsot, 3–22. Malibu: Undena, 1979
—. *The Muslim Concept of Freedom prior to the Nineteenth Century*. Leiden: Brill, 1960
Rotman, Youval. *Byzantine Slavery and the Mediterranean World*. Trans. Jane Marie Todd. Cambridge, MA: Harvard University Press, 2009
Rozbicki, M. J. 'To Save Them from Themselves: Proposals to Enslave the British Poor, 1698–1755.' *Slavery & Abolition* 22, n. 2 (2001): 29–50
Sabban, Rima. 'Encountering Domestic Slavery: A Narrative from the Arabian Gulf.' In *Slavery in the Islamic World*, ed. Mary Ann Fay, 125–53. New York: Palgrave, 2019
Ṣafadī, Khalīl b. Aybak. *Al-Wāfī bi'l-wafāyāt*. Ed. Aḥmad al-Arnā'ūṭ and Turkī al-Muṣṭafā. 29 vols. Beirut: Dār Iḥyā' al-Turāth al-ʿArabī, 2000
Sagaster, Börte. *"Herren" und "Sklaven": der Wandel im Sklavenbild türkischer Literaten in der Spätzeit des Osmanischen Reiches*. Wiesbaden: Harrassowitz, 1997
Sahmī, Ḥamza b. Yūsuf. *Tārīkh Jurjān*. Hyderabad: Dā'irat al-Maʿārif al-ʿUthmāniyya, 1950
Sakhāwī, Shams al-Dīn Muḥammad. *Al-Ḍaw' al-lāmiʿ li-ahl al-qarn al-tāsiʿ*. 12 vols. Beirut: Dār al-Jīl, 1992
—. *Al-Maqāṣid al-ḥasana*. Ed. Muhammad ʿUthman al-Khisht. Beirut: Dār al-Kitāb al-ʿArabī, 2004
Salamon, Hagar. 'Cow Tales: Decoding Images of Slavery in the Ethiopian Jewish Community.' *Slavery & Abolition* 29, n. 3 (2008): 415–35
Salau, Mohammed Bashir. 'Slavery in Kano Emirate of Sokoto Caliphate Recounted: Testimonies of Isyaku and Idrisu.' In *African Voices on Slavery and the Slave Trade*, ed. Alice Ballagamba, Sandra E. Greene and Martin Klein, 88–113. Cambridge: Cambridge University Press, 2013
Saleh, Walid A. *In Defense of the Bible: A Critical Edition and an Introduction to al-Biqāʿī's Bible Treatise*. Leiden: Brill, 2008
Samarqandī, Abū Layth. *Tafsīr*. Ed. ʿAlī Muḥammad Muʿawwaḍ et al. 3 vols. Beirut: Dār al-Kutub al-ʿIlmiyya, 1993
Ṣanʿānī, ʿAbd al-Razzāq. *Muṣannaf*. Ed. Ḥabīb al-Raḥmān al-Aʿẓamī. 11 vols. Beirut: al-Majlis al-ʿIlmī and al-Maktab al-Islāmī, 1983

Ṣanʿānī, Muḥammad b. Ismāʿīl Ibn al-Amīr. *Subul al-salām sharḥ Bulūgh al-marām*. Ed. Muḥammad ʿAbd al-Raḥmān al-Marʿashlī. 4 vols. Beirut: Dār Iḥyāʾ al-Turāth al-ʿArabī, 2005

—. *Taṭhīr al-iʿtiqād ʿan adrān al-ilḥād*. Cairo: Maktabat al-Salām, 1980

Santos, Ricardo Ventura, et al. 'Color, Race, and Genomic Ancestry in Brazil.' *Current Anthropology* 50, n. 6 (2009): 787–819

Sartain, Elizabeth. *Jalāl al-Dīn al-Suyūṭī*. 2 vols. Cambridge: Cambridge University Press, 1975

Schmid, Alex P. 'Terrorism – The Definitional Problem,' *Case Western Reserve Journal of International Law* 36, n. 2 (2004): 375–420

— and Albert J. Longman. *Political Terrorism*. New Brunswick, NJ: Transaction Publishers, 1988

Schneider, Irene. 'Freedom and Slavery in Early Islamic Time [sic] (1st/7th- 2nd/8th Centuries).' *Al-Qanṭara* 28, n. 2 (2007): 353–82

Searing, James F. *'God Alone is King': Islam and Emancipation in Senegal*. Oxford: James Curry, 2002

Sears, Christine E. '"In Algiers, the City of Bondage": Urban Slavery in Comparative Context.' In *New Directions in Slavery Studies*, ed. Jeff Forret and Christine E. Sears, 201–28. Baton Rouge: Louisiana State University Press, 2015

Seng, Yvonne. 'A Liminal State: Slavery in Sixteenth-Century Istanbul.' In *Slavery in the Islamic Middle East*, ed. Shaun Marmon, 25–42. Princeton: Markus Wiener, 1999

Shaarawi, Huda. *Harem Years: The Memoirs of an Egyptian Feminist*. Trans. Margot Badran. New York: The Feminist Press, 1987

Shāfiʿī, Muḥammad b. Idrīs. *Al-Umm*. 2nd edn. 8 vols. in 4. Beirut: Dār al-Maʿrifa, [1973]

Shafīq, Aḥmad. *L'Esclavage au point de vue musalman*. Cairo: l'Imprimerie Nationale, 1891

—. *Mudhakkirātī fī niṣf qarn*. 3 vols in 4. Cairo: Maktabat al-Adab, 2008

Sharʿānī, ʿAbd al-Wahhāb. *Al-Mīzān al-kubrā*. 2 vols in 1. Cairo: Maktabat Zahrān [no date]. Reprint of Cairo: Maktabat al-Kastiliyya, 1862

Shaʿrānī, Abū al-Ḥasan. *Nathr-i ṭūbī*. Ed. Muḥammad Qarīb. Tehran: Islāmiyya, [2002]

Shariati, Ali. *The Visage of Muhammad*. Trans. Abdalaziz Sachedina. Houston: Free Islamic Literature Inc., 1979

Shāṭibī, Abū Isḥāq. *Kitāb al-Iʿtiṣām*. Cairo: al-Maktaba al-Tijāriyya al-Kubrā, 1914

—. *Al-Muwāfaqāt*. Ed. Bakr ʿAbdallāh Abū Zayd and Mashhūr Ḥasan Salmān. 6 vols. Cairo: Dār Ibn ʿAffān, 1997

Shatzmiller, Maya. *Her Day in Court: Women's Property Rights in Fifteenth-Century Granada*. Cambridge, MA: Harvard University Press, 2007

Shawkānī, Muḥammad b. ʿAlī. *Nayl al-awṭār sharḥ Muntaqā al-akhbār*. Ed. ʿIzz al-Dīn Khaṭṭāb. 8 vols. Beirut: Dār Iḥyāʾ al-Turāth al-ʿArabī, 2001

Shaybānī, Muḥammad b. Ḥasan. *Al-Siyar al-kabīr*. Ed. Muḥammad Abū Zahra and Muṣṭafā Zayd. Cairo: Cairo University Press, 1950

Shaykhzāde, Muḥyī al-Dīn. *Ḥāshiyat Muḥyī al-Dīn Shaykhzāde ʿalā Tafsīr al-Bayḍāwī*. Ed. Muḥammad ʿAbd al-Qādir Shāhīn. 8 vols. Beirut: Dār al-Kutub al-ʿIlmiyya, 1999

Shayzarī, ʿAbd al-Raḥmān. *Nihāyat al-rutba fī ṭalab al-ḥisba*, published with Muḥammad b. al-Ḥasan al-Murādī, *Kitāb al-Siyāsa*. Ed. Muḥammad Ḥasan Muḥammad and Aḥmad Farīd al-Mazīdī. Beirut: Dār al-Kutub al-ʿIlmiyya, n.d.

Sheriff, Abdul. 'The Slave trade and its fallout in the Persian Gulf.' In *Abolition and its Aftermath in Indian Ocean Africa and Asia*, ed. Gwyn Campbell, 103–19. London: Routledge, 2005

—. 'Social Mobility in Indian Ocean Slavery: The Strange Career of Sultan bin Aman.' In *Indian Ocean Slavery in the Age of Abolition*, ed. Robert Harms et al., 143–79. New Haven: Yale University Press, 2013

—. *Slaves, Spices & Ivory in Zanzibar*. Athens, OH: Ohio University Press, 1987

—. '*Suria*: Concubine or Secondary Slave Wife? The Case of Zanzibar.' In *Sex, Power and Slavery*, ed. Gwyn Campbell and Elizabeth Elbourne, 99–120. Athens, OH: Ohio University Press, 2014

—, et al., ed. *Transition from Slavery in Zanzibar and Mauritius*. Dakar: CODESRIA, 2016

Shields, Christopher. *Aristotle*. London: Routledge, 2007

Shihadeh, Ayman. *The Teleological Ethics of Fakhr al-Dīn al-Rāzī*. Leiden: Brill, 2006

Shirbīnī, Shams al-Dīn Muḥammad b. al-Khaṭīb. *Mughnī al-muḥtāj*. Ed. Muḥammad Khalīl Aytān. 4 vols. Beirut: Dār al-Maʿrifa, 1997

Siddiqui, Mona. *The Good Muslim: Reflections on Classical Islamic Law and Theology*. Cambridge: Cambridge University Press, 2012

Ṣidqī, Muḥammad Tawfīq. 'Al-Dīn fī naẓar al-ʿaql al-ṣaḥīḥ.' *Al-Manār* 8, n. 19 (1905, Shawwal 1323 AH): 732–44

Simmel, Georg. *The Sociology of Georg Simmel*. Trans. Kurt H. Wolff. New York: Free Press, 1950

Sijpesteijn, Petra. *Shaping a Muslim State*. Oxford: Oxford University Press, 2013

Sobers-Khan, Nur. *Slaves without Shackles: Forced Labour and Manumission in the Galata Court Registers, 1560-1572*. Berlin: Klaus Schwarz Verlag, 2014

Sorenson, L. R. 'Rousseau's Liberalism.' *History of Political Thought* 11, n. 3 (1990): 443–66

Spaulding, Jay. 'Precolonial Islam in the Eastern Sudan.' In *The History of Islam in Africa*, ed. Nehemia Levtzion and Randall L. Pouwels, 117–29. Athens, OH: Ohio University Press, 2000

Sperling, David. 'The Coastal Hinterland and Interior East Africa.' In *The History of Islam in Africa*, ed. Nehemia Levtzion and Randall L. Pouwels, 273–302. Athens, OH: Ohio University Press, 2000

Spicq, C. 'Le vocabulaire de l'esclavage dans le nouveau testament.' *Revue Biblique* 85, n. 2 (1978): 201–26

Sprankling, John G. and Raymond R. Coletta. *Property: A Contemporary Approach*. 2nd edn. St. Paul, MN: West, 2012

Sreenivasan, Ramya. 'Drudges, Dancing Girls, Concubines: Female Slaves in Rajput Polity, 1500–1850.' In *Slavery & South Asian History*, ed. Indrani Chatterjee and Richard M. Eaton, 136–61. Bloomington: Indiana University Press, 2006

Stark, Freya. *The Southern Gates of Arabia*. [New York]: E. P. Dutton, 1936

Starratt, Priscilla. 'Tuareg Slavery and Slave Trade.' *Slavery & Abolition* 2, n. 2 (1981): 83–113

Steinberg, Guido. 'Jihadi-Salafism and Shi'is: Remarks about the Intellectual Roots of anti-Shi'ism.' In *Global Salafism*, ed. Roel Meijer, 107–25. New York: Columbia University Press, 2009

Stephens, W. O. 'Epictetus on Fearing Death: Bugbear and Open Door Policy.' *Ancient Philosophy* 34 (2014): 365–91

Stevenson, Brenda. *What is Slavery?* Malden, MA: Polity, 2015

Stuard, Susan Mosher. 'Ancillary Evidence for the Decline of Medieval Slavery.' *Past & Present* 149, n. 1 (1995): 3–28

Subkī, Tāj al-Dīn ʿAbd al-Wahhāb. *Al-Ṭabaqāt al-shāfiʿiyya al-kubrā*. Ed. ʿAbd al-Fattāḥ Muḥammad al-Ḥuluw and Maḥmūd Muḥammad al-Ṭanāḥī. 2nd edn. 9 vols. Cairo: Hujr, 1992

Subkī, Taqī al-Dīn ʿAlī. *Fatāwā al-Subkī*. 2 vols. Beirut: Dār al-Maʿrifa, n.d.

—. *Qaḍāʾ al-arab fī asʾilat Ḥalab*. Ed. Muḥammad ʿĀlim ʿAbd al-Majīd al-Afghānī. Mecca: al-Maktaba al-Tijāriyya, 1993

Suhrawardī, Abū Ḥafṣ ʿUmar. *ʿAwārif al-maʿārif*. Ed. ʿAbd al-Ḥalīm Maḥmūd and Maḥmūd al-Sharaf. Cairo: al-Īmān, 2005

Sutherland, Heather. 'The Makassar Malays: Adaptation and Identity, c. 1660–1790.' *Journal of Southeast Asian Studies* 32, n. 3 (2001): 397–421

—. 'Slavery and the Slave Trade in South Sulawesi, 1600s–1800s.' In *Slavery, Bondage and Dependency in Southeast Asia*, ed. Anthony Reid, 263–85. New York: St. Martin's Press, 1983

Suyūṭī, Jalāl al-Dīn. *Azhār al-ʿurūsh fī akhbār al-ḥubūsh*. Ed. ʿAbdallāh Muḥammad al-Ghazzālī. Kuwait: Markaz al-Makhṭūṭāt, 1995

—. *Al-Ḥāwī li'l-fatāwī*. 2 vols. Beirut: Dār al-Kitāb al-ʿArabī, n.d.

—. *Al-Jāmiʿ al-ṣaghīr*. Beirut: Dār al-Kutub al-ʿIlmiyya, 2004

—. *Al-Laʾālīʾ al-maṣnūʿa fī al-aḥādīth al-mawḍūʿa*. Ed. Ṣāliḥ Muḥammad ʿUwayda. 3 vols. Beirut: Dār al-Kutub al-ʿIlmiyya, 1996

—. *Miṣbāḥ al-zujāja*, printed in *Sunan Ibn Mājah al-muḥashshā*. Karachi: Qadīmī Kutubkhāne, n.d.

—. *Rafʿ sha'n al-ḥubshān*. Ed. Muḥammad ʿAbd al-Wahhāb Faḍl. Cairo: Muḥammad ʿAbd al-Wahhāb Faḍl, 1991

Syrett, Nicholas L. *American Child Bride: A History of Minors and Marriage in the United States*. Chapel Hill, NC: University of North Carolina Press, 2016

Tābanda, Sulṭān Ḥusayn Gunābādī. *Naẓar-i madhhabī bih iʿlāmiyya-yi ḥuqūq-i bashar*. Qum: Maṭbūʿātī-yi Ḥikmat, 1966

Ṭabarānī, Abū al-Qāsim Sulaymān. *Al-Muʿjam al-awsaṭ*. Ed. Ṭāriq ʿAwaḍ Allāh and ʿAbd al-Muḥsin Ibrāhīm. 10 vols. Cairo: Dār al-Ḥaramayn, 1995

—. *Al-Muʿjam al-kabīr*. Ed. Ḥamdī ʿAbd al-Majīd al-Salafī. 25 vols. Beirut: Dār Iḥyāʾ al-Turāth al-ʿArabī, [no date]

Ṭabarī, Muḥammad Ibn Jarīr. *Tārīkh al-Ṭabarī*. 6 vols. Beirut: Dār al-Kutub al-ʿIlmiyya, 2003

Ṭabāṭabāʾī, ʿAllāma Muḥammad Ḥusayn. *Al-Mīzān fī tafsīr al-Qurʾān*. 22 vols. Beirut: Muʾassasat al-Aʿlamī, 1997

Ṭabāṭabāʾī, Muḥammad Saʿīd al-Ḥakīm. *Fī riḥāb al-ʿaqīda*. 4th edn. n.p.: Dār al-Hilāl, 2004

Taftāzānī, Saʿd al-Dīn. *Sharḥ al-Arbaʿīn al-Nawawiyya*. Istanbul: al-Maṭbaʿa al-ʿĀmira, 1898

Tahānawī (Thānvī), Muḥammad Aʿlā. *Kashshāf iṣṭilāḥāt al-funūn*. Ed. Rafic Al-Ajam et al. 2 vols. Beirut: Libraire du Liban, 1996

Ṭaḥḥān, Maḥmūd. *Al-Ḥāfiẓ al-Khaṭīb al-Baghdādī wa atharuhu fī ʿulūm al-ḥadīth*. Beirut: Dār al-Qurʾān al-Karīm, 1981

Ṭarābulusī, ʿAlā al-Dīn ʿAlī b. Khalīl. *Muʿīn al-ḥukkām fī-mā yataraddadu bayn al-khaṣmayn min al-aḥkām*. Cairo: al-Maṭbaʿat al-Maymaniyya, 1892

Taşköprîzâde Ahmed Efendi. *Şerhu'l-Ahlâki'l-Adudiyye*. Ed. Elzem Içöz et al. Istanbul: Türkiye Yazma Eserler Kurumu Başkanlığı, 2014

Taylor, Michael. 'British Proslavery Arguments and the Bible, 1823-33.' *Slavery & Abolition* 37, n. 1 (2016): 139–58

Temperley, Howard. 'The Delegalization of Slavery in India.' *Slavery & Abolition* 21, n. 1 (2000): 169–87

—. 'The Ideology of Antislavery.' In *The Abolition of the Atlantic Slave Trade*, ed. David Eltis and James Walvin, 21–35. Madison: University of Wisconsin Press, 1981

Testart, Alain. 'The Extent and Significance of Debt Slavery.' *Revue Française de Sociologie* 43 (2002): 173–204

Thaʿlabī, Aḥmad b. Muḥammad. *Tafsīr*. Beirut: Mu'assasat al-Aʿlāmī, n.d.

Thesiger, Wilfred. *Arabian Sands*. New York: E. P. Dutton, 1959

Thomas, Edward. *Islam's Perfect Stranger: The Life of Mahmud Muhammad Taha, Muslim Reformer of Sudan*. London: I. B. Tauris, 2010

Thomas, Yan. 'Vitae Necisque Potestas: Le Père, La Cité, La Mort.' *Publications de l'École Française de Rome* (1984): 499–548

Thomson, Joseph. *To the Central African Lakes and Back: the narrative of the Royal Geographical Society's East Central African Expedition, 1878–1880*. 2 vols. London: S. Low, Marston, Searle and Rivington, 1881

Thornton, Thomas. *The Present State of Turkey*. London: Joseph Mawman, 1807

Tilimsānī, Ibn Maryam. *Al-Bustān fī dhikr al-ʿulamā' wa'l-awliyā' bi-Tilimsān*. Ed. ʿAbd al-Qādir al-Būbāya. Beirut: Dār al-Kutub al-ʿIlmiyya, 2014

Tobias, Carl. 'Interspousal Tort Immunity in America.' *Georgia Law Review* 23 (1989): 359–478

Toledano, Ehud. *As if Silent and Absent: Bonds of Enslavement in the Islamic Middle East*. New Haven: Yale University Press, 2007

—. *The Ottoman Slave Trade and its Suppression, 1840–1890*. Princeton: Princeton University Press, 1982.

—. *Slavery and Abolition in the Ottoman Middle East*. Seattle: University of Washington Press, 1998

Tor, Deborah G. 'The Political Revival of the Abbasid Caliphate: Al-Muqtafī and the Seljuqs.' *Journal of the American Oriental Society* 137, n. 2 (2017): 301–14

Toru, Miura and John Edward Philips, ed. *Slave Elites in the Middle East and Africa*. London: Kegan Paul, 2000

Trabelsi, Salah. 'Eunuchs, Power, and Slavery in the Early Islamic World,' in *Sex, Power and Slavery*, ed. Gwyn Campbell and Elizabeth Elbourne, 541–57. Athens, OH: Ohio University Press, 2014

Tsuda, Kaoru et al., 'Extensive interbreeding occurred among multiple matriarchal ancestors during the domestication of dogs: . . .' *Genes & Genetic Systems* 72 (1997): 229–38

Tsugitaka, Sato. 'Slave Traders and the Kārimī Merchants during the Mamluk Period.' *Mamlūk Studies Review* 10, n. 1 (2006): 141–56

Turley, David. 'Slave emancipations in modern history.' In *Serfdom and Slavery*, ed. Michael Bush, 181–96. London: Longman, 1996

Uchendu, Victor C. 'Slaves and Slavery in Igboland, Nigeria.' In *Slavery in Africa*, ed. Suzanne Miers and Victor Kopytoff, 121–32. Madison: University of Wisconsin Press, 1977

ʿUlwān, ʿAbdallāh Nāṣiḥ. *Niẓām al-riqq fī al-islām*. Cairo: Dār al-Salām, 2003

Urbach, E. E. *The Laws Regarding Slavery*. New York: Arno Press, 1979

Urbainczyk, Theresa. *Slave Revolts in Antiquity*. Berkeley: University of California Press, 2008

Urban, Elizabeth. 'Hagar and Mariya: Early Islamic Models of Slave Motherhood.' In *Concubines and Courtesans*, ed. Matthew S. Gordon and Kathryn A. Hain, 225–43. New York: Oxford University Press, 2017

ʿUthmānī, Muftī Muḥammad Taqī (Usmani, Muhammad Taqi). *Inʿām al-Bārī: durūs-i Bukhārī sharīf*. Ed. Muḥammad al-Nūr Ḥusayn. 4 vols. Karachi: Maktabat al-Ḥirā, 1962

—. *Takmilat Fatḥ al-mulhim*. 3 vols. Karachi: Maktabat Dār al-ʿUlūm Karātshī, 2004

Vassiliev, Alexei. *The History of Saudi Arabia*. New York: New York University Press, 2000

Verderame, Lorenzo. 'Slavery in Third-Millennium Mesopotamia.' *Journal of Global Slavery* 3 (2018): 13–40

Verlinden, Charles. 'l'Origine de *sclavus* – esclave.' *Bulletin du Cange: Archivum Latinitatis Medii Aevi* 17 (1943): 97–128

Vlassopolous, Kostas. 'Does Slavery Have a History?: The Consequence of a Global Approach.' *Journal of Global Slavery* 1 (2016): 5–27

Vogt, Joseph. *Ancient Slavery and the Ideal of Man*. Oxford: Basil Blackwell, 1974 (translated from German original)

Wadud, Amina. *Inside the Gender Jihad*. Oxford: Oneworld, 2006

Wagemakers, Joas. 'Reclaiming Scholarly Authority: Abu Muhammad al-Maqdisi's Critique of Jihadi Practices.' *Studies in Conflict and Terrorism* 34, n. 7 (2011): 523–39

Walton, Douglas. 'The Argument of the Beard.' *Informal Logic* 18, n. 2–3 (1996): 235–59

Walwāljī, ʿAbd al-Rashīd. *Al-Fatāwā al-Walwāljiyya*. Ed. Miqdād Mūsā al-Qaryuwī. 4 vols. Beirut: Dār al-Kutub al-ʿIlmiyya, 2003

Walz, Terence. 'Black Slavery in Egypt During the Nineteenth Century as Reflected in the Mahkama Archives of Cairo.' In *Slaves and Slavery in Muslim Africa II*, ed. John Ralph Willis, 137–60. London: Frank Cass, 1985

Wansharīsī, Aḥmad b. Yaḥyā. *Al-Miʿyār al-muʿrib wa'l-jāmiʿ al-mughrib ʿan fatāwī ahl ifrīqiyya wa'l-andalus wa'l-maghrib*. Ed. Muḥammad Ḥajjī et al. 14 vols. Rabat: Wizārat al-Awqāf wa'l-Shu'ūn al-Islāmiyya, 1981

Ward, Kerry. 'Slavery in Southeast Asia.' In *The Cambridge World History of Slavery*, Volume 3, *AD 1420–1804*, ed. David Eltis and Stanley Engerman, 163–86. Cambridge: Cambridge University Press, 2011

Ware, Rudolph T. *The Walking Qur'an: Islamic Education, Embodied Knowledge and History in West Africa*. Chapel Hill, NC: University of North Carolina Press, 2014

Watkins, Margaret. '"Slaves among Us": The Climate and Character of Eighteenth-Century Philosophical Discussions of Slavery.' *Philosophy Compass* 2017; 12:e12393. doi: 10.1111/phc3.12393

Watson, James L., ed. *Asian & African Systems of Slavery*. Oxford: Basil Blackwell, 1980

Wazzānī (also al-Wāzzānī), Abū ʿĪsā Sīdī al-Mahdī b. Muḥammad. *Al-Nawāzil al-jadīda al-kubrā fī-mā li-ahl Fās wa ghayrihim min al-badū wa'l-qurā / al-Miʿyār al-jadīd al-jāmiʿ al-muʿrib ʿan fatāwā al-muta'akhkhirīn min ʿulamā' al-maghrib*. Ed. ʿUmar ʿImād. 12 vols. Casablanca: Maṭbaʿat al-Faḍāla, 1997

Webb, William J. *Slaves, Women and Homosexuals*. Downers Grove, IL: InterVarsity Press, 2001

Weiner, Annette. *The Trobrianders of Papua New Guinea*. New York: Holt, Rinehart and Winston, 1988

Weitz, Lev. 'Polygyny and East Syrian Law: Local Practices and Ecclesiastical Tradition.' In *The Late Antique World of Early Islam: Muslims among Christians and Jews in the East Mediterranean*, ed. Robert Hoyland, 157–91. Princeton: Darwin Press, 2015

Wessels, Antonie. *A Modern Arabic Biography of Muḥammad: A Critical Study of Muḥammad Ḥusayn Haykal's* Ḥayāt Muḥammad. Leiden: Brill, 1972
West, Robin. 'Sex, Law, and Consent.' In *The Ethics of Consent*, ed. Franklin G. Miller and Alan Wertheimer, 221–50. Oxford: Oxford University Press, 2010
Westermann, William Linn. 'Enslaved Persons who are Free.' *The American Journal of Philology* 59, n. 1 (1938): 1–30.
—. *The Slave Systems of Greek and Roman Antiquity*. Philadelphia: American Philosophical Society, 1955
Westermarck, Edward. *The Origin and Development of the Moral Ideas*. 2nd edn. 2 vols. London: Macmillan & Co., 1912
Wheatcroft, Andrew. *The Ottomans: Dissolving Images*. London: Penguin Books, 1995; first published by Viking, 1993
Wheatley, Paul. *The Places Where Men Pray Together: Cities in the Islamic Lands*. Chicago: University of Chicago Press, 2001
White, Charles. *Three Years in Constantinople*. 3 vols. London: Henry Colburx, 1845
White, Jonathan R. *Terrorism and Homeland Security*. 6th edn. Belmont, CA: Wadsworth Cengage Learning, 2014
Williams, Eric. *Capitalism and Slavery*. Chapel Hill, NC: University of North Carolina Press, 1994
Willis, John Ralph, ed. *Slaves and Slavery in Muslim Africa*, Volume I, *Islam and the Ideology of Enslavement*. London: Frank Cass, 1985
—, ed. *Slaves and Slavery in Muslim Africa*, Volume II, *The Servile Estate*. London: Frank Cass, 1985
Winks, Robin, ed. *Slavery: A Comparative Perspective*. New York: New York University Press, 1972
Wirtschafter, Elise K. *Russia's Age of Serfdom 1649–1861*. Oxford: Blackwell, 2008
Wittek, Paul. '*Devshirme* and *Sharī'a*.' *Bulletin of the School of Oriental and African Studies* 17, n. 2 (1955): 271–78
Woolley, Morgan Lee. 'Marital Rape: A Unique Blend of Domestic Violence and Non-Marital Rape Issues.' *Hastings Women's Law Journal* 18 (2007): 269–93
Wright, Benjamin Fletcher, Jr. *American Interpretations of Natural Law*. New Brunswick, NJ: Transaction, 2016, originally published 1962
Wright, John. *The Trans-Saharan Slave Trade*. London: Routledge, 2007
Wyatt, David. *Slaves and Warriors in Medieval Britain and Ireland, 800–1200*. Leiden: Brill, 2009
Xenophon. *Memorabilia*. Trans. E. C. Marchant. Cambridge, MA: Harvard University Press, 1923
Yaḥyā b. Ādam al-Qurashī. *Kitāb al-Kharāj*. Ed. Ḥusayn Mu'nis. Cairo: Dār al-Shurūq, 1987
Yamanī, Najm al-Dīn ʿUmāra. *Al-Mustafīd fī akhbār Ṣanʿāʾ wa Zabīd*. Ed. Muḥammad ʿAlī Akwaʿ al-Jiwālī. Sanaa: Maṭbaʿat al-Saʿāda, 1976
Yaqoubi, Muhammad. *Inqādh al-umma: fatwā mufaṣṣala fī ithbāt anna dāʿish khawārij wa anna qitālahum wājib*. N.p.: n.p., 2015
Yazıcı, Abdurrahman. 'Osmanlı Hukûk-ı Âile Kararnâmesi (1917) ve Sadreddin Efendi'nin Eleştirileri.' *Ekev Akademi Dergisi* 19, n. 62 (2015): 567–84
Yilmaz, Gulay. 'Becoming a Devşirme: The Training of Conscripted Children in the Ottoman Empire.' In *Children in Slavery through the Ages*, ed. Suzanne Miers and Joseph C. Miller, 119–34. Athens, OH: Ohio University press, 2009
Yılmaz, Hüseyin. *Caliphate Redefined: The Mystical Turn in Ottoman Political Thought*. Princeton: Princeton University Press, 2018

Yosef, Koby. 'The Term *Mamlūk* and Slave Status during the Mamluk Sultanate.' *Al-Qanṭara* 34, n. 1 (2013): 7–34

Young, Walter. 'Stoning and Hand-Amputation: The pre-Islamic origins of the *hadd* penalties for *zinā* and *sariqa*.' MA thesis, McGill University, 2005

Zabīdī, Murtaḍā Muḥammad. *Itḥāf al-sāda al-muttaqīn bi-sharḥ Iḥyā' 'ulūm al-dīn*. 10 vols. Beirut: Mu'assasat al-Tārīkh al-ʿArabī, 1994

Zack, Naomi. *The Ethics and Mores of Race*. Lanham, MD: Rowman & Littlefield, 2011

Zamakhsharī, Maḥmūd b. ʿUmar. *Al-Kashshāf*. 2 vols. Cairo: al-Maṭbaʿa al-ʿĀmira, [1864]

Zarkashī, Badr al-Dīn. *Al-Baḥr al-muḥīṭ fī uṣūl al-fiqh*. Ed. Muḥammad Muḥammad Tāmir. 4 vols. Beirut: Dār al-Kutub al-ʿIlmiyya, 2007

Zayyān, Abū al-Qāsim. *Al-Bustān al-ẓarīf fī dawlat awlād mawlāya al-sharīf*. Ed. Rashīd al-Zāwiya. Rabat: Maṭbaʿat al-Maʿārif al-Jadīda, [1992]

Ze'evi, Dror. 'My Slave, My Son, My Lord: Slavery, Family and the State in the Islamic Middle East.' In *Slave Elites in the Middle East and Africa*, ed. Miura Toru and John Edward Philips, 71–80. London: Kegan Paul, 2000

Zilfi, Madeline C. *Women and Slavery in the Late Ottoman Empire*. Cambridge: Cambridge University Press, 2010

Zubayrī, al-Muṣʿab b. ʿAbdallāh. *Kitāb Nasab Quraysh*. Ed. E. Levy Provencal. 3rd edn. Cairo: Dār al-Maʿārif, 1982

Zuḥaylī, Wahba. *Āthār al-ḥarb fī al-fiqh al-islāmī*. 2nd edn. Damascus: Dār al-Fikr al-Islāmī, 1998, first published 1963

—. *Mawsūʿat al-fiqh al-islāmī wa'l-qaḍāyā al-muʿāṣira*. 14 vols. Damascus: Dār al-Fikr, 2010

Zurqānī, ʿAbd al-Bāqī and Muḥammad b. al-Ḥasan al-Bannānī. *Sharḥ al-Zurqānī ʿalā Mukhtaṣar al-Khalīl*. Ed. ʿAbd al-Salām Muḥammad Amīn. 8 vols. Beirut: Dār al-Kutub al-ʿIlmiyya, 2002

ISIS & RELATED SOURCES:

Al-Awlaki, Anwar. 'The Ruling on Dispossessing the Disbelievers wealth [sic] in Dar al-Harb.' *Inspire* 4 (January 2011): 55–60

ISIS Dīwān al-Buḥūth wa'l-iftā. *Al-Adilla al-jaliya fī kufr man nāṣara al-ḥamla al-ṣalībiyya ʿalā al-khilāfa al-islāmiyya*. [Raqqa]: Maktabat al-Himma, 2014

ISIS pamphlet. 'Al-Walā' li'l-islām lā li'l-waṭan.' [Raqqa]: Maktabat al-Himma, 2015

Al-Saby: aḥkām wa masā'il. [Raqqa]: Dīwān al-Buḥūth wa'l-Iftā', 2014

Umm Sumayyah al-Muhājirah. 'Slave-Girls or Prostitutes.' *Dabiq* 9 (May 2015): 44–49

Notes

INTRODUCTION: CAN WE TALK ABOUT SLAVERY?

1. William L. Burton, 'The use and abuse of history,' *American Historical Association Newsletter* 20, n. 2 (1982): 14 (cited from David Lowenthal, *The Past is a Foreign Country*, 263).
2. Quran 16:75.
3. See Anne Norton, *On the Muslim Question*; Roxanne Euben, *Enemy in the Mirror* (especially Chapter 5).
4. Kecia Ali, *Sexual Ethics and Islam*, 71.
5. See Chapter Four, notes 66 and 67. For an interesting case, see Jeffrey Fynn-Paul, 'Empire, Monotheism and Slavery in the Greater Mediterranean Region from Antiquity to the Early Modern Era,' 6. For the performative element here, see Walter Johnson, 'On Agency,' 120–21. Thanks to Bruce Hall for pointing me to this source.
6. Margaret Watkins shows brilliantly how we perceive many eighteenth-century philosophers' arguments against slavery as insufficient and even offensive; Margaret Watkins, '"Slaves among Us": The Climate and Character of Eighteenth-Century Philosophical Discussions of Slavery.'
7. Niall McKeown, *The Invention of Ancient Slavery?*, 11–29, 38–39, 159–60.
8. Jennifer Welchman, 'Locke on Slavery and Inalienable Rights,' 78–79.
9. See Walter Rodney, *West Africa and the Atlantic SlaveTrade.*
10. John W. Cairns, 'The Definition of Slavery in Eighteenth-Century Thinking,' 65; Indrani Chatterjee, 'Abolition by denial: The South Asian Example,' 151. The earliest person I have come across to refer to slaves holding positions of power in the Ottoman Empire as part of an argument over the morality of slavery was Gioviano Pontano (d. 1503); Joseph Vogt, *Ancient Slavery and the Ideal of Man*, 194.
11. Here I am speaking about Muslims, not Arabs, owing reparations. See Martin Plaut, 'Should Arab Countries Pay Reparations for Slavery Too?,' *New Statesman*, Aug. 21, 2013, https://www.newstatesman.com/international-politics/2013/08/should-arab-countries-pay-reparations-slave-trade-too; Rhoda Howard-Hassman, 'Reparations for the Slave Trade,' 427–54.
12. Najm al-Dīn ʿUmāra al-Yamanī, *al-Mustafīd fī akhbār Ṣanʿāʾ wa Zabīd*, 134.
13. The Hadith continues, '. . . and you are all more or less alike.' This Hadith, which mentions Bilāl as the person insulted and includes the Prophet's remarks on race and merit, appears in narrations in Abū Bakr al-Bayhaqī (d. 1066), *Shuʿab al-īmān*, 4:288 and Ibn ʿAsākir (d. 1176), *Tārīkh madīnat Dimashq*, 10:464. This rare Hadith is often conflated with another, much more common and widely attested Hadith in which the

Prophet upbraids his Companion Abū Dharr for insulting the mother of one of his (i.e., Abū Dharr's) slaves. This latter Hadith does contain invaluable ethical and legal material on the proper treatment of slaves, but it does not specify the slave as Bilāl, include any mention of Blackness or address the issue of race & merit; *Ṣaḥīḥ al-Bukhārī*: *kitāb al-īmān, bāb al-ma ʿāṣī min amr al-jāhiliyya* . . .; *Ṣaḥīḥ Muslim*: *kitāb al-īmān, bāb iṭ ʿām al-mamlūk mimmā ya'kulu* . . . A narration mentioned by Ibn Baṭṭāl (d. 1057) identifies the person insulted as Bilāl and the insult as denigrating his mother's Blackness (*sawād*); Ibn Baṭṭāl, *Sharḥ Ṣaḥīḥ al-Bukhārī*, 1:87.

14. *Musnad* of Aḥmad Ibn Ḥanbal (Maymaniyya printing): 5:411.

15. Ricardo Ventura Santos et al., 'Color, Race, and Genomic Ancestry in Brazil,' 787–819.

16. Abdullah Hamid Ali, 'The "Negro" in Afro-Arabian Muslim Consciousness.' See also Abū Isḥāq al-Iṣṭakhrī, *Masālik al-mamālik*, 40.

17. Terence Walz, 'Black Slavery in Egypt During the Nineteenth Century,' 140.

18. Merrill Perlman, 'Black and white: why capitalization matters,' *Columbia Journalism Review*, 6/23/2015, https://www.cjr.org/analysis/language_corner_1.php. Thanks to Su'ad Abdul Khabeer for this citation.

CHAPTER 1 DOES 'SLAVERY' EXIST? THE PROBLEM OF DEFINITION

1. http://www.imsdb.com/scripts/Matrix,-The.html

2. The narrative of Simonides and his status as a former slave of the House of Hur is much more complicated in the original novel. Returned to Judea, Ben-Hur seeks out the aid of his father's slave, now a prosperous merchant, hoping to call on his presumed-lost inherited birthright to ownership of the man. '. . . if Simonides had indeed been his father's slave. But would the man acknowledge the relation? That would be to give up his riches and the sovereignty of trade so royally witnessed on the wharf and river. And what was of still greater consequence to the merchant, it would be to forego his career in the midst of amazing success, and yield himself voluntarily once more a slave. Simple thought of the demand seemed a monstrous audacity. Stripped of diplomatic address, it was to say, You are my slave; give me all you have, and – yourself.' See Lew Wallace, *Ben -Hur*, Book 4, chapter 3.

3. Abdurrahman Yazıcı, 'Osmanlı Hukûk-ı Âile Kararnâmesi (1917) ve Sadreddin Efendi'nin Eleştirileri,' 580; Ahmed Yasin Küçüktiryaki, 'Sadreddin Efendi'nin Hukuk-ı Aile Kararnamesine İlişkin Görüşlerinin Değerlendirilmesi,' 112. Thanks to Said Kaymakci for this insight.

4. Christoph K. Neumann, 'Whom did Ahmet Cevdet represent?,' 117.

5. Nergiz Aydoğdu, 'Makyavelist Düşüncenin Türkiye'ye Girişi: Onsekizinci Yüzyıl Osmanlı Siyaset Felsefi,' 120. Thanks to Said Kaymakci for this insight. See also Ehud Toledano, *Slavery and Abolition in the Ottoman Middle East*, 120-121; Madeline Zilfi, *Women and Slavery in the Late Ottoman Empire*, 15 (the master/slave idiom was 'a cornerstone of Ottoman ideology'); Mohammed Ennaji, *Slavery, the State, and Islam*. For the Safavid adoption of this idiom, see Sussan Babaie et al., *Slaves of the Shah*, 6–19.

6. Pamela Kyle Crossley, 'Slavery in Early Modern China,' 200.

7. In a 1706 book, the British author Mary Astell argued that marriage qualified as slavery for women; Jacqueline Broad, 'Mary Astell on Marriage and Lockean Slavery,' 724, 726–27.
8. John Kells Ingram, *A History of Slavery and Serfdom*, 261.
9. http://www.imsdb.com/scripts/Fight-Club.html
10. Oliver J. W. Cox, 'Frederick, the Prince of Wales, and the First Performance of "Rule Britannia!,"' 931–54.
11. John W. Cairns, 'The Definition of Slavery in Eighteenth-Century Thinking,' 62. Kyle Harper writes, 'Slavery was a politically created reality, buried in the consciousness of late antique men and women . . . Slave status was part of the public order imposed by the Roman Leviathan.'; Kyle Harper, *Slavery in the Late Roman World, AD 275–425*, 355. See also ibid., 213.
12. In his *Kitāb al-ʿAyn*, the famous lexicographer Khalīl b. Aḥmad (d. *circa* 785) defines *riqq* as slavery (*al-ʿubūda*) and *ʿabd* as 'owned (*mamlūk*)' (i.e., a slave); Khalīl b. Aḥmad, *Kitāb al-ʿAyn*, 2:142, 3:83. I have asked Kecia Ali and Jonathan Brockopp, and neither of them knows of definitions for slavery (*riqq*) in the first three centuries of Islam. Franz Rosenthal remarks that 'the problem of freedom found little positive attention in [Muslim] legal works.'; Franz Rosenthal, *The Muslim Concept of Freedom prior to the Nineteenth Century*, 33.
13. Richard Robinson, *Definition*, 2–3.
14. Jonathan Wright, 'Tooth clinches identification of Egyptian queen,' *Reuters, Science*, June 27, 2007, https://www.reuters.com/article/us-egypt-queen/tooth-clinches-identification-of-egyptian-queen-idUSL2776273020070627.
15. Stephen A. Diamond, 'Is Depression a Disease?,' *Psychology Today*, Sept. 1, 2018, https://www.psychologytoday.com/blog/evil-deeds/200809/is-depression-disease.
16. Kathleen Weldon, 'Public Attitudes about Mental Health,' *Huffpost*, Dec. 6, 2017, https://www.huffingtonpost.com/kathleen-weldon/public-attitudes-about-me_b_7160960.html.
17. L. A. Rebhun, 'Culture-Bound Syndromes,' in *Encyclopedia of Medical Anthropology: Health and Illness in the World's Cultures*, ed. Carol R. Ember and Melvin Ember (Springer Science + Business Media, 2004).
18. For a reference to and adjustment of received opinion on this, see Annette Weiner, *The Trobrianders of Papua New Guinea*, 6, 51–64.
19. Robinson, *Definition*, 170–71.
20. James Mallet, 'A species definition for the Modern Synthesis,' 294–99; Brendan Kelley, Andrew Whiteley and David Tallmon, 'The Arctic Melting Pot,' 891; Kaoru Tsuda et al., 'Extensive interbreeding occurred among multiple matriarchal ancestors during the domestication of dogs . . .,' 229–38.
21. Drawing from Robinson, *Definition*, 156.
22. Wael Hallaq, introduction, and Ibn Taymiyya, *Ibn Taymiyya against the Greek Logicians*, xxix–xxxv, 7; Mohamed Ali, *Medieval Islamic Pragmatics: Sunni Legal Theorists' Model of Communication*, 98; Ovamir Anjum, *Politics, Law and Community in Islamic Thought*, 210–211. Cf. Ayman Shihadeh, *The Teleological Ethics of Fakhr al-Dīn al-Rāzī*, 182–83.
23. Robinson, *Definition*, 154.
24. https://en.oxforddictionaries.com/explore/is-a-tomato-a-fruit-or-a-vegetable
25. See Jonathan R. White, *Terrorism and Homeland Security*. Alex Schmid (2012) offered this definition: 'Terrorism refers, on the one hand, to a doctrine about the presumed effectiveness of a special form or tactic of fear-generating, coercive political

violence and, on the other hand, to a conspiratorial practice of calculated, demonstrative, direct violent action without legal or moral restraints, targeting mainly civilians and non-combatants, performed for its propagandistic and psychological effects on various audiences and conflict parties'; see http://www.terrorismanalysts.com/pt/index.php/pot/article/view/schmid-terrorism-definition/html. See also http://www.fbi.gov/stats-services/publications/terror_08.pdf; http://www.fbi.gov/stats-services/publications/terrorism-2002-2005; http://www.state.gov/s/ct/rls/crt/2003/31880.htm.

26. 'Alleged Halifax mass shooting plot "not culturally based" say police,' *CBC News*, Feb. 13, 2015, http://www.cbc.ca/news/canada/nova-scotia/alleged-halifax-mass-shooting-plot-not-culturally-based-say-police-1.2957446.

27. Anna Mehler Paperny, 'Halifax plot: So what is "terrorism," anyway?,' *Global News*, Feb. 14, 2015, https://globalnews.ca/news/1830795/halifax-plot-so-what-is-terrorism-anyway/.

28. Devin Neiwert, 'Huh? Since When is Attempting to Blow Up a Federal Building NOT an Act of Domestic Terrorism?' *Crooks and Liars*, Feb. 18, 2010, https://web.archive.org/web/20190317023152/https://crooksandliars.com/david-neiwert/huh-when-attempting-blow-federal-bui. More recently, a young, white, conservative Christian man was found to be behind a spate of package bombings in Austin, Texas. The White House spokesperson stated that the attacks has 'no known links to terrorism'; 'No known link to terrorism in Texas bombings: White House,' *Reuters, US*, March 20, 2018, https://www.reuters.com/article/us-texas-blast-whitehouse/no-known-link-to-terrorism-in-texas-bombings-white-house-idUSKBN1GW293.

29. Simon Mabon, 'Locating Terrorism Studies,' 5–17.

30. Jana Winter and Sharon Weinberger, 'The FBI's New U.S. Terrorist Threat: "Black Identity Extremists,"' *Foreign Policy*, Oct. 6, 2017, http://foreignpolicy.com/2017/10/06/the-fbi-has-identified-a-new-domestic-terrorist-threat-and-its-black-identity-extremists/; Timothy McGrath, 'Turns out people get angry when you say white Americans are terrorists, too,' *PRI*, July 8, 2015, https://www.pri.org/stories/2015-07-08/turns-out-people-get-angry-when-you-say-white-americans-are-terrorists-too.

31. Alex P. Schmid and Albert J. Longman, *Political Terrorism*, 3; Schmid, 'Terrorism – The Definitional Problem,' 375–420.

32. See Michel Foucault, 'The Order of Discourse,' 48–78.

33. See the work of Rémi Brulin, 'Le discours Américain sur le terrorisme: Constitution, evolution et contextes d'enonciation (1972–1992).' For an admission that US courts see using the label terrorist as 'prejudicial' for acts of violence carried out by White Americans, see Ryan J. Reilly, 'There's A Good Reason Feds Don't Call White Guys Terrorists, Says DOJ Domestic Terror Chief,' *Huffpost*, Jan. 11, 2018, https://www.huffingtonpost.com/entry/white-terrorists-domestic-extremists_us_5a550158e4b003133ecceb74?ncid=engmodushpmg00000004.

34. *Jacobellis v. Ohio*, 378 U.S. at 197 (Stewart, J., concurring).

35. David Brion Davis, *Slavery and Human Progress*, 8.

36. Joseph C. Miller, *The Problem of Slavery as History*, 12. Igor Kopytoff arrived at a similar question about the realism of 'slavery'; Igor Kopytoff, 'Commentary One [on Lovejoy's Indigenous African Slavery],' 62–76.

37. See Mabon, 'Locating Terrorism Studies,' 5–17.

38. James L. Watson, 'Introduction: Slavery as an Institution: Open and Closed Systems,' in Watson, ed., *Asian & African Systems of Slavery*, 3.

39. Shaun Marmon, 'Domestic Slavery in the Mamluk Empire: A Preliminary Sketch,' 13–14.

40. The translation 'gradual self-purchase' comes from Emily Berquist, 'Early Anti-Slavery Sentiment in the Spanish Atlantic World,' 184.
41. *Yik banda-yi meṭvāʿ bih az sīṣad farzand; kiʾīn marg-i pidar khwāhad va ū ʿumr-i khudāvand*; Niẓām al-Mulk, *Siyāsat-nāma*, 86.
42. See Erhan Afyoncu, 'Sokullu Mehmed Paşa,' *İslam Ansiklopesi*, at http://www.islam-ansiklopedisi.info/?idno=370357; G. Veinstein, 'Soḳollu Meḥmed Pasha,' in *Encyclopaedia of Islam*, 2nd edn; Zilfi, *Women and Slavery in the Late Ottoman Empire*, 143.
43. David Eltis and Stanley Engerman, 'Dependence, Servility, and Coerced Labor in Time and Space,' 7; Julia O'Connell Davidson, *Modern Slavery: The Margins of Freedom*, 68. In England this issue was governed by the Statute of Artificers, which the American colonies only adopted in a limited way.
44. http://transcripts.cnn.com/TRANSCRIPTS/0403/10/acd.00.html.
45. See Sophia Rosenfeld, *Common Sense: A Political History*, 244. See also, for example, Alasdair MacIntyre, *Whose Justice? Which Rationality?*, 250 ff.
46. For the extent to which nineteenth-century moral and colonial discourse in general and Western discourse on 'Islam and slavery' in particular, were shaped by the 'Atlantic slave trade,' even after it had been ended, see E. Ann McDougall, 'Discourse and Distortion: Critical Reflections on Studying the Saharan Slave Trade,' 202.
47. John W. Cairns, 'The Definition of Slavery in Eighteenth-Century Thinking,' 64.
48. For an interesting look at this issue, see Peter Kolchin, 'Review Essay: Putting New World Slavery in Perspective,' 279.
49. Anthony Reid, 'Introduction: Slavery and Bondage in Southeast Asian History,' in *Slavery, Bondage and Dependency in Southeast Asia*, 1.
50. Rodney Coates, 'Slavery' in *Blackwell Encyclopedia of Sociology*, ed. George Ritzer (Oxford: Blackwell, 2007). Blackwell Reference Online. 15 Feb., 2018 http://www.sociologyencyclopedia.com.proxy.library.georgetown.edu/subscriber/tocnode.html?id=g9781405124331_chunk_g978140512433125_ss1-125.
51. Ehud Toledano, *As if Silent and Absent: Bonds of Enslavement in the Islamic Middle East*, 33. This continues a conception of slavery as an asymmetric negotiation of power as described by John Blassingame in *The Slave Community: Plantation Life in the Antebellum South* and Eugene Genovese in *Roll, Jordan, Roll.*
52. https://www.dependency.uni-bonn.dc/cn/about.
53. Toledano, *Slavery and Abolition in the Ottoman Middle East*, 21.
54. https://itunes.apple.com/us/podcast/ottoman-history-podcast/id513808150?mt=2&i=378549385; last accessed January 2017. See also Nur Sobers-Khan, *Slaves without Shackles: Forced Labour and Manumission in the Galata Court Registers, 1560–1572.*
55. Igor Kopytoff and Suzanne Miers, 'African "Slavery" as an Institution of Marginality,' 7. See also a useful discussion by Laura Culbertson, 'Slaves and Households in the Near East,' 1–20. A more recent effort to define slavery as the deployment of the 'tools' of humans-as-property and domination in ever-changing contexts comes from Kostas Vlassopolous, 'Does Slavery Have a History?: The Consequence of a Global Approach,' 5–27.
56. Kopytoff and Miers, 'African "Slavery" as an Institution of Marginality,' 77.
57. Here I am building on Martin Klein's taxonomy. See Martin Klein, 'Introduction,' in *Breaking the Chains: Slavery, Bondage, and Emancipation in Modern Africa and Asia*, 4–5.
58. Moses Finley, 'Slavery,' 14:308.
59. See, for example, the Spanish Siete Partidas laws of the fourteenth century; Andrew T. Fede, *Homicide Justified: The Legality of Killing Slaves in the United States and the Atlantic World*, 25.

60. Aristotle, *Politics*, 1.1253b; idem, *Metaphysics* 1.982b (a free man is one who 'exists for himself and not for another'; '*Et libertas quidem est, ex qua etiam liberi vocantur, naturalis facultas eius quod cuique facere libet, nisi si quid aut vi aut iure prohibetur. Servitus autem est constitutio iuris gentium, qua quis dominio alieno contra naturam subicitur.*'; Corpus Iuris Civilis, *Institutes*, 1.3. Latin text is available at http://www.thelatinlibrary.com/justinian/institutes1.shtml.

61. Rosenthal, *Muslim Concept of Freedom*, 9–10, 23. Muḥammad Ṭāhir Ibn ʿĀshūr (d. 1973) states that the Arabic word for freedom (*ḥurriyya*) originally meant 'not a slave'; Ibn ʿĀshūr, *Uṣūl al-niẓām al-ijtimāʿī fī al-islām*, 160.

62. I have asked Kecia Ali and Jonathan Brockopp as well, and neither of them know of definitions for slavery (*riqq*) in the first three centuries of Islam. Franz Rosenthal remarks that 'the problem of freedom found little positive attention in [Muslim] legal works.'; Rosenthal, *The Muslim Concept of Freedom*, 33.

63. David Graeber, *Debt: The First 5,000 Years*, 204.

64. Suzanne Miers, 'Slavery: A Question of Definition,' 2.

65. Here quoting Youval Rotman, *Byzantine Slavery*, 19.

66. Rotman, *Byzantine Slavery*, 17–18.

67. Vaughan Lowe, *International Law: A Very Short Introduction*, 1.

68. Burhān al-Dīn al-Marghīnānī, *al-Hidāya sharḥ al-Bidāya*, 3:431; ʿAlāʾ al-Dīn ʿAbd al-ʿAzīz al-Bukhārī, *Kashf al-asrār ʿan Uṣūl Fakhr al-Islām al-Bazdawī*, 4:394 (*riqq* is a *ḍaʿf ḥukmī* that leads one to be the property of another); Shams al-Dīn Muḥammad b. al-Khaṭīb al-Shirbīnī, *Mughnī al-muḥtāj*, 3:36 (*ʿajz ḥukmī yaqūmu bi'l-insān bi-sabab al-kufr*); Muḥammad Aʿlā al-Tahānawī, *Kashshāf iṣṭilāḥāt al-funūn*, 1:870. See Marmon, 'Domestic Slavery in the Mamluk Empire,' 4–5. An interesting comparison arises with Victor Uchendu's definition of slavery as 'a continuum of status disabilities and the disabilities vary with the number of "commodity rights" in a person that are acquired.' See Victor C. Uchendu, 'Slaves and Slavery in Igboland, Nigeria,' 123. We also find a Persian saying of equivalent meaning, *bandegī bīchāregī*; ʿAlī Akbar Dekhodā, *Amthāl-o ḥekam*, 1:467.

69. Emma Goldman, *Red Emma Speaks*, 121; Isaiah Berlin, 'Two Concepts of Liberty,' in *Isaiah Berlin: The Proper Study of Mankind*, 191–242.

70. See Snake Plissken in *Escape from New York* (1981) and *Escape from L.A.* (1996), Jack Reacher, and Captain Pike from *Star Trek*'s first episode, 'The Cage' (1966).

71. The judge who turned Ibrahim Pasha away was the leading scholar *şeyhülislam* Fenārīzāde Mehmet Chelebi (d. 1548). See Mehmet Gel, 'Kanûnî Devrinde "Müftî" ile Rumeli Kazaskeri Arasında Bir "Hüccet-i Şer'iyye" İhtilafı Yahut Kemalpaşazâde-Fenârîzâde Hesaplaşması,' 72.

72. For the relatively recent date of 'negative freedom' as total autonomy and freedom from constraint, see Isaiah Berlin, 'Two Concepts of Liberty,' 201; Syed Naquib al-Attas, *Prolegomena to the Metaphysics of Islam*, 33, 59, 93; Ḥusayn b. Aḥmad al-Marṣafī (d. 1889), *Ru'ya fī taḥdīth al-fikr al-miṣrī*, 122.

73. Georg Simmel, *The Sociology of Georg Simmel*, 273–74.

74. Kopytoff and Miers, 'African "Slavery" as an Institution of Marginality,' 17; Kopytoff, 'Cultural Context of African Abolition,' 488-490. For an extended philosophical take on this issue, see John Christman, 'Analyzing Freedom from the Shadows of Slavery,' 162–84.

75. *Exodus* 21:6.

76. Freya Stark, *The Southern Gates of Arabia*, 64.

77. Reid, 21; V. Matheson and M. B. Hooker, 'Slavery in the Malay Texts: Categories of Dependency and Compensation,' 184–86.

78. Rotman, *Byzantine Slavery*, 97–98.
79. For an excellent example of this, see S. D. Goitein, 'Slaves and Slavegirls in the Cairo Geniza Records,' 4.
80. https://www.merriam-webster.com/dictionary/slave.
81. For other definitions of slavery centered on slave-as-human-property, see John K. Ingram, *A History of Slavery and Serfdom*, 262 (admitting the legal bent of his definition); H. J. Nieboer, *Slavery as an Industrial System* (a slave is someone who is the property of another, socially and politically lower than them and doing compulsory labor); Anthony Reid, 'Introduction: Slavery and Bondage in Southeast Asian History,' 2; Finley, 'Slavery,' 14:307–13 (the element of property is central to embodying the powerlessness of the enslaved); Watson, 'Slavery as an Institution: Open and Closed Systems,' 4; Paul Lovejoy, 'Slavery in the context of ideology,' 11–15; Jean Allain and Robin Hickey, 'Property and the Definition of Slavery,' 915–38. For a useful overview of slavery -as-property and criticisms of this view, which I found only after writing this chapter, see David M. Lewis, 'Orlando Patterson, Property, and Ancient Slavery: The Definitional Problem Revisited,' 31–54 (especially 40–48).
82. Plato, *Statesman*, 289d; Aristotle, *Politics*, 1.1253b.
83. See, for example, Cairns, 'The Definition of Slavery in Eighteenth-Century Thinking,' 63.
84. The text of these conventions is available at http://hrlibrary.umn.edu/instree/f3scas.htm.
85. Khalīl b. Aḥmad, *Kitāb al-ʿAyn*, 3:83; ʿAlāʾ al-Dīn al-Bukhārī, *Kashf al-asrār*, 4:394–95.
86. Edward Westermarck, *The Origin and Development of the Moral Ideas*, 1:671–2.
87. A. M. Honoré, 'Ownership,' 113. The definition of property as 'rights among people concerning things,' I take from John G. Sprankling and Raymond R. Coletta, *Property: A Contemporary Approach*, 25. For an early effort to theorize law of property, see Frederick Pollock, *An Essay on Possession in the Common Law*, 1–25. Stressing that the concept of ownership is more unified than diverse in mature legal systems, Honoré offers the (very vague) definition of ownership as 'the greatest possible interest in a thing which a mature system of law recognizes.' See Honoré, 'Ownership,' 108.
88. See Honoré, 'Ownership,' 145–46; Robin Hickey, 'Seeking to Understand the Definition of Slavery,' 220–41.
89. Miers, 'Slavery: A Question of Definition,' 2–3.
90. W. W. Buckland, *The Roman Law of Slavery*, 2–3.
91. Crossley, 'Slavery in Early Modern China,' 191. In Han and Tang times killing slaves without government sanction was a crime; E. G. Pulleyblank, 'The Origins and Nature of Chattel Slavery in China,' 213.
92. Ward, 'Slavery in Southeast Asia,' 171.
93. Lawrence M. Friedman, *A History of American Law*, 225.
94. The Ḥanafī and Zaydī schools only allowed the ruler/state to carry out Hudud punishments on slaves, while the other Sunni schools allowed masters to do it; Ibn al-Amīr al-Ṣanʿānī, *Subul al-salām*, 3:14–15; Muḥammad b. ʿAlī al-Shawkānī, *Nayl al-awṭār*, 7:137–38. All schools of law punished a free person for murdering a slave, but only the Ḥanafī school allowed execution as a punishment for this. It did so because the school read the Quranic verse 'a life for a life' (Quran 5:45) as superseding another verse stating 'a free person for a free person, a slave for a slave . . .' (Quran 2:178). The Ḥanafīs took this second verse as meaning any free person is the equal of any other free person, etc. The other schools of law assumed that 'a free person for a free person' meant that a

free person could only be executed for murdering another free person and concluded that this verse superseded the 'a life for a life' verse; Jonathan Brown, *Misquoting Muhammad*, 99–100. The Prophet and the caliph ʿUmar punished owners who either killed or burned their slaves with one hundred lashes, a year in exile, a loss of stipend and a requirement to free another slave in the first case and one hundred lashes and freeing the burnt slave in the second; al-Bayhaqī, *Sunan al-kubrā*, 8:66.

95. See Harper, *Slavery in the Late Roman World*, 232; William Westermann, *The Slave Systems of Greek and Roman Antiquity*, 115.

96. Buckland, *The Roman Law of Slavery*, 36–8.

97. Harper, *Slavery in the Late Roman World*, 232; Westermann, *The Slave Systems of Greek and Roman Antiquity*, 115.

98. Kenneth Morgan, *Slavery and Servitude in Colonial North America*, 35, 77; Ira Berlin, *Many Thousands Gone: The First Two Centuries of Slavery in North America*, 116; Paul Finkelman, 'Slavery: United States Law,' in *Oxford International Encyclopedia of Legal History*, 5:258–62; Friedman, *A History of American Law*, 225–6.

99. See Ibn Ḥajar al-ʿAsqalānī, *Fatḥ al-Bārī*, 9:379; al-Buhūtī, *Kashshāf al-qināʿ*, 5:491–2.

100. Yan Thomas, 'Vitae Necisque Potestas: Le Père, La Cité, La Mort,' 507; Catherine Hezser, *Jewish Slavery in Antiquity*, 134.

101. Kopytoff and Miers, 11.

102. Orlando Patterson, *Slavery and Social Death*, 22.

103. Miers, 'Slavery: A Question of Definition,' 6. The Roman emperor Antoninus, who introduced laws protecting slaves, also ruled that when Roman fathers sold their children off, those sales were invalid. Though fathers were not forbidden from doing so, if the child later wanted to challenge their slave status they could cite the invalidity of the original sale. The emperor Diocletian referred to this as a fixed principle of law. Later, in 391 CE, the emperor Valentinian II explicitly allowed selling children off temporarily for debt payment. In Late Antique Jewish law, the *Mekhilta* allowed fathers to sell their daughters but not their sons. See Justinian *Codex* 7.16.1 and 4.43.1, 4.10.12; Hezser, *Jewish Slavery in Antiquity*, 187–88, 190.

104. Cam Grey, 'Slavery in the Late Roman World,' 496; Rotman, *Byzantine Slavery*, 174–76.

105. Nasser Rabbat, 'The Changing Concept of the *Mamlūk* in the Mamluk Sultanate in Egypt and Syria,' 89, 97.

106. Indrani Chatterjee, 'Abolition by Denial: The South Asian Example,' 153.

107. Patterson, *Slavery and Social Death*, 22.

108. Patterson, *Slavery and Social Death*, 22; Harry D. Krause and David P. Meyer, *Family Law,* 100.

109. Davidson, *Modern Slavery*, 162.

110. Crossley, 'Slavery in Early Modern China,' 191.

111. Igor Kopytoff and Suzanne Miers, 'African "Slavery" as an Institution of Marginality,' 23.

112. Crossley, 'Slavery in Early Modern China,' 187; cf. Pulleyblank, 213.

113. Patterson, *Slavery and Social Death*, 7–8, 13.

114. Leslie Pierce, *Morality Tales*, 315; Toledano, *As if Silent and Absent*, 25; Zilfi, *Women and Slavery in the Late Ottoman Empire*, 26–28.

115. See Ali Yaycıoğlu, 'Wealth, Power and Death: Capital Accumulation and Imperial Seizures in the Ottoman Empire (1453-1839),' available at http://www.econ.yale.edu/~egcenter/Yaycioglu%20-%20Wealth%20Death%20and%20Power%20-%20November%202012.pdf.

116. Ebru Boyar and Kate Fleet, *A Social History of Ottoman Istanbul*, 147–48; M. Sukru Hanioglu, *A Brief History of the Late Ottoman Empire*, 21.
117. Dror Ze'evi, 'My Slave, My Son, My Lord: Slavery, Family and the State in the Islamic Middle East,' 75. See also Metin Kunt, 'Ethnic-Regional (*Cins*) Solidarity in the Seventeenth-Century Ottoman Establishment,' 233–39.
118. Veinstein, 'Soḳollu Meḥmed Pasha,' *Encyclopaedia of Islam*, 2nd edn.
119. Daniel Crecelius and Gotcha Djaparidze, 'Relations of the Georgian Mamluks of Egypt with Their Homeland in the Last Decades of the Eighteenth Century,' 326. See also Zilfi, *Women and Slavery in the Late Ottoman Empire*, 135.
120. Christine E. Sears, '"In Algiers, the City of Bondage": Urban Slavery in Comparative Context,' 203, 207, 211.
121. Rotman, *Byzantine Slavery*, 104.
122. It was in the Ottoman state's interest to keep this agricultural system stable; Y. Hakan Erdem, *Slavery in the Ottoman Empire and its Demise, 1800–1909*, 12–13, 15.
123. Ibn Qudāma, *Mughnī*, 12:502–3. The *umm walad* was freed on the death of her master based on a Hadith of the Prophet. See *Sunan Ibn Mājah*: *kitāb al-ʿitq*, *bāb ummahāt al-awlād*. For the early dispute over whether an owner could sell his *umm walad* and the eventual Sunni consensus that he could not, see Younus Mirza, 'Remembering the *Umm Walad*: Ibn Kathir's Treatise on the Sale of the Concubine,' 297–323.
124. Paul Lovejoy, 'Slavery in the context of ideology,' in *The Ideology of Slavery in Africa*, 11–15. See also Watson, 3–5.
125. See Kopytoff and Miers, 'African "Slavery" as an Institution of Marginality'; Finley, 'Slavery,' 308.
126. Claude Meillassoux, *The Anthropology of Slavery*, 28; A. Testart, 'The Extent and Significance of Debt Slavery,' 176.
127. Ruth Karras, *Slavery and Society in Medieval Scandinavia*, 156–66.
128. V. Matheson and M. B. Hooker, 'Slavery in the Malay Texts,' 182–208; John M. Gullick, 'Debt Bondage in Malaya,' 51–52 (extract from an original published in 1952). See also Bruce Hall, *A History of Race in Muslim West Africa*, 212.
129. See Gwyn Campbell, 'Introduction: Slavery and Other Forms of Unfree Labour in the Indian Ocean World,' in *The Structure of Slavery in Indian Africa and Asia*, ed. Gwyn Campbell, vii–xxxii. See also Kopytoff and Miers, 'African "Slavery" as an Institution of Marginality,' 20.
130. Davis, *Slavery and Human Progress*, 17–19; Brenda Stevenson, *What is Slavery?*, 8. See also David Wyatt, *Slaves and Warriors in Medieval Britain and Ireland, 800–1200*, 51–52; Eltis and Engerman, 'Dependence, Servility, and Coerced Labor in Time and Space,' 2 (slavery is regarded as 'the most extreme form of dependency and exploitation'), 13.
131. This list is inspired by Eltis and Engerman, 'Dependence, Servility, and Coerced Labor in Time and Space,' 3. See also Finley, 'Slavery,' 308.
132. Kerry Ward, 'Slavery in Southeast Asia, 1420–1804,' 165–66.
133. Richard Hellie, 'Russian Slavery and Serfdom, 1450–1804,' 276–77.
134. Grey, 'Slavery in the Late Roman World,' 484–6; Wendy Davies, 'On servile status in the early Middle Ages,' 232–38.
135. Henry Heller, 'Bodin on Slavery and Primitive Accumulation,' 53; Hellie, 'Russian Slavery,' 284, 292–93; Michael Bush, 'Serfdom in medieval and modern Europe: a comparison,' in *Serfdom and Slavery*, ed., Bush, 199–224; Christopher Dyer, 'Memories of freedom: attitudes towards serfdom in England, 1200–1350,' 278.

136. Eltis and Engerman, 'Dependence, Servility, and Coerced Labor,' 7; Davidson, *Modern Slavery*, 68.
137. Howard Temperley, 'The Delegalization of Slavery in India,' 179.
138. Miers, 'Slavery: A Question of Definition,' 5, citing Michel Boivin's unpublished paper 'La condition servile dans le Sindh.' See also Lionel Caplan, 'Power and Status in South Asian Slavery,' 170.
139. Isaac Mendelsohn, *Slavery in the Ancient Near East*, 23–25.
140. Reid, 11.
141. Hellie, 'Russian Slavery,' 279–80. The author notes the similarity between this Russian contract and the ancient Persian custom of *antichrisis* (as named by Greek authors).
142. Kenneth Morgan, *Slavery and Servitude in Colonial North America*, 8–9, 20; David Galenson, 'The Rise and Fall of Indentured Servitude in the Americas: An Economic Analysis,' 4.
143. Hellie, 'Russian Slavery,' 279–80.
144. Engerman's chapter on the similarities and differences between slavery and serfdom is useful but admittedly deals in generalizations, a fact that only confirms the point being made here. See Stanley Engerman, 'Slavery, serfdom and other forms of coerced labour: similarities and differences,' 18–41; Davies, 'On servile status in the early Middle Ages,' 227, 232, 236.
145. Reid, 4.
146. David Brion Davis, *Challenging the Boundaries of Slavery*, 17–18; Charles Verlinden, 'l'Origine de *sclavus* – esclave,' 128. The earliest attestation of the word *sclavus* for slave is probably from 937 CE; Michael McCormick, *Origins of the European Economy*, 737–39.
147. Eltis and Engerman, 'Dependence, Servility, and Coerced Labor,' 6. The question of whether the Scottish colliers were slaves or not was an issue of dispute in Scotland and England in the 1760s–90s, mostly because it was a matter of whether or not slavery existed or was allowed in Britain. There was some debate over whether colliers were or were not slaves on the basis of whether their children were born into that status, but mostly it has to do with the a *priori* question of whether or not slavery existed in the realm; see P. E. H. Hair, 'Slavery and Liberty: The Case of the Scottish Colliers,' 136–51.
148. Henry Heller, 'Bodin on Slavery and Primitive Accumulation,' 56–57; Cairns, 'The Definition of Slavery in Eighteenth-Century Thinking,' 65.
149. Pierre Bonnassie, *From Slavery to Feudalism in South-Western Europe*, 19.
150. Erdem, *Slavery in the Ottoman Empire and its Demise*, 12–13, 15.
151. Davidson, *Modern Slavery*, 33. See also Andrea Major, *Slavery, Abolitionism and Empire in India, 1772–1843*, 326.
152. http://www.ohchr.org/EN/ProfessionalInterest/Pages/SlaveryConvention.aspx; http://www.ohchr.org/EN/ProfessionalInterest/Pages/SupplementaryConventionAbolitionOfSlavery.aspx. Article 4 of the Universal Declaration of Human Rights states that 'No one shall be held in slavery or servitude; slavery and the slave trade shall be prohibited in all their forms.'
153. Robin Hickey observes that ownership of people has been abolished in the sense that a major aspect of ownership as understood in law is the recognition that the owner has the primary right to control, use, etc., of something and that this should not be interfered with (without some good reason). This has been prohibited in the case of owning human beings. But in terms of actual control, Hickey argues, it continues; Robin Hickey, 'Seeking to Understand the Definition of Slavery,' 233. For another advocate of Hickey's approach, see Lewis, 'Orlando Patterson, Property, and Ancient Slavery,' 40–48.

154. Honoré writes, 'A slave is a person who, in fact though not in law, is subordinate to an unlimited extent to another person or group of persons (who may be organised as a corporation or association) and who lacks access to state or other institutions that can remedy his or her inferior status.'; Antony Honoré, 'The Nature of Slavery,' 16.
155. Kevin Bales, *Understanding Global Slavery*, 52–54.
156. Davidson, 36.
157. See Kevin Bales, 'Testing a Theory of Modern Slavery,' [2], available at https://glc.yale.edu/sites/default/files/files/events/cbss/Bales.pdf; Davidson, *Modern Slavery*, 2, 36–7; Bales, *Understanding Global Slavery*, 57. See also the use of Bales' definition by the American Anti-Slavery Group http://www.iabolish.org/index.php?option=com_content&view=article&id=181:guarding-americas-first-right-freedom-from-bondage&catid=5:essays-on-slavery&Itemid=8.
158. Kevin Bales, *Disposable People: New Slavery in the Global Economy*, 29.
159. Bales, *Understanding Global Slavery*, 57.
160. http://www.iabolish.org/index.php?option=com_content&view=article&id=181:guarding-americas-first-right-freedom-from-bondage&catid=5:essays-on-slavery&Itemid=8.
161. Westermarck, *The Origin and Development of the Moral Ideas*, 1:671. See also Finley, 'Slavery,' 309.
162. Xenophon, *Memorabilia*, 2.1.13.
163. Crossley, 187. See also Sally McKee, 'Slavery,' 282.
164. Siliadin v. France, 333 Eur. Ct. H.R. 7, 33 (2005). Available at https://ec.europa.eu/anti-trafficking/legislation-and-case-law-case-law/siliadin-v-france-application-no-7331601_en.
165. Jean Allain, 'R v Tang: Clarifying the Definition of 'Slavery' in International Law,' 246–57.
166. https://www.thenation.com/article/new-abolitionism/.
167. Irshad Manji, *Allah, Liberty and Love*, 116–17, 235.
168. Davidson, *Modern Slavery*, 3, 6, 22–23, 37–39, 69, 169. See also Eltis and Engerman, 'Dependence, Servility, and Coerced Labor in Time and Space,' 13.
169. Davidson, *Modern Slavery*, 53.
170. See Zilfi, *Women and Slavery in the Late Ottoman Empire*, 102, 116.
171. Zilfi, *Women and Slavery in the Late Ottoman Empire*, 27–28.
172. Patricia Clark, 'Women, Slaves, and the Hierarchies of Domestic Violence: The Family of St. Augustine,' 109–29. The Dutch Orientalist Snouck Hurgronje observed, regarding the inhabitants of Mecca beating their slaves, that 'the Arab punishes his own son just as severely if he committed some fault'; Hurgronje, *Mekka in the Latter Part of the 19th Century*, 22.
173. Toledano, *As if Silent and Absent*, 49.
174. Harper, *Slavery in the Late Roman World*, 220–21; Stefano Fenoaltea, 'Slavery and Supervision in Comparative Perspective: A Model,' 635–68.
175. Claude Meillassoux, *The Anthropology of Slavery*.
176. Engerman, 'Slavery at Different Times and Places,' 481. For Westermarck, slavery by choice or temporary slavery were only an 'imitation of slavery true and proper.' See Westermarck, *The Origin and Development of the Moral Ideas*, 1:671.
177. Crossley, 'Slavery in Early Modern China,' 189.
178. Hellie, 'Russian Slavery,' 284, 293.
179. See Gwyn Campbell, 'Unfree labour and the significance of abolition in Madagascar,' 69–70, 77. This was also sometimes the case during Dutch efforts to

encourage emancipation in areas of indirect colonial control in Southeast Asia; Martin Klein, 'The emancipation of slaves in the Indian Ocean,' 204–205.

180. Johanna Ransmeier, 'Ambiguities in the Sale of Women at the End of the Qing Dynasty,' 319–44.

181. Sobers-Khan, *Slaves without Shackles*, 68, 161. See also Yvonne Seng, 'A Liminal State: Slavery in Sixteenth-Century Istanbul,' 29.

182. Bales, *Disposable People*, 35. For a critique of Bales' distinction between new and Old slavery, see Joel Quirk, 'The Anti-Slavery Project,' 579 ff.

183. *Global Estimates of Modern Slavery: Forced Labour and Forced Marriage* (Geneva: International Labour Office, 2017), 9, cf. 17.

184. http://www.ilo.org/dyn/normlex/en/f?p=NORMLEXPUB:12100:0::NO::P12100_ILO_CODE:C029.

185. http://www.ohchr.org/EN/ProfessionalInterest/Pages/SupplementaryConventionAbolitionOfSlavery.aspx.

186. Miers, 'Slavery: A Question of Definition,' 11. See also Quirk, 'The Anti-Slavery Project,' 584–95.

187. 'Florida prisoners plan Martin Luther King Day strike over "slavery",' *Guardian*, Jan. 15, 2018, https://www.theguardian.com/us-news/2018/jan/15/florida-prisoners-martin-luther-king-day-strike-slavery; Ed Pilkington, 'US inmates stage nationwide prison labor strike over "modern slavery",' *Guardian*, Sept. 21, 2018, https://amp.theguardian.com/us-news/2018/aug/20/prison-labor-protest-america-jailhouse-lawyers-speak.

188. See Daniel Harr, 'The New Slavery Movement,' *Social Policy*, 28-32; Whitney Benns, 'American Slavery, Reinvented,' *The Atlantic*, Sept. 21, 2015, https://www.theatlantic.com/business/archive/2015/09/prison-labor-in-america/406177/

189. Douglas Blackmon, *Slavery by Another Name*, 4, 7.

190. Davidson, *Modern Slavery*, 100.

191. Bales, *Understanding Global Slavery*, 58.

192. See Article 2 (c. of the 1930 ILO Convention, available at http://www.ilo.org/dyn/normlex/en/f?p=NORMLEXPUB:12100:0::NO::P12100_ILO_CODE:C029; *Global Estimates of Modern Slavery: Forced Labour and Forced Marriage* (Geneva: International Labour Office, 2017), 60-1. See also http://www.ilo.org/global/standards/subjects-covered-by-international-labour-standards/forced-labour/lang--en/index.htm.

193. Whitney Benns, 'American Slavery, Reinvented,' *The Atlantic*, Sept. 21, 2015, https://www.theatlantic.com/business/archive/2015/09/prison-labor-in-america/406177/; Emily Yahr, 'Yes, prisoners used to sew lingerie for Victoria's Secret — just like in "Orange is the New Black" Season 3,' *Washington Post*, June 17, 2015, https://www.washingtonpost.com/news/arts-and-entertainment/wp/2015/06/17/yes-prisoners-used-to-sew-lingerie-for-victorias-secret-just-like-in-orange-is-the-new-black-season-3/?utm_term=.43e3bf089f56;

194. https://ccrjustice.org/home/get-involved/tools-resources/fact-sheets-and-faqs/torture-use-solitary-confinement-us-prisons.

195. Ronald Sullivan, 'In New York, Prisoners Work or Else,' *New York Times*, Jan. 27, 1992, http://www.nytimes.com/1992/01/27/nyregion/in-new-york-state-prisoners-work-or-else.html; https://www.washingtonpost.com/news/arts-and-entertainment/wp/2015/06/17/yes-prisoners-used-to-sew-lingerie-for-victorias-secret-just-like-in-orange-is-the-new-black-season-3/?utm_term=.43e3bf089f56; Reese Erlich, 'Prison Labor: Workin' for the Man.'

196. Ta-Nehisi Coates, 'The Case for Reparations,' *The Atlantic*, June 2014. https://www.theatlantic.com/magazine/archive/2014/06/the-case-for-reparations/361631/.
197. https://www.womensmarch.com/march/.
198. https://www.theguardian.com/us-news/2018/jan/15/florida-prisoners-martin-luther-king-day-strike-slavery.
199. Casey Quackenbush, 'The Libyan Slave Trade Has Shocked the World. Here's What You Should Know,' *Time.com*, Dec. 1, 2017, http://time.com/5042560/libya-slave-trade/ ; Nima Elbagir, Raja Razek, Alex Platt and Bryony Jones, 'People for Sale,' *CNN*, Nov. 14, 2017, http://edition.cnn.com/2017/11/14/africa/libya-migrant-auctions/index.html.
200. Lila Abu-Lughod, 'Authorizing Moral Crusades to Save Muslim Women,' 11, 20–21. For good examples, see Andrew Wheatcroft, *The Ottomans: Dissolving Images*, 208–30.
201. Davidson, *Modern Slavery*, 31.
202. William Clarence-Smith and David Eltis, 'White Servitude,' 139, 144; Linda Colley, *Captives*, 56–65, 99–134.
203. https://www.springfieldspringfield.co.uk/movie_script.php?movie=the-spy-who-loved-me.
204. http://moderngov.rotherham.gov.uk/documents/s100912/CSE_The_Way_Forward_2015_18 Consultation Draft.pdf, last accessed 2/1/2017. See also www.thestar.co.uk/news/majority-of-rotherham-child-exploitation-suspects-are-white-claims-new-report-1-7392637. More recently, see Naz Shah, 'We need to dispel the dangerous myth that it's only Asian men who sexually assault young women,' *Independent*, Aug. 12, 2017, https://www.independent.co.uk/voices/newcastle-grooming-scandal-exploitation-victims-sarah-champion-race-a7890106.html; 'The usual suspects: Is grooming children for sex a disproportionally Asian crime?,' *The Economist*, Oct. 25, 2018, https://www.economist.com/britain/2018/10/27/is-grooming-children-for-sex-a-disproportionately-asian-crime.
205. 'Slave labour props up unexpected parts of Britain's economy,' *The Economist*, Aug. 2, 2018, https://www.economist.com/britain/2018/08/04/slave-labour-props-up-unexpected-parts-of-britains-economy?frsc=dg%7Ce.
206. See Carla Gardina Pestana, 'Comparing the Irish to African American Slaves is Prejudiced,' *Huffpost*, March 27, 2017, https://www.huffingtonpost.com/entry/irish-slaves-and-other-misuses-of-american-history_us_58d47fb4e4b0f633072b364d.
207. Liam Stack, 'Debunking a Myth: The Irish Were Not Slaves, Too,' *New York Times*, March 17, 2017, https://www.nytimes.com/2017/03/17/us/irish-slaves-myth.html.
208. Douglas Walton, 'The Argument of the Beard,' 235–59.

CHAPTER 2 SLAVERY IN THE SHARIAH

1. G. E. Daumas, *Le Grand Désert*, 219.
2. 'Ten Years On,' *The Economist*, 9/3/2011, https://www.economist.com/leaders/2011/09/03/ten-years-on.
3. Ovamir Anjum, 'Islam as a Discursive Tradition: Talal Asad and His Interlocutors,' 656–72.
4. Jonathan Brockopp, 'Islamic Origins and Incidental Normativity,' 28–43; Jonathan Brown, *Hadith*, 19–29.

5. J. Brown, *Hadith*, 71 ff., 99–104.
6. For a discussion of this tension, see Shahab Ahmad, *What is Islam?*, 32 and passim.
7. In these verses, *riqāb* is considered by most schools of law to mean *mukātab* slaves, with the Mālikī school limiting it to aiding slaves one has already freed and the Ḥanbalīs extending it to buying the freedom of any slave or Muslim prisoners of war; al-Qurṭubī, *al-Jāmiʿ li-aḥkām al-Qur'ān*, 4:512; Manṣūr al-Buhūtī, *Rawḍ al-murbiʿ*, 166–67. One famous Hadith promises that one of the three people that God has taken on the obligation to help is the *mukātab* seeking to complete their payments (along with the one fighting in the path of God and one trying to marry to preserve their chastity); *Jāmiʿ al-Tirmidhī: kitāb faḍā'il al-jihād, bāb mā jā'a fī al-mujāhid wa'l-nākiḥ wa'l-mukātab.*
8. *Ṣaḥīḥ al-Bukhārī: kitāb al-ṣawm, bāb idhā jāmaʿa fī Ramaḍān.*
9. Abū Bakr al-Bayhaqī, *al-Sunan al-kubrā*, 8:10–23; idem, *Shuʿab al-īmān*, 6:369–87; Abū Ḥāmid al-Ghazālī, *Iḥyā' ʿulūm al-dīn*, 2:1249–53; Ibn Ḥajar al-Haytamī, *al-Zawājir*, 2:176–85; Murtaḍā al-Zabīdī, *Itḥāf al-sāda al-muttaqīn*, 5:352–53, 6:321–28. For a useful translation of much of this material, see Muḥammad b. Ismāʿīl al-Bukhārī, *Al-Adab al-Mufrad*, trans. Adil Salahi (Markfield, UK: Islamic Foundation, 2017), 139–69.
10. *Ṣaḥīḥ al-Bukhārī: kitāb al-aymān, bāb al-maʿāṣī min amr al-Jāhiliyya . . .*; *Ṣaḥīḥ Muslim: kitāb al-aymān, bāb iṭʿām al-mamlūk mimmā ya'kulu wa ilbāsihi mimmā yalbasu . . .*; *Sunan* of Abū Dāwūd: *kitāb al-adab, bāb fī ḥaqq al-mamlūk*; *Jāmiʿ al-Tirmidhī: kitāb al-birr wa'l-ṣila, bāb mā jā'a fī al-iḥsān ilā al-khadam*; *Sunan Ibn Mājah: kitāb al-adab, bāb al-iḥsān ilā al-mamālīk.*
11. For the first Hadith, see *Ṣaḥīḥ Muslim: kitāb al-aymān, bāb iṭʿām al-mamlūk mimmā ya'kulu . . .*; for the second, *Ṣaḥīḥ al-Bukhārī: kitāb al-ʿitq, bāb idhā atāhu khādimuhu bi-ṭaʿāmihi.*
12. *Ṣaḥīḥ Muslim: kitāb al-faḍā'il, bāb mubāʿadatihi (ṣ) li'l-āthām . . .*; *Sunan* of Abū Dāwūd: *kitāb al-adab, bāb fī ḥaqq al-mamlūk*; al-Bukhārī, *Al-Adab al-mufrad*, 142.
13. *Sunan* of Abū Dāwūd: *kitāb al-adab, bāb fī ḥaqq al-mamlūk*; *Musnad Ibn Ḥanbal*, 5:173.
14. *Jāmiʿ al-Tirmidhī: kitāb al-birr wa'l-ṣila, bāb mā jā'a fī al-iḥsān ilā al-khadam*; *Sunan Ibn Mājah: kitāb al-adab, bāb al-iḥsān ilā al-mamālīk*; *Musnad Ibn Ḥanbal*, 1:7.
15. *Ṣaḥīḥ Muslim: kitāb al-aymān, bāb ṣuḥbat al-mamālīk wa kaffārat man laṭama ʿabdahu*; al-Khaṭīb al-Baghdādī, *Tārīkh Baghdād*, 8:158.
16. *Sunan* of Abū Dāwūd: *kitāb al-diyāt, bāb man qatala ʿabdahu aw maththala bihi a-yuqādu bihi.* For a judge ordering a woman who cut off her slave's nose to free her *c.* 60–80 AH in Egypt, see Muḥammad b. Yūsuf al-Kindī, *Kitāb al-Wulāt*, 317–18.
17. Al-Bayhaqī, *Sunan al-kubrā*, 8:66.
18. The first Hadith is found in *Ṣaḥīḥ al-Bukhārī: kitāb al-ʿitq, bāb mā jā'a fī al-ʿitq wa faḍlihi*; the second is in *Sunan* of Abū Dāwūd: *kitāb al-ʿitq, bāb ayy al-riqāb afḍal.*
19. *Jāmiʿ al-Tirmidhī: kitāb al-waṣāyā, bāb mā jā'a fī al-rajul yataṣaddaqu aw yuʿtiqu ʿind al-mawt*; *Sunan* of Abū Dāwūd: *kitāb al-ʿitq, bāb faḍl al-ʿitq fī al-ṣiḥḥa*; *Ṣaḥīḥ al-Bukhārī: kitāb al-ʿitq, bāb mā yustaḥabbu min al-ʿatāqa fī al-kusūf aw al-āyāt.*
20. *Ṣaḥīḥ al-Bukhārī: kitāb al-ʿilm, bāb taʿlīm al-rajul amatahu wa ahlahu.* When the scholars of Timbuktu were given slave girls by the ruler of Songhay in the sixteenth century many of them freed and married them; John Hunwick, 'Notes on Slavery in the Songhay Empire,' 27. A rare Hadith also encourages the man to give his newly freed wife a dower; Abū Nuʿaym al-Iṣbahānī, *Ḥilyat al-awliyā'*, 8:308.
21. *Ṣaḥīḥ Muslim: kitāb al-īmān, bāb tasmiyat al-ʿabd al-ābiq kāfiran.* Al-Nawawī explains that this Hadith means either that the act of fleeing is an action befitting an unbeliever, that such acts could lead to *kufr*, that it is ingratitude (*kufr al-niʿma*) or that

it means that the person in question considers the act to be *ḥalāl*, which would make them an actual unbeliever; Muḥyī al-Dīn al-Nawawī, *Sharḥ Ṣaḥīḥ Muslim*, 1/2: 417–18; *Sunan al-Nasā'ī*: *kitāb taḥrīm al-dam, bāb al-ʿabd ya'baqu ilā arḍ al-shirk* . . .

22. *Ṣaḥīḥ Muslim*: *kitāb al-aymān, bāb ṣuḥbat al-mamālīk wa kaffāra* . . .

23. *Sunan Ibn Mājah*: *kitāb al-diyāt, bāb man maththala bi-ʿabdihi fa-huwa ḥurr*. In one report the caliph ʿUmar freed a slave woman who had been burned by her owner; *Muwaṭṭa'*: *kitāb al-ʿitq wa'l-walā', bāb ʿitq ummahāt al-awlād* . . .

24. *Ṣaḥīḥ al-Bukhārī*: *kitāb al-mukātab, bāb ithm man qadhafa mamlūkahu al -mukātab* . . .

25. *Ṣaḥīḥ al-Bukhārī*: *kitāb al-nafaqa, bāb wujūb al-nafaqa ʿalā al-ahl wa'l-ʿiyāl; kitāb al-shahādāt, bāb shahādat al-imā' wa'l-ʿabīd*; *Musnad Ibn Ḥanbal*, 2:252, 2:527; Ibn Ḥajar al-ʿAsqalānī, *Fatḥ al-Bārī*, 9:626–27.

26. Ibn Saʿd, *al-Ṭabaqāt al-kubrā*, 3:213.

27. *Muwaṭṭa'*: *kitāb al-isti'dhān, bāb al-amr bi'l-rifq bi'l-mamlūk*.

28. Ibn Kathīr, *Musnad al-Fārūq*, 2:246–47.

29. Ibn Saʿd, *al-Ṭabaqāt al-kubrā*, 4:156.

30. Al-Haytamī, *al-Zawājir*, 2:184.

31. ʿAbdallāh Ibn ʿAbd al-Ḥakam, *Sīrat ʿUmar b. ʿAbd al-ʿAzīz*, 34, 121.

32. *Allāh Allāh fī-mā malakat aymānukum albisū ẓuhūrahum wa'shbiʿū buṭūnahum wa alyinū lahum al-qawl*; Ismāʿīl al-ʿAjlūnī, *Kashf al-khafā*, 1:220. For less reliable versions of well-attested Hadiths or mixed-up versions, see Jalāl al-Dīn al-Suyūṭī, *al-Jāmiʿ al-ṣaghīr*, #s 124, 125, 127. A good example is the 'Fear God regarding the two weak ones, the slave and the woman,' which seems to be a corruption of the better-known version specifying orphans and women; al-Suyūṭī, *al-Jāmiʿ al-ṣaghīr*, #126; *Sunan Ibn Mājah*: *kitāb al-adab, bāb ḥaqq al-yatīm*.

33. For example, 'The *umm walad* cannot be sold (*lā tubāʿu umm walad*)' and 'The *umm walad* is free even if [the child] is miscarried (*umm al-walad ḥurra wa in kāna siqṭan*); al-Suyūṭī, *al-Jāmiʿ al-ṣaghīr*, #1616, #9724.

34. Jonathan Brown, 'Even if It's Not True It's True: Using Unreliable Hadiths in Sunni Islam,' 1–52.

35. *Sunan Ibn Mājah*: *kitāb al-adab, bāb al-iḥsān ilā al-mamālīk*; Muḥammad Nāṣir al-Dīn al-Albānī, *Ḍaʿīf Sunan Ibn Mājah*, 300. Other examples of very weak and forged Hadiths on slavery include: 'However much you lighten the work of your servant will be a reward in your scales' (al-Bayhaqī, *Shuʿab al-īmān*, 6:378), 'Do not beat a slave, for indeed you do not know what you'll encounter (*lā taḍribū al-raqīq fa'innakum lā tadrūna mā tuwāfiqūn*)' (al-Albānī, *Silsilat al-aḥādīth al-ḍaʿīfa*, 5:70–71, #2051).

36. Abū Yaʿlā al-Mawṣilī, *Musnad*, 7:80: al-Bayhaqī, *Shuʿab al-īmān*, 6:378; al-Albānī, *Silsilat al-aḥādīth al-ḍaʿīfa*, 10:1:301–302 (#4757).

37. For the first Hadith, see al-Albānī, *Ḍaʿīf al-Jāmiʿ al-ṣaghīr*, 685; for the second (*Lā taḍribū imā'akum ʿalā inā'ikum fa'inna lahā ājālan ka-ājāl al-nās*), see Abū Nuʿaym al-Iṣbahānī, *Ḥilyat al-awliyā'*, 10:26; al-Albānī, *Silsilat al-aḥādīth al-ḍaʿīfa*, 2:343–44 (#938).

38. See al-Zabīdī, *Itḥāf al-sāda al-muttaqīn*, 6:323–24.

39. Abū al-Qāsim al-Ṭabarānī, *al-Muʿjam al-awsaṭ*, 9:96.

40. This Hadith originally appeared in the *Musnad* of al-Ḥārith b. Abī Usāma (d. 895–6) and was branded a clear forgery by al-Suyūṭī and Ibn Ḥajar; al-Suyūṭī, *al-La'ālī al-maṣnūʿa*, 2:306, 308, 310, 311.

41. *Sabbiḥī mi'at tasbīḥa ʿidl mi'at raqaba* . . .'; al-Bukhārī, *al-Tārīkh al-kabīr*, 2:234; al-Ṭabarānī, *al-Muʿjam al-awsaṭ*, 2:288.

42. The main version of this Hadith is '[Ibrāhīm] will have a wet-nurse in the Garden, and if Ibrāhīm had lived he would have been a faithful prophet, and if he had lived his maternal uncles would all be free and no Copt would be enslaved,' which includes a clause linking Ibrāhīm to his mother Māriya's people (*Sunan Ibn Mājah*: *kitāb al-janā'iz, bāb mā jā'a fī al-ṣalāt ʿalā ibn rasūl Allāh (s) wa dhikr wafātihi*). The notion that Ibrāhīm would have been a prophet is corroborated by an opinion narrated by the Companion ʿAbdallāh b. Abī Awfa in *Ṣaḥīḥ al-Bukhārī* (*kitāb al-adab, bāb man summiya bi-asmā' al -anbiyā'*). The first Prophetic report is considered *ṣaḥīḥ* by Ibn Ḥajar al-ʿAsqalānī, al-Albānī, and al-Haythamī (*rijāluhu rijāl al-ṣaḥīḥ*). Ibn ʿAbd al-Barr (d. 1070), by contrast, considered the Hadith to be unacceptable because it suggests that the children of prophets somehow inherit prophethood; ʿAbd al-Ra'ūf al-Munāwī, *Fayḍ al-qadīr*, 10:5098–99; Ibn Ḥajar, *Fatḥ al-Bārī*, 10:579; al-Albānī, *Silsilat al-aḥādīth al-ḍaʿīfa*, 1:387 (#220), 7:185–86 (#3202).

43. Elizabeth Urban, 'Hagar and Mariya: Early Islamic Models of Slave Motherhood,' 225.

44. Kyle Harper, *Slavery in the Late Roman World*, 500, 506, 509; Hugh Kennedy, 'Justinianic Plague in Syrian and the Archeological Evidence,' in *Plague and the End of Antiquity*, ed. Lester K. Little (Cambridge: Cambridge University Press, 2006), 87–99.

45. Walter E. Young, 'Origins of Islamic Law,' in *The [Oxford] Encyclopedia of Islam and Law, Oxford Islamic Studies Online*, http://www.oxfordislamicstudies.com/article/opr/t349/e0106 (accessed 10-Jun-2018).

46. *Corpus Iuris Civilis, Institutes*, 1:3; Westermann, *Slave Systems of Greek and Roman Antiquity*, 105. Diodorus Siculus (*fl.* first century BCE) mentions that in Egypt the father was seen as the sole agent of reproduction, and hence there were no such things as bastards, whether born of free or slave women. But this does not address the issue of whether the child born of a slave mother was free or a slave; Diodorus Siculus, *Diodorus of Sicily*, 1.80.3.

47. Muḥammad b. Idrīs al-Shāfiʿī, *al-Umm*, 4:268. An exception arose when a non-Muslim wife/mother embraced Islam. Only the Mālikī school of law held that her children followed her husband's religion. All others said they became Muslim like her. A case in tenth-century Cairo is instructive: a Christian woman converted to Islam, but her husband did not. The long-serving judge, a Mālikī scholar named Abū Ṭāhir al-Dhuhlī (d. 979), ruled that, though the mother wanted the couple's young son to be considered Muslim, he would still remain Christian. The 'people' were angered by this and voiced their displeasure. When it was mentioned that the opinion of the Shāfiʿī and Shiite schools was that the child could be declared Muslim, the judge changed his ruling. 'So the people prayed for him, and his ruling pleased them'; Ibn Hubayra, *Ikhtilāf a'immat al-ʿulamā'*, 2:67; Ibn Ḥajar al-ʿAsqalānī, *Rafʿ al-iṣr ʿan quḍāt miṣr*, 330; Ṣaḥnūn, *al-Mudawwana* (Beirut, 4 vols), 2:538.

48. Ibn Taymiyya, *Majmūʿat al-fatāwā*, 29:76.

49. Ibn Rajab, *al-Qawāʿid*, 301.

50. *Mukātaba* has parallels in Babylonian, Greek and Near Eastern Roman provincial slavery, and in the Mishna and the Syriac law code as well. Though the relationship of debt slavery for Israelites as mentioned in the Torah differed from *mukātaba*, the Torah's command that the owner should give the debt slave some of the harvest when setting them free (Deuteronomy 15:14–17) is a parallel to the Quranic command in 24:33. In the Shariah the slave's limited property rights resemble the Roman notion of the slave's peculium as well as Babylonian law and Old Testament law, although under the Shariah slaves had much more control over property given to them by their masters. The concept of *umm walad* goes back to the Code of Hammurabi, but the status is greatly improved in the Shariah. Justinian's *Digest* allowed the state to intervene and free slave girls who had been prostituted by their owner; Mendelsohn, *Slavery in the Ancient Near East*, 50–52, 67, 74; Crone, *Roman, Provincial and Islamic Law*, 64–76, 87; Brockopp, *Early Mālikī Law*, 170, 181.

51. Hezser, *Jewish Slavery in Antiquity*, 106–108; Westermann, 'Enslaved persons who are free,' 14.

52. *Ṣaḥīḥ al-Bukhārī*: *kitāb al-ʿitq, bāb*s 4–5. For the frequency of joint ownership of slaves, see Ghislaine Lydon, 'Slavery, Exchange and Islamic Law: A Glimpse from the Archives of Mali and Mauritania,' 133–35.

53. *Sunan* of Abū Dāwūd: *kitāb al-ʿitq, bāb fī-man aʿtaqa naṣīban lahu min mamlūk*; *Musnad Ibn Ḥanbal*, 5:74. See Ibn Ḥajar, *Fatḥ al-Bārī*, 5:199–200; Muḥammad b. ʿAlī al-Shawkānī, *Nayl al-awṭār*, 6:94–98.

54. ʿAbd al-Wahhāb al-Shaʿrānī, *al-Mīzān al-kubrā*, 2:228; Muḥammad b. Naṣr al-Marwazī, *Ikhtilāf al-fuqahā'*, 511. The reasoning on this issue expressed in the Hadiths seems to have inspired ʿAlī's ruling on what do with a child of unknown paternity; Wakīʿ Muḥammad b. Khalaf, *Akhbār al-Quḍāt*, 66–67.

55. It is worth noting that there are few Hadiths exhorting humane treatment of slaves via an ethics of reciprocity (i.e. the Golden Rule). Although one could argue that it is deeply implied in the Hadith seen as the basic text for the treatment of slaves ('Your slaves are your brothers . . . so feed them from your food . . .', etc.), the only Hadith I have found where it is explicit is much rarer and is commonly found only in texts written after the fourteenth century CE. In great part this is because its earliest known appearance is in al-Ghazālī's (d. 1111) influential *Iḥyā' ʿulūm al-dīn*, which was widely read, especially in West Africa. The bulk of the Hadith's text seems to be taken from better-known Hadiths, but it adds the reciprocity clause at the end. The Prophet allegedly says, 'Fear God concerning those whom you rightfully possess, feed them from what you eat, clothe them from what you wear, and do not burden them with work they cannot bear. As long as you like them, keep them. And when you do not like them, sell them. And do not inflict pain on the creation of God [thus far all material found in well-known Hadiths], for indeed God made you their owners, but if He had willed, He could have made them own you (*ittaqū Allāh fī-mā malakat aymānukum aṭʿimūhum mimmā ta'kulūn wa'ksūhum mimmā talbasūn wa lā tukallifūhum min al-ʿamal mā lā yuṭīqūn; fa-mā aḥbabtum fa'msikū wa mā karihtum fa-bīʿū, wa lā tuʿadhdhibū khalq Allāh fa'inna Allāh mallakakum iyyāhum wa law shā'a la-mallakahum iyyākum*).' It is also worth noting that, even when discussing this Hadith, prominent Muslim scholars do not interpret it as we would expect. Aḥmad Bābā (d. 1627) notes that the Hadith means that God has chosen to bless Muslims with Islam, but if He had so chosen He could have made them unbelievers subject to enslavement. All this is in contrast to the Torah's reminder for Jews to treat their own Jewish slaves well because the Jews were once slaves in Egypt (Deuteronomy 15:15; 16:12). The Quran's description of the Jews in Egypt is that of being 'oppressed (*yastaḍʿifu*),' not slaves (Quran 28:4). The Quran uses the same language of the oppressed to describe the Muslims during their time in Mecca (Quran 8:26). The Quran does use an ethics of reciprocity, however, in exhorting children to care for their parents, who had cared for them when they were young (Quran 17:24); al-Ghazālī, *Iḥyā' ʿulūm al-dīn*, 2:1249–50; al-Haytamī, *Zawājir*, 2:183; Aḥmad Bābā, *Miʿrāj al-Ṣuʿūd: Ahmad Baba's Replies on Slavery*, 35. See also Aḥmad Shafīq, *l'Ésclavage au point de vue musalman*, 39; Muḥammad Bayram al-Khāmis, 'al-Taḥqīq fī mas'alat al-raqīq,' 510; Muḥammad Yūsuf Aṭfayyish, *Sharḥ Kitāb al-Nīl wa Shifā' al-ʿalīl*, 5:218.

Though not a Hadith, another interesting report tells of a prisoner captured by a king. The king asks the prisoner how he would like to be treated, and the prisoner replies, 'Do with me what you'd want God to do with you.' The king released him; Ibn Abī al-Ḥadīd, *Sharḥ Nahj al-balāgha*, ('Īsā al-Bābī al-Ḥalabī ed.), 16:84 (available http://www.haydarya.com/maktaba_moktasah/07/book_16/index.htm). See Justin Parrott, 'The Golden Rule in Islam: The Ethics of Reciprocity in Islamic Traditions.'

56. Hezser, *Jewish Slavery in Antiquity*, 152; K. R. Bradley, *Slaves and Masters in the Roman Empire: A Study in Social Control*, 21–25.

57. Harper, *Slavery in the Late Roman World*, 206–207.

58. See, for example, John Hunwick, 'Falkeiana III: The *Kitāb al-Tarsīl*,' 181.

59. Harper, *Slavery in the Late Roman World*, 226–31, 236; Westermann, *Slave Systems*, 102, 105, 106 (*pace* Harper, Westermann understands reports of intense cruelty more as representative of general alarm over inhumane treatment than as indicative of the norm).

60. Al-Khaṭīb al-Shirbīnī, *Mughnī al-muḥtāj*, 2:311; Ibn Abī al-ʿIzz, *al-Tanbīh ʿalā mushkilāt al-Hidāya*, 4:455–56; Ibn ʿĀbidīn, *Ḥāshiya*, 4:87-88; Baber Johansen, 'Vérité et torture: *ius commune* et droit musalman entre le xe et le xiiie siècle,' 144–45.

61. Harper, *Slavery in the Late Roman World*, 206–208, 229.

62. Mullā Hüzrev, *Durar al-ḥukkām sharḥ ghurar al-aḥkām*, 2:75, al-Nawawī, *Sharḥ Ṣaḥīḥ Muslim*, 11/12:234; Ibn Ḍuwayyān, *Manār al-sabīl*, 2:182; Jonathan Brown, 'Taʿzīr,' *The [Oxford] Encyclopedia of Islam and Law. Oxford Islamic Studies Online*, http://www.oxfordislamicstudies.com/article/opr/t349/e0189 (accessed 24-Feb-2019).

63. See Jonathan Brown, 'Stoning and Hand Cutting – Understanding the Hudud and Shariah in Islam,' https://yaqeeninstitute.org/en/jonathan-brown/stoning-and-hand-cutting-understanding-the-hudud-and-the-shariah-in-islam/.

64. Kecia Ali, *Marriage and Slavery in Early Islam*, 172–73; Mona Siddiqui, *The Good Muslim*, 51; Abū al-Ḥasan al-Māwardī, *al-Ḥāwī*, 9:574–75.

65. Hammurabi Code, §8; Walter Young, 'Stoning and Hand-Amputation: The pre-Islamic origins of the *ḥadd* penalties for *zinā* and *sariqa*,' 128–30, 161.

66. Westermann, *Slave Systems*, 82; Brockopp, *Early Mālikī Law*, 137.

67. *Sunan al-Nasāʾī: kitāb al-qasāma, bāb dhikr ḥadīth ʿAmr b. Ḥazm fī al-ʿuqūl . . .*

68. Al-Khaṭīb al-Shirbīnī, *Mughnī al-muḥtāj*, 4:104; al-Qudūrī, *Mukhtaṣar*, 527; Mullā Hüzrev, *Durar al-ḥukkām*, 2:117.

69. Hezser, *Jewish Slavery in Antiquity*, 191–98, 386; Glancy, 'The Sexual Use of Slaves: A Response to Kyle Harper on Jewish and Christian *Porneia*,' 215–29.

70. Anson Rainey et al., 'Concubine,' *Encyclopaedia Judaica*, ed. Michael Berenbaum and Fred Skolnik, 2nd edn. (Detroit: Macmillan Reference, 2007), 5:133–36.

71. Judith Grubbs, *Law and Family in Late Antiquity*, 304, 306–308, 313–14; Kyle Harper, *From Shame to Sin*, 242--43.

72. Lev Weitz, 'Polygyny and East Syrian Law: Local Practices and Ecclesiastical Tradition,' 173–76.

73. One Abū Bakr al-Ṣabbāgh (d. 1032) had over 900 wives; Ibn al-Jawzī, *al-Muntaẓam*, 15:232; Franz Rosenthal, 'Fiction and Reality: Sources for the Role of Sex in Medieval Muslim Society,' 17; Basim Musallam, 'The Ordering of Muslim Societies,' 193–94; L. Veccia Vaglieri, 'al-Ḥasan b. ʿAlī b. Abī Ṭālib,' *Encyclopaedia of Islam.*

74. Brockopp, *Early Mālikī Law*, 137–38, 170.

75. Majied Robinson, 'Prosopographical Approaches to the Nasab Tradition,' 136-40; Mendelsohn, *Slavery in the Ancient Near East*, 50–52.

76. Westermann, *Slave Systems*, 135.

77. *Ṣaḥīḥ al-Bukhārī*: *kitāb al-buyūʿ*, *bāb ithm man bāʿa ḥurran*.
78. Though Schneider tries to make a case for continuity with pre-Islamic Near Eastern laws in the era before al-Shāfiʿī, she comes up with little evidence, and what she does offer is ambiguous. As Ibn Ḥajar suggested, the early ruling by the caliph ʿAlī that a person who admits they are a slave is a slave probably pertains to someone whose status is unknown, not to self-dedition. See Irene Schneider, 'Freedom and Slavery in Early Islamic Time [sic],' 353–82; Ibn Ḥajar, *Fatḥ al-Bārī*, 4:526.
79. John Hunwick and Eve Troutt Powell, *The African Diaspora in the Mediterranean Lands of Islam*, xv. Slave ownership between non-Muslims from outside the Dār al-Islām was assumed to be legitimate. If a non-Muslim slave got the better of his non-Muslim master in the Dār al-Ḥarb and made him his slave, and then they both came into the Dār al-Islām, the original 'slave' would be seen as the legal owner of the original 'master'; Ḥamd al-Khaṭṭābī, *Maʿālim al-sunan*, 2:265. There were certainly restrictions on matters like buying children from their non-Muslim parents outside the Dār al-Islām. But practical assumptions that goods being sold were legitimate, and deference to practices of enslavement among non-Muslims, meant that the mainstream of Islamic legal thought tended to assume that a slave being offered to a Muslim merchant in the Dār al-Ḥarb could be legitimately purchased. For more on this, see Chapter 5, note 52.
80. See, for example, the case of Egypt in 35AH/657CE; Muḥammad b. Yūsuf al-Kindī, *Kitāb wa Wulāt wa Kitāb al-Quḍāt*, 12–13.
81. The earliest I have found this principle stated is in the work of the Ḥanafī jurist al-Jaṣṣāṣ (d. 981): '*al-aṣl huwa al-ḥurriyya*' and '*ẓāhir aḥwāl al-nās al-ḥurriyya*'; Abū Bakr al-Jaṣṣāṣ, *Sharḥ Mukhtaṣar al-Ṭaḥāwī*, 8:148.
82. See Appendix 5 – Was Freedom a Human Right in the Shariah?
83. Ibn al-Mundhir, *Kitāb al-Awsaṭ min al-sunan wa'l-ijmāʿ wa'l-ikhtilāf*, 11:428. Thanks to my friend Omar Anchassi for this wonderful citation. I have interpreted the term used by Ibn al-Mundhir (*ḥ-ṣ-n*) as Form 2 (*taḥṣīn*). I translate it as 'fortify' and not 'make immune' because there were instances in which humans could be enslaved.
84. Westermann, *Slave Systems*, 156. For a broader examination, see Michael Cook, *Ancient Religions, Modern Politics*, 28. As Jeffrey Fynn-Paul has pointed out, both Islam and Christianity created massive 'no-slaving zones' by effectively prohibiting enslavement within Christendom and the Abode of Islam; Jeffrey Fynn-Paul, 'Empire, Monotheism and Slavery in the Greater Mediterranean Region from Antiquity to the Early Modern Era,' 5.
85. Unlike the Shariah, Jewish law going back as far the ordinances of the Old Testament allowed Jews to enslave other Jews, either as debt-slaves, as punishment for certain crimes, or if they chose to give themselves as slaves. Biblical law also clearly distinguishes Hebrew slaves from gentile ones, with Hebrew slaves accorded far better treatment (Exodus 21:20–21; Leviticus 25:43, 46) (though this distinction seems to have vanished into irrelevance by the rabbinic period, with all slaves being Jewish or converts; there is much debate over whether the practice of Jews enslaving other Jews had disappeared by the Second Temple period). The ways in which Jewish slaves should be treated are similar to the ethics in the Islamic tradition. Admittedly working in an Islamic context, Maimonides (d. 1204) writes that Hebrew slaves could not be worked 'relentlessly' (defined as work without time limit or constraint or busy work) or humiliated with overly servile tasks. Hebrew slaves should be treated like brothers or sisters. Gentile slaves, on the other hand, could be worked relentlessly. Maimonides exhorts, however, that even in their case benevolence and wisdom should lead the master to treat the slave with mercy and justice, not to overburden him and to make sure he has food and drink.

He praises the sages of old for sharing their food with their slaves and for being inspired by the example of by God's mercy (Psalms 145:9, Deut. 13:18); Maimonides, *Mishnah Torah*, The Law of Slaves, 1–3, 9. Thanks to Shlomo Pill for help with these citations. Though Midrashim sources do not require masters to provide food for their slaves, they recommend this, with rabbis like R. Yochanan used as exemplars who taught that the same God made slaves and free, with Abraham's treatment of Hagar as ideal. Probably following the Roman tradition of peculium, Talmudic law seems to have given Jewish slaves some limited rights to accumulate property particularly, in self-purchase; Hezser, 46, 153–55. Urbach writes that the respect for a human life shaped in the image of God applied to slaves and non-slaves alike, i.e., slaves could not be killed without just cause; E. E. Urbach, *The Laws Regarding Slavery*, 3–4, 93.

86. I have not found any scriptural anchor for this in the Quran or the Hadith corpus. It seems to have been an agreed-upon position from the earliest period, however. There was an opinion traced back to the caliph ʿUmar that Arabs could not be enslaved (*laysa ʿalā ʿarabī milk*), but this was outweighed in the eyes of most jurists by the sound Hadith describing the Prophet enslaving Arabs of the Hawāzin tribe. A Hadith, noted by al-Shāfiʿī, in which the Prophet allegedly alluded to a prohibition on enslaving Arabs, was seriously criticized for its *isnād*. See Yaḥyā b. Ādam, *Kitāb al-Kharāj*, 68–69; *Ṣaḥīḥ al-Bukhārī*: *kitāb al-ʿitq, bāb man malaka min al-ʿarab raqīqan . . .*; al-Bayhaqī, *Sunan al-kubrā*, 9:125; al-Shawkānī, *Nayl al-awṭār*, 8:9.

87. Muslim property captured by non-Muslim enemies is not considered to be legally owned by them according to the Shariah (though the Ḥanafī school acknowledged ownership if the non-Muslims took protective possession of that property); ʿAbd al-Wahhāb al-Shaʿrānī, *al-Mīzān al-kubrā*, 2:202; Mullā Hüzrev, *Durar al-ḥukkām*, 1:290. More research must be done on the question of whether Muslims who had been enslaved by non-Muslims considered themselves to be legally slaves according to the Shariah, if this impacted their behavior or actions, or whether formulating this question as such would have mattered at all to them. Manuel Barcia has argued that many of the African slaves in north-east Brazil and Cuba, a large portion of whom were Muslim and Hausa and Yoruba-speakers from West Africa, saw their rebellions in the first half of the 1800s as continuations of the West African jihads. Barcia suggests that they saw the Americas as simply an extension of the Dār al-Ḥarb. Margarita Rosa has discussed how leaders in the Brazilian Muslim slave community in Bahía organized the collection of Zakat, which legal Muslim slaves do not pay. Sylviane Diouf has shown how Muslims who had attained their freedom in certain Caribbean areas formed associations to systematically buy the freedom of other Muslims, suggesting that removing Muslims from slavery was a recognized, common mission. There are also examples of Ottoman soldiers taken prisoner by the Russian army after the Siege of Ochakov (1788) demanding that they be treated according to Islamic law; Manuel Barcia, *West African Warfare in Bahia and Cuba*, 71, 96–111; Margarita Rosa, 'Du'as of the Enslaved: The Malê Slave Rebellion in Bahía, Brazil,' https://yaqeeninstitute.org/en/margarita-rosa/duas-of-the-enslaved-the-male-slave-rebellion-in-bahia-brazil/#ftnt16; Sylviane Diouf, *Servants of Allah*, 104-105; Terry Alford, *A Prince among Slaves*, 46; W. Eton, *A Survey of the Turkish Empire*, 120–21. Interestingly, one Ḥanafī fatwa manual states that a Muslim slave, if he is captured by unbelievers in the Dār al-Ḥarb and escapes, is freed because they had become his owners and that ownership had ceased; ʿAbd al-Rashīd al-Walwāljī, *al-Fatāwā al-Walwāljiyya*, 3:149.

88. '*Al-Islām lā yanfī/yunāfī baqā' al-riqq*.' There were some notional exceptions. For example, if a non-Muslim outside the Dār al-Islām had a slave who converted to Islam, and then Muslims conquered that area, that Muslim slave would be free; *al-Fatāwā al-Hindiyya*, 1:573; Badr al-Dīn al-ʿAynī, *al-Ramz sharḥ al-Kanz*, 145b. In practice, of course, conversion to Islam could result in better treatment.

89. Ibn Ḥajar, *Fatḥ al-Bārī*, 6:208; Mullā Hüsrev, *Durar al-ḥukkām*, 1:290–93; Muḥammad b. Ḥasan al-Kawākibī, *al-Fawā'id al-samiyya sharḥ al-Fawā'id al-saniyya*, 1:391.

90. See, for example, the *Fatāwā al-Hindiyya*, 1:573.

91. Ibn Qudāma, *Mughnī*, 9:317–18. See also a ruling attributed to ʿUmar; Ibn Kathīr, *Musnad al-Fārūq*, 2:248.

92. *Tashawwafa al-shāriʿ li'l-ḥurriyya*; This concept can be found very early in Islamic history, in the *Kitāb al-Taḥrīsh* of Ḍirār b. ʿAmr (d. *circa* 815), where the author writes that 'God wishes freedom.' It is tied to a Hadith attributed (unreliably) to the Prophet, in which he says that, if a man says to his wife 'You're divorced, if God wills,' then she is not divorced. But if he says to his slave 'You're free, if God wills,' then he is freed. Al-Qarāfī (d. 1285) mentions *tashawwuf al-sharʿ li-maṣlaḥat al-ʿitq*. The occurrence of the maxim with the specific wording mentioned above, however, seems only to have appeared in the thirteenth century; Ḍirār b. ʿAmr, *Kitāb al-Taḥrīsh*, 127; al-Bayhaqī, *Sunan al-kubrā*, 10:81; Shihāb al-Dīn al-Qarāfī, *al-Dhakhīra*, 6:292; 7:97; Ibn Taymiyya, *Majmūʿat al-fatāwā*, 29:107; Muḥammad Ibn ʿArafa al-Mālikī (d. 1400), as cited in *Qurrat al-ʿayn bi-fatāwā ʿulamā' al-Ḥaramayn*, 286.

93. Ibn Taymiyya, *al-Qawāʿid al-nūrāniyya*, 291–2; idem, *Majmūʿat al-fatāwā*, 29:107; al-Ghazālī, *Fatawa*, 42 (noted as a *rukhṣa*).

94. This Hadith lists three things in which statements in jest are like those not in jest or in which joking is not allowed: entry into marriage, divorce, and *ʿitq*; Ibn Ḥajar, *Talkhīṣ al-ḥabīr*, 3:423; al-Ṭabarānī, *al-Muʿjam al-kabīr*, 18:304; al-Qudūrī, *Mukhtaṣar*, 416, 479; Muḥammad Nawawī al-Jāwī, *Qūt al-ḥabīb*, 295; Ibn Ḍuwayyān, *Manār al-sabīl*, 2:108; al-Marwazī, *Ikhtilāf al-fuqahā'*, 270–71.

95. Al-Qudūrī, *Mukhtaṣar*, 477; al-Buhūtī, *al-Rawḍ al-murbiʿ*, 357.

96. Ibn Qudāma, *Mughnī*, 12:234.

97. Based on the Hadith 'Whoever comes to own one close of kin (*dhā raḥim maḥram*), he is free.' See *Sunan* of Abū Dāwūd: *kitāb al-ʿitq, bāb fī-man malaka dhā raḥim maḥram*; *Jāmiʿ al-Tirmidhī: kitāb al-aḥkām, bāb fī-mā jā'a fī-man malaka dhā raḥim maḥram*.

98. Ibn Qudāma, *Mughnī*, 12:237; Muḥammad al-Bazzāzī (d. 1424), *al-Fatāwā al-Bazzāziyya*, printed on margins of *al-Fatāwā al-Hindiyya*, 1:572.

99. Al-Ghazālī, *Fatāwā*, 130.

100. Abū ʿĪsā Sīdī al-Mahdī al-Wazzānī (or al-Wāzzānī), *al-Nawāzil al-jadīda*, 10:319.

101. Al-Wazzānī, *al-Nawāzil al-jadīda*, 10:356; al-Wansharīsī, *al-Miʿyār al-muʿrib*, 9:218–19.

102. Al-Nawawī, *Sharḥ Ṣaḥīḥ Muslim*, 11/12:144; Ibn Qudāma, *Mughnī*, 9:314; al-Shawkānī, *Nayl al-awṭār*, 6:93–94. For an excellent discussion of how social realities and predominant legal structures distanced interpretation of the Sunna from its egalitarian impetus, see Ingrid Mattson, 'A Believing Slave is Better than an Unbeliever: Status and Community in Early Islamic Society and Law,' 80–125.

103. Ibn Ḥajar, *Fatḥ al-Bārī*, 5:219. Cf. Shaun Marmon, 'Domestic Slavery in the Mamluk Empire: A Preliminary Sketch,' in *Slavery in the Islamic Middle East*, ed. Shaun Marmon, 5.

104. Al-Qurṭubī, *al-Jāmiʿ li-aḥkām al-Qur'ān*, 6:532–33; Abū Bakr al-Jaṣṣāṣ, *Aḥkām al-Qur'ān*, 3:321; Ahmed El Shamsy and Aron Zysow, 'Al-Buwayṭī's Abridgement of al-Shāfiʿī's *Risāla*,' 348. For the irrepressibility of hierarchy, see Cook, *Ancient Religions*,

Modern Politics, 170. Al-Ṭabarī also considered *mukātaba* to be obligatory for the master to accept if the slave was worthy; Muḥammad Rawwās Qalʿajī, *Mawsūʿat fiqh al-Ṭabarī wa Ḥammād b. Abī Sulaymān*, 79.

105. Siddiqui, *The Good Muslim*, 51; Ibn Qudāma, *Mughnī*, 7:509. For the extreme rarity of a free man marrying a slave woman, see E. Ann McDougall, '"To Marry One's Slave is as Easy as Eating a Meal": The Dynamics of Carnal Relations within Saharan Slavery,' 144. The famous Sufi Abū Ṭālib al-Makkī (d. 996) quotes 'some jurists' saying 'The stupidest person is the free man who marries a slave woman, and the smartest is the slave who marries a free woman. Because the second one has part of himself freed, while the first has part of himself enslaved'; al-Makkī, *Qūt al-qulūb*, 2:240.

106. Hunwick refers to this as a 'don't ask don't tell' policy; Hunwick and Powell, *The African Diaspora*, xv.

107. Ibn Shaddād, *al-Nawādir al-sulṭāniyya*, 68–69. Thanks to Adnan Rashid for alerting me to this.

108. Yaʿqūb b. Sufyān al-Fasawī, *Kitāb al-Maʿrifa wa'l-tārīkh*, 3:390–91. The Companion in the story is named as Ḍirār b. al-Azwar, but it may have been Ḍirār b. al-Khaṭṭāb; al-Bukhārī, *al-Tārīkh al-kabīr*, 4:289.

109. Mu'ayyad-zāde [ʿAbd al-Raḥmān Efendī, d. 1516], *Risāla* (Bağdat Vehbi, 2052), 142a–b.

110. Burhān al-Dīn al-Marghīnānī, *al-Hidāya*, 3:431.

111. ʿAlā' al-Dīn al-Bukhārī, *Kashf al-asrār*, 4:399.

112. Taqī al-Dīn al-Subkī identifies this scholar as Tāj al-Dīn al-Fazārī, author of the *Rukhṣa al-ʿamīma fī aḥkām al-ghanīma*. Kātib Chelebī gives his full name as Abū Ibrāhīm/Ibrāhīm b. ʿAbd al-Raḥmān b. Ibrāhīm, so this may be the son of the more famous ʿAbd al-Raḥmān b. Ibrāhīm al-Fazārī Ibn al-Firkāḥ (d. 1291); Kātib Chelebī, *Kashf al-ẓunūn*, 2:165.

113. Taqī al-Dīn al-Subkī, *Qaḍā' al-arab fī as'ilat Ḥalab*, 539–48; idem, *Fatāwā*, 2:281–85 (his teacher, Quṭb al-Dīn al-Sunbāṭī [d. 1322], had seen some pious folk in Egypt pay the *khums* to the treasury to be safe when they bought a slave girl). Ibn Battuta states that the sultan of Kilwa on the east African coast would carry out jihad against the Zanj in the interior and then set aside the *khums* for visiting descendants of the Prophet; *The Travels of Ibn Battuta*, 2:380–81.

114. Shehzade Mehmet Korkud, *İslâm'da Ganimet ve Cariyelik*, 13, 20, 106, 109–10.

115. Toledano, *As if Silent and Absent*, 72, 112.

116. Ibn al-Qayyim notes an opinion among the Salaf that the slave could also be freed as a reparation for the physical harm he had suffered. He can definitely flee, an opinion also given by al-Thawrī; Ibn Qayyim al-Jawziyya, *al-Ṭuruq al-ḥukmiyya*, 138–39.

117. Ibn Qudāma, *Mughnī*, 4:256.

118. *Sunan* of Abū Dāwūd: *kitāb al-libās, bāb fī qawlihi ʿazza wa jalla qul li'l-mu'mināt . . .*; Ibn Qudāma, *Mughnī*, 7:459.

119. Ibn Qudāma, *Mughnī*, 10:408.

120. Al-Shirbīnī, *Mughnī al-muḥtāj*, 4:102.

121. *Sunan* of Abū Dāwūd: *kitāb al-diyāt, bāb man qatala ʿabdahu . . .*; *Jāmiʿ al-Tirmidhī*: *kitāb al-diyāt, bāb mā jā'a fī al-rajul yaqtulu ʿabdahu*; *Sunan al-Nasā'ī*: *kitāb al -qasāma, bāb al-qawad min al-sayyid li-mawlāhu.*

122. This is even phrased as an unreliable Hadith, '*lā yuqādu mamlūk min mālikihi*'; al-Bayhaqī, *Sunan al-kubrā*, 8:65–66. For the legal reasoning mentioned here, with an additional suggestion that, since *riqq* is caused by *kufr* and most scholars do not allow a Muslim to be executed for killing a *kāfir*, the same would follow for a slave, see Abū Bakr

Ibn al-ʿArabī, *ʿĀriḍat al-aḥwadhī*, 6:184. For the overlap with a parent not being killed for killing their child, see Brown, *Misquoting Muhammad*, 180–83.

123. Al-Qurṭubī, *al-Jāmiʿ li-aḥkām al-Qurʾān*, 1:638; al-Bayhaqī, *Sunan al-kubrā*, 8:65-66; al-Nawawī, *Sharḥ Ṣaḥīḥ Muslim*, 11/12:137–38. For evidence that discretionary punishment (*taʿzīr*) could be present even for minor injuries done to slaves, see Ibn Ḥajar al-Haytamī, *al-Fatāwā al-kubrā al-fiqhiyya*, 4:218.

124. Al-Qudūrī, *Mukhtaṣar*, 527; Mullā Hüsrev, *Durar al-ḥukkām*, 2:117.

125. Al-Shirbīnī, *Mughnī al-muḥtāj*, 4:104. Ibn Ḥazm sees (accurately) this whole discussion as scripturally baseless; Ibn Ḥazm, *al-Muḥallā*, 8:152–54.

126. Ibn Qudāma, *Mughnī*, 8:148.

127. Ibn Ḥajar, *Fatḥ al-Bārī*, 12:39.

128. Ibn Qudāma, *Mughnī*, 2:196; *Ṣaḥīḥ al-Bukhārī*: *kitāb al-jumʿa, bāb al-jumʿa ʿalā al -qurā wa'l-mudun*.

129. Ibn Qudāma, *Mughnī*, 10:468.

130. Ibn Qudāma, *Mughnī*, 2:29, 196.

131. ʿAbd al-Bāqī al-Zurqānī and Muḥammad b. al-Ḥasan al-Bannānī, *Sharḥ al-Zurqānī ʿalā Mukhtaṣar al-Khalīl*, 5:546; Muḥammad b. Jaʿfar al-Kattānī, *Salwat al-anfās*, 3:247; Ibn Ḥanbal, *Masāʾil Aḥmad Ibn Ḥanbal riwāyat ibnihi*, 54.

132. Ibn Qudāma, *Mughnī*, 12:375.

133. This is even the case in later Ibāḍī law, which cites the same explanations as the Sunni schools; Aṭfayyish, *Sharḥ Kitāb al-Nīl wa shifāʾ al-ʿalīl*, 14:329–30. See also Patricia Crone, '"Even an Ethiopian Slave": The Transformation of a Sunni Tradition,' 59–67.

134. Ibn Ḥajar, *Fatḥ al-Bārī*, 13:153.

135. Ibn Qudāma, *Mughnī*, 12:71.

136. Ibn Qudāma, *Mughnī*, 10:432.

137. See Ahmed Akgündüz, *Ottoman Harem*, 122–23.

138. Al-Khaṭṭābī, *Maʿālim al-sunan*, 2:262; Muḥammad b. Ismāʿīl al-Ṣanʿānī, *Subul al -salām*, 3:32–33; al-Munāwī, *Fayḍ al-qadīr*, 11:5928–29; Jalāl al-Dīn al-Suyūṭī, *Hāshiyat Sunan Ibn Mājah*, 162. The Hadiths include examples such as 'Whoever separates a mother and her child, God will separate him from his loved ones on the Day of Resurrection'; *Jāmiʿ al-Tirmidhī*: *kitāb al-buyūʿ, bāb mā jāʾa fī karāhiyat al-farq bayn al -akhawayn . . .*; *Sunan Ibn Mājah*: *kitāb al-tijāra, bāb al-nahy ʿan al-tafrīq bayn al-saby*; *Musnad Ibn Ḥanbal*, 5:412–13.

139. This created a duty that could only be created by agreement with the slave; al-Nawawī, *Rawḍat al-ṭālibīn*, 7:102; al-Buhūtī, *Kashshāf al-qināʿ ʿan matn al-Iqnāʿ*, 5:45; Marmon, 'Domestic Slavery in the Mamluk Empire,' 6.

140. Ibn Qudāma, *Mughnī*, 9:316, 7:459.

141. Ibn Qudāma, *Mughnī*, 8:150, 9:315–16.

142. Siddiqui, *The Good Muslim*, 51; Khalīl b. Isḥāq, *Mukhtaṣar Khalīl*, 112.

143. ʿAbd al-Raḥmān al-Shayzarī, *Nihāyat al-rutba fī ṭalab al-ḥisba*, 256. This concern is totally absent in the Christian physician Ibn Buṭlān's (d. 1066) treatise on how to buy a slave. Ibn Mujāwir's sardonic thirteenth-century description of Adenis buying and selling slave girls suggests that looking at their private parts was disgraceful. See Ibn Buṭlān, *Risāla jāmiʿa li-funūn nāfiʿa fī shirā al-raqīq wa taqlīb al-ʿabīd*, 1:351-389; Ibn Mujāwir, *A Traveller in Thirteenth-Century Arabia*, 162.

144. ʿAbd al-Razzāq al-Ṣanʿānī, *Muṣannaf*, 7:285–88.

145. '. . . *aw ʿayb fī farj* . . .'; Yūsuf Rāġib, *Actes de vente d'esclaves et d'animaux d'Égypte médiévale*, 3–15.

146. Mendelsohn, *Slavery in the Ancient Near East*, 50; Grubbs, *Law and Family in Late Antiquity*, 313–16. Unlike in Islamic law, Babylonian men could have sex with their wives' slave women too; Mendelsohn, *Slavery in the Ancient Near East*, 50; Kecia Ali, *Sexual Ethics and Islam*, 39–55.
147. Kecia Ali, 'Concubinage and Consent,' 149; Hina Azam, *Sexual Violation in Islamic Law*, 180.
148. See Kecia Ali, *Marriage and Slavery in Early Islam*, 31–39.
149. See Chapter 7 on Concubines and Consent.
150. See Kecia Ali, *Marriage and Slavery in Early Islam*.
151. Ehud Toledano, *As if Silent and Absent*, 84. As Elizabeth Elbourne writes, 'In many contexts, women in particular status groups had no choice but to provide coerced sexual labor, even if they were not considered slaves.' See Elizabeth Elbourne, 'Introduction: Key Themes and Perspectives,' 10.
152. Hina Azam, *Sexual Violation in Islamic Law*, 186.
153. *al-jāriya allatī lā tuṭīqu al-waṭ'*; al-Buhūtī, *Kashshāf al-qinā'*, 4:514.
154. The slave's limited property rights resemble the Roman notion of the slave's peculium as well as Babylonian law and Old Testament law; Brockopp, *Early Mālikī Law*, 181; Mendelsohn, *Slavery in the Ancient Near East*, 67, 74.
155. Al-Khaṭṭābī, *Ma'ālim al-sunan*, 4:79.
156. In the Maliki school, male slaves could actually own concubines; K. Ali, *Marriage and Slavery in Early Islam*, 165, 173.
157. Fisher and Fisher, *Slavery and Muslim Society in Africa*, 142–43.
158. Ibn Qudāma, *Mughnī*, 4:256.
159. Ibn Ḥazm, *al-Muḥallā fī al-āthār*, 8:159; 9:444–45.
160. On the basis of the Prophet's Hadith: *in kāna li-aḥadikunna mukātab wa kāna 'indahu mā yu'addī fa'l-taḥtajib minhu*; *Sunan* of Abū Dāwūd: *kitāb al-'itq, bāb fī al-mukātab yu'addī ba'ḍ kitābatihi fa-ya'jizu aw yamūtu*; *Jāmi' al-Tirmidhī*: *kitāb al-buyū', bāb mā jā'a fī al-mukātab idhā kāna 'indahu mā yu'addī*; Ibn Qudāma, *Mughnī*, 7:132.
161. Ibn Qudāma, *Mughnī*, 7:133 ff.; al-Nawawī, *Rawḍat al-ṭālibīn*, 6:30.
162. Toledano, *As if Silent and Absent*, 61, 72, 84–88; al-Kindī, *Kitāb al-Wulāt*, 317–18.
163. This had been prohibited in Roman law in the late first century CE; Westermann, *Slave Systems of Greek and Roman Antiquity*, 114.
164. Ibn Qudāma, *Mughnī*, 9:317; al-Khaṭṭābī, *Ma'ālim al-sunan*, 1:54. Exodus 21:26–27 tells masters to free slaves if they strike them severely. See also Bruce Hall, *A History of Race in Muslim West Africa*, 225–26.
165. See *Ṣaḥīḥ Muslim*: *kitāb al-aymān, bāb iṭ'ām al-mamlūk mimmā ya'kul . . .*; Ibn Ḥajar, *Fatḥ al-Bārī*, 5: 218–19. For this, see Joel Blecher, *Said the Prophet of God: Hadith Commentary across a Millennium*, 188–90.
166. Ibn Qudāma, *Mughnī*, 9:315; al-Zurqānī and al-Bannānī, 5:277; al-Buhūtī, *Kashshāf al-qinā'*, 5:477; al-Nawawī, *Rawḍat al-ṭālibīn*, 9:115–18; *al-Fatāwā al-Hindiyya*, 1:568.
167. Ibn Qudāma, *Mughnī*, 9:315.
168. Ibn Qudāma, *Mughnī*, 9:315; al-Nawawī, *Rawḍat al-ṭālibīn*, 9:115.
169. For the centrality of Islamic law to Islamic ethics, see Kevin Reinhart, 'Islamic Law as Islamic Ethics,' 186–203.
170. Aḥmad Miskawayh, *Tahdhīb al-akhlāq*, 368.
171. Taşköprîzâde Ahmed Efendi, *Şerhu'l-Ahlâki'l-Adudiyye*, 199.
172. 'Alā' al-Dīn al-Kāzirūnī (d. ??), *Şerhu'l-Ahlâki'l-Adudiyye*, 151–55; Taşköprîzâde, *Şerhu'l-Ahlâki'l-Adudiyye*, 195–201; Ismā'īl Mufīd Istanbūlī (d. 1802), *Şerhu'l-Ahlâki'l-Adudiyye*, 168–69.

CHAPTER 3 SLAVERY IN ISLAMIC CIVILIZATION

1. Abū Nuʿaym al-Iṣbahānī, *Ḥilyat al-awliyā'*, 10:166.
2. This definition of Islamic civilization follows roughly the periodization of Marshall Hodgson, *The Venture of Islam*, 1:96, 2:3.
3. Al-Iṣbahānī, *Ḥilyat al-awliyā'*, 10:173–74; Ibn Battuta, *Ibn Battuta in Black Africa*, 57–58.
4. Al-Kindī, *Kitāb al-Wulāt*, 317–18; Petra Sijpesteijn, *Shaping a Muslim State*, 69.
5. Ibn Mujāwir, *A Traveller in Thirteenth-Century Arabia*, 87-88; E. Powell, *Tell This in My Memory*, 62; Alexander Burnes, *Travels into Bokhara*, 2:57.
6. ʿAbd al-Qādir Badā'ūnī, *Muntakhabu-t-Tawārīkh*, 2:228; Shamil Jeppe, 'Leadership and Loyalties: The Imams of Nineteenth Century [sic] Colonial Cape Town,' 153.
7. Qāḍī ʿIyāḍ, *Tartīb al-madārik wa taqrīb al-masālik*, 3:334–35; Huda Shaarawi, *Harem Years*, 68–69.
8. Evliya Efendi, *Narrative of Travels in Europe, Asia and Africa in the Seventeenth Century*, 2:5; Linda Colley, *Captives*, 60.
9. Hunwick and Powell, *African Diaspora in the Mediterranean Lands of Islam*, 107; Leonard Andaya, *The Kingdom of Johor*, 270.
10. See, for example, the association between Islam and slavery in French colonial policy in West Africa; Christopher Harrison, *France and Islam in West Africa, 1860–1960*, 99.
11. Abdul Sheriff and Vijayalakshmi Teelock, 'Introduction,' 9–12; R. David Goodman, 'Demystifying "Islamic Slavery": Using Legal Practices to Reconstruct the End of Slavery in Fes, Morocco,' 153. See also McDougall, 'Critical Reflections on Studying the Saharan Slave Trade,' 203–205, 221–22, 227; Frederick Cooper, 'Islam and Cultural Hegemony: The Ideology of Slaveowners on the East African Coast.'
12. See Matheson and Hooker, 'Slavery in the Malay Texts,' 185.
13. I alter Lovejoy's list of features slightly here. See Lovejoy, *Transformations in Slavery: A History of Slavery in Africa*, 15–18. See also E. Ann McDougall, '"What is Islamic about Slavery in Muslim Societies",' 7–36; Gwyn Campbell et al., 'Introduction: Resisting bondage in the Indian Ocean world,' in *Resisting Bondage in Indian Ocean Africa and Asia*, 1; Matheson and Hooker, 'Slavery in the Malay Texts,' 192. For the commonness of *mukātaba* (called *murgu*) in the Sokoto Caliphate, see Lovejoy, 'Slavery in the Sokoto Caliphate,' 233–35; Polly Hill, 'Comparative West African Farm Slavery Systems,' 38. A papyrus document from 721 CE shows a woman making her property a pious endowment for her manumitted slave girl; Petra Sijpesteijn, *Shaping a Muslim State*, 69. Nineteenth-century manumission documents from Cairo show real concern on the part of owners for slaves who were being manumitted but lacked job skills or had no family to assist them; they often received large sums of money to help ease their way; Terence Walz, 'Black Slavery in Egypt During the Nineteenth Century,' 147.
14. Priscilla Starratt, 'Tuareg Slavery and Slave Trade,' 95–96.
15. Ibn Mujāwir, *A Traveller in Thirteenth-Century Arabia*, 35; Quran 24:33.
16. Khasnor Johan, 'The Undang-Undang Melaka: Reflections on Malay Society in Fifteenth-Century Malacca,' 131–50; Matheson and Hooker, 185.
17. Carolina López, 'The British Presence in the Malay World,' 20–21.
18. Hill, 'Comparative West African Farm Slavery Systems,' 37; Erdem, *Slavery in the Ottoman Empire and its Demise*, 12–13, 15.

19. See Hunwick and Powell, *African Diaspora*, 105–106; Fisher and Fisher, *Slavery and Muslim Society in Africa*, 143–48.
20. Though in the Nubian case this may have been because of periodic rebellions against Muslim rule. See Jay Spaulding, 'Precolonial Islam in the Eastern Sudan,' 119.
21. For an excellent selection of examples from the Sahel region, see Fisher and Fisher, *Slavery and Muslim Society in Africa*, 24–33; also Gwyn Campbell, 'Introduction: Slavery and other forms of Unfree Labour in the Indian Ocean World,' xvii–xviii.
22. Ertuğrul Düzdağ, *Ebussuud Efendi Fetvaları*, 138–39; Muḥammad al-Kawākibī, *al-Fawā'id al-samiyya*, 2:396; Ibn Kamāl Pāsha, *Majmūʿ rasā'il al-ʿallāma Ibn Kamāl Bāsha*, 5:457-461; Yanishehirli ʿAbdallāh Efendī, *Behcetül'l-Fetâvâ*, 189–92; Abdurrahman Atçıl, 'The Safavid Threat and Juristic Authority in the Ottoman Empire during the 16th Century,' 295–314; Erdem, *Slavery in the Ottoman Empire and its Demise*, 21; Guy Burak, 'Faith, law and empire in the age of Ottoman "Confessionalization,"' 1–23. See Appendix 6 – Enslavement of Apostate Muslims or Muslims Declared to be Unbelievers.
23. Vladimir Minorsky, *Medieval Iran and Its Neighbors*, Chapter 8: 'The Poetry of Shah Ismāʿīl'.
24. The Almohads frequently took their enemy's womenfolk captive and either sold them into slavery or kept them as slaves; Heather J. Empey, 'The Mothers of the Caliph's Sons: Women as Spoils of War during the Early Almohad Period,' 144, 148, 150, 153. See Appendix 6 – Enslavement of Apostate Muslims or Muslims Declared to be Unbelievers.
25. R. David Goodman, 'Demystifying "Islamic Slavery,"' 147; This was Sultan Sulaymān b. Muḥammad al-ʿAlawī (d. 1822); al-Kattānī, *Salwat al-anfās*, 3:285.
26. Mohammed Bashir Salau, 'Slavery in Kano Emirate of Sokoto Caliphate Recounted,' 92, 104.
27. French authorities in Senegal in the early twentieth century estimated that several thousand pilgrims a year were enslaved at or on the way to Hajj; Miers, 'Slavery and the slave trade in Saudi Arabia and the Arab states of the Persian Gulf,' 122, 126, 130; Ghislaine Lydon, 'Slavery, Exchange and Islamic Law: A Glimpse from the Archives of Mali and Mauritania,' 119; Roger Botte, *Esclavages et Abolitions en Terre d'Islam*, 122–26.
28. See Abdul Sheriff, 'Social Mobility in Indian Ocean Slavery: The Strange Career of Sultan bin Aman,' 145; Freya Stark, *The Southern Gates of Arabia*, 281–82.
29. Hunwick, 'Notes on Slavery in the Songhay Empire,' 19; idem, *Sharīʿa in Songhay*, 70.
30. Jeff Eden, *Slavery and Empire in Central Asia*, 33–34.
31. Mullā ʿAlī al-Qārī', *Majmūʿ rasā'il*, 6:357–63, 371, 381 (from his treatise *Shamm al-ʿawāriḍ fī dhamm al-rawāfiḍ*). One famous Ḥanafī scholar who had declared many of the lands of Central Asia and north-east Iran to be Dār al-Ḥarb 'after the strife of the Tatars' was al-Mukhtār al-Zāhidī (d. 1260), who hailed from Khwarazm. See Ibn Nujaym, *al-Baḥr al-rā'iq*, 3:230–31.
32. Burnes, *Travels into Bokhara*, 1:190, 343.
33. Eden, *Slavery and Empire in Central Asia*, 34. This figure may be the well-traveled Ottoman scholar Muḥyī al-Dīn Muḥammad b. ʿUmar al-ʿAjamī (d. 1531), whose grandfather had come from the region of Herat and who wrote extensively against the Safavids and promoted jihad against them in the courts of two Ottoman sultans; Taşköprîzâde, *al-Shaqā'iq al-nuʿmāniyya*, 247–48.
34. Mirzai, *A History of Slavery and Emancipation in Iran*, 75–78; Burnes, 1:343. See Appendix 6 – Enslavement of Apostate Muslims or Muslims Declared to be Unbelievers.
35. Jeff Eden, unpublished manuscript on the religious justification for enslavement in Muslim Central Asia; ʿAbdallāh Efendī, *Behcetül'l-Fetâvâ*, 189–92.

36. For a description of slavery in the elite homes of Rajput lords in 16th–19th-century Rajasthan that resembles closely 'Islamic slavery' in Istanbul or Cairo, see Ramya Sreenivasan, 'Drudges, Dancing Girls, Concubines: Female Slaves in Rajput Polity, 1500–1850.'

37. Lovejoy, *Transformation of Slavery*, 15–18; Mendelsohn, 121–22.

38. Cicero, *Philippics*, 8.32; Peter Hunt, *Ancient Greek and Roman Slavery*, 118–19; Toledano, *As if Silent and Absent*, 91; Walz, 'Black Slavery in Egypt During the Nineteenth Century,' 147. Patricia Crone and Nur Sobers-Khan have also noted a similar continuity between Byzantine and Ottoman patterns of slavery and manumission. See Crone, *Roman, Provincial and Islamic Law*, 66–69; Nur Sobers-Khan, *Slaves without Shackles*, 75–76.

39. See Clarence-Smith, *Islam and the Abolition of Slavery*, 12–16.

40. In early imperial Rome, the rate of biological replacement in the slave population was estimated at as high as 80 percent; Marek Jankowiak, 'What Does the Slave Trade in the Saqaliba Tell us about Early Islamic Slavery?,' 171. See also Erdem, *Slavery in the Ottoman Empire and its Demise*, 52; John Wright, *The Trans-Saharan Slave Trade*, 1, 23.

41. Walz, 'Black Slavery in Egypt during the Nineteenth Century,' 150–51; Wright, *Trans-Saharan Slave Trade*, 23.

42. Hunwick and Powell, *African Diaspora*, xvii. Miers notes how the Shariah practices of manumission led to a 'steady attrition' in the number of slaves and thus a need for constant resupply; Miers, 'Slavery: A Question of Definition,' 5. See also Clarence-Smith, *Islam and the Abolition of Slavery*, 9; Reid, 'Introduction,' 29; B. Lewis, *Race and Slavery in the Middle East*, 10.

43. Maḥmūd Kaʿtī Tunbuktī (d. 1593), *Tārīkh al-Fattāsh*, 120, 122.

44. Wright, *Trans-Saharan Slave Trade*, 2–3. Jeff Eden's research on testimony by slaves in Muslim central Asia in the mid-nineteenth century shows that, for the several dozen testimonies he has found, the mean period of enslavement was around twenty years; Jeff Eden, 'Beyond the Bazaars,' 927.

45. As cited from Abdul Sheriff, '*Suria*: Concubine or Secondary Slave Wife? The Case of Zanzibar,' 100; idem, 'The Slave trade and its fallout in the Persian Gulf,' 118.

46. Wright, *Trans-Saharan Slave Trade*, 1, 23; Gwyn Campbell, 'Introduction: abolition and its aftermath in the Indian Ocean world,' in *Abolition and its Aftermath in Indian Ocean Africa and Asia*, ed. Campbell, 7–8.

47. Thorkild Hansen, *Arabia Felix*, 221.

48. The pattern of ascending miscegenation in Islamic civilization is reminiscent of Montesquieu's fictional Persian narrator describing Rome's system of slavery, whereby 'the republic constantly renewed itself, allowing new families in as the old ones were destroyed'; Montesquieu, *Persian Letters*, 208–209 (letter 115).

49. Daniel Pipes, 'Mawlas,' 136, 141.

50. Chase Robinson, 'Slavery in the Conquest Period,' 161.

51. Al-Khalīlī, *al-Irshād fī maʿrifat ʿulamāʾ al-ḥadīth*, 17; al-Dhahabī, *Siyar aʿlām al-nubalāʾ*, 5:157. Al-Qāsim b. Muḥammad b. Abī Bakr and Sālim b. ʿAbdallāh b. ʿUmar, both major scholars of the Successor generation and grandsons of caliphs, were sons of slave-concubines; ʿAbd al-Malik b. Ḥabīb, *Adab al-nisāʾ*, 154–55.

52. J. M. B. Jones, 'Ibn Isḥāḳ'; J. Pedersen, 'Ibn Djinnī,' both in *Encyclopaedia of Islam*.

53. Claude Gilliot, 'Yāqūt al-Rūmī,' in *Encyclopaedia of Islam*.

54. Abū Nuʿaym al-Iṣbahānī, *Ḥilyat al-awliyāʾ*, 10: 129.

55. Ibn Battuta, *The Travels of Ibn Battuta*, 2:373.

56. Shams al-Dīn al-Sakhāwī, *al-Ḍawʾ al-lāmiʿ li-ahl al-qarn al-tāsiʿ*, 10:194. Al-Sakhāwī mentions that Maymūn died of starvation, but it is unclear whether this was related to his status as a slave or not. He was also seen as an ascetic.

57. Ulrich Haarmann, 'Joseph's Law – the careers and activities of Mamluk descendants before the Ottoman conquest of Egypt,' 61, 67, 73, 78–80; idem, 'The Sons of Mamluks as Fief-holders in Late Medieval Egypt,' 141–68.
58. Maurice Lombard, *Golden Age of Islam*, 198; Cristina De la Puente, 'The Ethnic Origins of Female Slaves in al-Andalus,' 127–28.
59. Paul Wheatley, *The Places Where Men Pray Together*, 493.
60. Lovejoy, 'Slavery in the Sokoto Caliphate,' 201; Hall, *A History of Race in Muslim West Africa*, 214.
61. Walz, 'Black Slavery in Egypt During the Nineteenth Century,' 146.
62. See J. M. Rogers and J. Jomier, 'al-Qāhira,' in *Encyclopaedia of Islam*.
63. Toledano, *As if Silent and Absent*, 14.
64. Anthony Lee, 'Africans in the Palace: The Testimony of Taj al-Saltana Qajar from the Royal Harem in Iran,' 103.
65. Heather Sunderland, 'Slavery and the Slave Trade in South Sulawesi,' 269; Reid, 'Introduction,' 29. See also Peter Boomgaard, 'Human Capital, Slavery and Low Rates of Economic and Population Growth in Indonesia, 1600–1910,' 84.
66. David Sperling, 'The Coastal Hinterland and Interior East Africa,' 278–80.
67. Sheriff, *Slaves, Spices & Ivory in Zanzibar*, 138, 230.
68. Hend Gilli-Elewy, 'On the Provenance of Slaves in Mecca during the Time of the Prophet Muhammad,' 164–67; Noel Lenski, 'Captivity and Slavery among the Saracens in Late Antiquity (*Ca.* 250–630 CE),' 248, 259.
69. M. Robinson, 'Prosopographical Approaches to the Nasab Tradition: A Study of Marriage and Concubinage in the Tribe of Muḥammad, 500–750 CE.'
70. Sijpesteijn, *Shaping a Muslim State*, 80.
71. Aḥmad b. Yaḥyā al-Balādhurī, *Futūḥ al-buldān*, 627.
72. See Fred Donner, *Early Islamic Conquests*, 240–41; Pipes, 'Mawlas,' 148–49; Taqī al-Dīn al-Subkī, *Fatāwā*, 2:381.
73. Yaḥyā b. Ādam, *Kitāb al-Kharāj*, 92.
74. Robert Hoyland, *Seeing Islam as Others Saw It*, 98–101, 197–98, 262–63, 531.
75. Arthur Jeffery, 'Ghevond's Text of the Correspondence between ʿUmar II and Leo III,' 325–26.
76. Sijpesteijn, *Shaping a Muslim State*, 55.
77. Daniel F. Caner, *History and Hagiography from the Late Antique Sinai*, 193. Thanks to Sean Anthony for alerting me to this source. See also Michael Penn, *When Christians First Met Muslims*, 90, 115.
78. Halil İnalcık, *An Economic and Social History of the Ottoman Empire*: Volume One, 307.
79. Michael McCormick, *Origins of the European Economy*, 755.
80. David Ayalon, *L'Esclavage du Mamelouk*, 7; İnalcik, *An Economic and Social History of the Ottoman Empire*, 284. For prices of domestic slaves and slave women in medieval Cairo, see S. D. Goitein, 'Slaves and Slavegirls in the Cairo Geniza Records.'
81. McCormick, *Origins of the European Economy*, 759, 775.
82. Wright, *Trans-Saharan Slave Trade*, 169.
83. Lombard, *The Golden Age of Islam*, 196–201.
84. Jankowiak, 'What Does the Slave Trade in the Saqaliba Tell us about Early Islamic Slavery?,' 170; *Hudūd al-ʿĀlam: The Regions of the World*, 115–16, 145, 160, 161; al-Iṣṭakhrī, *Masālik*, 318.
85. Jankowiak, 'What Does the Slave Trade in the Saqaliba Tell us about Early Islamic Slavery?,' 170; Thomas S. Noonan, 'Fluctuations in Islamic Trade with Eastern Europe during the Viking Age,' 237, 239.

86. Lombard, *The Golden Age of Islam*, 196–97; al-Iṣṭakhrī, 184.
87. Sato Tsugitaka, 'Slave Traders and the Kārimī Merchants during the Mamluk Period,' 144; Ayalon, *L'Esclavage du Mamelouk*, 3.
88. David Davis, *Challenging the Boundaries of Slavery*, 17–18.
89. İnalcık, *An Economic and Social History of the Ottoman Empire*, 283–85.
90. McCormick, *Origins of the European Economy*, 763–64, 768; Davis, *Challenging the Boundaries of Slavery*, 17–18; Lombard, *Golden Age of Islam*, 201.
91. Lombard, *Golden Age of Islam*, 198; McCormick, *Origins of the European Economy*, 734 ff.; Bernard S. Bachrach, *Early Medieval Jewish Policy in Western Europe*, 72–73.
92. Abdul Sheriff, *Slaves, Spices & Ivory in Zanzibar*, 33–76; Edward A. Alpers, *The Indian Ocean in World History*, 40–68.
93. Lombard, *Golden Age of Islam*, 200–201; Lidwien Kapteijns, 'Ethiopia and the Horn of Africa,' 232.
94. Sperling, 'The Coastal Hinterland and Interior East Africa,' 280.
95. Wright, *Trans-Saharan Slave Trade*, 20, 24, 27, 160–63, 167; *Hudūd al-ʿĀlam*, 165; B. G. Martin, 'Ahmad Rasim Pasha and the Suppression of the Fazzan Slave Trade,' 51–82; al-Iṣṭakhrī, 44.
96. See Spaulding, 'Precolonial Islam in the Eastern Sudan,' 118, 125.
97. Between Timbuktu and Gao, Ibn Battuta recounts meeting a wealthy nobleman who gives him a slave boy and himself has an Arabic-speaking slave girl from Damascus; Ibn Battuta, *Ibn Battuta in Black Africa*, 54.
98. See, for example, Ibn Mujāwir, 157, 162.
99. Scott Levi, 'Hindus Beyond the Hindu Kush: Indians in the Central Asian Slave Trade,' 281–83.
100. See Jeff Eden, 'Beyond the Bazaars,' 919–55; Heather Sunderland, 'The Makassar Malays: Adaptation and Identity, *c.* 1660–1790,' 399, 403, 416; Nordin Hussin, 'Trading Networks of Malay Merchants and Traders in the Straits of Melaka from 1780 to 1830,' 63.
101. Alpers, *The Indian Ocean in World History*, 83–84.
102. Kapteijns, 'Ethiopia and the Horn of Africa,' 232.
103. David Roberts, *Sketches in Egypt and Nubia*, 62.
104. William D. Phillips, *Slavery in Medieval and Early Modern Iberia*, 56; McCormick, *Origins of the European Economy*, 764; Jan S. Hogendorn, 'The Location of the "Manufacture" of Eunuchs,' 47–49.
105. Hunwick and Powell, *African Diaspora*, 99–101; Hogendorn, ibid.; Otto Meinardus, 'The Upper Egyptian Practice of the Making of Eunuchs in the XIII and XIX Century,' 50–51.
106. Hurgronje, *Mekka*, 106–109; E. W. Lane, *Manners and Customs of the Modern Egyptians*, 186–87; De la Puente, 'The Ethnic Origins of Female Slaves in al-Andalus,' 127–28; Matthew Gordon, 'Abbasid Courtesans and the Question of Social Mobility,' 34.
107. Patterson, *Slavery and Social Death*, 58; Bernard Lewis, *Race and Slavery in the Middle East*; Bruce Hall, *A History of Race in Muslim West Africa, 1600–1960*; Jonathon Glassman, *War of Words, War of Stones: Racial Thought and Violence in Colonial Zanzibar*; Chouki El Hamel, *Black Morocco: A History of Slavery, Race, and Islam*; Eve Troutt Powell, *A Different Shade of Colonialism: Egypt, Great Britain, and the Mastery of the Sudan.*
108. These include Ethiopians, East Africans (*zanjiyyāt*) and a group of Black Africans from the Sahara (*zaghāwiyyāt*); Ibn Buṭlān, *Risāla jāmiʿa li-funūn nāfiʿa*, 373–78. For a similar breakdown, see Ismāʿīl Mufīd Istanbūlī, *Şerhu'l-Ahlâki'l-Adudiyye*, 169.

109. Miskawayh, *Tahdhīb al-akhlāq*, 416–17.
110. El Hamel, *Black Morocco*, 62 ff.
111. Shams al-Dīn al-Sakhāwī, *al-Maqāṣid al-ḥasana*, 119–20; Ismāʿīl al-ʿAjlūnī, *Kashf al-khafā*, 1:262.
112. The report first appears in al-Bayhaqī's (d. 1066) *Manāqib al-Shāfiʿī*, 2:134–135. In this version, reproduced in later works like the *Manāqib al-Shāfiʿī* by al-Rāzī, the word for prison (*al-ḥabs*) appears as 'Ethiopians' (*al-ḥabash*), which makes no sense in the meaning of the story. The *isnād* to al-Bayhaqī is: al-Sulamī – Manṣūr b. ʿAbdallāh al-Harawī – al-Maghāzilī – al-Muzanī. Al-Harawī was regarded as a liar who narrated unknown material; al-Khaṭīb, *Tārīkh Baghdād*, 13:84–85.
113. Ibn Qayyim al-Jawziyya, *al-Manār al-munīf fī al-ṣaḥīḥ wa'l-ḍaʿīf*, 101.
114. El Hamel, *Black Morocco*, 62–71; David Goldenberg, *The Curse of Ham*, 172–74, 197.
115. El Hamel, *Black Morocco*, 70–86.
116. Al-Masʿūdī, *Murūj al-dhahab*, 1:26–27, 33.
117. Ibn ʿAbbās reportedly warned Muslims not to read the books of the People of the Book, since the Quran had not been corrupted as their books had; *Ṣaḥīḥ al-Bukhārī*: *kitāb al-shahādāt, bāb lā yus'alu ahl al-shirk ʿan al-shahāda wa ghayrihā*.
118. See Walid Saleh, *In Defense of the Bible*, 1–3; Younus Mirza, 'Ishmael as Abraham's Sacrifice,' 277–98. A Hadith of the Prophet summarizes the tension: 'If the People of the Book tell you something, do not believe them and do not disbelieve them. Say "We believe in God and His messengers." So, if it was true you did not disbelieve it, and if it was false you did not believe it.' In another Hadith the Prophet says, 'Narrate from the Children of Israel without discomfort.' As al-Khaṭṭābī explains, however, this is not permission to narrate falsehoods from them but, rather, that Muslims can narrate reports from the Biblical tradition without *isnād*s to those sources, since those *isnād*s did not exist. Al-Dhahabī explains that this means Muslims can take information such as medicine but not proofs for Islamic law and theology; *Sunan* of Abū Dāwūd: *kitāb al-ʿilm, bāb riwāyat ḥadīth ahl al-kitāb, bāb al-ḥadīth ʿan Banī Isrā'īl*; al-Khaṭṭābī, *Maʿālim al-sunan*, 4:187; al-Dhahabī, *Mīzān al-iʿtidāl*, 3:470; Ibn Ḥajar, *Fatḥ*, 13:412; 8:530. Al-Dārimī (d. 868) reports a Hadith in which the Prophet warns that it would suffice for Muslims to be led astray for them to turn away from their prophet and their book to the prophets and books of others; *Sunan al-Dārimī*: introductory chapters, *bāb man lam yara kitābat al-ḥadīth*.
119. The story is reported by Wahb, while ʿAbd al-Raḥmān al-Dāwūdī (d. 1074–5) said the story is unsubstantiated and heretical; Raif Georges Khoury, *Wahb b. Munabbih*, 1:68–81; Qāḍī ʿIyāḍ, *Kitāb al-Shifā*, 363–65.
120. By Torah, Muslim scholars generally meant the wider collection of biblical scripture, law and exegesis; Jonathan Brown, *Hadith*, 292.
121. Ibn Qutayba, *al-Maʿārif*, 25-26; al-Masʿūdī, *Murūj al-dhahab*, 1:27, 33.
122. Noah curses Ham's descendants with Blackness after he saw his father bathing nude; Ibn al-Mulaqqin, *Mukhtaṣar al-Mustadrak li'l-ḥāfiẓ al-Dhahabī*, 2:999; J. Brown, *Hadith*, 110.
123. ʿAbd al-Raḥmān Ibn ʿAbd al-Ḥakam, *Futūḥ Miṣr*, 17. The *isnād* of this report is fairly reliable from a Sunni Hadith perspective.
124. Al-Khaṭīb al-Baghdādī, *al-Jāmiʿ li-akhlāq al-rāwī*, 2:114; ʿAbd al-ʿAẓīm al-Mundhirī, *Jawāb al-ḥāfiẓ al-Mundhirī ʿan as'ilat fī al-jarḥ wa'l-taʿdīl*, 73–76; al-Dhahabī, *Mīzān al-iʿtidāl*, 2:266, 3:470.
125. Al-Ṭabarī, *Tārīkh*, 1:125–26, 129.

126. Al-Ṭabarī, *Tārīkh*, 1:13. Historians like al-Ṭabarī preserved lots of varied and contradictory material, some of which they disagreed with, while still shaping what they presented into a subtle narrative; Chase Robinson, *Islamic Historiography*, 35–36, 79.
127. Ibn al-Jawzī, *Tanwīr al-ghabash fī faḍl al-sūdān wa'l-ḥabash*, 35.
128. Al-Suyūṭī, *Rafʿ sha'n al-ḥubshān*, 271–72. Al-Suyūṭī also produced an abridgement of this work that actually adds some material; idem, *Azhār al-ʿurūsh fī akhbār al-ḥubūsh*, 19.
129. Ibn Khaldūn, *Tārīkh Ibn Khaldūn*, 1:105.
130. This book is cited as *The Book of Blacks and their Virtue over Whites* (*Kitāb al-Sūdān wa faḍlihim ʿalā al-bayḍān*) by Kātib Chelebī (d. 1657), but earlier scholars like al-Khaṭīb al-Baghdādī (d. 1071) have it as *Kitāb kalaf al-sūdān* (*The Book on the Pigment [?] of the Blacks*). See Maḥmūd al-Ṭaḥḥān, *al-Ḥāfiẓ al-Khaṭīb al-Baghdādī wa atharuhu fī ʿulūm al-ḥadīth*, 296; Kātib Chelebī, *Kashf al-ẓunūn*, 3:49.
131. Ibn al-Jawzī, *Tanwīr al-ghabash*, 29. See also Aḥmad Bābā, *Miʿrāj al-Ṣuʿūd*, 30–35.
132. Ibn al-Marzubān, al-Suyūṭī and Ibn al-Jawzī each included chapters on prominent Muslims, from Abū Bakr's son to al-Farazdaq, who fell in love with Black African women or considered them more beautiful than 'whites.' Many of the stories, however, contain elements of the men being rebuked for falling for the women; al-Suyūṭī, *Rafʿ sha'n al-ḥubshān*, 366-369; Ibn al-Jawzī, *Tanwīr al-ghabash*, 233–45 (almost the entire section is taken from Ibn al-Marzubān).
133. This is the Meccan Mullā ʿAlī al-Qārī' (d. 1606), *al-Asrār al-marfūʿa fī al-aḥādith al -mawḍūʿa*, 442; idem, *Sharḥ al-Shifā'*, 4:394.
134. Kātib Chelebī, *Kashf al-ẓunūn*, 3:49.
135. Al-ʿAjlūnī, *Kashf al-khafā*, 1:388.
136. Hunwick, 'Notes on Slavery in the Songhay Empire,' 22–25.
137. Nehemiah Levtzion, 'Islam in the Bilad al-Sudan to 1800,' 76.
138. Lovejoy, 'Slavery in the Sokoto Caliphate,' 204.
139. Hill, 'Comparative West African Farm Slavery Systems,' 37–41. The British explorer Hugh Clapperton said of Sokoto *circa* 1820 that the children of slaves were never sold unless they continued to be unmanageable even after repeated punishment; Fisher and Fisher, 73.
140. See McDougall's discussion, 'Critical Reflections,' 212–13. For the crafting of descriptions as part of the Abolitionist movement, see A. Adu Boahen, *Britain, the Sahara, and the Western Sudan 1788–1861*, 100–101. Miers, who can be trusted to push back against established narratives, confirms this trade route as 'particularly ghastly'; Miers, *Britain and the Ending of the Slave Trade*, 61.
141. Hunwick and Powell, *African Diaspora*, 53–54 (cited from R. R. Madden, *Egypt and Mohammed Ali*, London, 1841).
142. Griga describes how the eunuch of the chief died fighting the raiders; Hunwick and Powell, *African Diaspora*, 55–56 (cited from F. J. G. Mercadier, *L'Eslavage de Timimoun*, Paris, 1971).
143. See Hunwick and Powell, *African Diaspora*, 67–71, 176.
144. Fisher and Fisher, *Slavery and Muslim Society in Africa*, 77.
145. Thorkild Hansen, *Arabia Felix*, 89.
146. Hunwick and Powell, *African Diaspora*, 212–14.
147. Millingen, 'On the Negro Slaves in Turkey,' xcii–xciii.
148. Hurgronje, *Mekka*, 12–13.
149. Doughty, *Travels in Arabia Deserta*, 1:605.
150. Bruce S. Hall, 'How Slaves Used Islam,' 284.
151. Hunwick and Powell, *African Diaspora*, 209.

152. For a discussion of well-known slave vocations, see Ibn Buṭlān, *Risāla jāmi'a*, 385–389.
153. Muḥammad b. Ja'far al-Kattānī, *Salwat al-anfās*, 2:23.
154. Sobers-Khan, *Slaves without Shackles*, 163.
155. E. Powell, *Tell This in My Memory*, 117, 134.
156. Edward Thomas, *Islam's Perfect Stranger*, 9–10. Thanks to Omar Anchassi for pointing me to this.
157. Hunwick and Powell, *African Diaspora*, 89.
158. Paul Lunde and Caroline Stone, trans. and ed., *Ibn Fadlān and the Land of Darkness: Arab Travellers in the Far North*, 81. The original Arabic text can be found in César E. Dubler, *Abū Ḥāmid El Granadino y su Relación de Viaje por Tierras Eurasiáticas*, 30–31.
159. Al-Balkhī, *Kitāb al-Maqālāt*, 350.
160. Shaun Marmon, 'Domestic Slavery in the Mamluk empire,' 13. See also Bruce Hall, 'How Slaves Used Islam,' 286-292. For more examples, see Goitein, 'Slaves and Slavegirls,' 15–16.
161. Mohammed Bashir Salau, 'Slavery in Kano Emirate of Sokoto Caliphate as Recounted,' 95, 100. This is testimony from a ninety-year-old former slave in Kano in 1975.
162. Ibn Battuta, *The Travels of Ibn Battuta*, 1:149.
163. Al-Dhahabī, *Siyar a'lām al-nubalā'*, 14:538.
164. Al-Dhahabī, *Siyar*, 22:170.
165. This scholar was 'Abd al-'Azīz b. Abī Rawwād (d. 775); Abū Nu'aym al-Iṣbahānī, *Ḥilyat al-awliyā'*, 8:191–92; Rūmī, *Mathnavī*, 1:1547–50.
166. Freya Stark, *The Southern Gates of Arabia*, 142–43.
167. The two visiting scholars were Ibn Ḥanbal and Ibn Ma'īn; al-Dhahabī, *Mīzān al-i'tidāl*, 1:302.
168. Jacob Lassner, *The Topography of Baghdad in the Early Middle Ages*, 178; Ibn Ḥazm, *The Ring of the Dove*, 175.
169. Ibn al-Jawzī lists all the members of the ruling Quraysh tribe whose mothers were Black African concubines, including several Abbasid caliphs; Ibn al-Jawzī, *Tanwīr al-ghabash*, 246–47.
170. Julia Bray, 'Men, women and slaves in Abbasid society,' 134.
171. Ibn al-Sā'ī, *Consorts of the Caliphs*, 141.
172. E. Powell, *Tell This in My Memory*, 125.
173. Nadia El Cheikh, 'Revisiting the Abbasid Harems,' 6, 13; Julia Bray, 'Men, women and slaves in Abbasid society,' 135–37.
174. Pernilla Myrne, 'A *Jariya*'s Prospects in Abbasid Baghdad,' 58.
175. Al-Khaṭīb al-Baghdādī, *Tārīkh Baghdād*, 10:411–12.
176. De la Puente, 'The Ethnic Origins of Female Slaves in al-Andalus,' 128–29.
177. Al-Khaṭīb al-Baghdādī, *Tārīkh Baghdād*, 10:412–13.
178. '*. . . aw 'ayb fī farj . . .*'; Yūsuf Rāġib, *Actes de vente d'esclaves et d'animaux d'Égypte médiévale*, 3–15. Ibn Mujāwir describes, with a suspicious level of cynicism, buyers examining the anuses and vaginas of slave girls in Aden; Ibn Mujāwir, 162.
179. Toledano, *As if Silent and Absent*, 86–87.
180. See Toledano, *As if Silent and Absent*, 84.
181. Ibn Taymiyya, *al-Qawā'id al-nūrāniyya*, 293; idem, *Majmū'at al-fatāwā*, 29:103–104. Thanks to Kecia Ali for checking my understanding of this passage.
182. Fisher and Fisher, *Slavery and Muslim Society in Africa*, 108–109.
183. Al-Balkhī, *Kitāb al-Maqālāt*, 521; al-Yamanī, *al-Mustafīd fī akhbār Ṣan'ā' wa Zabīd*, 158.

184. Lane, *Manners and Customs*, 186–88

185. Walz, 'Black Slavery in Egypt,' 145.

186. A scandal on the opposite coast of the Red Sea in 1141 CE suggests similar social condemnation of disposing of pregnant slave women; Goitein, 'Slaves and Slavegirls,' 4.

187. Hurgronje, *Mekka*, 108–109.

188. *aḥmaq al-nās ḥurr tazawwaja bi-ama wa a'qal al-nas 'abd tazawwaja bi-ḥurra li'anna hādhā yu'taqu ba'ḍuhu wa dhālik yuraqqu ba'duhu*; Abū Ṭālib al-Makkī, *Qūt al -qulūb*, 2:240.

189. Rapoport, 'Legal Diversity in the Age of *Taqlīd*,' 218–219.

190. *Ittakhadhū al-sarārī fa-innahunna mubārakāt al-arḥām*; al-Mawṣilī says on this issue, 'There is nothing sound from the Prophet (s) on the issue of concubines'; 'Umar b. Badr al-Mawṣilī, *al-Mughnī 'an al-ḥifẓ*, 50.

191. Al-Suyūṭī, *al-La'ālī' al-maṣnū'a*, 2:138–39.

192. *Man ittakhadha min al-khadam ghayr mā yankiḥu thumma baghīna fa-'alayhi mithla āthāmihinna min ghayr an yanquṣa min āthāmihinna shay'*; al-Suyūṭī, *Raf' sha'n al -ḥubshān*, 384.

193. Bray, 'Men, women and slaves in Abbasid society,' 138; Elizabeth Sartain, *Jalāl al-Dīn al-Suyūṭī*, 1:23.

194. Kristina Richardson, 'Singing Slave Girls (*Qiyan*) in the 'Abbasid Court in the Ninth and Tenth Centuries,' 114.

195. See Pernilla Myrne, 'A *Jariya*'s Prospects in Abbasid Baghdad.'

196. Ibn al-Jawzī, *Muntaẓam*, 12:321–22; Nadia El Cheikh, 'Revisiting the Abbasid Harems,' 10; Bray, 144.

197. Al-Iṣbahānī, *Ḥilyat al-awliyā'*, 10:171.

198. See Appendix 1 – A Slave Saint of Basra.

199. Aḥmad al-Ghumārī, *al-Burhān al-jalī fī intisāb al-ṣūfiyya ilā 'Alī*, 63. In the case of the Ottomans and Mughals, the dynasties gradually inserted themselves into this mystical schema as well, with the sultans becoming the *quṭb*; Hüseyin Yılmaz, *Caliphate Redefined*, 146–49; Azfar Moin, *The Millennial Sovereign*, 184, 198.

200. The full version includes a second clause: 'Only a hypocrite would hate the *mawālī*.' Al-Dhahabī considered the Hadith insufficiently attested (*munkar*). See al-Dhahabī, *Mīzān al-i'tidāl*, 2:47; Ibn Ḥajar, *Lisān al-mīzān*, 2:457; al-Haytamī, *al-Fatāwā al-ḥadīthiyya*, 425.

201. 'Umar responded to the slave's refusal to convert by recalling the Quranic verse 'There is no compulsion in religion' and freed the slave on his death; Abū 'Ubayd al-Qāsim b. Sallām, *Kitāb al-Amwāl*, 43.

202. Ayalon, 'Preliminary Remarks on the *Mamlūk* Military Institution in Islam,' 50.

203. El Cheikh, 'The Qahramâna in the Abbasid Court,' 43.

204. Salah Trabelsi, 'Eunuchs, Power, and Slavery in the Early Islamic World,' 541–57.

205. El Cheikh, 44, 53; idem, 'Revisiting the Abbasid Harems,' 12; Ibn al-Jawzī, *Muntaẓam*, 13:180–81.

206. Ibn al-Jawzī, *Muntaẓam*, 13:322–29.

207. Sussan Babaie et al., *Slaves of the Shah*, 6–9.

208. Richard Eaton, 'Malik 'Ambar,' *Encyclopaedia of Islam*.

209. Mushirul Hasan, ed., *Seamless Boundaries: Luftullah's Narrative beyond East and West*, 185.

210. Levtzion, 'Islam in the Bilad al-Sudan,' 84; Lovejoy, 'Slavery in the Sokoto Caliphate,' 205.

211. Jeremy Jones and Nicholas Ridout, *A History of Modern Oman*, 57.

212. Paul Wittek, '*Devshirme* and *Sharīʿa*,' 274–77; Gelibolulu Muṣṭafā ʿĀlī (d. 1600), *Siyaset Sanatı: Nushatü's Selâtîn*, 392.
213. Erdem, *Slavery in the Ottoman Empire and its Demise*, 2–4.
214. Orlin Sabev, 'Enderun Mektebi,' *Encyclopaedia of Islam*, 3rd edn.
215. Muhammet Zahit Atçıl, 'State and Government in the Mid Sixteenth-Century Ottoman Empire: the Grand Vizierates of Rüstem Pasha (1544–1561),' 17–18, 28.
216. Gulay Yilmaz, 'Becoming a Devşirme: The Training of Conscripted Children in the Ottoman Empire,' 119–34; Gabor Agoston, 'Devşirme,' *Encyclopedia of the Ottoman Empire,* ed. Gabor Agoston and Bruce Masters.
217. Ayalon, 'Preliminary Remarks,' 44; Robert Irwin, *The Middle East in the Middle Ages,* 7. In the 1400s–1500s the Dutchy of Muscovy also had military slaves; Richard Hellie, 'Russian Slavery and Serfdom,' 281.
218. Patricia Crone, *Slaves on Horses: The Evolution of the Islamic Polity*.
219. Ayalon, 'Preliminary Remarks,' 44.
220. Irwin, *The Middle East in the Middle Ages*, 10.
221. Ayalon, 'Preliminary Remarks,' 46; Crone, *Slaves on Horses*, 75.
222. Hugh Kennedy, *The Armies of the Caliphs*, 117, 121, 134.
223. Kennedy, *The Armies of the Caliphs*, 115, 134.
224. Matthew S. Gordon, *The Breaking of a Thousand Swords*, 1–8.
225. Jere L. Bacharach, 'African Military Slaves in the Medieval Middle East: The Cases of Iraq (869–955) and Egypt (868–1171),' 477, 482.
226. Reuven Amitai, 'Continuity and Change in the Mongol Army of the Ilkhanate,' 47.
227. Deborah Tor, 'The Political Revival of the Abbasid Caliphate: Al-Muqtafī and the Seljuqs,' 301–14.
228. Linda S. Northrup, 'The Baḥrī Mamlūk sultanate,' 242–89; Jean-Claude Garcin, 'The regime of the Circassian Mamlūks,' 290–317.
229. This relationship to one's master even after manumission was present in Abbasid slave soldiery as well. See Roy Mottahedeh, *Loyalty and Leadership in an Early Islamic Society*, 84.
230. Ayalon, *L'Esclavage du Mamelouk*, 4, 10–12, 18–19, 21 21; Koby Yosef, 'The Term *Mamlūk* and Slave Status during the Mamluk Sultanate,' 28.
231. Yosef, 'The Term *Mamlūk* and Slave Status,' 14–21. Thanks to Rumee Ahmed for this citation. For the continued prevalence of slave origins for the continued Mamluk system under Ottoman rule, see Gabriel Piterberg, 'The Formation of an Ottoman Egyptian Elite in the Eighteenth Century,' 275–89.
232. Khalīl b. Aybak al-Ṣafadī, *al-Wāfī bi'l-wafāyāt*, 18:319; cf. Tāj al-Dīn al-Subkī, *Ṭababāt*, 8:206–207.
233. Peter Jackson, 'The *Mamlūk* Institution in Early Muslim India,' 341–45, 355; idem, 'Ḳuṭb al-Dīn Aybak,' *Encyclopaedia of Islam*; Ibn Battuta, *The Travels of Ibn Battuta*, 3:630.
234. Richard Eaton, 'The Rise and Fall of Military Slavery in the Deccan,' 122, 128.
235. Abū al-Qāsim al-Zayyān, *al-Bustān al-ẓarīf fī dawlat awlād mawlāya al-sharīf*, 1:171; Maurice Delafosse, 'Les débuts des troupes noires du Maroc,' *Hespéris* 3 (1923): 7–8; Aḥmad al-Nāṣirī al-Salāwī, *Kitāb al-Istiqṣā li-akhbār duwal al-maghrib al-aqṣā*, 7:58.
236. Hunwick, 'Notes on Slavery in the Songhay Empire,' 23–25.
237. Alexei Vassiliev, *The History of Saudi Arabia*, 307–308.
238. Freya Stark, *Southern Gates of Arabia*, 158, 204–205.
239. James Searing, *'God Alone is King': Islam and Emancipation in Senegal*, 147.

240. Toledano, *As if Silent and Absent*, 74, 79.
241. Alexandre Popovic, *The Revolt of African Slaves in Iraq*, 150; al-Ṭabarī, *Tārīkh*, 5:444; *Ṣaḥīḥ Muslim: kitāb al-aymān, bāb iṭʿām al-mamlūk mimmā ya'kulu . . .*; *Ṣaḥīḥ Bukhārī: kitāb al-aymān, bāb al-maʿāṣī min amr al-Jāhiliyya.*
242. Popovic, *The Revolt of African Slaves in Iraq*, 130–31, 133–34, 140–41.
243. Lovejoy, 'Slavery in Sokoto Caliphate,' 230.
244. Ira Lapidus, *Muslim Cities in the Later Middle Ages*, 95, 171–72.

CHAPTER 4 THE SLAVERY CONUNDRUM

1. ʿAbd al-Bārī ʿAṭwān, "Tijārat al-ʿabīd fī Lībyā . . .," Ra'y al-Yawm, 11/20/2017, https://www.raialyoum.com/index.php/%d8%aa%d8%ac%d8%a7%d8%b1%d8%a9-%d8%a7%d9%84%d8%b9%d8%a8%d9%8a%d8%af-%d9%81%d9%8a-%d9%84%d9%8a%d8%a8%d9%8a%d8%a7-%d8%a2%d8%ae%d8%b1-%d9%85%d8%a7-%d8%aa%d9%88%d9%82%d8%b9%d9%86%d8%a7%d9%87-%d9%81/
2. 'Lexington: Roy Moore: kickboxer, sacked judge, US Senator?,' *The Economist*, Sept. 21, 2017.
3. Lynn Vavreck, 'Measuring Donald Trump's Supporters for Intolerance,' *New York Times*, Feb. 23, 2016, https://www.nytimes.com/2016/02/25/upshot/measuring-donald-trumps-supporters-for-intolerance.html?smid=tw-share; https://d25d2506sfb94s.cloudfront.net/cumulus_uploads/document/ctucuikdsj/econToplines.pdf
4. *Tucker Carlson Tonight*, Fox News, Aug. 15, 2017, https://video.foxnews.com/v/5542205277001/?#sp=show-clips. A transcript is available at 'Tucker Carlson attempts to defend America's history by pointing out the Aztecs, Africans and Mohammed had slaves too,' *Media Matters*, Aug. 15, 2017, https://www.mediamatters.org/video/2017/08/15/tucker-carlson-attempts-defend-americas-history-slavery-pointing-out-aztecs-africans-and-mohammed/217649.
5. https://www.youtube.com/watch?v=Urk5u2kpJOI (last accessed Sept. 2017).
6. Alex Tizon, 'My Family's Slave,' *The Atlantic*, June 2017, https://www.theatlantic.com/magazine/archive/2017/06/lolas-story/524490/.
7. Therese Reyes, 'Filipinos are defending Alex Tizon from Western backlash to his story "My Family's Slave,"' Quartz, May 17, 2017, https://qz.com/985614/the-atlantics-my-familys-slave-cover-story-filipinos-defend-alex-tizon-from-western-backlash/.
8. M. Evelina Galang, 'What the Conversation around Alex Tizon's Atlantic Essay is Missing,' Slate.com, May 21, 2017, http://www.slate.com/blogs/browbeat/2017/05/21/alex_tizon_s_essay_is_particularly_painful_and_valuable_for_those_of_us.html.
9. Josh Shahryar, Twitter post, 5/16/2017, 10:35am, https://twitter.com/JShahryar/status/864534668284055553
10. Jesse Singal, 'It is Really Important to Humanize Evil,' NYMag.com, May 19, 2017, https://www.thecut.com/2017/05/it-is-really-important-to-humanize-evil.html
11. See, for example, 'Britain's Got Talent 2017: Simon Cowell SHOCKED by comedian Daliso Chaponda slave joke,' *Daily Express*, June 3, 2017, https://www.express.co.uk/showbiz/tv-radio/812507/Britains-Got-Talent-2017-Simon-Cowell-Daliso-Chaponda-slave-auction-joke-ITV; https://www.buzzfeed.com/justincarissimo/comedian-leslie-jones-criticized-over-saturday-night-live-sl?utm_term=.aoZd-8zLqL#.cd5dkKX2X.

12. Elyse Wanshel, 'School Apologizes for Asking Students to List "Positive Aspects" of Slavery,' Huffington Post, April 20, 2018, https://www.huffingtonpost.com/entry/school-texas-pros-cons-slavery-assignment_us_5ada30a5e4b01c279db434ca?ncid=engmodushpmg00000003.

13. This final speech seems to have been given artistic license by the writers, though in the published version of his arguments Adams does point to copies of the Declaration of Independence in asking, rhetorically, if it acknowledges the right to enslave captives. And he finishes his argument before the Court with a paean to the great and courageous Americans whom he, in his old age, recalls as having passed before him. See *Argument of John Quincy Adams, before the Supreme Court of the United States, in the case of the United States, appellants, vs. Cinque, and others . . .*, 88, 134–35.

14. Moses Frenck, 'Slavery wasn't really that bad for some slaves, says Fox News' O'Reilly,' DiversityInc.com, July 28, 2016, http://www.diversityinc.com/news/slavery-wasnt-really-bad-slaves-says-fox-news-oreilly/.

15. Bill Maher, Twitter post, June 1, 2015, 2:06pm, https://twitter.com/billmaher/status/616352233886584832?lang=en.

16. *Real Time with Bill Maher*, 'Episode 434,' HBO, 8/18/2017, opening monologue.

17. Matthew Yglesias, 'The huge problem with Trump comparing Robert E. Lee to George Washington,' Vox.com, Aug. 17, 2017, https://www.vox.com/policy-and-politics/2017/8/16/16154738/lee-davis-washington-jefferson.

18. 'After Charlottesville: Donald Trump's failure of character emboldens America's far right,' *The Economist*, Aug. 19, 2017.

19. http://gameofthrones.wikia.com/wiki/Slavery

20. Amina Wadud, *Inside the Gender Jihad*, 123–24.

21. *Musnad Ibn Ḥanbal*, 5:411.

22. David B. Davis, *The Problem of Slavery in the Age of Revolution*, 549.

23. Molly Oshatz, 'The Problem of Moral Progress: The Slavery Debates and the Development of Liberal Protestantism in the United States,' 234–35.

24. *Rubb kadhib mubāḥ li-maṣlaḥa*; Abū Ḥāmid al-Ghazālī, *The Fatāwā of al-Ghazzālī*, 79.

25. *Sherlock*, 'The Final Problem,' BBC Television, Jan. 15, 2018.

26. *Battlestar Galactica*, 'A Measure of Salvation,' Scifi Network, Nov. 10, 2006.

27. Augustine, 'Lying (*De Mendacio*),' 67–70.

28. Abū Ḥāmid al-Ghazālī, *Miʿyār al-ʿilm*, 122–23; Alan Watson, trans., 'Book One', in *The Digest of Justinian*, Volume 1, 1–39 (Philadelphia: University of Pennsylvania Press, 1998), 2–3; Anver Emon, *Islamic Natural Law Theory*, 114.

29. 'Fair and Square,' *The Economist*, Sept. 18, 2003.

30. Al-Balkhī, *Kitāb al-Maqālāt*, 343.

31. Karl Jaspers, *Kant*, 65–66.

32. Kant's approval of slavery comes from the same period in which he was formulating his Categorical Imperative; Pauline Kleingeld, 'Kant's Second Thoughts on Race,' 574, 577.

33. David Forman, 'Kant on Moral Freedom and Moral Slavery,' 1–32.

34. Alasdair MacIntyre, *Ethics in the Conflicts of Modernity: An Essay on Desire, Practical Reasoning, and Narrative*, 85–86.

35. Plato, *Crito*, 50a–b9. See also Alfonso Gómez-Lobo, *The Foundations of Socratic Ethics*, 58–59.

36. The first is the moral objectivism of the Muʿtazila, the second is the divine command of the Ashʿarī school of theology. See Sherman Jackson, *Islam and the Problem of Black Suffering*, 47–98.

37. See Aristotle, *Politics*, 1.1253b.
38. Cicero was a follower of the Academic school, but he was both highly influenced by Stoicism and an influential articulator of its views; Cicero, '*On Duties III*,' 163.
39. David Davis, *The Problem of Slavery in Western Culture*, 77–81. A. T. Raymer, 'Slavery – The Graeco-Roman Defense,' 17–21.
40. See Duncan Kelly, *The Propriety of Liberty*, 48–49.
41. Jean-Jacques Rousseau, *The Social Contract*, Book 1, chapters 2–4.
42. Naomi Zack, *The Ethics and Mores of Race*, 84.
43. The notion that the slave was property/chattel was a foundational feature of slavery in the Ancient Near East; Isaac Mendelsohn, *Slavery in the Ancient Near East*, 34. For the early modern and modern periods, see Kevin Bales, *Understanding Global Slavery*, 46.
44. Aristotle, *Politics*, 1.1253b–1255b; Christopher Shields, *Aristotle*, 369–71.
45. Jonathan A. Silk, 'Slavery,' in *The Encyclopedia of Buddhism*, ed. Robert E. Buswell (New York: Thomson Gale, 2004), 2:780–81.
46. See Howard Temperley, 'The Delegalization of Slavery in India,' 169–71; Indrani Chatterjee, *Gender, Slavery, and Law in Colonial India*, 5–6; Dharma Kumar, 'Colonialism, Bondage, and Caste in British India,' 113–14.
47. U. N. Ghoshal, 'On a Recent Estimate of the Social and Political System of the Maurya Empire,' 68; idem, *Studies in Indian History and Culture*, 327.
48. Mendelsohn, *Slavery in the Ancient Near East*, 123.
49. See also Exodus 21; Leviticus 25:42–49; Deuteronomy 15; 20:11–14. See also 1 Samuel 8:10–18, 1 Kings 10:2–5; Proverbs 12:9, 22:7; 29:19–21.
50. David Novak, 'Natural Law and Judaism,' 30–34. See *Tosefta*: Avodah Zarah 8.4; B. Sanhedrin 56a.
51. Novak, *In Defense of Religious Liberty*, 63.
52. Matthew 18:21–35.
53. See Luke 17:7–10, Titus 2:9, Ephesians 6:5, and 1 Timothy 6:1. See also 1 Corinthians 7:20–24, Ephesians 6:5–9; Andrew Wilson, 'The Best Argument for Trajectory Hermeneutic – and Where it Goes Wrong,' March 6, 2013, http://thinktheology.co.uk/blog/article/the_best_argument_for_a_trajectory_hermeneutic_and_where_it_goes_wrong, accessed 5/5/2018. It has been suggested that Paul urged obedience to the slave system because this was part of the 'petty affairs of a dying world,' to quote Jennifer Glancy, and that he was sure the Kingdom of God was close at hand; see Jennifer A. Glancy, *Slavery as Moral Problem in the Early Church and Today*, 46.
54. Pierre Bonnassie, *From Slavery to Feudalism in South-Western Europe*, 26; Augustine, *City of God*, 19:xv; Westermann, *The Slave Systems of Greek and Roman Antiquity*, 156.
55. Bonnassie, *From Slavery to Feudalism in South-Western Europe*, 28.
56. Joel S. Panzer, *The Popes and Slavery*, 34–37; Avery Dulles, 'Review of John Noonan, Jr., *A Church That Can and Cannot Change: The Development of Catholic Moral Teaching*,' *First Things*, October 2005. John Noonan, Jr. certainly disagrees with Dulles; see Noonan's seminal essay 'Development in Moral Doctrine,' 664–67. As does Ronald R. Conte, Jr. See Conte, 'Intrinsic Evil: Slavery and the Death Penalty,' at https://ronconte.wordpress.com/2010/12/30/intrinsic-evil-slavery-and-the-death-penalty/ 12/30/2010.
57. Henry Heller, 'Bodin on Slavery and Primitive Accumulation,' 55.
58. David Davis, *Slavery and Human Progress*, 107–108.
59. Muḥammad Ibn Jarīr al-Ṭabarī, *Tārīkh al-Ṭabarī*, 2:216–18.
60. The early Hadith transmitter Maʿmar b. Muthannā reported that the Prophet had four concubines; al-Ḥākim al-Naysābūrī, *al-Mustadrak*, 4:41; Ibn Kathīr, *al-Bidāya wa'l-nihāya*, 5:303–304.

61. Ibn Kathīr, *al-Bidāya wa'l-nihāya*, 5:303–304; *Sunan Ibn Mājah*: *kitāb al-ʿitq, bāb ummahāt al-awlād*.
62. David B. Davis warns that 'we must avoid the retrospective indignation that can only serve to congratulate the present world while obscuring our understanding of the past.'; Davis, *Slavery and Human Progress*, 122. R. Stephen Humphreys writes that 'It is natural but misleading to identify one moment as normative and to judge all other periods against that one.'; R. Stephen Humphreys, 'Egypt in the World System of the Later Middle Ages,' 445.
63. For example, on the issue of physical violence in disciplining children, see Glancy, *Slavery as Moral Problem*, 57, 84; Zilfi, *Women and Slavery in the Late Ottoman Empire*, 116; T. R. Hobbs, *A Time for War: A Study of Warfare in the Old Testament*, 17, 211 (on explaining how the Old Testament could order the slaughter of babies in Joshua 6:21).
64. Buck v. Bell, 274 U.S. 200 (1927).
65. Edward Gibbon, *The History of the Decline and Fall of the Roman Empire*, Chapter 2, Part 2; Chapter 53, Part 2, n. 38. This French scholar was Francois Guizot, who translated the work into French.
66. Shields, *Aristotle*, 369; Alasdair MacIntyre, *After Virtue*, 162. In the case of Plato, one scholar even suggested that Plato disapproved of slavery despite his extensive writing on and endorsement of the institution; Glenn R. Morrow, *Plato's Law of Slavery*, 130–131.
67. Malcolm Heath, 'Aristotle on Natural Slavery,' 243–44. A more historicized view comes from P. A. Brunt, who observes that 'Aristotle's defence of slavery is a defence of the exploitation of other men's labour; the circumstances in which he lived and wrote determined that it should be a defense of slavery'; P. A. Brunt, *Studies in Greek History and Thought*, 345. For similar expressions, see Zilfi, *Women and Slavery in the Late Ottoman Empire*, 97; Glancy, *Slavery as Moral Problem*, 8.
68. Yusuf Fadl Hasan, 'Historical Roots of Afro-Arab Relations,' 33; John Hunwick and Eve Troutt Powell, *The African Diaspora in the Mediterranean Lands of Islam*, x.
69. Vicente L. Rafael, '"My Family's Slave"- A UW professor weighs in,' Crosscut, May 17, 2017, http://crosscut.com/2017/05/my-familys-slave-can-alex-tizon-be-forgiven-for-his-sins/.
70. See https://yaqeeninstitute.org/en/jonathan-brown/the-problem-of-slavery/; Nathaniel Mathews, 'Slavery, Abolition and the Moral Horizon of the Prophet Muhammad: A Response to Jonathan Brown.'
71. For a useful commentary on this, see Peter Kolchin, 'Review Essay: Putting New World Slavery in Perspective,' 279.
72. See, for example, John Richter Jones, *Slavery Sanctioned by the Bible*, 8 ('The term slavery is as vaguely used as any word in our language').
73. This wording comes from Thomas Cobb (d. 1862), a defender of slavery in the antebellum South; Cairns, 'The Definition of Slavery in Eighteenth-Century Thinking,' 65; Chatterjee, 'Abolition by Denial: The South Asian Example,' 151.
74. Richard Roberts and Suzanne Miers, 'The End of Slavery in Africa,' in *The End of Slavery in Africa*, 12–13, 48; Banaji, *Slavery in British India*, 15–20. Andrea Major shows how the British East India Company helped create the image of slavery in India as complex, relatively benign and incomparable to slavery in the Americas in order to deflect abolitionist attention; Major, *Slavery, Abolitionism and Empire in India, 1772–1843*.
75. Toledano, *Slavery and Abolition in the Ottoman Middle East*, 113.

76. *Et libertas quidem est, ex qua etiam liberi vocantur, naturalis facultas eius quod cuique facere libet, nisi si quid aut vi aut iure prohibetur. Servitus autem est constitutio iuris gentium, qua quis dominio alieno contra naturam subicitur*; *Institutes*, Book I, Title III. On the nature of natural law and the law of nations, the *Institutes* adds, 'For wars have arisen, and captivity and slavery, which are contrary to natural law, have followed as a result, as, according to Natural Law, all men were originally born free; and from this law nearly all contracts, such as purchase, sale, hire, partnership, deposit, loan, and innumerable others have been derived.' http://www.constitution.org/sps/sps02_j1-1.htm Book I, Title II. Pope Gregory the Great (d. 604) used similar language as he arranged for both the manumission and purchase of slaves; Kyle Harper, *Slavery in the Late Roman World,* 497–98. See also Hugo Grotius, *De Iure Belli ac Pacis*, I.3.8 and also III.7.1; Gustaaf van Nifterik, 'Hugo Grotius on 'Slavery',' 233–44.

77. David Graeber, *Debt: The First 5,000 Years*, 204.

78. See Alan Watson, trans., 'Book One,' in *The Digest of Justinian*, 2–3. This was pointed out by the Dutch jurist Ulric Huber (d. 1694); Cairns, 62.

79. As Irene Schneider writes, 'The Roman jurists, too, did not develop a systematic [sic] of natural law *(ius naturale)* but used the term *ius naturale* in different contexts with different meanings. As a consequence, the institution of slavery on the one hand and the status of freedom of every man on the other hand were both seen [sic] founded in the *ius naturale.*' Schneider sees this as a useful comparison to the internal tensions in the Islamic tradition; Irene Schneider, 'Freedom and Slavery in Early Islamic Time [sic] (1st/7th– 2nd /8th Centuries),' 380-81; Stefan Knoch, *Sklavenfürsorge im Römischen Reich*, 35.

80. Robert M. Cover, *Justice Accused*, 10. See also Hugo Grotius, *De Iure Belli ac Pacis*, I.3.8 and also III.7.1.

81. Crossley, 'Slavery in Early Modern China,' 191.

82. See Scharfeld v. Richardson, 133 F.2d 340, 341 (DC Cir. 1942) ('It is an established principle of the common law that a dog is personal property . . .').

83. For example, Colorado, Hawaii, Mississippi, New Jersey, North Carolina, Ohio, South Dakota, Virginia.

84. For example, Delaware, DC, Florida, Maryland, Massachusetts, New Mexico, Oregon, Rhode Island, South Carolina.

85. Georgia, Minnesota, Nevada, North Dakota.

86. California, Louisiana, Pennsylvania, Oklahoma.

87. Alaska, Washington.

88. Alabama, Arizona, Arkansas, Indiana, Maine, Texas.

89. Delaware, Utah, Vermont.

90. Margaret C. Jasper, *Animal Rights Law*, 61–122, in particular, 67, 76–77, 88, 118. See Revised Code of Washington state, §16.52.207, available at https://app.leg.wa.gov/rcw/default.aspx?cite=16.52.207; Main Revised Statutes §4011, available at http://legislature.maine.gov/statutes/7/title7sec4011.html.

91. The Daily Heartbeat, 'Humans Reunited with Dogs,' Feb. 23, 2018, https://www.facebook.com/TheDailyHeartbeat/videos/359755377834933/

92. *Seinfeld*, 'The Dog,' NBC, 10/9/1991.

93. Gary L. Francione, 'The Abolition of Animal Exploitation,' 22, 83. See also https://www.prnewswire.com/news-releases/animal-rights-is-about-abolition-not-animal-cruelty-says-responsible-pet-owners-alliance-of-texas-300107739.html.

94. Paul Lovejoy, 'Slavery in the context of ideology,' 11–15. See also James L. Watson, 'Introduction: Slavery as an Institution: Open and Closed Systems,' in *Asian & African Systems of Slavery*, ed. James Watson, 3–5.

95. Ruth Karras, *Slavery and Society in Medieval Scandinavia*, 156–66. There were also so many levels of formal and substantive dependence/subordination in the Malay world from the 1400s through the early 1900s that one single distinction between slave and free is hard to identify, let alone endow with more meaning than any number of other distinctions. See V. Matheson and M. B. Hooker, 'Slavery in the Malay Texts,' 182–208. Gwyn Campbell speaks of 'webs of dependence' as being more definitive of slavery in the Indian Ocean world than the free-slave distinction. See Gwyn Campbell, 'Introduction: Slavery and Other Forms of Unfree Labour in the Indian Ocean World,' in *The Structure of Slavery in Indian Africa and* Asia, ed. Gwyn Campbell, vii–xxxii. See also Kopytoff and Miers, 'African "Slavery" as an Institution of Marginality,' 20.
96. Burke, *Reflections on the Revolution in France*, 58, 68, 89, 103.
97. Lorenne M. G. Clark, 'Women and John Locke; Or, Who Owns the Apples in the Garden of Eden?,' 702–703.
98. P. A. Brunt, *Studies in Greek History and Thought*, 344–45.
99. See Hanna Arendt, *On Revolut*ion, 21–23, 34.
100. http://www.iabolish.org/index.php?option=com_content&view=article&id=181:guarding-americas-first-right-freedom-from-bondage&catid=5:essays-on-slavery&Itemid=8
101. Joan Lockwood O'Donovan, 'The Theological Economics of Medieval Usury Theory,' 108.
102. Finley, 'Slavery,' 14:308.
103. Tanya Cariina Newbury-Smith, personal communication, March 2017. For a study on similar encounters, see Rima Sabban, 'Encountering Domestic Slavery: A Narrative from the Arabian Gulf,' 125–53.
104. Ogier De Busbecq, *Turkish Letters*, 69–70; George Keith, 'An Exhortation & Caution to Friends concerning Buying or Keeping of Negroes,' 269–70 (Christian slavery in the Americas gave terrible image in the Muslim world); Charles White, 2:297 ff.; Mirza Abu Taleb, 25 (This Indian Muslim from Lucknow describes the Dutch he encountered in Cape Town in 1799 as 'more oppressive to their slaves than any other people in the world.'); Thomas R. R. Cobb, *An Inquiry into the Law of Negro Slavery*, cxviii (a Georgian, Cobb wrote in 1858 that Ottoman slave owners were considered by European visitors to be much less cruel than Europeans and that *mukātaba* was routine; I thank Michael Muhammad Knight for this citation); Fisher, *Slavery and Muslim Society in Africa*, 83–85 (Gustav Nachtigal observed that, from Algeria to Zanzibar in the 1870s, 'Everywhere . . . Islam brings with it a mild administration of the institution of slavery.'); Gustave le Bon, *La Civilisation des Arabes*, 394–99 ('The condition of slaves in the Orient is effectively preferable to that of domestic servants in Europe.' [my translation]); Alex Burnes (d. 1841), *Travels into Bokhara*, 1:342–43 (Persian slaves among the Uzbeks are not beaten but are clothed and treated as part of the family); Jules Gervais-Courtellemont, *Mon Voyage à la Mecque*, 122–23 (visit to Mecca in 1894); Joseph Thomson, *To the Central African Lakes and Back*, I:17 (slaves in Zanzibar in 1878 'have ten times more real liberty than thousands of our clerks and shop-girls' but noting how conditions had been worse before); Hurgronje, *Mekka in the Latter Part of the Nineteenth Century*, 21–22 ('Taken as a whole the position of the Moslim slaves is only formally different from that of European servants or workmen.'); W. H. Macnaghten, *Principles and Precedents of Moohummudan Law*, xxxix ('In India . . . between a slave and a free-servant there is no distinction but in the name,' with the former not required to maintain himself); Hunwick and Powell, *The African Diaspora in the Mediterranean Lands of Islam*, 170 (Gordon Laing, a British explorer in

North Africa in the 1820s, notes that slaves in a Saharan town are 'treated with so much kindness and have so many privileges that the remark "that slavery is but a name" might almost apply here'); Harrison, *France and Islam in West Africa*, 202 (the French imperial explorer Louis-Gustave Binger 'doubted that the unemployed of metropolitan France were as well treated as the house slaves of African Muslims'); Wilfred Thesiger, *Arabian Sands*, 63–64 (Bedouin 'treat a slave, however black, as one of themselves' and honour them); Freya Stark, *Southern Gates of Arabia*, 34 ('they enter a household and become part of it'); Westermarck, *The Origin and Development of the Moral Ideas*, 1:687; S. D. Goitein, *Jews and Arabs*, 28–29; Vogt, *Ancient Slavery and the Ideal of Man*, 194; Howard Temperley, 'The Delegalization of Slavery in British India,' 174–75; Suzanne Miers, 'Slavery and the slave trade in Saudi Arabia and the Arab states on the Persian Gulf, 1921–63,' 121; Anthony Reid, 'Introduction: Slavery and Bondage in Southeast Asian History,' 15; John Wright, *The Trans-Saharan Slave Trade*, 1. For a contrasting view, see Thomas Thornton, *The Present State of Turkey*, 368–78; Emmeline Lott, *The English Governess in Egypt: Harem Life in Egypt and Constantinople*, 124, 128–29, 148. For competing narratives from two British consuls in two Moroccan cities, see Miers, *Britain and the Ending of the Slave Trade*, 66–67. Doughty's description of slaves in the Hejaz in the late nineteenth century is more nuanced, taking into account variations in treatment; C. M. Doughty, *Travels in Arabia Deserta*, 1:604–605.

105. Some scholars of US slavery have argued that Black churches sometimes accepted and helped promulgate pro-slavery understandings of Christianity (perhaps they had little choice but to). See Charles Irons, *The Origins of Proslavery Christianity*.

106. For an excellent discussion of adaptive preference, see https://plato.stanford.edu/entries/feminism-autonomy/#FemHarCas.

107. See Saidiya Hartman, *Scenes of Subjection: Terror, Slavery and Self-Making in Nineteenth-Century America*.

108. Bonnassie, *From Slavery to Feudalism*, 3, 28, 54. In 626–7 the Council of Clichy banned the sale of Christians to Jews or pagans. In the second half of the eleventh century the Bishop of Worcester issued a condemnation of English slave traders selling English slaves to Ireland from Bristol; Michael McCormick, *Origins of the European Economy*, 740, 748; Rosalind and Christopher Brooke, *Popular Religion in the Middle Ages*, 106.

109. As Mendelsohn discusses, slavery in the ancient Near East seems to have begun with foreign captives. But eventually most slaves were members of the in-group who had fallen into slavery due to debt or poverty; Mendelsohn, *Slavery in the Ancient Near East*, 1, 23–5.

110. Petronius, *Satyricon*, 81 (at 71,1).

111. Graeber, *Debt*, 202; Mendelsohn, *Slavery in the Ancient Near East*, 42.

112. That slavery was an effect of unbelief that persisted even after someone converted to Islam seems not to have been contested by Shāfiʿī/Ashʿarī scholars or Ḥanafīs in the mid-1000s CE, as demonstrated in a debate between Abū Isḥāq al-Shīrāzī (d. 1083) and Abū ʿAbdallāh al-Dāmaghānī (d. 1085) in Baghdad; Tāj al-Dīn al-Subkī, *al-Ṭabaqāt al-shāfiʿiyya al-kubrā*, 4:237–45.

113. The scholar in question is the Ḥanafī scholar al-Bābartī (d. 1314), *al-ʿInāya sharḥ al-Hidāya*, 4:458; al-Marghīnānī, *al-Hidāya*, 3:431.

114. See Mona Siddiqui, *The Good Muslim*, 48.

115. *Musnad* of Ibn Ḥanbal, 4:198–99, 4:204; al-Munāwī, *Fayḍ al-qadīr*, 5:2547.

116. See Abū Ḥāmid al-Ghazālī, *On the Boundaries of Theological Tolerance in Islam*,

126. These people were known as the *Ahl al-Fatra,* roughly translatable as 'People of Times of Vitiated Prophecy,' the term based on the wording of Quran 5:19 and the principle laid out in Quran 17:15, namely that 'No bearer of burdens will bear the burden of another, and We would not punish [a people] until We had sent a messenger.' That those who died in a time of weakened prophecy will be judged independently on the Day of Judgment is also affirmed in a Hadith referring to the *Ahl al-Fatra,* which is found in the *Ṣaḥīḥ* of Ibn Ḥibbān and other, less rigorous collections. Al-Suyūṭī considered its various narrations to be *ḥasan,* and al-Albānī ranked it as *ṣaḥīḥ;* Al-Suyūṭī, *al-Ḥāwī li'l-fatāwī,* 2:404; al-Albānī, *Silsilat al-aḥādīth al-ṣaḥīḥa,* #1434, #2468.

117. ʿAbd al-ʿAzīz al-Bukhārī, *Kashf al-asrār,* 4:395. For this legal ruling, see Yaḥyā b. Ādam, *Kitāb al-Kharāj,* 65.

118. See also Hugo Grotius, *De Iure Belli ac Pacis,* I.3.8 and also III.7.1.

119. ʿAbd al-ʿAzīz al-Bukhārī, *Kashf al-asrār,* 4:399. In a discussion between al-Shāfiʿī and Muḥammad b. Ḥasan al-Shaybānī (both his teacher and a founding figure in the rival Ḥanafī school), the two scholars debated what should be done if one party misappropriates (*ghaṣb*) some material (like a plank), then uses it in some construction (like a building), and then this is discovered. Al-Shaybānī's response is that the misappropriating party can choose between returning the material (thus damaging or destroying their building) or compensating the wronged party for their loss and keeping the material. Al -Shāfiʿi requires that the material be returned regardless of the consequences, provided this does not involving committing a prohibited act. Al-Shaybānī objects that the Prophet ordered that 'There be no harm nor harming (*lā ḍarar wa lā ḍirār*).' In other words, al-Shāfiʿī's reasoning would lead to harmful consequences. But al-Shāfiʿī replies by asking al-Shaybānī what he would do if a man misappropriated another man's female slave, had ten sons by her, 'all of whom learned the Quran, gave sermons on the pulpit and served as judges among the Muslims'; then, indisputable proof is provided that this slave woman was wrongly taken. How would al-Shaybānī rule?, asks al-Shāfiʿī. Al-Shaybānī replies that he would declare that the slave woman belonged to her original, actual owner, and that these sons were his slaves as well (since all schools of law agreed that the children of a free husband and a slave woman belonged to the mother's owner). But what is more harmful, retorts al-Shāfiʿī rhetorically, declaring all these sons to be slaves (who cannot be judges, etc.) or removing the plank from the building?; Abū Nuʿaym, *Ḥilyat al-awliyā',* 9:75–76.

120. Mohammed Bashir Salau, 'Slavery in Kano Emirate of Sokoto Caliphate Recounted,' 106. This is the testimony of a seventy-seven-year-old slave in Kano in 1975.

121. Mendelsohn, *Slavery in the Ancient Near East,* 1.

122. Mendelsohn, *Slavery in the Ancient Near East,* 5, 23; Miers, 'Slavery: A Question of Definition,' 6.

123. These three were Bishop George Berkeley (Irish) (d. 1753), Andrew Fletcher (d. 1716), and Francis Hutcheson (d. 1746). See M. J. Rozbicki, 'To Save Them from Themselves: Proposals to Enslave the British Poor, 1698-1755,' 32–39.

124. *Sunan* of Abū Dāwūd: *kitāb al-adab, bāb fī ḥaqq al-mamlūk; Sunan Ibn Mājah: kitāb al-waṣāyā, bāb hal awṣā Rasūl Allāh ṣallā Allāh ʿalayhi wa sallam;* Abū Ṭālib al-Makkī, *Qūt al-qulūb,* 2:252.

125. Muḥyī al-Dīn al-Nawawī, *al-Majmūʿ,* 16:514; al-Bābartī as cited in Shams al-Dīn Qāḍī-zāde Efendi, *Natā'ij al-afkār,* 8:324 (categorizing a child as a slave due to uncertainty about paternity is '*ḍarar ʿaẓīm*').

126. Muḥammad b. Aḥmad Ibn Rushd al-Jadd, *Masā'il Abī al-Walīd Ibn Rushd al-Jadd,* 1:217.

127. Ibn Qudāma, *al-Mughnī*, 12:233. This was repeated verbatim by noted later Hanbali scholars; ʿAbd al-Raḥmān b. ʿAbdallāh al-Baʿlī (d. 1778), *Kashf al-mukhaddarāt wa riyāḍ al-muzhirāt li-sharḥ Akhṣar al-mukhtaṣarāt*, 2:571; Ibn Ḍuwayyān (d. 1935), *Manār al-sabīl*, 2:107. See also note 119 above.

128. In two of his publications, Dr. Khaled Abou El Fadl has quoted the famous Muʿtazilite scholar Qāḍī ʿAbd al-Jabbār (d. 1025) saying that slavery was inherently repugnant/wrong (*qubḥ fī dhātihi*). But the author includes no reference for this quotation. I have not been able to locate it in ʿAbd al-Jabbār's *Mughnī*. Certainly, ʿAbd al-Jabbār describes slaves as suffering physical harm (meaning pain, suffering). But, as Sherman Jackson has pointed out, ʿAbd al-Jabbār explicitly states that, because God allows and even, on some occasions, commands slavery, it *must* be morally acceptable and serve some legitimate human interest; Khaled Abou El Fadl, *The War on Terror*, 200; idem, 'Cultivating Human Rights: Islamic Law and the Humanist Imperative,' 176; Sherman Jackson, *Islam and the Problem of Black Suffering*, 184. ʿAbd al-Jabbār's original wording is *'idhā kāna bi-ibāḥatihi (yaʿnī istikhdām al-ʿabīd) taʿālā wa amrihi bidhālika ʿalimnā ḥusn istikhdāmihim wa'l-iḍrār bihim'*; Qāḍī ʿAbd al-Jabbār, *al-Mughnī fī abwāb al-tawḥīd wa'l-ʿadl*, 13:465. It's also important to note the conception of rational moral objectivism (*ḥusn wa qubḥ al-ʿaqlī*, namely that acts have inherent moral rulings that could be discovered by reason alone and were binding on God because God had fused this moral dimension into their nature) as found in the early Muʿtazila of the eighth and ninth centuries CE became more complex in the tenth and eleventh centuries. By the time that ʿAbd al-Jabbār was writing in the late tenth/early eleventh century, Muʿtazila thinkers acknowledged that this inherent moral ruling could switch based on circumstances or modality. This was still moral objectivism, it just was determined by the interaction of acts with context. See Jackson, *Islam and the Problem of Black Suffering*, 60.

129. The argument that slavery offered a chance at salvation and civilization is old; Muḥammad b. ʿAlī al-Qaffāl al-kabīr al-Shāshī, *Maḥāsin al-sharīʿa*, 201–202; Shāh Walī Allāh, *Ḥujjat Allāh al-bāligha*, 2:515; ʿAlī Bāshā Mubārak, *ʿAlam al-dīn*, 2: 713–14; Ḥusayn al-Jisr, *al-Risāla al-ḥamīdiyya*, 427–28; Hall, *A History of Race in Muslim West Africa*, 230–34 (quoting Shaykh Bay al-Kuntī [d. 1929]); Aḥmad ʿAbd al-Razzāq al-Dawīsh, ed., *Fatāwā al-lajna al-dā'ima li'l-buḥūth al-ʿilmiyya wa'l-iftā'*, 16:570–72 (a 1977 fatwa signed by ʿAbd al-ʿAzīz Bin Bāz and others). There is also the Hadith that 'God is pleased with those people who enter the Garden in chains,' which has been understood as meaning those brought into Islam by slavery; *Ṣaḥīḥ al-Bukhārī*: *kitāb al-jihād wa'l-siyar, bāb al-asārī fī al-salāsil*.

130. Abū Suʿūd Efendī, *Tafsīr*, 6:172; al-Thaʿlabī, *Tafsīr*, 7:96; Ibn Ḥajar, *Fatḥ al-Bārī*, 5:241 (Ibn Ḥajar feels that none of the reports attributed to Ibn ʿAbbās on this verse are reliable).

131. Brockopp, *Early Mālikī Law*, 152; *Muwaṭṭa'* of Mālik: *kitāb al-ʿitq wa'l-walā', bāb ʿitq ummahāt al-awlād . . .*

132. Ibn Qudāma, *Mughnī*, 12:234. See also Ibn Ḍuwayyān, *Manār al-sabīl*, 2:107.

133. Xavier Burgin, Twitter post, 8/15/2017, 3:17pm, https://twitter.com/xlnb/status/897583167212724224.

134. Plato, *Republic*, 433d. For a detailed study of how Plato conceived of the laws of slavery, see Glenn R. Morrow, *Plato's Law of Slavery*.

135. Aristotle, *Politics*, 1255b 12–15. See Christopher Shields, *Aristotle*, 369-71. The most comprehensive discussion of Aristotle's view on slavery is P. A. Brunt, *Studies in Greek History and Thought*, 343–88.

136. Justin Buckley Dyer, *Natural Law and the Antislavery Constitutional Tradition*, 3.
137. Juan Ginés de Sepúlveda (d. 1573) relied heavily on Aristotle's natural slavery argument in his justification for the violent conquest of the Americas by the Spanish; Hanke, *Aristotle and the American Indians.* See also Hugo Grotius, *Commentary on the Law of Prize and Booty*, Chapter VI, Article V, Article II.
138. See Benjamin Fletcher Wright, Jr., *American Interpretations of Natural Law*, xx–xxi, 125–40.
139. Rousseau, *Social Contract*, 1.4. See Jimmy Casas Klausen, *Fugitive Rousseau*, 41–48. For a review and reconsideration of the vibrant disagreement on Rousseau's view on natural law, see L. R. Sorenson, 'Rousseau's Liberalism,' 456 ff.
140. Dyer, *Natural Law*, 2. Dyer summarizes arguments that even the public-reason-based liberalism of John Rawls would not have been able to prove the wrongness of slavery at the time it was being debated in the mid-nineteenth century because 1) Rawl's reasoning is premised on a) a notion of universal freedom and equality, which itself cannot be proven by Rawl's public reason, and b) a notion of justice that is not proven in our present-day culture but only assumed; 2) Rawl's theory of public reason bars recourse to metaphysical or religious arguments, which formed the core and most compelling elements of the abolitionist argument; Dyer, 167–74.
141. This has been pointed out in relation to MacIntyre's criticism of Aristotle's approval of slavery, which MacIntyre argues cannot be accepted under natural law. It was, indeed, seen as acceptable under natural law by centuries of that system's greatest thinkers. If slavery is both morally acceptable and morally unacceptable, that means that there must be multiple natural laws and thus multiple truths, which undermines the whole concept of natural law. See Rafael Ramis-Barceló, 'Alasdair MacIntyre on Natural Law,' 205–206.
142. MacIntyre, *Ethics in the Conflicts of Modernity*, 85–86.
143. H. L. A. Hart, *The Concept of Law*, 192–9. This is one reason that MacIntyre and others criticized Hart's conception of natural law for lacking moral content; MacIntyre, *Are There Any Natural Rights?*
144. Jacques Maritain, *Les Droits de l'homme et la loi naturelle*, 105, 107.
145. Thomas Aquinas et al., *Summa Theologica*, Supplement, Question 52: Article 1, available at http://www.newadvent.org/summa/5052.htm#article1; J. Fox, 'Ethical Aspect of Slavery,' *The Catholic Encyclopedia* (New York: Robert Appleton Company, 1912), available at http://www.newadvent.org/cathen/14039a.htm.
146. Joel Panzer argues that some types of just title servitude even included children inheriting this status, but he provides no examples or references; Joel Panzer, *The Popes and Slavery*, 3–4.
147. David Davis, *The Problem of Slavery in Western Culture*, 33.
148. Aristotle, *Politics*, 1.1253b.
149. Christopher Brooke, *Philosophic Pride: Stoicism and Political Thought from Lipsius to Rousseau*, 47. For a review of debates over whether Stoicism should or should not be credited with Roman legal and philosophical inclinations towards the conviction that slavery was unnatural and towards fair treatment of slaves, see Westermann, *The Slave Systems of Greek and Roman Antiquity*, 116.
150. Epictetus, 'Fragments,' 32 (#s 42–44).
151. Cicero, *On the Commonwealth* (De Republica), iii: 24–25.
152. Philo, *De Specialibus Legibus*, 2.123 (*Philo*, Loeb edition, 7:381); Westermann, *Slave Systems*, 159; Aristotle, *Politics*, 1253b.
153. Epictetus, 'Fragments,' 32.

154. Westermann suggests that the attitude expressed toward slavery from Paul to Augustine was strongly influenced by middle Stoicism, in this case by the idea that the legal status of slavery was meaningless to the truly wise or pious; Westermann, *The Slave Systems of Greek and Roman Antiquity*, 156.
155. David Forman, 'Kant on Moral Freedom and Moral Slavery,' 1–32.
156. *Al-ḥurr ʿabd mā ṭamiʿ wa'l-ʿabd ḥurr mā qaniʿ*; attributed to Bunān al-Ḥammāl (d. 928); ʿUmar al-Suhrawardī, *ʿAwārif al-maʿārif*, 300. One Sufi said 'Outward slavery but inner freedom is part of the ethics of the noble (*al-ʿubūdiyya ẓāhiran wa al-ḥurriyya bāṭinan min akhlāq al-kirām*)'; Abū Nuʿaym al-Iṣbahānī, *Ḥilyat al-awliyā'*, 10:345. This was also the leitmotif and main means of addressing the problem of slavery in the 2015 animated film *Bilal*.
157. Theresa Urbainczyk, *Slave Revolts in Antiquity*, 82; Barry Baldwin, 'Two Aspects of the Spartacus Slave Revolt,' 291; Alexandre Popovic, *The Revolt of African Slaves in Iraq*, 130.
158. See Robert Brady, 'The Role of Las Casas in the Emergence of Negro Slavery in the New World,' 43–55.
159. Lewis Hanke, *Aristotle and the American Indians*, 45–61 (especially 58).
160. Hugo Grotius, *Commentary on the Law of Prize and Booty*, Chapter VI, Article V, Article II; idem, *De Iure Belli ac Pacis*, I.3.8 and also III.7.1; Gustaaf van Nifterik, 'Hugo Grotius on 'Slavery',' 233–44; Jennifer Welchman, 'Locke on Slavery and Inalienable Rights,' 67–81; Vogt, *Ancient Slavery and the Ideal of Man*, 196, 199.
161. These reports come from Philo and Josephus; Glancy, *Slavery as Moral Problem*, 9. Josephus' report is very brief and vague. See Josephus, *Antiquities of the Jews*, 18.1.5.
162. Ilaria E. Ramelli, *Social Justice and the Legitimacy of Slavery*, 12–13, 83–87.
163. Ramelli, *Social Justice and the Legitimacy of Slavery*, 215, 247.
164. See Gregory of Nyssa's Fourth Homily on Ecclesiastes, in Stuart George Hall, ed., *Gregory of Nyssa Homilies on Ecclesiastes*, 73–75; and Maria Mercedès Bergadá, 'La condamnation de l'esclavage dans l'Homélie IV,' in ibid., 195.
165. Vogt, *Ancient Slavery and the Ideal of Man*, 193–94. Gioviano Pontano, 'De Obedientia,' in *Ionnis Ioviani Pontani Opera Omnia Soluta Oratione Composita* (Venice: Aldus, 1518), 23b–24b. At 24b he writes, '*Haec igitur tanta humani generis iniuria ius gentium effectum est.*'
166. Heller, 'Bodin on Slavery,' 55–57.
167. George Keith, 'An Exhortation & Caution to Friends concerning Buying or Keeping of Negroes,' 13:265–70. Available at http://www.qhpress.org/quakerpages/qwhp/gk-as1693.htm.
168. Robert M. Cover, *Justice Accused*, 15-16. See also Appendix 2 – Enlightenment Thinkers on Slavery.
169. Claudine Hunting, 'The Philosophes and Black Slavery,' 411.
170. For the conservative American intellectual Thomas Sowell this only proves the moral exceptionalism of the modern West; Thomas Sowell, 'Ending Slavery,' *Jewish World Review*, Feb. 8, 2005, http://www.jewishworldreview.com/cols/sowell020805.asp.
171. Ralph Ireland, 'Auguste Comte's Views on Slavery,' 559.
172. Daniel Carey, *Locke, Shaftesbury, and Hutcheson*, 11.
173. Davis, *Slavery and Human Progress*, 113.
174. Heller, 'Bodin on Slavery,' 53–4. For how economic and political changes in Southeast Asia led to the end of slavery there, see Reid, 'Introduction,' 33.
175. Howard Temperley refers to these two schools of thought as the economic and the intellectual diffusionist; Howard Temperley, 'The Ideology of Antislavery,' 26–27, 30.

176. David Turley, 'Slave emancipations in modern history,' 182–83.
177. Peter Kolchin, 'Some controversial questions concerning the nineteenth-century emancipation from slavery and serfdom,' 44–49. Brief Summary of the Debate: Eric William's landmark book *Capitalism and Slavery* (1944) landed a major blow to the Moral Awakening narrative, arguing that Anglo-American abolitionism triumphed in ending the Atlantic slave trade in 1807 because the rise of free trade and industrial production, along with the weakening of mercantilism, meant that the agricultural industries that depended on slavery had entered economic decline by that time. In short, slavery was no longer part of a good business plan. In his 1977 response, *Econocide*, Seymour Drescher showed that, far from being in decline, slave-based agricultural production in the Americas had actually entered its peak profitability in the early 1800s. Ending it was 'economic suicide' for a major chunk of the British/American economy. Moreover, slavery was totally compatible with industrial modes of production. The Moral Awakening narrative had been right, in effect. Drescher and others since have argued that abolition was brought about by a major change in Anglo-American public sentiment regarding slavery, sentiment that ran counter to economic interests. Other scholars have tried to counter the Drescher school. What Williams had introduced was more than the obsolete specifics of his 'decline thesis.' It was the notion that the end of slavery ultimately hinged on changes in material circumstances, not the idea of slavery-as-immoral driving history. They have offered several proposals for reconciling this Economic narrative with Drescher's critique. Thomas Haskell argued that the peak profitability of slavery-based production was ultimately marginal in light of the major economic changes afoot on the world stage. I find Temperley's explanation, which I rely on in this chapter, to be the most convincing. As Thomas Bender writes, 'Few historians today discount the possibility of some connection between capitalism and antislavery.' See Eric Williams, *Capitalism and Slavery*; Seymour Drescher, *Econocide*; David Eltis, *Economic Growth and the Ending of the Transatlantic Slave Trade*; Jeremy Adelman, *Sovereignty and Revolution in the Iberian Atlantic*, Chapter 2; Thomas Haskell, 'Capitalism and the Origins of the Humanitarian Sensibility, Part 1'; Thomas Bender 'Introduction,' in *The Antislavery Debate*, 2. David Davis' Foreword and Drescher's Preface to the second edition of *Econocide* are excellent summaries (if not impartial) of this debate. Drescher considers Temperley's explanation to be unthorough; Drescher, *Econocide*, xxvi.
178. See Seymour Drescher, 'The Shocking Birth of British Abolitionism,' 571–93.
179. Thomas L. Haskell, 'Capitalism and the Origins of the Humanitarian Sensibility, Part 1,' 107–35 (republished from *The American Historical Review* 90, n. 2 [1985]); Davis, *Slavery in the Age of Revolution*, 350.
180. Davis, *Slavery and Human Progress*, 155.
181. Davis, *Slavery and Human Progress*, 111.
182. As Condorcet wrote, 'We deprive the Negro of all his moral faculties and then declare him inferior to us, and consequently destined to carry our chains. This is a monstrous mixture of injustice and cruelty. No compassionate person could ever stop hoping for an end to this appalling situation, which contradicts all the laws of humanity.' See Condorcet, 'On Slavery. Rules for the Society of the Friends of Negroes (1788),' in *Condorcet: Political Writings*, 150.
183. See, for examples, Baer, *Studies in the Social History of Modern Egypt*, 179, 182–89; Miers, 'Slavery and the slave trade in Saudi Arabia and the Arab states of the Persian Gulf, 1921–63,' 124, 128; Roberts and Miers, 'The End of Slavery in Africa,' in *The End of Slavery in Africa*, 33–47; Wright, *Trans-Saharan Slave Trade*, 162–63.
184. Temperley, 'The Ideology of Antislavery,' 29.

185. Davis, *The Problem of Slavery in the Age of Revolution*, 535, 538.
186. Outram, *The Enlightenment*, 66. See also Michael Taylor, 'British Proslavery Arguments and the Bible, 1823–33,' 147–48; John Richter Jones, *Slavery Sanctioned by the Bible*.
187. Oshatz, 'The Problem of Moral Progress,' 238.
188. Samuel Fisher, 'Rusticus ad Academicos (The Rustic's Alarm to the Rabbis),' 33; Travis Frampton, *Spinoza and the Rise of Historical Criticism of the Bible*, 216–19.
189. J. William Frost, 'Why Quakers and Slavery? Why Not More Quakers?,' 31–32.
190. Davis, *The Problem of Slavery in the Age of Revolution*, 526–7. For the origins and development of the Western historical critical method, see Jonathan Brown, *Hadith*, 226–38.
191. See Glancy, *Slavery as Moral Problem*, 23–27.
192. Noonan, 'Development in Moral Doctrine,' 670–71, 676–77; Cardinal John Henry Newman, *An Essay on the Development of Christian Doctrine*, 171–72, 200, 363.
193. See, for example, Steve Holmes, 'Homosexuality and hermeneutics: creating counter-cultural communities,' Evangelical Alliance, Jan. 15, 2013, http://www.eauk.org/church/stories/homosexuality-and-hermeneutics.cfm, last accessed 5/5/2018.
194. Bishop Richard Watson (d. 1816) wrote, 'God cannot authorize injustice; but he did authorize slavery amongst the Jews; therefore slavery is not opposite to justice.' This was 'the one short argument, if there were no other, which proves that slavery is not as such opposite to justice.' James Griffith wrote in the early 1800s: 'If once it can be shewn that the Almighty ever did sanction the possession of bond servants or Slaves, the following unanswerable syllogism must be deduced . . . God never can or could sanction anything it itself unjust or wicked; But God did sanction the possession of slaves, with Abraham and among the Jews ... Therefore, it must necessarily follow, that, the Possession of Slaves cannot, in itself, be either unjust or wicked.'; Taylor, 'British Proslavery Arguments and the Bible, 1823–33,' 145. See also Davis, *The Problem of Slavery in the Age of Revolution*, 545. As Steve Holmes writes in response to trajectory hermeneutics (though not on the issue of slavery), 'Our understanding of the truth does not grow and develop and improve beyond the point in history when we once looked the Truth in the face; we do not know more of the works of God than when we saw God at work in the dusty streets of Galilee.' See Steve Holmes, 'Homosexuality and hermeneutics.' Contrast this with William Webb's assertion that remaining tied in any way to Biblical texts on slavery is absurd in our time. Instead of what Webb calls a static hermeneutic, he advocates a redemptive one; William J. Webb, *Slaves, Women and Homosexuals*, 36 ff.
195. Oshatz, 'The Problem of Moral Progress,' 229.
196. Davis, *Slavery and Human Progress*, 112. See also Oshatz, 'The Problem of Moral Progress,' 231, 233. As Davis notes, these defenders of biblical slavery argued it had not entailed 'total degradation'; Davis, *The Problem of Slavery in the Age of Revolution*, 552.
197. Oshatz, 'The Problem of Moral Progress,' 247–49.
198. Henri St. Simon, *Social Organization, the Science of Man, and Other Writings*, 19; Auguste Comte, *General View of Positivism*, 283, 338–39, 372.
199. Ahmed Khan, *Ibtāl ghulāmī/Tabriyat al-Islām ʿan shayn al-ama wa'l-ghulām*, 32-46; Avril A. Powell, 'Indian Muslim Modernists and the Issue of Slavery in Islam,' 271, 293. Khan was followed in his arguments by the Pakistani Islamic modernist Ghulam Ahmad Parvez (d. 1985), founder of what is known as the Parweziyya Quran-only movement. This case was fervently restated by a Pakistani scholar living in London, Hafiz Muhammad Sarwar Qureshi, in a book entitled *Nāmūs-i Rasūl* (*The Honor of the*

Messenger). A section from this book refuting the idea that Māriya was the Prophet's concubine was translated into English. A less dramatic version of this approach was taken by the Austrian Jewish convert to Islam and prolific author Muhammad Asad (d. 1992), who acknowledged that the Quran allowed slavery (abolishing it immediately would have been impossible, but abolition was always Islam's aim) but insisted that Islamic tradition had erred grievously in understanding that God allowed sex with slave women. The phrase 'those whom your right hands possess' in those verses that seem to permit sex with slave women (4:24, 23:6) should actually be read, Asad argues, as 'those whom you rightfully possess [in wedlock].' But Asad also acknowledges that the Quran also uses the phrase to mean female slaves (e.g., 4:25, 24:38). This overall argument is echoed by Muhammad Diakho; Ghulam Ahmad Parvez, *Islam: A Challenge to Religion*, 354–55; Muhammad Sarwar Qureshi, *The Qur'an and Slavery*, trans. Kaukab Siddique (no publication information); Muhammad Asad, trans., *The Message of the Qur'ān*, 36, 101, 106–107, 519, 545; Muhammad Diakho, *L'Esclavage en Islam*, 16–21.

200. Oshatz, 'The Problem of Moral Progress,' 230. One interesting question is why Christian scholars (and Muslims with the Quran) did not try harder to argue for an allegorical reading of slavery in the Old and New Testaments. Origen (d. 254 CE) had read the bloody Israelite conquest of Palestine under Joshua as allegory in which Joshua was Jesus vanquishing the forces of sin and evil from hearts. Perhaps the problems were that 1) slavery is not a passage or event described in these scriptures. It appears as a mundane thread throughout all of them, was ubiquitous in their contexts and is thus harder to reduce to allegory; 2) by the nineteenth century allegorization had lost much ground to historicization as a device for dealing with such problems; and 3) there were some instances in the Bible that Origen concluded were only figurative, i.e., they did not actually happen as described (for example, the Devil did not *actually* take Jesus up on a high mountain and show him all the kingdoms of the world, because that would be impossible), but that does not seem to be the case with the slaughter in Joshua. Origen does not seem to deny that the events occurred in history, he just feels their true, spiritual meaning is allegorical. Origen's reading of biblical warfare would thus not satisfy someone like Buber because his allegorical reading only adds a dimension to the events described in the text, it does not replace literal with figurative. It seems hard to imagine a reading of slavery in the Bible or the Quran that could manage that. It's interesting to note that Origen is worried not that the audience of his sermon would be shocked by the biblical bloodshed but, rather, that they would dismiss the battles described as irrelevant for them; Origen, 'On First Principles,' in *Origen*, 189–90; idem, *Homilies on Joshua*, 127; Anders-Christian Jacobsen 'Allegorical Interpretation of Geography in Origen's Homilies on the Book of Joshua,' 290. Thanks to my colleague Leo Lefebure for discussing this with me.

201. Susan Niditch, *War in the Hebrew Bible*, 9.

202. Martin Buber, 'Autobiographical Fragments,' 31–32.

203. Niditch, *War in the Hebrew Bible*, 41.

204. Qāḍī ʿIyāḍ (d. 1149) states that the *umma* has agreed that the Prophet was immune from Satan, that he was infallible (*maʿṣūm*) in delivering God's revealed message, and that there is consensus that, after the beginning of their prophethood, all prophets are immune (*ʿiṣma*) from grave sins and repugnant acts (*fawāḥish*); Qāḍī ʿIyāḍ, *Kitāb al-Shifā*, 326, 330, 346. Insulting (*sabb*, *shatīma*) or belittling (*istikhfāf*) the Prophet is *kufr* by *ijmāʿ*; Ibn Ḥajar al-Haytamī, *al-Iʿlām bi-qawāṭiʿ al-Islām*, 67–69; Mullā ʿAlī al-Qāri', 'Sharḥ alfāẓ al-kufr,' in *Majmuʿ rasā'il al-ʿallāmā al-Mullā ʿAlī al-Qāri'*, 7:121–22; idem, *Sharḥ al-Fiqh al-akbar*, 126; Muḥammad Anwar Shāh Kashmīrī, 'Ikfār al-mulḥidīn fī ḍarūriyyāt al-dīn,' in *Majmūʿat rasāʾil al-Kashmīrī*, 3:64–65; ʿAbdallāh al-Ghumārī, *Afḍal maqūl fī manāqib afḍal rasūl*, 73–75; idem, *al-Khawāṭir al-dīniyya*, 1:78.

205. Muḥammad Bakhīt al-Muṭīʿī (d. 1935), 'Kitāb Aḥsan al-kalām fī-mā yataʿallaqu bi'l-sunna wa'l-bidʿa min al-aḥkām,' in *Majmūʿat rasāʾil al-ʿallāma Muḥammad Bakhīt al-Muṭīʿī*, 30. Interestingly, the prominent Salafi scholar Muḥammad Nāṣir al-Dīn al-Albānī (d. 1999), wrote: 'Declaring a Muslim to be an unbeliever is not a light matter. Yes, someone who denies what has been established necessarily as part of the religion after proof has been presented to him, he is an unbeliever (*kāfir*), for whom the true meaning of the label *kāfir* applies. But as for the person who denies something due to it not being established according to his opinion, or due to some doubt regarding the meaning, that person is misguided, but not an unbeliever or apostate from the religion. His status is the status of anyone who denies any sound Hadith according to the scholars of knowledge.'; al-Albānī, *Silsilat al-aḥādīth al-ḍaʿīfa*, #1082. An example that appears in numerous respected works of Ḥanafī law after the twelfth century states that if someone says that a clear ruling from the Quran or the Prophet, such as the Quran allowing a man to have four wives, 'does not please' them, then this is *kufr*. See the *Fatāwā al-ʿAttābiyya* of Zāhid al-Dīn Aḥmad b. Muḥammad al-ʿAttābī of Bukhara (d. circa 1190), as cited by Farīd al-Dīn al-Dihlawī, *al-Fatāwā al-Tātārkhāniyya*, 7:291; *al-Fatāwā al-Hindiyya*, 2:261.

206. Ibn ʿĀbidīn, *Ḥāshiyat Ibn ʿĀbidīn*, 3:48. See also Kecia Ali, *Sexual Ethics and Islam*, 39. The Saudi scholar Ṣāliḥ al-Fawzān allegedly said on Twitter that taking female prisoners of war as concubines is *ḥalāl* in Islam and saying otherwise is *kufr*; http://musawasyr.org/?p=13328.

207. Badr al-Dīn al-Zarkashī, *al-Baḥr al-muḥīṭ fī uṣūl al-fiqh*, 3:247. For example, there is a well-known if admittedly unreliable Hadith in which the Prophet states that 'Of what is permissible, the most hated by God is divorce.' But there are also well-known reports that the Prophet divorced his wife Ḥafṣa, though he later retracted the divorce. The Shāfiʿī scholar al-Khaṭṭābī thus understands the hated aspects of divorce to be the negativities that generally lead to divorce, not divorce itself, which God permitted and which the Prophet once did. The Ḥanafī school holds that divorce should only be done if there is some pressing need for it. For the Hadith on Divorce as the Most Hated Thing via Ibn ʿUmar see *Sunan* of Abū Dāwūd: *kitāb al-ṭalāq, bāb fī karāhiyat al-ṭalāq*; *Sunan Ibn Mājah*: *kitāb al-ṭalāq, bāb*. For evaluations of its authenticity according to Sunni Hadith scholars, see al-Albānī, *Daʿīf Sunan Ibn Mājah*, 155; idem, *Daʿīf Sunan Abī Dāwūd*, 2:228–29; al-Ghumārī, *al-Mudāwī*, 1:78 ff.; al-Sakhāwī, *al-Maqāṣid al-ḥasana*, 25-26. See also *Sunan* of Abū Dāwūd: *kitāb al-ṭalāq, bāb fī al-murājaʿa*; *Sunan al-Nasāʾī*: *kitāb al-ṭalāq, bāb al-rajʿa*; al-Khaṭṭābī, *Maʿālim al-sunan*, 3:231; Ibn Kamālpāsha, *Rasāʾil*, 59.

208. Ibn Ḥajar al-Haytamī, *al-ʿUmda fī sharḥ al-Burda*, 286.

CHAPTER 5 ABOLISHING SLAVERY IN ISLAM

1. Tim Cahill, 'The Rolling Stone Interview: Stanley Kubrick in 1987,' 3/7/2011, https://www.rollingstone.com/culture/news/the-rolling-stone-interview-stanley-kubrick-in-1987-20110307.

2. Ali Shariati, *The Visage of Muhammad*, 12. The phrase 'oppressed in the land' is the language that the Quran uses to describe the condition of the Jews in Egypt, making 'oppression in the land' the Quranic equivalent of the Jewish enslavement by Pharaoh (Quran 28:4). The archetypal liberated slave Bilāl is also called 'one of the *mustaḍʿafīn* of the Muslims' by the early scholar ʿUrwa b. al-Zubayr; al-Suyūṭī, *Rafʿ sha'n al-ḥubshān*, 248–49.

3. Sayyid Qutb, *Milestones*, 45.

4. The New Testament often refers to the faithful as the 'slaves', *doulos*, of the Lord; C. Spicq, 'Le vocabulaire de l'esclavage dans le nouveau testament,' 204–206; Lorenzo Verderame, 'Slavery in Third-Millenium Mesopotamia,' 19–20; Brockopp, *Early Mālikī Law*, 128.

5. *Sunan* of Abū Dāwūd: *kitāb al-ḥudūd, bāb al-ḥukm fī-man irtadda*.

6. Qutb, *Milestones*, 81, 148. For the original report of Ribʿī b. ʿĀmir's meeting with Rostom, see Ibn Kathīr, *al-Bidāya wa'l-nihāya*, 7:39.

7. '*mudh kam taʿabbadtum al-nās wa qad waladathum ummahātuhum aḥrāran*'; this report appears in the ninth-century text of ʿAbd al-Raḥmān Ibn ʿAbd al-Ḥakam (d. 870), *Futūḥ Miṣr*, 290; Rashīd Riḍā, 'al-Raqīq al-abyaḍ wa'l-aswad,' 20; El Hamel, *Black Morocco*, 17; Abū Nāyif al-Tamīmī, 'Tafsīr qawlihi taʿālā aw mā malakat aymānukum li'l -shaykh ʿAbd al-ʿAzīz Fawzān,' YouTube video, 5/28/2014, https://www.youtube.com/watch?v=oPTLRtt1uXY, (interview on Risāla Network in 2014).

8. *Ṣaḥīḥ Muslim*: *kitāb al-īmān, bāb ṣuḥbat al-mamālīk wa kaffārat man laṭama ʿabdahu*.

9. *Ṣaḥīḥ al-Bukhārī*: *kitāb manāqib al-anṣār, bāb islām Salmān al-Fārisī*. Thanks to my friend Omar Suleiman for pointing me to this.

10. *Sunan* of Abū Dāwūd: *kitāb al-adab, bāb lā yaqūlu al-mamlūk rabbī wa rabbatī*; *Ṣaḥīḥ Muslim*: *kitāb al-alfāẓ min al-adab wa ghayrihā, bāb ḥukm iṭlāq lafẓat al-ʿabd wa'l-ama*... This is more than reminiscent of Paul's exhortation that masters not threaten their slaves, since they both have the same Master (*κυριος*) in heaven (Ephesians 6:9). The Greek *kyrios* here is essentially the same as the Arabic *sayyid* and the English master/mr.

11. Khalīl b. Aḥmad, *Kitāb al-ʿAyn*, 3:83.

12. Feridun M. Emecen, 'Osmanlı Hanedanına Alternatif Arayışlar Üzerine Bazı Örnekler ve Mülahazalar,' in *Osmanlı klasik çağında hanedan, devlet ve toplum* ([Istanbul]: Timaş Yayınları, 2011), 49. Thanks to my student Said Salih Kaymakci for this citation.

13. Though an impressive film, the emancipatory argument in *Bilal* was not based in the Quran or Sunna but, rather, in Stoic thought, just like the responses to slavery invoked by Christians like Augustine and, of course, Stoic philosophers. The real chains, Bilal's mother teaches him, are in his heart, not on his hands. Being a slave or free was really a matter of one's inner disposition and understanding. Physical slavery was immaterial.

14. Erdem, *Slavery in the Ottoman Empire*, 92; Baer, *Studies in the Social History of Modern Egypt*, 176, 183; B. Lewis, *Race and Slavery in the Middle East*, 156 (appearing at the end of an 1842 correspondence between British consular officials); Behnaz A. Mirzai, 'The 1848 abolitionist *farmān*: a step towards ending the slave trade in Iran,' 96–97, 99 (in 1848 the Shah did issue a decree prohibiting the trade of Black African slaves in the Persian Gulf).

15. William Ochsenwald, 'Muslim-European Conflict in the Hijaz: The Slave Controversy, 1840–1895,' 119–21; Toledano, *The Ottoman Slave Trade and its Suppression*, 132. There were also rumors that the Ottomans would ban the call to prayer, ban women wearing the hijab, give women the right to unilateral divorce, and that the Ottomans were seeking aid from European powers; Cevdet Pasha, *Tezâkir*, 1–12:133–35.

16. Muir offers this opinion for 'three radical evils,' namely slavery, polygamy and divorce; William Muir, *The Life of Mahomet*, 4:321.

17. Hurgronje, *Mekka in the Latter Part of the 19th Century*, 23.
18. John Hunwick observes that slavery in Islam was 'divinely sanctioned' and that humans could not abrogate its legality in the Shariah. Paul Lovejoy notes that in the Sokoto Caliphate 'strict adherence to law and tradition precluded any thought of abolition.' J. R. Willis urged us to remember that 'Muhammad, the Prophet of Islam, was at once a slaveholder and a practitioner of polygamy and concubinage . . .'; Hunwick and Powell, *African Diaspora*, xvi, 181; Lovejoy, 'Slavery in the Sokoto Caliphate,' 208; J. R. Willis, 'Preface,' in *Slaves and Slavery in Muslim Africa*, 1:viii–ix. See also Frederick Millingen, 'On the Negro Slaves in Turkey,' lxxxvii (it's an 'axiom' that 'slavery is inherent in the religious and social system of Mohammedanism'); Erdem, *Slavery in the Ottoman Empire*, 87 (British Ambassador to Istanbul Henry Elliot wrote in 1869 about this 'detestable social system which is part of the Mohemmedan religion . . .'); Humphrey J. Fisher, *Slavery in the History of Muslim Black Africa*, 14 ('Slavery is very closely woven into the fabric of Islamic religion and society.'); Murray Gordon, *Slavery in the Arab World*, 19; Lewis, *Race and Slavery in the Middle East*, 78 (Muslims cannot forbid what God has permitted); Wright, *The Trans-Saharan Slave Trade*, 58; Roger Botte, *Esclavages et Abolitions en Terres d'Islam*, 1–36. See also Malek Chebel, *L'Eslavage en Terre d'Islam*, which attempts to answer the question of whether Islam sought to end slavery or not.
19. Amina Wadud, *Inside the Gender Jihad*, 188; Abdullahi An-Na'im, *Towards an Islamic Reformation*, 174.
20. William Gervașe Clarence-Smith, *Islam and the Abolition of Slavery*, 19.
21. See, for example, Sir Syed Ahmed Khan, *A Series of Essays on the Life of Mohammed*, 20–21; Alexander Morrison, 'Twin imperial disasters: the invasions of Khiva and Afghanistan in the Russian and British official mind, 1839–1842,' 282–83; Jeff Eden, *Slavery and Empire in Central Asia*.
22. See, for example, ʿAbbās Maḥmūd al-ʿAqqād, 'Mas'alat al-riqq fī al-Islām,' 17. See Bruce Hall, *A History of Race and Slavery in Muslim West Africa*, 210; Kopytoff, 'Cultural Context of African Abolition,' 485.
23. Others who held this view include: Rashīd Riḍā, 'As'ila min Bārīs,' 743-46; idem, 'al -Raqīq al-abyaḍ wa'l-aswad,' 19–22; Syed Ameer Ali, *A Critical Examination of the Life and Teachings of Mohammed*, 254–62; Muhammad Iqbal, 'Islam as a Moral and Political Ideal - I,' 34–35; Muḥammad Abū Zahra, introduction to *Sharḥ al-Siyar al-kabīr*, 1:79–80, 84; Muḥammad Ṭāhir Ibn ʿĀshūr, *Uṣūl al-niẓām al-ijtimāʿī fī al-islām*, 166–68; ʿAllāl al-Fāsī, *Maqāṣid al-sharīʿa al-islāmiyya*, 242–43; Wahba al-Zuḥaylī, *Āthār al-ḥarb fī al-fiqh al-islāmī*, 442–43; idem, *Mawsūʿat al-fiqh al-islāmī*, 3:771; Fazlur Rahman, *Islam and Modernity*, 19; Muhammad Asad, *The Message of the Quran*, 36, 251 (on Quran 2:177, 8:62); Taha Jabir al-Alwani, *Shaykh Taha Jabir al-Alwani on Issues in Contemporary Islamic Thought*, 137–38; Farid Esack, *On Being a Muslim*, 117; An-Na'im, *Towards an Islamic Reformation*, 174; G. A. Parwez, *Islam*, 354–55; Muhammad Diakho, *L'Esclavage en Islam*, 16–21; Riffat Hassan, 'On Human Rights and the Qur'anic Perspective,' 59; Javed Ghamidi, *Islam*, 447; Feisal Abdul Rauf, *What's Right with Islam*, 31.
24. See Davis, *The Problem of Slavery in the Age of Revolution*, 535.
25. Riḍā, 'As'ila min Bārīs,' 744. See also Muḥammad Quṭb, *Shubuhāt ḥawl al-Islām*, 47.
26. Ameer Ali, *A Critical Examination*, 257–61; Avril Powell, 'Indian Muslim Modernists and the Issue of Slavery in Islam,' 265–69.
27. Aḥmad Shafīq, *L'Esclavage au point de vue musalman*, 32–34, 52.
28. See Aḥmad Shafīq, *Mudhakkirātī fī nisf qarn*, 2:2:269. ʿAbduh's mentor, the activist scholar Jamāl al-Dīn al-Afghānī (d. 1897), praised Shafīq's book after its publication; 'al -Riqq fī al-Islām,' *Ḍiyā' al-khāfiqayn* 1, n. 4–5 (1892): 181–82.

29. Muḥammad Tawfīq Ṣidqī, 'al-Dīn fī naẓar al-ʿaql al-ṣaḥīḥ,' 732–34. ʿAbd al-Raḥmān al-Kawākibī (d. 1902) also expresses that the 'free ulama of the Muslims' thank Europeans for ending slavery; al-Kawākibī, 'Tijārat al-raqīq wa aḥkāmuhu fī al-islām,' 859.
30. This figure was the Egyptian Aḥmad al-Maḥmaṣānī; Amal Ghazal, 'Debating Slavery and Abolition in the Arab Middle East,' 44. Interestingly, Maḥmaṣānī cites as his evidence a Hadith in which the Prophet says that Gabriel had counseled him on several matters, including, 'Gabriel did not cease counseling me to [be kind to] slaves until I thought he would set a time period for them after which they would be freed . . .'. For more on this Hadith see Chapter 6, n. 57.
31. Riḍā, 'As'ila min Bārīs,' 744.
32. See David Robinson, 'Un historien et anthropologue sénégalais: Shaikh Musa Kamara,' 99–100. Robinson's statement that Kamara 'took certain liberties' in following the Shariah should be read in conjunction with Diop's description of Kamara's and other leading West African scholars' justifications for their actions; Abdoul Malal Diop, 'Le vie et l'oeuvre de Cheikh Moussa Kamara de Ganguel (1864–1945),' 48 ff. Thanks to Bilal Ware for this dissertation.
33. Constance Hilliard, '*Zuhur al-Basatin* and *Ta'rikh al-Turubbe*: Some Legal and Ethical Aspects of Slavery in the Sudan as Seen in the Works of Shaykh Musa Kamara,' 160–80. Kamara wrote the *Zuhūr al-basātīn* between 1920 and 1925. For the report about Ibn ʿUmar, see Ibn Saʿd, *al-Ṭabaqāt al-kubrā*, 4:156; Shafīq, 36. See also Aḥmad al-Nāṣirī al-Salāwī, *Kitāb al-Istiqṣā li-akhbār duwal al-maghrib al-aqṣā*, 5:134.
34. Rudolph T. Ware, *The Walking Qur'an*, 118–19, 142; Ousmane Kane, *Beyond Timbuktu*, 72; Ghislaine Lydon, 'Slavery, Exchange and Islamic Law: A Glimpse from the Archives of Mali and Mauritania,' 129. Ibn Battuta describes a custom in Timbuktu of placing chains on the feet of youths *until* they had succeeded in memorizing the Quran, which *liberated* them; Ibn Battuta, *Ibn Battuta in Black Africa*, 47–48.
35. Ware, *The Walking Qur'an*, 103–104, 114–16.
36. Ware, *The Walking Qur'an*, 161.
37. Sean Hanretta, *Islam and Social Change in French West Africa*, 3, 141, 173–74, 178–79, 214–15. Shaykh Amadu Bamba (d. 1927), a much more influential Sufi leader in Senegal, fiercely resisted the enslavement of Muslims but did not oppose *riqq* in principle; Searing, *'God Alone is King': Islam and Emancipation in Senegal*, 247–48.
38. Aḥmad Bābā, *Miʿrāj al-Ṣuʿūd: Ahmad Baba's Replies on Slavery*; Marta García Novo, 'La doctrina mālikí sobre esclavitud y el Miʿrāŷ de Aḥmad Bābā,' 75–95 (thanks to Nathaniel Mathews for this second source). This continued to be an issue under the Sokoto Caliphate, whose leaders condemned it; Lovejoy, 'Slavery in the Sokoto Caliphate,' 210–12.
39. Ibn Ḥajar al-Haytamī, *al-Zawājir ʿan iqtirāf al-kabā'ir*, 2:176.
40. Aziz Abdalla Batran, 'The ʿUlama of Fas, Mulay Isma'il, and the Issue of the Haratin of Fas,' 1–15. For a discussion of Aḥmad Bābā, Jassūs and others, see John Hunwick, 'Islamic Law and Polemics over Race and Slavery,' 43–68. For a somewhat similar situation in nineteenth-century Sumatra, see Clarence-Smith, 'Islam and the abolition of the slave trade in the Indian Ocean,' 139. For a similar law in a fifteenth-century Malay legal text, see Liaw Yock Fang, *The Laws of Melaka*, 155.
41. El Hamel, *Black Morocco*, 163–74.
42. Ibn Battuta, *The Travels of Ibn Battuta*, 3:578–79.
43. ʿAbd al-Raḥmān Jāmī, *Nāmehā va Monšaʾāt-e Jāmī*, 149.
44. This problem is described by a contemporary as quite severe, with men selling their own female relatives as well. See Shaykh Jalāl al-Dīn Faqīh al-Ṣaghīr (Sjech Djilâl Eddîn),

Verhaal van den Aanvang der Padri-Onlusten op Sumatra, 8–9. Thanks to Muhammad Rofiq for his help with this text.

45. Bābā, *Mi'rāj*, 50. These Shāfi'ī scholars included Taqī al-Dīn al-Subkī and Shaykh al -Islām Zakariyyā al-Anṣārī; Taqī al-Dīn al-Subkī, *Qaḍā' al-arab fī as'ilat Ḥalab*, 539–48; idem, *Fatāwā al-Subkī*, 2:281–85; Shehzade Mehmet Korkud, *Islâm'da Ganimet ve Cariyelik / Ḥall ishkāl al-afkār fī ḥall amwāl al-kuffār*. An interesting Ḥanafī confirmation of this comes from Iftikhār al-Dīn Ṭāhir al-Bukhārī (d. 1147–8), who is reported to have married a Turkic slave girl he had bought (instead of having sex with her as a concubine) out of concern that she had been illegally acquired; W. H. Macnaghten, *Principles and Precedents of Moohummudan Law*, xxxiii.

46. A famine brought on by locusts in the Iranian province of Khurasan in 1904 led many families there to sell their children as slaves to Turcoman nomads; Mirzai, *A History of Slavery and Emancipation in Iran*, 79.

47. Andrea Major, *Slavery, Abolitionism and Empire in India*, 58, 65, 152–58; Eltis and Engerman, 'Dependency, Servitude, and Coerced Labour in Time and Space,' 15; John Marshall, *John Marshall in India: Notes and Observations in Bengal (1668–1672)*, 18, 125, 150.

48. This work, titled *Ibrāhīm Shāhiyya fī fatāwā al-ḥanafiyya*, was written by Shihāb al -Dīn Aḥmad Niẓām Gīlānī (or Kīkānī) (d. *circa* 1534); Kātib Chelebī, *Kashf al-ẓunūn*, 1:83.

49. 'Abd al-Qādir Badāyūnī, *Muntakhab al-tavārīkh*, 301, available here https://archive.org/stream/in.ernet.dli.2015.484970/2015.484970.Muntakhab-Ul-Tawarikh#page/n309/mode/2up; idem, *Muntakhabu-t-Tawārīkh*, 3:112.

50. Al-Badāyūnī, *Muntakhabu-t-Tawārīkh*, 2:405.

51. Chattopadhyay, *Slavery in the Bengal Presidency*, 81–83, 158–61.

52. The Ḥanafī jurists responding to the British were certainly being selective. One issue was whether Muslims could buy as slaves people sold by their non-Muslim families outside the Dār al-Islām. According to the main position in the Ḥanafī school, if a Muslim enters the Dār al-Ḥarb with the permission of its regime he cannot validly buy a child sold by parents there or buy any other family member they are selling, since *no one* can validly own (and hence sell) their child or any other close relative. There is, however, the position that this Muslim visitor could legally buy a non-Muslim who had previously been free but had been enslaved by another non-Muslim who was *not* their close relative, provided that enslaving free people was allowed in that non-Muslim culture. The prominent early Baghdad Ḥanafī jurist Abū al-Ḥasan al-Karkhī (d. 952) even held that Muslims visiting the Dār al-Ḥarb could buy the children of non-Muslims selling them if this was accepted in that culture. This is what al-Walwāljī (d. *circa* 1145) sees as correct, namely that essentially any sale deemed acceptable in that non-Muslim culture is valid for the Muslim buyer; 'Abd al-Rashīd al-Walwālījī, *al-Fatāwā al-Walwāljiyya*, 2:307. In Ibn 'Ābidīn's (d. 1836) influential writings, this is reduced to a blanket prohibition on buying such children; Ibn 'Ābidīn, *Ḥāshiyat Ibn 'Ābidīn*, 4:160. As concerns buying slaves from pagan (*mushrik*) Black Africans, the Ibāḍī scholar Aṭfayyish notes that it is disliked (*kuriha*) to buy the subjects of a ruler if he sells them, a wife being sold by her husband or someone being sold by their relative. As for buying a child from their parent, one opinion states that it is prohibited while another allows it. As for non-Black Africans (*sūdānī*), if selling a child is allowed in the people's religion then it is nonetheless either prohibited or disliked for Muslims to buy them. It is, however, permitted in the case of famine, though never from a non-Muslim living under Muslim rule (*dhimmī*, and a *muwaḥḥid* child cannot be sold); Aṭfayyish, *Sharḥ*

Kitāb al-Nīl, 8:265–68; Daddi Addoun, 'Slavery and Abolition in Ibāḍī Theology,' 235–36. Medieval Muslim travelers noted that the Slavs and pagan (i.e., non-Jewish or Christian) Khazars of the steppes sold their children into slavery in certain circumstances (such as payment for a fine or debt among the Slavs); César E. Dubler, *Abū Ḥāmid El Granadino y su Relación de Viaje por Tierras Eurasiáticas*, 24; Abū Isḥāq al-Iṣṭakhrī, *Masālik al-mamālik*, 223.

53. W. H. Macnaghten, *Principles and Precedents of Moohummudan Law*, xxx.

54. Taqī al-Dīn al-Subkī, *Fatāwā*, 2:285.

55. ʿAbd al-Qādir Khānī, *Waqāʾiʿ-i Khānī*, 285a-b.

56. Perhaps Bābā was more conservative on this point because the issue of enslaved people claiming to come from Muslim areas was a real phenomenon in his context and not a theoretical question; Aḥmad Bābā, *Miʿrāj al-Ṣuʿūd*, 28, 50. See also for the same position in the Shāfiʿī school, Muḥammad ʿAlī al-Mālikī, ed., *Qurrat al-ʿayn bi-fatāwā ʿulamāʾ al-ḥaramayn*, 338 (citing Muḥammad Ṣāliḥ al-Zubayrī [d. 1825], who says that, if a slave being sold protests that they were actually free, the presumption of human freedom supersedes the seller's property right). See also Hunwick, 'Notes on Slavery in the Songhay Empire,' 19; Hiskitt, *The Sword of Truth*, 77–8.

57. Rainer Osswald, *Sklavenhandel und Sklavenleben zwischen Senegal und Atlas*, 30, 38. The opinion accepting the slave's claim seems to be more prevalent the farther south one goes into the Sahel. See Bruce Hall, *A History of Race in Muslim West Africa*, 83–87.

58. For a similar conclusion, see Lovejoy, 'Slavery in the Sokoto Caliphate,' 210.

59. Hanretta, *Islam and Social Change in French West Africa*, 212.

60. Hanretta, *Islam and Social Change in French West Africa*, 210 ff.

61. Peter Kolchin, 'Some controversial questions concerning the nineteenth-century emancipation from slavery and serfdom,' 44–49; Thomas Bender, 'Introduction,' in *The Antislavery Debate*, 2.

62. Westermann, *Slave Systems*, 152 ff.; Harper, *Slavery in the Late Roman World*, 209–14.

63. McKee, 'Slavery,' 289; A. G. Kennedy, 'Cnut's law code of 1018,' 74. In the second half of the 1000s CE the Bishop of Worcester issued a condemnation of English slave traders selling English slaves to Ireland from Bristol; Rosalind and Christopher Brooke, *Popular Religion in the Middle Ages*, 106.

64. Sue Peabody, *There Are No Slaves in France*, 5.

65. Joseph Vogt, *Ancient Slavery and the Ideal of Man*, 171–77.

66. Sally McKee states that by the mid-twentieth century, historians had come to a consensus that slavery had ended in Western Europe by the ninth century. But serious disagreement remained. Bonnassie has shown that it lasted at least until the eleventh century in South-West Europe. Slavery seems to have lasted in Denmark and Sweden until the mid-twelfth century; McKee, 'Slavery,' 282, 284; Bonnassie, *From Slavery to Feudalism in South-Western Europe*, 1, 56; Karras, 137–8. See also David Pelteret, *Slavery in Early Medieval England*, 13–24.

67. Susan Stuard, 'Ancillary Evidence for the Decline of Medieval Slavery,' 3–28; Wyatt, *Slaves and Warriors*, 397.

68. Hunwick and Powell, *The African Diaspora in the Mediterranean Lands of Islam*, 72.

69. Ibn Maryam al-Tilimsānī, *al-Bustān fī dhikr al-ʿulamāʾ waʾl-awliyāʾ bi-Tilimsān*, 231.

70. Francione, 'The Abolition of Animal Exploitation,' 5, 8, 18, 22; https://www.prnewswire.com/news-releases/animal-rights-is-about-abolition-not-animal-cruelty-says-responsible-pet-owners-alliance-of-texas-300107739.html.

71. Francione, 83.

72. See Fazlur Rahman, 'Status of Women in the Qur'an,' 40. Interestingly, according to Riḍā, ʿAbduh blamed the Mongol influence on Arab-Islamic civilization for knocking Muslims off what he considered a very Arab track towards freedom; al-Kawākibī, 'Tijārat al-raqīq,' 858. The late Iraqi scholar Shaykh Taha Al-Alwani states that none of the great Muslim empires of the pre-modern period fulfilled the Quranic mission of abolishing slavery because they did not properly understand the Quranic text; al-Alwani, *Shaykh Taha Jabir al-Alwani*, 138.

73. For expressions of this approach, see: Riḍā, 'Su'āl ʿan al-istirqāq al-maʿhūd fī hādhā al-zamān,' 32; Ibn ʿĀshūr, *Maqāṣid al-sharīʿa*, 131–32; idem, *Uṣūl al-niẓām al-ijtimāʿī fī al-islām*, 166–68; ʿAllāl al-Fāsī, *Maqāṣid al-sharīʿa al-islāmiyya*, 242–43; al-Zuḥaylī, *Mawsūʿa*, 3:770–771. In an essay published after his death in *al-Manār*, ʿAbd al-Raḥmān al-Kawākibī (d. 1902) quotes a scholar, whom Riḍā identifies as ʿAbduh, in a long passage on abolishing slavery. In it this friend states that the Shariah 'called for the nullification (*ibṭāl*) of slavery' gradually; al-Kawākibī, 'Tijārat al-raqīq,' 856, 857; Ṣubḥī al-Maḥmaṣānī, *Arkān ḥuqūq al-insān*, 99-105; Muḥammad Quṭb, *Shubuhāt ḥawl al-Islām*, 44; Esack, *On Being a Muslim*, 117; Muḥammad Ḥusayn Faḍlallāh, 'al-Islām al-yawm fī qafaṣ al-ittihām,' http://arabic.bayynat.org.lb/DialoguePage.aspx?id=4490 (2005 CNBC interview). See also An-Na'im, *Towards an Islamic Reformation*, 173–74.

74. See Chapter 2, n. 92.

75. Muḥammad ʿAbduh, *al-Aʿmāl al-kāmila*, 4:415.

76. Ibn ʿĀshūr, *Maqāṣid al-sharīʿa*, 131–32.

77. See Omid Safi, 'What is Progressive Islam?', http://jsrforum.lib.virginia.edu/pdfs/SafiProgressive.pdf; idem, 'Progressive Islam,' in *Oxford Islamic Studies Online*, http://www.oxfordislamicstudies.com/article/opr/t343/e0202 (accessed 25-May-2018); Adis Duderija, *The Imperatives of Progressive Islam*.

78. Scott Siraj al-Haqq Kugle, *Homosexuality in Islam*.

79. See Kecia Ali, 'Slavery and Sexual Ethics in Islam,' 118.

80. Fazlur Rahman, *Islam and Modernity*, 18–19.

81. Rahman, 'Status of Women in the Qur'an,' 43–45.

82. Adis Duderija, 'A Case Study of Patriarchy and Slavery: The Hermeneutical Importance of Qur'ānic Assumptions in the Development of a Values-Based and Purposive Oriented Qur'ān-sunna Hermeneutic,' 84–85.

83. Kecia Ali, *Sexual Ethics and Islam*, 66. Amina Wadud mentions slavery in her book *Inside the Gender Jihad* (pp. 123–25). Her wording on the moral standing of the issue, however, is ambiguous, and I did not feel comfortable engaging her discussion without clarification. My attempt to seek clarification was not welcomed.

84. Mohsen Kadivar, 'Mas'ala-i barda dārī dar Islām-i muʿāsir,' http://kadivar.com/?p=1033; idem, 'Īḍāḥ-i naskh-i ʿaqlī,' http://kadivar.com/?p=14660. This has apparently now been translated into English at https://www.iqraonline.net/the-issue-of-slavery-in-contemporary-islam/.

85. ʿAbd al-ʿAzīz al-Bukhārī, *Kashf al-asrār*, 3:162.

86. Fakhr al-Dīn al-Rāzī, *al-Maḥṣūl fī uṣūl al-fiqh*, 3:74.

87. Kadivar, 'Mas'ala-i barda dārī dar Islām-i muʿāsir.'

88. An-Na'im, 170–74.

89. Ware, *The Walking Qur'an*, 116; Chattopadhyay, *Slavery in the Bengal Presidency*, 83, 189; Eden, *Slavery and Empire in Central Asia*, 169–71; Toledano, *The Ottoman Slave Trade and its Suppression*, 95–168, 226–36; Baer, *Studies in the Social History of Modern Egypt*, 177–89; Wright, *The Trans-Saharan Slave Trade*, 164; Miers, 'Slavery and the slave trade in Saudi Arabia and the Arab states of the Persian Gulf,' 128; Klein, 'The emancipation of slaves in the Indian Ocean,' 198–218; Roberts and Miers, 'Introduction,' in *The End of Slavery in Africa*, 10–15; Jeffrey Hadler, *Muslims and Matriarchs*, 125–26; Lovejoy, *Transformations in Slavery*, 290–94; Clarence-Smith, *Islam and the Abolition of Slavery*, 117; Daniel Field, *The End of Serfdom*, 8–50. Botte claims Morocco has never technically prohibited slavery; Botte, *Esclavages et Abolitions*, 145.

90. Maḥmūd b. ʿUmar al-Zamakhsharī, *al-Kashshāf*, 2:406; Fakhr al-Dīn al-Rāzī, *Tafsīr al-Fakhr al-Rāzī*, 30:42; 12:76.

91. '*Ḥalāl Muḥammad ḥalāl abadan ilā yawm al-qiyāma wa ḥarāmuhu ḥarām abadan ilā yawm al-qiyāma lā yakūnu ghayruhu wa lā yajīʾu ghayruhu*'; Muḥammad b. Yaʿqūb al-Kulaynī, *al-Kāfī*, 1:58.

92. Al-Kindī, *Kitāb al-Wulāt wa Kitāb al-Quḍāt*, 367.

93. Al-Rāzī, *Tafsīr*, 12:76, 30:42. See also Muḥammad b. Sirāj al-Andalusī, *Fatāwā Qāḍī al-Jamāʿa*, 223. In the Ḥanafī school, this principle of caution lay behind a ruling that, if a Muslim army conquered an enemy fortress with a large number of soldiers within, if there was even one unknown *dhimmī* among them, the Muslims could not kill any of them due to their duty to protect *dhimmī*s; Kamāl al-Dīn Ibn Humām, *Fatḥ al-qadīr*, 1:191.

94. See Shihāb al-Dīn al-Qarāfī, *The Criterion for Distinguishing Legal Opinions from Judicial Rulings and the Administrative Acts of Judges and Rulers*, trans. Mohammad Fadel, 263. Al-Nawawī writes that the ruler's authority is *mā yakhtaṣṣu bi-ḍabṭ al-bayḍa min iʿdād al-juyūsh wa jibāyat al-kharāj*; al-Nawawī, *Sharḥ Ṣaḥīḥ Muslim*, 11/12: 450. Al-Ṭarābulusī and al-Qarāfī concur but add that the dividing line between the jurists' purview and the ruler's is determined by local custom; al-Ṭarābulusī, *Muʿīn al-ḥukkām*, 12–14; al-Qarāfī, *al-Furūq*, 1:358. Al-Nawawī may have derived this language from the Andalusian Qāḍī ʿIyāḍ (d. 1149), see al-Nubāhī, *Tārīkh quḍāt al-andalus*, 21; Ibn Abī al-Wafāʾ, *al-Jawāhir al-muḍiyya*, 4:31–2; Abū Isḥāq al-Shāṭibī, *Kitāb al-Iʿtiṣām*, 2:121.

95. Although it is often stated that only the Ḥanafī school allowed rulers to require judges to rule by one school of law, the Shāfiʿī authority Ibn Ḥajar al-Haytamī (d. 1565) clarifies that this had been the position of his school as well for some time. He affirms the opinion of his predecessor al-Bulqīnī (d. 1403); Ibn Ḥajar al-Haytamī, *al-Fatāwā al-kubrā*, 4:331.

96. Samy Ayoub, '"The Sulṭān says": State Authority in the Late Ḥanafī Tradition,' 239–78.

97. Taqī al-Dīn al-Subkī, *Fatāwā*, 1:186 (*wa matā kāna shayʾ min al-mubāḥāt fa-huwa ʿalā mā huwa ʿalayhi min tamkīn kull ḥadd minhu wa ʿadam manʿ shayʾ minhu illā bi-mustanad . . .*). ʿAbd al-Ḥayy al-Laknawī (d. 1887) notes this principle and attributes it to Badr al-Dīn al-ʿAynī (d. 1451) in his *Ramz sharḥ al-Kanz*. I have looked through a manuscript of this work but have not been able to find the passage al-Laknawī was referring to; al-Laknawī, *Majmūʿat rasāʾil al-Laknawī*, 2:306.

98. Mullā Hüsrev, *Durar al-ḥukkām sharḥ ghurar al-aḥkām*, 1:335.

99. Amalia Levanoni, '*Takfīr* in Egypt and Syria during the Mamlūk Period,' 158, 171–72, 177.

100. Ayoub, '"The Sulṭān Says",' 262; Martha Mundy and R. S. Smith, *Governing Property, Making the Modern State*, 31–37.

101. This comes from the influential legal manual of the Tatar scholar Muḥammad b. Muḥammad b. Shihāb al-Bazzāzī (d. 1424), who explains that, in such a case, the judge is stretching his oversight powers too far; *al-Fatāwā al-Bazzāziyya*, on the margins of *al-Fatāwā al-Hindiyya*, 4:120. For the political will behind this ruling, see Yossef Rapoport, 'Royal Justice and Religious Law: *Siyāsah* and Shariʿah under the Mamluks,' 89–92.

102. Al-Wazzānī calls this valid *siyāsa shar'iyya*; al-Wazzānī, *al-Nawāzil al-jadīda*, 3:466–67.
103. See Ibn Taymiyya's fatwa that Muslims are being wronged when their ruler restricts access to otherwise permissible goods or resources; Ibn Taymiyya, *Majmū'at al-fatāwā*, 29:153. Muḥammad al-Ghazālī (d. 1996) expresses a similar position in *Fiqh al-sunna*, 336.
104. According to Samer Akkach, the first work, al-Nābulusī's weighty *al-Ḥadīqa al-nadiya*, was completed in 1091 AH. The second, *Ibāḥat al-dukhān*, was completed in 1092 AH (Samer Akkach, personal communication). See 'Abd al-Ghanī al-Nābulusī, *al-Ḥadīqa al-nadiya sharḥ al-Ṭarīqa al-muḥammadiyya*, 1:142–43; idem, *Risāla fī ibāḥat al -dukhān*, MS 5136 Ẓāhiriyya, 369a (thanks to Samer Akkach for this MS)(. . . *min ghayr an yakūna fī dhālik maṣlaḥa lanā min jalb manfa'a aw daf' maḍarra*); idem, *al-Ṣulḥ bayn al-ikhwān fī ḥukm ibāḥat al-dukhān*, 97–98; Ralph Hattox, *Coffee and Coffeehouses*, 102.
105. Bayram al-Khāmis, 'al-Taḥqīq fī mas'alat al-raqīq,' 583–84; al-Kawākibī, 'Tijārat al -raqīq,' 857; Riḍā, 'As'ila min Bārīs,' 745.
106. Ibn 'Āshūr, *Fatāwā al-shaykh al-imām Muḥammad Ṭāhir Ibn 'Āshūr*, 364–65; Muḥammad Taqī 'Uthmānī, *Takmilat Fatḥ al-mulhim*, 1:272.
107. Ismael M. Montana, *The Abolition of Slavery in Ottoman Tunisia*, 5, 7, 51, 82, 97. See also the useful study of Elisabeth C. van der Haven, 'The Bey, the mufti and the scattered pearls: Shari'a and political leadership in Tunisia's Age of Reform – 1800–1864,' in particular Chapter 2.
108. Here Aḥmad Bey is referring to a famous Hadith in which the Prophet instructs Muslims that your slaves are 'your brothers, whom God has put under your control, so feed them from what you eat, clothe them from what you wear, and do not burden them with work that overwhelms them. If you give them more than they can do then assist them.' See *Ṣaḥīḥ al-Bukhārī: kitāb al-aymān, bāb al-ma'āṣī min amr al-Jahiliyya . . .; Ṣaḥīḥ Muslim: kitāb al-aymān, bāb iṭ'ām al-mamlūk mimmā ya'kulu . . .*
109. For this section, see the work of Ahmad Bey's secretary and later a noted historian, Aḥmad Ibn Abī Ḍiyāf, *Itḥāf ahl al-zamān bi-akhbār mulūk tūnis wa'ahd al-amān*, 4:87–88. The Ḥanafī mufti was Muḥammad Bayram al-Rābi' (d. 1861), the Mālikī one Ibrāhīm al-Riyāḥī (d. 1850).
110. This letter was purportedly sent after the Emancipation Proclamation but long before the Thirteenth Amendment ended slavery in the US. For the text of Ḥusayn Pasha's letter, see Ra'īf Khūrī, *Modern Arab Thought*, 152-157. For a discussion about the authenticity of this exchange, see Toledano, *Slavery and Abolition in the Ottoman Middle East*, 118, n. 9.
111. See his *Mulāḥaẓāt siyāsiyya 'an al-tanẓīmāt al-lāzima li'l-dawla al-'aliyya* (1898), published in Moncef Ben Abdel Jelil and Kamal Omrane, *Bayram V: Bibliographie Analytique*, 259–62.
112. This dating comes from Bayram al-Khāmis' son in a biography he wrote of his father, included in M. Bayram al-Khāmis, *Ṣafwat al-i'tibār bi-mustawda' al-amṣār wa'l -aqṭār*, 1:57, 171. The treatise was published in 1891 in two parts over two months in consecutive issues of the Egyptian journal *al-Muqtaṭaf*. An obituary of the author, published in the subsequent issue, notes that the treatise had been published that year; 'al-Sayyid Muḥammad Bayram,' *al-Muqtaṭaf* 15, n. 10 (1891): 677.
113. Bayram al-Khāmis, 'al-Taḥqīq,' 505, 583–84. Slavery would be an ongoing concern for Bayram until his death. He reiterated the arguments made in the *Taḥqīq* in a December 8, 1887 issue of a weekly newspaper he started in Egypt, *al-I'lām bi-ḥawādith al-ayyām* (1885–88). He wrote about slavery on numerous other occasions in the paper

as well: 11/13/1887 (emancipating slaves in Bukhara), 2/10/87 (concern over pilgrims being illegally enslaved on the way to Mecca), 3/24/87, 5/12/87 (how claiming to be a slave does not exempt one from military service), 6/16/87 (the link between the Mahdist revolt in Sudan and the slave trade); Moncef and Omrane, *Bayram V*, 96, 99, 105, 111, 114, 132.

114. Bayram al-Khāmis, *'al-Taḥqīq,'* 509, 579–81, 583.

115. *Al-Manār* notes the death of his son in 1899 and praises Bayram as *al-ʿallāma al-muṣliḥ al-shahīr*; *al-Manār* 2, n. 39 (1899): 624. See also Arnold Green, *The Tunisian Ulama*, 147–48, 244–45, Moncef and Omrane, *Bayram V*, 23.

116. Accoring to Riḍā, the scholar being quoted was ʿAbduh; al-Kawākibī, 'Tijārat al-raqīq,' 857.

117. Toledano, *The Ottoman Slave Trade and its Suppression*, 107–108. The letter of the Ottoman Shaykh al-Islam to the Hijaz in 1856 insists that the Sultan would never prohibit owners buying and selling slaves as long as that ownership was 'legally sound'; Cevdet Pasha, *Tazâkir*, 1–12:134.

118. http://www.kff.com/ar/King-Faisal. See also Aḥmad ʿAbd al-Razzāq al-Dawīsh, ed., *Fatāwā al-lajna al-dā'ima li'l-buḥūth al-ʿilmiyya wa'l-iftā'*, 16:577.

119. Bernard Freamon, 'Straight, No Chaser: Slavery, Abolition, and the Modern Muslim Mind,' paper presented at Yale University, Nov. 2007, 66–67; idem, *Indian Ocean Slavery in the Age of Abolition*, 61–80); Hamka, *Tafsir al-Azhar*, 5:17.

120. See Afsaneh Najmabadi, *The Story of the Daughters of Quchan*.

121. Mirzai, *A History of Slavery and Emancipation in Iran*, 77, 132, 156–57, 167, 171–73.

122. Sulṭān Ḥusayn Tābanda, *Naẓar-i madhhabī bih iʿlāmiyya-yi ḥuqūq-i bashar*, 33–38 (also available at http://www.sufism.ir/books/download/farsi/nazare_mazhabi.pdf, pg. 20, accessed 5/11/18). See also Ann E. Mayer, *Islam and Human Rights*, 21.

123. Wilfrid Scawen Blunt, *Secret History of the English Occupation of Egypt*, 190, 193–94 (from a letter Blunt says ʿAbduh sent him on April 25, 1882). This accords with what al-Kawākibī quoted from ʿAbduh (allegedly); al-Kawākibī, 'Tijārat al-raqīq,' 858. Blunt wrote elsewhere about Islamic reformism: 'Again, slavery must, by some means, be made illegal; and a stricter interpretation of the Koranic permission be put on marriage, concubinage, and divorce.' See Blunt, *Future of Islam*, 153.

124. Blunt, 'Slavery in Egypt,' 91–92 (addressed March 17, 1882). This notion was also hinted at by Syed Ameer Ali, *A Critical Examination*, 260.

125. Al-Nāṣirī, *Kitāb al-Istiqṣā*, 5:131–34. Here al-Nāṣirī is referencing a famous Hadith that the true cause of jihad is fighting 'so that God's word might be supreme/elevated'; *Ṣaḥīḥ al-Bukhārī: kitāb al-ʿilm, bāb man sa'ala wa huwa qā'im ʿāliman jālisan*. The argument of blocking the means is also invoked by Bayram, as is the absence of legitimate jihad; Bayram, 'al-Taḥqīq,' 583. For a study of al-Nāṣirī see Kenneth Brown, 'Profile of a Nineteenth-Century Moroccan Scholar,' 127–48.

126. Riḍā, 'Su'āl ʿan al-istirqāq al-maʿhūd fī hādhā al-zamān,' 32; idem, 'As'ila min bārīs,' 743-44; idem, 'Ḥukm ʿabīd ḥaḍramawt,' 189–90; al-Jisr, *al-Risāla al-ḥamīdiyya*, 427. Bayram admits that there were some Muslim states engaging in legitimate warfare, giving the example of Bornu; Bayram, 'Taḥqīq,' 580.

127. Abū Zahra, ed., *Sharḥ al-Siyar*, 1:78; al-Zuḥaylī, *Āthār*, 444; idem, *Mawsūʿa*, 3:770–72; Muḥammad Quṭb, *Shubuhāt ḥawl al-Islām*, 55–56.

128. Riḍa, 'al-Raqīq al-abyaḍ wa'l-aswad,' 20.

129. Abū Zahra, ed., *Sharḥ al-Siyar*, 1:78. Al-Zuḥaylī followed Abū Zahra; al-Zuḥaylī, *Āthār*, 444; Faḍlallāh, 'al-Islām al-yawm fī qafaṣ al-ittihām,' http://arabic.bayynat.org.lb

/DialoguePage.aspx?id=4490 (2005 CNBC interview); Muṣṭafā al-Zarqā', 'Mawqif al-Islām min al-riqq,' appendix in al-Qaraḍāwī, *Fiqh al-jihād*, 2:1464–67.

130. Khan, *Essays*, 25–26; Bayram, 'al-Taḥqīq,' 508, 583. See also Shafīq, *L'Esclavage*, 35.

131. Riḍā, 'Su'āl ʿan al-istirqāq al-maʿhūd fī hādhā al-zamān,' 32. See, for example, ʿUthmānī, *Takmilat Fatḥ al-mulhim*, 1:264-265; Muḥammad Saʿīd Ramaḍān al-Būṭī, *Min al-fikar wa'l-qalb*, 85–94.

132. *Ṣaḥīḥ al-Bukhārī: kitāb al-jihād wa'l-siyar, bāb qatl al-asīr*...; *Ṣaḥīḥ Muslim: kitāb al-ḥajj, bāb jawāz dukhūl makka bi-ghayr iḥrām.*

133. *Ṣaḥīḥ al-Bukhārī: kitāb ṣalāt al-khawf, bāb al-tabkīr wa'l-ghalas*...

134. Al-Zuḥaylī, *Mawsūʿa*, 3:769–73; al-Māwardī, *The Ordinances of Government*, 145–52; Muḥammad b. Ismāʿīl al-Ṣanʿānī, *Subul al-salām*, 4:74–75; Aḥmad al-Ghumārī, *Masālik al-dilāla*, 167–68.

135. Riḍā, 'As'ila min bārīs,' 745.

136. Shafīq, *L'Esclavage*, 36; al-ʿAqqād, 'Mas'alat al-riqq fī al-Islām,' 18.

137. Riḍa, 'Su'āl ʿan al-istirqāq,' 32.

138. Al-Būṭī, *Min al-fikar wa'l-qalb*, 87-90; idem, *Hādhihi mushkilātuhum*, 54–63.

139. ʿUthmānī, *Takmilat fatḥ al-mulhim*, 1:272.

140. Yūsuf al-Qaraḍāwī, *Fiqh al-jihād*, 2:977–79.

141. Tamīmī, 'Tafsīr qawlihi taʿālā aw mā malakat aymānukum li'l-shaykh ʿAbd al-ʿAzīz Fawzān,' YouTube video, 5/28/2014, https://www.youtube.com/watch?v=oPTLRtt1uXY.

142. See Abū al-Ḥasan Shaʿrānī (d. 1974), *Nathr-i ṭūbī*, 1:186.

143. Mirzai, *A History of Slavery and Emancipation in Iran*, 139–42; al-Kulaynī, *Uṣūl al-Kāfī*, 5:114 (*sharr al-nās man bāʿa al-nās*).

144. This notion can be traced even farther back to 1827 in the East India Company's *Asiatic Journal*: 'Other sources of slavery practically exist, by fictions or and evasions of the law; but these are abuses.' See, 'On Slavery in the East,' *Asiatic Journal*, 447; Ameer Ali, 258–59. See also ʿAlī Mubārak, *ʿAlam al-dīn*, 2:715.

145. Abū Zahra, ed., *Sharḥ al-Siyar*, 84.

146. To my knowledge, one of the few Muslim scholars who has called drawn attention to this is Mohsen Kadivar. See http://kadivar.com/?p=1033.

147. Taqī al-Subkī, *Qaḍā' al-arab*, 541. In fact, if a slave got the better of his master in the Dār al-Ḥarb and 'enslaved' him, and then they both came into the Dār al-Islām, the 'slave' was the recognized owner of the 'master'; al-Khaṭṭābī, *Maʿālim al-sunan*, 2:265.

148. See note 52 above.

149. Al-Kawākibī, 'Tijārat al-raqīq,' 856.

150. Riḍā, 'Ḥukm ʿabīd ḥaḍramawt,' 190.

151. Bayram, 'Taḥqīq,' 583-584; Riḍā, 'As'ila min Bārīs,' 745.

152. Erdem, xx.

153. Al-Shāṭibī, *al-Muwāfaqāt*, 2:23.

154. This was reported to me by Ibn ʿUthaymīn's student Yasir Qadhi, who heard it from him.

155. Abū Zahra, *Fatāwā*, 725.

156. Ali Gomaa (ʿAlī Jumʿa), *al-Bayān li-mā yashghalu al-adhhān*, 72.

157. Alakhbarinfo, 'Al-Shaykh al-Dadaw: mumārasat al-riqq madʿāt li'l-fitna wa lā yuqurruhā aḥad,' YouTube video, 4/21/2012, https://www.youtube.com/watch?v=rsfnkbNH93A; see also http://www.elwassat.info/index.php/3amme/4543-2015-04-13-16-23-16

158. Exposed!, 'Ṣāliḥ al-Fawzān: ḥukm al-riqq (al-shar'ī) wa'l-jawārī wa'l-farq bayn al-taḥrīm wa'l-man',' YouTube video, 9/2/2013, https://www.youtube.com/watch?v=8hNMh32cuks. See also Muḥammad Mukhtār al-Qāḍī, 'Bayn al-Sharī'a al-islāmiyya wa'l-qānūn al-rūmānī: niẓām al-riqq,' 365-371. See also Faḍlallāh, 'al-Islām al-yawm fī qafaṣ al-ittihām,' http://arabic.bayynat.org.lb/DialoguePage.aspx?id=4490 (2005 CNBC interview).

159. A Tuareg slave trader defends *riqq* to a French general in 1839 by saying: European servants can change jobs, but they will always be servants and never integrated into a family, while in Islam slaves are. Slaves are also cared for in old age. In Europe, children born of mistresses are disgraces to be hidden, while a child born of a *jāriya* is legitimate and his mother is freed; Eugène Daumas, *Le Grand Désert* (Paris: M. Levy Frères, 1856), 220, quoted from Hunwick and Powell, *The African Diaspora*, 64. The 1864 revised edition has the sentence on children born of mistresses removed (p. 211). See also Shafīq, *L'Esclavage*, 20-27; al-Jisr, *al-Risāla al-ḥamīdiyya*, 420-428.

160. Khan, *Essays*, 24.

161. Iqbal, 'Islam as a Moral and Political Ideal – I,' 36.

162. Al-Jisr, *al-Risāla al-ḥamīdiyya*, 420-428; Mubārak, *'Alam al-dīn*, 2:712–22; Ghazal, 'Debating Slavery,' 142–43.

163. Muḥammad Taqī 'Uthmānī, *In'ām al-Bārī: durūs-i Bukhārī sharīf*, 1:459–60; al-Qaraḍāwī, *Fiqh al-jihād*, 2:974.

164. Islam Channel, 'Mas'alat al-riqq fī al-islām: al-Albānī,' YouTube, 8/6/2016, https://www.youtube.com/watch?v=lrpPaMRk6rE; Islam Channel, 'Mas'alat al-riqq fī al-islām 2 al-Albānī,' YouTube, 8/6/2016, https://www.youtube.com/watch?v=p6WF6XFLemI.

165. Abul A'la Maududi, *Purdah and the Status of Women in Islam*, 20, 212.

166. Here it's interesting to consider the hefty volume written by Mawlānā Sa'īd Aḥmad Akbarābādī, *Ghulāmān-i Islām* (n.p.: Nadwat al-Muṣannifīn, 1940), a biographical dictionary of all the great and notable freed slaves in Sunni history.

167. Maududi, *Human Rights in Islam*, 17–19.

168. Muḥammad Quṭb, *Shubuhāt ḥawl al-Islām*, 57.

169. 'Abdallāh Nāṣiḥ 'Ulwān, *Niẓām al-riqq fī al-islām*, 83–91.

170. Muḥammad Quṭb, *Shubuhāt ḥawl al-Islām*, 58–59.

171. 'Allāma Muḥammad Ḥusayn Ṭabāṭabā'ī, *al-Mīzān fī tafsīr al-Qur'ān*, 6:356.

CHAPTER 6 THE PROPHET & ISIS

1. See, for a study on Muslims in central Texas, Shehnaz Haqqani, 'Islamic Tradition, Change, and Feminism,' 145–63.
2. 'Abd al-Qādir Khānī, *Waqā'i'-i Khānī*, 285b.
3. Syed Ameer Ali, 249.
4. Abdul Sheriff, '*Suria*: Concubine or Secondary Slave Wife?,' 102–103; Hunwick and Powell, *The African Diaspora*, 64; Burnes, *Travels into Bokhara*, 1:296.
5. Toledano, *Slavery and Abolition in the Ottoman Middle East*, 117–34; Börte Sagaster, *"Herren" und "Sklaven": der Wandel im Sklavenbild türkischer Literaten in der Spätzeit des Osmanischen Reiches.*
6. Mirzai, *A History of Slavery and Emancipation in Iran*, 170.

7. Toledano, *Slavery and Abolition in the Ottoman Middle East*, 117.
8. Blunt, 'Slavery in Egypt,' 91.
9. For Ottomans playing on these ambiguities in discussions with European powers, see Toledano, *As if Silent and Absent*, 76-78, 110–11. In 1825 the British visitor in the sultanate of Bornu, Dixon Denham, reported that the ruler of the state admitted (allegedly) that the slave trade was against the tenets of Islam but that Arab merchants only accepted payment in slaves; Boahen, *Britain, the Sahara, and the Western Sudan*, 71.
10. Riḍā, 'al-Raqīq al-abyaḍ wa'l-aswad,' 20; idem, 'As'ila min bārīs,' 743.
11. This fair question is raised by the otherwise unenlightening Sam Harris in his *Islam and the Future of Tolerance*, 66.
12. Riḍā, 'As'ila min bārīs,' 745–46; idem, 'Ḥukm ʿabīd ḥaḍramawt,' 32.
13. Abū Zahra, ed., *Sharḥ al-Siyar*, 78; al-Zuḥaylī, *Āthār*, 444.
14. See, for example, Jonathan Brown, 'Is the Devil in the Details?: Tension between Minimalism and Comprehensiveness in the Shariah,' 464.
15. Al-Būṭī, *Min al-fikar wa'l-qalb*, 86.
16. ʿUthmāni, *Takmilat Fatḥ al-mulhim*, 1:268–72. See also Brockopp, *Early Mālikī Law*, 133.
17. Andrew Wilson, 'The Best Argument for Trajectory Hermeneutic – and Where it Goes Wrong,' 3/6/2013, http://thinktheology.co.uk/blog/article/the_best_argument_for_a_trajectory_hermeneutic_and_where_it_goes_wrong, accessed 5/5/2018.
18. Rahman, *Islam and Modernity*, 19. The question of how Muslims could replace the pious act of manumission was taken up by the nineteenth-century Ibāḍī scholar Muḥammad b. Yūsuf Aṭfayyish, who suggested that sacrificing a ewe could be a replacement, just as Abraham had replaced the sacrifice of his son with a sheep; Daddi Addoun, 'Slavery and Abolition in Ibāḍī Theology,' 239.
19. Batran, 'The 'Ulama' of Fas,' 12.
20. Bernard Freamon, 'Slavery, Freedom, and the Doctrine of Consensus in Islamic Jurisprudence,' 60–61.
21. Ḥamza b. Yūsuf al-Sahmī, *Tārīkh Jurjān*, 445. Muḥammad Zāhid al-Kawtharī considers this report to be a fabrication because, among other reasons, it omits mention of the Sunna. See al-Kawtharī's notes on Shams al-Dīn al-Dhahabī, *Manāqib al-Imām Abū Ḥanīfa*, 73.
22. Ibn Baṭṭāl (d. 1057) states, 'Nothing is infallible except what is in the Book of God, the Sunna of His Messenger (s) or in the consensus of the ulama about the meaning found in one of those two.' The Shāfiʿī scholar al-Khaṭṭābī (d. 996) explains that if a Muslim denies something on which there is consensus that is well known, such as that there are five daily prayers, the Ramadan fast, the prohibition on fornication, etc., then that person is no longer Muslim (unless he is a new Muslim who does not know these things). If it is a consensus that is well known only among scholars, however, such as the prohibition on marrying a woman and her aunt at the same time, then denying such a thing does not make one an unbeliever. Al-Ghazālī cautions readers not to be too hasty in declaring someone an unbeliever for denying something on which there is allegedly consensus, since 'affirming consensus is one of the most allusive of things.' Ibn Ḥanbal was quoted by his son as saying, 'Whoever claims consensus has spoken falsely, for indeed people could have differed.' Finally, ʿAbdallāh al-Ghumārī (d. 1993) criticizes those who mischaracterize Ibn Ḥanbal's quote as 'Whoever claims the existence of consensus has spoken falsely . . .,' since the original statement does not doubt the existence of consensus, only its frequency. See Ibn Baṭṭāl, *Sharḥ Ṣaḥīḥ al-Bukhārī*, 10:320; al-Khaṭṭābī, *Maʿālim al-sunan*, 2:9; Ibn Ḥajar al-ʿAsqalānī, *Fatḥ al-Bārī*, 12:249; al-Ghazālī,

On the Boundaries of Theological Tolerance in Islam, 118; al-Shāfiʿī, *Kitāb al-Umm*, 7:281; ʿAbdallāh b. Aḥmad, *Masāʾil al-imām Aḥmad Ibn Ḥanbal*, 439; Muḥammad b. Ismāʿīl al -Ṣanʿānī, *Taṭhīr al-iʿtiqād ʿan adrān al-ilḥād*, 38; ʿAbdallāh al-Ghumārī, *al-Rasāʾil al-ghumāriyya*, 78–79.

23. Muhammad Yaqoubi, *Inqādh al-umma*, 25–26.

24. Freamon uses the word *ḥarām*, while the Open Letter to Baghdadi uses the phrase '*taḥrīm al-riqq wa tajrīmihi*'; 'Al-Risāla al-maftūḥa,' 17–18 (available at http://lettertobaghdadi.com/pdf/Booklet-Arabic.pdf).

25. Bayram, 'al-Taḥqīq,' 583.

26. Al-Dawīsh, ed., *Fatāwā al-Lajna al-dāʾima*, 16:573.

27. Al-Qaraḍāwī, *Fiqh al-jihād*, 2:974.

28. It is pertinent and interesting to note that Arab Socialists used Islam's acceptance of slavery in order to make the argument that the Shariah had quite clearly only been meant to remain valid for a certain period of time. See Muḥammad Quṭb, *Shubuhāt ḥawl al-Islām*, 37.

29. Al-Būṭī, *Min al-fikar wa'l-qalb*, 85–94; idem, *Hādhihi mushkilātuhum*, 63.

30. An-Na'im, 170–174.

31. Online fatwas collected from ISIS show that they allowed taking women from the Shiite, Nusayri, Yazidi and other non-Muslim communities provided they had no treaty with ISIS. There was disagreement over whether the women of Sunni enemies of ISIS (called apostates) were permissible; http://www.aymennjawad.org/17879/the-archivist-unseen-islamic-state-fatwas-on.

32. See Loveday Morris, 'Islamic State says it is buying and selling Yazidi women, using them as concubines,' *The Washington Post*, 10/12/2014, http://www.washingtonpost.com/world/islamic-state-says-it-is-buying-and-selling-yazidi-women-using-them-as-concubines/2014/10/12/d904756d-10ab-47b9-889c-d3b00343470f_story.html; Rukmini Callimachi, 'ISIS Enshrines a Theology of Rape,' *New York Times*, 9/13/2015, https://www.nytimes.com/2015/08/14/world/middleeast/isis-enshrines-a-theology-of-rape.html; idem, 'To Maintain Its Supply of Sex Slaves, ISIS Pushes Birth Control,' *New York Times*, 3/12/2016, https://www.nytimes.com/2016/03/13/world/middleeast/to-maintain-supply-of-sex-slaves-isis-pushes-birth-control.html?_r=0.

33. Umm Sumayyah al-Muhājirah, 'Slave-Girls or Prostitutes,' 44–49; *Al-Saby: aḥkām wa masāʾil* ([Raqqa]: Dīwān al-Buḥūth wa'l-Iftāʾ, 2014).

34. Yaqoubi, *Inqādh al-umma*, 25–26.

35. 'Al-Risāla al-maftūḥa,' 17–18 (available See http://lettertobaghdadi.com/pdf/Booklet-Arabic.pdf). The Muslim feminist scholar Kecia Ali offers a short but sharp critique of the claims made here, see https://feminismandreligion.com/2015/02/24/isis-and-authority-by-kecia-ali/.

36. *Al-Saby: aḥkām wa masāʾil*, 17. Ibn Taymiyya certainly seems to build a case for the permissibility of taking polytheist/non-*kitābī* slave women as concubines in his *Fatāwā al-kubrā*, but in the material included in the *Majmūʿat al-fatāwā* he seems to support the vast majority position prohibiting it; Ibn Taymiyya, *al-Fatāwā al-kubrā*, 3:105-108; idem, *Majmūʿat al-fatāwā*, 31:227. His student Ibn Qayyim al-Jawziyya clearly allows it; Ibn Qayyim, *Zād al-maʿād fī hady khayr al-ʿibād*, 5:120–21. For evidence of consensus on the prohibition of taking non-*kitābī*s as slave-concubines, see Ibn Qudāma, *Mughnī*, 7:506–508. Taking non-*kitābī*s as concubines was not uncommon amongst the Muslim nobility in India, going back to the Delhi Sultanate in the late twelfth century; Peter Jackson, *The Delhi Sultanate*, 279.

37. *Al-Saby*, 6.

38. Kecia Ali, *Sexual Ethics and Islam*, 71.
39. Anwar al-Awlaki, 'The Ruling on Dispossessing the Disbelievers wealth [sic] in Dar al-Harb,' 56.
40. Avril Powell, 'Indian Muslim Modernists,' 273.
41. See, for example, Joseph S. Spoerl, 'Sex-Slavery and the Sharia in the Islamic State,' *New English Review* (Nov. 2014), http://www.newenglishreview.org/Joseph_S._Spoerl/Sex-Slavery_and_Sharia_in_the_Islamic_State/.
42. Nathaniel Mathews, 'The "Fused Horizon" of Abolitionism and Islam: Historicism, the Quran and the Global History of Abolition'; Freamon, 'Straight, No Chaser: Slavery, Abolition, and the Modern Muslim Mind.'
43. For a discussion of this even on the theoretical level, see Rowan Cruft et al., 'The Philosophical Foundations of Humans Rights: An Overview,' 21–22.
44. Samuel Moyn, 'The 1970's as Turning Point in Human Rights History,' 1–14.
45. https://www.independent.co.uk/news/world/asia/philippines-president-rodrigo-duterte-doesnt-give-a-s-about-human-rights-war-on-drugs-civilians-a7365156.html.
46. As John Gray writes, 'Whatever they are called, torture and slavery are universal evils; but these evils cannot be consigned to the past like redundant theories in science. They return under different names: torture as enhanced interrogation techniques, slavery as human trafficking.'; John Gray, *The Silence of Animals: On Progress and Other Myths*, 75.
47. ISIS pamphlet, 'Al-Walā' li'l-islām lā li'l-waṭan.'
48. ISIS Dīwān al-Buḥūth wa'l-iftā, *al-Adilla al-jaliya fī kufr man nāṣara al-ḥamla al-ṣalībiyya ʿalā al-khilāfa al-islāmiyya*, 22 ff.
49. During an 1847 rebellion in eastern Anatolia some Christian and Yazidi men and women were taken as slaves. Ottoman officials immediately issued a fatwa that they were *dhimmīs* who had to be released; Ahmed Akgündüz, *Ottoman Harem*, 102.
50. Cole Bunzel, 'Caliphate in Disarray: Theological Turmoil in the Islamic State,' 10/3/2017, http://www.jihadica.com/caliphate-in-disarray/.
51. Al-Qaeda leadership warned ISIS's predecessor organization, led by Abū Muṣʿab al-Zarqāwī, not to alienate Sunni communities and their leadership. A leading Salafi-Jihadi ideologue, Abū Muḥammad al-Maqdisī, also criticized al-Zarqāwī for attacking civilians and Shiites in Iraq who, even if sinful, did not deserve to die; https://ctc.usma.edu/harmony-program/atiyahs-letter-to-zarqawi-original-language-2/; Joas Wagemakers, 'Reclaiming Scholarly Authority: Abu Muhammad al-Maqdisi's Critique of Jihadi Practices,' 523–539.
52. Al-Albānī, *Fatāwā al-shaykh al-Albānī*, 247–49, 269–70, 274.
53. Alakhbarinfo, 'Al-Shaykh al-Dadaw: mumārasat al-riqq madʿāt li'l-fitna wa lā yuqirruhā aḥad,' YouTube video, 4/21/2012, https://www.youtube.com/watch?v=rsfnkbNH93A; Botte, *Esclavages et Abolitions*, 215, 354.
54. https://www.iraqbodycount.org/analysis/numbers/ten-years/
55. http://www.psr.org/news-events/press-releases/doctors-group-releases-startling-analysis.html.
56. Neta C. Crawford, 'The Cost of War: Human Cost of the Post-9/11 Wars,' https://watson.brown.edu/costsofwar/files/cow/imce/papers/2018/Human%20Costs,%20Nov%208%202018%20CoW.pdf.
57. This narration is rare and seems to oscillate around the *ḥasan* rating. It adds this slave clause to a Hadith via Aisha that is very well known, appearing in the *Ṣaḥīḥayn*. But the well-known Hadith mentions Gabriel urging caring for neighbors and does not mention slaves. Al-Bayhaqī, however, states that this slave clause, as narrated via Aisha,

is *ṣaḥīḥ*, which al-Haythamī confirmed. Al-Suyūṭī considered it *ḥasan*. There is another narration of this Hadith via Abū Hurayra, but Ibn Ḥibbān states it is totally unreliable (*bāṭil*). Aḥmad al-Ghumārī concludes that the narration mentioning slaves cannot be *ṣaḥīḥ* due to this disagreement in the *matn* as well as the omission of one narrator in the *isnād* of some versions. He seems to agree with al-Suyūṭī's *ḥasan* rating. Al-Albānī considers the slavery clause an anomalous addition not to be accepted (*ziyāda shādhdha munkara*); Ibn Sallām al-Ibāḍī (d. 887), *Kitāb fīhi bad' al-islām wa sharā'i' al-dīn*, 87; al-Bayhaqī, *Shu'ab al-īmān*, 6:369; idem, *al-Sunan al-kubrā*, 8:19; Ibn Ḥibbān, *Kitāb al-Majrūḥīn*, 1:280; al-Munāwī, *Fayḍ al-qadīr*, 10:5358; Aḥmad al-Ghumārī, *al-Mudāwī*, 5:475–76; al-Albānī, *Irwā' al-ghalīl fī takhrīj ḥadīth Manār al-sabīl*, 3:401. See also Abū Layth al-Samarqandī, *Tafsīr*, 1:354 (from Anas with no *isnād*, on Quran 4:36).

58. Ibn Rushd al-Jadd (d. 1126) of Cordoba notes that the compelled sale of a person's share of a co-owned slave when the other co-owner manumits his share is a restriction on the general rule that Muslims cannot be compelled to give up or sell their property against their will (Hadith: 'It is not permitted for a man to take the property of his brother without his right . . .'). In this case, the imposition may well be, says Ibn Rushd al-Jadd, for the benefit of removing the harm of slavery from the slave; Muḥammad b. Aḥmad Ibn Rushd al-Jadd, *Masā'il Abī al-Walīd Ibn Rushd al-Jadd*, 1:217; *Musnad Ibn Ḥanbal*, 5:425.

59. Thanks to Bilal Ware for this insight.

60. This is based on Gwyn Campbell's observations about general features of slavery in the Indian Ocean world and on discussions with my colleague Nathaniel Mathews; Campbell, 'Introduction: abolition and its aftermath in the Indian Ocean world,' in *Abolition and its Aftermath in Indian Ocean Africa and Asia*, ed. Campbell, 7–8; idem, 'Introduction: Slavery and other forms of Unfree Labour in the Indian Ocean World,' xiii–xix.

61. Ḍirār b. 'Amr, *Kitāb al-Taḥrīsh*, 127.

62. Sean Henretta asserts that some West African Muslim scholars opposed abolition, citing the case of Hajj 'Umar of Kete-Krachi, who, 'expressed outrage at British insistence on the legal equality of slaves and scholars.' I do not think this is an accurate reading of Hajj 'Umar's expressed sentiments. His poem speaks about the effects of colonization (in translation from Arabic):

> They said: 'There should be no slave trade; and no slavery.
> No confinement with fetters of ropes; no beating with painful punishments.'
> The freeborn became a slave to them; And slaves became noblemen.

Here Hajj 'Umar is not objecting to abolition but, rather, mourning how British rule had generally destroyed the indigenous order of his society. See Henretta, 226; Talatu Mustapha, 'Historiographical Study of Four Works of al-Ḥājj 'Umar ibn Abī Bakr of Kete-Krachi (*circa* 1850–1934),' (MA thesis, McGill University, 1970), 61, 110, 149.

CHAPTER 7 CONCUBINES AND CONSENT

1. Al-Ṭahṭāwī, *An Imam in Paris*, 206.

2. Muḥammad Ḥusayn Haykal's original *Ḥayāt Muḥammad* calls Māriya one of the *sarārī*, while the late Isma'il al-Faruqi translates it as wife; Haykal, *The Life of Muhammad*, 416. This discrepancy is also noted by Kecia Ali, *The Lives of Muhammad*, 132, 186. For

Haykal, the 'controversies' around the Prophet's family life were the Zayd/Zaynab affair and the jealousy of the Prophet's wives towards Māriya. Neither Aisha's age nor Māriya's status register; Antonie Wessels, *A Modern Arabic Biography of Muḥammad: A Critical Study of Muḥammad Ḥusayn Haykal's* Ḥayāt Muḥammad, 116–20, 141.

3. See Appendix 4 – Was Māriya the Wife or Concubine of the Prophet?

4. See Haqqani, 136, 154.

5. Fikret Karčić, *Kroz prizmu historije*, 239–42; http://www.stuff.co.nz/national/2828715/Call-for-reassurance-over-headscarves-in-court.

6. Johan Norberg writes, 'There can hardly be a stronger example of human progress than the fact that slavery, which existed in almost all countries as late as 1800, is now formally banned everywhere.' See Johan Norberg, *Progress: Ten Reasons to Look Forward to the Future*, 148; John Gray, *The Silence of Animals*, 75.

7. Norberg, *Progress*, 164–65.

8. See Avery Cardinal Dulles, 'Development or Reversal,' *First Things*, Oct. 2005, https://www.firstthings.com/article/2005/10/development-or-reversal.

9. Sherman Jackson, 'The Alchemy of Domination? Some Ashʿarite Responses to Muʿtazilite Ethics.'

10. 'Pet Food,' *The Economist*, June 20, 2015.

11. Herodotus, *Histories*, Book III: 38; Montaigne, *Essais*, Book 1:31; Blaise Pascal, *Pensées*, 17.

12. Grubbs, *Law and Family in Late Antiquity*, 155.

13. Nicholas L. Syrett, *American Child Bride*, 3–5, 45–46, 78, 81–85, 218.

14. Here I use Syrett's conclusions about the American South, but extrapolating to other regions today and adding life expectancy are my own additions; Syrett, *American Child Bride*, 218. Ralph Fitch, one of the first British to travel to and write about India, noted in 1588–91 that child marriage was common. He saw one marriage between a boy of nine and girl of six. Marriages happened at such a young age, he explains, because parents wanted grandchildren during their lifetimes; Mohammad Azhar Ansari, *European Travellers under the Mughals*, 20.

15. Rachel Herz, *That's Disgusting: Unraveling the Mysteries of Repulsion*, 205, 232–33. See Gregory Leavitt, 'Tylor vs. Westermarck: Explaining the Incest Taboo,' 46.

16. Al-Sakhāwī, *al-Maqāṣid al-ḥasana*, 374; *Muwaṭṭa'*, recension of Muḥammad al-Shaybānī: *bāb qiyām shahr Ramaḍān wa mā fīhi min al-faḍl.*

17. See *Ṣaḥīḥ al-Bukhārī*: *kitāb istitābat al-murtaddīn . . ., bāb man taraka qitāl al-khawārij*; *Ṣaḥīḥ Muslim*: *kitāb al-zakāt, bāb dhikr al-khawārij wa ṣifātihim.*

18. Stark, *The Southern Gates of Arabia*, 137–38, 143.

19. Jacques Maritain, *Les Droits de l'homme et la loi naturelle*, 105, 107.

20. In social praxis, the dependency involved in *riqq* could blend with other relationships of obligation and control. Polly Hill notes how the economic condition of slaves and free married sons was 'remarkably similar' in nineteenth-century Hausaland; neither could leave their village; Hill, 'Comparative West African Farm Slavery Systems,' 45.

21. Carl Tobias, 'Interspousal Tort Immunity in America,' 359–478; Henry Ansgar Kelly, '"Rule of Thumb" and the Folklaw of the Husband's Stick,' 341–65. British judges in India noted that Islamic law on the permissibility of husbands physically disciplining their wives was comparable to British law; A. A. A. Fyzee, *Cases in the Muhammadan Law*, 92–93, 102, 154.

22. See Goitein, 'Slaves and Slavegirls,' 6–8; idem, 'The Sexual Mores of the Common People,' 47–48; Haqqani, 154.

23. Sometimes a group of slaves was seen as so foreign and other that sex with them was considered reprehensible, as in the case of thirteenth-century Angkor and the mountain peoples that were enslaved there. See I. Mabbett, 'Some Remarks on the Present State of Knowledge about Slavery in Angkor,' 44–45.
24. Elbourne, 'Introduction: Key Themes and Perspectives,' 1.
25. In the Near East as far back as Hammurabi's Code (*circa* 1750 BCE) we find the notion that if a wife was barren she should provide a handmaiden to her husband; Hammurabi Code, §144–45; Exodus 21:7–11; Gen. 21:12–14.
26. See Joseph Fischel, 'What do we consent to when we consent to sex,' *Aeon*, Oct. 23, 2018, https://aeon.co/ideas/what-do-we-consent-to-when-we-consent-to-sex?fbclid=IwAR3R9am_3e2p1p5b-YvXOGCPLXoR9WwPSRZDHqTEske7q8Iyz6j0qM9I8_w.; Robin West, 'Sex, Law, and Consent,' 221–50.
27. W.O. Stephens, 'Epictetus on Fearing Death: Bugbear and Open Door Policy,' 381.
28. Vera Bergelson, 'Consent to Harm,' 177–80.
29. Syrett, *American Child Bride*, 20. See also Judith Butler, 'Sexual Consent: Some Thoughts on Psychoanalysis and Law,' 417–18.
30. For a useful discussion of the inconsistencies around the legal tests for the capacity to consent to sex, see Robin Mackenzie and John Watts, 'Capacity to consent to sex reframed,' 56–58.
31. Butler, 'Sexual Consent,' 421.
32. See Butler, 'Sexual Consent,' 418.
33. For a dated but still informative study on this trend, see William N. Eskridge, Jr., 'The Many Faces of Sexual Consent,' 47-67.
34. See Joseph J. Fischel, *Screw Consent: A Better Politics of Sexual Justice*.
35. Joseph J. Fischel, *Sex and Harm in the Age of Consent*, 10. See also Butler, 'Sexual Consent,' 423.
36. Fraidy Reiss, 'Why can 12-year olds still get married in the United States?,' *Washington Post*, Feb. 10, 2017, https://www.washingtonpost.com/posteverything/wp/2017/02/10/why-does-the-united-states-still-let-12-year-old-girls-get-married/?utm_term=.9edd3f8c07ee.
37. 'Statutory Compilation Shows How State Laws Permit Child Marriage to Persist in Present-Day America,' Nov. 18, 2016, Tahirih Justice Center, https://www.tahirih.org/news/statutory-compilation-shows-how-state-laws-permit-child-marriage-to-persist-in-present-day-america/.
38. See Andrew Buncombe, 'New Jersey governor refuses to ban child marriage because "it would conflict with religious customs",' *Independent*, May 14, 2017, https://www.independent.co.uk/news/world/americas/new-jersey-chris-christie-child-marriage-ban-fails-religious-custom-a7735616.html; idem, 'Virginia introduces law to stop 12-year-old girls getting married,' *Independent*, July 4, 2016, https://www.independent.co.uk/news/world/americas/virginia-introduces-law-to-stop-12-year-old-girls-from-getting-married-a7119091.html.
39. Butler, 'Sexual Consent,' 425.
40. Lila Abu-Lughod, *Do Muslim Women Need Saving?*, 217–19; idem, 'Authorizing Moral Crusades to Save Muslim Women,' 20–21.
41. Bales, *Understanding Global Slavery*, 48.
42. Johanna Ransmeier, 'Ambiguities in the Sale of Women at the End of the Qing Dynasty,' 319–44.
43. See Morgan Lee Woolley, 'Marital Rape: A Unique Blend of Domestic Violence and Non-Marital Rape Issues,' 269 ff.

44. Hina Azam, *Sexual Violation in Islamic Law*, 186.
45. Kecia Ali, 'Concubinage and Consent,' 149.
46. See, for example, ʿAbd al-ʿAzīz al-Ghumārī, *Mā yajūzu wa mā lā yajūzu fī al-ḥayāt al-zawjiyya*, 21–31.
47. Al-Buhūtī, *Kashshāf al-qināʿ*, 5:45; Mullā Hüsrev, *Durar al-ḥukkām*, 1:351; al-Nawawī, *Rawḍat al-ṭālibīn*, 7:102–103.
48. For example, al-Buhūtī, *al-Rawḍ al-murbiʿ*, 384.
49. Al-Kindī and Ibn Ḥajar, *Kitāb al-Wulāt wa kitāb al-Quḍāt wa Rafʿ al-iṣr ʿan quḍāt miṣr*, 584.
50. Al-Wazzānī, *al-Nawāzil al-jadīda*, 4:438, see also 474.
51. Al-Shāfiʿī, *al-Umm*, 5:189. In the contexts of husbands not actually being required to have sex with different wives provided they cared for each equally, al-Juwaynī (d. 1085) adds, 'it is not appropriate by the fine merits of the Sacred Law for sex to be forced for equal apportionment (*lā yalīqu bi-maḥāsin al-sharʿ al-ijbār ʿalayhi wa'l-taswiya*)'; al -Juwaynī, *Nihāyat al-maṭlab*, 13:247. Al-Māwardī adds that one cannot force sex because it comes from desire and love and cannot be 'manufactured' (*taṣannuʿ*); al-Māwardī, *al -Ḥāwī*, 9:572–73. Thanks to Justin Parrot for finding this quote.
52. Ibn Qudāma, *Mughnī*, 8:131.
53. Ibn Taymiyya, *Majmūʿat al-fatāwā*, 29:106; also al-Buhūtī, *al-Rawḍ al-murbiʿ*, 384. See, for example, al-Wazzānī, *Nawāzil*, 3:437–38, 4:502–504. Thanks to Tesneem Alkiek for this citation.
54. Ibn Qudāma, *Mughnī*, 8:127; Ibn Ḍuwayyān, *Manār al-sabīl*, 2:216; *al-Fatāwā al-Hindiyya*, 1:287.
55. Hurgronje, *Mekka*, 106–107.
56. *Hamlet*, ed. Edward Hubler (New York: Signet, 1963), 1, 5, 108 (act, scene, line).

Index

Bold page numbers indicate the most substantial discussion of a topic. 'Al-' is omitted from the first part of Arabic names, with the exception of regnal titles for caliphs. Transliteration follows the convention of the main text of this book.